NFL

SUPER STARS 2012

by Jim Gigliotti

SCHOLASTIC INC.

ISBN 978-0-545-43495-9

12 11 10 9 8 7 6 5 4 3 2 1   12 13 14 15 16 17/0

Printed in the U.S.A.   40
First printing, September 2012

TABLE OF CONTENTS

AARON RODGERS
QUARTERBACK, GREEN BAY PACKERS

The 2011 season was the Year of the Quarterback in the NFL. Never before had so many signal callers played such an important role. Among the best was Green Bay's Aaron Rodgers, who was named the league's Most Valuable Player that year.

Aaron was the Packers' first MVP since Brett Favre in 1997. Favre was the legendary quarterback for whom Aaron took over when he became the team's starter in 2008. At the end of the 2007 season, Favre had decided to retire. Then he wanted to come back. There was a lot of controversy among the media and fans, but there was no controversy for the Packers. Favre had a long and great career, but Green Bay knew it was Aaron's time. By his second year as a starter, Aaron led the team to the playoffs. In 2010, the team won the Super Bowl and Aaron was named MVP.

In 2011, Aaron posted some incredible numbers: club records of 4,643 yards and 45 touchdowns, with only 6 interceptions. His passer rating of 122.5 was the best in NFL history. Green Bay won 15 of 16 games during the regular season.

The Packers have had several amazing quarterbacks. But before his career is over, Aaron may surpass them all.

QUICK STATS

HEIGHT:
6-2

WEIGHT:
225

YEAR:
8TH

COLLEGE:
UNIVERSITY OF CALIFORNIA

HOMETOWN:
CHICO, CALIFORNIA

DRAFTED:
ROUND 1, 2005

TOM BRADY

QUARTERBACK, NEW ENGLAND PATRIOTS

It's hard to believe, but there was a time when people doubted that Tom Brady would be a star pro quarterback. In fact, Tom wasn't even a first, second, or third round pick in the 2000 NFL Draft.

It wasn't until the sixth round, with the 199th overall pick of the Draft, that the New England Patriots tabbed Tom. The Patriots figured Tom would back up star quarterback Drew Bledsoe for a few years. But when Bledsoe got hurt in the 2001 season, Tom stepped in and led the team to a surprise Super Bowl championship. Two more Super Bowls soon followed, and today Tom is considered one of the best quarterbacks in the history of the NFL. In 2011, in fact, he became just the sixth quarterback ever to pass for 300 touchdowns in his career.

Twelve years after he was drafted, Tom has thousands of fans and three Super Bowl championships. What more could he possibly want? A fourth Super Bowl ring, of course! Only two quarterbacks have led their teams to four Super Bowl wins. Tom's chance at another slipped through his fingers when the Giants edged the Patriots in Super Bowl XLVI in the 2011 season. But you can expect he'll have New England in the title chase again soon.

QUICK STATS

HEIGHT:
6-4

WEIGHT:
225

YEAR:
13TH

COLLEGE:
UNIVERSITY OF MICHIGAN

HOMETOWN:
SAN MATEO, CALIFORNIA

DRAFTED:
ROUND 6, 2000

DREW BREES

QUARTERBACK, NEW ORLEANS SAINTS

Some sports records seem unbreakable. In basketball, there's Wilt Chamberlain's 100-point game. In baseball, there's Joe DiMaggio's 56-game hitting streak. And in football, there's Johnny Unitas' amazing 47 consecutive games with a touchdown pass. Unitas' record has lasted since 1960 with no one coming close to beating it. Brett Favre's 36-game string that ended in 2004 is second on the list.

Now, though, Saints' quarterback Drew Brees is taking aim at Unitas' mark. He closed 2011 with 43 consecutive games with a touchdown pass. If he passes for a touchdown in his first five regular-season games in 2012, he will break one of the NFL's oldest records.

The last part's the toughest, but who's to say he can't do it? After all, in 2011, Drew broke another long-standing NFL record: the mark for passing yards in a season. That record had stood since 1984, when Miami's Dan Marino passed for 5,084 yards. Drew came close to breaking it once, when he had 5,069 yards in 2008. Last year, he broke the mark with one game still to play! By season's end, he had 5,476 yards.

Drew is sure to have all of the Saints' fans behind him in his quest for Unitas' record. Since signing with the club in 2006, he's helped build the Saints into one of the NFL's best franchises and gives back to the New Orleans community.

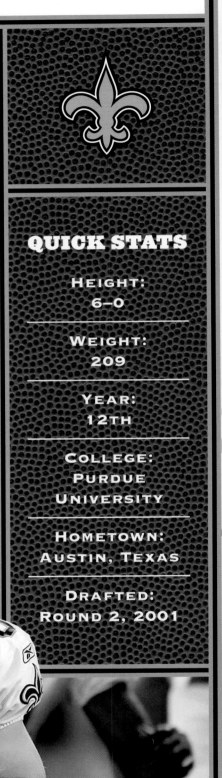

QUICK STATS

HEIGHT:
6-0

WEIGHT:
209

YEAR:
12TH

COLLEGE:
PURDUE
UNIVERSITY

HOMETOWN:
AUSTIN, TEXAS

DRAFTED:
ROUND 2, 2001

TIM TEBOW

QUARTERBACK, NEW YORK JETS

There was no quarterback more talked-about last year than Tim Tebow. Not Eli Manning, who led the Giants to a Super Bowl victory. Not even the Packers' Aaron Rodgers, who was the league's Most Valuable Player.

Tim began the year, his second in the NFL, on the bench. But when the Broncos struggled early in the season, the crowds in Denver began calling for him. "Te-bow! Te-bow! Te-bow!" they chanted. In the sixth game, with the Broncos' record just 1–4, head coach John Fox put Tim in the starting lineup. That week, he led the team to an amazing come-from-behind win over the Miami Dolphins. Two weeks later, the Broncos had a six-game winning streak that carried them to the playoffs.

Tim's passing statistics don't come close to those of Manning or Rodgers. But the number one job of a quarterback is to lead his team to victory. Tim knows how to do that—and usually it has fans on the edges of their seats.

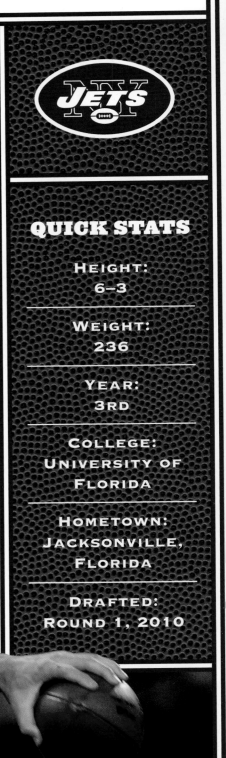

In 2012, the Broncos traded Tebow to the New York Jets after signing Peyton Manning as their starting quarterback. Fans are excited to see what Tebow brings to the Jets team.

QUICK STATS

HEIGHT:
6-3

WEIGHT:
236

YEAR:
3RD

COLLEGE:
UNIVERSITY OF FLORIDA

HOMETOWN:
JACKSONVILLE, FLORIDA

DRAFTED:
ROUND 1, 2010

ELI MANNING

QUARTERBACK, NEW YORK GIANTS

Ever hear the term *déjà vu*? It's the feeling that you've experienced something before. Well, the New England Patriots probably felt a little bit of déjà vu late in the fourth quarter of Super Bowl XLVI in the 2011 season. That's when Eli Manning and the New York Giants got the football at their own 12-yard line with 3:46 remaining and the Patriots ahead by two points. Eli completed a long pass to Mario Manningham. Several plays after that, the Giants scored a touchdown to win the game 21–17.

The fourth quarter of Super Bowl XLII in the 2007 season had a very similar outcome. The Giants got the ball late in the fourth quarter at their own 17-yard line with time for one last drive. The Patriots were leading by four points. But soon Eli completed a long pass to David Tyree, who made an incredible catch. Soon after that, the Giants scored a touchdown to win the game 17–14.

The 2011 victory was a memorable ending to Eli's best season. He passed for 4,933 yards, which was the most in a season in Giants' history, and had 29 touchdowns during the regular season in 2011. More important, the Giants were Super Bowl champs for the second time in five years.

And for the second time, Eli was named the Super Bowl's Most Valuable Player. Maybe he had a little sense of *déjà vu*, too!

QUICK STATS

HEIGHT:
6–4

WEIGHT:
218

YEAR:
9TH

COLLEGE:
UNIVERSITY OF MISSISSIPPI

HOMETOWN:
NEW ORLEANS, LOUISIANA

DRAFTED:
ROUND 1, 2004

CAM NEWTON

QUARTERBACK, CAROLINA PANTHERS

Some college draft picks take years to develop into successful starting quarterbacks. For the Carolina Panthers' Cam Newton, though, it took all of about eight plays into his rookie season to make an impact. That's when he tossed his first NFL touchdown pass: a 77-yard strike to Steve Smith in a game against the Arizona Cardinals on Kickoff Weekend.

He passed for 422 yards against the Cardinals in his debut. It was the most ever in a game by an NFL rookie. The next week, he broke his own mark with 432 yards against the Packers. By season's end, he became the first NFL player to pass for more than 4,000 yards (he had 4,051 yards) in his rookie season.

Cam was just as impressive with his feet as he was with his arm. He ran for a touchdown in each of his first two games. Later in the year, he ran for 3 touchdowns in a single game against Tampa Bay. By season's end, Cam ran for 14 touchdowns—the most in any season by any quarterback in NFL history.

With this unique combination of skills and his incredible rookie season, fans around the league will be keeping their eyes on Cam.

QUICK STATS

HEIGHT:
6–5

WEIGHT:
248

YEAR:
2ND

COLLEGE:
AUBURN
UNIVERSITY

HOMETOWN:
COLLEGE PARK,
GEORGIA

DRAFTED:
ROUND 1, 2011

RAY RICE

RUNNING BACK, BALTIMORE RAVENS

It used to be that almost every team had a starting running back who stayed in the game no matter the down and distance. The backup running back came in the game only when the first-string guy needed a rest or was injured. These days, though, some teams have one back to pound the ball between the tackles, and another to burn teams on the outside. Others have one back who helps move the ball down the field, while a different player comes into the game when the ball is near the goal line. In Baltimore, Ray Rice is all of those guys!

In 2011, Ray ranked second in the NFL in rushing yards (with 1,364), fourth in touchdowns (12), and first in yards from scrimmage (2,068 yards rushing and receiving). He also was second among all running backs with 76 catches.

For a long time now, defense has been the key to Baltimore's success. It is the main reason the Ravens have reached the playoffs eight times in the past 12 years. But Baltimore hasn't been to the Super Bowl since the 2000 season. And the Ravens know that to get back, the offense needs to do its share, too. Ray certainly does his share. Don't be surprised if one day soon he's one of the main reasons Baltimore makes it back to the Super Bowl.

QUICK STATS

HEIGHT:
5-8

WEIGHT:
212

YEAR:
5TH

COLLEGE:
RUTGERS UNIVERSITY

HOMETOWN:
NEW ROCHELLE, NEW YORK

DRAFTED:
ROUND 2, 2008

ARIAN FOSTER

RUNNING BACK, HOUSTON TEXANS

Houston running back Arian Foster is a fantasy-football owner's dream—and an opposing defensive coordinator's nightmare. Foster runs the ball just about as well as anybody in the NFL, is an excellent pass catcher, and scores lots of touchdowns, too.

It's hard to believe, but Arian wasn't drafted out of college. Through two days, seven rounds, and 256 players, Foster's name was never called at the 2009 NFL Draft. He ended up signing with the Houston Texans as an undrafted free agent, but at first, he didn't make the team and was cut. The Texans re-signed him to play for their practice squad, which means he worked out with the team during the week, but didn't suit up on game day. It wasn't until late in the season, after injuries to the Texans' other running backs, that he was signed to the 53-man roster.

Then came the first game of 2010. Most people still didn't know who Arian was, but he set a team record by rushing for 231 yards and 3 touchdowns in the Texans' upset of the Colts. That was just the beginning. By the end of the season, Arian led the NFL with 1,616 yards rushing, 16 touchdowns, and 2,220 yards from scrimmage (rushing and receiving). In 2011, Arian missed several games due to injury, but still ran for 1,224 yards. He helped the Texans make the playoffs for the first time in the history of the franchise.

And now, when Draft day comes each year— fantasy Draft day, that is—Arian's name is one of the first ones called.

QUICK STATS

HEIGHT:
6-1

WEIGHT:
229

YEAR:
4TH

COLLEGE:
UNIVERSITY OF
TENNESSEE

HOMETOWN:
SAN DIEGO,
CALIFORNIA

DRAFTED:
FREE AGENT, 2009

MAURICE JONES-DREW

RUNNING BACK, JACKSONVILLE JAGUARS

After his 2010 season-ending knee injury, Jacksonville Jaguars running back Maurice Jones-Drew knew he'd have his doubters in 2011. Plus, it wasn't just his knee. Maurice had injuries to his wrist, ankle, and abdomen, too. "Uh-oh," his critics said. "The Jaguars will have to cut back on his workload."

But they were proven wrong. Maurice not only increased his workload in 2011, but he also led the NFL with 343 carries. He topped the league in rushing yards, too, with 1,606. And he made the Pro Bowl for the third season in a row.

That may have ⬛⬛⬛⬛⬛ his critics, but, then again, Maurice's NFL career has been full of surprises. When MJD was drafted in 2006, many thought he was too short (he's 5 feet 7 inches) to make it. In his rookie season he scored 16 touchdowns. Then he added 24 touchdowns over the next two seasons. "Okay, but Fred Taylor handled the bulk of the Jaguars' carries those years. MJD won't be durable enough when he's the main man," the skeptics said. So in 2009, after Taylor left, MJD rushed for more than 1,000 yards in a season (he had 1,391) for the first time. Then came an excellent 2010 season, even injured (1,324 yards), and an even better 2011. And now, the critics have to admit that the little back has made it big.

QUICK STATS

HEIGHT:
5–7

WEIGHT:
208

YEAR:
7TH

COLLEGE:
UCLA

HOMETOWN:
CONCORD, CALIFORNIA

DRAFTED:
ROUND 2, 2006

JARED ALLEN
DEFENSIVE END, MINNESOTA VIKINGS

When an NFL coach talks about a player's "motor" he's referring to how hard a player works during practice and on game day. In today's NFL, there might not be a player with a motor quite like Minnesota Vikings defensive end Jared Allen.

During every game Jared is a non-stop flurry of activity. He encourages teammates, intimidates opponents, urges the fans to cheer louder, and, most important, he sacks the quarterback. At just 29 years old at the end of the 2011 season, he already ranked number 20 on the NFL's all-time list with 105 sacks in his career. In fact, Jared posted more sacks than any other player in the NFL in 2011. He had 22 sacks, just half a sack short of the league record, and he made the Pro Bowl for the fourth time in the last five seasons.

That's what the Vikings had in mind when they traded a first-round Draft choice and a pair of third-round picks to the Kansas City Chiefs in 2008 in order to obtain Jared. It was a huge price to pay for one player, but the Vikings felt that Jared was worth the cost.

Minnesota went on to win the NFC North in Jared's first season with the team, and in his second, too. Things haven't gone quite so well for the team since then. But you can't tell by watching Jared play. His motor has never stopped.

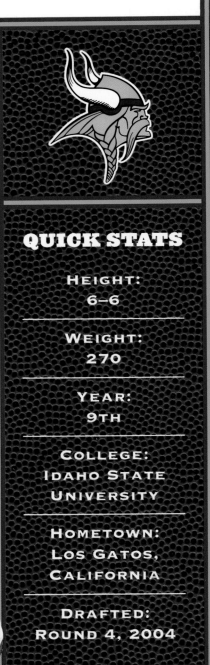

QUICK STATS

HEIGHT:
6–6

WEIGHT:
270

YEAR:
9TH

COLLEGE:
IDAHO STATE
UNIVERSITY

HOMETOWN:
LOS GATOS,
CALIFORNIA

DRAFTED:
ROUND 4, 2004

DEMARCUS WARE
LINEBACKER, DALLAS COWBOYS

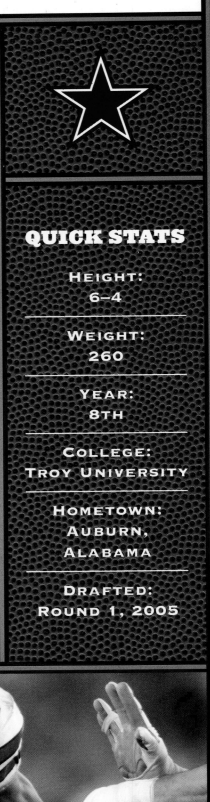

When DeMarcus Ware came out of college, NFL scouts labeled him "tweener." Now, seven years later, NFL scouts have a different label for Ware: "best pass rusher in the league." Ware posted 19.5 sacks in the Cowboys' 16 games in 2011. That gives him 99.5 sacks in just 112 regular-season games since Dallas selected him with the eleventh overall pick of the 2005 NFL Draft.

The "tweener" label was short for "in-between." Ware played defensive end in college, but at about 251 pounds at the time he was not big enough to play defensive end in the NFL. At 6 feet 4 inches, he was too big to be a conventional linebacker, either.

The Cowboys didn't care. They knew DeMarcus had a combination of strength and speed that was far too good to pass up when their turn came in the first round. And they've been happy with the choice ever since. Dallas placed DeMarcus at outside linebacker in their 3-4 defensive alignment—that means three down linemen and four linebackers—and told him to rush the passer. In his second season, DeMarcus posted 11.5 sacks and made the Pro Bowl. He's been an all-star every year since, too.

Only eight NFL players ever have posted as many as 20 sacks in a season, including DeMarcus, who led the league with 20 sacks in 2008. His next goal? Making 22.5 sacks in a season. That's the NFL record set by the New York Giants' Michael Strahan in 2001.

QUICK STATS

HEIGHT:
6-4

WEIGHT:
260

YEAR:
8TH

COLLEGE:
TROY UNIVERSITY

HOMETOWN:
AUBURN, ALABAMA

DRAFTED:
ROUND 1, 2005

JUSTIN SMITH

DEFENSIVE END, SAN FRANCISCO 49ERS

One of the best examples of what Justin Smith means to the 49ers' defense came during San Francisco's victory over New Orleans in the 2011 playoffs. On third down from deep in his team's territory in the fourth quarter, the Saints' Drew Brees dropped back to pass. He was protected on his blind side by Jermon Bushrod, a Pro Bowl left tackle. Bushrod squared up on Justin and didn't let the big defensive end get around him. So Justin just kept pushing Bushrod back . . . and back . . . and back some more—until both players were right on top of Brees! The Saints' quarterback threw the ball away, incomplete. New Orleans had to punt.

Nothing in the box score shows what Justin did to Brees on that play. He didn't get any personal statistic to his credit, but his teammates knew what happened. Television analyst Daryl Johnston, a former NFL fullback, called the play "relentless."

And that's just what Justin is. He's relentless in his pursuit of opposing quarterbacks. His massive strength makes him one of the biggest forces on defense in the NFL, even if he doesn't get to the quarterback. Of course, a lot of times he does get to him. Justin had 7.5 sacks in 2011 to make the Pro Bowl for the third season in row. More important, he was a key part of one of the best defenses in the NFL. That unit helped the 49ers win 13 regular-season games on the way to their first division championship in 11 years.

QUICK STATS

HEIGHT:
6-4

WEIGHT:
285

YEAR:
12TH

COLLEGE:
UNIVERSITY OF MISSOURI

HOMETOWN:
JEFFERSON CITY, MISSOURI

DRAFTED:
ROUND 1, 2004

DARRELLE REVIS

CORNERBACK, NEW YORK JETS

A shutdown corner is a cornerback who takes away—or "shuts down"—one entire part of the field for opposing pass offenses. His presence on one side of the field makes quarterbacks pass the ball to the other side. In the NFL today, the best shutdown cornerback is Darrelle Revis of the New York Jets.

In 2011, Darrelle made the Pro Bowl for his fourth consecutive season. He even was an all-star in 2010, when he didn't intercept a single pass. How could he be a Pro Bowl player if he had zero interceptions? It's because quarterbacks pretty much stopped trying to throw the ball his way—even when Darrelle was covering the opposing team's best receiver.

Apparently, that memo didn't reach Dallas quarterback Tony Romo when the Jets and the Cowboys played on Kickoff Weekend in 2011. With less that a minute to go in the game and the score tied 24–24, Romo tried to force a ball onto "Revis Island." The Jets' cornerback intercepted the pass and returned the ball 20 yards into Dallas territory. Moments later, New York kicked a field goal to win the game 27–24.

Ask most quarterbacks, and right away they'll tell you that Darrelle is the best cornerback in the NFL. Ask Jets head coach Rex Ryan, though, and he'll say, "Revis is the best player in football."

QUICK STATS

HEIGHT:
5–11

WEIGHT:
198

YEAR:
6TH

COLLEGE:
UNIVERSITY OF PITTSBURGH

HOMETOWN:
ALIQUIPPA, PENNSYLVANIA

DRAFTED:
ROUND 1, 2007

PATRICK PETERSON

CORNERBACK/KICK RETURNER, ARIZONA CARDINALS

Midway through the fourth quarter of his first NFL game, Patrick Peterson settled under a punt at the Arizona Cardinals' 11-yard line. He ran up the middle, burst past a couple of Carolina players before they could tackle him, and broke into the clear. Eighty-nine yards later, Peterson dove across the goal line to put an exclamation point on the second-longest punt return in Cardinals' history—which began in 1898! Even better, though, the touchdown broke a 21–21 tie and lifted Arizona to a 28–21 victory.

Patrick's big return was just the kind of play the Cardinals were hoping for when they selected him out of Louisiana State with the fifth overall pick in the 2011 NFL Draft. The team liked Patrick's size, speed, maturity, and work ethic, and they figured he would someday be a star. Little did they know it would be right away. His punt return against the Panthers on Kickoff Weekend was only the beginning. By the season's end, Peterson brought back 4 punts for touchdowns. That's more than any other player in Cardinals' history did in his entire career with the club. He was the first NFL player ever with 4 punt-return touchdowns in a season that covered more than 80 yards each.

Not surprisingly, Patrick made the Pro Bowl as a return man in his rookie season. Chances are, he'll soon be there as a cornerback, too. In fact, it seems he can do just about anything on the football field.

QUICK STATS

HEIGHT:
6–0

WEIGHT:
219

YEAR:
2ND

COLLEGE:
LOUISIANA STATE
UNIVERSITY

HOMETOWN:
POMPANO BEACH,
FLORIDA

DRAFTED:
ROUND 1, 2011

2011 NFL STANDINGS

AFC East
New England Patriots 13–3
New York Jets 8–8
Miami Dolphins 6–10
Buffalo Bills 6–10

AFC North
Baltimore Ravens 12–4
Pittsburgh Steelers 12–4
Cincinnati Bengals 9–7
Cleveland Browns 4–12

AFC South
Houston Texans 10–6
Tennessee Titans 9–7
Jacksonville Jaguars 5–11
Indianapolis Colts 2–14

AFC West
Denver Broncos 8–8
San Diego Chargers 8–8
Oakland Raiders 8–8
Kansas City Chiefs 7–9

NFC East
New York Giants 9–7
Philadelphia Eagles 8–8
Dallas Cowboys 8–8
Washington Redskins 5–11

NFC North
Green Bay Packers 15–1
Detroit Lions 10–6
Chicago Bears 8–8
Minnesota Vikings 3–13

NFC South
New Orleans Saints 13–3
Atlanta Falcons 10–6
Carolina Panthers 6–10
Tampa Bay Buccaneers 4–12

NFC West
San Francisco 49ers 13–3
Arizona Cardinals 8–8
Seattle Seahawks 7–9
St. Louis Rams 2–14

SUPER BOWL XLVI
NEW YORK GIANTS 21, NEW ENGLAND PATRIOTS 17

THE RACIAL COMPOSITION
OF THE HABSBURG POSSESSIONS

The Rise and Fall
of the
Habsburg Monarchy

VICTOR-L. TAPIÉ

Member of the Institut de France

The Rise and Fall
of the
Habsburg Monarchy

translated by
STEPHEN HARDMAN

PRAEGER PUBLISHERS
New York · Washington · London

Published in the United States of America in 1971
by

Praeger Publishers, Inc.
111 Fourth Avenue, New York, N.Y. 10003, U.S.A.
5 Cromwell Place, London sw7, England

Second printing, 1972

Originally published as *Monarchie et peuples du Danube*
© 1969 by Librairie Arthème Fayard, Paris
Translation © 1971 by Pall Mall Press Limited, London

Library of Congress Catalog Card Number: 77-137893

Printed in the United States of America

Contents

Preface

On the Piazza Navona in Rome stands the fountain carved by Bernini and adorned with four statues of rivers, each symbolizing a part of the earth. The statue of the Danube represents Europe. At the time when Bernini erected this monument, in the seventeenth century, a great part of the Danube's course passed through territories occupied by Islam; but further up-river, in the region known as Royal Hungary and in the Austrian duchies, the route along the valley of the Danube was still open: one more confrontation was possible in the struggle between Christendom and Islam. In 1683 Vienna suffered a last siege and the Christian armies emerged victorious. The Hungarian plain and Transylvania were then reconquered and the group of states over which the Habsburgs had begun to establish their dominion in 1526 became a great power in Europe, a power which endured until the end of the First World War, when the old monarchy made way for democratic states founded on the principle of self-determination.

In a study of this part of Europe in modern times, the two elements of monarchy and peoples cannot be dissociated: the Danubian monarchy was a royal power intent on uniting in common enterprises peoples who, while they refused to be merged into a single nation and preserved their own laws and languages, found themselves bound together by economic interests, cultural affinities and similar social structures, and who, in their common concern to defend themselves, accepted this form of association. The Danubian peoples, living in juxtaposition with one another but never unified in the manner of the great Western countries, thus formed a territorial complex which was eventually to assume an existence of its own.

The history of the countries of the Middle Danube was viewed by the nineteenth century either as the history of the individual nations, or in terms of the political system that united them. However, as a modern Czech historian has justly observed, the history of these countries 'has a richness and diversity that cannot be conveyed by systematically tracing the evolution of each particular country or nation of the Empire and then attempting to bring these separate elements together'.[1] That the structure of the Empire lasted for so long can only be explained by factors which extend beyond traditional territorial boundaries—the kingdoms of Bohemia and

Hungary, the archduchies of Austria and so on—and beyond the limits of national groupings.

Neither must these factors be reduced merely to the Habsburg dynasty's desire for power or its military strength. The historical reality assumed a variety of forms which, quite understandably, has always appeared disconcerting to Western minds accustomed to more precise and coherent habits of thought. In attempting to resolve the contradictions of Danubian history, it has been assumed out of laziness that everything could be explained in terms of a continual struggle between the House of Austria and its peoples: too often have historians been induced by their ideological inclinations to take one side or the other. Only a few years ago, it seemed impossible to take an interest in the history of a particular country without embracing all that country's national passions and adopting an attitude of hostility towards its neighbours; similarly, any attempt to be fair to the Habsburg monarchy was interpreted as evidence that the author was in favour of its restoration. The beginnings of modern historical science and frequent consultations between historians of different countries and different methods have made it possible to take a broader and, no doubt, a more accurate view of things. In the field of economic and social history, the analysis of an original civilization which, though many-sided, was rich in common elements, brings a clearer understanding of what might be termed a state of unstable equilibrium, in which centrifugal and centripetal forces clashed and which nevertheless endured for four hundred years.

This book is the result of nearly fifty years of study and has been inspired by the work of several generations of historians, including the most recent interpretations. The author has contributed the results of his own research on a number of questions. A deep feeling for the countries of the Danube, where people so often respond with friendliness and warmth when they realize that an interest is being taken in their past history, can help the historian towards a true understanding of his subject. The author would therefore like to express his great indebtedness to the Academies of Sciences, the professors past and present of the universities of Prague, Vienna, Graz and Budapest, and the many colleagues and personal friends who will all recognize the fruits of their co-operation throughout the pages of this work.

[1]Jurij Křížek—Historica XII, p. 73, Prague, 1966.

Part One

I

A Historical Survey of the Danube Countries up to 1526

ON 29 AUGUST 1526 the army of Louis II Jagellon, king of Hungary and Bohemia, was defeated by the numerically superior forces of Sultan Soliman II on the banks of the Danube, not far from the town of Mohács in Hungary. Louis himself was drowned in the marshes bordering the river as he fled from the battlefield. A few weeks later, on 22 October, his brother-in-law, the Archduke Ferdinand of Austria, was elected king of Bohemia in Prague, and on 17 December was elected king of Hungary in Pressburg. The Alpine territories of the House of Austria, with Bohemia and its incorporated provinces (Moravia, Silesia and the Lusatias) and Hungary, now came under the rule of a single prince, a member of the Habsburg dynasty which was to remain in control of these countries, through many changes of fortune, until the collapse of the Austrian Empire in 1918.

The year 1526—a memorable date, indeed—must first be set in the context of the period. In 1520, six years earlier, the papal bull *Exsurge Domine* had condemned the forty-one propositions of Luther: the confrontation between the Reformation and Rome was tearing Christendom asunder. Charles V had been emperor since 1519; he had defeated Francis I at Pavia and in January 1526 imposed on him the harsh treaty of Madrid, which France refused to accept. In America the Spanish Conquest was in full spate. A year later, in 1527, Rome was sacked and the Renaissance shaken to its foundations. Amid the mighty transformation which Europe and the world were undergoing, the beginnings of Habsburg domination in central Europe acquire a symbolical significance.

Austria, Bohemia and Hungary[1] formed a vast territory: the Alpine regions of Austria, the quadrilateral comprising Bohemia and the German provinces, the crescent of the Carpathians, the broad plains watered by the Danube and the Tisza, and the mountains of Transylvania to the east. But this particular form of

1

territorial regrouping had not been determined either by geography or by history. The Danube certainly provided a link between several of these lands, but the bridges which gave access to the trade-routes between Mediterranean Europe and northern Europe were mostly situated down-river. The Elbe and the Oder, the rivers of the kingdom of Bohemia, flowed northwards.

The populations of these countries were of diverse origin: the Alpine regions were inhabited by Germans and southern Slavs; Bohemia consisted largely of Slavs, but with some Germans in the mountains and the towns; in Hungary the Magyars, of Finno-Ugrian stock, lived mostly on the plain, while the Slavs were to be found in the mountains; Transylvania was inhabited by Germans (both in the towns and in certain rural areas) and by country peoples of Rumanian stock. Above all, each of the Danubian peoples had its own long history, its own laws and customs. The Danube had remained the frontier of the Roman world until the Barbarian invasion, whereupon the river had ceased to fulfil its old function. Christianity had brought Western influences back to these regions, which it had been slowly penetrating since the sixth century, initially through the efforts of the missionary monks and later through the monasteries founded in Carolingian times. In the ninth century Cyril and Methodius, Christian missionaries from Thessalonica, had preached in Slavonic to the tribes of Bohemia and Moravia, which were briefly united in the empire of Great Moravia. St. Wenceslas, a Christian prince of Bohemia, had suffered martyrdom at the beginning of the tenth century and legend had glorified him as the duke of the Czechs, their eternal protector who would never allow their race to perish. Later, a bishop of Prague, St. Adalbert, had converted Géza, the king of Hungary, and in the year 1000 Géza's son, St. Stephen, was crowned king by Pope Sylvester II and the emperor. Western Christianity had thus given the peoples of the Danube their first experience of a common culture that transcended ethnic differences.[2]

The other major feature of the historical evolution of the Danubian countries was their immediate proximity to Germany, which explains many of their institutions, technical achievements and customs. Austria had originally been Ostmark, the Eastern March, where the fortresses commanding the deep valley of the Danube prevented the Barbarian invaders from using the river as an access route.

Bohemia had become an imperial fief and in 1085 its prince had received the title of king. Yet there was no question of rigid subordination. The German Empire enjoyed the prestige of being the moral heir of Rome and aspired to universality. The kingdom of Bohemia, while forming part of the Empire, was the emperor's ally as much as his vassal. In the twelfth century the Babenberg dukes of Austria had succeeded, by means of the *privilegium minus*, in obtaining the right to choose their own successors and to dispense justice, and had also secured a reduction of their military responsibilities—concessions which each represented a step towards territorial sovereignty. In the following century (at Vienna, in 1208) Leopold VI Babenberg proclaimed himself 'by the grace of God, duke of Austria and Styria'. Hungary, for its part, had escaped all form of imperial vassalage and had been supported by the Holy See, which in return exercised the right of patronage over that country.

The political structure could not, however, diminish the Germanic influences that had slowly but steadily been permeating the life of the Danubian peoples. Although these influences did not create a common way of life (important local, economic and juridical differences remained), they did breed strong affinities. The populations of central Europe, originally nomads or shepherds, had gradually adopted an agrarian economy. The historian is here confronted with the problems of the ownership of land and the manner of its cultivation. It has long been considered that the Slavs in general led a communal existence, with families (in the broadest sense of the word) enjoying common ownership of fields and forests and having no individual possessions apart from their homes. Were these agrarian communities, which can be traced in the early history of the Slavs and also in Hungary (the *nagyczálad*), peculiar to the Slav world? The great Austrian medievalist Alfons Dopsch doubted this, for he had observed evidence of similar communities in the Alpine districts, among both Germans and Slavs.[3]

Is it not likely that the peoples of the Danube had simply reached a stage in the organization of economic and social life which all Indo-European societies experienced? At all events, as trade expanded and money replaced the system of barter, crop-growers and shepherds entered upon a more complex kind of economic life. The period from the eleventh to the fifteenth centuries is called the 'feudal' period, a term that has aroused debate among scholars in recent years, for the feudalism of central Europe differed from that of western Europe. The hierarchy of lords and vassals bound to them by military obligations was not characteristic of the whole of central Europe: here, it seems, to a greater degree than in the West, there still existed communities of free crop-growers whose only overlord was the prince of the medieval state, to whom they paid taxes in various forms. Moreover, the practice of using prisoners of war as slave labour continued until the eleventh or twelfth century, and even into the thirteenth century in Hungary, despite the teachings of Christianity.

The fief was, nevertheless, a common feature of central Europe: the prince would grant lands to his companions-in-arms, the men of the *družina*; these lands were either held for life or handed down to sons and then to grandsons, and in some cases, they were even awarded on a full hereditary basis. The monasteries (Benedictine or Cistercian) benefited from similar concessions of land. The most powerful of the feudal lords, who in both Bohemia and Hungary were called *barons* (a title that placed them above the other nobles), granted fiefs to their servants and administrators; in return the latter, not all of them originally freemen, assumed certain military responsibilities. At the same time, the landowners encouraged the development of individual holdings and villages on their estates.

Initially, freemen could be deprived neither of their personal independence nor of their possessions. According to the Czech historian Kamil Krofta, this explains why the earliest charters of cession include no mention of freemen: the first cultivators of seigniorial domains must have been slaves. However, freemen not only had to pay taxes, but were also liable to be summoned for military service when their prince was at war. Their desire to avoid such obligations coincided with the landowners' need to find labour for the farming of their estates. It was to the

3

advantage of the free peasantry, on the one hand, to have the immediate protection of a powerful lord; the lord, on the other hand, increased his revenues by converting the uncultivated parts of his domains into arable land. Under the agreements reached between the two parties, the peasants paid their lord a quit-rent and gave him part of their harvest. In return, they escaped the direct authority of the prince, for they were exempted from both taxes and military service. In Bohemia, land was divided into two categories: the *dominical* comprised that land which the lord kept for himself and which was cultivated by his servants (later, the peasants were given plots on the dominical, which thus extended over a wider area than the lord's own personal preserve); the *rustical* consisted of all the lands awarded to the peasantry, where villages were built. Individual property-ownership was established at the same time, for agreements were drawn up in the names of the contracting parties. On the rustical the peasant held possession of his own house and fields, and was entitled to pass them on to his heirs or to transfer possession to another, subject to his lord's approval. Only if his family became extinct did the law of mortmain take effect: the land then reverted to the lord.

The patrimonial character of the societies of the Danubian states was thus firmly established in the Middle Ages. Although free rural communities still existed and although the feudal hierarchy differed from that in the west, it is easy to see why historians have felt obliged to use the term 'feudal system', even if the relationship between lords and peasants was, strictly speaking, seigniorial rather than feudal in nature.[4] This relationship underwent subsequent modification as the peasant's obligations to his lord grew more burdensome and more precisely defined; whether these obligations changed in essence is not certain.

Soon, foreigners were being encouraged to immigrate, either because the local populations were not large enough and possibly lacked the skills necessary for clearing and cultivating large tracts of land, or because they showed a reluctance to move even a short distance from their old fields. In contrast, a large number of Germans were eager to join this colonizing movement. A great migration took place, to Upper Hungary in the twelfth century and to the valleys of the mountains encircling Bohemia in the thirteenth century. People came from afar—from Flanders, the lower valley of the Rhine and Westphalia—and entered into contracts with the barons, who gave them land; the contracts were arranged either directly with the landowner or through an intermediary, the *lokator* or colonizing agent. Communities of Saxons obtained lands and privileges in Transylvania. In the towns, which had come into existence with the extension of trading centres and workshops, the Germans settled in large numbers, often controlling the leading workshops and managing local affairs.

The presence of precious minerals in Bohemia and Upper Hungary constituted an important source of revenue, provided that efficient mining techniques were applied. The mining towns now began to play a major role in the economy of these countries, similar to that of the market towns, where the produce of the land (cereals and cattle) and handicraft articles were sold.

The patricians in the larger towns, where the Germans mingled with the native populations, often adopted the customs and even the dialects of Germany; much of the technical and craft vocabulary of the Slav and Hungarian languages was derived from German words. But to speak of Germanization would be misleading, since it was a question not so much of a deliberate and systematic campaign, as of a spontaneous social phenomenon. Nevertheless, as social distinctions became gradually superimposed over national differences, hostility arose between one group and another and in times of difficulty became very bitter.

No less significant was the contamination of local customs by Germanic customs. The old law of the Slav countries made way for German law, at first in the towns, but later also in the country regions. Some historians have even distinguished between the law of the rural areas and the law of the towns, as if it were only in the towns that Germanic law prevailed. Naturally, Germanic law in the Danubian states was by no means uniform. The law of Magdeburg applied in the region of Leitmeritz, in Bohemia, at Olmütz in Moravia and even in Prague itself, in the Little Town (Malá Strana), while the law of Nuremberg governed Eger and the old city of Prague. The mining towns also came under Germanic law. In the country areas, on the other hand, when the formulation of laws was initiated on the large estates, there can be no doubt that the old Slav traditions were preserved more generally.[5]

Another important point must be made: in Bohemia a distinction existed in the manner of cultivation of peasant lands, a distinction quite independent of the juridical division of land into the *dominical* and the *rustical*. Some lands were termed 'redeemed' and others 'unredeemed'. In the first case, the peasant enjoyed effective ownership of his house and land, and could hand them down to his heirs; though bound by numerous obligations, he retained a considerable measure of personal and economic liberty. The peasant farming unredeemed land found himself in an apparently less favourable position: he was merely the usufructuary or tenant of the land he occupied; the farm-buildings belonged to the lord and the peasant's feudal obligations appear to have been more arbitrary and less precisely defined. Historians still disagree about the origin and nature of these two categories of land. Some incline to the view that unredeemed lands, over which the lord wielded greater authority, came into existence at a later date and resulted from the harsh conditions that placed the peasantry at the mercy of the nobility in the sixteenth and, in particular, the seventeenth centuries. Others believe that the two categories represented a survival from an older feudal order and derived from the difference between Germanic law, which was more clearly defined and more favourable to the individual, and Slav law, which attached greater importance to practice and usage than to contract. The author has no intention of attempting to resolve this controversial question here. But it should be pointed out that all records concerning redeemed lands were entered in books kept by the village community (as a contemporary historian, Vladimir Procházka, has indicated, these books reveal only the life of the more prosperous peasant élite; records for unredeemed lands were kept in the lord's administrative registers). A fundamental distinction existed, then, between two categories of peasants: a distinction that not only divided the peasants into richer and poorer, but, even more important, affected the extent of their personal liberty.

On entering into the service of the lord, the peasants had at first escaped the vassalage of the State. But, as the State grew stronger, it began to reclaim authority over all its subjects and, since the barons succeeded in preserving their fiscal immunity for the *dominical*, the State's taxes henceforth fell on the lands of the *rustical*.

※

If the medieval State cannot be compared with the modern State, either in strength or in cohesion, it nonetheless constituted a solid reality. All the warrior-princes of central Europe were pursuing roughly similar policies, based on family and dynastic considerations. They aimed to extend their territories by conquest, by matrimonial alliances and by claiming hereditary rights. If they became sufficiently powerful, they could even make a bid for the imperial crown which, with its aura of universality, represented the apex of power.

In this game of alliances the princes of Bohemia fixed their sights not only on Hungary, but also on Poland, where political and social institutions in many ways resembled their own. The extinction of the Babenberg dynasty of Austria in the mid-thirteenth century (1246) aroused the same ambition in Ottokar II Přemysl, king of Bohemia, and Béla IV, king of Hungary—an ambition that was quite natural in the political context of the period. Ottokar wanted the territories of Austria so that he could extend his empire from the Elbe to the Adriatic, while Béla was anxious to obtain Styria. The two kings agreed to divide Austria between them, but then waged war against each other. Victory went to Ottokar, the Czech, a courageous horseman and a skilled tactician. But Ottokar was also a wise politician who attached as much importance to the administration and economic well-being of his peoples as to feats of arms. In both Bohemia and Austria he encountered the resistance of the nobles, whose privileges he was determined to restrict; at the same time he bestowed favours on the towns and encouraged colonization. He continued to receive the support of the Church and the German princes for a long time. However, when Ottokar laid claim to the Empire after the death of Richard of Cornwall, king of Germany, the prospect of his attaining this supreme goal provoked widespread concern. In 1273 Rudolf IV of Habsburg, a German prince who held vast domains in Alsace and Swabia, was elected (as Rudolf I) in his place. Ottokar contested the election and the new king banished his rival from the Empire. Rudolf assembled a powerful coalition army which brought together the duke of Bavaria, the German bishops of Salzburg, Passau and Ratisbon, the king of Hungary and the count of the Tyrol. Ottokar put himself at the head of a large force consisting of Czechs, Poles, Silesians and Germans from Misnia and Brandenburg. Behind the king of Bohemia, whose war-cry was 'Praga', lay northern Germany, while the Habsburg cry of 'Roma—Christus' already epitomized the Empire with its universality of character and its Italian links. A successful tactical move by Rudolf and the intervention of the Hungarian cavalry combined to defeat the army of the great Přemyslid, who was killed in combat on 26 August 1278, near Dürnkrut in the Marchfeld.[6]

Ottokar's empire perished with him. His son, Václav II, sought a reconciliation with Rudolf of Habsburg; then, backed by the growing wealth of Bohemia, where new silver-mines had been discovered, he intervened in Poland, where he was crowned king in 1300. When the Árpád dynasty of Hungary became extinct, he tried to secure that kingdom for his son, but the Papacy supported the candidature of another royal house, the Angevins of Naples. Václav III proved no more successful in his attempt to establish a lasting union of Bohemia, Hungary and Poland than his grandfather had been in trying to keep Austria as part of his great empire. He was assassinated in 1306.

This world of chivalry was marked by a curious contradiction: the kings, yearning for dynastic glory, sought the crowns of countries already strong enough to provide the means with which to promote their policies; but the nobles, representing landed wealth and old established authority, would accept as their king only a prince who was not powerful enough to make himself feared and who would respect their privileges. In the early fourteenth century, this situation led to a chaotic period of minor wars and rivalries, at the end of which relative stability returned: the Habsburgs, who came from Swabia, took over Austria from the extinct Babenberg dynasty, the Angevins ruled Hungary and a Western family, the Luxemburgs, rose to power in Bohemia.

The nobles of Bohemia chose as their king a very young man, John, son of the Emperor Henry VII, and married him to the sister of Václav III, Eliška Přemyslovna. John governed under the tutelage of the nobles, but he was interested in Bohemia only in so far as that country's resources would enable him to indulge in adventures elsewhere. In the struggle between France and England, he sided with the French king. At the battle of Crécy, in 1346, in spite of the fact that he was blind, he insisted on being led into the thick of the fighting so that he could prove his courage, and thus became the legendary king who, in the words of Chateaubriand, 'died for us at the time of our ancient misfortunes'. His son Charles, who succeeded him, revealed a quite different character and authority. The traveller of today who visits Bohemia, and in particular the city of Prague, cannot fail to marvel at the abundance of memorials to the king-emperor and the countless relics of a reign so happy and so vividly remembered that it might almost have ended yesterday—as if the minds of the people were haunted by nostalgia for that time of glory. Moreover, the Czech people's evident interest in France seems to have sprung from the French culture which Charles IV implanted on the banks of the Vltava. He had grown up at the court of the Valois. Of his four wives his favourite was a Frenchwoman, the princess Blanche. He cherished a lasting affection for the fleurs-de-lis. Yet France was not the keystone of his policy which, though essentially imperial, rested firmly on Bohemia itself.

The origins of Charles IV's Bohemian policy can be discerned in the deep attachment which he felt for his mother's native country. He loved Bohemia and the beauty of its landscapes, and he was proud of a lineage that associated him with the gentle figure of St. Wenceslas, whose relics he venerated and whose memory he glorified. Indeed, it was through his efforts that the cult of St. Wenceslas became forever identified with the kingdom of Bohemia and the Czech nation. Bohemia and its language, which he found 'noble and worthy of love', helped Charles IV

7

towards an understanding of the Slav tradition. The most significant proof of his interest in this tradition was the fact that he established in Prague a community of Croatian monks who had preserved the ancient liturgy and the Old Slavonic language. He gave them the monastery of Na Slovanech (Emmäus) and obtained permission from the Pope to have Mass celebrated according to the Cyrillic rite wherever he found himself in residence.

But the Empire was his chief preoccupation. After an election that had been contested, and not without reason, Charles had found great difficulty in obtaining recognition and in holding his own against his rival, Louis of Bavaria. The Empire was itself passing through a crisis, the final episode in its struggle with the Church. The king elected by the German princes only became emperor after being crowned in Rome. But the Pope was at Avignon. Who then was going to consecrate the emperor? In Rome, memories of ancient times were revived and some claimed that, as formerly, the Roman people should award the crown. Charles IV, whom German historians have criticized for neglecting the Empire and showing more interest in Bohemia, in fact strove to reinforce the authority of the Empire and the prestige of the emperor. After his coronation in Rome in 1355, an event that bore little resemblance to the brilliant cavalcade awarded to his grandfather, Henry VII, he convoked a Diet at Nuremberg and promulgated the Golden Bull, which fixed the constitution of the Holy Roman Empire for more than four hundred years. The Bull made no mention of Italy; the Empire, although the heir of Rome and still universal in theory, was to be centred on Germany and the emperor was to be chosen by the seven German electors, three ecclesiastical and four secular princes. By virtue of his royal dignity the king of Bohemia enjoyed primacy among the secular princes. The prerogatives with which the imperial electors were endowed—for example, the privilege of *non appellando*, which made them the supreme judicial authority within their territories—could be used with particular advantage by the king of Bohemia in his own state. Charles IV thus endeavoured to make his kingdom the centre and pivot of the Empire by extending his territorial power, strengthening his authority as king and promoting general prosperity.

He consolidated Bohemia's traditional links with Moravia and, by negotiation and purchase, annexed the duchies of Silesia, Upper Lusatia and Lower Lusatia. The king-emperor would have liked to expand his territories even further by adding Brandenburg and Bavaria. But he had at least created a strong Bohemian state (the kingdom and its incorporated provinces) that would endure the passing of the centuries. It was necessary for the king to impose his will on his subjects and even on the recalcitrant nobility, and so the royal tribunals were reinforced with royal charters. Charles IV's policy of expansion proved very costly; he had constantly to turn to the clergy and nobility for loans or special levies which, by the end of his reign, had practically become annual taxes. It was thus essential to his purpose that his country should be rich, and so he encouraged commercial activity (a subject that will be treated at a later stage). He wished to make Prague the meeting-point of the great international trade-routes linking the markets of western Europe with those of the Mediterranean world. The city's old bridge was rebuilt in stone with a watch-tower at each end. To the east a new quarter was built which extended beyond the line of the ancient ditch and shared the same privileges as the old city. Prague, which was both the capital of the most powerful state of the Empire and the residence of the emperor, was to be invested with the intellectual prestige of a city of learning, to which the best teachers would come and where students from all countries would be educated. In 1348 the university was founded. The creation of an archbishopric at Prague removed the clergy of Bohemia (but not the clergy of the incorporated provinces) from the jurisdiction of the German bishops. A new cathedral designed by a French architect, Matthias d'Arras, was built inside the walls of the royal palace.

As he felt old age advancing, Charles IV decided to pay a final visit to France and the surviving friends and relatives of his youth, and to make the acquaintance of the younger generations. He went to Paris, where he received a dazzling welcome; the royal family was happy to meet an illustrious relative again and the people were delighted by the sight of an emperor. But protocol was followed in scrupulous detail in order to dispel any impression that a suzerain was visiting his vassal: 'the emperor has no right to be called lord of all the world'. King Charles V, though moved by this meeting with his uncle, would not accord him the white horse which emperors were accustomed to ride in the cities of the Empire, 'so that no token of domination could be observed'. The states of the West appreciated the value of symbolism as a means of asserting the fullness of their sovereignty.[7]

The death in Prague of the Emperor Charles IV, in 1378, provides a convenient point at which to take a broad view of the Danubian countries.

Each of these states was already fully conscious of existing in its own right, with its own territory, laws and tradition. In the Christian society of the time—when Christianity had its sublime aspects and its blemishes, on the eve of the Great Schism—tradition expressed itself in the fervour shown to the patron-saints who were identified with the very history of each country: in Austria, St. Leopold; in Hungary, St. Stephen; in Bohemia, St. Wenceslas. The chronicles composed in the monasteries by clerics, who were the first, if not the only repositories of culture, had recorded legends that were now accepted as historical fact. The bishops had encouraged devotion to these saints who, when answers to prayers were interpreted as miracles, became real and living powers involved in public events and in the lives of individuals.

The spiritual power of the clergy was buttressed by great material wealth. By serving their princes as effective and much-feared counsellors and by using the superior techniques made available through access to a broader education, the monks had been able to establish themselves as great landowners. In Austria, Bohemia and Hungary they were among the most powerful proprietors of estates: Benedictines, Cistercians, Augustinians, Premonstratensians, Hospitallers and Templars, all bore the same marks of authority and wealth in each of these countries. Most of the monasteries survived into the period of the Counter-Reformation, when they acquired the Baroque ornamentation visible to the traveller of today, and many of them are still visited by the faithful. To single out Stams and Welten in the Tyrol, Admont and Seckau in Styria, Lambach, Melk, St. Florian, Klosterneuburg, Wilhering and Zwettl in Austria, Ossiach in Carinthia, Teplice, Vyšší Brod, Osek and Zbraslav in Bohemia, and Szentgothárd, Pannonahalma and Pétervárad in Hungary, can give only a vague idea of the abundance of monasteries and the influence they wielded; but each of these names epitomizes several centuries' experience of religious life, hard work and artistic activity. In these establishments famous manuscripts and psalters were patiently copied; in their churches were assembled the jewelled reliquaries of the early Middle Ages and the panels painted in the fourteenth and fifteenth centuries, the Bohemian madonnas on a gold ground, majestic in their tenderness, and the tormented works of the Danubian school.[8]

Similarly, landed property was the mainstay of the political authority of the great lords, and through this they were able both to check the power of the king and to impose their will on a minor nobility which, though less prosperous, was no less proud of its rank. Below the two classes of nobles, the peasantry, far from constituting a single social group, was divided into various degrees of economic well-being, from the prosperous farmer or owner of herds to the poorest cultivators and shepherds.

Meanwhile, the general economic expansion that had been taking place in Europe since the thirteenth century had stimulated the growth of workshops, which in some parts (Flanders and Italy) were beginning to specialize in particular crafts; merchandise was being transported along major trade-routes, through the intermediate towns, to the centres where the annual fairs were held. By the fourteenth century the towns engaged in craft-production and trade were already flourishing and had secured royal privileges which guaranteed them autonomy of administration and control of labour and justice, as in the Italian towns and the imperial cities. There were many of these royal cities in the kingdoms of Bohemia and Hungary, among them the mining towns, such as Kutná Hora in Bohemia, where the silver-mines were worked and coin produced, and also Beszterczebánya and Kolozsvár in Hungary.

The chief articles of commerce were textiles (woollen and linen cloth), which were manufactured in all parts of Europe, though the best cloth came from Flanders and Florence. Every country was a consumer of spices and wines, and the planting of vineyards in Hungary, in Austria and even in Bohemia did not prevent the importation of French and Rhenish wines. Finally, those countries with mines producing salt, iron (Austria and Poland), tin, gold and silver (Bohemia and Hungary) attracted merchants because these products were indispensable for general consumption, for the workshops and for striking coin.

The Danube, from Ulm to Buda in Hungary, was the principal line of communication from west to east. With its bridges at Ulm, Donauwörth, Ratisbon (Regensburg), Passau and Vienna, the river-valley provided the necessary links between Italy (Florence, Milan and Venice) and central Germany, between the Mediterranean world and the North Sea and the Baltic, the home of the Hanseatic

League. The chief overland routes ran from Cologne or Mainz (an intermediate point on the route from France and, in particular, the province of Champagne) to Frankfurt am Main, Würzburg, Bamberg and Nuremberg or Leipzig, and from there roads led into Poland through Saxony (Meissen and Dresden) and Silesia (Breslau). From Cracow there were routes to Lithuania and even Russia.

For reasons of distance and geographical accident, the Alpine valleys of Austria, the quadrilateral of Bohemia and the fertile plains of Hungary had no easy access to these major lines of communication. In the fourteenth century the Danubian countries prospered in so far as they could offer the European economy the products it needed. They neither dominated nor controlled this mercantile economy, in the manner of the great commercial cities of Germany. They did, however, reap the benefits of European trade: to meet the growing demands of customers, business houses had multiplied in these countries, thus guaranteeing the exchange of goods. The workshops, while not producing enough to export in large quantities, helped to satisfy the needs of regional customers, and especially the rural and middle classes. Both in Bohemia and in Hungary the leading firms were in the hands of foreigners, Germans and Italians, many of whom acquired the rights of citizenship. In the eleventh century Hungary had achieved union with the Slav kingdom of Croatia-Slavonia-Dalmatia,[9] thereby obtaining access to the Adriatic; but it was the Venetians and the Greeks who monopolized trade on the Adriatic. Although it thus had a seaboard and a fishing industry, Hungary was not a maritime nation. It traded with the West, both as supplier and as customer, but the problems of distance compelled Hungary to restrict its dealings to immediate neighbours. It is significant that in 1359, to attract the merchants of Ratisbon, King Louis of Anjou offered them a customs privilege to facilitate transport from the Moravian frontier to Buda. Austria and the Alpine counties, with their wooded mountains and valleys, did not possess the immense agricultural resources of the two neighbouring countries. But Vienna occupied an ideal position. Linked by river with Ratisbon and even with Venice, and with Graz, Judenburg and St. Veit an der Glan serving as convenient intermediate stages along the valleys of Styria and Carinthia, the city was a distribution-centre for both Bohemia and Hungary. Vienna had also been made an imperial city and was therefore more independent of its dukes than were the other capitals *vis-à-vis* their kings.

F. Graus has recently demonstrated that in the reign of Charles IV the mineral wealth and agricultural production of Bohemia placed that country in a particularly advantageous position without, however, preventing its trade from remaining largely passive. Bohemia imported salt, herrings, cattle and cheap Polish cloth for general consumption; exports comprised grain, wood, wax and hides, textiles (sent to Vienna) and, in particular, silver coin and tin.[10]

Thus, in order to supply the upper classes with luxury goods, which consisted chiefly of expensive textiles, table-wines, fabrics from the East, spices and high-quality manufactured articles, Bohemia depended on imports from abroad. Moreover, the outflow of strong currency (the gold that the Holy See exacted from the churches in the form of annates and various other dues, and the silver drained from the country by merchants and speculators) was hardly compensated by the influx of light coin from Saxony and Austria, the currency used in ordinary transactions. This situation was aggravated to some extent by Charles IV's policies, so beneficial to the country in other respects. The heavy expenditure involved in the acquisition of fiefs in German territories diverted large sums of hard currency from the kingdom of Bohemia. Furthermore, the king-emperor needed the support of the towns and especially that of the rich middle class of Prague, wealthy patricians (many of them naturalized Germans) who made their fortunes in the import business and had no desire to see an improvement in the volume and still less in the quality of local production. Consequently, Bohemian production lagged behind that of other countries, Germany in particular. Public opinion could not understand such things: the upsurge in consumption at all levels of society guaranteed the workshops of Bohemia a clientele large enough to induce a general feeling of progress and well-being. But Bohemia was in no position to capture the foreign markets. Finally, although control of the Elbe and Oder waterways should have facilitated Bohemia's relations with the Hanse towns and northern Europe, trading activity was obstructed along the lower reaches of these rivers by the Saxon towns and by Frankfurt-an-der-Oder, which demanded transit duties. Bohemia's commercial dealings were therefore concentrated in the regions that lay near its frontiers. The economy of the country was being pushed back in the direction of Brno and Vienna: its links were with the lands of the Danube rather than with northern Germany.

The advantages and disadvantages of Prague's situation were thus nicely balanced. The city was better placed to be the political capital of the Holy Roman Empire than to become its economic centre. In the splendour of its setting, with the tall outlines of the old city's Gothic churches—St. Mary Týn, St. James, St. Giles and St. Havel—the sober beauty of its patrician houses and, on the other side of the river, the castle towering above the Malá Strana, Prague owed its brilliance to its dual position as the seat of the university and the residence of the emperor. Not far away in his castle of Karlštejn, which served both as fortress and as palace, Charles IV assembled his collection of precious fabrics and gold and silver plate. On the walls of his palace he hung the striking portraits painted by Theodorik. Vienna, the capital of a less prosperous country of mountains and forestland, occupied a key position on the Danube, at the intersection of the continental trade-routes and a great waterway. A free city (though the duke of Austria had established himself in residence there), Vienna could also boast a university, created in 1365 by Rudolf IV Habsburg, the Founder. Finally, the city of Buda towered above the Danube at the most majestic part of the river's course. Inside the fortress the Angevin kings had built state rooms and a chapel in keeping with the grandeur of a royal residence and the life of a civilized court. This was a period of progress, which historians have called a Golden Age. Archaeologists are now clearing the ruins of the old palace and bringing to light other buildings dating from the reign of King Sigismund. The city stood on the fringe of western Europe and depended on the neighbouring countries for its share of prosperity; even then, the benefits it received were only partial and slow to take effect. Yet, as a result of the interweaving of Germanic and Italian influences and the impression made on local traditions by new ways of life, a civilization was blossoming which was common to the entire Danubian world and at the same time allowed individual peoples to preserve their own special character.

In the fourteenth century, Hungary enjoyed a commercial prosperity manifested by the activity of its markets and fairs and by the output of the craft workshops. The royal cities (Buda, Pest, Pozsony, Szeged) enjoyed a privileged status, while the smaller towns, many of which came under the jurisdiction of a landowner, noble or ecclesiastical, possessed fewer rights and sought promotion to the rank of royal city. At an early stage in its history the territory of Hungary had been divided up, in the German manner, into comitats or counties endowed with relative autonomy. In its political structure Hungary was already an aristocratic state whose elected king was merely the military chief, supreme judge and administrator accepted by the privileged order. Gradually the doctrine had been elaborated of a Mystical Body whose head was the Holy Crown of Hungary, the hierarchical symbol of the State, and whose members were the privileged. Only the prince elected by the Diet could claim to be king, and only from the moment he received the royal crown from the hands of the primate-archbishop. Since the time when the daughter of King Louis of Anjou had been recognized as *king* on the death of her father, in 1382, women had been eligible for the Holy Crown. The Diet comprised two chambers: the magnates (secular and ecclesiastical) and the delegates nominated by the counties. In accordance with the Golden Bull issued by Andrew II in 1222, the Diet had to be convoked annually by the king, who presided over the assembly, or, when this was not possible, by the palatine, who had originally been the lord chief justice but had become a kind of viceroy mediating between the sovereign and the Diet. The Diet voted taxes and also all new measures, which thereby acquired the force of constitutional laws. The Golden Bull had also recognized the *jus resistendi*, the right to oppose the king if he should issue a command contrary to written tradition. To enable people of different languages to understand one another, Latin had been made obligatory at the Diet and had assumed the status of the kingdom's official language; this does not mean, however, that by the end of the Middle Ages Hungarian (or Magyar) did not possess the characteristics of a civilized language.

In Transylvania the status of 'nation' had been granted to two groups, the Germans who had settled in the towns and the Szekels, a branch of the Finno-Ugrian race; but the term must not be understood in the modern sense or confused with the idea of nationality. The 'nations' were those groups recognized by the universities in the classification of teachers and students, and not all the members of these groups enjoyed the same advantages; only those privileged by wealth, juridical status and birth derived any real benefit. This system of laws was jealously guarded by those whose influence it served to maintain. It bore a certain resemblance to the constitution of the German Empire and to that of Poland. Yet, in spite of its immediate proximity, Hungary had retained complete independence *vis-à-vis* the Empire, though this was partially offset by the allegiance Hungary owed to the

Holy See in return for the support which it had received in the struggle against ambitious emperors.

The general history of Hungary up to the time of the Dual Monarchy can only be understood if one essential fact is remembered: this kingdom was never a fief of the Empire and always regarded the Empire as a foreign state to which it owed nothing.

❧

Two series of events had a decisive influence on the destinies of the countries of central Europe in the fifteenth century: the Hussite movement in Bohemia and the Turkish menace. The Hussite movement was one of the symptoms of the religious and social crisis through which the whole of Christendom was passing; for geographical reasons, the Turkish menace chiefly affected Hungary, a country with which Europe, preoccupied with its own troubles, was slow to recognize its deep bonds of solidarity.

The prosperity of Bohemia in the time of Charles IV and the intense activity of the University of Prague, with its four 'nations' (Bohemia, Saxony, Bavaria and Poland) enjoying the same rights, explain why these countries should have been caught up in one of the most serious upheavals in the history of Christianity. The author has no intention of tracing the course of the Hussite movement in detail, or of pronouncing a final judgement on a crisis which has provoked the same passionate controversy among later historians as it did at the time of the events themselves. It nevertheless remains profoundly true that, before acquiring political or social overtones, the protest of John Huss was religious in inspiration, an act of faith dictated by a Christian conscience.[11]

John Huss found his priest's conscience agonized at the sight of the evils that were infiltrating the Church and the Christian world. He was filled with the conviction of a man of learning intent on breaking the fetters imposed on him by the methods of scholastic theology. He placed his greatest hope in the renewal of the spiritual life, and in his preaching urged the people to join with him in this. He was scandalized by the excessive wealth of the Prague clergy and the ossification of a society in which the privileged orders clung ever more firmly to their rights. It so happened that, among the clergy as in the secular society of Bohemia, the positions of power had been monopolized by the Germans; the less fortunate strata of society consisted of the Czechs, including minor nobility and peasantry. Because they were poor and, consequently, closer to those whom Christ had specially favoured, the Czechs were the first to be invited by Huss to listen to the word of God.

Such, then, was the spiritual and social climate in which the great Hussite movement developed. John Huss, renowned as the first reformer of modern times and inspired with the ardour of the apostle and rebel, was a revolutionary neither in intention nor in fact. One of his more recent historians, Father de Vooght, is doubtless right in maintaining that, at a time when truth had been obscured and when there must have been a strong temptation to approach the problems of the day in

14

a revolutionary spirit, Huss should be given credit for having treated those problems in conformity with scripture and tradition, which indeed remained the very essence of his preaching. Above all, Huss revered St. Paul and St. Augustine, allowing them an authority he never conceded to Wycliffe, whose treatises he had studied, but whose opinions on the Eucharist and the true nature of the Church he was far from sharing.

In some of his bolder ideas and especially in his passion for scripture, Huss broke away from scholastic theology, but he continued to adopt its methods of thought and argument. Consequently, his teachings, both oral and written, betrayed an element of uncertainty and even contradiction. It seems improbable that Huss was condemned primarily because he was a realist, whereas the German theologians of Prague were nominalists, since neither of these positions was considered to involve a doctrinal truth and could not therefore be rejected as heresy. The real danger for Huss lay in the antagonism that existed between Germans and Czechs in Prague itself. This conflict resulted in the decree of Kutná Hora (1409) which reorganized the constitution of the university, allowing the Czech 'nation' three votes and the other three 'nations' only one vote. Huss was elected rector of the reformed university, whereupon some of the German teachers left the country and went to Leipzig to found a new establishment. Huss was anxious above all to purge the Church of its scandals; against the material wealth of the clergy, the interference of the civil power, and simony, he set the poverty preached in the Gospels. In his treatise on the Church he distinguished between the *congregatio fidelium* or organized Church and the *universitas praedestinatorum* of which Wycliffe had spoken, and which signified the assembly of the predestined and the pure in union with Jesus Christ. Immediately he found himself in collision with the Bohemian hierarchy, who excommunicated him and suspended him *a divinis*.

The intellectual and moral attitude of John Huss was nothing new in Bohemia. During the most prosperous years of Charles IV's reign the seeds of conflict had already been sown between the Bohemian hierarchy and the Roman Curia, on the one hand, and, on the other, a clergy of scholars, the religious orders who were the repositories of theological learning and who defended doctrine from a position untrammelled by worldly compromise. The emperor had been inclined in favour of the clergy of scholars. The controversy that sprang up around John Huss also reflected the antagonism between Czechs and Germans, an antagonism that was social as much as national in origin. Yet a number of Czech theologians, who had been disciples of Huss, were among his most active adversaries and were responsible for drawing up the list of errors that was to destroy him. Huss was irreproachable in his moral principles and in no circumstances would have wanted to break either with the Church or with the Pope. Although it is true that Huss, like Marsilio of Padua and William of Ockham before him, regarded the Papacy as subordinate to a General Council, he never questioned the necessity of the Pope's presence at the head of the Church.

But institutions could not be efficacious if their human representatives were not pure Christians. Huss therefore maintained that mortal sin and scandal deprived both Pope and bishops of their right to obedience from the faithful. The spectacle which the organized Church presented at this time was a cause for despair to a great many people throughout Europe. Since 1378 Christendom had been split by the Great Schism. There had been two popes, one at Rome, the other at Avignon, and when the Council of Pisa had attempted to restore unity to the Church by securing the submission of the two rivals and the election of a new pontiff, there were three popes instead of two. The so-called Pope John XXIII, successor to the pope elected at Pisa, offered indulgences for sale to collect the money he needed in order to wage war on the other two popes. Huss preached against the indulgences. He had such great faith in the necessity for reform and in the authority of scripture, as he interpreted it, that no sentence that might be passed on him could compel him to silence. He believed that, by submitting, he would himself have been guilty of sin.

The affair ended in tragedy. The Emperor Sigismund wanted to see religious peace restored in Europe, with one Church, one undisputed territory and one undisputed emperor. He persuaded John XXIII (who was hoping to be established as the true pope) to convene a council at Constance. Huss, whose excommunication had been lifted and who had been provided with a guarantee of safe conduct, agreed to attend the council and to defend himself. When the council condemned forty-five propositions of Wycliffe, Huss found himself in a dangerous position. He was confronted with a list of his errors and ordered to retract them. His theses had certainly been misunderstood and badly translated. However, far from diverting the fury of his enemies, he only succeeded in antagonizing the council by the manner in which he defended himself, obstinately declaring that he had never taught anything which could not be found in the Gospels and that no authority would prevent him from believing and spreading the word of Jesus. Gerson saw Huss as a rebel, whose rebellion was itself a form of heresy and who was aggravating the troubles in the Church at a time when both doctrine and discipline needed to be re-established. Huss was given over to the secular authorities and was sentenced to be burnt at the stake on 6 July 1415. His quiet courage surprised and moved those present at his death.

The news of his martyrdom aroused widespread indignation in Bohemia, where he had enjoyed great popularity. The nobles of Bohemia and Moravia—both the higher and the lower nobility—protested against the execution of the rector of Prague University. Theologians at the university insisted on the purity of his teachings which, they claimed, contained the only principles that could raise Christianity from its ruins. They demanded freedom in preaching, communion in both kinds for all the faithful (the chalice had hitherto been reserved for the clergy), the confiscation of monastery lands and punishment by the state authorities of mortal sins. King Václav IV, both weak and brutal, was quite incapable of pacifying this general uprising of his kingdom. He died in 1419. He was succeeded by his brother, the Emperor Sigismund, who had been present at the condemnation of John Huss. Sigismund, anxious to quell the agitation in Bohemia, persuaded Pope Martin V to place the kingdom under anathema and to issue a bull of crusade. The Czechs were becoming more and more indignant at these attacks against them and gathered together an army whose leader, Žižka of Trocnov, a member of the minor nobility, proved himself a redoubtable warrior. They defeated the army of crusaders. Although all classes of Bohemian society had taken part in the defence of their country with heroic fervour (further crusading expeditions in 1426, 1427 and 1431 also met with failure), differences of opinion began to appear within Bohemia. People were disturbed by the violent acts of the soldiers who had remained loyal to the memory of Žižka (he had died in 1424), by the fanaticism with which they attacked and destroyed monasteries and by the social reforms demanded by the Tábor party (named after the new town where Žižka had set up his army headquarters). It was not the well-to-do who were afraid, as has been suggested by historians who now view the Hussite wars merely as a class-struggle, but those people who still preserved the idea of a national state, who saw their country reduced to anarchy and terrorism and cherished the hope that the Church could be regenerated by the spirit of John Huss.

Prague, where cultivated men capable of moderation and political wisdom existed in large numbers, became increasingly opposed to the Taborite party. There were also many Catholics who had remained loyal to the Church. Learning from the failure of the crusades, the Pope and the emperor inclined towards a compromise solution. The Diet of Bohemia and the Curia entered into negotiations. At the Council of Basle the Hussite delegates, whose spokesman was the Utraquist priest John Rokycana, were allowed to put forward their theses and defend their cause without encountering the prejudice and bad faith which had brought about the downfall of John Huss. In 1434, on the battlefield of Lipany, the army of the Diet inflicted a decisive defeat on the Taborites. Two years later, at the Council of Basle, the *Compactata* were signed: the Czechs were readmitted into the Church with a guarantee that they would be allowed to retain their own rites and, in particular, receive communion under both kinds, *sub utraque specie*, to which they attached the greatest importance. This achievement would have seemed more complete if Rome had made Rokycana a bishop to erase any taint of heresy that might still be associated with the Hussites. In fact, there were henceforth two Catholic Churches in Bohemia: one, of Roman obedience, headed by the archbishop; the other, of the Utraquist rite, under Rokycana, parish-priest of the main church in the old city, St. Mary Týn. But peace appeared to have been firmly re-established between them and, indeed, throughout the country.

Meanwhile, the years of struggle against the foreign powers—namely the Curia and the emperor, which seemed to indicate that the principles of Church and Empire were becoming alienated from Bohemian territory—and the military effort which those years had produced, together with the social convulsions of this period, had kindled in the people's consciousness a sense of autonomy, of national solidarity, that was to give the Czechs a new moral strength. Even those who had detested and resisted the violence of the Taborites had cause to cherish the glorious memory of the one-eyed warrior, his bold and resolute soldiers and lieutenants with their fine war-chariots and their battle-song, the *Soldiers of God*. The Czech nation had forced itself on the attention of Europe. It had asserted itself in the face of 'the other', who might be the king (even if the king were also emperor), the Church (either pope or council) or a foreign neighbour (the

Germans, both in Bohemia itself and in the Empire). No doubt, the romanticism of the nineteenth century, in reviving and dramatizing memories of the Hussite troubles, exaggerated the extent to which the national spirit of the Czechs could be identified with the tradition of Huss or Žižka and the Taborites. Later, Tábor became the magic word (though used in a quite different sense) which symbolized the democratic programme of Thomas G. Masaryk and the socialist programme of Z. Nejedlý. But the exaggerations of subsequent ages would not have been possible if popular tradition had not, over the centuries, kept alive the memory of the tragic years when the Czechs broke away from the rest of Europe and endured great suffering on behalf of an ideal. Moreover, the Hussite crisis was soon followed by a return to hard work and a new surge of production in the towns. The economic structure changed: the corporations, whose growth had been checked by the merchant patricians, assumed greater power and the towns regained their former prosperity.

The confiscation of ecclesiastical properties had been to the advantage of the nobility: many estates remained in the hands of the barons, but a large number had also been acquired by the second order of nobles, the knights.

Bohemia's political reconciliation with the Emperor Sigismund did not last long, as the emperor died in 1437. He left as his heir a daughter, married to Albert, duke of Austria, whom he had seen crowned king of Hungary during his lifetime. In 1438 Albert was elected king of the Romans. Two parties now confronted one another in Bohemia. The Utraquists, led by Rokycana and the most influential noble of the group, Ptáček of Pernštejn, wanted the Diet to vote for the brother of the king of Poland; the Catholics, from the moment that Albert II promised to ratify the *Compactata*, thereby guaranteeing their religious status, agreed to vote for him in the belief that he was the candidate most likely to preserve the peace of the kingdom. The Catholics were victorious; for the first time a Habsburg prince found himself in possession of Hungary, Bohemia and Austria, and also the imperial crown. But the general situation made it impossible for Albert to embark on any kind of unified policy. He was merely the sovereign of juxtaposed territories.

The strange destiny of Albert's posthumous son Ladislas, who was born at Székesféhervár in Hungary, in 1440, and died at Prague in 1457, revealed during those seventeen years that the monarchic principle had not yet matured sufficiently to bind together peoples who, though ruled by the same king, recognized him as their natural prince only separately. The unfortunate Ladislas, who was by no means dull-witted, became the pawn and hostage of the nobles in each of the lands he ruled.

Ladislas was to become entangled in the history of Austria, Bohemia and Hungary and also in the family history of the Habsburg dynasty. As soon as he was born his mother had him crowned king, but subsequently the Hungarian Diet questioned the validity of the coronation and nominated another prince, Wladislas of Poland. Albert's widow then fled to Austria with the child-king and also the Holy Crown, without which no one could claim to reign legitimately in Hungary. Four years later, when Wladislas had been killed at Varna during the Turkish war, the

Hungarians once more recognized Ladislas as their sovereign; but neither Ladislas nor the Holy Crown was in Hungary. In Vienna, where Ladislas had inherited his father's duchies, the lawful regent was the nearest male relation, Frederick of Styria. Frederick realized the importance of the powers entrusted to him. In Bohemia, the Utraquist and Catholic nobles had clashed over the choice of a successor to Albert II. George of Podiebrad, an Utraquist lord, occupied Prague and secured the recognition of Ladislas as king, by virtue of the precedent favouring the son of the last monarch, although heredity was not admitted as an established rule. It was necessary that the king should be crowned in Prague and should take up residence there. Podiebrad negotiated with Frederick and succeeded in having Ladislas returned to Prague. The young prince thus grew up, disputed by his various states, quite incapable of governing any of them himself and therefore powerless to establish any kind of link between them. Podiebrad tried to use Ladislas in an attempt to extend Bohemia's alliances and the kingdom's prestige in Europe; in 1457, shortly after he had secured Ladislas' betrothal to Madeleine of France, daughter of Charles VII, the young king died of tuberculosis in his Czech capital.

After hesitating between various foreign sovereigns as candidates, the Diet of Bohemia gave a majority of votes to Podiebrad himself. The Bohemian throne was now occupied by a king who was both a Czech and a Hussite. But circumstances prevented Podiebrad from laying too much emphasis on either the national or the religious character of his reign. Measures of a provocative nature were out of the question. To maintain the upsurge in production and in the progress made by the towns, and to extend trade, it was essential to preserve peace with Bohemia's closest neighbours and in particular with the kingdom of Hungary. The public good of his realm—an ideal often invoked by Podiebrad—compelled him to seek alliances abroad, especially since his enemies at home would have no difficulty in finding their own allies. A man of Oldřich of Rožmberk's status could negotiate almost on a footing with the kings of Poland and Hungary.

Pius II, the humanist pope who knew the countries of the Danube by personal experience and had a special affection for Vienna, where he had stayed and whose culture he had helped to promote, regarded the *Compactata* as a salutary but temporary expedient which, he hoped, would bring the Utraquists of Bohemia back to the Roman rite. In parts of the country the peasants became converts to Illuminism; prophets sprang up and Rokycana had cause to fear schisms within the Hussite Church itself. He looked on Peter Chelčický's preachings for a return to the primitive Church as a dangerous revival of Taborism.

Finally, if George of Podiebrad wanted to preserve the integrity of his kingdom, it was vital that he should gain control over the towns of Silesia, the population of which was German. His policy was to be conciliatory, in order that Catholics and Utraquists, Czechs and Germans, should be persuaded to consider themselves all Bohemians and to contribute jointly to the prosperity of the kingdom. Bohemia's bonds with the Empire were numerous and practically indissoluble. The Empire's currencies were circulating in Bohemia simultaneously with the kingdom's own currencies, and so one of Podiebrad's advisers urged him to stabilize the situation by unifying the monetary system and granting large loans to merchants. Podiebrad was a peacemaker as much by necessity as by temperament. He sought to establish friendly relations both with Poland and with Hungary, and in 1464 sent messengers to King Louis XI with proposals for a treaty of alliance and a peace league. Henceforth the states of Europe would submit their differences to arbitration. Neither the Pope nor the emperor was to be involved in this organization. But Podiebrad had no intention of using it as a weapon against the emperor: on the contrary, he would have liked to become the emperor's deputy, and in Austria had supported him against the nobility. He also hoped that this association of European princes would exert an indirect influence on the Pope. However, the weakness of the Utraquist group and the spread of other sects in Bohemia encouraged the Roman Curia to put an end to divisions. The Curia demanded that the *Compactata* be abandoned and that the two Bohemian clergies be merged. Podiebrad could not consent to this without the risk of losing the support of part of the Czech nation, and at the same time the resistance of the Catholic nobles and the German towns was hardening. Furthermore, he was a sincere devotee of the Hussite movement. He had therefore to resign himself to war. Paul III excommunicated him and entrusted the crusade to the king of Hungary, Matthias Corvinus.

Despite his military successes, Podiebrad was forced to abandon Moravia, Silesia and Lusatia to Matthias, who had himself crowned king of Bohemia at Olmütz. George of Podiebrad did not believe that his sons would be able to wield the authority necessary to continue his work and to rectify his failures in a kingdom that had been reduced to the single territory of Bohemia. To prevent an interregnum he had his successor elected during his lifetime, choosing the son of the king of Poland, Wladislas Jagellon. Since he had been thwarted in his imperial ambitions, he wanted to be able to count on an alliance with a northern Slav prince. Podiebrad died in 1471.

᠅

The Turkish menace was the second dominant factor in the history of the Danubian countries in the fourteenth and fifteenth centuries. This was no prolonged brutal assault, despite the sieges and battles, but rather a process of gradual infiltration in which advantage was taken of the conditions peculiar to eastern Europe and of the religious and political crises in which the West found itself embroiled (the Hundred Years' War, the conflicts between Church and Empire, the Great Schism), and which prevented men from perceiving the danger that threatened Christendom. Even the successes of the Angevin dynasty in Hungary facilitated the Turkish advance by the rivalries they provoked.

Two Hungarian kings of French origin and Italian culture—Charles and, in particular, Louis I—conceived great schemes for their kingdom, conducting a policy of intervention in all directions. Among other things—and only among other things—they aimed at imposing their tutelage on the Balkan principalities, which lay between the kingdom of Hungary and the Greek Empire. Here, however, they were obstructed by the prince of Serbia, Stephen Dushan, who in the middle of the century subjugated Albania, Macedonia and Thessaly and proclaimed himself emperor of the Serbs and Greeks. Louis I, determined to retain Bosnia within his alliance, could not avoid conflict with Stephen Dushan. He defeated Dushan but then found himself at odds with Venice, which disputed Hungarian control of the Dalmatian coast.

During these years the Ottomans, who had consolidated their power in Asia, attempted to establish a footing in Europe, not by a violent invasion, like the Tatars whom they were fighting in the East, but by stealing their way gradually, taking advantage of the dissensions that were weakening the decadent Byzantine Empire and seeking allies among the Christians themselves. Their first success was in gaining a foothold at Gallipoli (1357), on the shore of the Bosporus opposite Constantinople; then they attacked Adrianople and made it the capital of a European territory; from there they had little difficulty in invading Bulgaria and Serbia. Their first clash with the Hungarians took place in 1366, but Louis I was far too preoccupied with events in Italy and Poland (where he was crowned king in 1370) to see this engagement with the Ottoman troops as anything more than an incident of the kind that had been common with the Serbs and Bulgars.

The Christian states of the Balkans differed from the Western countries in their religious attitudes. They did not make such a clear-cut distinction between the infidel and the heretic. They might well have resisted in a body, if they had been supported by a foreign army. The Ottoman policy presented them with a choice between an open war, which they could not hope to win, and a pact of expediency that offered important immediate advantages to compensate for its drawbacks. Admittedly, they had to pay tribute, but they were offered alliances and even guaranteed Ottoman protection against any close rival. In 1365 the little republic of Ragusa received confirmation of its commercial freedom in return for an annual tribute. When the occasion arose, the Greek emperor even became the ally of the Ottoman. At Constantinople, however, the Turkish menace was regarded with apprehension, although it was diverted whenever the incursions of the Tatars or the uprisings of subjugated populations called the sultan back into Asia.

At Adrianople the sultans organized their European kingdom. They created hereditary fiefs for their knights (the *spahis*) and on these domains the Christians (*raïas*) were allowed to keep the lands they cultivated and to hand them down to their sons. Those Christians who undertook to serve in the Turkish army were exempted from paying tribute. The Greek emperor insisted on appealing to the West for assistance. Pope Gregory XI proclaimed a crusade in 1373, but King Louis did not respond until 1377, and even then failed to take advantage of his military successes. After his death in 1382 the problems of the succession prevented Hungary from taking any further offensive in the Balkans.

In 1389 the tsars Lazar of Serbia and Simeon of Bulgaria decided that the moment had come to attack Sultan Murad; but they were both defeated. The Serbian defeat at Kossovo was all the more serious because Lazar had secured the alliance of Bosnia, Albania and Wallachia, and his troops far outnumbered those of Sultan Murad. When Louis I's son-in-law, Sigismund of Luxemburg, who had been recognized as king of Hungary in 1387, found himself with greater freedom to manoeuvre, he tried to halt Sultan Beyazit Ildirim, Murad's son and successor, in his advance into Bulgaria. Sigismund appealed to Pope Boniface VIII, to Venice and to the king of France, Charles VI. A great crusader army with contingents from all the Western countries, totalling some sixty thousand men, set off for the Danube. At Nicopolis, on the banks of the river, the crusaders suffered a defeat that instilled terror in the Western countries. Sigismund fled on a boat down the Danube and then went on to Constantinople; the commander of the French contingent, the count of Nevers (later to be John the Fearless), more fortunate than the ten thousand Christians who were beheaded, was granted his life. The sultan received him with courtesy and invited him to join a hawking expedition which was of such splendour that the count, accustomed to the luxury of Western courts, realized that the West could not match the ceremony of the East and that the Ottomans, reputedly a barbarous power, had in fact captured all the magnificence and refinements of the civilizations of Islam.

Turkish troops made incursions into Hungary and Styria, but their successes were short-lived. However, there could no longer be any doubt that the Turks had established themselves solidly in the Balkan peninsula and that, sooner or later, Byzantium would be theirs. The Danube once again became the *limes* between two worlds: this time it was on the north side of the frontier that the heritage of Rome and of Christianity awaited the onslaught of its adversaries. Hungary was the last great state to remain free: the fate of the rest of Europe might depend on the success or failure of its defence.

This defensive role was, admittedly, shared by Venice, but an alliance between two countries that were quarrelling over Dalmatia seemed fraught with difficulties. If the king of Hungary wanted to gain time (the Turks were not always reluctant to call a truce), he needed to placate the sultan with promises and gifts and to give his protection to the princes of Wallachia and Serbia, at least as long as they did not use him as a weapon against the sultan, or the sultan as a weapon against himself. But a policy of this kind, based on cunning and subterfuge, could offer only a temporary respite.

The alternative was to wage war. This state of perpetual alert, though its effects were felt only indirectly within the kingdom of Hungary, helped to foster a military spirit and a taste for adventure and individual prowess among the Hungarians and the Croats, and at the same time to make the Hungarian army into a first-class cavalry of high repute. The Turk was feared. The organization of the Turkish state had already acquired a flexibility and efficiency which could teach the European countries a great deal. Yet it was not this which most impressed itself on Hungarian opinion. Other influences were at work among the Hungarians, and it is not easy to see which was the most powerful. First of all, a religious ideal was at stake. The sultans led the Muslim peoples off to battle with proclamations of a holy war, pointing to the verses of the Koran in which Allah blessed the subjugation of unbelievers as a necessary and meritorious act. The confrontation was one between Christendom and Islam: in a mental climate in which ardour of faith brought fanaticism in its wake, political and economic interests were subordinated, even though they remained important and led to truce and compromise when the battle was over. Secondly, Hungary knew of the cruelties inflicted by the Turks both in battle and afterwards. The severed heads of Christian military chiefs taken prisoner (even if they did not all suffer this death), the humiliation and thirst for vengeance nurtured by the victims' families, the raids in which women were abducted to fill the Turkish harems (the Orientals were much attracted by Western womanhood), the plundering of harvests and cattle, the destruction of churches and mutilation of images in conquered villages—all this was indisputable fact and, although the historian can point to compensating factors which were not recognized at the time, endowed the Turk with the reputation of a fierce and implacable adversary to be resisted in a struggle to the death.

The Hungarian nobility thus assumed the role of champion of Christendom, destined to drive off the Turkish onslaught. The nobles, who held the effective power in the kingdom, committed themselves to a mighty and efficacious military effort embodied in the figure of Hunyadi János (John Hunyadi). Hunyadi was born around 1407 into a Wallachian family that had moved to Transylvania and had there been granted the fief of Vajadahunyad; after entering into the personal service of Sigismund, who sent him to be educated at the court of Milan, and firmly establishing himself in the aristocratic society of the kingdom by his marriage to a member of the Szilágyi family, this young noble was appointed commander of the fortress at Belgrade, with authority over the neighbouring regions, and then governor of Transylvania, where he routed a large Turkish offensive. He then set about preparing the great campaign of 1443, the purpose of which was to liberate Serbia and which proved successful until interrupted by the winter. Western Christendom believed that in Hunyadi it had found the much-needed saviour, and the Pope thought in terms of a crusade. But the fervour of the knights was frustrated by commercial interests: the Genoese Republic traded with the Turks and had no desire to break off relations. When they found themselves deprived of the support they had been expecting, the Hungarians wondered if it was really worth resuming the struggle. They concluded a truce. Hunyadi decided to break the truce and re-opened hostilities, insisting that King Wladislas ride at the head of the army. The Hungarians marched as far as Varna, in Bulgaria, but Sultan Murad attacked them with a large army that was all the more resolute for having been assigned the mission of punishing Hunyadi's perfidy. The Turks emerged victorious from a chaotic brawl and the head of King Wladislas, who was killed on the battlefield, was sent to Brusa as a trophy. The Diet of 1446 restored the throne to Ladislas the Posthumous; but, since the child-king had taken refuge in Austria, Hunyadi was made regent and it was he who exercised the real powers of kingship. The task of governing was not an easy one: in Austria, Bohemia and Hungary the nobles were challenging one another for dominance and forming rival factions; at the same time, each country wanted its young king to take up residence on its own territory. While this rivalry and confusion absorbed the attention of central Europe and prevented it from undertaking joint action against Islam, Scanderbeg was organizing an uprising in Albania. Then, in 1453, Mahomet II captured Constantinople. Pope Calixtus III launched a pathetic appeal to the Christian world. Every day at noon, throughout the West, church bells sounded, urging the people to pray for military success. The Hungarians had once again to bear the brunt of the war. In

1456 Hunyadi repulsed a Turkish assault on Belgrade: this encounter between a Christian army inspired by the eloquence of the Franciscan friar, John Capistrano, and a Muslim army waging a holy war was one of the momentous events in the confrontation of the two worlds. Christendom triumphed, but Hunyadi, exhausted by the effort, died a few days after his victory. Hunyadi was one of the rare men of his time, for whom the struggle against Islam had been both a chivalrous ideal and a political goal, both of which purposes held priority over all others. In the following year Ladislas the Posthumous died in his palace in Prague. Just as Podiebrad had finally succeeded in acquiring the throne of Bohemia, so the Diet of Hungary chose as its king Matthias, the second son of Hunyadi János.

Matthias Hunyadi Corvinus—the very name is a majestic symbol of tradition—was assuredly one of the most remarkable sovereigns of Hungarian history. He was destined by his family background to fight the Turk and he carried on the military achievements of his father by liberating part of Bosnia. He did not, however, make the struggle against Islam the chief purpose of his activities. It could even be said that he tilted Hungarian policy in the direction of the West, to the point of being momentarily tempted by the imperial crown. Moreover, the rejuvenation and interior consolidation of Hungary made an attack by the Turks more hazardous and therefore less probable.

It is possible that Matthias Hunyadi's shift of policy had its origins in his personal experience. After the death of his father, in the confusion caused by the rivalries among the great noble families, Matthias was taken away as a hostage and virtually held prisoner by King Ladislas, first in Vienna, then in Prague. In these two cities he witnessed a civilization that seemed more advanced than that of Hungary: more fine buildings, more evidence of wealth among the inhabitants, a more effective administration and a more coherent policy. In his eyes Hungary appeared a backward country whose resources were no longer being utilized to promote general prosperity or to make great enterprises possible. In Prague, Matthias was present at the celebrations in preparation for the young king's marriage and also at his death. When the Hungarian delegation came to tell him that the Diet was summoning him to ascend the throne, the young Hunyadi did not hesitate to promise the ransom which Podiebrad demanded in return for allowing him to leave; neither did he hesitate to accept Podiebrad's offer of his daughter's hand, a gesture which Podiebrad made as a token of alliance, though he hoped that his son-in-law would be his vassal. As soon as he had installed himself in Buda, Matthias made it known to the Hungarian nobles, and even to his uncle Szilágyi, that he intended to rule and to be obeyed, whereupon the nobles decided to reverse their vote and to nominate in his place the Emperor Frederick III. The emperor had in his possession in Vienna the Holy Crown of St. Stephen which Ladislas had entrusted to his care: Matthias was as yet only 'a king in a hat'.

After four years, thanks to the mediation of Pope Pius II, Matthias managed to come to an understanding with the emperor and paid him sixty thousand gold pieces. In return, Frederick, while retaining the dignity of king of Hungary among his titles, gave back the Holy Crown. Matthias was crowned and his power legitimized. But he felt that he would only be strong if he had a strong army. He did not believe that the cavalry of nobles, as it then existed, would prove effective enough; in 1458, therefore, he compelled the minor nobility to provide henceforth one knight for every twenty heads of family, and in 1465 one for every ten heads of family. These knights would serve for a period of three months, sometimes beyond Hungary's own frontiers. However, since the nobility was to be called up only in the event of war being declared and since he needed a permanent body of troops, Matthias formed an army of mercenaries, twenty thousand cavalry and ten thousand infantry, recruited among the foreigners most experienced in war, the Germans and the Czechs. The Black Army, as the new force was called, was to be one of the guarantees of the king's military success and his personal reputation. Matthias now needed the resources to maintain these forces and to support his bellicose policies. The Diet refused to vote new taxes, particularly because this would constitute a threat to the minor nobility, especially its poorest members: those nobles unable to provide knights for the king's service would be deprived of their fiscal immunity, hitherto their privilege and material safeguard. Matthias solved the problem by dispensing with the consent of the Diet. To succeed in this he needed to be able to rely on the loyalty of the officials in the comitats or counties, and to satisfy his people with an equitable judicial system. He therefore strengthened the authority of the *föispán*, his representative in the county, and also that of a college of judges where the members chosen by the nobles were outnumbered by the *homini regis*. Although the personnel employed were local nobles, this measure represented an attempt at centralization; appeals were heard by the *tabula regia judicaria* and the most serious cases were reserved for the king, assisted by members of his council. In this way, Matthias Hunyadi acquired the reputation of a champion of justice which made him a popular figure in the least privileged strata of society and which established his legend on firm foundations.[12]

The concepts of military power, princely authority and justice were not derived solely from Matthias' own innate practical sagacity. They had their roots in the humanism of the time, which, though by no means unfamiliar in Hungary, Matthias had been able to appreciate more fully in Vienna and Prague and which was radiating from Italy over Western Europe. Vitéz, the archbishop of Esztergom, whose predecessors had been Italians, had already established communication with Aeneas Sylvius Piccolomini (Pius II) and had gathered together a large library. By the end of his reign Matthias' own library comprised fifty-five thousand items—illuminated manuscripts, incunabula and all the literature of Greek and Latin antiquity then known to the world. The collection was dispersed after his death, which was perhaps fortunate, since the subsequent pillaging and burning of Buda would probably have destroyed the library and the world would thus have been deprived of the treasures that have survived to the present day. After the death of his Bohemian wife Matthias had no desire to marry a German princess. In 1476 he chose as his spouse a Neapolitan, Beatrice, whose refined culture and intelligent appreciation of the arts made the royal court of Hungary a centre of civilization.

Many Italians came to the court and one of them, Antonio Bonfini, wrote a history of Hungary. Bonfini attributed the family origins of the Hunyadis to Roman antiquity; after all, the Hunyadis had come from Transylvania, one of the lands of the 'Romanitas'. He traced their ancestry back to the consul Marcus Valerius Corvinus, whose patronym Matthias adopted, and derived Marcus Valerius' own mythical genealogy from a son of Zeus, enhancing the lustre of history with the magic of fable. But derivations of the historical ancestry of the Hunyadis were not restricted to Roman antiquity. The figure of Attila, always associated in the West with murder and carnage, acquired the aura of a powerful warrior and organizer, more Roman than barbarian, who stood as an example to his Hungarian descendant. Soon the humanists of Florence were establishing contacts with their disciples in Buda. Marsilio Ficino dedicated two of his works to King Matthias. The sciences exercised the same attraction as literature, history and neo-Platonic philosophy, and German astronomers came to stay at the residence of Archbishop Vitéz in order to study the calculation of eclipses and the configuration of the earth. From Germany also came the first printing-press. A university was founded in Buda and the construction of a great palace in which to house it was projected. Such was the cultural climate in which Matthias conducted his policies. In his own country he met with resistance among the nobility from which he himself had issued. Present-day Hungarian historians argue that Matthias, in his struggle against the ambitious 'barons', the representatives of the higher nobility, found his most reliable allies among the minor nobles, in the towns and villages, and among the peasants. The great nobles wished to secure permanent advantages for themselves at a time when the Hungarian economy was undergoing a transformation; in the ensuing conflict between the nobility and the monarchy, the nobility achieved victory by thwarting the enterprises of the king. But could it not also be argued that the personal factor began to play a decisive role once again and that the king, tempted by dreams of personal glory, committed himself to too many undertakings instead of first consolidating his power in Hungary? Matthias had to defend himself against two dangerous conspiracies. However, while not forgetting the Turkish menace, he was becoming increasingly preoccupied with his policies in the West. He was encouraged by Pope Paul II, who had received no support from the cautious and peaceable Emperor Frederick III in his clash with George of Podiebrad. It thus fell to Matthias to take the Catholic offensive against the Hussite kingdom. Before long, Moravia, Lusatia and Silesia, provinces of the kingdom of Bohemia, belonged to Matthias and were to remain in his possession for thirty years. He then had himself crowned king of Bohemia at Olmütz. After the death of Podiebrad in 1471, Prague and Bohemia proper, which Matthias had not annexed, passed to Wladislas Jagellon, which meant that two princes now bore the title of king of Bohemia. The emperor refused to agree to the investiture of Matthias as king of Bohemia, whereupon Matthias took up arms against him, capturing Styria, Carinthia and a part of Lower Austria, and established himself in Vienna, which he made his western capital. He died there in 1490, after five years' residence.

This gathering of several states under a single prince was not merely a matter of chance. If this was not the first time that neighbouring principalities in central Europe had found themselves united, the achievement of Matthias Corvinus was of a different kind, and indicated a maturing civilization. Obtained by force of arms, but without bloody conquest, his victory seemed to derive from the strength of his exceptional personality. His taste for knightly prowess nurtured a concrete political ambition conceived in the spirit of the Renaissance. The foundations of his power no doubt remained the kingdom of Hungary which he had transformed and consolidated, at least superficially. But in establishing himself at Vienna, nearer to the great international trade-routes and in a city with an already solid cultural tradition, Matthias showed how important a role the Austrian duchies might play in the construction of a great state that would have the Danube as its axis, would form part of the Holy Roman Empire and, at the same time, remain on the fringe of that Empire. He associated Hungary more closely with the German and Slav countries, and the agricultural regions with the craft centres and the mining towns. Even more important, he appeared on the scene at a time when the peoples of central Europe, benefiting from the general trend of cultural and economic progress, found themselves on the threshold of a new surge of activity and able to look forward to a common destiny.

Yet his project, which has been described as a first attempt at creating an 'Austrian Empire', but made by a fifteenth-century Hungarian prince, was premature and fragile because it depended too heavily on one man. Matthias Corvinus lamented the fact that he had no legitimate son to whom he could hand on such a heritage and could only offer his subjects a bastard son born of a German woman.

On his death his territories were dismembered. Maximilian, son of the Emperor Frederick, reconquered the Austrian duchies, while the Hungarian nobles, eager to avoid electing too powerful a king, nominated the same prince whom Podiebrad had chosen as his successor, Wladislas Jagellon, king of Bohemia. Neither in Bohemia nor in Hungary had the national monarchies survived their founders. The Diets preferred the foreign king, who would prove a more trustworthy arbiter between rival interests and whose personal initiative they had less reason to fear. At the same time, the union of Bohemia and Hungary under a single king might seem to maintain a territorial arrangement of central Europe in many respects similar to that achieved by Matthias Corvinus.

Such was not the case, however; in fact, the solution reached by the Diets had exactly the opposite effect. Matthias had represented the *prince* in the Roman manner, perhaps even more than he had himself realized, making himself responsible for satisfying the daily needs of his people so that he would be free to take important political decisions. King Wladislas Jagellon was scorned by his contemporaries because of his conciliating temperament and his habit of replying 'All right!', in whatever language might be appropriate, to proposals put forward by the representatives of his various kingdoms. He was no more than a figure-head, a puppet; the real power, both in Bohemia and in Hungary, lay in the hands of the nobles.

On the political plane, this meant a return to the past and to government by persons who, though tinged with humanism, were incapable of great actions or of seeing beyond the interests of their own order. This was particularly true in Hungary, during the quarter of a century between the death of Corvinus and the disaster at Mohács. Hungarians neither lacked the desire for national greatness nor were they unperturbed at the prospect of seeing their country dominated by foreigners (hence the hostility shown by the greater part of the nation to Maximilian of Austria, a possible candidate for the throne). Nevertheless, they allowed their country's military strength, the mighty Black Army formed by Matthias, to be dispersed. The same Diet that refused to sanction a treaty too favourable to Austria, concluded by Wladislas and Maximilian, took measures to increase to an unprecedented extent the lords' power over their peasants. This decision was influenced by the evolution of the economy. The growth of the home market, which created opportunities to send grain, wine and cattle to foreign parts, revealed the inadequacies of the traditional closed economy in which the peasant produced for his own subsistence, paying only light dues, and the lord was content with moderate revenues, having no great need to indulge in lavish expenditure. Taxes had therefore to be increased. The nobles were also afraid of no longer being able to find sufficient labour, for peasants in search of prosperity were being attracted to the towns, where they could supplement their incomes by taking on extra work, or were moving from one estate to another, to the detriment of their original landlord. One particular development resulted in a great peasant rebellion.

In 1514 the archbishop of Esztergom persuaded Pope Leo X to issue a bull of crusade against the Turks. An army was assembled which the peasants joined in large numbers. George Dózsa, a member of the minor nobility, was given command of the army. But the crusade was suddenly postponed, whereupon the army refused to disband until the measures taken against the peasants had been withdrawn and new guarantees had been given. Although the inhabitants of the royal cities made no move, the people in the small towns supported the uprising; in fact, the best soldiers in the rebel army were the shepherds from the great plain. The nobles deployed their full military strength against the insurgents; the minor nobility joined forces with the higher nobility, for they both needed peasant labour, despite the disproportion in the size of their estates. The battle proved a brutal affair and the reprisals that followed brought even greater atrocities. When Dózsa was taken prisoner a crown of hot iron was placed on his head, his body was tied to a red-hot mock throne and his companions were forced to bite his burning flesh. Shortly afterwards, the Diet decreed a series of inhumanly repressive measures: freedom of movement was totally suppressed, while the lord was empowered to extend the peasant's burdens and, in particular, the obligation to perform unpaid labour (the corvée).

The same Diet approved the code of law drawn up by the Hungarian jurist Verböczi, the *Tripartitum opus iuris consuetudinarii inclyti regni Hungariae*, which defined both the public and the private law of Hungary. The *Tripartitum* reaffirmed the character of the Hungarian monarchy: the source of all power, instead of residing in the person of the king, as the sovereigns, princes and jurists of the West were already inclined to assume, was to be found in the Holy Crown. The king possessed no legitimate authority other than that awarded on his election by the nobles and at his coronation. But the body politic comprised only the nobility—those persons or corporate entities (towns, 'nations') enjoying nobiliary privilege. The articles of the code which laid down that a noble could never be arrested without trial, that he recognized only the king as his suzerain, and that he had the right and the duty to resist the king if the latter should transgress the law, reflect a fundamental preoccupation with independence and liberty that has profoundly influenced the Hungarian nation throughout its history, imbuing its entire population with a horror of servitude—hence the numerous uprisings which, right up to present times, have resulted from the Hungarian people's tenacity in opposing any attempt at tyranny. The fact that the rank of noble was quite independent of personal fortune provided a safeguard which many other societies did not possess to the same degree. The code drawn up by Verböczi represented the victory of the minor nobility, the 'plebeians' of their class, both over the magnates, who had needed their support to defeat the great peasant revolt, and over the rebel peasants.

For the peasantry, however, the situation was the reverse: by the terms of the Hungarian constitution, only the nobility enjoyed juridical existence and the right to ownership of land. Henceforth, an ever-widening gap separated the nobles and the rest of the population. The peasants or *jobbágy*, who formed the majority of the population, found themselves helplessly cast into bondage. In comparison with other states of Europe, even those neighbouring states where the condition of the peasantry was to deteriorate into an increasingly harsh seigniorial system, the lot of the Hungarian peasant soon became the hardest and the closest to slavery.

Some Hungarian historians, convinced that the dramatic upheavals experienced by their country have derived to a very great extent from its social structure and the strangulation of its desire to develop, denounce the *Tripartitum opus* as the source of all evils: 'No king, dictator or tyrant could have achieved what a mere text accomplished: Hungary has not yet fully recovered from the damage caused by a book.' It must surely be admitted that the constant reaffirmation of the concepts of public liberty and individual rights, at least for the members of the most active sector of society, nurtured in the Hungarians a national pride and a spirit of sacrifice. Even those who had been enslaved felt proud to belong to a free nation. The hope of regaining total liberty induced them to follow the nobles when they rose up against a king or an invader. If the Diets of Hungary, like the Diets of Poland, gradually laid their country open to foreign oppressors, the indomitable Hungarian nation, winning the sympathy of other peoples by its resistance, enjoyed a prestige that remains one of the outstanding facts of political history and of the history of national consciousness.

This will appear something of a paradox, no doubt, but the Hungary of modern times can only be understood in terms of the economic backwardness of its masses and its general passion for liberty.

NOTES

1. During the nineteenth century a great many historical studies were devoted to the three great countries of the Danubian complex, Austria, Bohemia and Hungary; for further

detail readers should consult the guide by Richard Charmatz, *Wegweiser durch die Literatur der österreichischen Geschichte*, Stuttgart, 1912, and especially the excellent bibliography of Karl and Mathilde Uhlirz, *Handbuch der Geschichte Osterreichs und seiner Nachbarländer Böhmen und Ungarn* (four volumes published between 1927 and 1944). Naturally, these basic works need to be supplemented with others. The universities of Austria, Hungary and Germany have published a number of solid works of scholarship. In France, the little book by Louis Léger, *Histoire de l'Autriche-Hongrie*, was merely a résumé of events. Mention must be made of the work by A. Himly, *Histoire de la formation territoriale des États de l'Europe centrale*, Paris, Hachette, 1876 (two volumes) and, published after the First World War, J. Aulneau, *Histoire de l'Europe centrale*, Paris, Payot, 1926, which deals mainly with the problems of the nationalities and gives only a cursory view of the past.

The reader should at least be aware of the existence of the most recent historical syntheses concerning the Danubian region.

In Austria, Hugo Hantsch, *Geschichte Österreichs*, in two volumes (2nd edition 1953), is to be recommended for its scientific authority and its firmness of exposition, and Erich Zöllner, *Geschichte Österreichs*, 1961, one volume, is a concise work with a large and up-to-date bibliography. The book by Zöllner has been translated into French (Éditions Horvath, 1966).

For the history of the Austrian duchies, see Max Vancsa, *Geschichte Nieder- und Oberösterreichs*, Stuttgart, 1927.

Traditional Hungarian historiography prided itself in the great history by V. Homan and J. Szekfü, in Hungarian, *Magyar Történet*, six volumes, of which volumes IV and V (by J. Szekfü) are devoted to the sixteenth and seventeenth centuries. A new interpretation of the period from 1526 is to be found in the work by Elekes and Léderer, *Magyarország története*, 1961. In *History of Hungary*, London, 1959, Denis Sinor presents the evolution of the Hungarian state and its societies in a clear and stimulating manner, but the author omitted to add a proper bibliography, which would have been very useful. Although it does not trace the history of Hungary from its origins, the basic work by Louis Eisenmann, *Le Compromis austro-hongrois de 1867*, Paris, 1904, offers perspectives on the general evolution of political Hungary. The short *Histoire de la Hongrie* by François Eckhardt, Paris, 1932, largely political, remains an objective and elegant exposé written by one of the best historians of the liberal school.

After the 1914 war Czech historians published a collective work of synthesis devoted to the history of Bohemia and that of the Slovak comitats of Hungary, insisting on the interdependence of these two elements (vol. IV of the encyclopaedia *Vlastivěda*, entrusted to the best specialists of the period). After the Second World War the enterprise was resumed and given a Marxist orientation—*Československá Vlastivěda*, tome II, *Dějiny* (*History*), vol. I, 1963—under the auspices of the Academy of Sciences and under the direction of Josef Macek. Václav Husa (d. 1964) wrote a general history of Czechoslovakia (*Dějiny Československa*, 1961) which has the merit of presenting many aspects neglected by the old historiography (e.g. the working-class movement) and offering a new interpretation, but which on certain points sacrifices the kind of detailed development that would have been welcome.

Throughout the countries of central Europe the Academies of Sciences and the chairs of history at the universities are carrying out a programme based on team-work, publishing reviews and thus making an incontestable contribution to the progress of historical knowledge, in so far as their research is allowed to develop freely.

In 1960 the Academy of Sciences of Czechoslovakia published a critical bibliography under the title *Twenty-five Years of Czechoslovak Historiography, 1936–1960*.

2. On the introduction of Christianity into these countries: J. Cibulka, *Velkomoravský Kostel v Modré u Velehradu a začátky Křestánství na Moravě* ('The Church of Modra, near Velehrad, and the Beginnings of Christianity in Moravia'), Prague, 1959. Id., *Die Ankunft der Brüder Konstantin und Methodius*, 1965. Also, F. Dvorník, *Les légendes de Constantin et de Méthode vues de Byzance*, Paris, 1933; and *Sborník Svatého Václava* ('Collection of Studies on St. Wenceslas'), Prague, 1930.

   Lajos Nagy, *Die Geschichte des Christentums in Pannonien bis zum Zusammenbruch des römischen Grenzschutzes*, Leipzig, 1939.

3. Alfons Dopsch, *Die ältere Sozial- und Wirtschaftsverfassung der Alpenslaven*, 1909, and *Die ältere Wirtschafts- und Sozialgeschichte der Bauern in den Alpenländern Österreichs*, Oslo, 1930.

   On the constitution of feudal society, a subject that still gives rise to much debate, the reader should consult the bibliography in the above-mentioned work by Erich Zöllner (cf. note 1), p. 575 *et seq.*, and his references to the publications of the Institute for Austrian Historical Research (*Mitteilungen des Instituts für österreichische Geschichtsforschung*).

   The historical schools of the different countries have devoted their constant attention to the study of these problems. The *Revue des Études Slaves*, published by the Institut des Études Slaves in Paris, gives each year a bibliography of the works published in the Slav countries (Czechoslovakia, Poland and Yugoslavia).

   In this part of the chapter the author has made frequent use of three works in Czech: Kamil Krofta, *Přehled dějin selského stavu v Čechách a na Moravě* ('Outline of the History of the Peasant Class in Bohemia and in Moravia'), Prague, 1919, and new edition 1949; František Graus, *Dějiny venkovského lidu v Čechách v době předhusitské* ('History of the Peasant People in Bohemia in the pre-Hussite period'), 2 vols., Prague, 1955, an examination of the problem in terms of the class struggle; Vladimir Procházka, *Česká poddanská nemovitost v pozemkových knihách 16 a 17 stoleti* ('The Property of the Peasants of Bohemia in the Land Registers of the 16th and 17th Centuries'), Prague, 1963.

4. In *Twenty-five Years of Czechoslovak Historiography*, p. 149, F. Graus maintains that, whereas the historical schools of the West identify 'feudality with vassalage, Marxist historiography considers it as a socio-economic formation'. Without entering into the complexity of problems concerning the origins of feudalism, and without being convinced that the manner in which the Slav and Hungarian societies adopted the law and customs of the West has yet been fully elucidated, one can assume that the term 'feudal' is a sufficiently clear description of a society in which neither the land nor the peasant who cultivated it enjoyed complete freedom, and in which the privileges and immunities of the nobility and the Church obstructed the authority of the state.

5. On German colonization in Bohemia and the problem whether there really was colonization—i.e. an influx of German workers into Bohemia—rather than an economic growth of a population already settled in this country: B. Bretholz, *Geschichte Böhmens und Mährens bis zum Aussterben der Premysliden (1306)*, Munich, 1912, and *Geschichte Böhmens und Mährens I. Das Vorwalten des Deutschtums*, Reichenberg-Liberec, 1921.

   F. Graus (op. cit., II, p. 144 *et seq.*) has given a brilliant analysis both of the theories of Bretholz and of the interpretations of the Czech historians who were his predecessors—Krofta, Pekař and Chaloupecký; he sees Czech law and German law as stages of economic evolution rather than as opposed juridical systems.

6. On the struggle between Ottokar II Přemysl and Rudolf of Habsburg: O. Lorenz, *Deutsche Geschichte Ottokars von Böhmen*, Vienna, 1863; O. Redlich, *Rudolf von Habsburg*, Innsbruck, 1903; and a work by a Czech historian of great culture, J. Šusta, *Dvě knihy*

českých dějin, I, Poslední Přemyslovci a jejich dědictví ('Two Books of Czech History, I, the Last Přemyslids and their Heritage'), Prague, 1924.

Present-day Czechoslovak historians tend, in general histories of their country, to sacrifice political history to social history, to the extent of allowing only a few lines to this great sovereign whom Václav Husa has, however, singled out as 'one of the most powerful of the kings of Bohemia, extending his state as far as the Adriatic and making the kingdom of Bohemia the most important of the great powers of Central Europe'—*Dějiny Československa* ('History of Czechoslovakia'), p. 68.

On the Babenbergs: Erna Patzelt, *Österreich bis zum Ausgang der Babenbergerzeit*, Vienna, no date; Heinrich Fichtenau, *Von der Mark zum Herzogtum. Grundlagen und Sinn des privilegium minus für Österreich*, Vienna, 1958 (in the little collection *Österreich Archiv*).

7. There is no complete biography of Charles IV; consequently, as František Graus has indicated in his article (cf. note 10) in the Czechoslovak review *Historica*, II, 1960, p. 78, n. 2, the old monograph of F. M. Pelzel, an eighteenth-century Bohemian historian, is still of value: *Geschichte Kaiser Karls und seiner Zeit*, 2 vols., Dresden, 1783. Charles IV's personality, his achievement and the brilliance of his reign have been the subject of numerous studies: V. V. Tomek, *Dějiny města Praha* ('History of the City of Prague'), vol. II, 1871; E. Werunsky, *Geschichte Kaiser Karls IV und seiner Zeit*, Innsbruck, 1880; T. Lindner, *Deutsche Geschichte unter den Habsburgern und Luxemburgern*, 1890–3, 2 vols.; K. Burdach, *Vom Mittelalter zur Reformation*, 1892. J. Šusta, who had already published two volumes in the collection *České Dějiny* ('Czech History')—*Soumrák Přemyslovců a jejich dědictví* ('The Twilight of the Přemyslids and their Heritage'), 1935, and *Král cizinec* ('The Foreign King'), 1938—died before completing the great biography of Charles IV which he had planned to write. The following, however, were published: *Karel IV, otec a syn (1333–1346)* ('Charles IV, Father and Son'), 1946, and *Karel IV, Za cisařskou Korunu (1346–1355)* ('Towards the Imperial Crown'), 1948.

In the work by O. Schürer, *Prag*, 1939, the reader could consult the chapter entitled *Die Weltstadt Karls IV*, pp. 57–89. There are some stimulating pages by Zdeněk Kalista, an expert on the period and on the cultural currents between Prague and Italy, in his outline *Stručné dějiny československé* ('Short History of Czechoslovakia'), 1947, p. 72 *et seq.*

On the University of Prague: Václav Chaloupecký, *Université Charles à Prague de 1348 à 1409*, published on the occasion of the University's sixth centenary.

Aloís Kubiček-Josef and Alena Petráň, *Karolinum*, 1961.

The account of Charles IV's journey to Paris, published in *Les grandes chroniques de France*, vol. VI, and by R. Delachenal in vol. II of the *Chroniques de Jean II et Charles V*, has been translated into German and Czech (Jakub Pavel, Prague, 1937).

8. The catalogues issued for recent exhibitions contain introductions and commentaries which provide some valuable reinterpretations of the evolution of the arts: *Romanische Kunst* ('Romanesque Art'), Krems am Donau, 1964; *Die Kunst der Donauschule, 1490–1540* ('The Art of the Danube School'), Linz and St. Florian, 1965. For Bohemia, see the synthesis in *Dějiny vytvarného umění v Čechách* ('The History of the Plastic Arts in Bohemia'), vol. II, 'The Middle Ages', 1931, a collective work edited by Zdeněk Wirth.

9. The kingdom of Hungary comprised populations of diverse origin: Magyars, of Finno-Ugrian origin, and Slavs (Slovaks in the mountains of Slovakia and Croats in the kingdom of the king Tomislav, which was united with the kingdom of Hungary). Thus the foundations of the problem of the nationalities, which was to become so acute in the nineteenth century, were laid as early as the Middle Ages. Cf. the work by I. Szabó,

Ungarisches Volk; Geschichte und Wandlungen, Budapest, 1944. To build the entire history of central Europe around the history of the nationalities, as some historians have done, is a dangerous venture. The most important problem is that of the construction of the State at this period.

To these works of Hungarian history should be added the following: L. Makkai, *Histoire de la Transylvanie* and *Brève histoire de la Transylvanie* (The Academy of the Socialist Republic of Rumania, Bucharest, 1965), a French adaptation of the *History of Transylvania*, 2 vols., published in Rumanian and Hungarian under the editorship of Constantin Daicoviciu and Professor Miron Constantinescu.

For Croatia: Ferdinand von Šišić, *Geschichte der Kroaten*, I, Zagreb, 1917. The very solid work of Rudolf Kisling, *Die Kroaten*, 1956, deals only briefly with the origins of the Croats and concentrates on their development from 1526.

For Bosnia and Herzegovina: D. Mandic, *Bosna i Hercegovina*, I, Chicago, 1960.

The Academies of Sciences in the various states of the Federal Republic of Yugoslavia are at present centres for research where collections of texts are edited and reviews published.

10. A broad and stimulating article by František Graus, *Die Handelsbeziehungen Böhmens zu Deutschland und Österreich im 14. und zu Beginn des 15. Jahrhunderts*, in *Historica*, II, Prague, 1960, pp. 77–110.

11. It is not possible to provide here a bibliography of the numerous works on Huss and the Hussite period. In French, the study by Ernest Denis, *Huss et la guerre des Hussites*, 1878, 2nd edn. 1930, which in its time enjoyed an exaggerated reputation but had the merit of being a pioneering work, is now quite outdated.

There is a very good exposé in volume XIV^{II} of *Histoire de l'Église* by Fliche and Martin —*L'Église au temps du Grand Schisme et de la crise conciliaire (1378–1449)*—which takes the most recent studies into account. 'Heresy', the article says, 'eventually prejudiced reform. This reformist movement in the Bohemia of the late fourteenth century was full of promise and Huss had endowed it with the prestige of his evangelical ardour and his disinterestedness.'

Catholic historiography has become more favourable to John Huss and regrets the condemnation of Constance as a misunderstanding: Fr. de Vooght, *L'hérésie de Jean Huss*, Louvain, 1960, and *Hussiana*, 1960; J. Boulier, *Jean Huss*, 1958. The work of one of the best Marxist historians of Bohemia, Josef Macek, *Le mouvement hussite en Bohême*, Prague, Orbis, 1965, is a very up-to-date restatement of the subject; this little book, brief but brilliant, stresses the social conflicts and is a summary of the author's own works. Id., *Villes et campagnes dans le hussitisme*, pp. 243–258 of *Hérésies et sociétés dans l'Europe préindustrielle XIe-XVIIIe siècles* (Conference of Royaumont), Paris and The Hague, 1968.

Howard Kaminsky, *A History of the Hussite Revolution*, University of California Press, 1967.

Naturally, the principal works on the Hussite period have appeared in Bohemia itself. Since the great histories of the nineteenth century—F. Palacký, *Dějiny českého národu v Čechách a na Moravě*, 1848, and Tomek, *Dějepis města Prahy* ('History of Prague'), 1855–75—the most original work has been that of Josef Pekař, *Žižka a jeho doba* ('Žižka and his Time'), 1927–34, 4 vols.; Pekař's severe conclusions, not concerning Huss himself, but with regard to the movement that issued from his preaching and from the circumstances of his death, and in particular with regard to Žižka and the Taborites, created a scandal without provoking the discussion desired by the author.

The interpretations of present-day historians proceed from two different ideological schools: the liberal and Protestant school, represented by F. M. Bartoš, *Čechy v době Husově* ('Bohemia in the Time of John Huss'), Prague, 1947, and *Husitská revoluce I, Doba Žižková, 1415–1426* ('The Hussite Revolution, I, the Time of Žižka'), Prague, 1965; the Marxist school, represented by Josef Macek, *Tábor v husitském revolučním hnutí* ('Tábor in the Hussite Revolutionary Movement'), vol. I, Prague, 1952, vol. II, 1955; by the same author, the lecture in Italian entitled *Giovanni Hus e la riforma boema*, 1966; also, Zdeněk Nějedlý, *Dějiny husitského zpěvu* ('History of Hussite Song'), Prague, 1954–6, 6 vols., and the socio-economic study by František Graus, *Chudina městská v době předhusitske* ('Urban Poverty in pre-Hussite Times'), Prague, 1949; for the reign of George Podiebrad: R. Urbánek, *Věk Podebradsky* ('The Age of Podiebrad'), Prague, vol. I, 1915; vol. II, 1918; vol. III, 1930; vol. IV, 1962. O. Odložilík, *The Hussite King*, Rutgers University, 1965. Josef Macek, *Jiří z Poděbrad*, Prague, 1967.

12. The limits of the centralization of the Hungarian state and the strengthening of the regime of the orders, in spite of Matthias' efforts to free the power of the sovereign, are studied from a Marxist viewpoint by L. Elekes in an article in French in *Studia Historica*, 1960: *Essai de centralisation de l'état hongrois dans la seconde moitié du XVᵉ siècle*, which has a copious bibliography. By the same author: *Mátyás ës Kora* ('Matthias and his Time'), Budapest, 1956.

❧ 2 ❧

The Destiny of the Habsburgs

NEITHER OTTOKAR II Přemysl nor Matthias Corvinus had been able to maintain the association of the great Danubian kingdoms and states on a durable basis. The Habsburgs succeeded where they had failed. Habsburg sovereignty in these regions, established with the advent of Ferdinand in 1526, lasted for nearly four hundred years. Historians have often spoken of the 'domination' of the House of Austria, a word that should be avoided, for it is an insult to the nations of the Danube. Were these peoples so feeble, so lacking in institutions and national vigour that they remained bowed by the tyranny of one family for so long? And with what kind of extraordinary power was this family endowed, that it could achieve such a feat? It has been argued, no doubt, that the Habsburgs depended on the alliance they are supposed to have formed with the forces of repression: the nobility, the Church, commercial capitalism and then industrial capitalism. In the nineteenth century it was still being said that the Habsburg monarchy, threatened by the onslaught of nationalism, survived only by leaning for support on the army and on the essentially conservative sectors of society. But this is too simple an explanation, as will be seen. Should one then suppose that the princes of this family were invested, by some astounding piece of fortune, with a unique political genius? The name that first comes to mind is that of the most illustrious of them all, Charles V, whose ambition was to create a universal monarchy. But Charles V ruled neither Bohemia nor Hungary and appears to have had no clear understanding of the problems of the Danube. Nor must it be forgotten that in the nineteenth century there existed a quite opposite school of thought, which stressed the physical decadence of the Habsburgs, their sickliness and ugliness, the degeneration evident in the projecting jaw or the abnormally thick lower lip, the blood deficiency caused by inbreeding. To follow the biological evolution of a dynasty which reproduced itself with such persistence would be a fascinating and informative study, but one that should only be undertaken with sufficient medical knowledge and not be based solely on superficial observation. In this respect it should, however, be recalled that in the sixteenth and seventeenth centuries, when the territorial power of the Habsburgs was most solidly established and when the family had already provided princes who were among the finest political minds of the time, the dangerous practice of repeated marriages between first cousins and between uncles and nieces was rapidly paving the way for disaster—the sickly Charles II of Spain being the extreme example. When Charles II died, the western branch of the dynasty became extinct. But in Austria Leopold I's third marriage, to a princess of Neuburg who came from a family renowned for its perfect health, infused fresh vigour into the Habsburgs. The Emperor Charles VI, born of a strong and healthy mother, married a robust young German princess of dazzling beauty; though they were not fortunate enough to preserve their sons from the maladies of infancy, their daughter Maria Theresa was to become the mother of sixteen children. Finally, it must also be observed that the most unfavourable judgements on the Habsburgs, which have helped to darken the family legend, have been pronounced not so much by popular opinion, as by political writers and historians, mostly German.

A conflict between Francis I and Charles V laid the foundations for the hostility that developed between France and the House of Austria, with the result that it came to be taken almost for granted that neither could survive unless the other were humbled. Louis XIV himself held such a view. Over the generations Western opinion thus became convinced that the Habsburgs were aspiring to universal absolute monarchy and that the liberty of both the Empire and Europe must be defended. On the other hand, many nineteenth-century German historians saw the old order of the Empire as the chief obstacle to the political liberation of the German people and regarded the Habsburgs, who seemed to have attached themselves to the Empire, as the enemies of unity and, consequently, the betrayers of Germany's true nationality. Historians in the Danubian countries—Hungary, Bohemia and Rumania—have often reached the opposite verdict, censuring the aggressive Germanism of a dynasty that was German in its origins, employed a German army and German methods of administration, and conducted a policy which imposed German domination and German culture on the Slav and Latin peoples, depriving them of their own special genius and their liberty. By contrast with these divergent views, which all derive from a nationalist interpretation of history and lead to harsh and damning judgements, Austrian historians emphasize the supranational character of the Habsburg monarchy; in their opinion, the Habsburgs did not identify themselves with any one of the states or peoples they governed, but reconciled the aspirations of their subjects by maintaining a policy of common defence against external dangers (first against the Turks and later against France, in the time of Louis XIV and during the period of the Revolution, when France attempted to use its newly-found strength to extend its hegemony over Germany) and by establishing a common culture. Thus, these historians argue, the Habsburgs' ambition to create a rational form of association and peaceful collaboration among their peoples was fulfilled in an achievement which, though resisted and unrecognized, ought to have served as a model to the whole of Europe.

In view of the multiplicity of events and the diversity of general conditions which characterize this period, it is clear that none of the arguments put forward by either the critics or the defenders of the Habsburg monarchy is altogether lacking in cogency. But such interpretations are inspired by ideology, national or social in origin, and convey only one aspect of the situation. The frequent internal struggles, the rebellions followed by cruel and bloody repression, might seem to justify the argument that the permanence of the Habsburg monarchy was achieved by force and by the suppression of the weakest. On the other hand, the long periods of co-operation among the Danubian peoples, their demographic and economic progress in times of relative peace, and the development of a common civilization would appear to point to the opportuneness of their union under one sovereign and of the political system which that sovereign embodied.

Was this system something devised by men of experience and intelligence, or was it the product, perhaps not of chance, but of circumstances that had evolved over a period of many years—a system brought into being by the conjunction of diverse forces, both spiritual and material, and by the creation of an equilibrium which, though fragile, at least proved durable?

The history of the Habsburgs presents the rather rare phenomenon of a dynasty achieving enduring success in spite of upheavals, none of which proved irreparable until that of 1918. The Habsburgs' presence on the historical scene can be traced back to the eleventh century, when the family occupied the Habichtsburg, the Castle of Hawks, situated not far from the confluence of the Aar and the Reuss in what is today the Swiss canton of Aargau. The knights of the castle, who became the subject of many a legend, had already formed alliances with the lords of Alsace, the dukes of Lorraine, the Zollerns and the Zähringens (these last two families were to provide the rulers of Brandenburg and Baden). Soon, by entering into service or alliance with the German emperors they managed to involve themselves in the affairs of the Empire and to add much of modern Switzerland, Alsace and Swabia to their domains. Within three hundred years the family had become one of the most powerful in southern Germany, even to the extent of being able to stand surety for the loans of the young Emperor Frederick II. In return, the emperor agreed to be godfather to the grandson of Rudolf of Habsburg, in 1218. When Rudolf (the Elder) died in 1232, his possessions were divided among his sons, who took opposite sides in the conflict between Church and Empire: some joined the Guelphs, the others the Ghibellines. When Rudolf IV of Habsburg, the godson of Frederick II, came to power, the family reached a new landmark. Rudolf's achievement cannot be explained without taking into account his personal qualities. He was one of the great figures of his time: strong and handsome in physique, keenly intelligent, capable of both ambition and adaptability, with a yearning for grandeur and at the same time a desire to avoid excess. Above all, Rudolf was a sincere and convinced Christian whose faith encouraged him always to try to do better, to purify his political designs and not to be afraid of generous gestures. It was his personal qualities, his achievements and, in particular, the balance he had attained in territorial power and wealth (he was powerful enough to enhance the dignity of the Empire, but not yet powerful enough to be feared) which induced the German princes to elect him king (as Rudolf I) and the Pope to grant him his sanction. Rudolf was not, however, able to make the journey to Rome which alone would have allowed him to be crowned emperor and to bear the imperial title, nor was he able to secure the succession for his son by having him elected king of the Romans during his own lifetime.

Rudolf's election had unleashed a war with another candidate for the German throne, Ottokar II Přemysl, king of Bohemia, whom the electors had rejected because they thought him too powerful and possibly also because, in the eyes of the Germans, the Czech prince seemed more of a foreigner. The outcome of this conflict was that Austria, which had been ruled by the Babenbergs until Ottokar had conquered it, became a possession of Rudolf I. Thus the Habsburgs, having left the mountains of Switzerland and Alsace, were now established on the middle Danube in a state which the Babenbergs had already endowed with a measure of stability.

By fixing their roots in Austria, the Habsburgs were embarking on a policy that involved only a marginal relationship with the Empire and Germany: in other words, they were directing their ambitions for the future towards Bohemia and Hungary. These ambitions appeared to have been realized some fifty years later, when a Habsburg reigned briefly in Bohemia in 1307, and again in 1438, with the accession of Albert II as king of Germany, who was followed by Ladislas the Posthumous. It should be recognized, however, that these successes had only been made possible by the death of the great king of Bohemia, Ottokar II Přemysl, and that to obtain the wholehearted loyalty of the Czech peoples, who cherished the memory of their sovereign, the Habsburg kings would need to treat them with great tact.

Moreover, while Rudolf I had made the journey to Italy in his youth, in the company of the Hohenstaufens (to whom he had remained loyal), and had subsequently promised the Pope that he would not interfere any more in the peninsula's affairs, the possession of Vienna, situated on the Italy-central Germany trade axis, also played a decisive role in the absorption of Italian cultural influences. But these influences depended so much on the city itself, rather than on the person of the sovereign, that Rudolf was compelled to renew Vienna's privileged status of imperial city and to entrust it with its own destiny.

Another decision of great significance for the future of the dynasty, and later for the territories over which it ruled, was to grant the princes of the family undivided possession (*zur gesamten Hand*) of their fiefs. Although straightforward in principle, this decision proved highly complex in effect. The Habsburg domains became family possessions; when a prince died without heirs, his lands reverted to the surviving branches of the dynasty. In this way the principle of unity was established without precluding the rights of secundogeniture, since the head of the family (the eldest) retained overall control of his territories. Not all the princes, however, possessed a sufficiently mature intelligence to appreciate the political importance of this decision, which the wiser members of the family understood fully. As a result, strife and armed conflict constantly broke out between the princes of the dynasty; fratricidal war (*Bruderzwist*) became a regular occurrence in Habsburg history, and one cannot be certain that it did not leave its mark even on the present century. Yet the tradition of unity remained strong, and family solidarity, reaffirmed in successive statutes (*Hausordnungen*), was preserved, so much so that the whole of Europe was alarmed when Habsburg power became really solidly established. At the Diet of Augsburg in 1282, with the consent of the German princes, Rudolf I invested his two sons, Albert and Rudolf, with the duchies of Austria and Styria (formerly a Babenberg state). In the following year, at Rheinfelden, a family decree was issued making Albert sole ruler of Austria on the condition that his brother received compensation. Later, however, because this compensation had not been forthcoming, Rudolf's son John killed his uncle, King Albert, with his own hands (1308), a deed that earned him the opprobrium of being known in history as John the Parricide.

King Rudolf I died in 1291. He was buried in the cathedral at Speyer. He had been above all a German of Swabia and an emperor. Although he had not ruled for long enough to become a 'Danubian', he had laid the foundations on which the greatness of his family was to be built: the duchies of Austria and the claim to the imperial crown, the symbol of a supremacy which, though universal, assumed a specifically Germanic character whenever it was wielded by a German prince.

The death of this great Habsburg was followed by troubled times. In Switzerland, where the Habsburgs were counts of Aargau, Thurgau and Zürich, they failed to prevent a number of cantons, over which they claimed to exercise suzerainty, from obtaining immediate dependency on the Empire. When Leopold I attempted to restore the authority of his house, the armies of mountain-dwellers, who were trained and formidable warriors, defeated him at Morgaten (1315). Seven years later, in conflict with Ludwig of Bavaria, his rival for the imperial crown, Duke Frederick of Austria lost the battle of Mühldorf (1322) and was forced to renounce hopes of becoming emperor.

The task of preserving unity among the family for the sake of the future fell upon Albert II the Wise, brother of Leopold and Frederick, who was a peace-loving prince haunted by the family crime that had cost his father, Albert I, his life. He made his four sons, Rudolf, Frederick, Albert and Leopold, swear an oath that they would govern their territories in unison and that they would at all times behave 'virtuously and in brotherly fashion'; he also made his vassals sanction this family decree (1355). The inheritance of the eldest son, Rudolf IV, was nonetheless ambiguous: suzerainty over Switzerland was vigorously contested, Carinthia was secured with great difficulty on the death of Duke Henry, but the Tyrol had been denied him; any ambitions with regard either to Bohemia or to the imperial crown were frustrated, as Charles IV of Luxemburg was already solidly entrenched.

Yet, when the Golden Bull of 1356 gave the Empire a new constitution, it would have been quite in the normal course of things for the duke of Austria to be made an imperial elector. The privileges granted to the electors—the transmission of domains by primogeniture, the exercise of royal rights and juridical supremacy within their states—would have strengthened the dynasty. Rudolf IV possessed a certain grandeur of spirit, but he was also not without guile. To compensate for not having been nominated an elector, he demanded the implementation of certain provisions in ancient charters which would have endowed his house with exceptional privileges, giving him a special position in the Empire and quasi-sovereignty within his own territories.

The document in question was the *privilegium majus* or 'great privilege', composed of letters written by the emperors Henry IV, Frederick Barbarossa and

Frederick II. If the document was not a complete forgery, it had at least been cleverly reshaped in Rudolf's chancellery. A number of oddities survived in the document: for instance, the invocation of the rights of the Roman emperors 'Julius Caesar and Nero'! Rudolf had the *privilegium majus* taken to the Emperor Charles IV, whose daughter he had married, and begged him to promulgate it. Charles IV was too cultivated a man not to recognize the implausibilities of certain affirmations contained in the document, but he consulted his friend, the poet and humanist Petrarch, who could only confirm his doubts. Charles therefore took great care not to give the strange text his ratification. His reserve was to have important consequences. The need to obtain recognition of the *privilegium majus* and thereby to secure a position of eminence among the princes of the Empire was seen by the Habsburgs as one more reason for laying claim to the imperial crown. In fact, when Rudolf's grand-nephew became the Emperor Frederick III a century later, he ratified the dubious document and made it a law of the Empire. Moreover, since the imperial electorate had been withheld from Austria, the duke of that country had good reason to seek this privilege in some other state of the Empire. Neighbouring Bohemia, with which Austria had numerous links, thus became the prime objective of the Habsburgs' territorial policy. After the Hussite revolt Albert of Austria, son-in-law of the Emperor Sigismund, succeeded in obtaining both the imperial crown and the kingdom of Bohemia. The time was not yet ripe for the permanent establishment of Habsburg power, but this nonetheless remained a necessity.

During his brief reign (1358–65)—he died at the age of twenty-six—Duke Rudolf showed himself to be one of the outstanding princes of his time and one of those who sowed the seeds of the future greatness of Austria and, in particular, Vienna. He ordered the reconstruction of the cathedral of St. Stephen in a Gothic style and in 1365 persuaded Pope Urban V to issue a bull for the endowment of a university which was to be open to four 'nations': Austrian, Saxon, Rhenish and Hungarian. It was clearly his intention to provide his country with replicas of the cathedral of St. Guy and the University of Prague, the great achievements of his father-in-law, Charles IV. In accordance with the *privilegium majus*, the manner in which the duke of Austria received his investiture from the emperor implied an assertion of sovereignty (the duke presented himself on horseback, wearing the ducal cap). Among the legacies inherited from the princes of Carinthia was the title of archduke, borne by no other prince of the Empire. Henceforth, all members of the Habsburg family enjoyed the use of this title, which was of great value as a symbol of the spirit of the age.

Finally, Rudolf IV had the good fortune to settle the thorny problem of the Tyrol. This territory, a possession of the dukes of Carinthia, had been disputed by the Habsburgs and the House of Bavaria. In 1363 the last countess of the Tyrol, the adventurous and bellicose Margaret Maultach (Maultach was the name of one of her domains), made wiser by age and the failure of her policies, ceded her country to Rudolf. She then retired to a castle at the gates of Vienna, where a long street in that city is named after her. The Wittelsbachs of Bavaria renounced all their rights. With the acquisition of the Tyrol, all the routes leading from Germany to Italy passed through Habsburg territory. Along these routes the beautiful fabrics, cloth, velvet and silk from the workshops of Florence and the warehouses of Venice were transported northwards, while the cloths made in Germany moved southwards, together with salt, copper and iron. Rudolf strove to revive the commercial activity of Vienna, offering special guarantees to foreign merchants, despite the privileged position of the corporations. He was especially tempted by Italy and promised the patriarch of Aquileia his support in return for suzerainty over ecclesiastical domains in Styria, Carinthia and Carniola. He was seeking an alliance with the duke of Milan when he died in that city, in 1365. By a family decree of 1364 he had attempted to reconcile primogeniture, which he realized was of great importance for the future of the Habsburg territories, with a permanent alliance of the princes of the family and equality of rights among them.

After Rudolf's death the flames of the *Bruderzwist*, fanned by the local nobilities, spread once again among his brothers. The nobles were determined to preserve the privileges they enjoyed in their own countries, and they were afraid of being drawn by their princes into a policy of co-operation that would benefit only the ruling dynasty. In Prague, Charles IV observed these fratricidal wars with amusement. There was no need for him, said Charles, to spend his energies undermining the Habsburgs, since they seemed to be taking this task upon themselves. In 1379 the crisis resulted in a division of territories and the separation of the dynasty into two lines: the Archduke Albert III, the eldest of the princes, received Austria above and below the Enns and also a number of important towns; the Archduke Leopold III, the youngest and most adventurous of the brothers, was given Styria, Carinthia, Istria, the Tyrol, Vorarlberg and the domains of Alsace. Yet the principle of a family alliance was still safeguarded: all princes were to carry the same armorial bearings, even the emblems of territories newly acquired by one or other branch of the dynasty; no prince was permitted to enter into an alliance with the enemies of the other branch; and inheritances reverted initially in the male line to the princes of the other branch, to the exclusion of female members of the family except in the event of the male line becoming extinct. If in either branch an inheritance passed to a minor, tutelage would be exercised by the adult princes of the other line.

The balance between the principle of undivided possession (*zur gesamten Hand*) and that of secundogeniture was thus maintained; later, the application of this second principle led to a division by which the Tyrol passed to Frederick, the last son of Leopold III; but whenever the heir was in his minority (a frequent occurrence), tutelage was exercised by the other archdukes. It has already been seen how Ladislas, the posthumous son of King Albert II, became the ward of Frederick, a member of the line of Leopold, in Austria. On the death of Ladislas, Frederick succeeded to his inheritance (1457).

Before discussing the Emperor Frederick III, a contemporary and rival of George of Podiebrad and Matthias Corvinus, it would be useful to trace the growth of Habsburg territorial acquisitions, some of which were scattered far and wide, while the others formed a compact group. In the west, although the Habsburgs had lost all their possessions in Switzerland after the battle of Sempach against the Cantons, a battle in which Duke Leopold III was killed (1386), they succeeded in maintaining a firm hold on southern Alsace. They also secured the landgraviate of Upper Alsace and thereby assumed responsibility for the delegation of power among the local nobles. On the other side of the Rhine, they gained a foothold in the Breisgau. The town of Freiburg im Breisgau wanted to buy its independence from its overlord, the count of the Breisgau; the Habsburgs provided the town with the necessary funds. Possession of Freiburg carried with it the exercise of the landgraviate of the Breisgau. When the Emperor Charles IV approved the town's emancipation, he had promised that the count of the Breisgau would not be deprived of the landgraviate. But when Freiburg, unable to pay its debt, accepted the suzerainty of the Habsburgs in order to extricate itself from its difficulties, Leopold laid claim to the landgraviate on the pretext that his office was legally inseparable from possession of the town (1368). Leopold also obtained the provostship of Swabia in mortgage and then converted this into a hereditary possession; meanwhile, in this same region the family had acquired the county of Nellenburg and the landgraviate of Hegau.

Another region, present-day Vorarlberg, consisted in the fourteenth century of a cluster of imperial seigniories. In 1375 Leopold III obtained from Count Rudolf of Montfort-Feldkirch the succession to the seigniory of Feldkirch, which included the whole of the Bregenzer Wald except for the town of Bregenz, on the shores of Lake Constance. After Leopold's death his sons obtained prospective possession of the town of Bludenz and the vale of Montafone (Sankt-Anton). Patience was needed to add the final touches to this policy of territorial aggrandizement: in 1451 Sigismund of the Tyrol received from the margravine Elizabeth of Hochberg the half of the town of Bregenz which belonged to him, but the other half was not acquired until a century later (1523), by Archduke Ferdinand, brother of the Emperor Charles V.

The Habsburgs acquired yet another indispensable territory: Trieste. In 1382 Duke Leopold III, whose skill in conquest and varying fortunes have been outlined above, provided the Austrian territories with this window on to the Adriatic.

But Switzerland was well and truly lost: the peasants' desire for independence and their military valour had proved unconquerable. The luckless son of Leopold III, Frederick 'of the empty purse', was banished from the Empire for having helped the anti-pope, John XXIII, to escape from Constance. He then lost the seigniory of Badenweiler and the canton of Aargau, where the Habsburgs had retained their old title of count. Yet, despite these losses, the campaign of territorial expansion had proved an astounding success—a success achieved partly by conquest, but primarily by negotiation and money, and one to which all the archdukes, whether on good or on bad terms with each other, had made their contribution. At this point a figure already encountered in the first chapter reappears on the scene.

On the death of King Albert II the imperial electors chose as king of the Romans the head of the Styrian branch of the family, Frederick V. His father, Ernest 'of Iron', had been the first of the Habsburgs to confront Islam on the battlefields of Hungary; his mother was a Polish princess, Cymburka of Masovia, who has wrongly been supposed to have handed down to her descendants the characteristic heavy lower lip of the Habsburgs. Frederick did not bear the title of emperor or the name of Frederick III until twelve years later, when he was crowned by the Pope in Rome. No prince of his family had yet made the journey to Italy, but no emperor after him was to be consecrated in Rome. During a reign of fifty years this resolute prince encountered the severest difficulties of government, both in Germany and in his hereditary states, but he nevertheless succeeded in preserving his imperial function and in preparing the future greatness of his house. He was profoundly conscious of his dynastic rights; the ambitious device A.E.I.O.U., which has been variously interpreted (*Austriae est imperare orbi universo.—Alles Erdreich ist Österreich Unterthan.—Alea electa juste omnia vincit.*), clearly expressed the belief that a great destiny awaited his family provided that it retained the imperial throne. Such an affirmation of power seems absurd when one realizes that Frederick III was never loved in his own states and that he was on the worst of terms with the nobles of the various hereditary territories, and especially with the people of Vienna, who regarded a Styrian as a foreigner. In the Empire, Frederick III never received the financial and military support that would have enabled him to embark on ambitious policies. The major event of his reign was the fall of Constantinople in 1453. Frederick III thus became the sole emperor of Christendom. A humanist and politician like Poggio, then in his declining years, thought that in this situation Frederick was under an obligation to undertake a crusade, a suggestion that ignored practical problems: the necessary financial resources were lacking, and Frederick III knew this better than anyone. Similarly, various persons both in the Church and outside it expected him to initiate religious reform, the necessity for which was becoming ever greater. He preferred, however, to enter into prudent negotiations with the popes, in order to increase his authority over the clergy of his personal states; he obtained the right to recommend candidates for the bishoprics of Brixen, Chur, Gurk and Trieste, and later the creation of bishoprics at Laybach, Vienna and Wiener-Neustadt. He also secured the canonization of his great Babenberg predecessor, Leopold III, enhancing still further the prestige of the House of Austria and the Austrian duchies. His imperial office enabled him to confirm the *privilegium majus* in 1459 and to strengthen the moral authority of his house. The family decrees gave him tutelary authority over the young Ladislas, heir to King Albert II in Austria, who had been elected king in both Bohemia and Hungary. It has already been seen how Frederick maintained control over the person of the prince, how he welcomed the arrival in Vienna of the crown of St. Stephen and how, with his authority thus strengthened, he was able to negotiate with the rulers of the two kingdoms, Podiebrad in Bohemia and Matthias Corvinus Hunyadi in Hungary. But, when Ladislas died, Frederick was not able to prevent the election of the two 'national' kings. At first, he benefited from alliances with these kings: the intervention of the king of Bohemia saved him in 1462, when he was besieged in the fortress of Vienna by the people of the city and the army of his brother, Duke Albert VI. Later, he became embroiled with Podiebrad and was attacked by Matthias Corvinus Hunyadi, who drove Frederick from his capital for five years. These reverses jeopardized Frederick's power in the Empire. One German faction contemplated deposing him. There was no shortage of candidates for the succession: Podiebrad and Corvinus were eager to assume the function of deputy emperor, Frederick's brother Albert VI was ready to supplant him and the greatest duke of the West, Charles the Bold of Burgundy, who had no royal title, would have looked on the imperial crown as the consummation of his power. Relations with the Burgundian took a strange course.

Sigismund, the Habsburg prince of the Tyrol, had found himself in a difficult position as a result of differences with Switzerland and because he had been obliged to pledge his lands to the duke of Burgundy. He proposed a rapprochement between the two houses: Charles the Bold would be nominated as regent of the Empire and would receive the imperial crown after Frederick III; in return, Charles would guarantee that the crown was inherited by Frederick's son, the Archduke Maximilian, born in 1459. A marriage between Maximilian and Charles' heiress, Mary of Burgundy, would seal the alliance. Frederick approved the scheme and went to Trier in 1473 to meet the duke of Burgundy. Another aspect of his policy becomes clear at this point: *Bella gerant alii, Tu, felix Austria, nube* (Let others wage wars, you, happy Austria, marry).

The partners to the scheme could not reach immediate agreement. Charles the Bold insisted that the question of the imperial succession be settled before the marriage, while Frederick wanted the marriage to be celebrated first. When Charles died in 1477, the marriage at last took place. Although he realized there would inevitably be difficulties with France, Frederick recognized the importance of the Burgundian inheritance, while the advisers of the young Mary appreciated how valuable the support of the Empire might be in the future. In 1486 the electors named Maximilian king of the Romans. Frederick had thus succeeded in keeping the imperial crown in the House of Austria. Apart from the brief four-year reign of the Wittelsbachs in the eighteenth century, the crown was never to leave Austria. The policy of Frederick III showed a remarkable ingenuity, an ability to rebuild just when everything seemed in ruins, and suggests a comparison with his contemporary, Louis XI. But the two men were of very different natures. Frederick III loved pomp, fine palaces and the display of luxury. His residence at Wiener-Neustadt, where he felt more at ease than in recalcitrant Vienna, was filled with beautiful books, jewels and *objets d'art*.

Frederick was a man of great culture and continued to broaden his education under the influence of an Italian priest, Aeneas Sylvius Piccolomini, whom he made his secretary, his political adviser and then his historiographer, waiting for the opportunity to have him made a cardinal, the first step towards Piccolomini's election as Pope Pius II. This friendship had great consequences for the destinies both of the Habsburgs and of the Empire. Piccolomini was convinced of the importance of the imperial office for the public good and of the advantages of keeping that office within the same family: *in una domo caesari succedere caesarem et post patrem eligi filium*. Vienna, still rough and medieval in appearance, but with a university where important theologians such as Ebendorfer taught and where the humanists of Bohemia, Poland and Hungary could meet, was gradually becoming a centre of civilization and was already a Renaissance city in spirit.

The Empire and the House of Austria were associated in the most perceptive minds not with a general spirit of crusade, but with the more concrete purpose of defence against the Turk. When he made the journey to Rome for his coronation, Frederick III had married a Portuguese princess, Eleanor, daughter of King Edward VI. Eleanor brought new ideas and a broader view of the world into the House of Austria. She came from a country with a thriving economy founded on sea exploration and the acquisition of gold and spices. Eleanor realized that her Christian name, which was not common in Germany, might not be acceptable there, and so she offered to change it to Helena. Had not another Helena been the discoverer of the True Cross and the mother of the founder of Constantinople? She would have gladly given her son, born in 1459, the name of Constantine. Frederick preferred the name George, also evocative of a liberating saint. Their final choice, Maximilian, was inspired by the memory of the Croatian lord, Maximilian of Cilli, who had died in the wars against the Turk. The intention behind the choice of name remained the same.

However, the immediate problems were too numerous to allow this great project of the defeat of the Turk to be realized. In moments of crisis the empress reproached Frederick III with faint-heartedness. Yet the emperor's willingness to adopt the role of a peace-loving prince was by no means detrimental to the success of the great dynastic design. No satisfactory answer has yet been given to the problem posed by Frederick III. As far as can be seen, he was quite without support, whether political, religious or social. He was resisted by his nobles and unloved by his peoples. Popular preachers condemned him for having drained the life from all classes of society by his fiscal impositions which, they claimed, had benefited no one. He has been accused of being the emperor of the Jews. Is it possible that he was buttressed by the financiers in his moments of gravest peril and that, in the Empire, he took personal advantage of the prestige attached to his imperial dignity? Whatever the truth may be, this temporizing monarch, content to preserve the *status quo* over a period of half a century, stands as an intermediate figure between the great Luxemburg emperors, his predecessors, and the great Habsburgs of his own line, his son Maximilian and his great-grandson Charles V. Frederick was the first Habsburg to establish a durable alliance between his family, the Empire and the Danubian countries. The destinies of each were henceforth interwoven and were to attain new heights in the reign of Maximilian—though not without problems or hazards, for the Burgundian marriage had brought with it the era of conflict with France.

In the domains of Charles the Bold, an oddly-assorted but compact assemblage of territories, part of Flanders and the whole of Burgundy were fiefs of France which Louis XI was anxious to repossess. Maximilian was compelled to take up arms and then, in negotiations with France, to consent to certain sacrifices. By the treaty of Arras (1482), he renounced Artois and Franche-Comté, but retained Flanders. When Mary of Burgundy died, leaving him to care for their two children, Philip and Margaret, Maximilian agreed to allow his daughter to be brought up at the French court and to marry the dauphin Charles at some future date.

But the peace was not sincere. The claims which both sides laid to the Burgundian territories engendered a rivalry between the kingdom of France and the

House of Austria which, transmitted from the two princes to their subjects, became the cause of endless wars. The enemies of the one automatically became the allies of the other. Maximilian secured the support of the duke of Brittany, Francis II, who was also a semi-emancipated vassal of the king of France and who, though less powerful than Charles the Bold had been, occupied a similar role at the other end of the kingdom. When Francis II died, Maximilian married by proxy his heiress, the young duchess Anne, whom the Bretons were already calling the empress. However, Maximilian's French marriages had little success. When his wife was threatened by the king of France, he was not able to come to her assistance in time. To preserve the independence of her duchy, Anne of Brittany had no choice but to marry Charles VIII, who soon sent Margaret back to her father. Maximilian then married an Italian princess, Bianca Sforza, whose dowry doubtless proved more useful to his extravagant policies than had the co-regency of Brittany. Henceforth, his sights were set on Italy, but even here he found himself competing with the ambitious Valois. In order to secure the inheritance of Naples, Charles VIII had restored Artois and Franche-Comté in the treaty of Senlis, but a treaty was no more than a truce and the rivalry between France and Austria soon reappeared everywhere.

Yet marriages were a means of confirming alliances, even if the alliances were only temporary. To win the friendship of the Spanish king and queen, Ferdinand of Aragon and Isabella of Castile, Maximilian agreed with them that two marriages should take place: his daughter Margaret would marry their heir, Don Juan, and his son Philip the Fair, their daughter Juana. As a result of unforeseeable circumstances (the death of Don Juan, leaving his wife childless, and then that of the queen of Portugal, Ferdinand and Isabella's eldest daughter, who had succeeded to her brother's inheritance), Juana was left the sole heir of Spain. She was never to ascend the throne herself. Driven to despair by Philip's death in 1506, she went mad and was interned in the castle of Tordesilhas. Her inheritance passed to her children.

Maximilian and the king of Aragon made plans for the children's future: the elder son, Charles (the future Charles V), would be brought up in Flanders under the care of his aunt Margaret, who was entrusted with the government of the Netherlands, while the younger son, Ferdinand, was to remain in Spain. Maximilian's matrimonial policy had proved much more fruitful than he could have imagined at the outset, for it had secured for the Habsburgs not only the Burgundian territories, but also the future possession of Spain and, before long, the New World.

As soon as Maximilian was elected king of the Romans, he turned his attention away from the West and resumed his policies in Germany and Austria. He managed to persuade his cousin Sigismund to cede him the Vorländer and the Tyrol during Sigismund's lifetime. He had thus gathered together under his personal authority all the territories of the Habsburgs, when the death of his father in 1493 gave him control of the Empire. He did not, however, bear the title of emperor until his coronation in Trent in 1508. It now remained for Maximilian to settle the disputes with Bohemia and Hungary by reaching an agreement with Wladislas Jagellon, whose election as king of those countries he had been unable to prevent. In a treaty concluded in 1491 Maximilian and Wladislas declared themselves allies and agreed that, if Wladislas should die childless, his inheritance would revert to the House of Austria. In fact, Wladislas was ceding something that did not belong to him: it will be seen later how the Diets of Hungary and Bohemia refused to accept that the prince whom they elected could dispose of crowns and countries as if he owned them, when he merely held them in usufruct.

When Wladislas died, Maximilian tried to consolidate and extend the alliance. He took Wladislas' nine-year-old son under his protection. In 1515, in Vienna, at a sumptuous ceremony attended by the king of Poland, head of the Jagellon family, two extraordinary child-marriages were celebrated. The little King Louis married the Infanta Maria, one of the daughters of Philip the Fair and Juana. Then the emperor led to the altar the young princess Anne Jagellon, sister of King Louis, and married her by proxy to one of his two grandsons, but without specifying which of the two.

It could be said that the sacrament was merely a symbol and the recipients merely puppets, for the true marriage was the mystical union of Austria (and, to a certain extent, the Holy Roman Empire) with Bohemia and Hungary. Maximilian had adopted the child-king Louis; was he not thereby designating his grandson-in-law as a successor to the imperial crown and the future master of central Europe? Louis had been born and bred in these parts, whereas Maximilian's two grandsons were growing up in foreign lands: Charles in Flanders, already a French-speaking Burgundian, and Ferdinand in Spain, already a Castilian.

The name of Anne Jagellon's betrothed had to be announced within the year: the choice fell upon Ferdinand. Maximilian's matrimonial policy was preparing the territorial configuration and dynastic system which were to exercise such a great influence on the destinies of the peoples of central Europe, and even of Europe as a whole. One branch of the Habsburg dynasty was to dominate both eastern France (including the Netherlands and Franche-Comté) and the Iberian peninsula with its overseas colonies, while the other branch implanted itself in the heart of central Europe and was to monopolize the imperial crown.

Thus the reign of Maximilian can be seen to have been a turning-point in the history of Europe. The marks of his astounding personality are to be found everywhere. A man of tradition who also looked to the future, Maximilian owed many aspects of his character to the spirit of chivalry which informed the closing Middle Ages, and at the same time established himself as one of the first and most remarkable of Renaissance princes. In 1959 an exhibition was organized in Vienna to celebrate the fifth centenary of his birth. Numerous portraits, both paintings and engravings, were displayed. Albrecht Dürer's portrait showed him with eyes half-closed under the great velvet hat, one elegant hand clutching the pomegranate, symbol of immortality; Ambrogio da Predis of Milan caught the animated profile and the extraordinary intelligence of the half-smile. On the miniatures and medallions one could follow the changes which age brought to his face, right up to the last portrait of him, by an anonymous artist of Wels: the sunken flesh, the vacant eyes and half-closed lips of the dead emperor, a shattering image, Christian in its inspiration, with no insignia other than the silver cross on the black sheet drawn over the chest. Among the objects that belonged to Maximilian, the armour and damascened swords evoked the battles in which he had personally taken part against France and the engagement in which he nearly lost his life, during a war he had fought against Bavaria for possession of Kuefstein and Kitzbühl, the final additions to the territory of the Tyrol. The emperor had been a collector and a patron of the arts, as can be seen by his collection of precious books now in the National Library of Vienna. But most extraordinary of all was his personal library, which contained works by scholars and men of letters illustrated by artists of Maximilian's choosing, in which the greatness of his dynasty and the adventures of his life were recounted under the thin veil of fiction. Obliging genealogists, perhaps caught at their own game, abandoned the Roman origins which had long been attributed to his family and instead made Priam and the Trojans his ancestors. Writers composed at his dictation those astonishing books: *Freydal, Theuerdank* and the *Weisskunig* (the king in this latter work was an idealized representation of Maximilian himself). The horoscopes of astrologers discovered the signs of his destiny in the course of the stars. The emperor also kept a diary in which he would sometimes make entries in secret characters. All this is indicative of the poet and magician in a man of action ever haunted by the prospect of greatness. In his last years, twice widowed and preoccupied with his personal health, which he strove to protect by penance and an ascetic life (he renounced the company of naked women), Maximilian imagined he might take holy orders, become pope, and then, after his death, be glorified at the altars of Christendom. It is tempting, in this present age, to wonder if he suffered from delusions or even madness, but this would be to fail to recognize that the very mixture of cosmic ambition and practical sagacity makes Maximilian the authentic personification of the transition from the medieval spirit to the intellectual revolution of modern times. The wisdom manifested in the political institutions with which he endowed the Holy Roman Empire and his own states provided the counterpoise to the extravagance of his imagination.

Maximilian's prestige did not give him complete authority over the various countries which, directly or indirectly, came under his rule. In the Netherlands local institutions were strong, as he had discovered at the time of the revolt of the Flemish towns. He entrusted the government of these countries to his son, Philip the Fair, to whom he gave full freedom of decision, and then to his daughter, Margaret of Austria, who ruled in the name of the little Archduke Charles. In the exercise of their power, Philip and Margaret treated local institutions with respect and showed a readiness to compromise. The emperor could only play the part of experienced counsellor and head of the family, supervising the co-ordinated activity of his children.

Conditions in Germany were no less difficult. Landed property there was held by the nobles on a feudal basis. Disputes over fiefs were constantly occurring, among both princes and knights. The most powerful lords—ecclesiastical and secular—were seeking to strengthen their authority over their subjects. These vassals of the Empire were demanding investiture by the emperor: though bound to him by military and financial obligations, the lords aspired to complete sovereignty in their own lands (*Landeshoheit*) in matters of justice, military organization and taxes. The general economic situation was reducing the knightly class of nobles, whose estates were mostly of limited extent, to an increasingly archaic social level. The real wealth was to be found in the towns, where the houses of the patricians were being rebuilt in the Renaissance style. The towns were proud of their municipal halls and their opulent churches, maintained by the generosity of the faithful. Commercial capitalism flourished, bringing prosperity to the great bankers of Augsburg, Leipzig and Nuremberg, for it was they who made possible the circulation of goods, the great transactions of the international fairs, the transfer of funds from person to person, necessary for the supplying of goods to tradesmen and for the settlement of debts, and the operations in monetary exchange. Only the upper bourgeoisie could lend the princes the money they needed for their personal expenditure and the execution of their policies, which always exceeded their own resources.

The workshops were producing the high-quality arms and iron goods that established the reputation of German techniques. However, strife broke out constantly between the corporations of artisans and the merchants: the corporations stubbornly refused to allow any modification of their privileges, while the merchants impatiently sought new markets abroad and new techniques to increase their wealth. The condition of the ordinary people, both the urban and the peasant populations, was wretched; it was they who had borne the brunt of natural disasters, such as famine and epidemic, at a time when the means of rectifying or preventing these evils did not exist. Revolts occurred frequently; the poor struggled against the rich, and were provoked not so much by extreme poverty, as by the threat of one more burden being added to an already hard existence. The great peasant rebellion in Carinthia in 1478 was caused by the introduction of a new tax and a new monetary system. Certain parts of Germany witnessed an unparalleled surge of prosperity and all the external signs of solidly-founded wealth, while other regions suffered poverty of atrocious and barbaric proportions. The old feudal order had been shaken and people were clamouring for reform. In the humanist regions of the Rhineland and Swabia, where Roman law was regaining favour, the reorganization of the Empire was urged. The medieval notion of an emperor as the temporal and military head of Christendom, just as the pope was its spiritual head, was being replaced by a new concept: an emperor who was sovereign of the German nation and arbiter of order and justice in the Empire.

Maximilian had the wisdom to introduce reforms and the prudence to keep them in proportion to his actual powers. He defined more precisely the organization of the imperial Diet, which was divided into three 'colleges': the college of electors, the college of princes (itself divided into three chambers: the archbishops, bishops, abbots and abbesses, then the dukes and landgraves, and finally the counts, barons and burgraves) and the college of towns. All decisions assumed the character of agreements between emperor and Diet, and only thus did they acquire the force of law. However, the execution of a law depended on the goodwill of each Estate.

The emperor was responsible for justice. An Imperial Chamber (*Kammergericht*) was instituted in 1495, as a court of first instance for those nobles who were the immediate subjects of the emperor and a court of appeal for other suits; the emperor nominated the president, but the Estates appointed the councillors. Soon afterwards, in 1498, Maximilian created an Imperial Council (*Reichshofrat*), the members of which he was free to nominate himself, on the condition that foreigners were not admitted.[1] This Council heard causes involving fiefs and privileges and was also the criminal court for immediate subjects of the Empire. In this way, the personal justice of the emperor complemented and on occasion modified the exercise of justice in the courts of the Empire. Clashes between these two institutions were not infrequent and were aggravated by the fact that the Imperial Council sat where the emperor was in residence, while the Imperial Chamber was permanently established first at Speyer (from 1527) and then, much later, at Wetzlar. In reality, the Empire and its emperor had no capital. Maximilian lived by preference at Innsbruck, which he found conveniently situated for the route over the Alps and the route along the valleys of the Danube. The Imperial Chancellery was controlled by the archbishop of Mainz, but the departmental officials followed the emperor wherever he went. Maximilian reorganized the Chancellery (*Reichshofkanzlei*), which he established at his own court, entrusting it with responsibility for administrative correspondence and empowering it, at least in theory, to see that imperial decrees were put into effect. The Chancellery needed at its head an official who would wield the effective powers of chancellor without infringing on the theoretical authority of the archbishop of Mainz. A vice-chancellor was appointed by the emperor, who submitted his choice for the approval of the chancellor. A greater measure of order was thus introduced into the administration of the Empire. The personal authority of the emperor had undoubtedly been strengthened. It is therefore not true to say that he held no power in Germany and was simply the temporary head of a republic, as was claimed in the West. His unique imperial dignity ensured him a mighty prestige; German opinion already associated the national ideal with its pride at seeing its sovereign occupying the highest monarchic function in Christendom. But it would be a mistake to think that his reforms made him a powerful monarch, placing all the Empire's resources at his disposal. Maximilian remained an organ of that Empire and its supreme overlord, but he was far from wielding the authority of the ancient Roman emperors.

Maximilian was also direct ruler of a group of territories extending from the Vosges to Lake Neusiedl and crossed by the royal waterway of the Danube. Here, too, he attempted to bring greater cohesion and order to the administration of juxtaposed principalities, following the example of the dukes of Burgundy whose highly effective methods of government he much admired. He sought to constitute within the Holy Roman Empire a personal empire under his own immediate control, but he did not make a very clear distinction between the two notions. There was no question of his attaining the authority wielded by the king of France at this period, although even the king of France was still far from being an absolute monarch.

In each of the countries which the emperor ruled directly, the Estates, composed of the nobles, the knights and the representatives of the towns (and even peasants in the Tyrol), might accept the transmission of the supreme authority by primogeniture and might even derive a certain satisfaction from the realization that the territorial power wielded directly by their 'natural' prince, who enjoyed the same status in the neighbouring countries, enhanced his prestige and his fitness to assume the imperial function. But they would never have consented to entrust everything to his care, to accept him as their supreme master with authority to dispose as he wished of their military forces, their rights and their money. Maximilian succeeded nevertheless in reorganizing in three 'governments', each with its own administration (*Regiment*), the countries henceforth known as the 'hereditary states'. Lower Austria (*Niederösterreich*) corresponded historically to the lands formerly ruled by the Babenbergs, then by the Habsburg line of Albert III; geographically it comprised the present-day provinces of Upper and Lower Austria (the terms 'Austria above the Enns' and 'Austria below the Enns' were in use at this period), Carniola, Styria, Carinthia and the recently annexed county of Göritz. Upper Austria comprised the county of the Tyrol, parts of which jutted into Italy, and also Vorarlberg. The Austrian foreland (*Vorlande* or *Vörderösterreich*) included the territories of Alsace, Swabia and the Upper Danube.

The administrative capitals were Vienna (Lower Austria), Innsbruck (Upper Austria) and Ensisheim (Alsace). However, since the Diets remained at Linz and Graz, those cities were still the capitals of their respective regions, maintaining a role which continued to exercise a powerful appeal among the local inhabitants, nobles, bourgeois and peasants. Each of these regions would have wished its prince to take up residence in its capital, but the emperor could not be in more than one place at a time. Henceforth, the temporary authority of those who, in the past, had been appointed to represent him in his absence was in each case replaced by a permanent institution. It was here that the effectiveness of Maximilian's great innovation lay. The three governments consisted largely of nobles. The activities of each naturally came under the supervision of the Imperial Chancellery and a special exchequer was set up to control the revenues which the emperor received from his hereditary states.

As the imperial crown was never again to leave the House of Austria (except for the brief reign of Charles VII), the Reichshofkanzlei, Hofrat and Hofkammer became institutions of great importance both in the Empire and in the hereditary states.

The fact that these hereditary lands had preserved their individual autonomy in the process of reorganization meant that Austria, though a distinct territorial entity, was not yet a single state. The name Austria, which really belonged only to the former domain of the Babenbergs where the Habsburgs had established themselves quite recently, now extended to all the hereditary possessions. By virtue of those possessions the House of Austria (Haus Österreich, Casa d'Austria) secured its position in Europe. At the same time, Austria occupied a special place in the Empire, even if it was not an electorate (an unsuccessful attempt was made at the Diet to secure this honour for Austria), and was consequently better able to enter into association with great kingdoms like Bohemia, a fief of the Empire despite its indestructible independence, or neighbouring Hungary, which did not form part of the Empire. To Western Europeans, accustomed to identify one country with one dynasty, such a situation might appear disconcerting. Yet it was a perfectly logical situation brought about by the natural evolution of history. The dynasty had been essential to the success of territorial union and the credit for this achievement could be attributed to the skilfulness of particular princes. But their authority alone would not have sufficed. It was necessary that the various states should give this authority their consent, recognizing the value of association and confident that they would not lose their individuality. At this stage Austria was a *de facto* association of territories, and no more. Many years were to pass before this association acquired the organic, 'perennial' character with which it has been credited. Finally, it should be said that the institutions created by Maximilian shared a collegial status which became a normal feature of Austrian government and eventually imposed on the administration of that country an unwieldiness that was to be the cause of many a grievance. At the time, however, collective government seemed to offer advantages of uniformity and efficiency. Since the members of the various governing bodies exercised a kind of controlling influence over each other, it was thought that the interests of the prince would be better served thereby. Measures were taken to clarify the distinction between justice, on the one hand, and administration and finance, on the other. Yet complete specialization remained an impossibility and the monarchies of the West, which had been striving towards this end, proved no more successful. Local traditions continued to play an important role in the Austrian countries, obstructing the imposition of uniformity and preserving a certain patriarchal quality that has never ceased to be a part of Austria's way of life and methods of government.

Maximilian died in 1519. The terms of the family decree gave joint possession of his territories to his two grandsons, Charles, already king of Spain, and Ferdinand. But his successor to the imperial throne had not been nominated. The election of an emperor remained open to all and there was no German candidate. A foreign prince could therefore lay claim to a crown which was universal as much as Germanic. An especially strong claim was that of the young king of France, Francis I, who boasted of his victory at Marignano and distributed large quantities of gold. However, the Fuggers, the banking family of southern Germany, backed the candidature of the king of Spain and secured his election as Charles V. The young emperor then embarked upon a family settlement. In 1521 he reserved for himself the old Burgundian inheritance which lay closest to his heart, but ceded to his brother the Austrian domains, with the exception of the Tyrol and Swabia, which he handed over in the following year.

Ferdinand, brought up in Spain while his brother had lived in Flanders, had therefore to go to Vienna, where he found his fiancée of 1516, Princess Anne of Bohemia and Hungary, who now became his wife. The presence of a Habsburg in Austria was thus maintained. But Ferdinand was not yet a German; like his brother Charles, he spoke none of the German dialects. The new ruler of Austria had been educated at the court of his maternal grandfather, King Ferdinand of Aragon, and was very much a Spaniard; moreover, he brought with him as his adviser Salamanca, the man in whose shadow he had spent his youth. It would have been impossible to find a prince more alien to the Austrian countries and their peoples and less prepared for the successive responsibilities that were to fall upon him: first the government of Austria, then the administration of the Holy Roman Empire and later the imperial crown itself, and finally, as king of Bohemia and Hungary, the founding of the great Danubian empire which was to give new strength to the House of Habsburg.

NOTE

1. The terms *Hofrat* (Aulic Council) and *Reichshofrat* (Imperial Council) for practical purposes have the same meaning. The former refers to Austria, the latter to the Empire, but Maximilian I treated them as a single institution for the administration of justice in both Empire and hereditary states (though not Hungary).

✣ 3 ✣

The Turkish Threat, the Reformation, and the Great Domains

A FOREIGNER from Spain had been recognized as king of Bohemia and Hungary: his election enabled Ferdinand I to found the Danubian empire of the Habsburgs, one of the most important political structures of modern times and one which native-born princes had tried to erect, but without lasting success. A survey of the political and social system of this period reveals four major features: Ferdinand's efforts towards centralization, the Turkish peril, the alliance between the Habsburg dynasty and the Catholic Church, and the consolidation of an agrarian system which strengthened the economic and social power of the nobility.

These four currents, though not in themselves interrelated, converged naturally around the figure of the Habsburg monarch. Ferdinand himself was chiefly concerned with pursuing the policy of dynastic power inherited from his ancestors, whose patient efforts to this end have already been outlined, and he showed great political sagacity, prudence and perseverance. Circumstances were such that, in devoting his energies to the hereditary cause, he contributed to enterprises affecting the destinies of a large part of mankind. Would Europe be submerged by Islam? Would Christianity remain obedient to Rome, adhering to the dogmas defined by the Council of Trent (1545–63), or would it come to mean fidelity to the Gospel alone? Would the omnipotence of the prince, in the tradition of Roman law, replace the particularism that had characterized medieval societies? How would economic life evolve? As European and world markets became more accessible, would production be based on the craft and manufacturing industries, to the advantage of the towns, or on agriculture? Who would enjoy the rewards of labour and the capital that had already been accumulated: the controllers of the enterprise, the producers themselves or the State, whose needs were increasing with the growth in expenditure both at the court and in the public sector as administrative departments multiplied and the cost of maintaining armies and fighting wars became greater?

Every aspect of society was thus affected. The statesmen of the period were not fully aware of the magnitude of the problems confronting them, and Ferdinand proved no exception. The royal function was, by its very nature, guided by expediency; its primary tasks were to avoid catastrophes and to overcome any obstacles that might hinder the exercise of kingly authority, an authority which the monarch believed to be both legitimate and salutary.

Ferdinand's programme of centralization, however far-reaching its consequences, appears to have been dictated solely by practical necessity. Since he was both sovereign of several countries and administrator of the Holy Roman Empire, he found himself obliged to co-ordinate similar affairs of different states in certain departments and to seek assistance from Councils, in order that uniformity of policy might be achieved. By the terms of the great decree of 1 January 1527, the Aulic Council (*Hofrat*) enabled the prince to dispense justice in matters concerning fiefs and to take administrative decisions involving all the countries of the House of Austria and the Holy Roman Empire. The Privy Council (*Geheime Rat*) comprised only a few persons, who enjoyed the special confidence of the sovereign and usually occupied high positions at court; subsequently, the extension of their political powers restricted the role of the Aulic Council to judicial matters. From 1525 a royal exchequer (*Hofkammer*) controlled the inflow of revenues from the various royal domains, using the money to meet the needs of general expenditure— in other words, the personal policies of the sovereign. In 1527 a second exchequer was introduced in Bohemia to administer that kingdom's finances. The fact that this institution was subordinate to the general Hofkammer provided a further practical example of centralization. But its very existence betrayed a desire on the king's part to wield greater authority in Bohemia. It encountered the disapproval of the Bohemian Estates, who wished to remain the real rulers of their country and showed an aversion for supervisory bodies. There can therefore be no doubt that a central administration did exist, but it was always of a practical character and never appeared likely to become solidly established.[1] The financial reforms which Francis I introduced in his kingdom during these same years sprang from a similar desire to improve the administration of the country and to reorganize the inflow of revenues from the provinces; henceforth the taxes gathered by the treasurers and collectors of the *généralités* were sent to a superior authority, the Trésor de l'Epargne. These practical measures produced by no means all the desired results. Yet the king of France was master of his kingdom. His will was law, as the jurists and even the Estates-General admitted, while Ferdinand, who possessed no title higher than that of natural prince of each of his states, constantly found his own authority limited by that of the local Diets. The very manner of his succession to the thrones of Bohemia and Hungary proved this clearly. In Bohemia he was confronted with the terms of the Constitution decreed by Wladislas Jagellon in 1500, and in Hungary with the *Tripartitum opus* approved by the Diet in 1514. The agreements reached between his grandfather Maximilian I and his father-in-law Wladislas Jagellon were merely personal agreements between sovereigns. Ferdinand was elected by a majority of votes at the Bohemian Diet because he had accepted the conditions enumerated in his proclamation of accession on 15 December 1526: to maintain the *Compactata*, to appoint an archbishop of Prague who would respect them, to grant offices of state only to Bohemians, to preserve the privileges of all the orders, to allow no alienation of territory and not to reduce the value or weight of the currency without the consent of the Diet.[2]

At the cathedral in Prague, in the St. Wenceslas chapel where the statue of the young saint, carved by Peter Parléř, stood above the altar against a wall encrusted with amethysts and agates, the famous chorale had resounded, invoking the founder's eternal protection of his people:

> *Saint Wenceslas, duke of the Czech land,*
> *Our prince,*
> *Remember your race,*
> *Do not let us perish, us and our descendants!*

Ferdinand's marriage to Anne Jagellon had helped him to secure election. The Prague Diet was not a general Diet of the kingdom and its incorporated provinces. The Moravians convened their own Diet and elected Ferdinand on the strength of the hereditary rights of his wife, the sister and daughter of the last two Bohemian kings. Queen Anne showed great devotion to her native land and helped to resolve the difficulties which arose between her husband and the Bohemian Estates. She loved the palace in Prague and had the delightful balconied pavilion, the Belvedere, built by Italian architects (della Stella, Spatio). Chateaubriand, who saw the pavilion during his travels of 1833, observed what a pity it was that 'it could not be put in a hothouse in winter, with the palm-trees. I always imagined how cold it must have been at night.'[3]

When Queen Anne, already in her forties, died in childbirth in January 1547, her last words to Ferdinand were to urge him to be kind to his people. A chronicler, Dačický, called her 'the true mother and Esther of the Czech nation', which expresses the sentiments of the Czechs quite appropriately. In their queen they found a protector and compatriot whose assistance they needed constantly in defending their privileges against the policies of the king. In the transept of Prague cathedral the visitor will find the tomb of Ferdinand and Anne decorated with a frieze of medallions commemorating the former sovereigns of Bohemia, including Podiebrad. That the first Habsburg king of Bohemia should have wished to associate himself with the country's dynastic tradition is significant, serving to counterbalance the harshness with which he treated his Bohemian subjects on several occasions.

As a Czech historian has recently observed, the tomb in Prague also commemorates a political reality. The use of the term 'Austria' to describe the whole group of Habsburg states as constituted in the sixteenth century[4] is a misleading anachronism. Its natural resources, the composition of its population and the force of national consciousness at all levels of society made the kingdom of St. Wenceslas the most important element of the Habsburg structure at this period. Ferdinand felt no hostility towards the Bohemians. Like all monarchs of his time, he would not permit his subjects to defy their prince and he crushed resistance pitilessly. Yet his punishment of rebels never aroused public indignation. Many of the measures decreed by Ferdinand strengthened the internal cohesion of the kingdom of Bohemia—for instance, the restoration of the Lusatian provinces, which had been handed over to the elector of Saxony, or the creation in Prague of a court of appeal which also covered the incorporated provinces. Henceforth, appeals previously heard by tribunals of German towns (Leipzig, Magdeburg) were brought before Bohemian judges. Ferdinand refused to impose on the independent kingdom of Bohemia the imperial military and financial obligations demanded by the Reichstag at Augsburg. In the matter of religion, he kept the promises he had made at his coronation: he restored the archbishopric to Prague and showed his very keen appreciation of public opinion by persuading the Council of Trent and Pope Paul IV to allow communion under both kinds.[5]

The problems confronting Ferdinand in Hungary were much more serious and were aggravated by the Turkish menace. The defeat at Mohács had been all the more disastrous because Turkey was now ruled by one of the most remarkable sultans in history, Soliman the Magnificent, whose policy was not motivated solely by a thirst for conquest. Soliman had a wide understanding of the Western world and was determined to take advantage of its dissensions to extend his own empire, where he was already succeeding in establishing a sound administration.[6]

The incredible stubbornness of the Germans and the Bohemians in refusing to believe that their countries faced the same danger that threatened Hungary, their unwillingness to grant their princes subsidies for the expenses of war, and their facile claim, reiterated whenever they encountered difficulties with their own government, that the domination of the sultan could not be any worse, resulted in the Turkish invasion and the conquest and devastation of Hungary, which became one vast battlefield. After the battle of Mohács the young widow-queen, Maria, invoking the dynastic decrees, had demanded the election of her brother Ferdinand as king. A section of the nobility, returning to the ideal of a national king, nominated the voivode of Transylvania, John Zápolyai, who was crowned at Székesfehérvár on 10 November 1526. His election was contested by other nobles and a month later, on 17 December at Pressburg, a Diet claiming to be no less legitimate than the first elected Ferdinand. Finally, the nobles of Croatia, asserting the privileges of their ancient kingdom, convened their own Diet at Cetin on 1 January 1527 and proclaimed Ferdinand their king. They had no intention of severing their bonds with Hungary, but were quite prepared to choose for themselves between the two rivals and to support the non-Hungarian candidate. Hungary now had two elected kings. A few weeks after Mohács, Soliman reached Buda, which he occupied and pillaged. He stayed only briefly in the city, for a revolt in Cilicia necessitated his return to the East; but he was there long enough to receive a delegation of Hungarians and to promise his support for and an alliance with the candidate of their choice. Soliman's assurance at first helped the cause of Zápolyai; however, when it was not reinforced with more positive aid, Ferdinand and his supporters assembled a large army which marched on Buda and captured the city in the summer of 1527.

In the following November, Ferdinand received the crown of St. Stephen from the hands of the same archbishop, Peter Perényi, who had placed it on the head of Zápolyai the year before. Hungary now had two crowned kings, apparently with equal claims to legality. Zápolyai fled to Poland and from there went to England and then to France. King Francis I welcomed him at Fontainebleau and promised him an alliance, for Zápolyai was both the enemy of a Habsburg and the ally of the sultan.

It would be a mistake to interpret this succession of events merely in terms of the haphazard activities of ambitious rivals, when in fact deep-rooted interests and forces were at work. The Turks had revealed the full extent of their power. The battles had been hard: no one under-estimated the cruelty of the Ottoman armies or the dangers confronting the conquered populations, who were taken away as hostages or slaves if they were unable to pay their ransom.

The national awareness of the Hungarians cannot be called in question, even if the patriotism of the two opposing camps seemed to lead to conflicting policies. All Hungarians shared a common grief at the prospect of the ruin that threatened shortly to overcome the prosperous kingdom of Matthias Corvinus. Yet it must be realized that on two occasions, at the Diet of Speyer (1523) and the Diet of Nuremberg (1524), Hungarian delegates had gone to beg for military assistance from the Empire and that each time the Germans had dismissed their request, at least for the time being. Belgrade had fallen in 1521, then the Hungarian army had been routed at Mohács and the sultan had occupied Buda in person. In such circumstances was it reasonable to look for salvation to the prince of Austria and Bohemia, who would sooner or later be tempted to withdraw into his other territories?

As long as Europe as a whole refused to regard the Turkish advance as a threat to all Christendom and to oppose it with mass intervention, the Hungarians could count only on themselves. They would therefore have to accept the Turks as their neighbours and come to terms with them. At the governmental level, at least, the Turks were not barbarians. Soliman and his viziers were wise politicians and were prepared to negotiate. Consequently, agreement on the conditions of a *modus vivendi* was not impossible: everything would depend on the Turks' terms. Since Hungary was no longer able to survive alone, to obtain from the sultan a guarantee of peaceful co-existence was neither an unreasonable nor a dishonourable solution. By offering terms through her king, who spoke in the name of the Diet and thus on behalf of the nation, would not Hungary be encouraging the sultan to look upon the kingdom of St. Stephen as a power with which it would be in his interests to negotiate, instead of subjecting it to annihilation?

Since the Empire had spurned its plea for help, was not Hungary entitled to turn to other European states, to Poland, England or France? Of all the kingdoms of Europe, France held the greatest appeal, for its power was solidly founded and it was renowned for the quality of its armies and for its wealth. Hungary could now invoke its past affinities with that country, recalling those princes who had brought the fleurs-de-lis from Naples and had left the Hungarian people with memories of a golden age. From France the Hungarians could hope for some kind of moral guarantee to support the agreements which their country might make with the Porte. France, for its part, had already discovered that resistance to the House of Austria was a political necessity, and would therefore benefit from an alliance with the enemies of the Habsburgs. It was easy to argue that the Zápolyai faction stood for Hungary's traditional right to choose a king of Hungarian birth, and since Hungary did not form part of the Holy Roman Empire, the people's refusal to be subjected to the most powerful of the German princes, who would absorb their country into his own states on the pretext of defending it, was quite legitimate. But how great a sacrifice would France be prepared to make for the sake of her ally, and how far would she be deceived into thinking that the malcontents of Hungary would not, in the event of defeat, be compelled to seek reconciliation with their enemies?

A pattern now emerged which was to reappear in the centuries ahead: a Hungary isolated by the Ottoman conquest, courageous in battle and in resistance to oppression, but incapable of victory; a Turkish power whose fundamental aim was to conquer the whole of Europe in a holy war, but which was wise enough to grant its nearest adversary periods of respite, truces and pacts; a France which, in its struggle against the emperor or against the Holy Roman Empire, sought a pretext for a diversion in the East and found such a pretext in the malcontents of Hungary, but was unable to make maximum use of this alliance owing to the problem of distance and its own internal difficulties; and, finally, a king of Bohemia who was both duke of Austria and emperor and who, because of the strategic situation of his states, was more aware than others of the extent of the Turkish menace and needed Hungary as a bulwark to protect his other domains from invasion. This interplay of forces was to produce a constant ebb and flow in the affairs of central Europe.

Throughout this period the Hungarian plain remained a battlefield; hence the economic decline and social stagnation of a country with a soil so rich and varied, so well suited to agriculture, stockbreeding and vine-growing that, from the twelfth to the fifteenth centuries, it had proved itself capable of emulating the great states of Europe. Responsibility for these misfortunes cannot be laid on a particular social class, or even on the policies of any one government. The country faced a dilemma: either Europe would unite to liberate her, or Hungary, caught between several evils, would submit to each of them in turn, extricate herself as best she could and astound everyone simply by the fact of having survived.

In the spring of 1529 Soliman reappeared at the head of an army of two hundred thousand men. At Mohács he had a meeting with Zápolyai, who asked for his protection, kissing his hand and making him gifts which included a diamond ring that had belonged to Matthias Corvinus. A few weeks later, Buda was captured in spite of the resistance offered by a member of the Hungarian high nobility, Thomas Nádasdy; Zápolyai resumed power in the city and then accompanied the Turkish army in its march on Vienna. The Austrian capital was defended by a small garrison of sixteen to eighteen thousand men, Austrians, Bohemians and Spaniards, under the command of the count of Salm. The defenders set fire to the suburbs of the city to obstruct the progress of the enemy. The Turks then set up a regular siege and a flotilla made its way up the Danube. After several weeks of fighting had failed to produce a result, Soliman, disturbed by rains foreshadowing an early winter, ordered his army to retreat. The army moved off with its tents, camels and all the exotic equipment which had been striking terror into the populations of Europe. When he reached Constantinople, the sultan boasted that his show of strength had been successful. For several weeks Zápolyai governed the greater part of Hungary, but public opinion began to murmur against him, reproaching him with the humiliations of the defeats suffered at Mohács and Buda.

Ferdinand, elected king of the Romans in 1531, continued to appeal to the Holy Roman Empire for support and to insist that the reconquest of Hungary was necessary for the safety of Christian Europe.[7] His family was convinced of this. Before she died, Margaret of Austria, ruler of the Netherlands, wrote to her nephews: 'You, the heads of Christendom, cannot reap at home the honour you have lost by failing to pursue the Turks.' Charles V himself realized that the struggle against the Turk involved the whole of Christendom; the king of Spain and Naples had all the more reason to be aware of this fact because the trading activities of his subjects in the Mediterranean were being disorganized by Turkish naval power.

In 1532 Soliman resumed the offensive, this time along the valley of the Drave. As they advanced northwards, the Turks encountered unexpected resistance in the little town of Köszeg or Güns, defended by a Croat, Nicholas Jurivić. Meanwhile, Charles V, who had succeeded at the imperial Diets in restoring peace between Catholics and Protestants, had assembled a powerful army which he led to Vienna. This was the only visit that Charles V ever made to the city. The Turks had already penetrated into Styria, but the sultan made no attempt to undertake another siege of the capital. The emperor now had to make a momentous decision. Since the Turkish army was heading back into Hungary, was not this an opportunity to pursue the enemy and to transform its peaceful retreat into a rout? Were not the mighty Imperials, who were better able than the Orientals to endure the winter already breaking in this late September of 1532, in a position to win a victory over the one who claimed to be Invincible? Ferdinand hoped so; as Hugo Hantsch has commented, he would thus have proved the Habsburgs' vocation as kings of Hungary.[8] But, as soon as the territories of the Empire had been rid of the enemy, the German and Bohemian troops considered their mission accomplished. 'They are determined only to guard Germany and not to move into Hungary, if the Turk withdraws at all points,' Charles V was told by his adviser, Croy. And the emperor himself, weighing the situation carefully and knowing how little money he possessed, had no desire to embark on a hazardous venture. He declared that it was not reasonable 'to maintain such a large army'. At the beginning of October he set off along the valleys of Styria and Carinthia, via Graz and Sankt Veit an der Glan, heading for Italy from where he could return to Spain; at the same time the Germans began to make their way back home. The twentieth-century reader can doubtless follow the course of these events without emotion. But what must have been the conclusion drawn in 1532 by the Hungarians, both lords and serfs, when they were denied assistance in this manner, and what must they have thought of declarations of Christian unity which time and again dissolved into empty promises?

Soliman remained the arbiter of Hungary's fate, but he realized that it would take him a long time to conquer both Austria and Germany and that a truce would be the best solution. The two kings, Ferdinand and Zápolyai, negotiated with him. They then came to terms with each other. By the treaty of Várad (1538) it was decided that Zápolyai should continue to rule his provinces as king, but that on his death Hungary would be reunited under Ferdinand or one of his successors. Zápolyai, however, married the sister of the king of Poland and when a son, John Sigismund, was born to him, he changed his mind and made preparations for the throne to be handed on to his heir. Zápolyai, who had not anticipated the imminence of the transfer of power, died in 1540. Soliman stood to gain by maintaining a weakened Hungary divided between two princes and he therefore recognized the child John Sigismund as king. Ferdinand made war once again, but failed to capture Buda, which Zápolyai's supporters defended; it was the Turks who finally secured possession of the city (1541). Shortly afterwards, the Turks announced that all the territories which they then occupied (the Hungarian plain from Transdanubia to Transylvania) would be incorporated in the Ottoman Empire as pashaliks. At the court of Zápolyai's widow was a strange figure of Croatian origin who had entered holy orders under the name of Friar George and who, instead of his father's name, Utissenić, bore that of his mother, Martinuzzi. Friar George was too intelligent and too patriotic not to desire the reunification of his country and he felt that, if all Hungarian troops were mobilized, they would still be able to drive the Turks out. He negotiated with Ferdinand for Bohemian and German auxiliaries. Soon a large imperial army, commanded by Joachim, margrave of Brandenburg, arrived at the city of Buda; but, instead of launching an assault, the German forces scattered. In the following year the Turks seized more Hungarian towns. Ferdinand then reopened negotiations with the Porte and in 1547 obtained a truce. He had to promise to send the sultan a yearly gift of thirty thousand pieces of gold; the Turks regarded this sum as a tribute and claimed that any delay in its payment gave them the right to break the truce. For a brief moment in 1551 it seemed that Zápolyai's secession might be ratified, but negotiations were halted when Friar George Martinuzzi was assassinated by some of Ferdinand's Spanish officers.

The most serious outcome of all these rapid changes of fortune was the long-term dismemberment of 'indivisible' Hungary into three sections. A part of Croatia to the west, a strip of territories extending as far as Pressburg, and the comitats or counties in the mountains of the north (Upper Hungary or Slovakia) remained under the rule of Ferdinand and his successors and were known as Royal Hungary.

Royal Hungary, stretching from the Adriatic to the Carpathians, formed a territorial barrier protecting the routes to Vienna. In 1566, two years after the death of Ferdinand, Soliman seemed determined to resume his offensive against the imperial city. This time, however, he wanted to attack it from the south-west and to capture the important fortress of Sziget, not far from the Drave. A few years previously an Italian engineer had restored the fort's defensive system, adding the latest type of bastion. Owing to the lack of expert manpower, however, the new fortifications had been erected by local peasants summoned for statute labour, and they had only been able to build stockades packed with mud. Even so, the town and its citadel held out for several months, from spring to autumn. One of the richest lords of the region, Nicholas Zrinský, a Croat whose name took the form of Zrinyi in Hungarian, and who was general of Transdanubia, resolutely entrenched himself inside the fortress to await the arrival of the imperial army. But the imperial troops, numbering between twenty and twenty-five thousand men and commanded by the Emperor Maximilian II, son and successor of Ferdinand, halted at Györ, the last fortress before the Danube. The Turks bombarded Sziget, gradually destroying its defences until eventually Nicholas Zrinský, abandoning all hope of assistance from outside, made a final sortie with side-arms and was killed along with his remaining companions. Sziget was henceforth controlled by the Turks, who fortified it with solid brick walls and built mosques in the town. Soliman had died during the siege and there was therefore no immediate danger of a new offensive against Vienna. Despite its tragic end, the battle of Sziget soon became a legend, for it had stirred men's hearts both in Hungary itself and in the Empire. The memory of Nicholas Zrinský was long honoured among Hungarians and Croats. A descendant of the hero composed the poem *Szigeti Veszedelem* (*The Disaster of Sziget*, 1645), one of the masterpieces of baroque literature in the Magyar language. Even today one of the main squares in Zagreb bears Zrinský's name.[9] Less than two years after the siege of Sziget, the treaty of Adrianople, formulated in accordance with earlier treaties, established an eight-year truce which was subsequently renewed until 1593.

It was only to the north, in the mountains of Slovakia, that Royal Hungary extended beyond the narrow limits of the corridor formed by the frontier of the Holy Roman Empire and the arbitrary line marked by the halt of the Turkish advance. Yet, even though its area had been thus diminished, Hungary continued to occupy a position of importance both in the Habsburg structure and in Europe. It had not been subordinated to the authority of its sovereign, but retained its own institutions, its county assemblies and its Diet; Pozsony was its capital. The king reigned only from the moment of his coronation; in theory, he was represented in Hungary by the palatine, the intermediary between himself and the Diet, but in practice this office was exercised by a governing Council.

The Hungarians declined to accept the two seats on the Aulic Council which the Emperor Ferdinand had offered them on his accession, because they were reluctant to allow the affairs of their kingdom to be debated by an external organization common to other states. It was the nobles who ruled Hungary, in the county assemblies and in the Diet, and it was they who represented the 'nation'. The political consciousness of that nation was truly Hungarian, whether it expressed itself in Latin or in the various native languages that had already evolved sufficiently to attain high literary forms: Croat, Magyar, Czech and the Slovak dialects. This diversity of origins caused no conflict among the different ethnic groups, for pluralism coincided happily with the spirit of the age.

The eastern counties of Royal Hungary (the Slovakia of the present day) lay adjacent to the principality of Transylvania, an autonomous group of Hungarian counties under Turkish suzerainty. After John Sigismund, who retained the royal title until his death in 1571, the king of Hungary no longer ruled over Transylvania. The prince of that country bore the title of voivode, like the princes of the Rumanian provinces who were also vassals of the sultan. He was elected by the Diet of Transylvania, which comprised the nobles and the privileged communities of Szekels and Saxons. The Diet always chose a Hungarian noble and their decision was often influenced, directly or indirectly, by the Porte. Only the sultan could grant the royal investiture. The prince of Transylvania could not make war nor enter into an alliance without the sanction of his suzerain, to whom he paid a tribute which initially was less than the 'gift of honour' exacted from Royal Hungary. Transylvania thus remained autonomous. The ordinances of the princes, who inclined towards centralization and absolutism, and the decisions of the Diets, which ensured that the liberties of each community were preserved, gradually created an aristocratic regime in which the privileged exerted a controlling influence over each other. This regime successfully introduced a policy of co-existence between different nations and religions, though it bore no resemblance to modern liberalism.

The rest of Hungary was incorporated in the Ottoman Empire. Transdanubia, with Szekésféhervár and Györ (Raab), the valley of the Danube, with Esztergom (Gran) and Buda, the plain of the Tisza, the vast expanse stretching beyond it to the Transylvanian frontier, and, finally, the Banat of Temesvár all formed Turkish pashaliks. The pashalik of Buda, governed by a vizier, enjoyed primacy. The frontier artificially fixed in the treaties concluded between the sultan and the emperor underwent many local modifications over the years, as the Turks advanced along the Save or negotiated the cession of fortresses and fragments of counties.

It was now necessary to create a military security zone to the east of Carniola, extending beyond the Save and the Drave where new fortresses were built (Carlstadt, or Karlovac, and Warasdin). Such a zone was essential for the protection of Royal Hungary and, beyond, the hereditary states of the Habsburgs and the Empire itself; but its very existence and the special powers wielded by its administration aggravated the territorial dismemberment of Hungary. Even when Hungary was not engaged in open war with the Turks, incursions were constantly being made across her frontiers by bands of Turkish soldiers, who raided villages, carried off produce and cattle, and even abducted women and young girls for the slave markets. On the other hand, when war was actually declared, the imperial armies composed of Germans, Bohemians, Spaniards and Neapolitans serving in the Hungarian counties behaved just as if they were in a conquered country. Admittedly, plundering armies were a normal feature of war at this period. But the temptations of pillage and violence were all the greater in a country as disorganized as Hungary. The result was a series of tragic misunderstandings between the government in Vienna and the Hungarian nation. The Hungarian Diet complained that, instead of defending the nation, the troops were indulging in extortion on no less a scale than the Turks: indeed, their behaviour was even more scandalous because they were Christians. The imperial government was disconcerted and offended by the attitude of the Hungarians, who, far from appreciating the help they were receiving, never ceased voicing their grievances. Such a situation could only breed misunderstanding and even hatred between peoples whose fundamental interests were the same. The Hungarians realized more than ever that they could rely only on themselves. Their collective psychology underwent a transformation, both for better and for worse. They acquired a greater aptitude for personal valour and a greater skill in counter-attack. They produced a first-class infantry with exceptional powers of endurance and a cavalry which achieved wonders with its daring thrusts and lightning retreats. But these proud people were undisciplined and easily discouraged. They found ever greater difficulty in carrying out a sustained action and disheartened their allies by their indecision. As a result, insurrections against the Habsburg kings occurred frequently in Royal Hungary and the malcontents were in constant collusion with Transylvania. Close affinities still existed between the two regions: they had a similar economic structure and a similar political system based on privilege, including religious privilege. At the same time, certain great lords in Royal Hungary showed themselves more receptive to neighbouring Western influences; moreover, they admired the great power of their prince and his methods of centralized administration. Two parties destined to play an enduring role in Hungarian history were thus formed during the sixteenth and seventeenth centuries: the *labanc* or pro-Habsburg loyalists, mostly Catholic, and the *kuruc* or 'crusaders', who were in fact the 'malcontents' and who resorted to armed revolt. However, these bodies had nothing in common with the parties of a modern parliamentary monarchy, in spite of the tendency of Hungarians, evident even in the nineteenth century, to claim similarities between their traditional political system and the liberalism of countries where enfranchisement depended on a tax-qualification.

The circumstances which induced people to join one party or the other revealed all manner of contradictions. For example, one of the most formidable conspiracies against the Habsburgs was planned by a group of Croatian lords, who were subjects of Royal Hungary and Catholics. Yet perhaps it would be true to say that, on the whole, there existed stronger grounds for becoming a *labanc* in Royal Hungary and, conversely, a *kuruc* in Transylvania. The creation of the Ottoman pashaliks posed other problems. Many nobles and peasants left the subjugated regions and took refuge in the mountains of Slovakia and Transylvania. But the population of the plain, though diminished by these migrations, remained mostly of native origin. Economic conditions varied from one region to another. Although the majority of Hungarians continued to gain their livelihood by agriculture, and although the royal cities were everywhere in decline, the lands of the nobility in Royal Hungary and Transylvania were administered and cultivated by methods similar to those prevailing in Poland and Bohemia. The cities and the smaller towns, even if impoverished, largely preserved their traditional appearance.

Turkish Hungary presented a quite different picture: here the physical aspect of places changed. The buildings of the Gothic and Renaissance periods, with their statues and extravagant decoration, scandalized the Turk, who considered them idolatrous and systematically destroyed them; those that were spared fell slowly into decay. This is why the Hungarian plain today seems strangely bereft of monuments of ancient Western civilization: only the ruins remain. The splendour it had attained before the Turkish conquest is now forgotten. Edifices of a kind alien to Europe suddenly appeared. The old Gothic spires were replaced by the minarets and domes of mosques, while hitherto unknown forms of secular architecture also made their appearance. Everywhere the East imposed on Hungary an architecture which in itself marked the distance between two worlds. Historians admit that some small towns enjoyed a surge of prosperity with the shifting of markets and the demands of a new clientele. But even these assumed an Oriental character; though the number of craft establishments increased, the majority of tailors and shoemakers working in them were Muslims. In the country areas the Hungarian people, even more wretched under the Turkish yoke, cultivated the land and tended flocks for the benefit of the conqueror.

The migrations of peasants from the central region multiplied. Some followed their lords into Slovakia or Transylvania, or, wherever conditions seemed likely to prove at all tolerable, attached themselves to new masters, accepting what was almost a state of bondage. Others formed a new social group, already in evidence by the sixteenth century, which was to become famous and which, in its origins and the nature of its activities, presented certain affinities with the Cossacks of the Don and Volga plains. The *hayduks* were refugees from the great plain who had organized themselves along military lines. They had been well prepared for their new role by their earlier way of life and the traditional methods of Hungarian stockbreeding and cattle-trading. It had never been the practice in Hungary to drive herds back into sheds each day. When a cattle-owner wished to sell his animals, which sometimes meant sending them to distant markets, he had them rounded up and taken to their destination by herdsmen. The caravans, travelling along the valley of the Danube, took several months to reach the German towns. As they were liable to be attacked by brigands on the way, these herdsmen had become accustomed to carrying arms and were able to defend themselves or forestall an attack. In the confusion that followed the Turkish invasion many of them refused to become serfs and take up a fixed abode; instead they preferred to occupy abandoned or unguarded lands along an ill-defined frontier. They formed small bands which, over the years, were continually swollen by the arrival of newcomers from all parts of Hungary. Their first objective was to attack the Turks, to retaliate with raids against those who had raided them. Soon, however, they began to offer themselves for hire as mercenaries and in return demanded guarantees and privileges for their settlements and villages. The Hungarian nobility tried to disperse them and the Diets issued measures against them, but both the emperor and the princes of Transylvania engaged their services. The term 'hayduk', like the terms 'hussar' and 'Croat', acquired a more general usage. Hayduks were to be seen at official ceremonies in Prague, rather like the Swiss Guard of the popes, but they were merely show-figures. The true hayduks lived in colonies along the frontier, in villages protected by privileges; their number had risen to several tens of thousands. Some of them had, however, settled on the great seigniorial estates as serfs.[10]

The result of the Turkish invasion had thus been to reduce Hungary, for nearly two hundred years, to territorial dismemberment and an ever greater remoteness from the political and social structures of the rest of Europe. This state of affairs was to persist until the beginning of the eighteenth century and the great liberating campaigns of Prince Eugene of Savoy.

※

While the Turkish war subjected Hungary to a long period of national humiliation and increasing misery, other problems confronted the rest of the Danubian region.

First of all came the religious crisis of the sixteenth century, which not only convulsed the Holy Roman Empire, but contributed to the birth of modern Germany within that Empire. There was initially no question of breaking with Catholicism; the aim was rather to purify the Church and to compel a recalcitrant Papacy and Curia to introduce the reforms which they were still promising, but which they seemed unwilling to put into effect. Christendom was to be rejuvenated with the true spirit of the Gospel, through the preachings of Luther. The Germans had been the first to rediscover the true faith: would a German Messianic movement bring about the spiritual regeneration of the world? But at the roots of the German Reformation lay reawakened memories of John Huss and the Council of Constance. Many of Luther's demands—communion under both kinds for the faithful, the renunciation of wealth by the clergy, a simpler form of worship in keeping with the spirit of early times—coincided with the reforms urged by Huss and his followers. 'We are all Hussites,' Luther declared. For national and sociological reasons, however, Lutheranism found no easy link with the Hussite tradition. Its influence was widespread in Bohemia, initially among the middle class, for the towns maintained regular commercial and spiritual relations with Saxony.[11] As long as the archiepiscopal see was not occupied by a Roman archbishop who recognized the existence of the *Compactata*, the Calixtines came under the authority of the consistory of Prague and its administrator (the term 'Calixtine', emphasizing devotion to the chalice, is more appropriate here than 'Hussite'). There were two opposing factions at the consistory. One of the factions, more influenced by Lutheran teachings and by hatred for Rome and the Holy See, gained the upper hand in 1524 when Havel Carera, an admirer of Luther, became administrator. The other faction had its revenge in the following year, placing one of its members at the head of the councils of the city of Prague. For this group, the most important thing was to preserve the *Compactata*, thereby guaranteeing the faithful the use of the chalice and at the same time ensuring the consecration of the clergy by Roman bishops. But it failed to prevent the infiltration of Lutheran ideas, which had the advantages of being novel and well-expounded.

A form of crypto-Lutheranism thus evolved in Bohemia, among both Hussites and Catholics. Many people were waiting to see what would be the outcome of the reform movement in Germany. Would a council be convened at last? Would reforms be introduced in such a way as to satisfy the disciples and allies of Luther? If there was no council, could not the emperor convoke a German synod whose decisions would have the force of law? Luther still spoke of his 'dear Emperor

Charles', even after the break with Rome and the organization of the Protestant movement at the Diet of Speyer in 1529.[12]

Yet twenty years of uncertainty elapsed before the towns of Bohemia declared their support for the elector of Saxony in the struggle between the Protestants of the Empire and the emperor. This very uncertainty encouraged the most diverse spiritual tendencies. The intellectuals welcomed the Erasmian view which denounced the superstitions and pessimism of medieval faith without subscribing to Lutheran theology. In the fifteenth century a group of zealous reformers who wanted to detach themselves from the world had broken away from the official Hussite movement. Their preacher was Peter Chelčický, a mystic whose exemplary life, ideal of simplicity and practice of total poverty held a great appeal for the ordinary folk who became the first converts to his teachings. But these 'Brothers' had not been able to stand entirely aloof from the world. They had admitted that the performance of administrative functions or military service, provided these were derived from a legitimate authority, did not prevent people from gaining their salvation or practising the basic virtues. On the other hand, in their eyes neither commerce, because of the elements of profit and usury, nor art, because of its sensuality, could be commended. They were people of the earth who were content with little and served their masters well, but they would have faced martyrdom rather than renounce their faith. They were concentrated mainly in the region of Litomysl. It is easy to see how, amid the general turbulence which then affected men's minds and hearts, they succeeded in spreading their influence among the minor nobility of knights and in the Mladá-Boleslav region even obtained the protection of powerful lords such as the Krajk, who helped them to open schools and print Bibles.[13]

Much still depended on the princes, and in particular Ferdinand. As early as 1521, Charles V had thought of leaving Germany to reside in Castile, 'for Castile is not accustomed to being without its king'. He handed over the hereditary lands to Ferdinand and entrusted him with the administration of the Empire. Charles V was deeply attached to the Roman faith and clung with all his might to the oath he had taken in the cathedral of Aix-la-Chapelle after his election, when he had sworn always to give to 'the Holy Father the Roman Pope and to his Church the submission which is their due'. But he had admitted Erasmians to his Council. The emperor distinguished between fidelity to the Church and to Roman doctrine, on the one hand, and submission to papal policies, on the other. He had waged war on the Pope and his troops had pillaged Rome savagely. It was his opinion that the voices of the German theologians should be heard at a Council of the Church. Ferdinand was no more a fanatic than Charles. But his Spanish education had endowed him with greater intransigence in matters of doctrine. In 1527 he promulgated a general edict against Lutheranism. At the Diet of Speyer in 1529 he presented in the name of the emperor a text for the restoration of religious peace which had not in fact issued from Charles V, but which he had drawn up himself; Ferdinand's text provoked the 'protest' of the princes and cities of the Empire, who were determined to secure the right to reform the Church themselves within their respective territories. But the Protestants were far from being united doctrinally.

Their chief concern was communion under both kinds, which they regarded as of much greater significance than the subtleties of theology. The Utraquist reformers of Bohemia now became close allies of the Protestants of the Empire.

Saxon influence had an increasingly important effect among the middle classes of Bohemia. When war broke out between the emperor and the League of Schmalkalden, led by the prince of Saxony, Ferdinand encountered resistance from the Bohemian towns as he prepared to go to his brother's assistance. The towns assembled an army to support the League, but failed to intervene in time to prevent the Saxons from suffering a crushing defeat at the battle of Mühlberg (1547). Bohemia was punished by its king for this act of resistance.

Bohemia was not alone in its adherence to heresy. In Austria, Lutheran propositions had been preached in the cathedral of St. Stephen in Salzburg; one after the other the families of the Austrian nobility, Dietrichstein, Khevenhüller, Zinzendorf, Starhemberg, Puchheim, joined the ranks of the Reformation.[14] It has been said that, if the sovereign had not had the reputation of being a staunch Catholic, the movement would have been less widespread, since opposition was inspired to some extent by political motives. But the Reformation cannot be explained by what was only one of many causes.

The interruption of the Council of Trent, prolonged uncertainty and the extension of the schism in Germany where, despite the authority of Melanchthon and his attempted reconstruction of doctrine in the Augsburg Confession, new Churches were appearing in profusion, heedless of the threat of papal anathema—all these factors help to explain the great religious transformation that now took place in the countries of the Danube. Sectarian movements similar to those in Bohemia were occurring in the Austrian duchies and in the Tyrol. Among these sects were the Anabaptists or *Hütterischen Brüder*, whose eschatological doctrines, held in check as long as ecclesiastical authority had remained firm, spread rapidly amid the general spiritual disorder of the time, as religious and social structures came under assault. Hungary was also involved. When Charles V, on the death of his aunt Margaret, decided to entrust the government of the Netherlands to his sister Maria, queen of Hungary, she had to clear herself of her reputation for holding Erasmian views. Maria insisted that she had always remained a good Catholic, but it was none the less true that reformers—and perhaps even Protestants—had been members of her entourage. The new religion thus flourished in Hungary and Transylvania just as it had done in Bohemia and Austria. In these countries national differences still counted less than privilege and social rank. It would be an exaggeration to say that the Germans were fated to adopt Lutheranism and the non-Germans, the Magyars and Slavs, the doctrines of Zwingli and Calvin. Yet some distinction of this kind must inevitably be made: the German towns embracing Lutheran ideas, the nobility and peasantry rallying to Western Protestantism. These divergences cannot, however, be attributed solely to nationality. In this period of reform, each group was primarily concerned to preserve its privileges and thereby maintain its freedom.

Churches multiplied, mingling the old sectarian traditions with the new theology of the Reformation. The arrival of refugees from Germany and Switzerland, the welcome they received in the homes of the nobility, where the Renaissance had nourished a love of books and of learning, and, above all, the independent spirit of Hungary and the absence of a strong royal power led the Hungarian counties to assume a diversity of religious positions. But the most obvious consequence of the religious crisis was that, by the mid-sixteenth century, although Catholicism was still strong in each of these countries, the Danubian region as a whole had become Protestant, despite its prince's loyalty to the Catholic faith. Although the Emperor Ferdinand remained a Catholic, he always preserved a clear under-standing of the general situation. The period of the Council of Trent was one of constant struggles between the Habsburgs and the Papacy. When Charles V abdi-cated and handed over the government of the Empire to Ferdinand, king of the Romans and his representative in the Empire for more than a quarter of a century, Pope Paul IV was at first unwilling to recognize the new emperor, whom the Curia accused of having shown complaisance towards the Reformation. Pius IV was more conciliating. During the final sessions of the Council of Trent, the imperial ambassadors and the German bishops maintained, probably quite rightly, that to allow the faithful communion under both kinds was the surest way of halting the Reformation and bringing a large number of dissidents back to the Church. In the minds of many people, communion under both kinds was merely the fulfilment of the command given by Christ himself at the Last Supper: 'He took the chalice into his venerable hands and said: Drink of this, all of you.' In vain the theologians invoked the traditional practice of the Church or insisted that the grace received through one kind was no less than that received through both. According to the Articles of Schmalkalden (1536), this was a sophistical doctrine (*doxosophia ista*); even if the argument were sound, communion under one kind could not represent in its entirety the institution ordained by Christ.

While the majority of the faithful was incapable of fully appreciating subtleties of dogma, many of them would be satisfied if they were allowed to partake of the chalice; in this way they would be sure of finding salvation within the old Church and might even be happy to remain within the fold. The emperor, the duke of Bavaria, the German princes and the bishops of the Danubian countries (among them the bishop of Pécs, in Hungary) urged the Council of Trent to accede to this request. But the Spanish, Portuguese and Italian theologians were afraid of encouraging a heretical interpretation of the Eucharist and of jeopardizing the entire doctrinal achievement of the Council by making an imprudent concession that might prove to be only the first. In September 1562 it was decided to leave the matter to the Pope, who would decide which countries should be granted com-munion from the chalice.[15]

Although the archbishop of Prague was not one of those most in favour of communion under both kinds, and although some Latins held no strong opinions on the subject, this debate provoked a confrontation between the religious worlds of northern Europe and the Mediterranean. This was not a question of national conflicts, for Slavs and Germans were united in demanding communion under both kinds. What now emerged was a more mystical and troubled religious sensibility that had been slowly evolving before the crisis of the sixteenth century.

Furthermore, the political and social structure of the Empire was an agglomeration of distinct elements, each determined to safeguard its own particular interests without wishing to undermine the solidarity of the whole. The Latins manifested a more rigorous concern with uniformity. They looked to absolute values, liturgical disciplines and a doctrinal unity which would permit no divergence of opinion. Certainly, they recognized the impossibility of totally suppressing diversities of regional and cultural origin; but they were not deterred from their pursuit of an ideal order, a unified and universally recognized system of established practice.

What was to be the outcome of the confrontation? Having failed to obtain a liturgical concession that had no bearing on essential doctrine, the emperor and his bishops had to accept the Catholic Reformation and its Ultramontane principles. They received powerful support from the Jesuits and from the great reforming campaign of Peter Canisius, the new Pope Boniface. It would be a mistake to imagine that the resourceful Society of Jesus conducted a policy of coercion everywhere; on the contrary, the Jesuits began at an early stage to seek recruits to their Order in the countries they visited and attempted to channel each nation's traditions and modes of thought towards their purpose of restoring obedience to Rome. But clashes were to become more frequent between the Catholic Reformation, which had to overcome an increasing number of obstacles in order to gain converts, and the Protestant Reformation, which was forced to adopt a defensive position and to see its churches divided one from another. The sovereign princes, having failed to secure ecclesiastical reforms from the Council of Trent or from a national council, clung firmly to their right to impose on their subjects the particular doctrines of their own theologians, a right which they regarded as one of the attributes of their *Landeshoheit*. The nobles, who claimed an authority over their domains almost as great as that which the princes wielded over their territories, were to prove zealous champions of one faith or the other, according to circumstance and personal conviction.

In their efforts to bring populations back to the Church the Catholic missionaries were themselves quite prepared to turn to princes and lords for support. The great religious crisis thus resulted in a strengthening of individual authority in central Europe. In such conditions, once it became clear that neither the Catholic nor the Protestant camp would be able to suppress the other by force, the only possible solution was compromise.

Ferdinand I, who as king of Hungary was continually on his guard against the Turkish menace, found it necessary to humour the imperial princes. He granted them religious concessions in return for subsidies to fight his war. However loyal to the Church he might be, there could be no question of Ferdinand defeating the Protestants by arms; in the face of the Turkish peril the Christian armies of the Empire would have to present a united front and, when the danger became extreme, the same sacrifices of men and money would be expected of all.

Under his son, Maximilian II (emperor 1564–76), the situation remained the same in Austria and Bohemia and in those countries where Ferdinand had considered it prudent to establish his younger sons as rulers. The position in each country varied according to the personal whims of its prince. Maximilian II, described by one historian as the 'enigmatic emperor', appears either to have inclined towards Lutheranism or to have desired some form of universal religion uniting all the followers of Christ. Unable to achieve his object, Maximilian granted numerous concessions to the Germans and the Bohemians, who adopted the Confession of 1575. In the Tyrol, Ferdinand, who, by his marriage to a patrician, Philippine Welser, had set the precedent for the morganatic marriages of the Habsburgs, established the Jesuits at Innsbruck. The Tyrol, where the towns and market centres contained many Protestants, but where the nobility and the rural population had remained Catholic, thus became a bastion of the Counter-Reformation. The Archduke Charles, who had been allotted the provinces of Innerösterreich or Inner Austria (Styria, Carinthia, Carniola and Trieste), was the most Catholic of the Habsburgs. But Styria was likely to be the first to suffer from the Turkish threat and Charles was therefore forced to come to terms with the Protestant nobles and to issue new pacificatory edicts. Under the pretext of maintaining its religious liberties, the local aristocracy merely strengthened its political independence from the *Landesfürst*. On the other hand, the unity of the dynasty had been preserved: Maximilian had to send his sons to Spain, to the court of Philip II, so that their education could be completed in an environment far removed from the dangers of heresy.

❧

Although in the Middle Ages the feudal and seigniorial system of the West and that of the Danubian region may have been dissimilar in certain respects, they had not been fundamentally different. In the fifteenth century, however, a distinction began to emerge which became increasingly marked in the sixteenth century, with the result that the two systems were eventually totally alien in their economic and social structure.

In the West, the seigniorial system continued to exist and 'feudal' rights were still invoked, but the peasants had established their personal freedom; seigniorial rights, though still sufficiently irksome to provoke frequent discontent and even rebellion, were not an overwhelming burden. Opportunities for social advancement not only existed, but were relatively varied. In the Danubian countries, on the other hand, the seigniorial system became harsher. The personal servitude of the peasant was greater than ever; though he had not lost his right to the hereditary use of his holding or plot, he was now bound by the particularly exacting obligation of performing the corvée[16] or unpaid labour on his lord's private demesne. This phenomenon extended from the hereditary lands of the House of Austria to Hungary, Poland and even Russia (though in Russia special factors were involved). It has even been taken for granted by historians that agrarian Europe was divided into two distinct worlds separated by the Elbe. To distinguish between a free Europe, on the one hand, and a Europe in bondage, on the other, would be an exaggeration. But it can certainly be said that in one half of Europe feudalism (or, more exactly, the seigniorial system) was in decline and capitalism was expanding, while in the other half the great seigniorial domains had increased in area and the peasant found himself under ever stricter obligations to his master. It is doubtless true that in the West, to quote the words of Pierre de Saint-Jacob, a great historian of rural life, 'the seigniory remained the framework of agrarian life',[17] and that the lot of the peasant became harder wherever private ownership expanded to the detriment of communal lands. But the peasant of the West enjoyed advantages that were increasingly rare in the Danubian countries—freedom of movement and opportunities for possessing his own land. In central Europe the seigniorial domain had become a semi-independent little principality. J. Pekař wrote: 'There can be no doubt that the seigniory resembled a small state with its own order, its own administrative and economic system. If a subject passed beyond its boundaries, he entered upon foreign soil where conditions were often utterly different. The life of the peasant was contained almost entirely within the limits of the seigniory. Across the frontier lay another world, another Empire.'[18]

This contrast between two forms of economic and social structure was reflected in the contrast between two political systems that might at first appear similar because both were monarchies. In the West, however, and especially in France, monarchy meant government by the king and his officers: the law resided in the royal will. This sometimes led to despotic acts, but despotism was not inherent in the institution of kingship. On the contrary, absolutism was the source of public well-being and of juridical arbitration between the Estates or between different social groups.

In central Europe the king, whether elected or hereditary, was merely an organ of the state. The real legislative power belonged to the Estates and in particular to the great lords, who derived their strength from their vast domains. The prince who bore the awesome title of emperor, whose ambitions for hegemony in Europe were denounced by publicists when he waged war against the king of France, and who was able to assemble large armies and conduct the policy of a great power, at least for a time, was in reality no more than archduke of Austria and king of Bohemia and Hungary. In none of these countries was he an absolute king; any such pretensions he might have were thwarted. In each of his lands he had to come to terms with the Diet, the assembly of great lords. The policy of the king of France was inseparably linked with the French state, both territory and people. Habsburg policy, which remained primarily dynastic, required the consent of each of the national Diets in turn. Certainly, the nobles of each country served as the instrument of this dynastic policy, in that they provided the counsellors and military leaders necessary for its execution. But, at the same time, the nobles constituted a barrier between the sovereign and his peoples. By resisting unification and administrative centralization, they were able to maintain the power of the Estates, thereby protecting their own interests and limiting the effective authority of the prince in each of his territories. It will be seen later how the realities of seigniorial power were to influence events. One question arises immediately: how did the great lords come to possess the vast domains that formed the basis of their power? The studies of Polish, Czech and Hungarian historians have made it possible to trace the evolution of the seigniorial domain.

In the thirteenth and fourteenth centuries, landowners had found it more profitable to abandon the old system by which rents were paid in kind or by labour and instead to demand payment in money. The practice of emphyteusis, by which land was granted on a long lease in return for an annual rent, proved highly successful in Bohemia. The new system offered advantages to all concerned: the landowner now dealt in money, which the peasant had to obtain by selling more of his produce on the market. The success of the system doubtless depended on increased demand resulting from the growth of the urban population, and also on the use of improved farming techniques to provide a higher yield. Money soon began to lose its value, however, partly owing to the monetary measures introduced by governments. Since the purchasing power of money was reduced, it was no longer to the advantage of the landowner to receive fixed rents. Henceforth it was in his interest to produce foodstuffs which he could sell, and consequently to extend the area of his estate which he cultivated on his own behalf. Thus, when he found himself impoverished by his dependence on fixed rents, he decided to become a producer, thereby reversing the previous trend: the payment of rent by labour, the peasant corvée which he had only recently abandoned, acquired a new significance. The historian František Graus has analysed the reasons for this return to the methods of the past in Bohemia.

All landowners, however great or small their domains, realized that they would profit by reintroducing obligatory peasant labour, which henceforth featured more frequently in new contracts. The knights, who possessed only a few villages and small farms, were no less determined than the others to demand labour from their peasants. The discontent which they aroused sometimes resulted in peasant revolts, but the local Diets were disinclined to halt a process which was benefiting the entire noble class, and especially the upper nobility. A lord who owned a large estate, or who was able to extend his land by purchase or by recovering the plots awarded to the peasants, found himself in a position to produce for a wider market and to sell to foreign customers.

This trend was evident in several regions of central Europe by the fifteenth century, but had not yet become generalized. Historians of Poland have observed its signs along the banks of the Bug and the Vistula, where fields of rye and wheat appeared.[19] The crops were sent to Danzig, where the ships of the Hanse collected them for distribution to Germany and even more distant parts; soon Dutch ships were also engaged in transporting the crops. The great estates of the landowner-producers were enlarged at the expense of medium-sized holdings; the proportion of owners of manses (the unit of landed property necessary for the subsistence of a large family) to small farmers was reversed. The first category diminished because the lands of the peasant proprietors (*rolníki*) had gradually dwindled with the growth of the great seigniorial domains; the second category increased because many impoverished peasant proprietors were relegated to the ranks of the small tenant-farmers. The trend discernible in Poland was also to be observed in Bohemia and Hungary, in other sectors of agricultural production.[20]

In the late sixteenth century the landowners of southern Bohemia began to breed fish on their estates, possibly owing to an increase in food consumption caused by a rise in the urban population. In this humid region of marshland, dams and then ponds were constructed. Fish-breeding became more widespread after the Hussite wars and as activity returned to the towns, where demand was greater.

On the home market the salted fish imported from the Hanse towns came into competition with the fresh fish caught in the ponds of Bohemia. Soon the Bohemian carp were more popular than the herrings of the north and became a regular part of the nation's food consumption; for centuries to come, carp was a national dish in Czech homes. When the fish were caught, they were weighed in large wooden pails with handles (*džber*) which had a capacity of some thirty litres, and were then put in baskets which floated behind rafts. They were taken along the Vltava to Prague, or to Vienna and along the Danube to Passau. Production for 1524 on the estate of Krumlov (Krummau), on the banks of the Vltava, was 934 pails, sold for 2,178 Meissen *Becher* (a silver coin slightly lower in value than the imperial florin, according to the monetary regulations of 1559). The total revenue for fish production, including the sale of pike and of spawn, was 2,302 Meissen Becher. Twenty years later, on the estate of Třeboň, production amounted to 4,771 Meissen Becher. Ponds became more numerous and the income derived from them helped to make the fortunes of the great seigniorial families of southern Bohemia, such as the Hradec and the Rožmberk; the very presence of these ponds changed the aspect of the Bohemian countryside for a long period.

The brewing of beer was an equally profitable enterprise on seigniorial estates. In the sixteenth century, society as a whole still depended for its sustenance on a very limited number of foodstuffs, mostly consisting of boiled cereals. It was therefore a matter of importance if one drink proved more nourishing than another. The polluted waters in the flat country around the villages revolted even those who were not normally squeamish. Hydromel and wine were both drinks and foods, but many peasants and town-dwellers still drank only sour concoctions made with wild fruits. Beer would provide a wholesome alternative. Good breweries already existed in the towns, but not in large numbers. The landowners of Bohemia therefore set up breweries on their estates, certain of finding a clientele in the neighbouring towns and even in the villages, where they secured a monopoly in the sale of beer to the peasants. A high proportion of the revenues recorded in seigniorial accounts, about one-third of the total, came from the fisheries and breweries. For the year 1559–60, on the estate of Jindřichův-Hradec (Neuhaus), the revenue from the old seigniorial rights was still as high as 38 per cent, but the fisheries and breweries each produced 29 per cent. The breweries were eventually to prove the more successful: in the following century the revenue which they brought to landowners was about 60 per cent of total receipts. The capitalist enterprises of these powerful lords rested on compulsory peasant labour (the corvée): it was in this that the great economic and social transformation of central Europe lay.

To find the workmen needed for the upkeep of the ponds, catching fish, making beer and transportation, it was necessary either to have recourse to paid labour or to extend compulsory labour. Moreover, the growth of breweries meant that more hops and barley had to be cultivated. If one traces the agrarian evolution of Hungary in the works of I. Szabó and Z. Pach, it can be seen that in that country also seigniorial domains increased in area during the sixteenth century. The estates of the Nádasdy, Dobó, Forgásch and Drugeth families produced larger quantities of corn. In other regions, stock-raising progressed and cattle were sent to the markets of Vienna and Venice. Some great landowners joined together to form a cattle-trading association; others, extending the privilege of *educillatio* which gave them control of the sale of their wine, now demanded a part of the vine-harvest from their peasants and acquired a monopoly of the trade.[21] The use of the peasant corvée spread throughout Danubian Europe, rising from one to two or even three days a week. The extension of the corvée was evident both in Bohemia and Moravia, and also in Austria, though not to the same degree. It was now taken for granted that peasant labour was permanently at the lord's disposal. In certain Hungarian manorial registers (that of the abbey of Tapolca, for example) it is written that peasants must perform any service their lord might require of them— *ad omnia servitia pro libitu domini compellantur* (1570).[22] In Austria the peasants of one estate were obliged to travel as far as Styria to fetch furniture for the lord's castle.[23] These are not isolated cases, but the signs of a growing trend. At the same time, the Diets, in which the entire system of contemporary jurisprudence was reflected, adopted increasingly severe measures against the liberty of the peasants, depriving them of the right to leave the lord's domain and refusing to allow grievances against their lord to be heard at a royal tribunal. Henceforth, each seigniory was to settle its own internal conflicts. Thus in the sixteenth century seigniorial authority, evolving from forces which František Graus believes can be discerned even before the time of the Hussite wars, strengthened its hold over both land and men.[24]

The great lords were now able to lead a more luxurious existence. The old seigniorial dwellings, austere fortresses standing on high ground, were transformed into fine residences by the addition of new buildings and a skilful re-arrangement of rooms. Daily life assumed a greater style. Around the inner courtyards ran Italian arcades, elegant colonnades which caught the sun on its too rare appearances and brought the grace of the Latin world to these countries of the north. Furniture, tapestries and mirrors, brought from Italy and Germany or made in the country itself by foreign craftsmen or their pupils, showed a greater profusion and variety. Beautiful books and rare fabrics were collected. Carriages were made with better suspension and more attractive exteriors. The quality and ornamentation of armour and weapons acquired a new luxuriousness and horsemen selected pure-bred animals of stamina and spirit. Great value was attached to the cultivation of the mind and the life of the soul. The reading of the Bible, the singing of psalms among Protestants, a new attention to liturgy among Catholics, the decoration of churches in accordance with the instructions of the Council of Trent and, on both sides, familiarity with the works of ancient Greek and Latin culture, enabled the élite to pursue an interior life of subtle refinement.

Yet this was the lot of only a minority. It must not be thought that society was suddenly split into two, a landed aristocracy controlling vast domains and sub-jecting the peasants of its villages to excessive obligations of labour and, at the opposite extreme, an enslaved rural population. The great seigniorial estate producing for a wide market could not be established just anywhere.[25] It was practicable only in fertile regions or in areas where waterways and roads were easily accessible (southern Bohemia was not originally a fertile region). How could new techniques be applied in the mountainous forestlands or on the lands of the small farmer, in areas where the soil was so poor that the inhabitants were barely able to obtain their daily subsistence? Here, the number of labourers available was of much less significance than the quality of techniques handed down through the ages and developed by experience, the special skills possessed only by the most expert. This was true of the vineyard regions, for instance. Furthermore, although the towns attracted labourers from the rural areas, they also helped to maintain traditional forms of agrarian life in their immediate environs, where the small or medium-sized estates depended on their regular custom. A certain traditional rhythm of exchange, unaffected by the temptations of change, continued to operate at the level of small-scale production. The Hungarian historian, Z. Pach, has shown how the agrarian evolution of Hungary in the sixteenth and seventeenth centuries caused an ever-widening breach between the Hungarian economy and that of western Europe. But he admits that, at the end of the sixteenth century, two agrarian systems still existed. In one, paid labour was the dominant factor; the more prosperous peasant employed his less fortunate neighbours to cultivate his lands. This more exalted stratum of the rural population was ready to assume middle-class status. In the other system, compulsory labour became more widespread as the great seigniorial domains continued to absorb small peasant holdings. It was not yet clear which of the two systems would prevail.[26]

Moreover, as the corvée system spread through Poland, Bohemia, Austria and Hungary, it appeared in two distinct forms: the wealthier peasants, who can be compared with the peasant proprietors of the West, had to bring their own animals, while those who had no animals of their own and little or no land simply gave their labour. The first of these categories was generally the more exacting; eventually it meant that carts, draught-animals and farming implements were permanently at the lord's disposal, whereas the second category merely involved extra labour at the peak of seasonal activity. But the very fact that peasants of the first kind were able to provide animals and tools for use on the lord's demesne showed that they possessed the resources necessary for their purchase and maintenance. Thus there existed a class of peasants, either farming their own hereditary holdings or occupying land hired to them by their lord on a money-lease, who were subjected to the requirements of the corvée, but who were nevertheless able to devote a large part of their energies to the cultivation of their own land, which they held by virtue of the obligatory labour that they performed on the lord's preserve. Strictly subjected to the authority of the lord, and in particular to his bailiff, they led a joyless existence under the seigniorial system, but did not suffer the extremes of poverty—those who encountered hardship soon vanished. Although the very existence of the great domain presupposed some form of agrarian capitalism, this was subordinated to the general administration of the estate.[27] Furthermore, these peasant proprietors did not enjoy complete personal liberty; on the contrary, their freedom was curtailed by new obstacles. They were brought under the jurisdiction of their lord and prohibited from marrying without his permission or outside his estate. They had no control over the education of their children. The extent of these restrictions, which weighed heavily both on the person of the peasant and on his land, has induced historians to speak of a new serfdom, a second feudal age.

These three factors—the Turkish war, the religious revolution and, although by the sixteenth century it had not reached its full development, the growth of the great domain—paved the way for the decline of the towns, and especially the royal cities. Yet, at the time of the formation of the Danubian complex of states, the situation of the towns did not appear unpromising.

On the contrary, historians always stress the need for precious metals which made itself felt in the second half of the fifteenth century, and which inspired the voyages of the Portuguese around Africa and the search for a route to the West undertaken by Columbus and the Spaniards, all looking for gold and spices. But, before the European economy was convulsed by the arrival of metals from America, feverish mining activity in central Europe itself provided the European market with a small quantity of gold and a much larger quantity of silver, used for striking coin to facilitate commercial transactions. Although much detailed study is still necessary before these problems can be fully understood, it would seem that the growth of the great seigniorial estate was accompanied by a parallel increase in the production of the workshops, more marked in the western territories of the Habsburgs than in Hungary. Textiles made progress in Bohemia, Moravia, Silesia, where the soil was unsuited to agriculture, and Lusatia. At all events, during the sixteenth century, and especially in the latter half, as prices rose generally throughout Europe to the advantage of the large producers and to the disadvantage of wage-earners, the upper classes of society increased their demand for luxury articles—fabrics, furniture, jewellery, paintings and books—which could not be produced locally in sufficient quantities.

Throughout the Danubian region, in Bohemia, Hungary, Styria and Carniola, mineral deposits were discovered: silver, a little gold, iron, copper, tin, lead and mercury, products indispensable to the Western economy. Rock-salt was found in abundance in the mountains of Austria, making it unnecessary to import sea-salt or salt from Poland. In Bohemia there were two outstandingly successful silver-mines. One was situated on the lands of the Šlik family at Joachymstal, on the inner side of the Sudetic mountains. The coin which this family struck, the thaler, was accepted as imperial money in 1566 (the name of the coin, from *Tal* meaning 'valley', is the origin of the present-day 'dollar').

The other silver-mine was at Kutná Hora. This town, which began as a mining centre, flourished in the fourteenth and fifteenth centuries and became the second most important in the kingdom. The entire population—royal officials, Italian technicians, the middle-class patriciate and even the corporation of miners—contributed to the erection of monuments and churches. The most beautiful of these churches, dedicated to St. Barbara, patron saint of miners, is a masterpiece of the Flamboyant Gothic style. Inside, the ribs run up the pillars to cross on the vault in a series of interlacings in which illuminated blazons are set, as if a fantastic stone tapestry had been hung above the nave. The wall-paintings represent characters from the Bible in fifteenth-century costume and, suggesting a series of portraits, the familiar figures of the citizens and the miners in their white smocks, woollen hoods and leather aprons. While the lines and figures have a Florentine delicacy and precision, the richness of the colouring indicates a predilection for splendour and brilliance. This artistic achievement, which still enchants the visitor, did not prevent frequent social strife from tearing the city apart. The miners' daily task was exhausting, and they all succumbed to illness after a few years' work. The riots provoked by poverty and misery were mercilessly suppressed.[28]

Neusohl or Besztercebánya, in the Slovakian region of Hungary, also acquired a great reputation. The work of Georgius Agricola, *De re metallica*, illustrated with picturesque and faithful engravings, taught the mining techniques used in central Europe. England and soon America sought the services of the technicians of these mining towns. The other towns—the craft and market centres—came into more frequent contact with the country nobles and at the same time were their constant rivals, both economically and politically. As the nobles gradually established themselves as merchants and producers, their trading interests and then the workshops which they set up on their estates came into competition with the towns. In theory, each could have reserved a particular field of activity for itself: the nobility controlling the land, the towns controlling the workshops. But in fact their interests continually overlapped, for the middle class wanted to own land in the low-lying areas and the nobles were penetrating into the towns, where they bought premises but were unwilling to share the citizen's tax burdens. The corporations of master-craftsmen were becoming an increasingly closed world to which journeymen had only limited access; a journeyman could not open a workshop of his own unless he married the widow or daughter of a master-craftsman.

To avert the threat of competition, the corporations clung to their long-established regulations and obstructed innovations. As a result of changing techniques, some of the old crafts, such as parchment manufacture, dwindled in importance, while others progressed (arms manufacture, printing, clock-making). Foreigners were feared, though they continued to flock into the towns whenever their knowledge of new manufacturing processes was needed.

Most historians are nowadays severe in their treatment of the corporations, holding them responsible for retarding production and thereby depriving an expanding market of goods, either in their own country or abroad, and for leaving the small wage-earners in a precarious situation. To justify such a charge, it would be necessary to demonstrate that a much larger market in fact existed, either in the environs of the towns or over a wide radius. Certain regions which lacked agricultural and mineral resources were able to manufacture textiles for the foreign market. Silesia was one such country. The Silesian weavers employed peasants, who worked in their own homes; this marked the beginning of a tradition that only reached full development with the progress of manufacturing production. In the towns, where society was more mobile and intellectual activity more intense, the new religious ideas found a ready welcome and opportunities for propaganda. Since they remained centres of wealth, controlling currencies and the primitive accumulation of capital, the towns bore the brunt of royal taxes and loans—hence the clashes in which the Emperor Ferdinand was involved with the towns of his different kingdoms. When he encountered hostility to his policies, Ferdinand appointed royal officers to take charge of administration and justice. He tried to crush the power of the patricians by suppressing the corporations, which stubbornly reconstituted themselves at once. When the towns resisted his demands for money to fight the German Protestants and the Turks, their urban privileges were withdrawn.

Finally, the imperial government, alarmed by the continual rise in the cost of living and unable to discern its underlying causes, hoped to remedy the situation by decrees which fixed prices and wages, but which indirectly discouraged production.

The stagnation and decline of the towns were aggravated by circumstances which did not depend on the decisions of the government: the arrival of precious metals from America, which deprived the central European mines of their former importance, the more rapid prosperity of the countries of western Europe, which had seaboards on the Atlantic, and various local accidents, such as the flooding of the principal mine at Kutná-Hora, the Esel ('the Ass'). The 'ass', it was now said, had stopped braying. The towns of Hungary were inevitably impoverished by the general disorganization of the country and by the Turkish occupation of the great plain. Even if the towns retained a position of importance in the economy and the general life of the Danubian countries, their role was no longer the same. They were destined neither to activate nor to benefit directly from the agrarian, seigniorial capitalism which was now evolving and which was to characterize the general economy.

Linz remained the most important city, owing to its international market. Two cities, Vienna and Prague, the successive victims of royal reprisals (they were deprived of their privileges and subjected to fiscal exactions), nevertheless experienced a new phase of prosperity when each in turn became the sovereign's place of residence. Maximilian II lived in Vienna from 1564 to 1576; his son and successor, Rudolf II, resided in the royal castle of Prague, the Hradčany. Since both bore the imperial title, it was essential that they should have around them members of the imperial administration and representatives of their 'governments'. The prolonged presence of an emperor revitalized the life of a city: the number of inhabitants, and therefore of consumers, increased and their needs became more diversified. Since the emperors were Catholic princes, they bestowed favours on the religious orders, and especially the Jesuits. For Prague, at the turn of the century, the reign of Rudolf II was a period of prosperity. The emperor had attempted to return to Vienna at the time of the restoration of the Corpus Christi procession in 1578, but the ceremony had degenerated into a riot on the central square, the Graben. Clearly, the Hradčany, built on a hill outside the three towns of Prague, offered greater security than the Hofburg, situated in the heart of the Austrian capital. Rudolf loved this group of royal and seigniorial dwellings and churches, which formed a little town in itself, protected by fortified walls and ditches. On his walks he could easily reach the gardens of his grandmother Anne, and the menagerie, stables and riding rooms. In a lane that ran along the walls he installed laboratories and dwelling-houses for his alchemists and astronomers. The vast and beautiful Wladislas room, built in the Flamboyant style by the last of the Jagellons, was open to merchants when the Diet was not in session. The nobility of Bohemia and travellers from abroad came to admire the display of luxury: fine fabrics, jewellery, books and engravings. Prague produced little for export (only felt hats), but was an important supply centre for the entire kingdom and had to satisfy the needs of a clientele of nobles who were constantly buying and borrowing. Consequently, a great many foreign merchants—from Saxony, Nuremberg and Italy—settled in little colonies within the city-walls and were granted privileges for their corporations and for building their churches. According to their place of residence, they also obtained citizenship of one of the three towns of Prague: the Old Town, the New Town or the Malá Strana (Little Town). Powerful Jewish families established themselves in a ghetto—the Bassewi from Verona, who were both suppliers and bankers, and the Meyzl, who were given permission to build a palace.[29]

On both banks of the river, linked by the famous stone bridge with its two towers, the cosmopolitan society which had thus been superimposed on the native Czech patriciate and proletariat brought a colourful vitality to the city. What did it matter if the emperor had earned a reputation for neglecting the affairs of the Empire and the kingdom of Bohemia, and preferred to be in the company of scholars amid his collections of paintings, among them Albrecht Dürer's *Festival of the Rose garlands*, which was supposed to have been carried by hand all the way from Venice? Among the scholars were semi-magicians like the rabbi Loew, who constructed a mechanical figure known as the Golem, and scientists such as the Dane, Tycho-Brahé, and Kepler, expelled from Styria because of his suspect opinions, who found the freedom to pursue their researches under Rudolf's patronage. Prague was enjoying a period of respite before the troubles that lay ahead.[30]

NOTES

1. For the organs of centralization:
   T. Fellner, *Zur Geschichte der Österreichischen Zentralverwaltung 1493–1848*, M.I.Ö.G., vol. VIII, pp. 258–301; Ernst C. Hellbling, *Österreichische Verfassungs und Verwaltungsgeschichte*, Vienna, 1956; Václav Vaněček, *Dějiny státu a práva v Československu* (for the court of appeal). In *Dějiny Československa*, p. 116, Václav Husa considers that the creation of the court of appeal restricted the juridical autonomy of the towns. This was true, but, on the other hand, it also reinforced the autonomy of the kingdom, since previously appeals could be made to foreign courts.
2. The proclamation is given in the Czech text translated from the original Latin by Karel Doskočil, *Listy a listiny z dějin československých* ('Documents of Czechoslovak History'), 1938, and reproduced by Václav Husa in *Naše národní minulost v dokumentech* ('Our National Past in Documents'), 1954, p. 202.
3. Chateaubriand, *Mémoires d'Outre-Tombe*, ed. M. Levaillant, vol. IV, p. 248.

4. František Kavka, *Die Habsburger und der böhmische Staat bis zur Mitte des 18°. Jahrhunderts*, in *Historica*, VIII, pp. 35–64, an article to be recommended for its thoroughness and shrewdness. However, the author, applying the Marxist method, attempts to pass a value judgement on the Habsburgs' government in Bohemia, in terms of the efficacy of its economic policy for the well-being of the country. He demonstrates clearly the government's fiscal intentions, which, however, were common to all governments at this time.

5. For all aspects of Ferdinand's policy in Bohemia—in addition to the works of the old Czech historians such as F. M. Pelzel, whose *Geschichte der Böhmen* contains some excellent pages—the two Czechoslovak encyclopaedias, one published in 1932 (vol. IV, 'History') and concerned more with the narrative of events, the other in 1963, of a more sociological character (chapter by J. Macek), offer an exposé of the facts and a wealth of observation.

6. On Soliman the Magnificent: R. B. Merriman, *Soliman the Magnificent*, Cambridge (Mass.), 1944, and Albert H. Lybyer, *The Government of the Ottoman Empire in the Time of Suliman the Magnificent*, Cambridge (Mass.), 1913.

7. K. Brandi, *Charles-Quint et son temps*; Hugo Hantsch, *Die Kaiseridee Karls V*, 1958, and the article *Le problème de la lutte contre l'invasion turque*, pp. 51–60, in *Charles-Quint et son temps*, Paris, Centre National de la Recherche scientifique, 1959.

8. Hugo Hantsch, op. cit., p. 60.

9. In 1966 the fourth centenary of the battle was made the occasion of a very interesting commemoration at Sziget itself, where the fortifications have been partly restored. An exhibition there offered an abundance of factual information about the siege: the war material used by the two armies, German engravings and Turkish miniatures.

10. These last few pages owe much to papers delivered by Cinkovics and Kálmán Benda, professors at the University of Budapest, and Jean Bérenger, assistant professor at the Sorbonne, during a programme of seminar studies on modern Hungary held at the Sorbonne in 1965–6.

11. The organization and operation of mines involved constant exchanges between northern Bohemia, Slovakia and Saxony. Georgius Agricola, the author of the celebrated treatise *De re metallica*, was of Saxon origin.

12. K. Brandi, *Charles-Quint*, French translation, 1951, p. 321.

13. Joseph T. Müller, *Geschichte der Böhmischen Brüder*, I, Herrnhut, 1922. Victor-L. Tapié, *Une église tchèque au XVᵉ siècle: l'Unité des Frères*, 1934.

14. E. Zöllner, *Geschichte von Österreich*, p. 112. Grete Mecenseffy, *Geschichte des Protestantismus in Österreich*, Graz-Köln, 1956.

15. For the early sessions of the Council of Trent: H. Jedin, *Geschichte des Konzils von Trient*, 2 vols., 1949–57.

16. The corvée or forced labour performed by the peasant on the lord's land was commonly known by the Slav word *robot* ('work') throughout the Habsburg monarchy, even in the non-Slavonic countries.

17. P. de Saint-Jacob, *Les Paysans de la Bourgogne du Nord au dernier siècle de l'ancien régime*, Dijon, 1960, p. 50.

18. J. Pekař, *Kniha o Kosti*, vol. II, p. 3.

19. J. Rutkowski, *The Great Domain in Poland*, a basic work. In a study of the crisis of feudalism in the sixteenth and seventeenth centuries, published in the Czechoslovak Historical Review (ČSČH) of 1964, pp. 347–64, Miroslav Hoch and Josef Petráň state and discuss the theses of the Polish historians Malowist and Maczak.

20. A pioneering article of major importance by Aloís Mikai, 'Great Landed Properties in Southern Bohemia from the 14th to the 18th Centuries', *Sborník historický*, 1952, from which the figures quoted have been taken. For Hungary, the works of István Szabó, *Tanulmányok a magyar parasztság történetéböl* ('Studies in the History of the Magyar Peasantry'), Budapest, 1948, and Zs. P. Pach, *Die ungarische Agrarentwicklung im 16.-17. Jahrhundert*, Budapest, 1964 (no. 54 of the collection *Studia Historica*, 164 pages). The first chapter of this latter book has been translated into French and published in no. 6 of the *Annales* (Nov.–Dec. 1966) under the title *Hongrie au XVIᵉ siècle*. István Szabó recalls that, from 1543 to 1553, in thirty-seven comitats, 75 per cent of the land belonged to the great domains and that, during the civil wars and the wars against the Turks, it was in the interest of the lords to increase the production of cereals in order to supply the armies.

21. Pach, op. cit., p. 18 *et seq.*

22. Ibid., p. 57.

23. G. Grüll, *Die Robot in Oberösterreich*, Linz, 1952, pp. 67 and 68.

24. The fine book by František Graus, *Dějiny venkovského lidu v Čechách v době předhusitské* ('History of the Rural People in Bohemia in pre-Hussite Times'), I, II, Prague, 1957, seeks the origins of this phenomenon in the distant past. But this vigorous analysis throws much light on the later period.

25. Josef Petráň contrasts the great domains of the Rožmberks (southern Bohemia), the Smiřický and Trčka families, which embraced several hundred villages and thousands of peasants, with the small estates of the knights, which comprised few villages (from one to five) and, consequently, a relatively small number of peasants.

26. Pach, op. cit., p. 33. See also the article by I. Sinkovics, *Le servage héréditaire en Hongrie aux XIV-XVIIᵉ siècles*, pp. 47–99, in the collective work *La Renaissance et la réformation en Pologne et en Hongrie*, Budapest, 1963.

27. The condition of these peasants, to which the authors of all pre-1914 works of agrarian history (Krofta, Pekař, Šimák) refer, is clearly defined in three recent books in Czech: Otto Placht, *Lidnatost a společenska skladba českého státu v 16–18 stoleti* ('Population and Social Structure in the Bohemia of the 16th–18th centuries'), 1957, p. 121 *et seq.*; Vílem Procházka, *Česká poddanská nemovitost* ('The Landed Property of the Subjected Bohemian Peasants'), Prague, 1963; and Josef Petráň, *Poddaný lid v Čechách na prahu třicetileté valky* ('The Subjected People of Bohemia on the Threshold of the Thirty Years' War'), 1964, which also shows the obstacles that faced the great domain and prevented it from becoming the sole determining factor in the production of goods.

    J. Petráň, in an article entitled 'The movement of the subjected population and it, juridical condition [*jeho osobní právní vztahy*] in Bohemia before the White Mountain's published in the review *Československý Časopis Historický*, V, 1957, 1 and 3, has shown that the great lords sought to retain both the settled rural population, which possessed lands, and the non-established population, which was admitted temporarily on to the domain, for both categories of peasant came under his judicial and fiscal authority. The corvée (*robot*) was still not general and the non-established population provided a source of wage-earning labour at the height of the season, although these peasants were also sought by the towns. The towns were supposed to employ only those bearing a letter of release from their landlord. In fact, the regulations of 1517, 1530 and 1567, authorizing the lord to reclaim fugitive peasants, should be seen rather as the assertion of a principle than as proof of its application.

28. On the particular case of Kutná Hora, see the study by Václav Husa, *Výrobní vztahy v českém mincovnictví v XV a XVI století* ('Mining Conditions in Bohemian Coin Manufac-

ture in the 15th and 16th Centuries'), Prague, Academy of Sciences of Czechoslovakia, 1955, 45 pages.

29. J. Janáček, *Řemeslná vyroba v českých meštech v 16 stoleti* ('Craft Production in Czech Towns in the 16th Century'). An ample bibliography concerning the towns of Austria in Erich Zöllner, *Geschichte Österreichs*, pp. 598–9.

30. For Rudolf II, the good Austrian histories of the mid-nineteenth century remain authoritative works: Anton Gindely, *Rudolf II und seine Zeit*, 1868, 2 vols.; Peter Ritter von Chlumecky, *Karl von Žerotín und seine Zeit*, 1862–79, 2 vols. See also in Oscar Schürer, *Prag*, 1935, the chapter entitled *Die Kunstkammer Europas*, p. 149, and in *Dějiny Prahy* ('History of Prague'), 1964, a collective publication edited by J. Janáček, chapter VIII, 'Prague before the White Mountain', pp. 279–323, written by Janáček himself. The latter two texts are accompanied by some fine illustrations.

J. Janáček, *Dějiny obchodu v předbělohorské Praze* ('History of Commerce in Prague before the White Mountain'), 1958.

4

The Thirty Years' War

WHERE SHOULD the historian seek the remote, deep-rooted causes of the Thirty Years' War which, beginning in the Danubian countries, and more precisely in Bohemia, spread first to Germany and then to the whole of Europe, modifying its political and social equilibrium? Like all great upheavals, this war has been differently explained according to the individual viewpoints of historians and the preoccupations of their age. Since the present trend is towards an economic and social interpretation of history, many authors consider the Thirty Years' War to have been the result of a crisis provoked by the transition from an agrarian economy to a commercial capitalism supplying vast markets, and by the blow thus delivered to the seigniorial system, which defended itself and, with the support of the Catholic Church and the princes, emerged triumphant in central Europe.

In reality, by the end of the sixteenth century the various factors analysed earlier —the Habsburg policy of maintaining supremacy over the Danubian countries and retaining the imperial crown, the struggle against the Turks, the unresolved confrontation between Catholics and Protestants, and the rise of the landed aristocracy—had combined to create an instability and unrest which, under the pressure of events that were in themselves of secondary importance, degenerated into crisis and general war.

The Empire still aspired to a settlement of the religious question, hoping for a stable peace which, though it might halt the process of secularization, would guarantee the Protestants possession of the lands that they had acquired. Rather than await such a settlement, Rome, supported by the kings of Spain, attempted to lay the foundations of the conversion of Germany by placing proved Catholics in the most important administrative posts in both the Empire and the kingdom of Bohemia.

The Papal Court sometimes wondered if elected sovereigns would not have been preferable to unreliable Habsburgs, since Poland, where the Diet chose the king, was setting an example of Catholic fidelity. In 1588 the papal legate Aldobrandini, the future Clement VIII, exchanged some curious table-talk with one of the Lobkowicz family: 'Vivat futurus pontifex! Vivat futurus rex Bohemiae!'[1] But this was a highly hazardous solution. A more effective plan, it seemed, was to remove the Protestants from high positions and to replace them with resolute Catholics whose personal wealth invested them with great power. In the countries ruled by the secondary branches of the dynasty—the Tyrol and Styria—had not

84

princes committed to a policy of conversion succeeded in bringing the Protestant nobility and people back to the Roman Church? Admittedly, this had been achieved only by numerous banishments and to the detriment of the country's economic stability. If Bavaria had become a citadel of Catholicism, it owed its position to the firmness of its neighbours, the bishops of Salzburg, to the activities of the Jesuits of Ingolstadt and, in no less a measure, to the personal initiative of its Wittelsbach kings, Albert V and Maximilian. Thus, the Protestant aristocracy of both the Empire and the Danubian countries, though numerically the stronger, might well feel that its faith and worldly interests were being threatened by a minority of Catholic princes and lords.

The extension of compulsory peasant labour and the growth of the great seigniorial estate, together with the new taxes imposed to finance the Turkish war, provoked the rural populations to armed rebellions which caused general alarm. Each side claimed that the revolts had been caused by the behaviour of its adversaries: the Catholics were accused of using too violent methods of conversion, the Protestants of setting an example of contempt for the laws of the Empire and indulging in dangerous innovations.[2]

At the same time, the Turkish threat had been revived. After a long war against Persia, the Turks had resumed the offensive in 1593, first from Bosnia and then from Belgrade. There was empty talk of retaliation by the West, a mighty Christian coalition uniting the Empire, Venice, Poland and Russia. But the West was the prisoner of internal rivalries. Soon, famine, foreign invasion and troubles over the succession were to submerge Russia, robbing it of the benefits of the stability which had been achieved by the harsh but effective policies of Ivan the Terrible. The war thus passed into Hungary, where towns were reconquered only to be lost again. The Turks gained only one important victory, at Keresztes in 1596. In 1598 the town of Györ-Raab was reconquered by a German general, Adolf von Schwarzenberg, who received the insignia of the Golden Fleece from the emperor himself. In Transylvania a Hungarian prince, Sigismund Báthory, nephew of the king of Poland, and a Wallachian lord, Michael the Brave, each in turn succeeded in establishing an autonomous state, but not for long. The brutal reprisals made by the imperial armies, and in particular the army of General Basta, led to a rebellion by a Hungarian lord named Bocskaj, supported by the hayduks. Bocskaj soon made himself master of Transylvania, even to the extent of carrying with him the Protestant nobility of Royal Hungary. Thus in 1606 the only possible solution seemed to be to bring a halt to war by making concessions to the enemy: to have done with Bocskaj by granting religious liberty to the Protestants of Hungary, and to have done with the sultan by taking advantage of his difficulties with the Persia of Shah Abbas, even if this meant accepting the principle of *uti possidetis.*

Such were the implications of the agreements reached with the Hungarians at Vienna, in June 1606, and with the sultan at Sitva-Torok, in the following November. Although the sultan retained the towns of Erlau, Kanisza and Esztergom, he renounced the annual tribute in return for a payment of 20,000 gulden. For the first time, the sultan was making peace not by a unilateral decision of his own authority, but by negotiating with the emperor on equal terms, in the

Western manner. For reasons which remain obscure, Rudolf II delayed the ratification of the agreements indefinitely. On the advice of the Pope and the king of Spain, his brothers and cousins in Styria decided to entrust the direction of the dynasty's affairs to Archduke Matthias, the eldest of the emperor's brothers, a rather colourless figure, who had already involved himself in political rivalries in the Netherlands and in Poland. Family dissension, the *Bruderzwist*, was once again dividing the House of Habsburg. In 1608, Matthias secured recognition as king of Hungary at Pressburg, after confirming the privileges of the kingdom; then he granted religious liberty to the Protestants of Austria, raised an army, advanced into Moravia where he obtained that country's support, and marched on Prague. Matthias and his advisers—among them Cardinal Khlesl, bishop of Vienna—hoped thereby to forestall a general uprising of the provinces against the dynasty. To their great surprise, Bohemia remained loyal to Rudolf. The emperor remained in possession of the kingdom, but had to cede Hungary and the two Austrias to Matthias (the peace of Libeň, 1608). He rewarded the loyalty of the Bohemians by granting them a religious charter, the Majestát. Proclaimed eleven years after the Edict of Nantes, the Majestát was another of those compromises which were necessary in order to arrest the conflict between the two religious camps. But the Edict of Nantes had been a concession made by a strong king who was master of a country reconciled under his authority. The Majestát gave the Utraquists of Bohemia, who had defined their doctrinal position in a new confession of faith, a number of important privileges: freedom of worship, extended even to the peasantry, the right to build churches, free access to the University of Prague, the right to convoke a special Diet in which only the Protestants of the three Estates would sit, and the right to elect commissaries who, as defenders of the faith, would ensure that the terms of the decree were observed.[3] To an even greater extent than the agreements which Matthias signed with the Protestants of other countries, the Majestát accorded to Bohemia represented the victory of the nobility over the sovereign. The endeavours of the Catholic minority had been thwarted. The Bohemian chancellor, Zdeněk Lobkowicz, the champion of royal authority against the rights of the Diets and a zealous Catholic, refused to give his counter-signature to the Majestát. But he did not resign his office.[4]

After an attempt by the Archduke Leopold, bishop of Passau, to bring Rudolf military assistance and restore his authority, the emperor was compelled to renounce the government of Bohemia in favour of Matthias. He died in 1612. Matthias then received the imperial crown and established himself at Prague; but he wielded little power and was incapable of containing the struggle which broke out once again between Protestants and Catholics. Since no son had been born of his marriage with his cousin Anne, daughter of the second marriage of Ferdinand of the Tyrol, the problem of the succession presented the two camps with the opportunity to measure their strength. The candidate proposed by the Catholics was the Archduke Ferdinand of Styria, thirty-seven years old, son of a Bavarian princess, an intelligent and courageous prince who had been educated by the Jesuits and who, in his extreme religious fervour, regarded the royal function as an apostolate. In Ferdinand's eyes, election to the throne of Bohemia was merely a means of attaining the imperial crown, so that Germany could be brought back to the Roman faith either freely or by force. The Protestants and Catholics of the Empire had recently organized themselves in two rival leagues, the very existence of which testified to the weakness of the imperial power. In 1608 the Evangelical Union was formed under the leadership of the Elector Palatine; in 1609 the Catholic League was created, under the duke of Bavaria.

Two surprising facts must here be considered: that at the Diet of 1617 the Protestants of Bohemia, despite their large majority, should have allowed themselves to be intimidated by the Catholic dignitaries into electing the Archduke Ferdinand; and that Europe, and in particular France, admittedly unaware of the agreements reached between the archduke and the king of Spain, should have looked favourably upon the success of this intransigent prince, when they wanted a peaceable, temporizing emperor to succeed Matthias.

The Calvinists of Germany were alone in perceiving the extent of the threat presented by the election of Ferdinand as king of Bohemia, which they realized was merely the prelude to his election as emperor. They attempted, if not to persuade the Bohemian Protestants to reverse their vote, at least to rouse them to rebellion in order to secure a reaffirmation of their privileges before it was too late. For several years an argument had been raging over Protestant churches built on ecclesiastical estates, which the Protestants claimed were royal lands and consequently public territory. The religious authorities had had these buildings demolished and the Protestants were demanding reparation. The dispute provided the pretext for a new clash with the government when the emperor left for Vienna and Pressburg, where he wished to obtain the election of Ferdinand as king of Hungary. In May 1618 a small group of conspirators who had gathered together in Prague decided, after failing to find Lobkowicz himself, to arrange a mock trial for two of the Catholic dignitaries who were administering the kingdom in Ferdinand's absence: the two men, Slawata and Martinic, were pronounced traitors by the Protestant Estates, convened for this purpose at the Hradčany, and by way of immediate punishment were thrown through a window of the chancellery 'in accordance with the ancient custom of the realm and the example of the Bible and Roman history'. This was the Defenestration of Prague (23 May 1618). It is necessary to pause briefly here. In the nineteenth century the episode was so frequently interpreted as signifying the revolt of a free people against a foreign sovereign that this false view became generally established and is still accepted today by many educated persons. If it is true that hostility between Germans and Czechs had always existed in Bohemia, it certainly did not play a primary role in these events—indeed, it could almost be said to have played no part at all. German-speaking nobles were to be found among the most zealous of the conspirators and the two victims were Czech lords. The rebel government which was formed in Prague after the Defenestration remained loyal to Matthias, who was as much a German as Ferdinand, and the affair was on the point of being settled by the arbitration of German princes when it was suddenly revived by the death of Matthias, in the spring of 1619.

The rebel government of Prague, led by thirty Bohemian directors, both

Germans and Czechs, had few troops at its disposal, but the duke of Savoy provided it with a contingent of German mercenaries commanded by the illegitimate Count von Mansfeld, which he had employed in a recent war against the duchy of Milan. Ferdinand, who now was legally king of Bohemia, also had an army, which occupied the south of the country and routed von Mansfeld at the battle of Záblatí. But these skirmishes were of minor significance, for the death of Matthias had brought the question of Bohemia on to the international plane.[5]

Other Habsburg territories decided to free themselves from their subjection to the dynasty. In May, Moravia, which had hitherto remained loyal under the Protestant Charles Žerotín, one of the leading nobles of the margraviate, rose up in revolt, driving out the Jesuits and forming an alliance with the Bohemians. A noble of Upper Austria (Austria above the Enns), George Erasmus Tschermbl, a Calvinist steeped in the ideas of the Genevan movement and the author of a treatise, *Concerning the resistance of subjects against their prince*, persuaded his compatriots to refuse homage to Ferdinand on the ground that the Estates of Upper Austria had not been invited to recognize his rights as successor to Matthias: since Ferdinand had merely been designated by a predecessor and had not received the sanction of the Diet, there was no archduke of Austria! Even in the Hofburg at Vienna, Ferdinand was threatened, just as Frederick III had been in former times, and owed his deliverance only to the arrival of a regiment of dragoons.

The entire kingdom of Bohemia detached itself from the Habsburgs. Moravia, Silesia and the Lusatias decided to join with Bohemia in forming a *Confederatio bohemica*. Henceforth, when the throne became vacant, the local Diets would assemble in a general Diet which alone would be empowered to choose the new king, and it would never appoint a successor during the king's lifetime. The Confederation undertook to defend any of the associated provinces in the event of its religious and political privileges being threatened by the royal government. The Majestát became a fundamental law of the realm for Bohemians.

The Society of Jesus was permanently banished from the territory of the Confederation, but there was no prohibition of other religious orders, nor of Catholic worship. The sovereign no longer had sole control of the armed forces, since he could not place a garrison in the fortresses without the permission of the Estates; although he still appointed officials, he had to choose these from a list presented by the Estates.

The nobility, the majority of which was Protestant, had thus subordinated the prince's authority to its own. It was the nobles who benefited from a system based on the seigniorial principle and directed against the interests of the towns. The most that can be said is that the new constitution, however unfavourable to the middle class of the towns, did not impede the future development of that class.[6] The victory of the nobility in Bohemia, it seemed, might be repeated in other Habsburg states. There existed no obstacle, either racial or national, which prevented the *Confederatio bohemica* from concluding an alliance with the nobles of Austria and Hungary. Was not the same aristocratic ideal to be found everywhere? It was even conceivable that these countries would agree on the choice of a common sovereign. A Danubian empire would then have existed which was no longer subject to the

Austrian dynasty. A contemporary Austrian historian, Hans Sturmberger, has shrewdly posed this question: 'Could not the state which was subsequently created by the dynasty have risen, at this moment in history, out of the common will of these countries, to form a whole, *ein Totum*, as Prince Eugene of Savoy later said?'[7] But things never reached this stage. Each country remained too jealous of its independence and the *Confederatio bohemica* was unable to bring its neighbours into a closer association with its own system. It had to be content with alliances, as if with foreign powers; only the alliance with Upper Austria was of a more solid kind.

In Hungary, the malcontents were ready to reverse the election of Ferdinand. The Calvinist prince of Transylvania, Bethlen Gábor, a man of ability and personal ambition, was the likely leader to whom they would rally.

It was necessary, however, to seek alliances further afield. Many Bohemian Lutherans and many Germans in the kingdom regarded the elector of Saxony as their natural protector. The Utraquists looked rather to the Evangelical Union and maintained regular contact with the ministers of its leader, the Elector Palatine. They even had reason to hope that through these ministers, who were in correspondence with their co-religionists in France, they might win sympathy in that country. There was also the duke of Savoy, whose thoughts sometimes turned to the imperial crown and who imagined that the troubles in Bohemia would indirectly favour his ambitions. Nevertheless, the most desirable and effective alliance appeared to be with the United Provinces of the Netherlands. This state, whose independence had been recognized by the other countries and provisionally by Spain since the twelve-year truce signed in 1609, was undoubtedly the most advanced exponent of large-scale commerce and capitalism in the world. Its ships distributed merchandise to all parts of Europe and beyond; consequently, it dominated the flow of currencies and had perfected monetary exchange operations by the creation in 1609 of the Bank of Amsterdam, initially a clearing bank. Although the local nobility provided the officers for the federal army, the predominant sector of society was the merchant middle class. Institutions were of a republican character and the spiritual climate was favourable to freedom of religious opinion. Admittedly, outbursts of fanaticism were not unknown in the United Provinces, for fanaticism belonged to the spirit of the age and was not the monopoly of any particular Church.

There can be no doubt that the Constitution of the United Provinces exercised a powerful influence on the authors of the *Confederatio bohemica*, to such an extent that one of the directors of the Confederation, Peter Myllner z Mylhauzu, a highly cultivated Czech knight with a keen understanding of the ideas of his time, had suggested that it was not perhaps necessary to provide for the election of a king of Bohemia and that an elected Council could fulfil the functions of the sovereign. In recent years some Czech historians have admitted that the most serious weakness of the Bohemian revolution was the lack of a sufficiently large and organized middle class of native Bohemians, which would have strengthened the alliance with the United Provinces. Although the Provinces supplied both men and money, there was never any close association of ideals and interests which would have provided

Bohemia with another means of support in economic progress and in its struggle against Spain and the Catholic Church.

Against the fragile alliances available to the Bohemian Confederation, King Ferdinand could count on the support of Spain and the Papacy, although financial assistance from Spain depended on its galleons returning from America. Disastrous delays occurred in the delivery of their cargoes and Ferdinand needed money immediately to pay his armies. In France the young Louis XIII had assumed effective power two years previously. His old ministers advised prudence in foreign policy, for the kingdom was still troubled by the activities of the nobility and the demands of the Protestants. The king of England, James I, an Anglican who believed in a strong royal power which he considered inconceivable without the support of a strong ecclesiastical hierarchy, felt little sympathy for a nobility in revolt against its king. He was disposed, moreover, towards a political *rapprochement* with Spain. Thus, neither side was to receive the assistance which it needed in order to gain a rapid victory over its adversary. This explains the strangely contradictory events of the summer of 1619.

Ferdinand was elected emperor at Frankfurt, but the Diet of Bohemia proclaimed his deposition from the Bohemian throne and elected a new king. No doubt, the electoral college which nominated the emperor was not necessarily representative of German opinion. In the Empire, however, the middle classes of the towns were afraid, above all, of upheavals that would undermine commerce and draw the whole of Germany into new civil wars. Conservative Germans showed a certain complaisance towards the tradition of electing a Habsburg, provided that he was not the king of Spain or too fervent a Catholic. They were either misjudging Ferdinand's character or merely pretending to have been duped. The possible candidatures of other Catholic princes, such as the duke of Bavaria or the duke of Savoy, were not taken seriously.

Despite the sterile protests of delegates at the Bohemian Diet, the archbishop of Mainz, the imperial chancellor, declared that Ferdinand, as the king elected by a Diet in 1617, was thereby invested with the electorate of Bohemia and would take part in the vote. Ferdinand was duly nominated by the unanimous decision of the seven elector-princes or their proxies, including the representative of the Elector Palatine, who was determined to join the majority, even if this meant supporting Ferdinand.

But in Bohemia the introduction of the new constitution invalidated the election of 1617, which had been secured only at a Diet of the kingdom. A general Diet was therefore convoked to elect a new king. The choice fell on the Elector Palatine, Frederick V, who appeared the most promising candidate, since he was leader of the Evangelical Union and son-in-law of the king of England. In Prague, however, the elector of Saxony, the traditional patron of the Lutherans and Germans of Bohemia, would have been preferred. Frederick V could have refused this dangerous honour, as he was advised to do by Germans and foreigners. The French minister Puysieulx, who had been Henry IV's counsellor, declared that the late king would have offered the very same advice. Yet, in a world of princes susceptible to prestige and honour, the attraction of a crown proved too strong. Frederick accepted and went to Prague. The choice was not a happy one for Bohemia: Frederick was an inexperienced, frivolous young man who knew nothing of his new kingdom; he was ignorant of the Czech language, the noble traditions of Bohemian history, the social structure of the country and its customs. Whenever his subjects approached him, he provoked misunderstanding or offended their pride. It was quite probable that Ferdinand, who had returned to Vienna and had consolidated his position a little in Austria, would seek to reconquer the kingdom. Moreover, since he now possessed the imperial crown, he could claim that the behaviour of the Elector Palatine constituted rebellion by a vassal. War was inevitable. To conduct a war, Frederick was compelled to impose new levies on his subjects, to raise troops at home and to hire mercenaries from abroad. The middle class and the Jews of Prague displayed great reluctance to provide money. The general discontent resulted in peasant uprisings on the royal domains: when the rural population and the poor inhabitants of the towns found themselves reduced to an even more wretched condition by new taxes, what did it matter whether the sovereign was Protestant and elected, or Catholic and hereditary? Publicists were spreading their pamphlets of propaganda all over Europe. Frederick's supporters attempted to conceal these troubles and spoke only of defending privileges and liberties; at the same time, the imperial Catholic party insisted on respect for the crown, and emphasized the dangerous example of rebellion and the peril which threatened the Catholic Reformation throughout central Europe if the Protestants remained the masters in Bohemia.

The Germans came to the conclusion that the war was going to spread to the Empire, and so the two leagues resumed their activities, each convinced that its security depended on its own strength. At the end of 1619, since assistance from Spain had been delayed, Ferdinand appealed to Louis XIII in the name of solidarity between kings against rebellious subjects and the common interests of Catholic monarchs. This was the occasion of one of the most disastrous mistakes in French foreign policy.[8] In fact, neither the victory of the Protestant king and the local aristocracy, nor the triumph of the emperor, would have been without its dangers for France in the European situation prevailing at this period. But when the king of France found himself solicited by both parties, he could have taken advantage of the opportunity to impose his arbitration. Instead, Louis XIII followed his own inclinations and promised to give Ferdinand military aid. When he discovered that, for reasons of distance, the troops which he was to provide were to be used against the princes of the Evangelical Union, the allies of France, rather than against the rebels in Bohemia, he realized the rashness of his promise. Instead of the expected reinforcements, Louis sent an official embassy of inquiry and conciliation. To promise aid and then withhold it was futile. This gave the disappointed Ferdinand time in which to receive the assistance expected from Spain and the Pope. Arriving at Ulm at the beginning of July 1620, the French embassy found the armies of the Union and the Catholic League face to face and ready to engage in battle. The ambassadors thought they had achieved success when they persuaded the commanders of the two armies not to fight there and then on German soil. The

Protestant army moved off northwards, in the direction of the Palatinate, which was being threatened by the Spanish forces led by Spinola. The Catholic army marched back down the Danube and into Bohemia, where it joined the imperial army commanded by Buquoy. At the White Mountain (*Bílá Hora*), near Prague, the combined Catholic armies gained a victory that soon placed the whole of Bohemia at the mercy of the emperor (8 November 1620).

The battle of the White Mountain was of no great military importance by comparison with other battles fought during the Thirty Years' War: barely forty thousand men were involved in all and no new strategic or tactical dispositions were employed. Its consequences might not even have proved decisive if, as was urged by one of the former Bohemian directors, the Protestant Václav Budovecz Budova, resistance had been attempted in the city itself. But the battle had immense political and psychological repercussions.

The victory was of deep significance: the army of the Catholic League, commanded by Tilly and spurred on to combat by a Carmelite preacher, Dominico di Jesù Maria, had displayed a crusading fervour. The opposing army of Frederick V was composed of mercenaries, who fought badly; only the Moravian regiments showed any fierce resistance. In contemporary opinion the battle of the White Mountain was given a place among the series of great military victories over heresy: its fame equalled that of Lepanto. In Rome, the church of the Carmelites built by Soria was dedicated to Santa Maria della Vittoria. In Prague, the same name (Panná Maria Vitězná) was given to a new church originally intended for the Lutherans, in which, as an *ex voto* offering, the emperor placed a statue of the Infant Jesus which bore a crown in imitation of the imperial crown.

Bohemian Protestantism had thus been crushed. A tradition was soon to be established which identified the entire Czech nation with the vanquished army, which made the White Mountain the symbol of the humiliation of a whole people, and which in Bohemia endowed the emperor and his dynasty with the reputation of foreign conquerors. The national passions of the nineteenth century were to be nurtured by these memories. It was quite true that the armistice of Ulm, arranged by the French ambassadors, had enabled the troops of the Catholic League to give Ferdinand the advantage; consequently, the Protestants of Germany were henceforth mistrustful of French intervention. As for the emperor, he entertained no feelings of gratitude towards Louis XIII; on the contrary, he could think only of the military aid which had been promised and then withheld. Ferdinand remained an enemy of France for the rest of his life, either openly or secretly, according to circumstances. The hostility between Habsburgs and Bourbons was thus intensified.

What wise minds had foreseen was now accomplished: Ferdinand, as king of Bohemia, punished his rebellious subjects as an example to others; as emperor, he deprived the Count Palatine, his rebel vassal, of his electoral dignity and his personal territories. If the German princes and Protestants attempted to oppose his action with armed resistance, there would be war in the Empire. It was just at this time (1621) that the twelve-year truce between the United Provinces and

Spain expired, with the result that territorial and religious war now spread over the whole of Europe.

※

Bohemia was to be punished. The elector of Saxony, whose hopes had been frustrated by the election of the Calvinist Frederick V at Prague, had entered into an alliance with the emperor. Although his troops did not take part in the battle of the White Mountain, he was allowed provisionally to occupy the Lusatias in recompense for his services. The duke of Bavaria received the administration of Upper Austria in pledge. Ferdinand thus had to reward his allies by mortgaging his provinces. In Prague, responsibility for restoring royal authority was entrusted to a great Moravian lord, Liechtenstein. This former Protestant who had been converted to Catholicism, and whose treatment of his former co-religionists was therefore all the harsher, established a regime of terror. A special court was created which dealt first with the rebel-leaders. In June 1621, twenty-one persons, including only three great lords (the rest were knights and citizens), were executed in the square of the Old Town; their bodies were mutilated, their heads and limbs exposed for years on the gates of the city's bridge. The severity of their punishment was atrocious, but in accordance with the customs of the time. These executions cannot justify the legend which later grew up and which supposed that the entire Bohemian nobility was destroyed by the axe to make way for a foreign nobility of Germans or Italians.

Another measure was taken which was hardly less severe: the estates were confiscated of all those who, whether Protestants or Catholics, had in any way compromised with the government of Frederick V, either by serving him in political posts or by paying him taxes.[9] A commission of inquiry determined whether the whole or only a part of an estate was to be confiscated. The lands in question were taken from their owners and became the property of the Hofkammer, which offered them for sale and issued warrants equivalent in value to that part of the estate which had not been confiscated. The result was a vast expropriation of the land of Bohemia.

The final decision, however, belonged to the king, who could reduce the penalties of confiscation or grant a pardon. Important persons whose support was desired were pardoned; their past was not investigated and they were allowed to remain in possession of their domains. Among the great lords, Jan Rudolf Trčka retained his vast estates; his wife, Madeleine Lobkowicz, whose father had been condemned to life imprisonment for rebellion, was accorded the privilege of remaining a Protestant. She was one of the leading purchasers of confiscated property, buying land to the value of 539,664 gulden, which she paid largely in the form of silver plate. The intercession of a powerful person could prove efficacious: Izalda Pětipeská, *née* Vojkovská z Milhostic, an old woman of a good knightly family, had lost her castle and eight farms and had been reduced, so she said, to living almost as a beggar 'in the dirt of the village and in the company of menials'. She addressed a humble request to Polyxena Lobkowicz, the wife of the great chancellor, and was granted a life annuity calculated in detail to guarantee her the comforts of her former condition and the help of a maidservant.[10]

Cases such as these, even if isolated, reveal the attitudes of the times and the habits of the nation. Who were the beneficiaries of expropriation? In the early years not many estates were acquired by foreigners, and even these were granted by way of reimbursement or reward. In southern Bohemia the emperor's Austrian adviser, Eggenberg, received part of the lands of the Rožmberks (Rosenbergs), which had escheated; Buquoy obtained the seigniory of Nové Hrady (Gratzen) which he had conquered by arms during the war. The most advantageous position was that of the Catholic lords who already owned vast estates, for their revenues and their freedom to borrow enabled them to seize the best opportunities. Families such as the Lobkowicz (the chancellor and his wife Polyxena), the Slawatas, the Liechtensteins and the Černíns greatly extended their domains and were raised from the order of knights to that of lords. Many of the knights, who formed the second category of the nobility, were ruined because the confiscation of even a part of their estates was enough to deprive them of adequate resources.

Soon, the economic situation of the entire country was jeopardized even further by a gigantic and highly dubious monetary operation. In 1621 Ferdinand found himself in need of six million gulden to pay his armies and his most urgent debts. He came to an agreement with a consortium of some twenty persons, nobles and merchants, which included the prince of Liechtenstein, a Dutch merchant, Hans de Witte, who had become a citizen of Malá Strana, a young Moravian officer, Albert von Wallenstein, who already had illustrious connections, and a rich Jew from Verona, Jakub Bassewi, who had settled in Prague before the war. By a treaty of 18 January 1622, the consortium promised to provide the sovereign with the necessary funds and in return was granted the exclusive right to strike coin in the kingdom of Bohemia, Austria below the Enns and Moravia.

The Czech writer Paul Stranský, in the work which he devoted some years later to the State of Bohemia (*Respublica bohemica*, 1634), observed that money had already been debased in Germany and in the kingdom of Bohemia, during the reign of Matthias, by the striking of coins which contained a higher proportion of copper (7/16) and that, with the revolution, the practice had been introduced of drawing up accounts in imperial kreutzers instead of the Bohemian 'gros'. For the issue of the six million gulden, the contract fixed the double gulden at 150 kreutzers, the gulden at 75 kreutzers and the half-gulden at $37\frac{1}{2}$ kreutzers. A Bohemian silver mark of 16 carats was valued at 79 gulden. But successive monetary decrees modified these rates. The consortium paid only 32 gulden per silver mark to the mines of Bohemia, Bassewi bought processed silver at 25 gulden per pound, while private persons received only 22 gulden per pound if they wished to convert their silver into currency. The most favourable rate was offered to the members of the consortium. The money put into circulation ('long' money) thus caused inflation, but enabled the emperor to honour his debts and guaranteed high profits to those with large sums of money at their disposal. Furthermore, a difference in the real value of the Prague pound, which was of an inferior fineness, and the Viennese pound enabled discerning persons to indulge in fruitful speculation. At the same time, the old coins had been withdrawn from circulation; holders of these coins were forced to exchange them for the new coins, but at a very low rate. The most apparent consequence of this monetary operation was an immediate rise in the cost of all commodities and immediate hardship for the majority of the population, especially for people of small means. At the end of a year the contract was not renewed: it had produced its effects, good and bad. Although the members of the consortium had greatly enriched themselves, they did not seem to want to press their advantage further. The emperor reassumed control of the striking of coin (21 March 1623). After a few months he declared a state of bankruptcy (*kalada*) and introduced a new currency which was nearer to the old one, with the thaler at 90 kreutzers. In their turn, the coins introduced during the monetary experiment were declared no longer valid for transactions, neither were they to be accepted by the exchequer in payment for confiscated properties. But this 'long' money, which was circulating all over the country, had to be withdrawn. A low rate of reimbursement was fixed, but the operation could not be completed as quickly as had been hoped and it was necessary to extend the time-limit for the exchange of currencies until 1625.

In 1627 Ferdinand published two decrees. One of these renewed the constitution of the hereditary kingdom of Bohemia and thus represented a modification of the constitution of King Wladislas. The decree declared that the crown of Bohemia was to be transmitted hereditarily, within the ruling house, until the dynasty was totally extinct in both the male and female lines. Only in these circumstances would the nation regain the right to elect a king. The king became the very source of the law and enjoyed the right to promulgate the law (*jus legis ferendae*). Consequently, only he could propose a law for the sanction of the Diet, but this sanction remained necessary and the Diet preserved the right to vote taxes, which acquired legal force only by its approval. The composition of the Estates was modified by the establishment of a fourth order, the clergy. The chancellery remained (it was hardly likely to disappear, since Lobkowicz had progressively extended its activities); but, since it could only perform its duties where the king was in residence, it was transferred to Vienna. At the beginning of the eighteenth century, one of the finest Baroque edifices in the city was built to accommodate its various departments.

Prague did not, however, lose its status of capital. The Diet could not be held outside the kingdom's frontiers and the royal palace of the Hradčany remained the sovereign's Bohemian residence. In punishment of its rebellion the kingdom was deprived of some of its former privileges: the Majestát was annulled and the original parchment was symbolically lacerated with two dagger-blows. The first text of the constitutional decree was published in German, from which it has often been assumed that the Czech language had lost its primacy and had been replaced by German as the official language of the realm. Indubitably, German henceforth occupied a position of advantage. A law of 1615 had prohibited from public office anyone not speaking Czech. This condition no longer applied to public officials. The members of the court of appeal were obliged to have a knowledge of German and even in cases heard by Bohemian courts German was used. However, the preliminary investigation of a case had to be conducted in the language of the accused. Imperialism of language, which was so powerful a force in the nineteenth century and is waning in the present century, was inconceivable in the seventeenth century. Moreover, written German—still a clumsy medieval German—was far removed from the Germanic dialects in use in the different provinces and even in Vienna. It is nevertheless true that, especially in aristocratic circles where the fashionable languages were Italian and, to a lesser extent, Spanish and French, it became customary to regard the Czech language merely as a patois a little more incomprehensible than others. Czech was even further discredited for having been the language of numerous heretical works. This was a sociological phenomenon rather than a political decision.[11]

Yet the second important decree of 1627, concerning religion, was based on an appeal to Bohemian traditions. In an insidious fashion this decree maintained that the kingdom had never at any other period enjoyed prosperity and greatness of the kind experienced in the reign of Charles IV, who had been the defender of religious unity and had authorized no faith other than the 'holy and apostolic Roman faith', the only instrument of salvation preserved without interruption in the kingdom since its emergence from paganism. The memory of this great past, which was peculiar to Bohemia and part of its historical development, was thus invoked to justify the prohibition of any religion other than Catholicism. Commissaries were appointed and given a period of six months in which, either by their own efforts or through persons designated for this purpose, to convert those members of the seigniorial and knightly orders who had embraced the Protestant cause. At the end of this period, which was judged sufficient for their enlightenment, the Utraquists would be obliged either to become converts or to leave the kingdom.[12]

But, in order that no one should believe that the government was seeking yet another opportunity to levy taxes or to confiscate domains, the decree specified that the departure of a landowner would not entail the imposition of any tax and that exiles would be able to sell their properties to Catholic relatives, whom they could invest with powers of attorney for the collection of their revenues or capital and the recovery of moneys from debtors. There was here no question of expropriation, which had been exercised in a variety of brutal forms during this period. In this rural society the principle of the patrimony was respected. Confiscation had been a punishment inflicted by virtue of the royal prerogative of chastising rebels; moreover, when it was not extended to an entire estate, the owner had been reimbursed for the land that remained. Even if a great many people were none the less ruined, this could be explained by economic circumstances—the congestion of the market and the collapse of the currency—which aggravated the effects of a measure conceived not without concern for equity in the matter of family property and the patrimonial rights of relations.

The year 1628 saw a massive emigration of the upper nobility, the knightly class and even the middle class. Some nobles left with large sums of money which enabled them to live in the grand style once again and to wield political and social influence in the country of refuge. One such noble was Vilem Kinský, a member of the conspiracy of 1618 and the son-in-law of Jan Rudolf Trčka; Kinský took up residence in Dresden. Most of the others, however, and in particular the knights, had no substantial means of existence. Their last resort was to enlist as officers in the mercenary armies pursuing the war in Germany: the armies of von Mansfeld, Christian von Brunswick-Wolfenbüttel, the margrave of Baden-Dourlach and the foreign sovereigns who in turn assumed the offensive against the emperor (the king of Denmark and, a few years later, Gustavus Adolphus of Sweden). All longed to go back to Bohemia, not because they wished to reinstate the Elector Palatine, whom they regarded as of little importance, or to restore the *Confederatio bohemica*, but because they hoped, in the security of a free pardon, to return to their old domains and to regain their position in the country. The two Bohemian societies which thus existed—one abroad, stout-hearted but impecunious, the other remaining in Bohemia, submissive and resigned, but humiliated and miserable—were by no means isolated one from another. Only a modern police system can close frontiers, intercept and confiscate correspondence, and keep a constant track of individuals. It was not that the seventeenth century was more humane; it simply lacked the technical means for this kind of inhumanity. Consequently, endless intrigues were contrived which are by no means all known to history; even if a recital of such events might seem to savour of anecdote, it would throw light on the mental attitudes of the time. It is possible that the pressure exerted by these emigrants played a part in the military offensives directed against Bohemia, where invading armies must have been regarded by many rather as liberating armies.

As long as war persisted in the Empire, the re-establishment of the Habsburgs in Bohemia remained uncertain and attainable only by intimidation. Catholicism itself resumed its old positions or secured new ones only with great difficulty and with no guarantee of lasting success. In their colleges and professed houses the Jesuits faced a formidable task in educating a generation of pupils who would remain loyal to them. The peasant population was always ready to revolt.

Events in Upper Austria proved this. Upper Austria had been provisionally entrusted to the duke of Bavaria. The governor, Adam Herbertstorff, acted with extreme severity. The emperor had granted an amnesty, but only after imposing heavy indemnities on the rebel nobles and compelling the towns to drive out Protestant pastors and school-teachers and to permit only Catholic worship within their walls. The reading of the Bible, the singing of Protestant psalms and the celebration of Protestant services continued secretly in manor-houses and villages. In 1626 peasant armies were formed and a great insurrection took place in the Mühlviertel and the Trauenviertel, around the Trauensee.

The uprising planned for Whit Sunday, 31 May, broke out a little earlier as the result of a clash between Austrians and Bavarians in the small town of Lambach. The army of peasants hoisted its flags and sang improvised hymns:

> From the yoke of Bavaria and its tyranny,
> From its great butchery,
> Deliver us, dear Lord God.
> He who values his soul and his possessions

He too must pay with his life and blood.
O Lord, give us the strength of the Heroes:
This must be!

The peasants were defeated at Frankenberg, where reprisals assumed an atrocious form: persons of influence in the villages and officers of the local militia were assembled on the town square and forced to throw dice, and the losers were hanged (the *Frankenberger Würfelspiel*).

But the government was compelled to compromise, to grant the rebels religious freedom if they surrendered and to reduce war levies. Several noble families had to sell their possessions and move to the countries of the Empire. The Bavarians evacuated Upper Austria in 1628: the return to Habsburg obedience seemed to restore tranquillity.[13] In Lower Austria a number of Protestant nobles were exiled. In the towns, Catholic worship alone was authorized. In Vienna, Protestant physicians were driven from the city and the university was entrusted to the Jesuits, who began building their beautiful church there. Protestantism nevertheless survived, albeit surreptitiously. Ferdinand II had distinguished only between Catholics and Protestants and had treated the Austrians no better than the Czechs. There could be no question of acting similarly towards the Hungarians. Bethlen Gábor, who had been elected king of Hungary, had taken care not to have himself crowned, thereby making it possible to reach a reconciliation with Ferdinand. He took up arms again with the intention of organizing an offensive against Vienna to coincide with the movements of the Protestant armies, but accepted peace terms as soon as he saw that he was exposing himself by pursuing the war. Poland was the emperor's ally and seized control of Transylvania from the rear. By the armistice of Nikolsburg (1624) and the peace of Pressburg (1626), Bethlen contented himself with Transylvania and the cession for his lifetime of the two Silesian principalities of Oppeln and Ratibor. Royal Hungary had thus been restored to Habsburg domination. By contrast with his treatment of Bohemia, Ferdinand acted with moderation. He gave his fullest support to the reforming activity of the Jesuits and the clergy, which was recruited in the country itself. Peter Pázmány, a prelate of great culture and strong character who had been born a Protestant, was the leading figure behind the patient and fruitful reconquest of Royal Hungary by the Catholic Church. He was to become a cardinal and archbishop of Esztergom, but, since that city was in Turkish hands, he had to reside in Trnava, where he founded a university. Such were the changes introduced in the Habsburg countries. In the Empire itself, without convening the Diet, the emperor had deprived the Elector Palatine of his dignity and confiscated his territories simply by summoning a commission of electors and princes, the *Deputationstag* of Ratisbon. The electoral dignity was provisionally transferred to the duke of Bavaria, who occupied the Lower Palatinate, while the Spaniards received Frankenthal in the Upper Palatinate by way of surety. But the Protestants of the Empire regarded the treatment of Frederick, who had been divested of authority without having been allowed to defend himself even before the Deputationstag, as a denial of justice, and armies were raised on his behalf. Western Germany now saw Catholics and reformers at war—a war of atrocities and fanaticism in which monasteries were raided and churches and towns sacked, and in which each side attempted to convince public opinion of the justness of its cause and the loyalty of its conduct, blaming the enemy for all the iniquitous acts that were perpetrated. Another war was being waged, between Spain and the United Provinces. The most zealous sought to merge these two wars into a single conflict, but neither the Empire nor the United Provinces wished to become involved in a state of open war.[14]

Rather than enter into a detailed account of the Thirty Years' War, it would seem more appropriate to single out its main features and to concentrate on certain problems.

Until the intervention of Gustavus Adolphus of Sweden, who brought with him new weapons and new military tactics, the levying of troops and the conduct of operations followed the old-established methods. The army chiefs recruited their mercenary soldiers among the men of the towns and the rural communities—people without employment and with a taste for adventure, who responded to the call to arms and accepted a certain measure of discipline as long as they were assured of being paid and of enjoying a degree of impunity in their treatment of the civilian population, despite the fact that the army had its own judges. A force of twenty thousand men, equipped with pikes and arquebuses, constituted a powerful army. The cavalry supported the attacks of the infantry and attempted to break the enemy's formations by its charges. Armies possessed little in the way of artillery, but had enough cannon to attack towns, which were poorly fortified and gave little resistance; municipal authorities hastened to reach honourable terms of surrender. Sometimes, in circumstances of invariable confusion, troops resorted to pillage, either in defiance of their officers' instructions or with their complaisance. The sack of Paderborn by the army of Christian von Halberstadt and the extortions of von Mansfeld in Alsace were examples of such behaviour. A pamphlet entitled *Acta Mansfeldica* and written by one of von Mansfeld's former officers, who had joined the Catholic camp, enumerated all the horrors committed in Alsace: 'In the churches they left not a single stall intact: altars were knocked down, images broken and missals torn up. Baptistries were so defiled that it would have been no miracle if the earth had opened to swallow these demons alive. How could Almighty God give his blessing and grant good fortune to such monsters, men who are not soldiers but assassins and Turkish dogs?'

The exiled king of Bohemia, Frederick V, anxious to preserve the dignity of his cause, wrote to the Senate of Strassburg, which intended to preserve the neutrality of the city and the bridge over the Rhine: 'We do not bear the responsibility for all the horrors that have been committed, it is our adversaries who have caused all this disorder.' He boasted that he would himself lead a 'free army for the liberty of all Germany, against the Pope, Spain and the House of Austria'.[15] When the imperial army commanded by Tilly routed the Protestant generals one after the other, the Circle of Lower Saxony organized its own defence and in 1625 entrusted the command of its forces to the king of Denmark, who had already concluded an alliance with the king of England and with Holland, both of which countries were at this time allies of France. A coalition thus seemed to have been formed that would halt the progress of the House of Austria in Germany. In reality, however, the whole of northern Europe was ablaze. Christian IV of Denmark, a Protestant prince, was intent on acquiring the bishopric of Bremen, between the Elbe and the Weser, and was all the more determined to strengthen his authority over the lands adjacent to his kingdom because he felt his mastery of the Baltic threatened by new rivals. Ships entering or leaving this sea had to sail along the Sund strait, both banks of which were the territory of the king of Denmark, who exacted tolls. Christian IV thus controlled the movements of the Dutch, the leaders of international sea traffic, and the transportation of Polish grain, Swedish copper and even products from Russia (wood, flax, cinders, saltpetre and furs). Sweden was a sparsely populated country but rich in minerals. Its ambitious sovereign, Gustavus II Adolphus, had concluded peace with Russia and was still at war with Poland, but he hoped to dominate traffic in the Baltic. King Christian intended to contain the Swedish king's ambitions, for he did not wish to see Gustavus Adolphus intervening in his place in the affairs of the Empire. He was consequently the first to come forward as the protector of the Protestants of the north against the imperial army of Tilly, which had already defeated von Mansfeld and Halberstadt. The intervention of Denmark, which was receiving subsidies from England and Holland for the upkeep of an army, rekindled the war just when Ferdinand believed it was about to end. Even the grand duchy of Muscovy was indirectly involved, for during these years it had been increasing its supplies of grain to Denmark in the hope of securing an ally against its own adversary, Poland.

These events seem far removed from the Danube. But the extension of the conflict had implicated all the countries of Europe in the baleful war that had begun in Prague; it was no mere chance that the support which Ferdinand needed to resist Denmark should have come from Bohemia itself.

Albert von Wallenstein, who has already been mentioned in connection with the consortium of 1622, offered to raise on the emperor's behalf a force of fifteen thousand infantrymen and six thousand cavalrymen under his personal command, on condition that the army was paid and supplied at the expense of the imperial treasury. Ferdinand accepted. Why should it be that such epithets as 'adventurer' and '*condottiere*' are always applied to Wallenstein? The use of such terms tends to conceal the extent to which the customs of the time and the conditions peculiar to his native country were reflected in the personality of the man, even when he appeared to rise above both by assuming an international role.

In the writing of history, the German form of his name, Wallenstein, has prevailed over the Czech forms of Valdštejn or Valdštýn.[16] He was born in 1583 in Moravia, into a family of genuinely noble stock; his mother, a Protestant Smiřická, was of ancient Czech lineage. His early education was acquired in Protestant schools in Bohemia and in the Empire; he then travelled in Germany, France and Italy, as was customary for wealthy young gentlemen seeking to broaden their knowledge and their culture. He served against the Turks in the imperial army commanded by Basta and became a colonel in 1606, at the age of twenty-three. It was at this date that Charles Žerotín, the husband of Wallenstein's eldest sister, recommended him personally to the court of the Archduke Matthias. The family link between Žerotín and Wallenstein only serves to clarify the difference between two generations, which was accentuated by the general crisis of society. Žerotín represented the humanist aristocracy nurtured on *belles-lettres*, an aristocracy whose deep religious faith was tinged with a certain stoicism. Quite apart from temperamental disposition, this may perhaps explain the disenchanted attitude of Žerotín, who seemed to withdraw into himself during the events of this period, remaining heroically faithful to his Church, the United Brethren, and to his legitimate sovereign, the Emperor Ferdinand. By contrast, Albert von Wallenstein, who had been an early convert to Catholicism but was also interested in astrology, was primarily concerned to further his ambitions by utilizing forces both concrete and occult; he never gives the impression of having been a Christian or of having entertained any sentiments of personal attachment and loyalty towards his princes.

In a letter to a gentleman-in-waiting at the court of the Archduke Matthias, dated 5 February 1607, Charles Žerotín wrote: 'My brother-in-law, Baron Albert von Waldstein . . . this young lord full of good and praiseworthy qualities who has given signal proof of his worth on more than one occasion . . . desires to be received into the Chamber of His Highness the Archduke Matthias as much to satisfy a particular ambition to serve this prince as to have a master whose authority and greatness would serve as a support and ladder for his advancement.' Must not this sagacious humanist have smiled in writing these words? 'Moreover, he is well-born, as you know, and has connections with the principal families of Bohemia, he is well-educated and wise . . . for his youthful age, and although I know that His Highness is not accustomed to making religious distinctions [a reference to the prince's policy of pacification and concession towards the Protestant nobility of his various countries] I must inform you also that he goes to Mass.'[17] This was the first stage in the career of a young opportunist. From the service of Matthias, Wallenstein passed to that of Ferdinand of Styria and took part in the war against Venice.

In 1609, at the age of twenty-six, he married not a rich old woman, as his detractors claimed, but a beautiful and virtuous young woman who had inherited her wealth from her first husband—*forma, moribus et maxime divitiis egregia*. When she died in 1614, she left her possessions to Wallenstein. When the revolution reached Moravia in 1619, Wallenstein was therefore very rich. Like Žerotín, but perhaps for less noble reasons, he sided with Ferdinand; by way of booty he brought with him to Vienna the funds of the Moravian Estates, one hundred thousand thalers, an act which scandalized the intransigent but virtuous emperor. After the battle of the White Mountain, Wallenstein quickly established himself in Bohemia, at Jičín. He laid claim to the possessions of his maternal uncles, the Smiřický, in order to protect them from the threat of confiscation; having strengthened his position by joining the consortium of 1622, he purchased a great many domains in the region. By the grace of the emperor this group of lands became the duchy of Friedland, with Jičín as its capital, and Wallenstein received the dignity of prince of the Empire. Within the kingdom of Bohemia he wielded considerable territorial power. He immediately organized the country's administrative, judicial and fiscal systems and the development of a capitalist economy, opening cloth and leather works and foundries, calling in foreign craftsmen (weavers, armourers and Italian silk-workers) and even attempting to introduce the cultivation of the mulberry-tree on the open slopes of Bohemia. Wallenstein can thus be said to have been one of the founders of the industrial economy of northern Bohemia.

Wallenstein's links with the Bohemian aristocracy and his prestige in the circles of government were strengthened by a second marriage, to Isabella Harrach, daughter of Ferdinand's counsellor and sister of the archbishop of Prague, a marriage which was in no way surprising, if one considers the equality of their respective pedigrees, but which at the same time was of very real advantage to Wallenstein. It now seemed quite natural that he should take command of the new army. He did not restrict the recruitment of troops to Bohemia alone, but the army's provisions came from the land and labour of Czech peasants; with this Czech lord as his intermediary, Ferdinand was to receive his principal support from the kingdom which he had reconquered, but which his policies had reduced to economic and social disorder.

The astounding outcome of the years 1626–7 was the victorious war against Denmark and the occupation of the duchies of Mecklenburg, the princes of which were placed under the imperial ban. At the beginning of 1628 the emperor, who already owed vast sums to Wallenstein for the wages which he had advanced to the troops and the war materials which he had supplied, entrusted him with the administration of these duchies and then invested him as their prince. The German princes, however, were unwilling to recognize Wallenstein's promotion. Although he had failed to occupy Stralsund, which he had promised to capture even if it were surrounded 'by a wall of iron and attached to the sky by chains of diamond', Wallenstein landed troops on the island of Rugen. His army, which had grown significantly, was said to number a hundred thousand men. The emperor awarded him the title of captain and admiral of the Atlantic and Baltic. The court of Vienna negotiated with the court of Madrid, offering to cede to it a part of the conquered territories of Denmark. Was the House of Austria, whose power in the Empire had been on the point of collapse a few years earlier, henceforth to dominate the coasts of the North Sea and the Baltic? It was now said that even the power of Charles V had never attained these heights. Wallenstein was credited with the startling suggestion that the imperial dignity passed by right to the emperor's son, and that it was no longer necessary to seek the votes of the electors. Once his master's authority in the Empire was secure, he even spoke of waging war against the sultan and establishing the emperor in Constantinople. Yet his triumph lacked the solid foundations necessary for lasting conquest. Either through wisdom or motives of expedience, Wallenstein mitigated the Draconian terms which the emperor's ministers were thinking of imposing on the king of Denmark. By the peace of Lübeck, Christian IV was re-established in his kingdom in return for a promise not to interfere again in the affairs of the Empire.

In March 1629 Ferdinand II, faithful to his intention of restoring the power of the Catholic Church, issued the Edict of Restitution demanding the return into Catholic hands of all monasteries not under the immediate authority of the Empire which had been alienated since the treaty of Passau, and of all imperial properties seized by the Protestant princes since the peace of Augsburg. Although the Catholic princes considered the edict to be founded in justice, they opposed it on the ground of its impracticability. How could the whole system of fiefs be moved back seventy years? A great many concessions and sales of land had taken place: the present owners—many of them Catholics—could not be held responsible for the changes of earlier times and were in danger of finding themselves unjustly ruined.

It is easy to see why the prestige of the House of Austria should have appeared so great that the Empire had become its personal possession and the emperor an absolute sovereign. Amid such upheavals everything seemed possible. But this was an illusion. The princes of the Empire, both Protestant and Catholic, valued their independence too highly to consent to such a situation and they still possessed the means of resisting Ferdinand, especially if they felt that they could count on support from outside. They considered that France, whose revival was now becoming evident, would not tolerate such power in Habsburg hands. During the day of the electoral assembly convened at Ratisbon in 1630, the envoys sent by Richelieu as observers in fact encouraged the electors in their opposition. Ferdinand was hoping to secure the election of his son as king of the Romans. The electors laid down as their first condition the disbanding of Wallenstein's army, which was useless now that peace had been made with Denmark; having obtained satisfaction on this point, they then adjourned, thereby provisionally denying the emperor the election he had requested.

By contrast with the crusading ambition of their sovereign—for the emperor, at least, it was not a question of personal power—the majority of German princes were preoccupied with the desire for peace, a general settlement that would include the confirmation of their privileges. As well as the princes, the various peoples of the Empire longed for a return to order. But the Edict of Restitution had still not been withdrawn and the threat of its execution remained a cause for alarm.

It was for this reason that Gustavus Adolphus advanced into Pomerania. His position strengthened by a treaty with France, which granted him subsidies in return for a promise to spare the Catholic countries and Bavaria, the king launched a broad offensive in 1631 which ended with his victory over Tilly at Breitenfeld (17 September). Gustavus Adolphus had put himself at the head of a national army staffed with strict officers and trained to respond to discipline; he also possessed a superior artillery and an excellent cavalry. He secured as his allies the electors of Brandenburg and Saxony, who would have remained loyal to the emperor if he had agreed to rescind the impracticable Edict of Restitution.

❦

The conspiracy of Wallenstein has been the subject of numerous studies, the most prominent of which are to be found in the classic works of great historians, but no definitive interpretation has yet been provided. Did Wallenstein entertain any coherent scheme of action? Did the man who had hitherto been regarded as the most powerful figure in Europe believe that he had at last found his match and co-partner, and that, if he were to come to an understanding with the king of Sweden, they would together be able to impose peace on Europe and found a durable order there? Was he inspired by imperial patriotism and did he truly seek the preservation of German liberties? Or was he embittered by the disgrace to which he had been subjected and simply pursuing a plan of vengeance, anxious to make 'the emperor and all his house feel the painful price of insulting a noble-man'? Or, yet again, in his increasing obsession with astrology, did he foresee some fantastic destiny for himself? Finally, had a premature decline in health re-duced him to an invalid or even disturbed his mind, so that he was incapable of carrying an enterprise to its conclusion and deprived of the intellectual and moral mastery which had made him a good military tactician? These are questions to which no definite answer can be given. The irritating mystery of Wallenstein remains, but to penetrate this mystery is not, perhaps, the most important thing. What does matter is that Wallenstein, even in the very contradictions of his actions, reveals the deep conflict between the authority of the sovereign and the desperate determination of the imperial princes and great lords to preserve the primacy of their position, or at least not to be reduced to a secondary role. Thus is laid bare the weakness of a central power which, unlike that of the king of France, had not succeeded in channelling the resources of its peoples for the furtherance of its policies.[18]

It is a striking fact that Bohemian aristocrats should have been the first to make contact with Gustavus Adolphus, using Wallenstein's name and employing for this purpose Czech emigrants who were serving as officers in the army of the king of Sweden. The aristocrats in question were members of the Trčka family, who maintained constant liaison with their emigrant relatives, the Kinskýs. Thus, throughout the conspiracy the restoration of a Bohemian monarchy was regarded as an essential condition for the overthrow of the House of Austria; there can be no doubt that the secession of the kingdom would have irremediably dislocated Ferdinand's dynastic empire.

The idea of secession had long been mooted in the chancelleries. However, no document has yet been produced proving that Wallenstein ever declared this to have been his own intention: his emissaries merely repeated that he wished to become king. He let this be known even at the French court. He probably yielded readily to the temptation, and internal conditions in Bohemia at this time made such an enterprise quite possible.

By the agreement reached with the emperor at Göllersdorf, Wallenstein con-sented to raise an army which he would command himself on unprecedented conditions: military operations were to depend no longer on the decisions of the War Council, but on his own initiative, and he was to be empowered to negotiate armistices with Saxony. The destinies of both the emperor and his states were now in Wallenstein's hands. By this time, secret negotiations with Saxony had reached an advanced stage and he was therefore obliged to make his excuses to his partners, explaining that he was reassuming command out of necessity, but that his plans had not changed.

Wallenstein staffed this army, the very source of his strength, with foreign officers from Italy who came seeking their fortunes and had little interest in the fate either of Bohemia or of the Empire. In fact, not much is known about the attitude of these officers or that of the army itself. The death of Gustavus Adolphus, who fell at the battle of Lützen, where Sweden nonetheless emerged victorious, rid Wallenstein of an adversary, or at least a partner on whom he could not rely. But at the end of the winter he made no effort to seek a decisive battle. A succession of armistices was reached with Saxony and from Dresden the conspiracy was hatched with the governments of Sweden and France. There is no doubt that neither Oxenstierna nor Richelieu refused to promise Wallenstein their support in the event of his adopting the cause of the 'public good'.[19] There came a moment of great emotion for the Czech people when the Protestant armies, with the emigrant nobles impatient to return to their country, were approaching the kingdom's frontiers, while Wallenstein's army, reorganized and apparently reconfirmed in its loyalty to its chief by the oath taken at Pilsen, awaited his decision to engage the Protestants in battle or to join forces with them. Had Wallenstein joined their cause, a mighty military power would then have marched on Vienna (January 1634).

By this time, however, the emperor was convinced of the treachery of his generalissimo. He was stunned by the denunciation of one of Wallenstein's lieutenants, Piccolomini, who was not acquainted with all the details of the conspiracy (no one could claim to have penetrated such a complex web of secrets), by the evident misgivings of the Spanish camp and by Wallenstein's startling refusal to engage in new battles in the Empire and to join with the approaching army of Cardinal Infant. It seems that Ferdinand recognized the need to act in order to avert a catastrophe. He ordered another general, Gallas, to take command of the imperial troops and capture the duke of Friedland, dead or alive. Once again the all-powerful general was to be deprived of his army. His pride deserted him. Followed by a few loyal Czech officers, Wallenstein fled from the Swedish army of Bernard of Saxe-Weimar, who was then at Ratisbon. Now that he had been stripped of his military strength, how could he hope to impose his authority on his former adversaries by reputation alone and persuade them to place him at their head? At Cheb an inglorious death awaited him. He was killed by the troopers of the garrison, after his officers had been massacred in an ambush.

The immediate result of this unhappy episode was to aggravate the misery of the Czech people. The possessions of Wallenstein and the Trčka family were confiscated and either sold or given to foreign families, whose arrival in the kingdom was to modify even further the composition of the Bohemian aristocracy. Vienna grew more deeply mistrustful of a nation where rebels seemed to be rising up at every instant. The tragic conflict between a sovereign and his people is reflected in a passage from the writings of the Czech Jesuit, Bohuslav Balbín, which is full of the pain and humiliation of his country: 'It seems to them [the enemies of the Czech nation] that the forests and the woods, the deep valleys and even the leaves and branches of the trees are murmuring "rebellion! rebellion!", and that it is necessary to resort to the advice of Machiavelli and on this mistrusted land destroy everything, raze fortresses, allow the walls of towns and villages to crumble into decay and treat this nation as the enemy of tomorrow.'[20]

With Wallenstein dead and the army henceforth under the supreme command of the emperor's son, the king of Hungary, the fortunes of war returned to the House of Austria. After the victory over the Swedes at Nördlingen, Saxony and then Brandenburg abandoned the foreign alliances into which they had been compelled to enter and sought to make peace with the emperor. There could no longer be any question of maintaining the fateful edict of 1629: Ferdinand had to seek a reasonable compromise between Protestants and Catholics. When it was decided to adopt the *status quo* of 1627, Ferdinand, whose scruples were allayed by a commission of theologians, accepted with resignation. He had to agree that the Imperial Chamber should be divided between Catholic and Protestant judges and that the army, henceforth the army of the emperor and the Empire, should be employed only in the service of their common interests. On these terms peace was signed at Prague on 31 May 1635 between the emperor and the elector of Saxony and was extended to all those princes who had not yet become reconciled; the elector of Brandenburg then signed the treaty and was soon followed by other princes of the north. It now seemed that national sentiment had overcome religious rancour in the hearts of men, as if the peoples of Germany, exhausted by suffering and violence, desired only the end of war, the departure of foreign troops and the restoration of peace in the Empire. They had seen too many towns burned and pillaged, too many estates abandoned and too many epidemics and famines!

The armies of both sides had generally followed the river valleys, but they had penetrated into the hinterland when they needed fresh provisions and the lure of booty had drawn troops into every kind of excess. Frequently they indulged their sadistic inclinations by torturing the peasants, with the same wicked stupidity which uncouth people of this period showed towards animals. The book by Grimmelhausen, *The Adventures of Simplex Simplicissimus*, presents an authentic picture of these horrors which is corroborated by the revelations of historical documents. It is true that some regions were spared and that merchants and speculators had found opportunities to make their fortunes by supplying arms and hides, harvesting and marketing corn (cereals and oats) and selling horses.

The possibility of a general peace in the Empire alarmed the powers at war with Spain. France had started the war, at the very time of the peace concluded at Prague, but Richelieu and, in particular, Louis XIII were convinced that they had merely prevented an imminent Spanish attack on the kingdom. Despite internal difficulties, the inadequacy of revenues, the indebtedness of the treasury, the revolts of the nobility and riots by the masses, Richelieu considered it essential that Sweden should not withdraw from the struggle. He concluded numerous treaties of subsidy, not all of which were honoured, and gave promises of military co-operation. In western Germany the Spanish armies were able to take the Rhine route and lead the troops levied in Italy right up to the frontiers of France and the Netherlands. France, which already possessed garrisons in Lorraine and several strongholds in Alsace, was also anxious to maintain under its protection the German princes of the Union of Heilbronn, which was in alliance with Sweden. Thus, far from coming to a halt as had been hoped, the war and all its inevitable evils continued in the Empire for another thirteen years. Henceforth, the emperor (after Ferdinand II, his son Ferdinand III) enjoyed the support of Saxony, Brandenburg and Bavaria. At the assemblies which he convened, even at the Diet of Ratisbon in 1640, Ferdinand III permitted discussions to be held on a general amnesty and the conditions of territorial sovereignty (*Landeshoheit*), even granting the princes the right to take part in the peace negotiations. A book written by a German publicist, Hippolytus a Lapide, entitled *Dissertatio de ratione status in imperio romano*, argued that the emperor was merely an organ of the Empire, to which he was subordinate: *Imperator minor imperio*. The author went even further, revealing his hostility to the House of Habsburg (*Haec certe familia Germaniae nostrae fatalis est*[21]), which he accused of having transformed the imperial crown into a dynastic apanage. He recommended that in future no more than two emperors should be chosen from the same family. Finally, to strengthen the sovereign authority of the Diet, he proposed the constitution of a *Reichsregiment*, an imperial government which, between the sessions of the Diet, would maintain a check on the activity of the emperor and take over responsibility for appointing garrison-commanders.

During the thirteen painful years separating the peace of Prague and the treaties of Westphalia, the House of Austria encountered many perils. There could be no question of it establishing absolute power in the Empire and the threat of its hegemony over Europe was finally removed.

France was struggling against Spain, but managed to reoccupy a number of key positions in the region of the Rhine: after the towns of Alsace, Brisach on the right bank of the river and the forest towns of the upper valley were taken. From there the French armies attempted to co-ordinate their movements with those of the Swedish forces for a campaign against the hereditary possessions of the Habsburgs. Swedish garrisons had been established in the cities of the Empire and were to be found from the Baltic to Lake Constance, at Augsburg and at Olmütz, an oddly scattered network that left the whole of Germany in bewilderment; meanwhile, the negotiations begun in 1645, with the Catholic powers at Münster and with the Protestants at Osnabrück, guaranteed Westphalia and the port of Hamburg a degree of neutrality.

The German princes had obtained the right to take part in the Congress. As a result, by the treaty of Münster signed on 24 October 1648, the Empire ratified the cession to France of the seigniories and rights possessed by the House of Austria in Alsace. The Emperor Ferdinand III had soon resigned himself to losing some of his more remote provinces, so that he might consolidate his position in the Danubian region, which was essential to the maintenance of his authority. All the contracting powers guaranteed the religious and political constitution of the Empire, which was fixed by the treaty of Osnabrück and recognized the religious freedom of Lutherans and Calvinists.

French historians, especially in the nineteenth century, have presented the treaties of Westphalia as an outstanding achievement of royal diplomacy, maintaining that these treaties brought about the dismemberment of the Empire and, by confirming the independence of the princes, destroyed for a long period the emperor's real power in Europe. Such a view is justified, provided that neither the novelty of the result nor the defeat of the House of Austria is exaggerated. If the power of the emperor had been diminished within the Empire, it was now more independent than ever in the hereditary states; the clause restoring immediate and mediate fiefs to their condition of 1624 concerned neither Bohemia nor Austria. Admittedly, the benefit of the amnesty was not withheld from former subjects of the kingdom of Bohemia, but the condition was made that they could return only if they submitted to the laws in force in that country, which meant adhering to the Catholic faith. Possessions confiscated immediately after the battle of the White Mountain were not returned. The Swedes had insisted that the restoration of all confiscated properties be authorized, but an article of the treaty of Osnabrück said: 'Although the Swedish plenipotentiaries insisted firmly and at length . . . it has not been possible to make any such stipulation to His Imperial Majesty, because of the constant opposition of the Imperials and because the states also considered that to pursue the war on this account would not be in the interest of the Empire.'[22]

Lusatia remained detached from the kingdom of Bohemia and annexed to Saxony, in accordance with the treaty of Prague. The duchies of Silesia received special privileges for their Protestant population, but the other territories (Bohemia and Moravia) were rejoined to Austria and the Alpine duchies to form a dynastic complex over which the sovereign imposed religious unity. The native-born nobility, the defenders of privilege and of the old constitution, was henceforth balanced by a new nobility which had been established too recently to forget that it owed its good fortune to the dynasty, and which was thus ready to offer its loyalty in return for new wealth and greater prestige.

To claim that the kingdom of Bohemia had been annihilated and its people enslaved to foreign masters is to allow truth to be distorted by passion. In correcting this extreme interpretation, however, it should not be forgotten that many things had indeed changed and that the long war, which had begun in Prague with the Defenestration and had ended in Prague at the gates of the Charles Bridge, had brought victory to the Habsburgs and had prepared the ground for a Danubian empire that was to have Vienna, rather than Prague, as its capital.

Royal Hungary protected this Habsburg empire on the east, serving as a bulwark, but Catholic influences were exerted there with increasing intensity: the Hungarian population, in its fierce attachment to its traditional liberties, regarded events in Bohemia as a warning, an ill omen that seemed to justify fears for its own future.

NOTES

1. Karel Stloukal, *Papežská politika a cisařský dvůr pražský na předělu XVI a XVII věku* ('Papal Policy and the Imperial Court of Prague at the Turn of the Sixteenth–Seventeenth Centuries'), Prague, 1925.

   Aldobrandini was passing through Prague on his way to Poland, where he was to restore peace between the new king, Sigismund Wasa, nephew of Stephen Bàthory, and his rival, the Archduke Maximilian, brother of the emperor.

2. All these questions are, in reality, closely linked one with another. The revolt of the peasants of Lower Austria in 1597, studied by P. Friess in *Die Bauerenaufstand in Nieder-österreich*, 1897, appears to have been caused chiefly by an attempt at conscription (one man in thirty, then one in ten and finally one in five) for the Hungarian war, but also by the extension of the corvée. The insurgents tried to form a league and extremists went so far as to demand the emancipation of the peasantry. Hardly any act of violence was committed against the nobles. Yet the Diet of Lower Austria demanded the punishment and execution of some of the ring-leaders. Although these rebel leaders appear to have included no Protestant pastors or Catholic priests, Canon Khlesl, later to become cardinal-archbishop of Vienna and the minister of the Emperor Matthias, attributed the responsibility for social troubles to the Protestant Reformation. (Paper by M. Jean Bérenger.)

3. Concerning all these events, in addition to the old but by no means superseded works of Hammer-Purgstall, *Geschichte des osmanischen Reiches*, 1835, and Khlesls, *Des Kardinals Direktors des geheimen Kabinett Kaiser Mathias Leben*, 1847, Gindely, *Rudolf II und seine Zeit*, 1868, and Peter von Chlumecky, *Karl von (Zerotín) und seine Zeit*, 1862, already mentioned, the reader could consult the studies by G. Lenz, *Der Aufstand Bocksays und der Wiener Friede*, Debrecen, 1967, Kamil Krofta, *Majestát Rudolfa II*, 1909, and J. Pekař, *Bílá Hora*, 1922.

4. On the centralizing role of Lobkowicz: Karel Stloukal, *Česká Kancelář dvorská* ('The Bohemian Court Chancellery'), 1931.

5. For the general history of the Thirty Years' War, see the work by Georges Pagès, *La Guerre de Trente Ans*, 1937, which should be supplemented with the little book by G. Livet, *La Guerre de Trente Ans* (in the collection *Que sais-je?*), and the course delivered by the author (Victor-L. Tapié) at the Sorbonne in 1962–4, published by the Centre de Documentation Universitaire.

   For a narrative account of the war there is the solid study by Gindely, *Geschichte des Dreissigjährigen Krieges*, 1869–80.

   For the confederation of 1619: R. Stanka, *Die böhmischen Confederationsakte von 1619*, 1932, and the lively study by Hans Sturmberger, *Aufstand in Böhmen*, Munich and Vienna, 1959. Also, J. Polišenský, *Tričetíletá válka a český národ* ('The Thirty Years' War and the Czech Nation'), 1960.

6. F. Kavka, *Historica*, VIII, pp. 35–64.

7. Hans Sturmberger, op. cit., p. 48.

8. Victor-L. Tapié, *La politique étrangère de la France et le début de la guerre de Trente Ans (1616–1621)*, 1934, translated into Czech by Z. Kalista under the title *Bílá Hora a Francie*, 1936; and *La France de Louis XIII et de Richelieu*, 2nd edn., 1967.

9. A mine of information is provided by *Dějiny Konfiskací v Čechách po r. 1618* ('History of Confiscations in Bohemia after 1618'), Prague, 1882, the material for which was taken from the archives of the Confiscation Commission. This work is a detailed list of all persons whose possessions were confiscated, with the number and value of these posses-

sions; it remains a basic source of information and, in a long preface, traces the history of the Confiscation Commission and of the instructions under which that body acted.

10. Letter published in Husa, *Naše minulost v dokumentech* ('Our Past in Documents'), Prague, 1954, p. 287. The article in *Dějiny Konfiskací* concerning the old lady's son, Vodolan Pětipeský (vol. I, p. 431), gives the curious details and consequences of this affair. In the royal instructions given to the Commission, a special case had been made for widows or female guardians who had not been able to resist the orders of the Estates and the king of Bohemia; perhaps it was accepted that elderly women had a right to some indulgence.

11. This point has been very justly made by Kavka in the article already mentioned (*Historica*, VIII, p. 59): seigniorial administration used the Czech language until the last decades of the eighteenth century and even later, even on estates owned by lords of foreign origin.

12. The decree of 1627 concerning religious conversion is published in Husa, op. cit., p. 293.

13. Julius Strnadt, *Der Bauernkrieg in Oberösterreich*, Wels, 1930.

14. On French policy, the author suggests that readers consult his book *La France de Louis XIII et de Richelieu*, 2nd edn., 1967.

15. The king of Bohemia at the Senate of Strassburg. Archives Strasbourg AA.

16. Some years ago (1934) W. Wostrý, professor at the German University of Prague, declared that the number of books written about Wallenstein was surpassed only by those devoted to Napoleon and since then new works have constantly appeared. Since the book by Ranke, *Geschichte Wallensteins*, Leipzig, 6th edn., 1910, two works of fundamental importance have been published: H. von Srbik, *Wallensteins Ende*, 1st edn., 1920, 2nd edn., 1952; and J. Pekař, *Valdštejn*, Prague, 1934, 2 vols. (German edition entitled *Wallenstein 1630 bis 1634, Tragödie einer Verschwörung*, 1937). Both authors make use of the numerous documents published by the historians Irmer and Hallwich in the nineteenth century. The most recent work is that written by Suvanto, a Finnish historian: *Wallenstein und seine Anhänger*, Helsinki, 1963.

17. Žerotín's letter appears in F. Dvorský, *Dopisy Karla st. z Žerotína, 1591–1610*, vol. XXVII of the collection *Archiv Český*, Prague, 1904, pp. 302–3.

18. In the opinion of the Austrian historian H. von Srbik, Wallenstein sought peace in the Empire and only detached himself from the Emperor because Ferdinand and his pro-Spanish entourage stubbornly persisted in the too close alliance with Madrid and remained intransigent on the religious question. The viewpoint of J. Pekař is particularly interesting because he illuminated the importance of the Czech problem and the strength of the traditions of the Bohemian nobility. H. von Srbik recognized the force of these arguments without being wholly convinced. But J. Pekař considered that Wallenstein's desire for vengeance dominated his entire conduct, that he could satisfy his desire only by re-establishing the independence of the kingdom, but that his state of physical and mental health prevented him from undertaking a more coherent plan of action.

19. The expression 'bien public' is found in a letter dated 3 January 1633 which Louis XIII sent to Wallenstein. The king of France had learnt that the duke of Friedland cherished 'worthy sentiments with regard to the public good' ('bons sentiments pour le bien public': *Lettres et négociations du marquis de Feuquières*, vol. I). Wallenstein's relations with France have not been the subject of a special study. In the opinion of the author, they appear to have been based on misunderstandings on both sides—inadequate information concerning the adversary's desires and the assistance he could offer, and thus mutual mistrust.

20. The Latin text has been translated into Czech by A. Pražák, *Národ se branil* ('The Nation

has Defended Itself"), Prague, 1945, p. 71. Pražák offers an excellent analysis of the famous work by Balbín, *Defence of the Czech Language*.

21. Hippolytus a Lapide (Chemnitz), *De ratione status in imperio romano-germanico*.

22. On 11 October 1648, Comenius sent to the chancellor, Oxenstierna, a letter of solemn entreaty in which he expressed the grief of the Czech emigrants who had been abandoned by their allies in the negotiations at Osnabrück (text of letter in Husa, *Naše Minulost*, p. 309). It seems that the German Protestant princes, who were anxious to rid themselves as quickly as possible of the Swedes, their redoubtable allies, were even less inclined than the Catholics to prolong the debates of the congress in order to satisfy the demands of the emigrants. As early as April 1648, the elector of Saxony, John George, who had acquired a piece of the kingdom of Bohemia, complained that the Czech rebels had never been willing to listen to his advice and declared that there could no longer be any question of prolonging the war and the enfeeblement of Germany. See the article by Sindelář, discussed by Toegel, in *Historica*, V, pp. 7–107.

Part Two

❧ 5 ❧

Dark Age or Baroque Glory?

THE TREATIES of Westphalia had not resulted in the defeat of Habsburg absolutism or the impotence of the Empire. They had indeed preserved the House of Austria and confirmed its dual vocation as head of the Empire, even if it did not wield a decisive influence there, and as the sovereign authority of juxtaposed states, some of which formed part of the Empire, while others lay outside its frontiers. The Empire had retained its medieval structure, although it had become more open to modern influences through the diversity of its Churches, the increased power of certain states (Saxony, Brandenburg, Bavaria) and the opportunities of economic progress; at the same time, the guarantee clause enabled France and Sweden, but not Spain, to intervene in the internal affairs of the Empire and to play a part in its destiny.

It is essential to have a clear understanding of this complicated political situation in order to follow the subsequent development of history. For the House of Austria was still powerful and was obliged to maintain this power if it wished to survive. It had therefore to be careful to preserve the prestige of the imperial crown.

During the lifetime of Ferdinand III his son, Ferdinand IV, was elected king of the Romans, but he died before the throne became vacant. When Ferdinand III died in 1657, the second son, Leopold I, became emperor. Mazarin had not dared to propose the candidature of the young Louis XIV and had been content to take soundings, which proved that circumstances would not permit the king of France to become an emperor, despite his influence in Germany.[1] Neither was the time yet ripe for a conflict between the Habsburgs and the Hohenzollerns. But the elector of Brandenburg at this period was Frederick William, who was to go down in history as the Great Elector; the grandfather of Frederick II, whom in certain respects he foreshadowed, Frederick William was also intent on increasing his territories and the authority of his house. Already a certain pattern could be discerned: a Protestant Germany to the north, separated by the valley of the Main from a Catholic Germany to the south with the valley of the Danube as its geographical axis. From the map it can be seen how the House of Austria, though it had sacrificed Alsace and the left bank of the Rhine, had retained the Breisgau on the right bank and possessed seigniories in the upper valley of the Danube which served as outposts. The Danube, after crossing through Bavaria and the bishopric of Passau, became the river of the Habsburgs right into Hungary. On each side of the Austrian valley lay the two great networks of states: the kingdom of Bohemia and its incorporated provinces on one side, the Alpine duchies and Innerösterreich on the other, with Trieste as a window on to the Adriatic. This territorially compact ensemble, with Royal Hungary as an appendage, constituted the patrimonial empire of the Habsburgs. In the political language of the time this empire was described as the 'hereditary states'—clearly a misnomer, if one takes Hungary into account—but historians of the present day can almost be excused for their frequent use of the anachronism 'Austria' as a convenient single term by which to refer to a territorial reality. Indeed, the emperors depended to a very real extent on this complex, for it provided them with the resources indispensable to their foreign policy, which was primarily dynastic, and even to their authority within the Empire itself, the struggles in which they were involved with France, on the Empire's behalf, and the ever necessary defence against the Turk.

It is tempting to think that, within this complex, the emperor was his own master and an absolute ruler. But the word 'absolutism' must be used in its strict sense. According to the tradition of Roman law and the interpretation of jurists, absolutism signifies the fusion of all powers—justice, finance and administration—in the person of the prince; it means the will of the prince making laws on his own undisputed authority, to which his subjects must remain in obedience. In the territories ruled by the Habsburgs there existed no such clearly defined power. The idea of the patrimony and the family predominated to such a degree over that of absolute kingship that the Habsburg monarchs had to accept the division of their lands by secundogeniture.

On his accession to power in Bohemia and Austria, Ferdinand II had brought Styria and the neighbouring duchies under the authority of one prince, but at the same time he had granted hereditary administration of the Tyrol, Vorarlberg and the Vorländer (Alsace) to his brother Leopold (1625). This was a tactic of expediency often employed by the Habsburgs: countries jealous of their independence were flattered at having their own princes, whom they regarded as the guarantors of their privileges, but they continued to form part of the complex.

The Tyrol, situated somewhat apart from the other states, an Alpine rather than a Danubian country and a transit route between Italy and the Empire (but well outside the orbit of Vienna), was proud to have Innsbruck as its capital and the place of residence of its prince, whose presence stimulated local commerce. When this regional dynasty became extinct in 1665, with the death of the third count, Sigismund Franz, the Tyrol was left with such a feeling of nostalgia that, thirty years later, the arrival in Innsbruck of a governor-prince, Duke Leopold of Lorraine, married to an archduchess, was enthusiastically welcomed as signifying a return of honour and prosperity. Yet the cohesion of the dynasty remained a constant cause for concern. The House of Austria believed that it could strengthen its power in Europe by marriages between near cousins and between uncles and nieces. Ferdinand III had as successive wives his first cousin Maria Anna of Spain, sister of Anne of Austria and Philip IV, and his other first cousin, Maria Leopoldina of the Tyrol. The Emperor Leopold, his son, also married two first cousins, Margaret Theresa of Spain and Claudia Felicitas of the Tyrol; his sister, the archduchess Maria Anna, was married to their uncle, Philip IV. The Spanish branch soon exhausted itself, but the German line was regenerated by beautiful, healthy and fertile outsiders, such as Eleanor of Neuburg, the third wife of Leopold, and the wives of Joseph I and Charles VI. Such a marriage policy, with its inevitable blunderings and hazards, was motivated by a medieval pragmatism; it was a question of employing any available means in order to ensure that the dynasty retained its territories and that the prospects of succession were safeguarded.

Thus, it was a matter of power, authority and prestige, but not of true absolutism. The prince strove nonetheless to render his authority more effective in each country, employing various methods for this purpose, though the conflict was essentially one between the rights of the *Landesfürst* and the claims of the Estates. The *Landesfürst* reserved the right to demand taxes and to increase his demands in proportion to his general needs, in other words the needs of the court and the army.

The Estates, which existed in each country, were still proving recalcitrant and even in Bohemia, which was supposed to have been reduced to silence, their administrative departments distinguished between those revenues that lay at the sovereign's personal disposal, such as confiscated properties, the revenues of the country itself, which the sovereign was expected to employ in the interests of his kingdom,[2] and the contributions voted by the Diet for military expenditure.

The religious question depended on the personal authority of the sovereign: in a territory over which he exercised sovereignty he could not be denied what the *Constitutio Westphalica* had recognized as the right of all princes of the Empire, an attribute of the *Landeshoheit*. He was thus able both to purge his administrative personnel and to favour the Catholic Church. This was evident even in Hungary, where the Estates were still keenly conscious of their authority and better able than in other countries to protect that authority. In Bohemia there can be no doubt that opposition had been weakened by the demise of Utraquism and the introduction of a nobility which, though it had shed its foreign origins by obtaining 'naturalized' status, had greater reason than the old nobility to hope for favours from the prince. The necessary elements of organized opposition no longer existed. By co-ordinating the benefits derived from a strengthening of his authority in each of his states, the emperor was able to support his policies with resources that his predecessors had lacked. The Aulic Council (*Hofrat*) was the organ of administration and justice; in order that it should not become the personal instrument of the emperor in matters of 'general' interest, the recruitment of its members was supervised by the Imperial Diet. The Privy Council or *Geheime Rat* and, in the reign of Leopold I, the Privy Conference or *Geheime Konferenz*, which exerted great influence on foreign policy, had gradually become detached from the Aulic Council. Above the individual chambers which administered the revenues of each state, the *Hofkammer* or Court Chamber collected the revenues deriving from regalian rights and the contributions voted by the Diets. The *Hofkriegsrat* or Court War Council, for a long time established at Graz which lay nearer to the Turkish frontier, controlled the finances of war. It also had command of fortresses and responsibility for the direction of military operations; for a time, as has already been mentioned, the powers of the Hofkriegsrat were subordinated to Wallenstein. There was thus no shortage of general organs of government, and it is possible to speak of a certain degree of centralization. Yet, in order that centralization should be effective and easily controlled, it was essential that the Empire, like France at this same period, should have a Council relatively small in number, composed of persons who were both experienced and trustworthy and who would devote themselves solely to the service of the prince; or, alternatively, a chief minister chosen by the prince (like Richelieu and then Mazarin, in France), or a sovereign such as Louis XIV, determined to govern himself. Instead, the various imperial Councils shared a collegial status and, although their members included jurists and representatives of the middle class, the majority belonged to the upper aristocracy. These men held high offices similar to those which Louis XIV tried to abolish, excluding their holders from his Councils. In theory there was no chief minister, but in practice the chancellor of each state assumed this role; sometimes the functions of chief minister appeared to fall to the Grand Master of the Court or Obersthofmeister, Portia. When Portia died in 1665, the Dowager Empress Eleanor advised her stepson, the Emperor Leopold, who valued her counsels, to declare his intention to tolerate no more chief ministers. By acting thus, he would have been able to reserve this role for himself. However, the existing system was such that reform was quite out of the question and the emperor continued to grant his 'Placet' to the decisions of the various collegial bodies responsible for the general affairs of the Empire. Under his patronage and in his name, the central government was exercised by a juxtaposition of Councils, just as the territory of the dynasty itself comprised a juxtaposition of autonomous kingdoms and principalities. This was an empirical system: the structure of the State was not yet complete.[3]

It was incomplete because in the seventeenth century, though sovereigns and their ministers were striving to build this structure, efforts were being concentrated on bringing together the resources of several different states to further the dynastic policy of their common sovereign. It is therefore a mistake to speak of the despotism, centralization and deliberate Germanization of the system, or to present this unorganized territorial complex as the skeleton of a supranational state whose liberalism could serve as a model to Europe. Both of these views are false, for they correspond neither to the ideal of the rulers of the period, nor to the resources which they had at their disposal. The person of the sovereign was regarded as the sign, the embodiment of Empire, to such an extent that there could be no capital other than the place of his actual residence, where the various chancelleries were established. It will be seen later what were to be the consequences for the future of Vienna. In the meantime, Vienna was far from being the city *par excellence* or symbol of the Empire: neither Prague, Innsbruck, nor even Graz was abandoned and after the conclusion of peace Ferdinand III wondered if Prague, situated on the banks of the Vltava, which joined the Elbe and carried it along towards Germany, might not prove a more convenient place of residence from which the emperor could exercise his dual function of head of the Holy Roman Empire and dynast of the 'hereditary' or patrimonial states.

But in the mid-seventeenth century the territories of both Empire and hereditary states bore the marks of endless war. The armies had returned time and again to the same places, destroying all that had been achieved by way of reconstruction during the intervals of war. If the Alpine states and the valley of the Danube had, on the whole, been spared, almost all of Bohemia, and also Silesia and Moravia, had suffered the interminable waves of Swedish and imperial forces which, whether friendly or hostile, had brought with them nothing but calamity and epidemic. Before the battle of the White Mountain the population of the kingdom of Bohemia was about 4,000,000: a little over 1,700,000 in Bohemia itself, 800,000 in Moravia and roughly 1,500,000 in Silesia; over a territory of roughly 44,000 square miles, this represents a high density of about 90 inhabitants per square mile. The extent of the kingdom's population losses can be measured by the fact that around 1650 there were only 930,000 inhabitants in Bohemia and 600,000 in Moravia. There are no reliable figures available for Silesia, but the German historians Franz and Keyser, who have studied the population statistics of the Thirty Years' War, place it amongst the most severely affected countries, estimating a loss of 33 to 66 per cent of its former population. It must be remembered that the two Lusatias had been detached from the kingdom and ceded to Saxony. Certainly, war had not been solely responsible for the slump in the population, for emigrations had also played a large part.[4]

The countryside itself had changed; where cultivated land had once existed, brambles and weeds now grew in profusion; forests had been abandoned or plundered. Lands that had been deserted by their tenants were occupied by neighbours, with the result that some peasants farmed larger areas than before the war. Livestock had dwindled, probably to a considerable extent, though precise information is not available. The richest, most fertile and most industrious provinces of the patrimonial states had thus fallen into ruin. Inevitably, it was the seigniorial system that was to provide the basis for recovery, although this does not mean that the great lords set about the restoration of their country by the conscious application of economic principles, or that the methods used were in themselves a guarantee of success. Nevertheless, the more prosperous were soon able to reorganize farms originally leased to tenants, but which they now cultivated themselves, resuming the role of producers which some of them—even women, such as Sylvia Černín, to name but one of many—had maintained with heroic efforts during the times of greatest crisis; eventually whole estates were brought back under cultivation. With the termination of the war, no new system had been introduced. What took place now was a second phase in the development of the great domain, the extension of an economic phenomenon that had been evident throughout central Europe since the sixteenth century, and which the restoration of peace merely served to advance. The material and moral benefits of this progress were enjoyed principally by the established aristocracy, both old and new.

The order of knights found its numbers diminished, both by emigration and by social promotion (the more prosperous had risen to the order of great lords), and domains of medium size were absorbed into the large seigniories, not by force, but by economic necessity: since their owners were unable to maintain these lands, they had no choice but to offer them to more wealthy neighbours. In 1659 a certain widow who was not able to keep her fifty-acre farm, 'because of the too heavy taxes and other difficulties', offered it to the lord of Kost. The purchase price, fixed at 1,600 Meissen florins, was to be paid in annual instalments: 600 florins within four years, the remainder at a rate of 50 florins a year. At the end of eight years (1667) the vendor demanded the immediate payment of 400 florins and relinquished the rest of the debt; it would appear that she received only 1,000 florins in all. A similar fate befell the former lands of Wallenstein, at Houska, which the emperor had confiscated so that he could partially reimburse his officers for the upkeep of their regiments or arrears of wages. The new proprietors had to pay the difference; but, since passing armies had reduced these lands to the final stages of ruin, they were only too anxious to be rid of them, at however low a price.[5] In this way the great domains continually increased in area: the seigniory, whether or not it formed a compact group, became an important economic unit.

The old law had distinguished between seigniorial land, the dominical, which was exempt from taxes, and common land, the rustical, which bore the fiscal impositions of the State. In acquiring the lands of the rustical, the lord often attempted to absorb them into his own demesnes. This abuse was prohibited in 1654. The lords continued to acquire peasant lands, but were obliged to pay the traditional taxes. The peasantry was divided into two categories: 'redeemed' peasants and 'unredeemed' peasants. Much discussion has been devoted to the origins and juridical nature of the two groups; it seems that 'redeemed' peasants were the effective owners of their lands, while 'unredeemed' peasants belonged rather to the category of temporary tenants and appear to have been the more numerous during the period immediately following the Thirty Years' War.

The great lords reorganized their estates, which they cultivated once again as productive enterprises and which provided them with large revenues for their commercial activities. Compulsory labour, the corvée, remained their chief resource.[6] In order to obtain labour, the lord strengthened his hold on the personal freedom of his subjects. The Diets of Bohemia, Moravia and Silesia—for this was the concern of the Diets, and not of the king-emperor—had reached a mutual agreement on the return of fugitive serfs. The *jus emigrandi* was not extended to the peasantry. Protestant Silesia, however, which had benefited from the influx of reformers, decided that residence of at least ten years gave a peasant prescriptive rights. The corvée either included the use of the peasant's own draught-animals, carts and implements or simply required his labour. As has been pointed out in an earlier chapter, 'draught labour' presupposed that the peasant possessed, either as tenant or as leaseholder, land sufficiently profitable for him to be in a position to supply his own equipment. This superior class of peasants (*sedláci*), similar to the *laboureurs* in France, formed the more prosperous section of rural society. Some Czech economists, such as the Jesuit Fišer, writing in 1679, considered that 'draught labour' could not have produced the expected results, since the peasants sent their poorest implements and their least efficient workmen. The second category of the corvée, involving simply labour, applied to the large numbers of peasants holding small plots or sometimes merely cottages adjoining a hemp-field or a few acres of land. The grievances of the Bohemian peasantry were directed largely at the corvée: the increase in the number of days of labour, the practice of transporting peasants long distances to work on other estates belonging to their lord, far from the estate on which they lived, and the obligation of shifting wood and stone for the construction of manors and churches. Discontent grew and eventually provoked the great peasant revolt of 1679–80 in northern and western Bohemia.[7] On the whole, it was not the principle of obligatory labour that was questioned, but the abuses of its application. The authority of ancient custom was constantly invoked, either for tactical reasons or from a genuine conviction, the effect of a collective mood nurtured by nostalgia for a supposedly happier past rather than by the hope of progress in the future. In 1680 Leopold I, alarmed when peasants refused to work and resorted to armed rebellion, issued a charter regulating the conditions of the corvée, in an attempt to put an end to the exactions of lords and their bailiffs; he, too, was seeking a return to order by the observance of long-established agreements which had been flouted.

The life of the seigniory seemed quite isolated from that of the rest of the country; on its territory the lord controlled the persons of his subjects no less than their possessions. The peasant, rich or poor, was subject to his lord in every aspect of his existence: he came under the judicial authority of the lord, could not marry without his consent or marry a girl from another estate; he was not permitted to send his children to work or to serve an apprenticeship outside the estate, nor was he entitled to contract a loan or to sell, mortgage or purchase property without the lord's authorization and the payment of taxes. The lord was the natural guardian of peasant orphans and in recompense for his tutelage demanded that they spend the period of their orphanhood in his service. This was soon extended as a general obligation binding all young people to perform some kind of service, just as in the nineteenth century conscription was introduced summoning all young men for military service.

The peasants were also compelled to submit to the various monopolies exercised by the seigniory, to consume only the products which it supplied and to buy their beer from the lord's brewery or at the taverns in the towns built on the lord's estate. They complained frequently of being obliged to buy animals which they had reared on their own lands, which had then worked on the lord's private demesne and which came back to them in a poor state; they also objected to having to buy back for their own sustenance spoiled produce which they had delivered fresh. All this helps to explain the view often expressed abroad, or by travellers, that the condition of the Bohemian peasantry was one of cruel and scandalous servitude.[8]

Nevertheless, during the seventeenth century and the first decades of the eighteenth century, the population of Bohemia increased, suggesting that extreme poverty could not have been the general rule. The rise in the population was very rapid. In Bohemia alone it reached 1,267,241 in 1672, 1,408,531 in 1682 and 1,560,423 in 1692; there was a gain of altogether 936,021 inhabitants within fifty years; by 1722 the population of the kingdom as a whole had reached and even passed the figures for the beginning of the seventeenth century. On the eve of the War of the Austrian Succession, which brought destruction once more to the kingdom of St. Wenceslas, Moravia numbered 900,000 inhabitants and Silesia, which was coveted by Prussia for this very reason, had 1,109,000 inhabitants. The proportions of Germans and Czechs should be taken into account, although this was not a preoccupation of the times. Silesia had a predominantly German population and Moravia, a transit route between Silesia and Austria, must have included many Germans. But, in the case of Bohemia, the highest rates of population growth for the years 1672–1722 are provided by districts with a Czech majority: 188 per cent in the Circle of Slany, 156 in that of Rakovník, 131 in that of Kouřím and 157 in that of the Vltava. These figures justify the observation of a statistician, Otto Placht, who maintained that the repopulation of Bohemia was the achievement of the Czech districts, while the German districts on the periphery did not reach the same high rate of growth.[9]

Much has been said of the decline of the towns during this period. The decline of the royal cities is indisputable; they had lost both their wealth and their moral authority. They were no longer the prime movers of the economy. Almost everywhere, though not simultaneously, the seventeenth century experienced monetary deflation, a fundamental cause of which was a reduction in the consignments from American mines. In central Europe the crisis was aggravated by the effects of the war and, as writers observed at the time, by competition from the Western countries, which were better equipped. As demand increased in the non-agricultural sector—by which is meant both the luxury expenditure of the upper classes and the taxes levied by the State—there was no corresponding rise in production in each country.[10] On the other hand, the towns which the lords had been able to build on their domains grew rapidly, becoming outlets for the surrounding region and centres of social advancement, where merchants could make their fortunes and peasants' sons could acquire a little education. Among these expanding towns were Jindřichův-Hradec on the estate of the Černín family, Český-Krumlov on the estate of the Eggenbergs, which was inherited by the Schwarzenbergs, Turnov in northern Bohemia, Náchod, which passed from the Trčka family to the Piccolomini, and the towns of Prachatice and Pardubice.

Would it not then seem that the great domain guaranteed the Czech people a degree of natural protection? The suppression of the peasant's freedom of movement, the necessity of marrying within the estate, the uninterrupted continuity of natural environment and custom, must certainly have nurtured and strengthened the Czech consciousness, which expressed itself in the traditional Czech language. Men's characters were shaped by the conditions of their existence. The peasant virtues (and, of course, the defects which are their inevitable counterpart), the astounding capacity for devotion, for fidelity—later to be represented by the motto *věrnost za věrnost*, 'fidelity for fidelity's sake'—the warm-heartedness of the Czech people and even the rough exterior which, for the casual visitor, the foreigner, conceals the true essence of the Czech, must surely have evolved from the stability of environment which characterized the generations of the period of the great domains.

But, as the historian directs his attention once again to the Danubian empire, it becomes equally clear that, although these countries had been brought together under one prince, the economic structure and customs of the seigniorial system served to maintain the differences which separated them, making them reluctant to mingle and suspicious of each other.

The seigniorial regime had split society into microcosms. In Austria, with its mountain regions, pastureland and forests, natural conditions were ill-suited to the formation of large producing estates. The feudal estate, as opposed to the domanial estate, still flourished there: the *Grundherrschaft* had survived and had not evolved into the *Gutsherrschaft*. An Austrian historian, H. Feigl, is no doubt justified in presenting the first half of the eighteenth century as the golden age of the feudal landowner in Austria.[11] Many domains were owned by the clergy, which meant that their administration was in the more patriarchal, if not more paternal hands of abbots who, while not disdainful of a luxurious style of living, were mostly of peasant origin and therefore felt affinities with the land; to the management of their estates the clergy applied methods developed by long experience, without involving themselves in the excessive expenditure which in court circles was absorbed by gaming, women and the prodigality of sons and sons-in-law. In Lower Austria the seigniory exacted tolls, customs dues, duties on transactions, quit-rents and numerous other taxes; it maintained a vigilant eye on the observance of forest or mining legislation, dispensed justice and needed a competent administrative personnel. In Austria, also, the seigniory required compulsory labour, but for less onerous tasks and for fewer days in the year; in fact, among lawyers the Austrian corvée was renowned for its moderation. When Maria Theresa announced that the maximum should not exceed 104 days per year (i.e. two days per week), very few peasants derived any marked benefit from her decision.[12]

In Hungary conditions varied from county to county, as regards both juridical and actual status. It has already been seen that the great domain had been established in Hungary since the sixteenth century, and even earlier, and that the peasants had long been deprived of their freedom of movement. In those parts of the country where the great domain had been organized in the manner prevailing in Bohemia and Poland, the lot of the peasant was one of extreme poverty and squalor. But there existed a large class of minor nobles who were entitled to sit at the county assemblies and to elect deputies to the Diet, and who thus enjoyed a quite different relationship with the upper nobility: they were in fact the political protégés of the great lords. In the region of the great plain and even in the areas bordering the mountains, the population, both nobles and peasants, had another reason for constant anxiety: the Turks, without declaring war, and even when no state of war existed between the sultan and the king, were continually raiding and sacking villages and taking prisoners—beautiful women destined for their harems, lords for whom a high ransom could be demanded and even peasants, for it was obviously in their master's interest to buy them back. Among the lower orders of the Danubian societies there thus existed such a great diversity of juridical status and of living conditions, and so many different causes of suffering, that even neighbouring regions represented quite separate worlds. The central government would have achieved a miracle if it had succeeded in imposing uniformity on these countries. The most it could expect was that each should contribute towards the cost of the foreign policy of which it remained sole arbiter.

❧

At least, conditions both general and particular, and the absence of a strong standing army, did not permit of an aggressive foreign policy. By the terms of the treaty of Westphalia, the emperor was compelled to remain neutral during the war between France and Spain, which ended in 1659. To the east, a new cause of discord had brought a resumption of hostilities between Poland and Russia. The head of the Cossack republic of the Ukraine, Bogdan Schmielnitsky, although of Polish culture, had solicited the protection of Russia. The emperor intervened to restore peace between Poland and Russia, but it was France which, several years later, pacified the north by the treaty of Oliva (1660), signed by the powers of the Baltic (Denmark, Sweden, Brandenburg and Poland). Despite the formation of the Rhenish League by the Rhenish princes and Louis XIV, the House of Austria had little to fear from France in the Empire, at least until the war over Holland. The principal external threat came from the Turks. During the Thirty Years' War the Turks had remained relatively peaceful, for their advances into Hungarian territory can be regarded as frontier incidents rather than as infringements of the truce. The whole situation changed, however, when the Turks invaded Transylvania in 1660 and when the prince of that country, George Rákóczi, appealed for assistance from the emperor.

Henceforth, the House of Austria had to regard as its virtual allies those other powers which found themselves threatened by the Ottoman Empire, or which could guarantee their security only by liberating former possessions that had fallen into Turkish hands. The powers concerned were Poland, still close to the Austrian countries in its social structure and its religion, Venice, which for several years had been at war with Turkey in an effort to safeguard Crete, and finally Russia, a country of which little or nothing was known in the West, but which, under the rule of the Romanov princes, was gradually reorganizing its administration and its army and thereby preparing itself for the great role that it was to play in the East. From 1660 to 1740 the Turkish war was to be the mainspring of the foreign policy of the House of Austria, determining its alliances, necessitating a new status for the imperial army and thereby exerting an influence on internal policy. If the fiscal impositions of the State became heavier during the seventeenth century, and if, as the great Czech historian Pekař has demonstrated, they formed a higher proportion of the peasantry's tax burden than seigniorial dues, it was because of the war with the sultan, which until 1683 proved a hard struggle with no positive results, but which then, with the campaigns of Prince Eugene of Savoy, brought victory and conquest. The expenditure of the court undoubtedly absorbed a large part of these revenues, but it is nevertheless true that the House of Austria, with the blood, sweat and money of its peasant populations, took upon itself the role of protector of Christendom against Islam. It did not, however, rely solely on the troops levied in the Habsburg states and maintained by fiscal contributions; the Holy Roman Empire provided its own contingents, thus strengthening the ties of solidarity between the emperor and Germany.

Political relations with France also depended on the vicissitudes of the Turkish war. When the sultan attacked Hungary in 1664, the king of France, as a member of the Rhenish League, sent his troops (six thousand men commanded by the Comte de Coligny) to join the imperial army led by Montecuccoli.[13] The French army played a major part in the Christian victory of St. Gotthard, named after the Cistercian monastery near the village of Morgersdorf in Burgenland, where the main assault took place. This association was followed by a period of close under-standing, evident at the time of the War of Devolution. The emperor, far from supporting his sister, the queen regent of Spain, prepared the ground for a possible division of the Spanish succession with Louis XIV. But when the emperor was drawn into the conflict between the Empire and France (1673-9), and then into resistance to the 'reunions', after the treaty of Nijmegen, France used the Turkish offensives as a diversion. To placate her ally, Poland, she sought to turn the Turks against the emperor's non-imperial states. France made the mistake of underestimat-ing the magnitude of the great Turkish offensive of 1683 and, instead of leading an army of liberation herself, left to the king of Poland, John Sobieski, and the imperial armies the honour of raising the siege of Vienna and saving Western Christendom.[14]

☙

These thirty-five difficult years (1648-83) present something of a paradox. Hungary was insecure and frequently in a state of war. Since existing local forces and the conscription of nobles (*insurrectio*) were insufficient to ensure the country's military defence, it was necessary to appeal to the emperor's army. German contingents then came to occupy the Hungarian fortresses, bringing with them the inevitable risk of friction between the *miles extraneus*, the foreign soldier, and the people of the country which he claimed to be defending.

Complaints against the garrisons appeared repeatedly in the *Gravamina*, the grievances voiced by the Diets.[15] In Bohemia, the privileged class of earlier times was disturbed and even scandalized by the changes that had come over society, for privileges had been extended to a much greater number of persons. Everywhere, even in Austria, the imposition of new burdens on the rural populations, the grow-ing fiscal demands of the State, and the contrast between the luxury enjoyed by the upper classes and the modest condition or even extreme poverty of the lower orders, fostered a social malaise.

In connection with Bohemia, in particular, historians have spoken of a 'dark age', the *Temno*, an expression that recalls the Time of Troubles or *Smutnoye Vremya* of Russian history, the harsh years of famine and of civil and foreign wars between the reign of Ivan the Terrible and the accession of the first Romanov.[16] But, in contrast, it should be remembered that this period also witnessed the building of churches and palaces, a transformation of the urban and rural scene, the erection of votive columns and statues in market-places, the activity of artists' and craftsmen's workshops, theatrical performances of great splendour, the advent of triumphal arches and all the machinery erected for religious and civic festivals, and the development of music of dazzling quality, both sacred and profane. This Baroque glory was the counterpart of the *Temno*. But wherein lay the true character of this society? How could two contradictory orders have co-existed?

The word 'Baroque' was not in use at this period, but it seems a convenient term by which to describe a form of civilization in which the values of sentiment and sensibility prevailed over intellectual values and rational ethics, and in which the cult of the marvellous and the external diverted men's minds and hearts from the values of harmony and balance and from the observation and representation of reality.

The Danubian basin, understood in the broad sense of the term and extended to include the Poland of the Cracow region, was the meeting-point of influences from the north and the advancing Mediterranean culture. The Renaissance, and the Mannerist movement which derived from it, a scientific attitude in which mathematical reasoning and experiment were mingled with occultism and a scholarly magic, astronomical observation conducted side by side with the study of the transmutation of metals and the search for signs betokening individual destinies—these were the manifestations of the general effervescence of society and also, undoubtedly, of its spiritual restlessness.

For this mood of restlessness the Church had its own answer, which its most convinced members and its fanatics attempted to impose. The Pope protested because certain clauses of the treaties of Westphalia had granted legal status to the reformed churches. Moreover, the introduction of the directorial year, enforcing the restoration of places of worship and estates to Protestants, seemed to block the further progress of Catholicism. But, in fact, peace was to prove favourable to the revival and extension of the Counter-Reformation. In the countries subject to the authority of the emperor, both in the Empire and in the patrimonial states, this revival was palpable and rapid.

In 1650, Ferdinand III ordered the restoration throughout the Empire, within a period of two months, of 'the crosses and the prayer-columns which Christians now deceased had erected at crossroads and in various other places, on roads and thoroughfares, in honour of God and in thanksgiving, and which were demolished during the war'. Two German states diffused the spirit of the Council of Trent and the Catholic Reformation over the neighbouring countries: Bavaria, where the Jesuits were strongly entrenched at Ingolstadt, and Salzburg, where the university founded in 1620 became the school of Benedictine theologians whose influence spread over Bavaria, Swabia and the western regions of the Habsburg states. The archbishops Wolf Dietrich, Marcus Sitticus and Paris Lodron commissioned the Italian architect Santino Solari to build there a magnificent cathedral with dome and towers, the first great Baroque edifice to be erected in these countries.

In Austria, the great abbeys rediscovered their old vitality: the Benedictines at Melk, Kremsmunster, Lambach, Altenburg and Göttweig, the Cistercians at Wilhering, the Premonstratensians at Geras, the Augustinians at St. Florian, St. Pölten and Herzogenburg. In Bohemia the monasteries of Osek, Zlatá Koruna and Zbraslav became active once again and the Jesuit colleges flourished in Prague, Kutná Hora, Jičín and at Olmütz in Moravia. Pilgrimages were made once more to venerated shrines and the multitudes of earlier times flocked to Maria-Taferl in the Danube valley, not far from the Strudel, the country of the Nibelungen, as if the impulse of a remote ancestral religion was needed to revive the faith of the Middle Ages and enlighten it with the Tridentine spirit; pilgrims also made their way to Mladá-Boleslav in Bohemia and to Svatá Hora, whose silver altar and resplendent sanctuary was described by Balbín.[17] To ensure that the practice of the faith was observed and that churches were attended regularly, the authorities took administrative measures which they judged no less necessary than those relating to censuses and land-surveying. In Austria, reform commissions were appointed which consisted of representatives of the Diet and of the secular clergy, and which often included members of the regular clergy, who were better trained for this kind of work. The commissions sent missionaries into the Protestant regions and, after a short period of instruction, gave the inhabitants the choice between conversion and exile. But the formalities of departure (permission to leave the estate, payment or recovery of debts, the necessity of finding a replacement in order not to leave land vacant) were so complicated that it seemed simpler to become a convert. Nonetheless, the Austrian historian Hugo Hantsch observes that, between 1647 and 1652, forty thousand persons left Austria for Germany.[18]

In Bohemia, two bishoprics were established: one at Leitmeritz in 1655, the other at Hradec Králové in 1660. Parish priests were ordered to keep a register of Easter confessions. But they needed to be educated men conscious of their responsibilities; the task of conversion thus fell largely on the religious orders and in particular the Jesuits, many of whom, like Father Bridel (1619–80), at the order of their superiors, left their teaching work in the colleges to join the missionaries. In Royal Hungary, the reforming archbishop of Esztergom, Cardinal Pázmány, was convinced that the Jesuits were the most skilful in effecting conversions.

The return to Catholicism of populations which had only recently been committed to the Reformation brought a change of sensibility and a different way of life that were evident even in daily behaviour. Primacy of position was henceforth guaranteed to a ritual, figurative religion characterized by the collective manifestation of religious sentiment, and by a richness of ornamentation far removed from the less expressive spirit of Lutheranism or the rigid austerity of Calvinism and the Hussite tradition. The way was clear for a revival and extension of Baroque art. It is a profoundly significant point of detail that people now acquired the habit, still common even today in the countries of central Europe, of making the sign of the cross when passing churches and crucifixes and of giving pious expression to the most banal daily greeting: 'I hail you in God, God be praised! *Grüssgott! Pochvalen bud'Pan Ježiš Christus!*' Finally, deep-rooted sociological causes restored the numerical predominance of the two traditional classes, the aristocracy and the peasantry, and led to an increasingly narrow hierarchy on the seigniory, where social mobility became more and more restricted; the independent middle class faded into the background.

The peasant populations conformed to the religion of their lords and bailiffs.

Wherever the lords had remained Protestant and failed to put the edicts into practice, adherence to the Reformation persisted. Wherever they were the zealous champions of conversion, Catholicism reappeared and gathered strength from generation to generation. The Catholic faith thus became one of the major elements of the Baroque movement.

It is worth pausing to consider some of the achievements of Baroque architecture; as the ornamental aspect of town and countryside changed, it influenced the men who lived there and permeated their sensibility. Even before 1650, Italian taste had begun to inspire those who built and decorated churches, both Lutheran and Catholic: the churches conceived in the tradition of Vignola, the two-storeyed façades of St. Mary of Victory (begun by Protestants) and of San Salvator, which was subsequently adorned with an elegant narthex and a terrace. Near the Charles Bridge in Prague an Italian architect, Lurago, built a Jesuit college, the Clementinum, with a row of Corinthian pilasters providing a vertical effect to correct the rather massive and monotonous aspect of this long edifice. Later, some time after 1670, J. B. Mathey, a Roman architect of Burgundian birth who had been brought to Prague in the service of Archbishop Wallenstein, introduced a new style that broke away from the tradition of northern Italy and revealed the noble dispositions of Bernini. The church of St. Francis Seraph stands beside the river, near San Salvator and the Clementinum: the movement of the embossed façade, the graceful strength of the columned drum, the oval cupola and the ribs which meet around the lantern, gave the Baroque architecture of Prague a hitherto unknown quality of plenitude and serene majesty.

The bird's-eye view of Prague sketched by Wenceslas Hollar during his travels of 1636, and engraved three years later at Antwerp, is a precious document which helps towards an understanding of the evolution of civil architecture. On the side of the Hradčany hill, where old fortified residences can still be seen, lies the central square of Malá Strana. The house of the Smiřický family, the Ů Montagů, provides an example of the architectural solution adopted in the sixteenth century: noble families acquired a number of buildings from middle-class citizens and converted them into one large dwelling in the Renaissance style. A little further away rises the imposing mass of the Wallenstein palace.[19] An entire district had to be razed so that the palace could be built. This first example of Prague's Baroque architecture stands witness to the extraordinary success of a great lord who was able to provide himself with magnificent surroundings fit for a sovereign prince—perhaps the first of the emperor's subjects to be more grandly accommodated than his master. Undoubtedly, the regular façade and the roof with its skylights have the traditional German heaviness. But, in this palace designed by the Italian architects Peroni and Spezza, the enchantment of Italy is to be found in the *sala terrena*, a superb loggia with triple arcades facing on to the gardens which calls to mind the Palazzo del Tè in Mantua, and in the gardens themselves where the avenues, decorated with bronze statues by the Flemish sculptor Adrian de Vries, extend as far as the walls covered with *rocaille* work. The hall of state and the chapel occupy two floors; on the ceiling of the hall of state is a fresco by the Italian artist Bacco Bianchi which depicts the master of the house as the god Mars on a chariot.

A generation later, Prague was embellished with another magnificent edifice: the palace erected by Francesco Caratti, another Italian architect, for Count Humprecht Černín, the boyhood friend of the Emperor Leopold. The count had visited Italy frequently, unlike Wallenstein, who was not familiar with that country. The palace represents the application on a massive scale of the architectural principles of Palladio: colossal columns rise high above a powerful substructure of embossed masonry, giving rhythm to the enormous façade. Completed only in 1692, this building, in which the family fortune was believed to have been sunk, is much more sumptuous than the Wallenstein palace, reflecting both a new stage in the evolution of society and a new aspect of the Baroque: on the one hand, the ostentation of aristocratic pride in a solidly established family; on the other, the appearance of the triumphal style. There was a greater degree of measure and harmony in the archbishop's palace which Mathey built on the Hradčany square and in the other palace, at the end of the same square, to which he added an attic and two little belvederes situated in the axis of the portals framing the central part of the building. This palace, named the Tuscan Palace by subsequent owners, is reminiscent of one of Bernini's last works, the façade of the Odescalchi palace, on the Piazza Santi Apostoli in Rome. The tradition of Baroque architecture which had thus been established in the Bohemian capital was to survive there for nearly a century, until the time of Maria Theresa, who restored the royal palace after the War of the Austrian Succession.[20]

The painters and sculptors of Bohemia must also be mentioned. In the mid-1630s an expatriate, Karel Škréta, returned to his city from Italy, where he had been converted and where his artistic style had been formed. In Italy he had become familiar with the works of the Renaissance, the schools of Bologna and of Caravaggio. His paintings, of an eclectic and personal nature, showed a diversity of subject and included portraits and religious scenes. His finest achievement was without doubt the St. Wenceslas cycle, which he painted for the Augustinian monastery of Zderaz, in Prague itself. This is also his most moving work, for the quality of the composition, the beauty of the lines and the sober solidity of the colours are enhanced by a tenderness for the Czech countryside, evoked in the background, and a fervour for the national tradition which no foreign artist could have expressed with such poetic effect. Italian art in the service of Bohemian inspiration—this was no longer merely a question of an artistic manner, for an authentic Czech Baroque style had been born.[21]

In 1650 a column was erected in honour of the Immaculate Conception in the square of the city hall in Old Prague. The column was stupidly demolished in 1919 on the erroneous pretext that it commemorated the victory of the White Mountain, with which it was in fact quite unconnected. The sculptor of the monument, J. J. Bendl, who also carved the equestrian statue of St. Wenceslas, was an artist of provincial inspiration, but nonetheless a precursor of the new style. The group of St. Anne and the Virgin by Jäckel was the first of the series of effigies of saints which made the Charles Bridge one of the great show-places of Baroque statuary.[22]

The suggestion which has so often been made, that this Baroque art was imposed on Prague by foreigners and by the Jesuits in an attempt to stifle the traditions of the country, is a misconception that can hardly be excused by the poverty of artistic knowledge of nineteenth-century political historians. What happened in Bohemia can be seen more clearly by comparison with the evolution of the arts in France at this same period. The masters of style and technique were initially Italians who left their country and came to France. It then became a tradition for French artists to go to Italy to study the masterpieces and to work in the famous studios of the time. Eventually, as artistic talents and vocations grew more abundant, French artists free of earlier influences became creators and masters in their turn. It is true that Prague no longer enjoyed the balance of relationships which, in the time of Rudolf II, had existed between artists, the urban patriciate, the corporations and foreign merchants. The economic life of artists was now entirely dependent on the commissions they received from the nobility and the Church. Nevertheless, the aspect of the city was transformed by their activity; some of these artists were natives of the kingdom of Bohemia, while others had come from the various Habsburg states and, for the most part, had been granted the rights of residence and citizenship. At the same time, an entire local artisan class of high quality— carpenters, metal-workers, joiners, cabinet-makers and decorators—depended for its subsistence on this surge of artistic activity, which it thus served to complement.

Vienna, enclosed within its walls, was still a medieval city. It had been almost wholly spared by the war and, as the population gradually became converted to Catholicism, new churches were built by the religious orders. Here, too, the style of post-Tridentine Italy prevailed: two- or three-storeyed façades with pediments and volutes, differing only in the elaborateness of their decoration; the Paulaner-kirche, austere and simple, the Dominican church reminiscent of the Gesù in Rome, the Jesuit church flanked by two towers, which conveys a more upward-reaching impression and bears an eloquent inscription: *Deo Victori Triumphatori, optimo, maximo, trophaeum hoc in memoria B.V. Mariae, Ignatii et Francisii Xavierii Ferdinandus imperator statuit*. The date is 1627, the year in which the Constitution of Bohemia was renewed. Where new buildings were not erected, old buildings were transformed. The aisles of the church of St. Stephen and of the old churches of the city assumed a different aspect as altars in the Roman style were added, with altarpieces of sumptuous materials, reliquaries, statues and wreathed columns. Italian architects, Marco Spazio and C. Antonio Carlone, refashioned the church of the Benedictines, the Schottenkirche, and Italian stucco-workers decorated it with their rosettes and a rich variety of motifs. In 1632 the same architects, working on the church of the Nine Choirs of Angels, the Am Hof, began the construction of an exquisitely delicate façade with a terrace lying between two projections.

Little advance had yet been made in secular architecture. Portia lived in a small and rather dull Renaissance palace, not far from the Hofburg. Even the emperor found himself cramped for room in the old fortress. He had a new wing built (the 'Leopold Wing', regular and sober in design) to connect with a palace situated to the west which had been built for Rudolf II in the sixteenth century, and which was subsequently named the Amalienburg. The group of buildings placed along the line of the fortifications lacked the space which facilitated the layout of the buildings and gardens around the Hradčany in Prague. If the festivals of Vienna were inspired by the festivals of Paris and Versailles, the Habsburg capital remained modest by comparison with the Bourbon capital. After all, did not the king of France have greater resources at his disposal than his cousin?[23]

Music possibly contributed as much as politics to guide the destiny of Vienna, which had become the emperor's permanent residence and, consequently, the virtual capital of the Danubian empire. Leopold I was a man of very simple personal tastes (on one occasion, a foreign ambassador who had been ushered into the emperor's presence at first took the small figure dressed in black to be a secretary), but he had a passion for music, like his stepmother the Empress Eleanor. In his correspondence with Humprecht Černín, he inquired about the theatres and concerts in Venice. When he married the Infanta Margaret Teresa, his niece, in 1668, the austere rooms and narrow courtyards of the Hofburg were filled with royal concerts, ballets and carousels. On the site of the present-day library, the emperor had a theatre built where the opera by Cesti, *Il Pomo d'Oro*, was performed with quick-change scenery by Burnacini. The opera was a novelty in Vienna, but it also represented a new stage in musical art because of the important position it gave to the arias, several of which had been composed by Leopold himself. Music was, moreover, the art preferred by Baroque society. The operas of Venice and the oratorios of Rome were highly esteemed. The composer Giacomo Carissimi (1605–74) and his pupils enjoyed repeated successes. It had not been possible to find performers of quality in the Danubian countries; as a result, a great many Italians came to Austria, Bohemia and Hungary to direct or to improve the production of their works. Then it was discovered that the genius of the Slavs and Magyars was suited to singing and the playing of instruments. The great lords of the preceding century had been primarily humanists, collectors of precious objects and book-lovers; those of the second half of the seventeenth century were drawn more towards music. Jindřichův-Hradec, the domain of the Slawata family, became a little capital of musical art. Adam Michna z Otradovic (1600–76) had started by composing hymns based on Czech poetry; then, studying the Italian scores obtained for him by the Jesuit library, he extended his style and composed the celebrated *St. Wenceslas Mass* in honour of the national saint. In the works of his contemporary, the Cistercian Alberic Mazak (1609–61), greater importance was given to wind-instruments than to strings. Music written for theatre, church or chamber groups required an ever greater number of instruments: organs, lutes, clavichords, harpsichords, spinets, viols of different sizes, clarinets, flutes and the sonorous trumpets which added so much brilliance to solemn compositions.[24]

In assessing a culture that was undoubtedly based on artistic rather than intellectual values, should the historian set against the brilliant successes of Baroque art a decline of intellectual and literary life sufficiently marked to justify the term *Temno* or 'dark age'?

The use of German (a clumsy, heavy German) spread throughout the Danubian countries to the detriment of the Slav languages, especially among the aristocracy, who adopted German because of their frequent relations with the court and the predominance of foreign families in their ranks. Historical literature contains several references to the case of Frederick Ulrich Kinský, chancellor of Bohemia, who in 1670 admitted that he had quarrelled with his German wife and had given her two hefty blows with the elbow, because she had been making fun of his Czech.[25] But the Jesuit colleges, far from proscribing the language of John Huss, were anxious to use it to propagate Catholic doctrine and made every effort to ensure that it was correctly taught; hence the work of their grammarian, Father Drachovský (1577-1644), entitled *Grammatica boemica in V libros divisa*, which was not, however, published until 1660. Between 1704 and 1753, there appeared six editions of the *Grammatica linguae boemicae* which Václav Jandit (who was not a Jesuit) had dedicated to his pupil, the Grand Duke Jean Gaston of Tuscany, who had acquired a palace in Prague and lands in the provinces. In the preface to this work, the usefulness of the Czech language is demonstrated by stressing the inconvenience of having to use an interpreter in order to communicate 'with people one meets constantly, people with whom one shares the same air and bread'. Moreover, in the colleges numerous theatrical performances were given in Czech. Slawata, lord of Jindřichův-Hradec, strove to preserve on his estates the practice of preaching in Czech. Evidence of this kind gives the lie to the suggestion that there was a general campaign of persecution against the national idiom. But, at the same time, it proves that the Czech language was in great peril. The Jesuit Bohuslav Balbín (1621-87) composed a *Defence of the Czech language* which, belatedly published in the eighteenth century at the time when the language was most severely threatened and the first efforts were being directed towards its revival, enjoyed a great success and a possibly exaggerated reputation.[26] Balbín came to be regarded as the archetype of the Czech patriot, the outstanding embodiment of his time, his religion and his order. But this was not so. It was simply that his superiors feared that certain assertions made by Balbín in his historical studies might displease or offend the circles of government, even though he had taken care to dedicate one work to Ferdinand III, in which he praised the emperor's piety towards the Virgin Mary. His *Miscellanea* are full of fervour for the past history of his Bohemian homeland, but they lack a critical perspective and reliability. At the beginning of this century Arne Novák, who was one of the first to 'discover' the Czech Baroque movement, shrewdly observed that Balbín should be judged rather by comparison with the sixteenth-century chronicler Hajek than as the precursor of the more erudite Benedictine school and Dobner. In both thought and style he was distinctly inferior to his compatriot, Pavel Stranský, a Protestant exile who published the *Respublica bohemica*, in the Elzevir collection. Neither did Balbín possess the charm, the poetry or perhaps even the culture of another Czech Jesuit, Father Bridel, whose poems and canticles drew their inspiration both from the German lyric poets Angelius Silesius and Opitz and from the French spiritual writers of his time. In his 'God-centred' fervour Bridel resembled Father Boudon, archdeacon of Évreux, who was very popular in France and whose work entitled *Dieu seul!* was translated into Czech by another Jesuit, Father Karel Rosenmüller.

The most celebrated Czech writer of this period was a pastor of the United Moravian Brethren, Jan Amoš Komenský or Comenius (1592-1670).[27] Should Comenius be excluded from the Baroque movement simply because he was a Protestant? His moral and didactic works are full of ingenious ideas and new methods

for the teaching of languages and for pedagogy in general; in the face of the upheavals that shook his country, they showed a great spiritual exaltation. Out of
the vicissitudes of his career there emerges a human type thoroughly representative
of the period. From the early years spent in his Moravian birthplace until his death
at Naarden, he followed all the great crises of the Czech Reformation. He was the
protégé of great lords such as Charles Žerotín, a Protestant who remained loyal
to the emperor, Sigismund Rákóczi, the Hungarian 'malcontent', and Leszczynski
in Poland; he then enjoyed the patronage of the de Geerts, the rich merchants of
Amsterdam who financed the publication of his works. Comenius thus led a
wandering existence which took him into different countries and among different
social groups, but he always found the protection of some illustrious and powerful
patron. In 1650 he settled for four years on the estate of Sigismund Rákóczi at
Sárospatak, below the Carpathians.

At Sárospatak stood a medieval castle whose wild aspect was barely softened by
the refurbished Renaissance rooms of the interior. The Rákóczi family took an
interest in intellectual life and had installed a printing-works in the town. The
simple arcaded building which housed the school can still be seen today. Comenius
taught in the school and wrote some of his books there: the *Schola pansophica* and
the *Orbis pictus*. The residence of the prince of Transylvania also stands witness to the
spirit and manners of the Baroque age; here, the prophetic sage and the adventurous
magnate joined in a common effort to hold their own against emperor and pope,
offering their services and advice to a coalition of the Protestant powers of the
north and west—Sweden, the United Provinces and even Cromwell's England.

The Baroque literature of the Austrian countries, eloquent and persuasive rather
than rational and deductive, displays the same inspiration and the same rhetorical
characteristics from one language to another. Its purpose was always to move men's
hearts rather than to convince their minds by intellectual arguments. Images are
deployed in dazzling fashion and sentences follow one another in a jingle of allitera-
tion which cannot be conveyed in translation, but which leaves the listener both
stunned and enchanted. Such was the oratorical style of Cardinal Pázmány,
archbishop of Esztergom (1570–1639), and, in the next generation, the Augustinian
friar Abraham a Sancta Clara, preacher at the court of Vienna, whose rare imaginative power developed these techniques to the peak of their effectiveness. The
great lord and the man of the people, using the same methods, both wrote in the
manner of poets and prophets; but Abraham a Sancta Clara possessed a particular
gift for embracing the mundane in order to rise to the sublime, the art of seizing an
event and then drawing from it the most glorious lessons, so that the natural and
the supernatural became merged into one. At the time of the third marriage of
Leopold I, when it was essential that the future of the dynasty should be safeguarded
by the birth of a male heir, as yet awaited in vain, his moving accents implored
heaven to grant the emperor 'as much happiness as there are trees in the forest,
grass in the fields, drops of water in the fountain, sand in the sea, stars in the sky ...'
and 'treasures and fortresses, victory and glory, joy and friendship, provinces and
princes'. During the plague of Vienna the language of the preacher assumed
Biblical tones. On the eve of the siege of the city he launched his great appeal:

'Arise! Arise, O Christians!', as if it was his task to set the Empire, Italy and France in motion and to drive their populations to the defence of Christendom and the West.[28]

Vienna was becoming the Habsburg capital and the time had passed when the Viennese regarded their neighbours from Graz or Innsbruck as foreigners. Although the Danube was not easily navigable in the region surrounding the city, the river valley provided the natural route between Hungary and the Empire. It will be seen in a later chapter how the economists of the time proposed to free Vienna from the limitations of an agricultural centre and orientate its activity towards European production. But, before attaining this new destiny, the city was to suffer two tragic ordeals: the plague epidemic of 1679 and the siege of 1683.

The epidemic, in its suddenness and sheer intensity, struck the city like a cataclysm. Neither science nor the conditions of hygiene of the time had made it possible to anticipate the plague and offered no means of eradicating it. Death or survival seemed to be purely a matter of chance. Abraham a Sancta Clara gave the disaster a religious significance, interpreting it as a terrible warning by Providence. A wise and learned physician, Sorbait, the rector of the university, was able to observe and analyse the spread of the epidemic, even though he could not diagnose its causes, and he took practical measures to halt the process of contagion by isolating the areas affected. During this time Prince Ferdinand Schwarzenberg set an example of personal composure by remaining in the city, helping the sick and having the dead buried.

The siege of Vienna was itself a terrible national catastrophe. The inhabitants, exhausted by famine, made efforts to maintain their spirits. They witnessed the heroism of the governor, Count von Starhemberg, and his Czech lieutenant, Kapliř z Sulevic, the nephew of one of the condemned men of 1621, and the courage of their burgomaster Liebenberg, whose sad fate it was to die before the deliverance of the city. Each morning they hoped that the support army would arrive before the end of the day, but the weeks slipped by without its appearance. They waited and waited, but for what? Events in the outlying districts of the city could have left no one under any illusion. If the Turkish army were to occupy the capital, there would be wholesale pillage and, for the inhabitants, either massacre or slavery. The author has been shown the testament of an old woman named Maria Pöckhin who lived at Enzersdorf, near Vienna.[29] It is dated 1694, eleven years after the siege. The person in question, though a subject of one of the estates of the Liechtensteins, had a number of possessions to bequeath: her house, some vines, pewter plate, linen, a small amount of money and reserves to pay for her burial and for three masses a week to be said for twenty-three years by the Franciscans of Enzersdorf. She entrusted this inheritance to a neighbouring relative so that it could remain for another ten years at the disposal of her five daughters, Maria Barbara, Maria Elizabeth, Anna Maria, Maria Catharina and Maria Regina; all five girls, together with their aunt Regina Kaiserin, had been abducted by the Turks or the Tartars during the siege and nothing had been heard of them since that time. This document, in which the long martyrdom of a mother and the humble resignation of a Christian are reflected, is a most touching echo from history.

One of the most expressive monuments of the Danubian Baroque style is still to be seen right in the heart of Vienna, on the Graben. Perhaps the Plague Column nowadays produces a rather bizarre effect amid the clutter of the Graben with its parked cars. The lesson it offers is less easily appreciated today than it was in the seventeenth century, when everyone understood its significance and could recall the memory of recent sufferings and hopes.

The emperor had wanted the monument as a votive offering and had himself, with the help of a Jesuit, Father Manegatti, decided its general theme: the unity of God in three Persons. By the intention of the divine wisdom, the power of the emperor rests in its turn on three patrimonial kingdoms: Austria, Bohemia and Hungary. Heaven calls for a threefold prayer: to praise God in his omnipotence, to implore his mercy at times of distress and to celebrate by thanksgiving the benefit of his mercy. The nine choirs of Angels (three times three) are the messengers of prayer. God created a happy world, but permitted its disruption by sin and physical evil. The Deluge attested by Holy Scripture is the essential catastrophe, but is renewed in the successive tribulations of the generations. The Word has redeemed man and overcome evil, so that the entire Cosmos participates in a threefold rhythm of fundamental good, accidental evil and peace regained by the Redemption. Thus, the terrible ordeal of Vienna had its place in the providential order of the world, but had also given yet another sign of God's inexhaustible mercy, since the scourge had come to an end.

The architect J. B. Fischer von Erlach, the painter Burnacini and the sculptors Frühwirth, Kracker, Gunst, Rauchmüller and Paul Strudel, all masters of their art, were invited to translate this broad profession of faith into a monument decorated with figures. They erected the column and adorned it with images charged with significance. The obelisk of triangular section is enveloped in clouds with the angels rising to the group of the Trinity and the rays of eternal glory. The monument is in keeping with the style of scenography that was so widespread at the time. It resembles the ephemeral structures which were erected on squares and in churches for festivals sacred and profane (expositions of the Blessed Sacrament, funerals, triumphal entries, the birth of a prince or a marriage) and which were often known as 'theatres'. The Plague Column is indeed a kind of theatre, but not one of illusion, fantasy or mirage. Transcending the dramatic and lyrical aspect of the figuration, concrete truths are here expressed: the afflictions of the terrestrial world, the religion of redemption and reassurance and, uniting the one with the other, monarchy incarnate in the person of this Christian prince kneeling to give thanks: 'I, Leopold, thy humble servant', says the prayer of thanksgiving; *Ego Leopoldus humilis servus tuus.*

In both general effect and detail, the monument is a fine specimen of plastic art. The transition from the geometric base, solid but not massive, to the lissom, soaring lines of the clouds and the fullness of the group of the Trinity suggests an ascent towards light. The angels of Paul Strudel are of a charming delicacy and harmony. The predominant colour, white, is itself symbolic, for it contributes to an impression of freshness in which the soul finds reassurance and new hope.[30]

It would be a mistake to consider this symbolism complicated or rarefied, since it conveys powerful but simple notions. There is here no recourse to fable and hardly even to allegory (only the statues of the Plague and of Faith). The symbolism has the simplicity of the catechism; consequently, even the most humble folk would not have found it overpowering or obscure, especially since the monument was only inaugurated after the siege of Vienna, which had brought misfortune back to the city, but had ended in deliverance. The figure of the kneeling emperor showed that his power was secondary, merely a reflection of the one true power; it thus set an example of humility and, despite its majesty, conveyed a sense of familiarity. In modern terminology the Plague Column merits the description 'Baroque', but this is a Danubian Baroque which presents characteristics different from those of Roman Baroque. The influence of the Renaissance or of antiquity is here less evident than the traditions of a patriarchal, rustic society. The technique of the artists proves that they were worthy heirs to the great tradition of the Roman *seicento*. But the profundity of this monument becomes clearer in the light of the following observation made by a modern Czech writer: 'It was the Renaissance alone that caused a rupture between the people and the world of art and poetry, because its scholarly inspiration was drawn from antiquity and because, in its rationalist exclusiveness, it claimed to reserve art for the culturally privileged. This was an episode of brief duration, however, for soon the Baroque rediscovered the way to reach the hearts of the people, not only by taking its inspiration from the people, but by giving them something in return, through the burning emotion of pathos.' The pathetic and the popular—these were the essential characteristics of Danubian Baroque, even in works that demanded of the artist both mastery of technique and culture. A study of the Plague Column (Pestsäule) reveals one of the most striking demonstrations of this style and helps one to appreciate that, in comparison with Italian Baroque, it possessed a greater intensity, a more vibrant and grief-laden spirituality. To give something through the emotion of pathos, when reason brought no solace or not enough to overcome the inevitability of misfortune, was to offer hope and, through hope, joy.

Historians sometimes fear lest the appeal of Baroque art should cause the many tragedies of this period to be forgotten: the misery of peoples, the extortions of armies, the short span of human life, incurable maladies, epidemics, peasant revolts and social inequalities. These evils were the consequences of the general economic structure and ideology of the time, rather than the signs of a sinister destiny peculiar to the Danubian countries. They may have been more acute in these countries; but, even so, they serve as the measure by which to judge the compensations provided in the Baroque ideal.

The column on the Graben is only one of many monuments which express the profound character of Danubian civilization. The plague returned on many subsequent occasions. The frequency of calamity led to a profusion of images of reparation. Other columns were erected in the squares of cities and towns, in Austria, Bohemia and Hungary; in each of these countries the columns were of a similar kind, bearing effigies of the Trinity and the Virgin and the figures of local patron saints such as St. Florian and St. John Nepomucene, or the saint-kings Wenceslas, Stephen and Leopold, all of them mediating and protecting saints.

The cult of St. John of Nepomuk, which originated among the aristocracy and the rural population of Bohemia, but then spread through the entire kingdom, is one of the most revealing manifestations of religious consciousness in the Baroque period. As legend accumulated around a rather slender basis of historical fact, the saint came to be honoured as the martyr of the secrecy of the confessional and the protector against the perils of the waters (disasters caused by floods and accidents suffered by individuals). His image, placed on bridges and rivers all over the country, became a part of the didactic iconography of abbeys and parish churches, as the symbol of the sacrament of penance. A special liturgy was authorized by Rome. The canonization, proclaimed in 1729, was celebrated with great festivals in Prague: it sanctified a devotion of a popular, sentimental and practical character which had also acquired a doctrinal value.

Although the Turks did not resume hostilities after 1683, the wars which were undertaken to drive them from the Danubian plain continued for many years, costing much blood and tears. The struggle against France was also pursued, on both the imperial and the Italian fronts—a struggle for dynastic prestige which, though of no real importance for the Danubian populations, was cruel nonetheless. Yet the date 1683 was a turning-point, not so much because of economic changes, which were still barely discernible, as in the consolidation of the political system, the achievement of great military successes and the extension of imperial renown. Danubian Baroque art reflected this evolution. Artists were invited to extol new values—power and glory. Their works, covering a cycle of some sixty years, assumed a triumphal character.

NOTES

1. See the article by G. Zeller, 'Les rois de France candidats à l'Empire', in *Aspects de l'ancien régime*, Paris, 1963.

2. For the nature and evolution of institutions in the different countries, see Hellbling, op. cit. (in chapter 3, note 1), and the large work by T. Fellner and H. Krestchmayr, which is divided into two parts: exposition and collections of texts. For the modern period, consult: *I. Abteilung. Von Maximilian I bis zur Vereinigung der österreichischen und böhmischen Hofkanzlei, 1742:* Volume 1, *Geschichtliche Übersicht,* 1907; Volume 2, *Aktenstücke, 1491–1681,* 1907; Volume 3, *Aktenstücke, 1683–1749,* 1907. For Hungary: J. Szekfü, *État et nation;* for Bohemia: the works by V. Vaněček and Kapras already mentioned.

3. O. Redlich, *Weltmacht des Barock,* 4th edn., 1961. After Portia, Wenceslas Lobkowicz wielded a dominant influence and was sacrificed in 1674 in a return to an anti-French policy. After him, Hocher, the chancellor of Austria, although in name merely a privy councillor, was in practice the chief minister from 1674 to 1683.

4. The demographic consequences of the Thirty Years' War were studied by C. Oestreich, *Der Blutverlust des deutschen Bauerntums im dreissigjährigen Kriege (Archiv für Bevölkerungswissenschaft und Bevölkerungspolitik,* VI, 1936).
   G. Franz, *Der dreissigjährige Krieg und das deutsche Volk,* Jena, 1940. Emil Keyser, *Bevölkerungsgeschichte Deutschlands,* 2nd edn., Leipzig, 1941. The evolution of Bohemia has been studied in a work of great value by Otto Placht, *Lidnatost a společenská skladba*

českého státu v 16–18 stoleti ('The Population and Social Structure of the State of Bohemia from the 16th to the 18th Centuries'), Prague, 1957.

5. The first case is quoted by J. Pekař, *Kniha o Kosti*, vol. II, p. 30, and the second by J. Šimák, *Kniha o Housce* ('The Record Book of Houska'), vol. I, p. 238 *et seq.*

   Otto Placht, op. cit., p. 217, observes that the 900 families constituting the order of knights in Bohemia in 1557 had been reduced to 460 by 1615 and to a mere 238 by the time of Leopold I; of the 69 families representing the order of great lords, only 20 remained. But the order of great lords had been swollen by the promotion of numerous knights and by the influx of 'naturalized' foreign families.

6. Václav Černý, *Hospodářské instrukce* ('Manorial Instructions'), Prague, 1930, studied and published the administrative regulations and the rules of labour applied on the great domains.

7. The collection of texts entitled *Deutsches Bauerntum*, vol. II, *Neuzeit*, no. 49, contains the complaint made by the peasants of the seigniory of Friedland against their lord, Francis Ferdinand Gallas, concerning the obligation to provide carts for the construction of the church of Haindorf (art. 9), the obligation to let their lord's young cattle graze on their pastureland (art. 3), and the new methods 'which did not exist in the time of our gracious lordship, the deceased father of the present lord'.

   No. 50, *Robotpatent* of 1680 for Bohemia. For the revolt of 1680 and an appraisal of the patent, the reader should consult the interesting pages written by J. Kočí, *Československá Vlastivěda, Dějiny*, vol. I. The author declares (p. 473) that the causes of the uprising are to be seen clearly enough in the conditions of the time—plague and poverty—and that they should not be attributed to the intervention of secret agents from France, Hungary and Saxony, as certain exponents of the old school of bourgeois historiography suggested. However, M. Livet, *L'intendance d'Alsace au temps de Louis XIV*, p. 479, points out that on 1 October 1680 Louvois awarded a sum of 224 imperial florins, payable by the town of Sélestat, to a certain Meusnier, a former ensign who had made a journey to Bohemia in the service of the king—a minor detail, but disturbing. On the other hand, the map of the revolt given on p. 433 of the book is highly significant: the rebellion, concentrated in the north, the west and on the frontiers of Moravia, spared the greater part of the kingdom and in particular the Czech region in the south, where large estates were owned by the Slawata, a family devoted to the national tradition. Finally, while the patent undoubtedly did not prevent the continuance of abuses and even though its effect was to make labour obligations uniform in all areas, and therefore more harsh than before in certain regions (p. 479), the intention of the king-emperor to establish his right of dispensing justice, even against the great lords, cannot be questioned. In conclusion, however, this comment by M. Livet should be borne in mind (p. 479): 'Above all, there existed no force capable of restraining the lords from exceeding the limits of exploitation specified by the patent.'

8. It is indeed difficult, allowing for the general mentality of the times, to assess the harshness of the seigniorial regime. It varied from one estate to another and often even on the same estate, depending on the attitude of the bailiffs and overseers rather than on the personality of the lord himself.

   With regard to the general economy, Miroslav Hoch and Josef Petřán have discussed the influence of the European and world situation on the development of neo-feudal structures, in a good article in ČSČH, XII, 1964, no. 3, pp. 267–364.

9. Otto Placht, op. cit., p. 371.

10. Hungarian historians put forward an interesting theory as a working hypothesis which

might well be verified in detail in later studies: in their view, general economic difficulties had repercussions on central Europe, which found its outlets blocked; this external factor was thus added to the local causes of economic recession (cf. the discussions of the conference of March 1968 at Budapest, between the Hungarian Academy of Sciences and the École des Hautes Études, section 6). Also, the hitherto unpublished study by Vera Zimanyi, 'Aspects of the Economic and Social Regression of the 17th Century'.

11. Helmuth Feigl, *Die niederösterreichische Grundherrshaft vom ausgehenden Mittelalter bis zu den theresianisch-josefinischen Reformen*, 1964, p. 320.

12. Ibid., p. 93.

13. The Italian Montecuccoli was one of the best generals in the service of Leopold, as long as the imperial army retained its old and inadequate organization. He fully realized that. small garrisons could not ensure the permanent defence of the system and recognized the danger of not being able to co-ordinate the movements of the imperial army with those of the 'noble levy' in Hungary. Montecuccoli's memoirs were published in Italian at Cologne in 1704 and translated into French in 1725. For the campaign of 1664 and the peace of Vasvár, the reader should consult the recent work by G. Wagner, *Das Türkenjahr 1664, eine europäische Bewahrung*. Also, Eisenstadt, *Burgenländische Forschungen*, 48, 2 vols., which J. Bérenger has reviewed in *Revue historique*, vol. CCXXXVII, January-March 1967.

14. In considering the progress made by the Danubian system towards the role of an international great power (a subject excellently treated by O. Redlich, *Weltmacht des Barock*, mentioned previously), one must take into account the evolution of the two neighbouring states: Russia which, hitherto alien to the West but not Asiatic, as has been unthinkingly suggested, was gradually becoming more conscious of her destinies (cf. Victor-L. Tapié, *La Russie de 1659 à 1689*, Centre de Documentation Universitaire, the author's course of lectures at the Sorbonne in 1954) and Poland, the ally of Austria and France (cf. the study by K. Piwarski, *Miezdy Francia a Austria*, 'Between France and Austria', Cracow, 1933). Russia and Poland found themselves, like Austria, the adversaries of Turkey, but they were traditional enemies and, moreover, rivals for the domination of the southern steppes. These regions, though sparsely populated, were inhabited by Slavs and effective power there was wielded by the Tartars, the subjects of the Porte.

Relations between the House of Austria and France were marked first of all by the *rapprochement* of 1668 (the most recent study of this question is by Jean Bérenger, 'Une tentative de rapprochement entre la France et l'Empereur, le traité de partage secret de la Succession d'Espagne du 19 janvier 1668' in *Revue d'histoire diplomatique*, 1965). For the siege of Vienna in 1683 and its international significance, consult the important article by W. Platzhoff, 'Ludwig XIV, das Kaisertum und die europäische Krisis von 1683', in *Historische Zeitschrift*, 1920, 3rd series, vol. 25. Ferdinand Stöller, *1683*, Vienna, 1933. Thomas M. Barker, *Double Eagle and Crescent: Vienna's second Turkish siege and its historical setting*, New York, 1967. Richard F. Kreutel, 'Kara Mustafa von Wien', in *Osmanische Geschichtsschreiber*, vol. I, Graz, 1955. Victor-L. Tapié, 'Europe et chrétienté', in *Gregorianum*, XLII, vol. 2, Rome, 1961. M. Parlebas, one of the author's students, wrote an unpublished thesis in 1960 entitled *L'opinion française et le siège de Vienne en 1683*.

15. The Diet of Hungary (i.e. of Royal Hungary—Transylvania had its own Diet, while the regions reduced to Turkish pashaliks had none) was rarely convened by the sovereign, but, since the Hungarian state remained autonomous, it was necessary to assemble it in grave circumstances. The Diet of 1655 elected Leopold king of Hungary and denounced the poor state of the garrisons and the Turkish attacks against Kassa and Tokaj.

16. The literature on the *Temno*, which sprang from the polemics waged during the time of the first Czechoslovak republic between those who erected this interpretation of history into a State dogma and those who questioned it, could provide a whole bibliography in itself. It is sufficient to mention the recent work by A. Klima, *Čechy b období temna*, Prague, 1959, 2nd edn. 1961. With the publication in 1915 of his fine essay 'Baroque Prague', the Czech writer Arne Novák (d. 1939) established himself as one of the most brilliant analysts of the Baroque spirit and of its literary and artistic manifestations in Bohemia.

17. B. Balbín, *Diva Montis Sancti seu origines et miracula magnae Dei Rominumque matris Mariae quae in sancto monte regni Bohemiae . . . adetur et colitur*, 1670.

18. Hugo Hantsch, *Geschichte Österreichs*, II, p. 15.

19. The drawing by Wenceslas Hollar, an emigrant Czech painter who went to England and entered the service of the earl of Arundel, dates from 1636, the year in which the artist accompanied his patron on a visit to Bohemia, but the engraving was made in Antwerp in 1639. A good biography of Hollar, by Borovský, is to be found in *Allgemeines Lexikon der Bildenden Künstler*, vol. XVII, 1924.
   The Wallenstein palace escaped confiscation because the duke of Friedland had mortgaged it to his family; it was not nationalized until 1945. It is interesting to note that in 1945 a Countess Wallenstein was given permission, owing to her great age, to occupy a small apartment in the palace, where she died in 1955, over a hundred years old (cf. Johanna, Baronin Herzogenburg, *Prag, ein Führer*, Munich, 1966, p. 131).

20. It is not possible to give here a complete bibliography of Baroque art. A few basic works are: the volume (VII) devoted to art (*Umění*) in the first *Československá Vlastivěda*, 1935; chapters IX (*Central Empire*) and X (Imperial Baroque) of the author's *The Age of Grandeur*, London, 1960; the books on Prague by Schnürer (in German, 1935), Swoboda (also in German, 1939) and Jakub Pavel, and the invaluable guide (in Czech) by Emanuel Poche and Josef Janáček, *Prahou krok za krokem* ('Prague Step by Step'), 1963. But to follow the results of the most recent research, the reader should consult the excellent review *Umění* ('Art'), published every two months under the editorship of Jaromir Neumann.

21. On Karel Škréta, the work by Jaromir Neumann (*Karel Škréta*) and, in the review *Umění* (year XIV, 1966, vol. III, p. 305), the article by Jiří Dvorský on the Zdéraz cycle.

22. O. J. Blažíček, *Sochařství baroku v Čechách* ('Baroque Statuary in Bohemia'), Prague, 1936. For Bendl's family origins, see the article in the review *Das Münster*, X, 1957.

23. This fever of religious building can be traced in an eighteenth-century album entitled *Vera et accurata delineatio tam residentiae et successuum caesareorum quam variorum ad Principis et Comites spectanticum . . . qui partim in Caesarea sede Vienna, partim in adjacentibus suburbiis et proximis territoriis oculis occurrunt*. The most recent modern studies are by Ann Tizia Leitich, *Vienna gloriosa, Weltstadt des Barock*, Vienna, 1963, and Fred Hennings, *Das Barocke Wien*, I (1620–1683), II (1683–1740), Vienna, 1965, the latter in an elegant collection intended for the educated but non-specialist public. For information of a strictly scientific kind, see the manual by Dehio, *Wien*, 4th edn., 1964, brought up to date by Anton Macku and Erwin Neumann, and the collective work by B. Grimschitz, R. Feuchmüller and Wilhelm Mrazek, *Barock in Österreich*, 1960.

24. On the music of central Europe, now accessible to music-lovers through the numerous concerts and recordings of the present day, see Andreas Lies, *Wiener Barockmusik*, 1946.

25. J. Muk, *Po stopách národního vědomí české šlechty pobělohorské* ('In the Steps of the National Consciousness of the Czech Nobility after the White Mountain'), 1931, p. 119.

Z. Kalista, *Uvod do politické ideologie českého baroka* ('Introduction to the Political Ideology of the Czech Baroque'), Brno, ed. Moravan, 1934.

26. J. Vašica, *České literární baroko* ('Literary Baroque in Bohemia'), Prague, 1938, a basic work.

Z. Kalista, *Bohuslav Balbín*, 1948. The works of Balbín published during his lifetime (i.e. excluding the *Defensio linguae bohemicae*, published by Pelcl in the eighteenth century) were the *Miscellanea Historia regni Bohemiae* (1679), an uncritical collection of numerous legends, and the *Diva Montis Sancti* (1670), in which the author invokes the special protection of the Virgin Mary for the kingdom.

27. The works of Jan Amoš Komenský, *Opera didactica omnia*, were re-issued in Prague in 1957 on the occasion of the third centenary of their original publication. Komenský has been the subject of countless works and there exists an active society for Comenian studies.

Josef Polišenský, *Jan Amoš Komenský a jeho doba* ('Comenius and his Time'), Prague, 1957.

Jean Amoš Comenius, 1592–1670, selected pages with an introduction by Jean Piaget, published by UNESCO, 1957, and the very useful catalogue for the 1957 exhibition: *Jan Amoš Komenský—Život-dílo-doba* ('The Life, Work and Time of Jan Amoš Komenský'), edited by Bohumil Novák.

28. On Austrian Baroque literature: A. Tibal, *L'Autrichien*, Paris, 1936. J. Nadler, *Literaturgeschichte Österreichs*, 1946.

Robert A. Kann, *A Study in Austrian Intellectual History*, New York, 1960; also, the works of Abraham a Sancta Clara: *Sämmtliche Werke*, Passau, 21 volumes, 1835–47, of which volume VIII contains the dissertations and sermons.

29. The author would like to thank his pupil, M. Jean Bérenger, for showing him this text, which he found in the course of his patient research in the Archives of Vienna.

30. An anonymous Latin work, *Vienna Gloriosa*, describes the Plague Column and the inauguration of the monument by the emperor, on Trinity Sunday 1692, during the war of the League of Augsburg. The archbishop of Vienna gave a triple benediction in the presence of a crowd struck with admiration and astonishment. 'The burning torches around it and the constant presence of a guard of honour, changed regularly, enhance the majesty of the monument in no small degree' (*Ardentes circum lampades et constans alternantium militium custodia operis non modice augent majestatem*). Obviously, the changes that have taken place in urban life since 1692 have made it impossible to preserve the original setting of the monument on the Graben.

6

The Monarchy as ein Totum

HOW WAS THE policy of a great power to be conducted by a state which was as yet incomplete and which in fact consisted of a juxtaposition of different states? In the year 1684, when the capital had just been saved from the gravest peril that it had faced since the time of Ferdinand I and the emperor found his prestige thus strengthened in the Empire, was it possible to draw up a balance-sheet of the situation? What, in fact, did the term 'state' signify? In each country it represented an historical territory which possessed its own special institutions. Even Austria below the Enns (the Lower Austria of the present day), with Vienna as its principal city, retained its regional autonomy. How much stronger must this sentiment have been in those countries proudly conscious of their long history and still possessing a constitution—Bohemia, where the sovereign enjoyed extensive rights, and Hungary, where his authority was limited by the privileges of the Estates. But the same prince reigned over these different lands. In practice, he had some control of the army and foreign policy depended on his will alone. By virtue of his imperial function, this foreign policy was closely bound up with that of the Empire. It was the Empire that had drawn Leopold I into the war against France, in Holland. Louis XIV and his ministers were henceforth convinced that, by causing the emperor problems in the patrimonial states, they would make him more accommodating in his imperial policy and persuade him to accept the 'reunions' of imperial territories which Louis XIV claimed as his own, according to his juridical interpretation of the treaties of Nijmegen. The king of France thus followed with interest the activities of the malcontents in Hungary, regarding them as his potential allies.[1]

Discontent in Hungary dated from the years following the peace of Vasvár, when Hungarian and Croatian nobles, humiliated by the cession of fortresses to the Turks and readily deceiving themselves with exaggerated hopes of support from the king of France, had entered into intrigues with the French ambassador in Venice, who had not encouraged them.[2] A conspiracy was nevertheless hatched, but was thwarted by the deaths of the ring-leaders, the Count Palatine Wesselényi and the archbishop of Esztergom, Lippai. Another plot had subsequently been organized by the president of the Aulic Council, Nádasdy, and the Croatian nobles

Peter Zrinyi and Frangepany (Zrinyi's brother-in-law). Even a Styrian noble, Count von Tattenbach, had joined the plotters. Like its predecessor, this conspiracy of magnates was a premature affair. It was brought to the emperor's attention, either by spies or by a denunciation from the Porte. With nothing to hope for but the emperor's clemency, the conspirators presented themselves in Vienna to seek his pardon. They were imprisoned, brought before a special court instead of being tried in their own country and in accordance with Hungarian law, and then executed on 30 April 1671, Nádasdy at the Rathaus in Vienna, his associates at Wiener-Neustadt. Their properties were confiscated and Frangepany's widow, deprived of her fine estates on the coast of Croatia, fled to Rome where she entered a convent.

The Hungarian Constitution was suspended and the office of palatine remained vacant. A military regime headed by a German, Ampringen, now governed Hungary and imperial regiments occupied the fortresses. Ruthless reprisals were made against the *kuruc* or 'malcontents' who revolted in Upper Hungary, but the young and valiant rebel-leader Imre Tököli reassembled the forces of the Hungarian and Slovakian counties in the region of Munkács and persevered in the struggle.

Leopold was much too conscious of the paternal character of his monarchy to nurture hatred towards his subjects. But he could neither permit their disobedience nor omit to punish rebels, especially if these were persons of high standing who should have set an example: 'Although I am ordinarily not at all cruel, I must be on this occasion, by necessity.' (*Obwohlen ich sonsten nit gar bös bin, so muss ich es diesmal per forza sein.*) Above all, Leopold was inclined not to take decisions alone; he was influenced by a circle of advisers who, though for various reasons, all tended to advocate severity. Over the rebellions of the Hungarian nobility there hovered the shadow of the Bohemian insurrection of 1621. In the minds of many, the two ideas of revolt and the Protestant religion were associated. Prince Lobkowicz, a Czech and, in the family tradition, both a loyalist and a Catholic, and the chancellor Hocher, a German of the Empire who had entered the service of the emperor in his personal states, were not centralists; but they were authoritarians and advised against making terms with rebels. A broadly similar view was held by those Hungarian lords who had become converted to Catholicism, or whose fathers had been converted. Yet it would be mistaken to think that these nobles would have sacrificed their country's privileges: on the contrary, they fully hoped that, with a return to a normal regime, they would find themselves occupying high offices in the kingdom. They were all the more resentful towards Protestants and rebels for obstructing their ambitions. Some regarded the suppression of the rebellion as an opportunity to put an end to heresy and to grant legality to the Catholic faith alone. The conversion of Hungary could not be achieved without the help of the Jesuits, for only they were capable of organizing an effective pastoral campaign amid the general chaos prevailing in the parishes. But the laws of Hungary had prohibited the Jesuits from holding any property in the kingdom; the juridical status of the colleges which they had founded and the lands which they had acquired was therefore precarious. All these considerations led to unprecedented measures being taken against Protestant pastors, who were compromised as often as possible by the authorities in the trials of rebels; they were ordered to leave their parishes and those who refused were taken on a long death-march to the kingdom of Naples, where they were put on the Mediterranean slave-ships. It would not be fair to suggest that such cruelties were peculiar to the Germans, for in France, during these same years, Protestants were being sent to the galleys. However, the subjects of the kingdom of Hungary, whether Magyars or Slavs, henceforth nursed feelings 'of unbelievable hatred for the German government'³ and probably also for the Czechs, who were to be found in large numbers among the officers and ranks of the imperial army. Historians who have failed to take a broad view of their subject, or to study it in depth, have often spoken of national hatred in the Danubian countries as if this hatred was directed exclusively at the emperors and the House of Habsburg. If this had been true, would not the peoples of the Danube have found the means of uniting in a struggle for liberation? In fact, events prompted each nation to direct its hatred at its neighbour, which it believed to be the instrument of the government's policies. Sooner or later, moreover, the desire to be rid of his soldiers and officials rekindled hopes of a reconciliation with the emperor. This interweaving of political history was in fact the product of a logic inherent in collective attitudes and sensibilities. But, when the emperor thus became reconciled with one of his peoples, he did not thereby succeed in strengthening his sovereign authority over the territories as a whole, an assumption often made by Austrian historians, writing from the viewpoint of Vienna—indeed, this had been a quite common illusion in the capital. In reality, when a country came to terms with the emperor, at the same time standing by its ancient laws, it was in order to win him to its own cause, to make him a more truly national figure associated with its own particular destiny, regardless of and even in spite of the common interests of other countries.

It was in this spirit of reconciliation, and in accordance with Leopold's own deep-seated desires, that counsels of moderation first proffered around the year 1680 finally led to an official truce at Sopron in 1681. On this occasion, the initiative came from two Czechs, the Bohemian chancellor Nostitz, who wanted peace, and General Kaplíř, who held the Hungarian nobility in great affection and hated the Jesuits. At the Hungarian Diet, in the presence of the 'king', it was decided to restore the office of palatine. The royal cities were granted permission to open Protestant churches and the nobles to hold Protestant services in their manors.⁴ The palatine, elected unanimously, was Paul Eszterházy of Galanta, a resolute *labanc* and a devout Catholic, who possessed an immense fortune and whose family owned the seigniory of Kismarton, in the Burgenland, where the first Hungarian Baroque manor-house was built.

Peace had, however, been made only with a part of Royal Hungary, since the insurrection was still alive in the northern counties (present-day Slovakia). Instead of seeking a reconciliation with the emperor, Tököli maintained secret communication with the prince of Transylvania and with the Porte. The Turks recognized him as prince of Hungary, but not as king, which meant that the kingdom was now divided into four: the Hungary of the Habsburgs, the territory controlled by

Tököli, Transylvania and the Turkish pashaliks.⁵ Tököli's alliance with the Porte
reinforced the great Ottoman offensive of 1683. After all that has been said of this
memorable siege, it is easy to understand the sentiments cherished by the people
of Vienna and Austria as a whole towards the Hungarian rebels: *'gens dura et
perdica'*.

In 1684 general conditions in the Danubian region and in the rest of eastern
Europe began to undergo a transformation. The imperial armies undertook what
neither Ferdinand nor even Charles V had dared to attempt, when Soliman's
onslaught had been contained at the gates of Vienna: they pursued the retreating
Turkish army in order to drive it out of Hungary.

A solemn alliance in the form of a Holy League was concluded under the Pope's
patronage, between the emperor, the king of Poland, the republic of Venice and the
tsar of Russia. All those states which had suffered the Turkish yoke on their
territories made common cause in the great war of liberation. The emperor's
army now functioned as the army of a private power. The contingents supplied
by the different parts of the Holy Roman Empire (Brandenburg and Bavaria)
and by Europe (Sweden, Italy, Catalonia) doubtless gave it the appearance of an
international army; but its commander-in-chief was answerable only to the
emperor and operations depended on the decisions of the War Council, the
Hofkriegsrat, which was based at Graz so as to be nearer to the theatre of war.
Leopold entrusted the command of his army first to his brother-in-law, the duke
of Lorraine, who had distinguished himself at the siege of Vienna as commander
of the relief contingents, and then to his son-in-law, the elector Max Emmanuel of
Bavaria.

The presidency of the War Council was exercised for some time by the margrave
of Baden. These men were good military leaders who had been trained in the
school of Montecuccoli and showed great qualities as strategists and tacticians. They
put into practice the lesson learnt from their master: 'Hungary belongs to whoever
occupies the Danube line.' But fortresses had to be recaptured one by one and
several years were to pass before the Imperials once again became masters of the
Danube. If reconquest proved a laborious process, it demonstrated to a surprised
public the calibre of the new army, which was more efficiently recruited, provisioned
and equipped and was under effective leadership. The fortresses of Esztergom and
Ersekujvár, the cornerstones of Ottoman power in Hungary, fell one after the other
in spite of being fiercely defended. Finally, on 2 September 1686, after a siege of
several months, Buda was recaptured. An inscription still visible on the walls of
the ancient citadel, *Buda e servitude in libertatem restituta*, reminds the visitor
of today how important this event seemed to Europe at the time and how great a
prestige still attached to the city of the Arpáds, the Angevins and Matthias Corvinus.
Soon, Pécs, Szeged and Mohács, where the might of Hungary had crumbled in
1526, were liberated in their turn. In 1688 Max Emmanuel of Bavaria, known as
the 'blue king' from the colour of his family's arms, reconquered Belgrade.
It even seemed possible that the Christian populations of the Balkans could be
stirred to revolt and the peninsula liberated. But the war which the League of

Augsburg was waging against France forced the emperor to fight on two fronts and prevented him from concentrating all his efforts against the Turks.

⚜

The epic tale of reconquest had its darker aspects. The officers and soldiers of the imperial army behaved with outrageous cruelty towards the populations whom they liberated, extorting ransom and plunder and, strange though it may seem, giving them frequent occasion to wish for the return of the Turks. The *kuruc* rebellion had been punished by atrocious reprisals, although an amnesty granted in 1684 had brought numerous submissions. At Eperies, General Caraffa instituted a special court which acquired a bloody reputation. More than ever before, the Hungarians held the Germans in execration.

Yet the reconquest of the kingdom posed grave problems. Liberated Hungary had been depopulated and reduced to extreme poverty. The imperial government was confronted with a disorganized society and expanses of vacant land which in parts had reverted to marsh and scrub, and where it was necessary to establish titles of ownership, bring back men and livestock and restore agriculture. Such problems concerned both the Hungarian people throughout the kingdom and the emperor's government. At Vienna, in the various Councils—the Geheime Rat, the Hofrat, the Hofkammer—there were experienced administrators and politicians open to the ideas of the time and capable of taking the measure of the task which confronted them. The Hungarian aristocracy itself was not without men of ability. The nobles considered that the time was ripe for new agreements with the sovereign, whose obvious strength might prove to be an asset, and that the Hungarian nation itself, now freed from the invader, was in a position to define its privileges and secure their confirmation.

The Diet of 1687 was consequently one of the most important in the history of Hungary. It recognized the crown as the hereditary possession of the House of Habsburg: the Hungarians promised that henceforth they would designate as their king the eldest son of the preceding king and the same prince who succeeded to the patrimonial states. Only in the event of the dynasty becoming extinct would the crown revert to the disposal of the nation. An amnesty was granted to the rebels. Religious and fiscal privileges were preserved as fundamental liberties of the kingdom. The Hungarian nation agreed to abandon Article 31 of the law of 1322, thereby sacrificing its right to resist the king.

The hereditary right to the crown of Hungary and the permanent association of that country with the other Habsburg states represented a mighty victory for the dynasty, one stage reached in the construction of a compact Danubian empire. Yet what had been obtained was no more than a new contract. The young Archduke Joseph, aged nine years, received the crown of St. Stephen from the old primate Széchenyi and took the traditional oath to respect the laws of the kingdom and to defend its territory. In accordance with custom, the Diet had presented Leopold with the *Gravamina*, the grievances of the comitats or counties. These grievances covered a diversity of problems—religion, the economy, justice, personal affairs—but put forward no coherent programme. They were received with due consideration, but the programme of reforms drawn up by the 'king' was to find its inspiration elsewhere.

Leopold sought the advice of a commission, formed under the presidency of the Obersthofmeister Ferdinand von Dietrichstein and composed of his habitual Austrian and Czech councillors (among them Count Kinský, chancellor of Bohemia) and a few Hungarian high officials. To one of these, Cardinal Kollonics, bishop of Györ, who in 1689 became archbishop of Kalocsa, he entrusted the task of forming a sub-commission and presenting a plan of reform. The cardinal, of a Croatian noble family, was a man of character and deep culture. His attachment to his country cannot be questioned, in spite of the unjust judgements of contemporaries and historians. He abhorred Caraffa and the brutal methods of the soldiery. But he had been president of the Hungarian Chamber for eight years and cherished no illusions about the economic state of his country, even in those regions which had escaped Turkish occupation; he appreciated the ineffectiveness and dangers of the old system and was fully aware that the liberties of the nobility had been preserved for the sake of selfish privilege and deep-rooted habit. He was a *labanc*, a convinced Catholic and an advocate of a strong royal power as the necessary condition of Hungary's prosperity. Within a few months the painstaking and zealous sub-commission over which he presided completed a plan of reform, which was accepted by the original commission and then by the emperor.

This plan (*Einrichtungswerk*) in many respects reflected the influence of the German jurists (Grotius and Puffendorf) and the new theoreticians of economic science.[6] It was practical in its inspiration and aimed at reforming institutions, reorganizing the conditions of agrarian labour and redistributing taxes more effectively. The Hungarian Chancellery was to become a central ministry based at the royal court. The army, which had caused so much misery, was no longer to live off the local population, but would take up its quarters after an agreement had been reached between the military commissaries and the commissaries appointed by the comitats. Proposals were made to draw up new religious boundaries and re-arrange parishes in proportion to the numbers of inhabitants, to restore the old practice of diocesan synods and episcopal visitations, in accordance with the instructions of the Council of Trent, but also to maintain a royal commissary in surveillance over religious assemblies. The religious privileges of the nobles were not, however, contested. The great problem was the repopulation of the country; among Leopold's circle of advisers there had been several persons of absolutist convictions who held the view that the liberated territory belonged to the king by right of conquest and that he could dispose freely of that territory, without concerning himself with any claims that might be put forward by former landowners.

Such persons could be given the opportunity to vindicate their claims, but the important thing was to attract foreign colonists to Hungary and to guarantee their complete personal freedom *vis-à-vis* the great lords. These settlers would be exempted from obligatory labour and taxes for a certain number of years.[7] The peasants on the estates would have to perform obligatory labour for no more than three days per week. Land-taxes were to be imposed on all domains, with the exception of ecclesiastical properties and those of the minor nobility, and the redistribution of taxes was to be carried out by representatives of the counties and the towns. The Court Chamber would ensure that regalian rights and state monopolies were safeguarded. When the proposals concerning justice, education and hospitals are also considered, it will be seen that this was indeed a constructive programme which, if implemented, could have given new life to Hungary. But circumstances were not favourable. The commission overstepped its powers by publishing the decrees itself; moreover, local authorities remained free to enforce or oppose them.

The Hungarian aristocracy immediately regarded as suspect any good intentions which issued from Vienna. Furthermore, an unfortunate sentence in the text of the decrees spoke of the arrival of German colonists 'to Germanize the Hungarian nation, to temper with German blood the blood of Hungary, too inclined to revolution and disorder, and to arouse fidelity and love for the natural king'. Letters patent issued on 11 August 1690 authorized persons claiming ownership of estates on the reconquered territory to make good their claims before 1 February 1691; those whose rights were recognized would be able to recover their hereditary lands on payment of a tax. The time allotted was too short and the tax too high. The result was rather similar to what had happened in Bohemia after the confiscation of properties: native-born families who already owned large estates, and whose records were better preserved, were able to assemble vast areas of land on the Hungarian plain; the situation was less favourable for the impecunious minor nobility, and in particular for those who had taken refuge in the counties of the Slovakian mountains. Many foreign military families to whom the emperor was in debt were given land or allowed to purchase it at a low price; some settled permanently in Hungary, while others resold their estates to the Hungarian upper aristocracy, which thus grew even more rich and powerful. Yet it is worth recalling the comment on the Hungarian aristocracy made by the historian Szekfü: 'This fact was of capital importance for the subsequent history of the country, for if, over large territories, foreign landowners had dominated foreign serfs, the Hungarians would eventually have vanished altogether in these regions and the political consequences would have been beyond imagination. On this occasion the nobility, by its very existence and by asserting its material rights, rendered a great service to the nation.'[8]

In effect, the most successful of the projects of the Kollonics commission was that which resulted in the entry of vast numbers of foreign settlers, whose arrival produced a widely mixed population. The settlers came from the German parts of Bohemia (northern Moravia and Silesia) and from the Empire (Swabia); they established themselves, with their own religion, customs and language, not far from Magyar or Slav villages, thus giving the area of the Hungarian plain a curiously variegated ethnic character. The newcomers comprised not only Germans. The lure of a new and reputedly rich land attracted Slovak peasants who had been vegetating in the mountain regions. A rise in the population of the Balkan peninsula, observable at the turn of the eighteenth century, caused a migration of

Rumanian peasants from the overpopulated regions of their own country to the less densely inhabited lands of Transylvania. Finally, Serbs who had joyfully welcomed their liberation by the imperial armies, but feared Turkish reprisals when the armies withdrew, settled in southern Hungary: thirty-nine thousand families were taken there by the patriarch Cernojević. The emperor granted them religious freedom and exempted them from the payment of tithes to the Catholic Church. At the time of these events it was impossible to foresee their consequences. The kingdom of Hungary, both in the feudal fragmentation of the comitats and under a more strictly centralized regime, rested on territorial and juridical principles which took no account of the ethnic origin or language of its inhabitants. Privileges were not simply advantages granted to some to the detriment of others, but guarantees awarded to each group within the framework of the political unity of the kingdom. Differences between social groups bore no relationship to national differences. It has already been explained how, among the privileged German nations of Transylvania, political rights were enjoyed only by the upper classes. The Slovak-speaking comitats had a native nobility which sometimes used Czech and sometimes Magyar. These nobles were concerned primarily with the concept of lordship and the institutions of the comitat which rooted that concept in the kingdom of Hungary. The diversity of groups, the confused babel of languages which was to make such a striking impression on the minds of the nineteenth and twentieth centuries, had been accentuated during this period by the process of reconquest and repopulation. The relative failure of the programme put forward by the Kollonics commission, the strengthening of seigniorial authority and the growth of the great domain under the protection of constitutional guarantees, the repeated blunders of officials and the inadequacy of military organization resulting from the wars in the West, combined to foster anarchy and to stimulate the Hungarians' traditional propensity for discontent and revolt—hence the great insurrection of Rákóczi several years later.

Nevertheless, the royal power, even if it had not been able immediately to turn all the benefits of reconquest to its own account, nor to regenerate Hungary by linking that country more closely with it, had been indirectly consolidated within the limits of the Hungarian Constitution by the recognition of its hereditary right to the crown. Soon, the military reconquest of Transylvania, which followed the battle of Salankenen (1691), and the death of Prince Apafi made a solution of the Transylvanian question possible. At a time when Caraffa, unconvinced of the evil of his brutalities, was recommending the introduction of authoritative rule even in Transylvania, the diploma issued by Leopold on 4 December 1691 recognized the autonomy of this country, at the same time declaring it to be an integral part of the kingdom of Hungary: Transylvania would thus have its own Diet and chancellery and would enjoy religious liberty.[9] By the end of the seventeenth century the House of Habsburg had re-established its sovereignty over immense territories. This complex was now more compact and its member-countries more closely associated, but it was by no means unified; however, in compensation for the guarantees which Hungary and Transylvania had secured, the Germano-Czech group of countries, from Trieste to the Giant Mountains, appeared to be assuming a greater cohesion.

꽃

Danubian society still derived its principal resources from agriculture; in the towns, even the towns of the great lords, the corporations jealously guarded their monopoly of craft production. Although the standard of living was rising, as can be observed from the increase in food consumption and in the activity of various sectors, especially that of building, and although the commerce in cereals and live-stock was beginning to extend beyond the boundaries of the Danubian states, the economy as a whole remained essentially patriarchal, a juxtaposition of individual economies. But there were men acquainted with what was happening in the West, who understood the Dutch system with its international and even world-wide connections and who had observed the efforts of contemporary France to establish manufacturing industries, so that the French people would no longer be dependent on foreign imports, but capable of offering their own products to the outside world. It is hardly surprising that such men should have aspired towards something other than stagnation and routine. It was their belief that a government desirous of attaining power in Europe should no longer be content with the old methods of production and should not depend, for the revenues essential to the luxurious life of the court, the maintenance of armies and the payment of officials, solely on taxes levied from the peasant, who was often reduced thereby to poverty, or on tolls which were so numerous that they obstructed the circulation of goods and caused prices to rise.[10]

The government should devote its energies to making the state rich, by making better use of the opportunities offered by agricultural and mineral resources and by the size and labour potential of the population. Such was the argument of the work published at Frankfurt in 1668 by Hans Joachim Becher, under the title: *Politischer Discurs von den eigentlischen Ursachen des Auf und Abnehnens der Städtl, Länden und Republicken; in specie, wie ein Land volkreich und nahrhaft zu machen und in rechte sociatatem einlem zu brengen* ('A political discourse on the particular causes of the decline or the rise of towns, countries and republics; how to make a populous country lucrative and transform it into a just civil society'). A just civil society, the author explained, could be defined as one in which there existed a harmony between population and production. Becher, who has been described as the inspired initiator of mercantilism in Austria, was a German of the Empire, a native of Speyer, who thought first and foremost in terms of the Empire, rather than the patrimonial states of the emperor. But he directed his attention to the imperial court as the motive power of a general economic system which involved the entire German nation and which was capable of freeing it from French domination. His chief concern was to put an end to a paradoxical situation which he decried with both passion and humour: 'We Germans find that French razors are better than others for cutting our beards; French scissors and pincers are better than our own for cutting nails and hair; our watches go better if they were made by Germans in

Paris than if the same watchmakers had made them in Augsburg. This must be because the air is better over there.'[11] In the central government of Vienna he hoped to find the instruments of an economic policy. Many aspects of economic affairs were the responsibility of the Hofkammer, since this body controlled the revenues which the emperor was entitled to use for his 'general' expenditure, outside his personal states. During these years the Privy Conference (*Geheime Konferenz*), entrusted with matters of major importance, had been formed as a body quite distinct from the Privy Council, which had grown too large. Similarly, side by side with the Hofkammer, another council was to be created with exclusive responsibility for commerce. The Council of Commerce was founded under the direction of the president of the Hofkammer, Georg Ludwig von Zinzendorf (1616–80); whatever its failings, this council was the first institution to be entrusted with the common economic interests of the patrimonial states. Becher was one of its members. His ideas were influenced by the Dutch and the models from which he drew his inspiration consequently related to a different kind of society. Even in Vienna there were merchants interested in international trade, but they were Italians and Jews. The leading members of the Council of Commerce belonged to the upper nobility and the world of officialdom; they brought their own financial ambitions and bureaucratic habits into the new organization, without any clear appreciation of the broader interests which should have been its primary concern. Inquiries should have been conducted so that, in full knowledge of the facts, regulations could have been introduced for the supervision and development of industry and a more effective organization of commerce. The working sessions of the council were supposed to take place every week, but in fact they became increasingly irregular. Furthermore, the members of the council received no fixed salary. Becher was paid one thousand gulden by the Hungarian Chamber. When the secretary, Prückner, asked for an increase from the Hofkammer, Leopold gave the request his 'placet', but added this note in the margin: 'I do not see the council meeting often *in corpore* as it should and so it seems to me that its work cannot be very important.' The emperor was no economist and none of his advisers ever explained these problems to him. Becher himself, who possessed an inventive and truly powerful intellect, indulged too wide a variety of unconnected interests. He had studied medicine and the sciences and was absorbed by alchemy, the search for gold-bearing sands and dreams of mechanical constructions for flying in space and travelling under water. During the war in Holland he had attempted to halt the importation of French goods into the Empire, by seeking the enforcement of the imperial edicts of 20 June 1674 and 7 May 1676, which had prohibited French imports. However, this would only have been practicable if the goods produced by France, the hereditary states or even Italy and Switzerland, could have been made in German factories. The time was approaching when Brandenburg would perceive the advantages of thus extending its production, but only for its own gain. In the meantime, the German towns concentrated on their traditional trading activities and the needs of their immediate clientele. The merchants considered that it would not be possible to supply home-manufactured products quickly enough, in sufficient quantities and at low enough prices to replace imported French goods.

The men and women of the court had no intention of sacrificing comfort to patriotism; in Vienna the ladies of the aristocracy were prepared to pay any price for shoes made in France. In vain had Becher argued, in the *Politischer Discurs*, that nothing could be more harmful to powers, states and peoples, nor bring about their ruin more effectively, than the vast and unnecessary expenditure of courts: for the upper classes and their suppliers, such expenditure remained indispensable and they would not sacrifice it in the general interest. Becher's judgement showed shrewdness on many points, but he was too far in advance of his time. He advised that workshops with royal privileges be opened; several workshops of this kind were soon established, but confusion arose immediately. For example, Zinzendorf was granted the royal privilege for a silk factory on his personal domains at Walpersdorf. Instead of buying Italian silk goods, he would import only the raw material from Italy and the fabrics would then be made at Walpersdorf by Italian workmen. Zinzendorf thought only of the profits which his factory produced; in his eyes, the Council of Commerce existed solely for the purpose of protecting his establishment. Other attempts to set up workshops were made. In 1672 Christian Sind, a merchant of Linz, was awarded the royal privilege for the manufacture of woollen fabrics, but the conditions attaching to the privilege hindered the progress of the enterprise from the outset: the factory was to use only wool from 'Austria above and below the Enns' and was not to undermine the interests of the merchants, weavers and dyers of the region. On the other hand, Sind received a guarantee that no factory would be allowed to compete with his in Upper Austria.

In Trieste and Fiume the Habsburg states possessed two windows on to the Adriatic. Becher proposed the development of trade with the East, but sufficient capital was not available and it would have also been necessary to reconcile the interests of the different countries, the western provinces with the Diets of Croatia and Hungary. The members of these Diets were little inclined to consider the general problems of the Danubian region and for this they could hardly be blamed. They had to sell agricultural produce and livestock and were already encountering great difficulties in doing so. The Diet of Hungary protested against the erection of customs posts beyond their frontiers, in particular the tolls along the Danube. The Austrians made it quite clear that Hungarian products were reserved for their own use and that Hungary would not be permitted to trade freely with the rest of Europe. Another constant factor in the subsequent history of the Danubian countries was already beginning to emerge.

Meanwhile, in 1667 Lilio de Luca, a merchant of St. Guy in Carinthia, founded a company for trade with the East which would have had nine ships on the Danube, exporting German merchandise such as metal objects from Nuremberg and other parts of the Empire, iron from Styria and fabrics from Silesia, and bringing back to the Habsburg countries cotton, raw silk, camel-hair and ostrich-feathers. All this was in keeping with the ideas of Becher, who had conceived a circulation of goods along a network formed by the rivers Danube, Rhine and Main. But trading with Turkey alarmed the Hofkriegsrat, which considered that to supply the Ottoman Empire with iron and steel was to risk providing an enemy with materials that could be used for war.

It would seem that, in the Danubian lands ruled by the emperor, the government faced an impossible task in attempting to control the parallel or contradictory interests of the different states, to elaborate and put into effect a comprehensive economic policy: all its efforts were wasted in short-lived enterprises. A contemporary historian, Erna Patzelt, has observed that economic policy depended not so much on the sovereign as on the Estates—one might add, even on the individual members of the Estates. Another exponent of mercantilism was Wilhelm von Schröder, also a German of the Empire, who came from Thuringia as an adviser to the court of Vienna and was there employed in the financial department. The work which he published at Leipzig in 1686, *Fürstlich Satz und Rentkammer*, affirmed that the wealth of a prince rested on the wealth of his people and that the fiscal structure should develop in harmony with the economy. In fact, the fiscal structure remained the weak point of the whole system. In addition to what he received from the Diets by way of royal revenues or war contributions both ordinary and extraordinary, the emperor should have obtained substantial revenues from certain sectors reserved for his personal use—his rural domains, comprising both hereditary and confiscated lands, and also a number of regalian rights: the tolls on the Danube, the output of the iron mines, the salt of the Salzkammergut, the mercury of Idria in Carniola and the copper of Besztercebánya (Neusohl) in Hungary. But many landed properties had been sacrificed by way of gifts to the religious orders or to individuals, in recompense for services rendered to the emperor. This procedure was all the more deplorable because the State had then been compelled to borrow large sums from the persons whom it had enriched at its own expense. In an excessive application of the fiscal principle, it was considered that all goods in circulation should bring some yield to the treasury, the amount varying according to the place through which they passed. This was a geographical and rather limited conception of the function of the toll. In contrast, Becher had recommended a general system of excises, that is to say, taxes graded according to the quality of the goods: it was supposed that the purchaser would consent to pay these taxes, preferring a small increase in the cost of the desired article to the inconvenience of doing without it. Becher estimated that the excises would yield double the amount provided by State taxes and that the different countries would feel the benefit. Excises were in fact introduced, but in a largely experimental manner. The majority of State tolls and monopolies were farmed out, in accordance with the practice prevailing in the West. The same persons who administered these taxes controlled the manufacturing industries and the large companies. They were therefore well placed for purposes of speculation and rapidly acquired large fortunes. Not all were dishonest like Zinzendorf, whom the emperor surprisingly retained as president of the Hofkammer. Some even recognized and defended the true interests of the State. Mittermayer brought the mercury mines under the control of the treasury. These mines were offered as security for the loans negotiated with Holland during the wars of the League of Augsburg and the War of the Spanish Succession; without the money provided by the Dutch, the emperor would not have been able to finance his armies.

Owing to the fragility of the economic structure and the constant lack of money, the Hofkammer was forced to have frequent recourse to private citizens. In times of urgent need the great Jewish merchants served as bankers; those who had evaded the edict of expulsion of 1669, imposed on the emperor by the jealousy of the corporations, and who had remained in Vienna, lent money to the treasury at high rates of interest (as much as 20 per cent). The most prominent and active of these men was Hans Samuel Oppenheimer, *Kaiserlicher Kriegsoberfaktor und Jud* ('Imperial Overseer for War and Jew'), whose resounding downfall nearly dragged the whole State into bankruptcy.

Though Becher had been more German than Austrian and had wished to use the emperor as the instrument of an economic reorganization of Germany, his relative and pupil, Hans Wilhelm von Hörnigk, secret adviser to the bishop of Passau, presented a more strictly Danubian programme. A year after the siege of Vienna, as if he perceived one of the major consequences of that event—the birth of a great Austria—Hörnigk published a work which was destined to be re-issued several times during the eighteenth century. On the economic plane, if one takes into account the experiments made by the states of western Europe, this treatise reveals none of Becher's originality of thought. But the title of his book is in itself a most illuminating discovery: 'Austria above all others, if only she so desires' (*Österreich über alles, wann es nur will*). Writing at this period, Hörnigk found it necessary to explain the term which he was the first to sanction. 'By Austria, I mean all the hereditary countries and kingdoms of the archducal house of German Austria, whether or not they form part of the Roman Empire. In isolation, each of these countries is helpless. Together, they constitute a natural body. What one lacks can be compensated by what the other possesses—a little world in itself which can be self-sufficient not only for the necessities, but also for the comforts of life.'

From this principle other mercantilist ideas were derived: as little as possible should be bought from abroad and production should be stimulated in order to attract foreign customers and check the outflow of gold and currencies. Such a vision was still premature, especially since the restoration of order in the re-conquered Hungarian territory presented the problems described earlier. But economic solidarity between the western group of Danubian states and the kingdom of St. Stephen was to prove necessary, as a complement to their political association. Ideas were changing. In 1699, the Bohemian Chamber demanded the formation of a reconstituted Council of Commerce with responsibility for all the territories of the emperor; six years later, in 1705, a commission of the Bohemian Diet repeated this demand, insisting that the proposed council, which was to be composed of financial advisers and merchants, should devote its energies to uniting all the hereditary states and provinces in a single body.

There was no question of denying each country's rightful existence as a separate state, nor of abandoning individual privileges and liberties. Yet this call for a

Gesamtösterreich revealed the dawning consciousness of a common economic interest, a solidarity of peoples for the sake of their material good.

※

Circumstances were all the more favourable for the consolidation of a Danubian empire through economic solidarity, because populations were now increasing throughout Europe. But the spirit of the times and the state of general knowledge prevented governments from recognizing and utilizing such factors as a basis for policy. The power of a state was always measured by the extent of its territory, the conquering prowess of its armies, its skill in causing divisions in a rival or hostile state and the glory that success appeared to bring. It was inevitable that the prestige which the emperor derived from his victories in the East should give offence to Louis XIV and his ministers. In 1684 the recognition of the 'reunions' for a period of twenty years, by the treaties of Ratisbon, had confirmed French political supremacy in Western Europe. With the annexation of Strassburg and with France henceforth closed to the Germans—*Clausa Germanis Gallia*—French expectations seemed to have been fulfilled. But Versailles was not mistaken in suspecting that, in the Empire, the settlement was not regarded as definitive and that there were those in Vienna who would call it in question as soon as the imperial armies had finished their task in the East. The Eastern Question—the undermining of Ottoman power under the pressure of the Austrians, the Poles and, in particular, the Russians who were advancing on Azov—was in itself sufficiently grave to occupy all the energies of the interested powers and to prevent them from intervening in other regions. In one respect Russia enjoyed a position of advantage, since she was able to concentrate on the struggle against the Tartars in the Crimea and thus maintain her campaign against the Ottoman Empire; she was not yet being pressed by Sweden. The emperor, on the other hand, remained a German prince constantly involved in the affairs of the Empire. His dynastic prestige was a consideration of fundamental importance. His policy towards the Empire depended on the crown being retained by his family. He had his elder son Joseph elected king of Hungary in 1687 and three years later, at Augsburg, the king of Hungary was elected king of the Romans. The over-riding interests of his house thus drew the emperor's attention back to Germany—intimately involved with Habsburg destiny—and compelled him to take a part in the Empire's system of internal alliances so that treaties might be observed and opposition to the king of France maintained. French diplomacy and imperial diplomacy engaged in a struggle for influence at the German courts, expending for this purpose a great deal of money, time, talent and guile. As far as the Empire and Germany were concerned, the king of France and the emperor were seen to be irreconcilable adversaries. Versailles and Vienna stood face to face.[12] But the general situation in Europe was deteriorating for other reasons. In the time of the Stuarts, the British government had seemed to move in the orbit of the king of France. For reasons that were religious and commercial as much as political, the situation began to change from the time of the English Revolution of 1688. The alliance between Great Britain and the United Provinces, achieved by the ingenuity of William III, became a determining factor in international relations. To hold France in check on the continent, the maritime powers had need of the emperor's armies. In the war of the League of Augsburg, which lasted from 1689 until 1697, France and the House of Austria confronted one another. Historians have not studied the repercussions that this war may have had on public opinion within the hereditary states and on the growing consciousness of the Danubian peoples. The evolution of religious life and the multiplication of its spectacular aspects—processions, appeals for divine protection and the intercession of the Virgin Mary against the dangers facing the emperor and his Empire in the struggle—suggest a strengthening of 'Austrian' solidarity. Admittedly, differences were becoming more accentuated between the Protestant Germany of the north (Saxony, Brandenburg and Hanover) and the largely Catholic Germany of the south (Swabia and Bavaria). But is it not likely that the people of Austria and even of Bohemia now felt themselves drawn more closely to Catholic southern Germany? With the slow but undeniable progress of commerce and of artistic and intellectual exchanges, a period of peace would have allowed a greater flexibility in the relations between peoples and enabled a pattern of reciprocal influences to be established throughout Europe. A long period of war, on the other hand, encouraged the growth of myths, the legend of the despotic king of France who was the enemy of Christendom, with the result that peoples everywhere gathered more closely round their natural prince, the emperor.

In the western states of the House of Austria the wars of the League of Augsburg and, later, the War of the Spanish Succession probably fostered rather than weakened a common feeling of loyalty. Furthermore, the imperial armies included numerous German contingents and were commanded and staffed by German generals. It is difficult not to believe that military society, through the very conditions of its existence, was being impregnated with Germanism and that it wielded a much more effective and formidable influence than governmental edicts which were relatively easy to evade or ignore.

After the capture of Belgrade, Leopold would willingly have sought peace with the sultan, but he was prevented from concluding a treaty by the tenacity of his allies and their hopes of new victories. To wage war on two fronts was beyond the emperor's financial resources, even if it was not beyond the human resources of his states. The maritime powers lent him money, thereby subordinating him even more firmly to their own enterprises. One of the principal stakes in the struggle, on the imperial side, was the restoration of the treaties of Westphalia; but the House of Austria also hoped to regain Alsace and European opinion wished the duke of Lorraine to be re-established in his duchy. Not only were there two fronts, but the western front lay scattered far and wide: the armies were fighting in Flanders, on the Rhine, in Italy and even in Catalonia, into which the French had advanced. The king of France, supported by the excellent army that the Louvois administration had organized, succeeded in containing the forces of the coalition. Peace, which was mooted at an early stage in the war, was not signed until 1697, at Rijswijk. Judged as a whole, this was one of the most reasonable and positive peace-treaties to have been concluded in Europe. Although the king of France renounced the 'reunions', he retained Strassburg and his kingdom was henceforth protected by a solid frontier. He no longer had a motive for conquest.

In the imperial army there had emerged a young officer of outstanding personality, Prince Eugene of Savoy, who was to exert great influence on the destiny of the imperial states and assume the reputation of a national hero: *der edle Ritter*, 'the noble knight'.[13] His paternal grandfather was Thomas, prince of Carignano-Savoy, and his paternal grandmother a Frenchwoman, the last of the Bourbons of Soissons; he was the son of Olympia Mancini, a niece of Mazarin. Born in Paris and brought up in France, Eugene of Savoy had left the court of Louis XIV in somewhat confused circumstances, possibly impelled by a chivalrous desire to take part in the battle of Vienna. At the time he was twenty years of age and played only a minor part in the battle. He then served his military apprenticeship under his kinsman, the margrave of Baden, in the reconquest of Hungary. During the war of the League of Augsburg he was awarded the rank of field-marshal and successfully commanded operations in Savoy, where his cousin, Duke Victor Amadeus II, participated in the coalition against Louis XIV. There can be no doubt that Prince Eugene was driven by the desire to take personal vengeance on the king of France and to humiliate the country which had refused to accord him his rightful position. His conception of personal honour and his princely pride inevitably call to mind the figure of Wallenstein. But half a century separated the two men and the distance in time throws light on their differences of ideal and culture.

Wallenstein had never revealed the qualities of a statesman; his vision could not extend beyond the kingdom of Bohemia and the Empire, nor his political activity transcend the religious conflict between Protestants and Catholics or the political rivalry between emperor and Estates.

Sometimes, Prince Eugene gave his signature the curious form 'Eugenio von Savoie', evoking the three countries with which he was associated: the country of his family origin and his military glory, the country of adoption in which he mostly served, and the country where he was born and educated. Once he had entered the service of the emperor, he never left it, identifying his own glory with that of the House of Austria in Europe. Indeed, it was he who was chiefly responsible for reviving Habsburg glory; one day, Louis XIV declared to Villars: 'For a long time now I have regarded Prince Eugene only as a subject of the emperor; in this capacity, he has done his duty.' Having no need to feel affection for the person of the sovereign in order to serve him unfailingly, sparing neither generals, civil ministers nor allies in the reports which he sent to his master, but preserving an irreproachable courtesy even in his most harshly critical moments, he was the perfect incarnation of the European *grand seigneur* of the eighteenth century. In appearance he was small, ugly and yet majestic. From the humanist tradition his interests passed to the sciences. He was concerned not to explore the unknowable, but to study new methods illuminated by mathematical and experimental reasoning. Few men of his time possessed such a diversity of equally fertile talents: on the battlefield he was not only the strategist, but also the combatant who risked his own skin; as a politician, he showed an intelligent appreciation of all the forces at work in Europe at this period; as a patron and lover of the arts, he was endowed with fine taste. Although his only protégé among French writers was J. B. Rousseau, he was the friend of Leibnitz and enchanted Montesquieu by the quality of his conversation and his detailed knowledge of the problems of the day. He was a loss to the France of Louis XIV, although in France he might have found more competitors and certainly would have had a less exalted career; but at the court of the ageing Leopold he seemed to be the one man capable of raising a confused amalgam of states and institutions into the great power of modern Austria.

Since the treaties of Rijswijk had brought a halt to the war in the west, all efforts could be concentrated once more on Hungary and the advance along the rivers. To the south of Szeged, Prince Eugene crushed the Ottoman army at the battle of Zenta and peace was signed at Carlovtsi in 1699. The terms of the treaty brought advantage to the entire coalition: the Poles recovered Podolia and the Venetians regained Morea, but Russia remained at war because she had failed to obtain the territories for which she had hoped. The emperor recovered Transylvania and the Hungarian plain as far as the Maros; the Banat of Temesvar remained in the hands of the sultan.

With the liberation of nearly the entire kingdom of Hungary and the consequent territorial aggrandizement of the House of Austria, the Danubian empire occupied an area of hitherto unparalleled extent. Among the stipulations of the treaty, the articles relating to the Danube were significant not only in their immediate effect, but, to an even greater degree, in their possible consequences for the future. The commercial traffic permitted by the state of the river at this period could not have contributed much to the general economy of the Empire and Europe. But, in defining the conditions of this traffic, the negotiators established two principles: freedom of navigation along the Danube and the importance of this waterway for the countries of the Habsburgs and the Empire.

The merchant ships of the countries subject to His Imperial Majesty (that is to say, both the hereditary states and the countries of the Empire—in fact, all ships using the navigable course of the Danube from Ulm) could pass from the Maros into the Tisza and from the Tisza into the Danube without any obstruction, on both the downward and the upward route; the same freedom was accorded by reciprocal agreement to the Ottomans and was extended to fishing-boats and ferry-boats. It was laid down that neither the erection of water-mills nor the development of irrigation should interfere with the movements of the emperor's merchant ships. Two problems which were to assume such an important place in the general policy and life of the monarchy now began to emerge: the economic penetration of the East via the Danube and the international use of the river.[14]

It seemed that peace had been restored in Europe. But one question remained unsolved: the Spanish succession. On this point, the interests of dynasties no longer coincided exactly with the interests of their peoples; the traditional ideas of power and glory were to prevail over the more recent notions of internal reform and prosperity. It was essential that there should still be a king of Spain and the best solution for all would have been the perpetuation in Madrid of the senior branch of the Habsburgs, which had become increasingly remote from the junior branch of Vienna. But Charles II of Spain died without an heir and his two nearest relatives, the Emperor Leopold and King Louis XIV, who in 1668 had agreed on an equitable division of the succession, now put forward opposing claims. For a long time Leopold had cherished hopes that his second son, the Archduke Charles, born in 1685, would be adopted by Charles II, the archduke's godfather. After the peace of Rijswijk, Louis XIV had the great wisdom to mitigate his claims; on condition that certain provinces passed to his kingdom, he agreed to leave to a prince of Bavaria, and then to the Archduke Charles, a Spain whose European territories had barely been diminished and which was still mistress of her colonial empire in America. However, the two treaties of partition (1698-9) had been accepted only by the maritime powers, anxious not to leave to the mercy of France their vital interests in trade with the Spanish empire of America. Leopold refused to subscribe to the treaties, hoping to the end that the king of Spain would bequeath his kingdom to the Archduke Charles. When the king died in 1700, he had just named as his heir a grandson of Louis XIV, the duke of Anjou.

Louis XIV may have believed that, by accepting the testament, he was not jeopardizing the peace of Europe, since he was acting in accordance with the wish of the Spanish nation, which was wedded to the concept of an indivisible monarchy, and since he was acquiring no territory himself. Nonetheless, it appeared as if the whole of Spain had passed under his protectorate and the maritime powers were scandalized by the flouting of the treaties of partition; with the emperor and his Empire they formed the Grand Alliance of September 1701 which was to lead to a new struggle in Europe, the War of the Spanish Succession, which lasted for thirteen years.

France was brought to the brink of ruin, but the House of Austria also experienced its tragic moments, for in Hungary it was confronted with the most violent of the *kuruc* rebellions, instigated by Francis II Rákóczi. This young lord, who was the son, stepson and grandson of former rebels, seized advantage of the discontent of the nobility and of popular uprisings directed partly against the seigniorial system, but primarily against the impositions of the military and the fatigue-duties exacted by the imperial army. His mother was Helen Zrinyi, whose second husband was Imre Tököli and who, until 1688, had continued her resistance from a fortress at Munkács, in the Carpathians. Meanwhile, Francis Rákóczi had been brought up in Austria, where he was converted to Catholicism and acquired a thorough familiarity with Western ways of life and thought. He was therefore hopeful that Louis XIV would come to his assistance. By skilful propaganda he attempted to rouse French opinion to sympathy for the Hungarian cause. He wanted subsidies and even military aid: troops were either to be sent across Poland, another ally, or to be landed on the Adriatic coast. But these were fanciful notions. At certain stages of the conflict it seemed possible that Rákóczi might triumph. In 1704, at the Diet of Alba Julia, he was elected prince of Transylvania. In contravention of the diploma issued by Leopold in 1691, the independence of the principality was restored and its new ruler joined the ranks of the European sovereigns, at least in the eyes of those princes who recognized him: the king of Sweden, the tsar and the king of Spain, Philip V, who awarded him the Golden Fleece (1708). The conditions peculiar to Hungarian society explain his success: he enjoyed direct possession of domains which, though scattered throughout the kingdom, were all of considerable extent, totalling roughly one million acres; he gathered round him both the nobles, fired by the old ideal of national independence, and peasants, to whom he promised personal freedom and the use of the land if they joined his army. In his residence at Sárospatak he held an assembly of representatives of the comitats and proclaimed a confederation. By 1705—the year in which Leopold died—the greater part of the territories reconquered since 1683, the comitats of Upper Hungary (present-day Slovakia), where the Turks had never penetrated and which had remained an integral part of Royal Hungary, and Transylvania itself were under the authority of Rákóczi. The new emperor, Joseph I, was left with a narrow strip along the Austrian frontier and a few towns. Not many Hungarian nobles remained on his side; among them was General Pálffy, one of the commanders of the imperial army, who, it was hoped, by his example and exhortation, might win back some of his compatriots. In 1707, at Onod, the confederates proclaimed the deposition of the House of Habsburg. Without difference of order, social class or religion, Hungary appeared to have rallied to the *kuruc* leader.[15]

In the meantime, Prince Eugene had secured the presidency of the Hofkriegsrat and membership of the Privy Conference, which made him a truly powerful minister. He urged the suppression of the Hungarian revolt by force and advised against any negotiation with the rebels. But he was himself involved in another direction: the struggle against France. Assisted in London by a very trustworthy Czech friend, Count Wratislaw, chancellor of Bohemia, he obtained from the Allies the financial and military support which he needed. Sharing the command of the army with the Duke of Marlborough, he gained the victory of Blenheim against the French and their Bavarian allies, in 1704. He then succeeded in liberating Turin, which the French were besieging (1707), and advanced into Provence. Moving from one field of battle to another, he set about the conquest of Flanders, capturing Audenarde and then Lille: the road to Paris seemed open.

A British ship had transported the Archduke Charles to Spain. The anti-king of Spain had entered Madrid on two occasions, but without being able to establish himself there: for reasons of national pride and in a shrewd appreciation of their economic interests—trade with France—the Castilians preferred Philip V. But Catalonia had adopted 'Charles III'. From Barcelona, his capital, Charles ruled as king of the Catalans for several years.[16] In the spring of 1709 the situation of France appeared so grave that Louis XIV resigned himself to seeking peace. At the Congress of The Hague, Prince Eugene presented conditions that would have nullified all the successes attained by France since 1648; the severity of his demands was so insulting and unjust that the French negotiators preferred to depart and Louis XIV then resumed the struggle. This was one of Prince Eugene's greatest political blunders, for he had lost the opportunity of restoring Strasbourg to the Empire and rendering the kingdom of France vulnerable once more on its eastern frontier.[17]

He showed greater wisdom and reason in Hungarian affairs: despite his former views, he no longer opposed Pálffy's negotiations with the insurgents. A heavy defeat at Trenčin in 1708 had not disheartened the *kuruc*, but they needed external help in order to hold their ground, and even more so if they were to abandon their defensive position and launch an offensive on Austrian territory. To await assistance became increasingly futile. France was incapable of supplying troops herself and was no longer managing to maintain a battle-front to harass the Imperials from the rear: Sweden, after overwhelming Poland, had lost the advantage by engaging its army in the pointless venture against Peter the Great. In Rákóczi's absence one of his lieutenants, Károlyi, negotiated peace terms with the emperor's generals at Szattmár (1711); the treaty was then ratified by the Hungarian Diet. Far from resulting in the total submission of the rebels, the war had led to a new pact of reconciliation between equals, yet another synallagmatic contract between the dynasty and the Hungarian nation. The 'king' granted an amnesty to all Hungarians and Transylvanians: magnates, nobles, citizens of the towns, militiamen and peasants. The nobility regained all its prerogatives, even the right to bear arms (except against the emperor). The soldiers of the lower ranks obtained a guarantee that they would not be forcibly conscripted into the imperial army; after taking an oath of loyalty, they could return in freedom to their homes, so that they might resume their work and live in peace (*ut ad suas aedes discedant ibique oeconomiam colant ac quiete sese continuant*). Future Diets would retain the right to present their grievances (*Gravamina*) and the freedom to vote, in order that there might be no doubt 'of the desire of His Imperial Majesty to preserve the laws of the kingdom of Hungary and of Transylvania, or of the determination of the Hungarians and the Transylvanians to yield to no other nation in fidelity to the king'.[18]

The military forces of Hungary would thus once again be at the disposal of the emperor when the time came to resume the struggle against the Turks. Joseph I died during the negotiations at Szatmár. The heir to his states, his brother Charles III of Spain, was elected emperor without difficulty, as Charles VI. But he had inherited such great power in Europe (his Catalan troops were pursuing the struggle) that it was no longer in the interests of Great Britain and Holland to continue the war for his advantage. Therefore, if Louis XIV and Philip V would accept a reasonable compromise, the best course was to make peace with them. At Utrecht, in 1713, Philip V consented to the loss of the Belgian and Italian territories conquered in the name of 'Charles III'. But he was recognized as king of Spain, including recalcitrant Catalonia and all the colonies, on condition that he granted Great Britain commercial preference. France now had only the emperor as her enemy and the fortunes of war changed in her favour after the victory gained by Villars at Denain and the recapture of Landau. Soon negotiations were opened at Rastatt between the two great adversaries, Villars and Prince Eugene. Even at the height of the conflict the two men had always held each other in mutual esteem, maintaining a friendship of long standing. Their negotiations were arduous, but, in spite of the resistance of their governments, they were together able to establish the broad lines of a future policy founded on the reconciliation of the two monarchies. France was to keep Landau. Belgium and the provinces of Milan and Naples would belong to the emperor. With Germany and Italy neutralized and continental Europe pacified, France could develop her maritime trade and the emperor resume his advance along the Danube, extending his frontiers at the expense of the Turkish

Empire. Such a prospect encouraged hopes of a new Europe in which dynastic rivalries and territorial ambitions would cease to be the mainsprings of policy, and in which a better understanding of the advantages of economic progress would enable nations to indulge in peaceful competition. The programme was nobly conceived and, before he died, Louis XIV believed it to be feasible. However, there were too many traditional forces at work obstructing its success and Europe soon returned to its former habits. Although it was claimed that the old quarrels in Germany had been settled, the Empire never ceased to be a cause of rivalry between the two monarchies. Because of the imperial crown, it was not possible for the House of Austria, and in particular Charles VI, to stand aloof from the Empire.

New powers had emerged there, all potential rivals of the emperor: Prussia, where the elector of Brandenburg had secured the royal title, the electorate of Hanover, whose prince was to succeed to the throne of England, and Saxony, where the elector had embraced the Catholic faith to become king of Poland. Austria, unable to turn its back on German affairs, found itself involved in conspiracies and intrigues which, in turn, alarmed the French.[19]

The freedom of manoeuvre obtained at Rastatt had made it possible to resume the struggle with Turkey. In a dazzling campaign that lasted less than two years, Prince Eugene captured Peterwardein and then Belgrade. By the peace of Passarowitz, concluded with the Turks on 21 July 1718, the emperor received the Banat of Temesvár, a part of Serbia which included Belgrade and, to the south of Transylvania, the region of Little Wallachia extending to the Aluta.

From a strategic point of view, these territories served as bulwarks protecting the kingdom of Hungary and completed the defensive system established between the Drave, the Save and the Danube, the military frontiers of Hungary. The economic clauses concerning navigation on the Danube were no less important. The Black Sea, encircled by Ottoman lands, was still inaccessible to ships other than those of the sultan; but the emperor's ships could sail along the Danube and through Ottoman territory as far as the trading-stations of the delta, where merchandise was transferred to caiques and other craft designed for navigation on the Black Sea; it could then be transported without hindrance to Constantinople, the Crimea, Trebizond or Sinope.

Austria thus had open access to the trade-routes of the East. But there were also open routes to the Mediterranean and the West. From his experiences in Catalonia, Charles VI had acquired knowledge of international relations and of the potential of sea-borne trade. Never had the power of his house been established to such advantage at the crucial points of Europe: Milan, Naples and present-day Belgium. From these centres, provided that he could find the necessary capital and ships, the emperor could enter into competition with the maritime powers, France and Spain, on the Mediterranean and Atlantic routes.

A company was founded at Ostend for trade with the East Indies and another received preferential rights for trade with Portugal, which was regaining importance as a result of the discovery of gold in Brazil. On the Adriatic coast, Trieste and Fiume were declared free ports where goods could be exchanged without being subject to customs duties. Within a few years the population of Trieste rose from five thousand to thirty thousand; to strengthen the city's links with Vienna and the Austrian interior, the emperor had the road built over the Semmering pass, which diverted traffic from the Brenner pass and thereby conflicted with the interests of the Tyrol. The road was considered to be a great constructional achievement and was as highly esteemed by contemporaries as the tunnels cut through the Alps in the following century. Austria was laying the foundations that would enable it to become a great power in the world economy, just as it was already a great territorial and military power in Europe. But its very structure was to reveal the most dangerous contradictions. In the political conditions of the time the dynasty was, without doubt, the bond necessary to maintain in a common association territories that lay scattered far and wide. It was essential to guarantee the transmission of the whole to a single person, which did not present too many difficulties when there was a male heir. In 1713 the Emperor Charles VI, who still had no son, promulgated from Vienna a Pragmatic Sanction reserving the rights of the direct female line against the rights of his nieces and aunts.[20] This was a most wise precaution, since it anticipated the possibility of the emperor dying without a male heir and thus placed the royal succession beyond all dispute. But the Pragmatic Sanction was merely a family provision: to be valid in the different countries ruled by the House of Austria it required the approval of the regional Diets, and to become part of the public law of Europe it needed the consent of the foreign powers. The various Diets willingly recognized the Pragmatic Sanction—even Hungary proved amenable, in 1723—but in return they obtained new privileges. Although the emperor had secured a dynastic advantage, he was thus limiting the authority which he needed for a more resolute general policy. Concessions also had to be made to the European powers and many of the advantages gained at Rastatt and Passarowitz were sacrificed in return for their approval. It is not possible here to enter into a detailed account of the diplomatic negotiations which took place over a period of twenty years, and which revealed that the Danubian monarchy, because of its very diversity, remained a fragile structure.

In the decades that followed, territorial grandeur and hopes of economic power had to be sacrificed to the Pragmatic Sanction. The Ostend Company was suppressed in the interests of Great Britain, which feared the effects of competition on her own companies. Such was the price which London demanded for recognition of the decree. After the War of the Polish Succession, in which Austria had become unhappily involved, the kingdom of Naples was ceded to a younger son of the king of Spain, Don Carlos, in exchange for the duchies of Parma and Piacenza, which were of little importance. Even a part of the duchy of Milan was lost in a cession of territories to the king of Sardinia. Finally, the alliance with Russia forced the House of Austria into a premature resumption of the war against Turkey. A new danger presented itself when the Russian troops advanced into Moldavia as far as Jassi. It was becoming clear that Russia, which Peter the Great had raised to the rank of a great European power and which was already taking the place of Sweden as the dominant force in the Baltic, would no longer be satisfied with an outlet on the Sea of Azov or with the northern shore of the Black Sea: she evidently intended to enter into competition with Austria in the Balkans and to ensure that Austria was not the only country to benefit in the event of the collapse of the Ottoman Empire. But the collapse of Turkish power no longer appeared imminent. On the contrary, the government of the Porte, taking advantage of the advice offered by France and the assistance of French technicians, had reorganized its army, while the Austrian army had begun to show signs of decline during the latter years of Prince Eugene's command (he died in 1736). The war proved much harder than expected and ended disastrously with the treaty of Belgrade (1739), in which Austria lost most of her conquests of 1718. Belgrade became Turkish once again, while Serbia and Little Wallachia were evacuated. In such circumstances it is understandable that Count Frederick Harrach, the governor of the Netherlands, should have written in the following terms to a friend in Vienna, towards the end of 1739: 'Meanwhile, here we are without allies and without advisers, after having lost part of the state of Milan, the kingdom of Naples and Sicily, Lorraine, Barrois [in fact, Lorraine and Barrois had never belonged to the Habsburgs, but they were now guaranteed as the future possessions of France], Serbia, Wallachia, a part of the Banat and terrain two leagues in width extending all along the Save.'[21]

Towards the end of his life Prince Eugene confessed his lack of confidence in the international agreements guaranteeing the Pragmatic Sanction. He recommended that the vast and noble monarchy of His Imperial Catholic Majesty be made into 'a whole', *ein Totum*,[22] that inefficiency be eliminated in both the civil and the military spheres and that all resources be concentrated in readiness for times of crisis. A good army of one hundred and forty thousand men provided the only sure guarantee and would avert all possibility of dispute. Without money, there could be no army: without an army, the hereditary states of the emperor could not be preserved.

But how was this to be achieved? Prince Eugene did not possess the imagination of a reformer. A great lord devoted solely to the monarch and the monarchy, equally at home in Austria or Hungary, in one or other of his sumptuous residences, he belonged to a seigniorial order offering economic advantages of which he availed himself personally, although he recognized their perilous consequences for the monarchy as a whole. 'A government of democratic and aristocratic tendencies, in which everyone has his privileges and customs, presents the most serious obstacles to the exercise of sovereignty. Subjects seek to limit that sovereignty by setting against it their own privileges and liberties which, though a mere semblance of words, are so dear to them that they strive to create and preserve a foundation for something which, in reality, they do not possess. If they are asked to provide subsidies, they raise a great protest; and yet the liberties and privileges which they cherish more than anything in the world could not be preserved without the assistance of the troops who alone ensure their safeguard.'[23]

This was the reasoning of a monarchist, a man who had always respected the authority of the prince, even an enemy prince, and who believed a strong central power to be the necessary condition of the greatness of a monarchy as 'a whole'. Prince Eugene thus regarded the army as indispensable to internal peace and prosperity. He had not, however, been able to maintain the army as the same effective weapon which it had proved up to 1718, in the wars against the Turks and in the West. Before he died, he had to admit that the weapon had been blunted.

૭૩

Yet war had not returned, at least not in the central region (Bohemia and the hereditary states). Armies fought on more distant battlefields. The security of peace enjoyed by this territory was one of the factors that contributed to the blossoming of an artistic, if not intellectual civilization which can be counted among the most original of modern Europe. It seems unnecessary to insist on fixing precisely the chronological limits of this civilization. The Baroque Exhibition held in Prague thirty years ago—a moving attempt to revive an awareness of past values, on the eve of upheavals that were to prove much graver than that of the White Mountain —suggested the dates 1600–1800, which cover too broad a period and also include the Mannerist and Rococo phases, and even Neo-Classicism.[24] Perhaps the dates 1684–1740 would be preferable: from the deliverance of Vienna to the War of the Austrian Succession, which convulsed the economic system and brought a halt to numerous enterprises. But 1740 merely marks a pause in a tradition that was soon to be re-established. Should it then be assumed that there existed a general artistic mood, a common sensibility that would entitle the historian to speak in terms, if not of a 'Danubian school', at least of a 'Danubian style'?[25] The important thing is to recognize that, over the course of a century, an intense artistic activity in these regions produced a multiplicity of manorial halls and churches, works of sculpture and painting in a wide variety of forms: fresco decoration on ceilings and vaults, painted altarpieces, statues of wood, stone and stucco, atlantes supporting balconies and staircases. Mention must also be made of the innumerable works in which local master-craftsmen displayed their skills and their delectable sense of realism. This wonderfully rich flowering of art is to be seen in the achievements of major figures such as J. B. Mathey, who in Prague built several palaces and a domed church for the Knights of the Cross in the latter decades of the seventeenth century; Fischer von Erlach and Hildebrandt, who transformed the Vienna of Leopold I, Charles VI and Prince Eugene; Prandtauer, who built the incomparable abbey of Melk on a spur overlooking the Danube; the sculptor Matthias Braun, in Bohemia, who with the Brokoffs and the Jäckels carved the statues on the Charles Bridge; the Dientzenhoffers, who were responsible for a number of churches in Prague; the painters Gran, Rottmayr, Tröger and Altomonte, who worked in the monasteries of Austria; and finally, two artists of the second half of the eighteenth century: Kracker, whose luminous compositions covered the vault of St. Nicholas in Malá Strana and the main hall of the Jesuit college at Eger, in Hungary, and Maulbertsch, who also moved from one country to another, painting with virtuosity, in pleasing bright colours and with a power of suggestion. These men were true princes of art. But the list is incomplete, almost unjust in its brevity. Although these artists did not form a single school, they shared common ground in two important respects. In the first place, while evolving with the times and absorbing new influences, they learnt their art from one another. They drew their inspiration from the architects, painters and sculptors of Baroque Italy—Bernini, Borromini, Caravaggio, Pozzo and Tiepolo—whose style so captivated central Europe in the second half of the eighteenth century. In the capitals, Vienna, Prague and even Pressburg, permanent studios existed and in 1705 an academy was opened in the imperial capital.

Secondly, these artists served the same clientele. In an aristocratic and ecclesiastical society, they obtained their commissions from the great lords and the religious orders, who were the beneficiaries of revenues from landed property and the possessors of vast individual fortunes. A taste for grandeur and ostentation governed architecture and decoration. In structures of huge proportions shimmering with gilt and colour, and in which space seems to have been manipulated, divided and multiplied, stability was subordinated to movement, to an indefinable but fundamental quality which is neither frenzy nor emotional ardour, but rather a sense of perpetual motion.

A widespread taste for music was an inseparable element of this culture. Churches and state chambers, designed with a painstaking concern for their acoustical properties, served as a setting for solemn high masses, cantatas and concerts, enhancing the brilliance and emotional power of such occasions with the character of their decoration. But this civilization of musicians was concerned less with the ideal of permanence than with the pleasures of the passing moment. Danubian art possessed such a subtlety of nuance that it is difficult to arrive at a true appreciation. Was this an imperial art? Certainly, in Vienna the Emperor Leopold I, whose simple personal tastes have already been mentioned, sought architectural grandeur and beauty as a means of affirming his imperial dignity and the glory of his reign. He instructed Fischer von Erlach to draw up plans for the embellishment of the Hofburg, but these were not realized until later. He wanted a palace to be built at Schönbrunn that would rival Versailles; instead, in the reign of Maria Theresa, the simple but graceful little palace of Paccassi was erected. Leopold was interested chiefly in his musicians. Charles VI, benefiting from his experiences in Spain, was more devoted to building. At Klosterneuburg he hoped to erect an Escorial, only a fragment of which exists. In his capital he had a church built by Fischer von Erlach and dedicated to his patron saint Charles Borromeo, in thanksgiving both for the abatement of a new plague in 1713 and for the restoration of peace in 1714. This church is one of the finest achievements of European Baroque, a synthesis in which are intermingled reminiscences of the façade of St. Peter's in Rome, Santa Maria della Salute in Venice and the designs of French architects. Rising from a central plan the beautiful ovoid cupola, resting on a drum and pierced with oculi, crowns a majestic and subtle composition. Rottmayr decorated the interior with a fresco celebrating the intercession of St. Charles Borromeo on behalf of the countries of Austria. On the façade tall columns harmonizing with the dome call to mind their Roman models, Trajan's Column and the colonnade of Antoninus, and symbolize the imperial virtues, Constantia and Fortitudo.

Yet Danubian art was seigniorial rather than imperial. The more one studies the period, the clearer it becomes that the seigniory constituted its focal point. It was within the framework of the seigniory that populations led their daily life. It was the seigniorial system which provided the resources for the enterprises of art patrons and stimulated rivalry among the great noble families, all of whom, in addition to their palaces in Vienna, Prague, Pressburg, Buda or Agram, wished to possess a residence in the country with its own park and woods, surrounded by their subject towns and villages extending beyond the horizon. Thus the seigniory, which was the real foundation of the social and political system, rather than the State, was also the determining factor in the flowering of the arts.

Vienna was indubitably the capital of the monarchy, but the architectural commissions of emperors were equalled, if not surpassed, by those of the great lords. In the 1690s one of the Liechtensteins had commissioned D. Martinelli to build a palace worthy of Rome and Padre Pozzo to decorate a ceiling in his summer residence at Rosau; later, Marshal Daun employed Hildebrandt to design one of the most attractive façades in the city, on the Freyung. But none of these buildings can be compared with those commissioned by Prince Eugene—the Himmelpforte-gasse palace, begun by Hildebrandt and completed by Fischer von Erlach, and the Belvedere with its two edifices, the magnificent and delicate upper palace joined by terraced gardens to the modest and homely lower palace. In Vienna, let it be remembered, Montesquieu found the emperor's subjects more comfortably accommodated than their sovereign.

Prague possessed a character of its own. The charm of Malá Strana was enhanced by façades with ovals (the Lobkowicz palace designed by Alliprandi) and with powerful but graceful decorative motifs, such as the eagles carved by Braun on the Thun palace and the figures of Day and Night carved by F. M. Brokoff on the Morzin palace. One senses the spirit of emulation that lay behind the decoration of these palaces. The traditional repertory of allegorical representation—the Iconology of Cesare Ripa—was still used by artists, but each building reveals the personal tastes of the founder and a specific concern with his genealogy. It was at this period that the statues commissioned by the religious orders made the Charles Bridge the supreme show-place of Baroque sculpture: here Jäckel, the Brokoff brothers from Slovakia and Matthias Braun, a Tyrolean, placed their tall figures and lifelike groups, the most moving of which is the ecstasy of St. Luitgarda with the unforgettable gesture of Christ half detached from the Cross. In churches and palaces, frescoes and altarpieces were painted in profusion. Halwax tried to found an academy, but artists continued to be influenced, directly or indirectly, by Italy. Some of Brandl's compositions had the power of sculpture, and it is rather strange that V. V. Reiner should have been his pupil. Without knowing the Venetians, he absorbed the qualities of suppleness and light from their works. Among the churches of Malá Strana one in particular, the Jesuit church of St. Nicholas, between the royal castle and the towers of the bridge, assumes a particularly striking aspect when viewed from the other side of the river. This church must be mentioned here, even though its construction, begun before 1710, and its interior decoration occupied several decades and were not completed until the 1770s. Although he was doubtless not responsible for drawing up the original plans, it was Kilian

Ignatius Dientzenhoffer who endowed St. Nicholas with its architectural character. The façade comprises three orders, but with curves that suggest the undulations of a piece of fabric; set back on a high drum, the magnificent copper-roofed dome is balanced by the light, rounded bell-tower. In the nave, divided into three bays without aisles, the chapels are in the form of conches and the high pillars of grey and pink marble form an oblique line, while the galleries curve inwards. Along the pillars, at the angles of the short transept and on the altar stand huge statues of the Judges, the martyrs and the Fathers of the Greek Church which convey an impression of frenzy; on the drum of the dome, statues of the Virtues restore a sense of calm. The vault is covered by a composition by Kracker which extends as far as the transept. In the centre is depicted the apotheosis of St. Nicholas of Myra in a sky filled with light; along the edge of the nave runs a scene of a coastal town with its towers and harbour quays and the bustle of travellers and merchants. The vast church of St. Nicholas (200 ft. long, 85 ft. wide, dome 260 ft.) is one of the finest expressions of the great period of seigniorial and religious art, the supreme flower of Baroque architecture in Prague.

Prague was certainly the capital of the kingdom, but its political life had been curbed, not so much by the will of the emperor as by the negligence of those who represented the Bohemian state but rarely attended the Diet. Instead, the city became the seigniorial capital, the favourite place of residence of the great lords, whose immense domains made them the rulers of principalities. These lords gathered in the city to enjoy the pleasures of social life more freely than was possible in Vienna. Prague, not destined to be an economic capital, now existed solely for the benefit of the noble families and the religious orders. The commercial middle class was almost non-existent in the city; activity was dominated by the numerous studios of artists, clerical workers and tradesmen who provided for the needs of the aristocratic clientele. The patient research undertaken by Jaromir Neumann has thrown light on the careers of artists whose names had been forgotten and who, born in Prague or coming there from other parts, received the rights of citizenship in the city which they transformed and embellished. The visitor of today who finds enchantment in Prague owes them a debt of gratitude.

Prague was thus not merely the subsidiary of Vienna. Its studios were sufficiently numerous to satisfy the city's needs, although they were so overwhelmed with commissions that a sculptor such as Braun could not possibly have been solely responsible for all the statues attributed to him; the painters Brandl, Halwax and Reiner also had many assistants.

Each domain, or more exactly each patrimony (certain estates were inalienable properties held in trust for the lifetime of the occupier, who was merely the usufructuary), had to have its own country seat. According to the wealth or taste of the master, this might be either an old building with a scantily refurbished interior or a new edifice, spacious, lavish and comfortable. In these vast and graceful new structures the central motif was sometimes a circular or oval pavilion around which the various wings were arranged, such as the residence of the Kinskýs at Chlumec, designed by the ingenious architect Santini Aïchel; in other cases, the wings were built along two sides of the main courtyard, in the French manner (the country home of the Kaunitz family at Slavkov, in Moravia, and that of the Lobkowicz family at Roudnice, in the Elbe valley). At Kuks, Count Sporck, an unconventional patron of the arts, had a hospital built in a rustic setting; the architect Alliprandi erected an elegant Baroque chapel and in front of the hospital buildings, on the terrace, a long row of statues carved by Matthias Braun and his colleagues was erected, a moving representation of the Beatitudes, the Virtues and the Vices. In the woods around Kuks the same artists carved scenes from the Gospel out of the living rock.[26] In these mansions costly furniture, tapestries from Flanders, Italy and France and pictures from the studios of Bohemia decorated the rooms which filled with guests in the hunting season and on special family occasions, celebrated with dancing and concerts.

The towns of Hungary, where the *kuruc* war had interrupted the first flowering of Baroque art, did not yet possess the same abundance of churches and palaces. But at Pressburg, where the castle above the Danube was still simply a fortress, churches were being built in a new style and soon a palace of noble proportions was erected for a great Croatian lord, Grassalkovich. Eventually, the liberation of the country and the return of peace made possible a renewal of the general architectural aspect of Hungary. At Kismarton, the beautiful palace of the Eszterházys, its façade adorned with busts, was modified to suit the tastes of successive generations. On the land which the emperor had granted him at Ráckeve, to the south of Budapest, Prince Eugene instructed Hildebrandt in 1702 to build a new palace which was repaired in 1708, after the rebellion. In the large central pavilion the grand hall occupies both floors; projecting from the façade is a huge, curved portico with graceful arcades and, in front, a terrace which has a balustrade decorated with statues; at the rear of the palace, gigantic armorial bearings fill the pediment. The whole is crowned by an octagonal dome; the wings enclosing the courtyard have pavilions at the angles and lead to a magnificent iron gate beside the river.[27]

The civil architecture of many small towns in Bohemia and Austria assumed a new aspect. Even with the progress of modern urban development, these towns have preserved their Baroque houses, built on the main square for local magistrates, seigniorial officials and merchants. The painted façades are generally decorated with holy statues.

Győr, a Hungarian town not far from Austria, provides one of the best examples of a fortified town which, as soon as the Turkish menace had been removed, was transformed into a Baroque city by adapting itself to the role of a regional capital: it was in such circumstances that the beautiful parish churches, the churches of the religious orders and the residences of the minor nobility and the middle class were built. Similarly, Veszprém and Székesfehérvár, towns of pacified Royal Hungary, now acquired their splendid palaces.

At Agram-Zagreb, on the slopes of the hill of Grić, new buildings were erected around the church of St. Mark: the noble dwellings of the Zrinyi (Zrinský) family and the single-storey palaces which form the graceful ensemble of the Dvory. The more limited resources of the Croatian nobles prevented them from using the services of the greatest architects, but they were nonetheless determined to express their consciousness of belonging to a historic country and their pride in possessing their own capital.

Finally, the peasantry, even while protesting against the corvée and resorting to rebellion in the years of severest hardship, had secured a certain degree of material comfort. The same taste for splendour and colour pervaded modest dwellings, reflecting what the peasants saw in church and in their lord's mansion: hence the household objects, pottery, pewter tankards, furniture, beds and chests painted in vivid colours and with floral decorations; hence, also, the costumes of women and men, bodices and shirts composed of white masses of stiff linen, embroidered skirts, the ribbons and pearls worn on the head, all the rustic glitter of popular Baroque which was flaunted in local processions, behind the banners and chasubles, and in the dances held at village festivals.

NOTES

1. In his article, 'Les relations franco-hongroises pendant la conjuration du Palatin Wesselenyi 1664–1668', in the *Review of the Hungarian Academy of Sciences,* Jean Bérenger recalls what Louis XIV said in 1666: 'I was still maintaining secret communication with Count Serin, in order to create a disturbance in Hungary if I were to enter into war with the emperor.'

   This is a most striking statement of the diversionary policy maintained by France and in which the Hungarian question was subordinated to that of friendship or hostility towards the House of Austria.

2. For the Hungarian revolts, see Oswald Redlich, *Weltmacht des Barock,* the whole of the second book entitled *Ungarn und die Türkenkriege bis 1668,* pp. 158–324; H. Bidermann, *Geschichte der Gesamtstaatsidee, 1526–1804,* 1867, 2 vols.; Louis Eisenmann, *Le Compromis austro-hongrois de 1867,* the first part of which traces the evolution of the Hungarian Constitution; consult also the history by Katona, *Historia regnum Hungariae,* Pest, 1779–1802, vols. XXXIII and XXXIV; D. Sinor, *History of Hungary,* London, 1959, chapter 20, 'Liberation'.

3. Speaking of Hungary as a whole, a French traveller in 1671 observed: 'Grievances have left in the heart of this bizarre and extravagant nation an unbelievable hatred of the German government which makes them desire a king from their own nation, claiming that their privileges give them the right to elect such a king.'

   The sufferings of the Hungarian pastors, condemned despite their innocence, are evoked in a contemporary work by Abraham van Poot, *Naauwkeurig Verhaal van der Vervolginge Aangerech tegens de Evangilse Leeraanen in Hungarien, Nevens een bewijs van der selver onschuld aan de rebellie,* Amsterdam, Tinotheus von Hoorn, *boekeverkooper,* 1684.

4. Yet another complication, serious in its consequence: in the absence of the palatine, the primate-archbishop prince of Esztergom became the first person of the realm. Grémonville, the French ambassador in Vienna, considered that the archbishop would not readily consent to the election of a palatine who would push him back into second place. Paris A.E. *Autriche,* vol. L, f° 168, 4 June 1681.

5. D. Sinor, op. cit., p. 205.

6. The full title of the project was *Einrichtungswerk des Königsreiches Hungarn in Sachen des status politici-cameralis et bellici unter Leitung von Bischof Kollonitsch.*

O. Redlich gives a detailed and pertinent analysis of the project. In the various Austrian and Hungarian histories, the reader can follow the two opposing points of view: a rational defence (H. Hantsch) or a bitter criticism of the Kollonisch project. D. Sinor is moderate in his judgement (op. cit., p. 214): 'Kollonisch was a man of integrity, but something of a theoretician.' Apropos of the famous sentence in the report recommending that Germans be brought into the country to stimulate devotion to the lawful king, Sinor maintains that the tragedy of the Habsburgs was that the Hungarians, despite their independent spirit or perhaps because of it, were the loyal people *par excellence*. It was not the Hungarians, he declares, but the favoured Slavs ('the cherished Slavonic populations') who in the twentieth century became the instruments of the Empire's disintegration (p. 215). But Slav historians do not feel that their nations were ever the favoured ones.

7. Colonists who rebuilt houses and restored land to cultivation were exempt from taxes for five years, if they were Germans, and for three years, if they were Hungarians. This provision brought protests from the Hungarians, but the Commission considered that the Germans were involved in heavier investment expenditure.

8. J. Szekfü, *État et Nation*, French edn. of 1945, *Presses Universitaires de France*, p. 179.

9. L. Makkai, *Histoire de Transylvanie*.

10. On the mercantilists, consult the solid study by H. Hassinger, *Johann Joachim Becher, 1635–1682*, Vienna, 1951. H. von Srbik, *Adriapolitik unter Leopold I*, 1929, and *Der Staatliche Exporthandel Österreichs von Leopold I bis Maria Theresia*, 1907, and the stimulating article by Arnošt Klíma, 'Mercantilism in the Habsburg Monarchy—with special reference to the Bohemian Lands', *Historica*, XI, 1965, pp. 95–119.

11. *Politischer Discurs*, ch. X.

12. H. von Srbik, *Wien und Versailles, 1692–1697*, has given an informative account of the dealings which took place between the governments in the course of the war.

The history of these events is clearly described in the works in German by O. Redlich, H. Hantsch and E. Zöllner, and in French by L. André and G. Zeller (in *Histoire des relations internationales*, under the editorship of Pierre Renouvin). It is not easy, however, to reach a just appreciation of the various interpretations put forward by these authors.

13. There exists an abundance of books on Prince Eugene. See B. Böhn, *Bibliographie zur Geschichte des Prinzen Eugen von Savojen und seine Zeit. Veröffentlichungen der Kommission für neuere Geschichte*, AÖG, vol. CXV, 1943. Two basic works are the old biography by Alfred von Arneth, *Prinz Eugen von Savoyen*, 3 vols., 1858–64, and the recent study by Max Braubach which presents the subject in a new light, *Prinz Eugen von Savoyen*, 5 vols., 1960–5.

Since the First World War the figure of Prince Eugene has been studied from diverse viewpoints. At the time of the two hundredth anniversary of his death (1736–1936), there was a tendency to look on him as the precursor of German unity, the founder of Greater Germany, the champion of Germanism against the ambitions of the Latin world and the Eastern peril, the initiator of *Drang nach Osten*.

Rössler, *Der Soldat des Reiches: Prinz Eugen*, Oldenburg, 1934; W. Schlüsser, *Prinz Eugen von Savoyen, Meister der Politik*, II, 1922; R. Lorenz, *Prinz Eugen von Savoyen* in *Neue deutsche Biographie: die Grossen Deutschen*, vol. II, 1935; H. von Srbik, *Aus Österreichs Vergangenheit, von Prinz Eugen zu Franz Josef*, Salzburg, 1949; Roland Krug von Nidda, *Eugen von Savoyen*, Vienna, 1963.

In Italian: C. Assum, *Eugenio di Savoia*, 1933; V. Adami, 'Eugenio di Savoia, Governatore di Milano 1706–1716', *Nova Revista storica*, 9, 1925.

In English: Nicholas Henderson, *Prince Eugene of Savoy*, London, Weidenfeld, 1964.

14. *Histoire des relations internationales* (ed. P. Renouvin), vol. III, *Les temps modernes* by Gaston Zeller, 2nd part, p. 79. The text of the treaty of Carlovtsi is reproduced in Du Mont (the treaty is drawn up in Latin):

    'Navigatio navium germanicarum aut aliorum subditorum caesareorum nullo possit in cursu suo ultra citroque incommodari, sed libere atque commodiccime fiat ubique in praedictis duobus fluviis' (these two rivers forming the frontier); and further on . . . 'ne diversione aquarum in Marusio cursus caesarearum navium incommodum aliquod petiatur; nullatenus permittetur ut sive molendinorum, sive alia occasione ex Marusio aquae alio deriventur, seu deducantur.'

15. A recently prepared map is exhibited in the museum of the manor of Sárospatak (Hungary). It illustrates in striking fashion the extent of the revolt and the peril confronting the eastern part of the monarchy. The work by Béla Köpeczi, *A Rákóczi-Szabadságharc és Franciaország* ('Rákóczi's War of Liberation and France'), Budapest, 1966, supported by an abundant documentation, throws new light on the history of the revolt and Rákóczi's difficult relations with France.

16. On the reign of Charles III in Catalonia, consult the works of Pedro Voltes Bou, *El Archiduque Carlos de Austria, rey de los Catalanes*, Barcelona, 1952; *Barcelona durante il gobierno del Archiduque Carlos de Austria*, Barcelona, 2 vols., 1963 (documents); and Pierre Vilar, *La Catalogne*.

17. Victor-L. Tapié, 'Aspects de la politique étrangère de Louis XIV', *Revue de travaux de l'Académie des Sciences morales et politiques*, 1966, 1st semester (ed. Sirey), pp. 89–92, in which the author has presented the results of his personal research in Vienna (Staatsarchiv) and Paris (Affaires étrangères) on the negotiations at The Hague and at Rastatt.

18. Text of the peace of Szattmár in Du Mont.

19. Max Braubach, *Prinz Eugen von Savoyen*, vol. IV.

20. The text of the Pragmatic Sanction, preserved in the Staatsarchiv in Vienna, is published by Otto Frass, *Quellenbuch zur Österr. Geschichte*, 2, p. 226.

    For an interpretation, consult G. Turba, *Geschichte des Thronfolgerechtes 1156–1732*, Vienna, 1903; *Die Pragmatische Sanktion*, Vienna, 1913, etc.; Louis Eisenmann, *Le Compromis austro-hongrois*, p. 9.

21. Victor-L. Tapié, 'Contribution à l'étude des relations entre la France et l'Autriche avant la guerre de Succession d'Autriche', in *Österreich und Europa, Festgabe für Hugo Hantsch zum 70 Geburtstag*, p. 142 (Vienna, Staatsarchiv, Frankreich Varia 16: F. Harrach to Liechtenstein, 6 October 1739).

22. Alfred von Arneth, *Prinz Eugen*, vol. III, p. 547, from the protocol of 27 January 1726. Cf. Frass, op. cit., p. 247.

23. Ibid., p. 248.

24. Catalogue *Pražské baroko 1600–1680*, Prague, 1938.

25. A full bibliography of Danubian Baroque would require too much space to be included here. However, the following biographies of the great architects should be mentioned: Hans Sedlmayr, *Johann Bernhard Fischer von Erlach*, Vienna, 1965; Bruno Grimschitz, *Lukas von Hildebrandt*. On the palaces: Bruno Grimschitz, *Wiener Barock Palaste* ('The Baroque Palaces of Vienna'), 1947. On sculpture: V. V. Štech, *Die Barockskulptur in Böhmen*, 1959. On painting: Klara Garas, *Franz Anton Maulbertsch, 1724–1796*, Budapest, 1960.

26. The case of Count Franz Anton Sporck, a freemason of Jansenist sympathies whom the Jesuits prosecuted for heresy, was studied by Heinrich Benedikt, *Franz Anton Graf Sporck (1662–1738)*, Vienna, 1923, and the artistic décor at Kuks is the subject of a monograph by Jaromir Neumann and Josef Prošek, *Matyáš Braun-Kuks*, Prague, 1959.

27. The link between the mental attitudes of the nobility and artistic activity in the Danubian countries is clearly recognized by modern historiography. Cf. Jaromir Neumann, op. cit., p. 13. Although less exclusive, because of competition from the middle-class clientele, the role of the aristocracy in the commissioning of works of art continued beyond the revolution of 1848 and the abolition of the feudal system.

At the time of the first timid agrarian reform of 1919 in Czechoslovakia, the historian Pekař, in a highly stimulating work, opposed the provisions of the reform on several grounds, one of which was the danger of the country's artistic patrimony being squandered—Josef Pekař, *Omyly a nebezpečí pozemkové reformy* ('Errors and Dangers of Agrarian Reform'), 1923, p. 56. For a number of reasons, the bourgeois republic found itself embarrassed by the consequences of the reforms which it introduced. The more radical solution of the socialist republic provided more effective means, in the form of museums, for the restoration and preservation of the artistic riches which the great lords of the eighteenth century had gathered together.

❦ 7 ❦

The Era of Reform and Enlightenment

WHEN, ON 20 OCTOBER 1740, the Emperor Charles VI died at the ripe age of fifty-five in the palace of La Favorite at Vienna,[1] after an illness lasting several days, the internal difficulties of the monarchy, its external reverses and the weakness of its government presented a strange contrast to the progress achieved in certain sectors of the economy. Moreover, rural society was still characterized by the old inequality of conditions.

With the permanent establishment there of the court, the chancelleries and the various administrative departments, Vienna had become an active city of one hundred thousand inhabitants which served as the common capital of the Danubian countries, without holding this status officially. The abundance of goods in its markets, the transactions carried on within its walls, the arrival of travellers from the other Habsburg states and from abroad, the spectacle provided by the reception of ambassadors and the religious processions that filled the streets on great festivals, all helped to create an atmosphere of genuine animation. The decorative aspect of the city was continually changing, as new churches and palaces were erected; in the narrow streets of the medieval city construction sites appeared everywhere. The old enclosure-walls had been preserved and the glacis repaired and strengthened, but the new buildings extended beyond this zone. Amid the greenery of the outlying districts stood the summer palaces of the nobility and, not far away, the textile and porcelain factories which had been granted the royal privilege. The Danube was one of the chief communication-routes for trading activity; the river encircled the city and on its quays, in front of the Rotenthurm, ships coming down from Germany or up from Hungary unloaded their merchandise. In the surrounding countryside vineyards were cultivated; the citizens of Vienna liked to visit the picturesque vine-growing villages for their Sunday relaxation and on their numerous public holidays. The forests in the distance were used for hunting, the favourite pastime of the court and the nobility.

The reconquest of Hungary meant that within a few miles of the city, instead of the vaguely defined frontier of the Turkish Empire, there now lay a vast, free country which was in the process of re-establishing itself. The era of national revolts in Hungary seemed to be at an end. Charles VI had respected the religious, political and fiscal privileges of the Hungarian nation; the wealthy great lords, the minor nobles of the comitats and the middle class of the towns were equally satisfied in this respect. At the same time, he had maintained the effective separation of Transylvania which, though in theory it remained an integral part of the kingdom of Hungary, possessed its own Chancellery in Vienna and enjoyed a genuine autonomy in the administration of its affairs.

The economic condition of Hungary continued to favour the proprietors of large estates and to ensure the servitude of the peasants, the *jobbágy*. The majority of the population was engaged in agriculture and stock-raising. However, activity was returning to the mining towns of Slovakia (Besztercebánya and Zips). Perhaps the most striking feature of the Hungarian economy was its subordination to the Viennese market. The merchants of Vienna controlled Hungary's exports and imports. Hungarian producers were not themselves in a position to have their cereals and livestock delivered to distant markets, but were compelled to use the Viennese, and often Jewish merchants, as intermediaries. On the other hand, Hungarian industry produced little. Local and home-based craft-production was sufficient to meet the requirements of peasant families; in their own homes the peasants made the beautiful costumes with leather ornaments and delicate em-broidery which were worn for festivals; at the markets in the small towns they bought the brightly coloured earthenware jugs and pots made by local artisans, who possessed the technique and stylistic talent for such work. But all other com-modities, and in particular those sought by the wealthy classes, were supplied by the warehouses and firms of Vienna, which were able to offer in abundance every-thing that the Hungarians could not provide for themselves. There can thus be no doubt that Hungary was closely dependent on the Austrian economic system, almost reduced to the status of a colony exchanging its agricultural produce for manufactures and luxury articles.

In the hereditary states, also, agriculture remained the backbone of the economy and was still dominated by the great seigniorial domain. But, whereas the lords of the sixteenth century had enriched themselves by organizing fish-ponds and breweries on their estates (breweries continued to provide their owners with substantial revenues),[2] some Bohemian lords were now attempting to establish factories on their lands and to produce for the international market. The abbey of Osek set up workshops for the manufacture of cloth and stockings in 1697. The cloth factory opened in 1715 by Count Jan Joseph Waldstein (Wallenstein) proved more successful and thirteen years later was employing four hundred workmen. The factory was of a distinctly modern kind; its workshops were equipped with good looms, and women and children were employed for dressing the yarn supplied by the local peasants. The French traveller Freschot, writing in 1704 of the Bohemian glass industry, talks of 'glass-works which are so profitable, we are assured, that a prince of Aversberg [Auersperg] alone received roughly one hundred thousand florins every year from his establishments'.[3] But these were still isolated cases, foreshadowing the rise of capitalism. The majority of nobles derived their greatest revenues from their estates and the corvée. In Bohemia, 50·6 per cent of the peasantry were holders of land, of which 63 per cent had land ranging between

5 and 20 hectares and 22 per cent possessed land exceeding 20 hectares. Peasants who held no land of their own worked as wage-earners for the more prosperous farmers. As the burden of increasing taxation was added to that of compulsory labour, despite the reluctance of the Diets to approve the taxes, widespread discontent became evident in rural society. There were peasant revolts in the region of Chrudim in 1711, in the region of Kolín in 1713 (an uprising by the peasants of Červená Pečka whose lord, Count Breda, was renowned for his great cruelty and earned himself the nickname of 'Breda-Běda', *běda* meaning 'misery') and in the environs of Čáslav in 1716. The rebel-leaders were tried and condemned to death.[4] In its patents of 1717 and 1738 the royal government attempted to restore order, harking back to the equitable provisions of the patent of 1680. Although gatherings and leagues of peasants, formed with the purpose of taking justice into their own hands, were prohibited as punishable offences, the peasants were invited to take their grievances to the authorities of the Circle and even to the emperor himself. The maximum for draught labour remained fixed at three days per week, from sunrise to sunset with a pause of two hours for a meal and a rest. During the long summer days labour was not to exceed ten hours, though it was conceded that these limits could not be rigorously observed in the haymaking and harvesting season. The patent of 1738 also advised landowners to regulate the corvée, by agreement with their peasants, according to the amount of work to be done rather than on a time basis. The peasantry detested the corvée as a crushing and humiliating obligation that left everything to the whim of the bailiff; they demanded its total suppression, a reform which succeeding generations were to await in vain until 1848. The belief thus grew up, especially abroad, that the peasants of Bohemia were grovelling in abject slavery and were not even masters of their own bodies (which was not quite true, but referred to the prohibitions preventing peasants from moving to another estate and the conditions attaching to apprenticeship). Yet farmsteads in many regions had an air of prosperity unknown in the previous century. The emperor derived large revenues from Bohemia. Land-taxes were assessed only on arable land and not on the entire area of the estate. Poverty certainly did not prevail everywhere and there were some very fertile regions: the hops of Žatec and Leitmeritz were highly esteemed by the brewers of Bavaria. On the other hand, there were few lords who, like Prince Ferdinand Schwarzenberg, could hand down to their children both their *Paterna monita*, or recommendations concerning the efficient administration of the estate, and at the same time an improved and enlarged patrimony.[5] Many nobles, unaware of the true state of their fortune, incurred expenses without either forethought or funds to back them up and hardly ever handled money except at the gaming-table; when they died, they owed large sums either to the treasury (if their administrators had not paid the peasant taxes for which they were responsible) or to individuals. Confiscations of estates as the result of judicial rulings were not infrequent.

The barrier which the aristocracy formed between the sovereign and the subjects of his different states continued to hinder the administration of the monarchy and made it impossible to bring each country's resources into harmony with general policy. Since the demise of Prince Eugene, who had never been able to attain either the official status or the effective power of a prime minister, the functions of government had remained divided among the traditional collegial institutions, each of which was primarily concerned not to allow the others to trespass on its own domain.

Consequently, military affairs still came under the joint control of the Hofkammer, which handled the sovereign's various revenues and from which army chiefs received the funds necessary for the upkeep of their regiments, the Hofkriegsrat, which was responsible for operations, and the General War Commissariat, entrusted with army administration and discipline. The Deputation, created in 1697 to co-ordinate the activities of these three bodies, had rapidly become a fourth military council on an equal footing with the others. A similar situation existed in the field of finance. Although the treasury had increased the war contributions levied from the Diets and also the indirect taxes imposed on consumer-goods, it had never been able to meet its liabilities; the debts of the State, contracted with foreign banks and with private persons, rose from year to year. In the reign of Leopold I an attempt had been made to provide the Hofkammer with the support of a Viennese bank which, by way of security, was authorized to collect indirect taxes and would thus absorb the government's debts. The bank was supervised by a government commission, the *Ministerial-Banco-Deputation*. Charles VI decided to go one step further by creating a State Bank, the *Bankalität* (1714), which was directly linked with the government and would support the Hofkammer. No one doubted that the emperor's government had solid sources of revenue at its disposal, provided that they were efficiently administered, and efforts were made to win the confidence of the public and persuade people to place their affairs in the hands of the State Bank. The new system, crowned by a Council of Finance or *Finanz-konferenz*, produced disappointing results. The most effective institution remained the Viennese bank, which was excellently administered for thirty-five years by Count Gundacker von Starhemberg and which succeeded in extinguishing a part of the old debt.[6] The Privy Conference retained control of general affairs and foreign policy. During his reign of six years, Joseph I, an intelligent and perceptive prince who was not afraid to introduce reforms, believed that he could render this body more effective by dividing it into two sections, one of which would have sole responsibility for external affairs. But these experiments in specialization had little effect, since the chancelleries remained jealous of their prerogatives. Moreover, there now existed four chancelleries: the Austrian (with two chancellors), the Bohemian, the Hungarian and the Transylvanian; in addition, there were departments (*Zentralstellen*) responsible for the affairs of Italy and the Netherlands. Each of these separate ministries claimed universal jurisdiction in matters concerning its own country. There could be no question of depriving the different countries of this autonomy; indeed, the House of Austria was far from exercising within its territories the despotism which has so often been attributed to it. But, in order to conduct a general policy, which, after all, would have benefited the Danubian countries as a whole, it would have been necessary to create some superior authority, guided by a prince assured of his resources who was capable of taking quick decisions and imposing them without contradiction. To an increasing degree, foreign policy was of interest only to the dynasty and aroused little concern among the masses, who merely felt the burdens which that policy entailed without understanding its underlying purpose. At the beginning of 1740 the French ambassador in Vienna, Mirepoix, who was a shrewd observer, wrote to Amelot: 'The hereditary states have been drained of men, especially Bohemia, which up to the present has had to provide the best recruits for the emperor's armies.'

Nevertheless, even in Vienna, whose general prosperity ought to have been a cause for satisfaction, the setbacks suffered by the imperial army and the surrender of Belgrade (1739) provoked discontent, a mood of wounded honour: 'The animosity and insolence directed against the government is growing at every moment. Everywhere the most insulting and impudent things are said aloud and publicly against the emperor and his ministers.'[7]

The 'ministers' mentioned were the high officials with whom the emperor had the most frequent contact, such as the senior chancellor of Austria, Count Philip Ludwig von Zinzendorf, Count von Starhemberg and the Bohemian chancellor, Count Kinský. They also included a representative of the middle class, the aulic councillor Bartenstein, who possessed 'the total confidence of the emperor'. Bartenstein's credit with the emperor caused him 'to have little fear of offending all the nobles individually, but it was a different matter when the nobility was assembled in a body and he dared do nothing which might arouse a general clamour against him'. Thus the government, by its weakness, had succeeded in exposing itself to the immediate threat of a nobility whose independence had already made it a formidable body within the different states, but which in Vienna, where it occupied high positions in the Councils, now opposed reforms simply through scepticism, indifference and lack of vision. Was the French foreign office, headed by Le Dran, sincere or simply blind when it persisted in declaring the House of Austria capable of posing a threat to France and of obtaining the submission of the Empire, at a time when a vigorous policy could be expected from other states? This applied to Prussia in particular, where the Soldier-King, Frederick William 1, had organized a first-class army and had just handed on to his successor, Frederick II, a solid financial legacy which had been built up without exhausting his country's fiscal potential.

The death of the emperor posed two problems which were not unrelated. His heir was the elder of his two daughters, the Archduchess Maria Theresa, born in 1717 and married to Francis, formerly duke of Lorraine, who had just exchanged Lorraine for Tuscany and now reigned at Florence. Firstly, would the Pragmatic Sanction be respected and put into force, so that the archduchess might take possession of her kingdoms? Secondly, since the imperial throne was not open to women, would the grand duke of Tuscany be elected emperor, so that the Empire might remain within the family?

The question of the succession presented no difficulty within the interested countries; only outside these countries was it a subject of dispute. Frederick II, whom many believed to be a frivolous young prince incapable of maintaining his father's achievements, immediately laid claim to Silesian duchies which in the past had been possessed by members of his family, but as fiefs of the kingdom of Bohemia. The courts of Europe wondered if this was not an opportunity for bargaining and if the new queen of Bohemia and Hungary might not consent to sacrifice a part of her territories in order to secure for her husband's election as emperor the vote of the king of Prussia, elector of Brandenburg. In reality, this was quite out of the question. When the Austrian army was defeated at Mollwitz and Silesia was occupied by Prussia, Maria Theresa proved indomitable. She knew the economic value of this province which had been incorporated in the kingdom of Bohemia, with a population of one million and a flourishing linen industry famous throughout the world, and which the king of Prussia coveted because of its very prosperity and because its annexation would enable him to round off his adjacent territories. 'Never will the queen agree to divest her other hereditary states of this tariff country. It would be better to have the Turks outside Vienna, to give the Netherlands to France, to make any concession to Bavaria or Saxony, than to renounce Silesia.'[8]

However, Bavaria and Saxony were to put forward their own claims. The elector of Bavaria and the elector of Saxony, who was king of Poland, had married the two daughters of the Emperor Joseph I. A rather enigmatic sentence in the pact of mutual succession established in 1705 between Leopold and his two sons, the king of the Romans and the king of Spain, could possibly be interpreted to mean that, in the event of the male lines becoming extinct, the rights of Joseph's two daughters would have priority over those of Charles VI's daughters. But, at the time of their marriages, the princesses had renounced all claims to their uncle's inheritance. The elector of Bavaria based his claim not on the rights of his wife, but on those which he held directly from his distant ancestress, the elder daughter of Emperor Ferdinand I, on the principle that the descendants of the first person to acquire rights (*primi acquirentis*) should enjoy priority over the descendants of the last person to possess those rights (*ultimi possidentis*). The Elector Charles Albert was apparently convinced of the legitimacy of his claim, which seemed plausible enough in the climate of juridical sophistry which still characterized European chancelleries in the eighteenth century. But this was merely a pretext devised to further his own interests. Charles Albert was looking beyond the kingdom of Bohemia and the electoral vote appertaining to its monarch, to the imperial crown which had so often been offered to his ancestors and which none of them had dared to accept. The elector of Saxony hoped to obtain the districts of northern Bohemia, which also boasted a strong textile industry and maintained regular trading relations with Saxony, despite the narrowness of the passes in the Elbe valley which provided communication between the two countries. Three German princes now looked on the kingdom of Bohemia as their prey which they were preparing to dismember for their own advantage, because they knew that the dynasty was weakened and that the monarchy was almost incapable of defending itself.[9]

However, the activities of these princes must be viewed in the broad context of European and even world affairs. The chancelleries spoke of European equilibrium;

writers in the tradition of Leibnitz believed in the existence of a Europe, at least a spiritual Europe, which was being torn asunder by futile wars between states, and the Abbé de Saint-Pierre had put forward the prospect of a perpetual peace and an equitable settlement of conflicts. But societies had imperceptibly entered the age of capitalist competition—albeit a commercial capitalism, for technical progress had not yet brought about the birth of industrial capitalism. The principal trade-routes lay across the Atlantic, the South Seas and the Pacific, which gave access to China and Japan. The bankers and merchants of London exerted their strength at the expense of the Spanish Empire and in competition with the growing activity of France, in the Indies and in Canada. At the beginning of the century gold and diamonds had been discovered in Brazil, a Portuguese colony; Portugal had been closely associated with Great Britain since the treaty of 1703. Great Britain thus regarded the events on the Continent as a canker which absorbed the attentions of France and Spain, especially the former, and prevented these countries from devoting all their fiscal and military efforts to the colonies. But Europe, with its vast population of one hundred and thirty millions and conscious of its political maturity, its obligation to uphold the heritage of its past, its refined civilization, the undeniable progress of its economy over thirty years and the general rise in its standard of living, was sufficiently confident of its strength to remain preoccupied with its own problems.

The era of hegemonies had drawn to a close, inasmuch as no state was any longer in a position to impose its law on others. But each country strove to protect its own independence and progress, by not allowing its neighbour to grow too strong and by seeking alliances with countries whose interests coincided roughly with its own. In conducting such a policy, states, or rather governments, were not primarily concerned with the well-being of their peoples, who were expected to obey their princes in accordance with the time-honoured order and to supply them with soldiers and money; it was nonetheless true that, in so far as the military strength of a state guaranteed the inviolability of its territory and averted war, its inhabitants were ensured a greater measure of happiness in their daily lives.

※

Though by no means bereft of prestige, the imperial dignity was no longer of much significance for the Germanic peoples and a realist such as the king of Prussia, skilled in the art of lying, may well have been speaking the truth when he said to the French ambassador Valory that it did not matter to him who was emperor and that he would act only in his own interests. It was more to his advantage to acquire a province of Bohemia. It was said that Frederick II would have no difficulty in raising thirty thousand troops in Silesia within a few months and bringing the total strength of his armies to one hundred and seventy thousand. At this time he certainly bore no hatred towards the Habsburgs and had no reason to oppose the election of the grand duke of Tuscany as emperor. He may even have hoped to find the dynasty more complaisant. France still occupied a key position in continental Europe and had recently acquired prospective possession of Lorraine. The French

Ministry of Foreign Affairs expressed the fear that the grand duke, once he was elected emperor, might be able to stir the body of German states into action and to reclaim his former duchy of Lorraine. This may have been the grand duke's intention, but only in the event of a general war would it have proved practicable.

Cardinal Fleury, the head of the French government, was also vexed by the naval war between Great Britain, a latent adversary of France, and Spain, France's ally, and by the complaisance which Charles VI had shown to Great Britain with regard to the war. In his latter years Prince Eugene considered that Austria could expect nothing positive from France and that the wisest course was to cultivate the friendship of the maritime powers, Great Britain and the United Provinces. It is thus easy to see the reasoning behind Cardinal Fleury's attitude towards Maria Theresa. While courteously expressing his regret at having to uphold interests opposed to her own, he observed that 'the princes find themselves engaged in foreign liaisons which oblige them to go further than they would themselves wish if they were entirely free'. In other words, it was not in the interests of France to uphold or even to respect the rights of the queen, for the simple reason that she was the ally of Great Britain.[10]

In consequence, the French faction, which was committed to the fundamental and insurmountable hostility of Habsburgs and Bourbons, and represented by Chauvelin and Marshal de Belle-Isle, was able to ensure that France supported the claims of the Elector Charles Albert of Bavaria, in the illusion that to have an emperor elected from among the princes under her protection would constitute a victory (treaty of Nymphenburg, 1741). Without declaring war immediately on Maria Theresa and under the pretext of defending the more just dynastic cause, France sent her troops on an expedition along the Danube which brought Charles Albert first to Linz and then into Bohemia, as far as Prague. The city resisted and the students of the university took up arms, following in the tradition of their predecessors of 1648 who had fought against the Swedes commanded by Koenigsmark. But Prague was captured in a surprise assault on 26 November 1741.

These events aroused a divergence of opinion within the kingdom of Bohemia. Coaxed by skilful propaganda and undivided by national distinctions, the peasant masses welcomed the elector of Bavaria, imagining that he would immediately abolish serfdom and in particular the corvée. The hope of social liberation had undoubtedly been kindled. The middle class of Prague was ambiguous in its attitude. As in 1619, because of the trading relations which they were establishing with Saxony along the Elbe, many wished to see the elector, already king of Poland, also chosen as king of Bohemia. Under the auspices of France, a partition treaty had been concluded between Bavaria and Saxony by which Saxony had secured the right of duty-free passage through the territories of northern Bohemia, in order to ensure communication with Moravia. Saxon contingents had taken part in the capture of Prague and had then set up their quarters in the provinces.

The Bohemian nobility was even more hesitant. In the Austrian army which had fought half-heartedly under the command of the grand duke and had failed to halt the advance of the French and the Bavarians, there were Czech generals such as Lobkowicz and Khevenhüller. The Bohemian chancellor, Count Kinský, remained in Vienna, loyal to the dynasty. On 7 December, Charles Albert, who had been established in Prague for two weeks, issued a proclamation in which he laid claim to the Bohemian crown and summoned the Estates to swear the oath of homage. Three stages were fixed for the ceremony: members of the Estates residing in Prague were to take the oath on 19 December, those living in distant parts of the kingdom on 8 January, and those resident abroad on 8 February. Any members of the Estates who evaded this obligation would have their possessions confiscated. Manderscheid, the archbishop of Prague, of Rhenish origin and an opponent of the Habsburgs, boasted of having rallied the greatest number of deputies to the cause of Charles Albert and indeed the ceremony of 19 December proved to be the most solemn and the best attended of the three: some four hundred deputies (about half the total representation of the Estates) were present. The traditional ritual was observed: the sounding of the great bell of St. Guy, Sigmunt, followed by the assembly in the Wladislas Room for the royal election and the acts of homage. The sequel to this great occasion was less brilliant. The king left Bohemia for Frankfurt to make preparations for his election as emperor, which took place in that city in January 1742. He had entrusted the government of his kingdom to a delegation of seven members under the presidency of Count Philip Kolowrat. The Estates were forced to approve heavy fiscal contributions which they found difficulty in paying. Bohemia found itself subjected to levies from all sides: the French, the Saxons, the Prussians and the Austrians.

Only twenty-four lords and forty-six knights attended the ceremony of homage on 8 January. Some nobles resorted to the ambiguous expedient of sending representatives to the ceremony and at the same time justifying themselves to Maria Theresa on the ground that their properties were in danger of confiscation. Undoubtedly, the ruling classes of Bohemia were no more enthusiastic towards the new regime than they were loyal to the queen. The upper aristocracy had lost its old sense of pride in the kingdom of Bohemia; the time of conspiracies was past and the country no longer possessed men of intrepid character from whose ranks would emerge a national leader to oppose hereditary claimants to the throne. The sole concern of the great nobles was to preserve individual fortunes and their attitudes were determined by considerations of convenience. Perhaps greater courage and loyalty were to be found among the minor nobility and the officers of the Circles, such as Mladota, captain of the Circle of Kouřim, who remained stubbornly faithful to his queen and who, when arrested by the French, was compelled by them to translate the conversation in Czech which he had exchanged with his wife. The young people in the colleges (moulded, admittedly, by the Jesuits) showed 'much ill will against the emperor'.

Throughout 1742 the Czech population of Bohemia, which only wanted to work in peace as it had done for nearly a century, had to bear the heavy burden of occupation by foreign troops, placed on its territory because of rivalries between great powers none of which took any interest in its fate. The question of improving the condition of the peasantry was, however, raised. The government of Charles Albert, king of Bohemia, whom Marshal de Belle-Isle served as an adviser, and the government of Maria Theresa entered into a bidding contest in which each thought it could turn peasant unrest to its own advantage. In Vienna, the president of the Hofkammer and the high officers of the government lost no time in holding discussions with the Bohemian chancellor, Joseph Philip Kinský, on the advisability of abolishing serfdom. Kinský maintained that serfdom was in no way connected with the punishment inflicted on the Bohemian nation after the White Mountain, but was a long-established *conditio rusticorum* peculiar to the Slavs; but he admitted that landowners often showed great harshness and that, without tampering with the basic principle of serfdom, it would be possible to grant personal liberty to peasants who were willing to join the army. Such was the general purport of the patents issued by Maria Theresa on 29 April and 28 May 1742, promising enfranchisement to those peasants who agreed to serve in the Austrian army for a period of three years. In retaliation, and in spite of the reticence of Bohemia's governing delegation, Marshal de Belle-Isle, commander of the French forces, decided to publish on 13 July a patent in the name of Charles Albert, promising freedom to all peasants willing to take up arms against Austria. This was the signal for a popular insurrection. Karel David, a Czech who rallied to the emperor and the French, tried to form a peasant army. But the army was not able to achieve much or to gain sufficient public sympathy to instigate a liberating revolution. Even Karel David, raised to the rank of count of the Empire by the Emperor Charles VII, did not refuse to take part in discussions with the emissaries of the Austrian general, Königsegg.

On 24 June the Austrian army had begun the siege of Prague. The French army, immured within the city, was compelled to take stricter measures for its defence. During the previous six months the quartermaster-general, Séchelles, had earned the reputation of a ruthless administrator. The military authorities succeeded in maintaining discipline and preventing serious disorder, but the French were accused of being 'a vain, ambitious and irreligious nation bent on extending its domination over the whole earth'. On several occasions Belle-Isle attempted to come to terms with the Austrian generals so that his army could make an honourable withdrawal from Bohemia. His hopes of deliverance then turned to the army of Maillebois, which entered Bohemia via Eger but failed to reach Prague. In December he made a heroic decision: evading the blockading army, he managed to lead the greater part of his troops (fourteen thousand men) out of the city and as far as Eger. The retreat from Bohemia was regarded as a great feat of military prowess at the time. Belle-Isle had left a small garrison in Prague under the command of Colonel Chevert, who negotiated the terms of capitulation and emerged with the honours of war. The Austrian army re-entered the city, whereupon Archbishop Manderscheid, unperturbed by the fact of having been one of the most ardent collaborators of the Franco-Bavarian regime, summoned the faithful to a *Te Deum*. But as he intoned the words 'Salvam fac, Domine, reginam nostram', people looked at one another and murmured. At the coronation of the queen on 18 May it was, significantly, the archbishop of Olmütz who officiated.

In her reconquest of Bohemia, where she took care not to indulge in futile reprisals, Maria Theresa owed her success to two factors. One was the attitude shown by Hungary, or rather the force which the concept of statehood and the autonomy of the political class still held in that country. In the desperate situation in which she found herself, Maria Theresa decided to appeal to the Hungarian nation's sentiment of honour and chivalry.

Respectful of the tradition of her father and of the Hungarian Constitution, she lost no time in going to Pressburg for her coronation at the Diet (June 1741). She appeared there in all the grace of her youth, even more appealing because of her recent misfortunes and because of the presence in her arms of a new-born child, Joseph, her first son (her first three offspring had been girls, two of whom had died). If one considers that at the present time, under a socialist government and in a period ill-disposed to expressions of romantic tenderness for the past, a bridge in Budapest still bears the name of Elizabeth of Bavaria, queen of Hungary, and the statue of the Archduke Joseph still stands on one of the city's squares, one can appreciate the collective sensibility of the Hungarian nation: the people of Hungary, who even today value their tradition of independence above all else, were never engulfed or enslaved under the Habsburg dynasty, but faithfully honoured the memory of those sovereigns who behaved honourably towards their country. The offering of life and blood to 'King' Maria Theresa—'Vitam et sanguinem pro rege nostro Maria Theresia'—was thus no empty gesture, but a reflection of the national temperament.

The nobles of Hungary, because they had remained more independent, both of Vienna and in the conditions of their daily existence, less involved in the capitalist system of the West and more susceptible to simple and lofty emotions, responded to the appeal of Maria Theresa. Between the nobility and the queen a spirit of true and chivalrous concord was established. In return for the confirmation of religious and fiscal privileges, the Diet granted the queen six regiments for use outside the kingdom and also settled the insurrection within the kingdom. Never before had a Hungarian army fought for any purpose other than the defence of its own territory. Admittedly, Hungarian soldiers had been enlisted in the imperial regiments but henceforth a small Hungarian army stood permanently at the disposal of the sovereign: as one historian has judiciously observed, Hungary, once a bulwark protecting the hereditary states against the Turks, had become a reserve from which the government drew both men and money for its operations in the West, in defence of the hereditary states and the entire monarchy. It was with the assistance of Hungary that the Austrian army achieved the occupation of Bavaria in 1742 and the liberation of Bohemia in 1743. Through a decision rendered no less effective by the length of the negotiations which preceded it, Hungary had saved the House of Austria.[11]

Returning chivalry for chivalry, Maria Theresa promised never to interfere with Hungary's privileges. The necessity of observing her pledge made it difficult for her to undertake the internal reforms which she recognized to be urgent. Under her reign, Hungary was to remain indubitably poorer than the other Danubian countries, but at the same time enjoyed a greater freedom and was always loyal.

In a sense, this indomitable particularism of Hungary within the Danubian complex provided a foundation for the association of two states which differed in their constitutions and their political regimes, foreshadowing the advantages and dangers of the Dual Monarchy as a solution to the problems of the following century.

The second factor contributing to the reconquest of Bohemia had a less glorious basis: the need to restore peace with the king of Prussia in order to divert from the struggle an adversary less dangerous than France. Maria Theresa had no choice but to cede the greater part of Silesia and, in the mountains, the county of Glatz, by the treaties of Breslau and Berlin. Only the regions of Teschen and Opava remained. According to the ideas of the time, however, a territorial renunciation of this kind could not be regarded as wholly sincere. Maria Theresa never ceased to look for an opportunity to recover this vital province which had been snatched from the kingdom of Bohemia.

It was in the hope of obtaining Silesia by an international settlement that Maria Theresa allowed herself in 1743 to be drawn by Great Britain into the war against France, in which her armies threatened Metz, Lorraine and Alsace, rekindling hostility between Bourbons and Habsburgs to no purpose. Since Prussia was in alliance with France, Frederick II invaded Bohemia and occupied Prague in an attempt to divert the Austrian armies. The Emperor Charles VII died in 1745. His son, the new elector of Bavaria, cherished no ambitions concerning the imperial crown. After reaching a reconciliation with the elector, by the peace of Füssen, Maria Theresa withdrew from Bavaria. The new emperor was her husband, Francis I, grand duke of Tuscany. Maria Theresa had thus become empress and it now remained for her to reconquer Bohemia yet again. In the course of the war the Austrian army had regained some of its old vigour: it fought well, but could not have been maintained without British subsidies. Indeed, British policy continued to dominate Europe. Great Britain was alarmed by the French successes in the Low Countries (the battle of Fontenoy, in 1745, the last great victory of the French monarchy), the support which France was giving to the Stuart pretender and the danger of a Prussian advance into Hanover, the personal domain of the British king. In this context the conflict between Austria and Prussia on account of Silesia was of a secondary, local character. Great Britain and Prussia then exchanged guarantees and Maria Theresa found herself compelled to sign the peace of Dresden with Frederick II; by the terms of the treaty she recovered Bohemia but not Silesia. Three years later, by the peace of Aix-la-Chapelle (1748), Maria Theresa regained Belgium, which the British were reluctant to leave in the possession of its French conquerors. Silesia remained under the control of Prussia. France and Austria, with no deep cause for conflict between them, had engaged each other in combat for indirect reasons of rivalry between the maritime powers.

The peace of Aix-la-Chapelle was a bitter disappointment to Frenchmen and the victor of Fontenoy, Marshal de Saxe, protested against the result achieved, at the cost of much bloodshed, by the tortuous policy of departments and ministers. In Vienna it was observed that the alliance with Great Britain had involved the deaths of a great many Austrian, Czech and Hungarian soldiers on the battlefields of Germany and Italy, without their sacrifice achieving the restoration of Silesia to the kingdom of Bohemia. In such circumstances, the last great idea of Louis XIV might seem to possess a new cogency: if the two strongest powers on the Continent were to be reconciled, who would be able to disturb the peace of Europe? A reversal of alliances was imminent. Since the time of Louis XIV, however, two other European states had grown to maturity: Prussia and Russia. Even if it had nothing to fear from France, Austria could never permit these neighbouring countries of eastern Europe to extend their territories without compensation for its own power. Another possibility was emerging, more remote but decisive in its importance. If Poland, weakened and badly governed, was one day to cede provinces to Russia and to Prussia, and if Prussia was then to refuse to give back Silesia, it would be necessary for Austria to take its share of the shameful plunder in order to maintain equilibrium. As war gave way to bargaining, territorial combinations were arranged the sole justification for which rested on the manoeuvrings of chancelleries and the purely political conception of a balance of power. But it was essential for the dynasty to base its strength on the reality, both material and spiritual, represented by the association of Danubian states: Austria, Bohemia and Hungary. During the respite of peace provided by the Congress of Aix-la-Chapelle, the dynasty faced the task of transforming this group of countries into a great power by improving their administration, making better use of their resources and judiciously promoting their prosperity.[12]

The crowns of the two kingdoms of Bohemia and Hungary and the archducal cap of Austria, which had fallen to Maria Theresa of Habsburg, and the crown of the Holy Roman Empire, awarded to Francis of Lorraine, shed their lustre around this royal couple who still seem familiar to us today, thanks to the careful studies of historians and an abundance of royal portraits. Within her states Maria Theresa enjoyed primacy of position. Her husband, for whom she had secured the status of co-regent in Austria in case she should leave a minor as her heir, 'sat at her left side'.[13] Invested with the highest dignity in Europe, Francis was not merely a prince consort. In addition to the Imperial Chancellery, he supervised his own private chancellery in the Kaiserhaus, on the Wallnerstrasse not far from the Hofburg. There he concerned himself with his personal states and patrimony—Tuscany, the county of Falkenstein in the Rhineland and the revenues from Lorraine which he received in compensation for the duchy. An excellent administrator, Francis was the founder of the Habsburgs' private fortune, as distinct from the revenues provided by their states, and he was thus in a position to make advantageous loans to the treasury when it found itself in difficulties.

Their marriage had been a love-match, especially for Maria Theresa, captivated by the young prince of Lorraine who had come to Vienna to be educated. Although Francis I was not always irreproachable in his conduct, the couple enjoyed the best of relationships, as is evident from the birth of sixteen children between 1737 and 1756.

A robust and handsome pair (Maria Theresa had the physique of her mother, a Wolfenbüttel, rather than that of the Habsburgs), neither lived into old age, the result of neglecting their health. Though above the ordinary in both intelligence and character, they lacked a basic education and were incapable of speaking or writing any language correctly. Maria Theresa expressed herself in Viennese dialect; on the reports in German which she received from her officials she made notes in her own distinctive French. The emperor gave the impression of being a Frenchman when speaking German and a German when speaking French.[14] It often happened that princes were both illiterate and cultured, because in their early years their education had been constantly interrupted by official functions and hunting, which made any sustained study impossible, and then in later years, as curiosity was awakened, their minds were nurtured by conversations with educated persons and scholars and by an interest in libraries and collections. Francis I possessed a keen appreciation of the life of the spirit. His religious, even mystical preoccupations, uncomplicated by dogma and theology, smoothed the way for his initiation to freemasonry.[15] Maria Theresa was a pious woman deeply attached to the practice of her religion, generous in her alms-giving and in her donations to shrines of pilgrimage. She shared the intolerance of her time, but had no taste for persecution. Quite simply, she believed that she was doing right: 'I must show no spirit of persecution, but, even more important, no spirit of tolerance, nor recognize all religious opinions as of equal worth. I must conduct myself thus as long as I live, until the moment when I shall descend into the crypt to join my predecessors, with the hope that my son will be as great and as religious as they.'[16] This fidelity to tradition and the fervent attachment to the memory of a father who, in her eyes, represented the model of kingship, did not prevent her from undertaking reforms. Maria Theresa was far too intelligent not to have perceived the chaotic state of the government when she came to the throne, and was keenly aware of the abuses constantly uncovered by the inquiries which she ordered; moreover, convinced of her responsibility towards the least of her subjects, conscious of her royal calling and very industrious, she had no faith in the efficacy of spectacular reorganizations of the kind undertaken by Peter the Great, Frederick II or Catherine II. In her blend of peasant simplicity and dignity, qualities characteristic of a genuine aristocrat, Maria Theresa belonged to the Baroque age rather than to the century of the Enlightenment, whose scholarly principles she admitted were beyond her comprehension. She was the *Landesmutter*, the mother of her lands and peoples. She was never guilty of self-seeking complaisance towards any person, however great or rich, but intended to be obeyed by each and every one of her subjects. 'If anyone does not wish to obey, let him be left in peace, but let him never appear again before my eyes.' From the obedience and fidelity both of individuals and of communities, she derived a sweet and subtle satisfaction. A woman could not be head of the army, but Maria Theresa loved the military spirit of devotion and sacrifice. During the journey for the imperial election in 1745, she stopped at Heidelberg to inspect her army, which was then in Germany. Since her pregnant condition prevented her from appearing on horseback, she rode in a carriage past her assembled troops and was enchanted by their fine demeanour. Later, to Marshal Daun, who on 18 June 1757 had gained the victory over Prussia at Kolín—the greatest victory of her reign—Maria Theresa addressed the following message, which both echoes the Middle Ages and presages the Romantic era, the gesture of the lady to the knight who has fought in her honour: 'On 18 June, the anniversary of the monarchy . . . the monarchy is beholden to you for its safety and I am beholden to you for the existence of my fine and cherished army. As long as I live, this will never vanish from my heart and from my memory; on the contrary, it seems to me that, as the years go by, the sentiment will grow more fresh and more intense. May God long preserve in the service of the State, the army, the military domain and my own person, my best, my true and loyal friend. And I am for ever his most dear lady!'[17]

Such was the woman who, both for the glory of her royal dignity and for the welfare of her subjects, took it upon herself to transform her hereditary lands into a modern state. She was encouraged in this purpose by a Silesian administrator, Count Haugwitz, 'the man with no other ambition than the ideal, once recognized, of total personal disinterestedness and unswerving devotion to his sovereign', who feared neither enlightenment nor the hatred of those whose interests he thwarted.[18] The practice followed throughout the two Silesian wars, which had consisted of rectifying defects in the administration by reforms of expediency, had produced no tangible results. In the individual states the Diets, even though they had largely accepted the government's fiscal demands, failed to ensure that taxes were efficiently collected by their officials; the regional administrations were in debt and the result was general confusion.

At the higher administrative level, in Vienna, the functions of the principal organs of government (the Hofkanzlei, the Hofkammer and the Hofkriegsrat) were in constant conflict. For Haugwitz, reform could not be partial. In his view, it was necessary to ensure the efficacy of the sovereign's authority, since she held sole responsibility for the territories as a whole and needed assurance that her exchequer would receive the funds necessary for the upkeep of the army, general expenditure and the public weal. It was essential, therefore, to develop the function of the sovereign in the direction of absolutism and to make the juxtaposed states operate as a single entity. Haugwitz drew his inspiration from the example of Prussia and from what he thought he knew of French institutions. He declared that his ideas were supported by all the publicists, and in particular Wilhelm von Schröder, the theoretician of mercantilism. Did not Schröder consider it to be the duty and fundamental right of the sovereign to provide for the maintenance of his army and to improve the economic system throughout his territory in order to increase fiscal revenue? Haugwitz had first tested his theories in Opava, in what remained of Silesia, and had then been sent to Carniola and finally to Carinthia. Everywhere he had encountered the same administrative and financial chaos: governments in debt, pensions awarded for no good reason to high dignitaries, even in the Councils at Vienna, and an unjust distribution of taxes. The nobles and the clergy escaped taxation, causing this burden to fall on their subjects, whose only refuge was in evasion and fraud, some paying too much and others too little. In all three countries, Haugwitz had succeeded in restoring order and rapidly improving the yield of taxation, by appointing new officials responsible solely to the sovereign. Maria Theresa, converted to his methods, decided to reform the administration of her hereditary states along the same lines. She allowed Hungary, the Netherlands and the duchy of Milan to retain their ancient constitutions; in fact, the methods by which taxes were distributed and collected in the duchy of Milan seemed to produce fruitful results and could even serve as a model.

At the beginning of 1748 Haugwitz declared that the essential thing was to provide for the upkeep of an army of one hundred and eight thousand men and that this would only be achieved by abandoning the old practices. In the case of Bohemia, the principles of the Constitution of 1627 would not be touched, but their application would be radically modified. A system of administrative and fiscal absolutism would be introduced of a kind which had never existed previously. It is true that, in the kingdom, the captains of the Circles had been appointed by the sovereign since 1627 and bore the title of 'royal captain', and that they had been empowered, if necessary, to compel the great lords to apply the corvée patents of 1680, 1717 and 1738. But these 'royal captains', recruited among the local nobility (two captains for each Circle, one from the order of lords, the other from the order of knights), paid by the Diet and inevitably caught up in the extraordinary complexity of administrative departments, had no direct contact with the sovereign who appointed them and whom they represented. The absolutism of Ferdinand II had been predominantly religious in character, a means of bringing the country back to Catholicism, protecting the lands of the Church, and uprooting and discouraging Protestantism. Considerations of this kind had long lost their importance: the people had been converted and even appeared to be fervent Catholics in most regions. What mattered now was that, in the fiscal and administrative field, the authority which the constitution recognized as belonging to the sovereign should be effectively exercised. The Estates would not be deprived of their right to vote ordinary military contributions and to administer the revenues of the royal domain within the country (*cameralia*), but responsibility for distributing and levying military contributions would be entrusted to direct agents of the sovereign. Two methods of government were in conflict: the old, aristocratic, and the new, absolutist. A special royal council held in Vienna on 29 January 1748 examined the problem: beside the empress sat her husband and her brother-in-law, Prince Charles of Lorraine, the chancellor of state (since 1742 the minister for foreign affairs), the chancellor of Bohemia, representatives of the Imperial Chancellery, the Ministerial-Banco-Deputation and the General War Commissariat, and also Haugwitz and Bartenstein. All, even the chancellor of Bohemia, Frederick Harrach, admitted that the financial departments were in total chaos and that reform was necessary. The partisans of tradition considered that the task should be entrusted to the Estates, which alone were entitled to introduce reforms. When Haugwitz explained his proposals, he boldly asserted that 'if it is desired to place a country in peril, all that is necessary is to leave the Estates free to act as they choose'. Everyone gave his opinion and the majority was opposed to Haugwitz. But the empress, unruffled, pronounced in his favour. The emperor then drew the necessary conclusion. 'Since the empress had made her opinion known so clearly and distinctly, everyone had now to submit to that opinion and could no longer oppose, either directly, indirectly, secretly or publicly, the execution of her will.' Thus, personal fidelity to the sovereign compelled these aristocrats to accept the principle, and soon the application, of a reform which considerably diminished the authority of their social group within the individual countries, and in particular within Bohemia. The Estates had been defeated and were in retreat before the power of the prince.[19]

It was now possible to introduce the great reforms of 1749. The Chancellery of Bohemia was suppressed (but not the office of chancellor) and the administrative and financial institutions were merged into a single authority in Vienna, the *Directorium in publicis et cameralibus*. The lieutenancies which had represented the sovereign in each country were replaced by a council, the *Representation und Kammer*, answerable to a Court Commission based in Vienna. In each of the Circles of Bohemia there would henceforth be only one 'captain', nominated and remunerated by the queen. Each captain was to be responsible to the Representation und Kammer and was to establish his department in a public building (previously, the captains had conducted their affairs from their own private dwellings). In a sense, this was the birth of Cis-Leithan Austria, which was to survive until 1918. The hereditary states seemed to have been reduced to the condition of provinces. A peaceful revolution had been accomplished by a woman. At the time, there were no upheavals, but Czech historians have since denounced the reforms of 1749 as a most cruel violation of the historic rights of their country, a defeat more terrible than that of the White Mountain. Vienna, and no longer Prague, was to decide the fate of the Bohemian nation, both Czechs and Germans. The Czech state had lost what freedom it had been able to preserve in the management of its own affairs.[20]

An Austrian historian with an expert knowledge of constitutional law observes: 'The great significance of these measures for the future of the monarchy cannot be shown more clearly than by recalling that, in the constitutional programme which they put forward in the nineteenth century, the Czechs saw the reform of 1749 as the fundamental cause of their loss of independence.'[21] This is to recognize that the events of 1749 had even more far-reaching implications than contemporary observers appear to have realized. Hitherto, the Habsburg monarchy had possessed the character of an association of states. Now, in its western part, it was becoming a centralized, unified state. The Chancellery had represented in Vienna the lawful existence of the different countries and their acceptance of association. As Josef Pekař has written: 'The Bohemian Chancellery was the expression of the administrative and juridical autonomy and, in a general manner, the independence of the Czech state.' It was this which was foundering.

Undoubtedly, the reforms of Haugwitz were of an aggressive character. However, it was not the countries themselves or their peoples that he was attacking, but the system of privileged orders, government by the nobility. The minister of the queen-empress, in his desire to make the monarchy strong, had come into collision with a body of men who clung to local customs and were incapable of taking a broad view. The past cannot be changed by supposition, but if the role of this Silesian bureaucrat had been assumed by a chancellor of Bohemia or of Austria, some high official of Moravia, Carinthia or the Tyrol, who could have devised a programme of reforms to prove that within the Danubian states there still existed forces capable of restoring order to the House of Austria, history would have taken a different course. In this way, the centres of action could have remained within the individual states, whereas in 1749 the whole territory suddenly gravitated towards Vienna. The city on the Danube, for so long merely one among others, and then the residential capital of the dynasty, was now confirmed as the political capital and sole activating force of the entire monarchy.

Haugwitz thought only in terms of general administration: the individual rights of the Estates were of no interest to him, arousing neither his affection nor his antipathy; he was not concerned with the importance of their contribution to the life of the Netherlands, the duchy of Milan or Hungary. He simply observed that in Silesia, Carniola and Carinthia he had found disorder to be a natural consequence of administration by the departments of the Estates and their agents. It was time to put an end to such negligence. If the privileged orders wished to retain the right of voting taxes, there was no objection to their being allowed this honour, on condition that they 'freely' accepted the figure fixed by the central government and that the distribution and collection of taxes were entrusted to agents of the central government, and not to agents of the Estates.

The question of ethnic origin or language was not involved at this stage. Both the Germans of Bohemia and the Czechs were equal subjects of the kingdom. They all came under its laws without distinction. It has often been said that Maria Theresa did not cherish towards the kingdom of Bohemia the same feelings of warmth inspired in her by Hungary. In view of the events of 1741, this would have been quite natural. But it is often forgotten that she had the royal palace in Prague restored and extended[22] and also ordered the reconstruction and transformation of the castle in Buda. At the Hradčany she founded a chapter of canonesses recruited among the young ladies of the Bohemian nobility and appointed one of her daughters as their abbess; the *Damenstift* or *Šlechticen ústav* existed until 1918 and the last abbess died in 1961.[23] The queen knew full well how great a contribution the kingdom made to her Empire by providing money, soldiers and merchandise. It was not in her interests to humiliate Bohemia. Moreover, was she not determined to recover Silesia, a province of the kingdom? At the same time, she had no desire to revive the special prestige of the realm of St. Wenceslas at the risk of provoking public opinion in the other countries. Already, in the fresco painted by Altomonte in the church of St. Florian, the monarchy was represented only by two figures: Austria and Hungary. In the allegorical decoration of the Schönbrunn galleries the place allotted to Bohemia is small.[24] Imperceptibly, it was being admitted that the kingdom was subordinate to Austria, like the Alpine provinces, or more exactly, rather as the kingdom of Croatia was associated with but also subordinate to the kingdom of Hungary.

Since fiscal considerations dominated the whole programme of reform, it was necessary to provide the tax structure with a solid basis. Haugwitz arranged for taxes to be granted by the Estates for a certain number of years (ten years in Bohemia) and for rates to be then revised. It has already been seen how in 1654, on the conclusion of the Thirty Years' War, an ordinance was issued prohibiting in Bohemia the practice of confusing the lands of the dominical and the rustical in claiming tax-exemption for seigniorial properties; a first census of the rustical had also been undertaken. At that time, however, declarations were required only for arable land under cultivation. What was needed was a more comprehensive survey of properties that could be taxed. Maria Theresa's first cadastral survey was made in 1749, but applied only to the rustical; in 1755 a second survey was taken and extended to the dominical, which was to be taxed, but at a lower rate than the rustical. The taxable unit was established arbitrarily as a certain area of land, which might consist of the property of one or of several taxpayers. The first survey reduced the number of taxable units, but increased the rate of contribution from fifty-four to sixty gulden. The important thing was that taxes should be paid regularly.[25]

Inevitably, the great domain was to remain untouched. The only difference was that royal officials possessed greater authority to intervene in conflicts between peasants and the seigniorial administration. Justice had been separated from the other functions of government by the creation in Vienna of a High Court, which survived until 1848. In each country a tribunal was established to hear the causes of subjects, who would be able to obtain the free assistance of advocates nominated by the Representation und Kammer. The intention was a noble one, but its realization proved difficult owing to the reluctance of the peasants to expose themselves to the rancour of the lord's bailiff.

Although the problems of the land, both economic and social, were the most urgent, owing to the general importance of agricultural production and the large proportion of the population involved, the government took a keen interest in industry. Manufactures were encouraged and a central organization was created, the *Universalkammerzdirektorium*, a kind of general ministry of commerce, which was subsequently attached to the *Directorium in publicis et cameralibus*. The ideas of economist writers were widely put into practice and the great landed proprietors, both ecclesiastical and lay, were invited to open factories on their estates. The most suitable regions for these experiments seemed to be the environs of Vienna and, above all, Bohemia, where labour was cheap. Textiles were the most favoured sector, because the government was anxious to compensate for the loss of the Silesian linen industry. Count Harbuval de Chamaré, to whom the Emperor Francis I (always a shrewd investor) entrusted funds, was a Silesian contractor. At Potštejn, in Bohemia, he established a large linen factory with annexes for bleaching and dyeing. In order to reach as wide a clientele as possible, within the country and abroad, cloth of every quality was made, from the commonest fabrics to the most elegant fine linen. In addition to linen factories there were wool factories and spinning-mills. A Viennese merchant, J. M. Schmidt, came to Nové Kdyně to set up a wool factory which was to enjoy prolonged prosperity. Industrial capitalism was dawning. A part of the peasantry now depended for its livelihood on manufactures, working either at home, where it provided yarn, or in the harsh conditions of the factory, where the working day extended throughout the daylight hours. Was the corvée really more terrible? The peasants employed in the factories were recruited mostly from among those with little or no land, the vagrants and the dispossessed, all who lacked the solid foundations of landed property. The labouring class was thus split into two categories: some sought their living from arable land and the results of their own independent effort, even if this effort was hindered and undermined by serfdom and the corvée; the others depended on wages, the reward received for directed effort of an increasingly rigorous nature. The government did not interfere in the matter of wages, except in the glass-works, whose reputation and production were rivalling those of Venice, in both the internal and the external markets. The glass-works lay along the periphery of Bohemia and it was feared that the workmen might leave if foreigners offered them better wages. It was important that the Austrian glass industry should continue to produce its beautiful cups with their incomparable colouring, finely cut like cameos, miracles of art the perfection of which has enchanted successive generations.[26]

A well-conceived system of customs legislation (1753) protected the hereditary states, providing for the reduction of tolls and the harmonization of the territories as a whole. Commerce and industry contributed to the interplay of interests and already, however slowly, were creating a common fiscal structure, a pattern of exchange which foreshadowed the developments of the future and made the combination of Bohemia-Austria a human association advancing along the path of progress. Vienna found more frequent opportunities for contact with the southern regions of the kingdom and with Moravia than with the Tyrol or Vorarlberg; in many of its activities the capital was beginning to reap the benefit of the labour and the virtues of the Czech population.

※

Since Frederick II insisted on retaining Silesia, the relationship between himself and Maria Theresa, even with the restoration of peace, could only be one of potential hostility. Frederick realized this and clung to the alliance with France. He shrewdly observed that Silesia and Lorraine were two sisters, one of whom had married the king of Prussia and the other the king of France. In other words, these were precarious possessions and it was in the interests of their owners to remain friends.

In the event of war, the king of Prussia could come to the aid of the king of France by attacking Hanover, a possession of the king of England and therefore an ally of Austria. But, in return, he needed a guarantee that Russia, another ally of the House of Austria, would not attack him on his eastern frontier, which was easily accessible via Poland. An agreement between Great Britain and Russia, requiring Russia to attack Prussia if Hanover was threatened, alarmed Frederick II. He decided that the wisest course was to arrange a pact himself, directly with London. He promised to respect the neutrality of Hanover, if Great Britain agreed not to intervene on behalf of Austria (treaty of Westminster, 1756).

The fear that the monarchy might find itself isolated and therefore all the more exposed to an offensive by Prussia induced Prince Kaunitz, one of Maria Theresa's most valuable advisers, who had negotiated the treaty of Aix-la-Chapelle and had been made ambassador in Paris and finally chancellor of state in 1753, to recommend a *rapprochement* with France. The enterprise proved difficult to realize, for there were too many prejudices on both sides: in France, Austria was regarded as the traditional adversary, while the court of Maria Theresa was convinced that the French court remained its worst enemy and also cherished a certain dynastic nostalgia with regard to Alsace and Lorraine.

But a reconciliation was in the interests of both powers. Reforms had been introduced which restored the effectiveness of the Austrian army. A military academy founded at Wiener-Neustadt, in 1752, ensured a better training for officers. Although the Prussian army was still a powerful and well-trained force, excellently equipped, the combination of the French army and a regenerated Austrian army could modify the balance of power. The guarantee which Frederick II had sought from the British finally led to a reversal of alliances: two treaties in succession were signed by Maria Theresa and Louis XV. The objectives envisaged in the treaties were the recovery of Silesia by Austria and the annexation by France of the Austrian Netherlands, which were to be ceded to the infante of Parma, the son-in-law of the French king.

At sea, however, in Canada and India, France was engaged in the struggle against Great Britain, which would not have tolerated the cession of Belgium to a prince who was the relative and protégé of the king of France. The author does not intend to trace in detail the changing military fortunes of the Seven Years' War (1756–63). Briefly, the war was set in motion by the king of Prussia, who launched an offensive against Saxony as a preventive measure; but Frederick II was confronted with the coalition of Russia, France and Austria and, although at first it seemed that he might be able to repeat his former successes in Bohemia, he was very rapidly made to realize the extent of the Austrian military revival. For family reasons the command of the coalition armies was entrusted to an incompetent nuisance, Prince Charles of Lorraine, who suffered a succession of defeats, but other generals showed qualities as leaders and strategists: Daun, for instance, who liberated Prague by his brilliant victory at Kolín, and generals like Laudon and Lacy. The allied troops fought well and, when fortune did not favour them, their endurance and discipline mitigated their failure. Frederick II defended himself fiercely, gaining victories (against the French at Rosbach in 1757) and suffering setbacks alternately. Austrian detachments arrived in Berlin; Silesia and the county of Glatz were reoccupied. As the war dragged on and as diplomatic complications presented themselves (in particular, a further reversal of alliances caused by the death of the Tsarina Elizabeth, a faithful ally of France and Austria, and the defection of Russia under its new tsar, a German prince, Peter III, who joined forces with Frederick), both camps began to seek the conclusion of peace.

Great Britain, which acquired practical possession of France's colonial empire by the cession of influence in India and territories in Canada, also secured the continued presence of Austria in the Netherlands. On the other hand, Silesia was not wrested from Prussia. Maria Theresa could only hope that one day her successors would be able to recover the province. She was ready to consider any policy that would enable her to leave the way open for this eventuality. Consequently, she persisted in the alliance with France: seven years after the conclusion of peace, she gave her youngest daughter, Marie-Antoinette, in marriage to the heir of the French king.

Among the reasons that had induced her to sign the treaty of Huburtusburg with Prussia, on 15 February 1763, was a dynastic consideration. Frederick II agreed to give his vote to elect the Archduke Joseph as king of the Romans. The emperor was by no means an old man and still enjoyed excellent health, but it was necessary to look to the future. The king of Prussia, practical as ever, considered that the preservation of Silesia was well worth a second vote for the Lorrainers. He did not think that the time had yet come when he would 'share the Empire with the emperor', as Antony and Octavius had once shared Caesar's inheritance. Yet his very presence robbed the imperial function of its reality. The emperor was no longer the sole arbiter of the affairs of the Empire; his vassal had become his rival. In certain respects, the rise of the Hohenzollerns had resembled that of the Habsburgs: it had been achieved by the same patient annexation of territories and the same accumulation of military successes. Geographically, the Hohenzollern power extended over northern Germany, which was Protestant and, in certain regions, already engaged in industrial capitalism; behind the Habsburgs lay the Catholic countries of the south and a vast territory foreign to the Empire: Hungary.[27]

The difficulties of the Seven Years' War had encouraged criticisms of the system devised by Haugwitz. Prince Kaunitz, a great lord of cosmopolitan sophistication, with an appreciation of literature and the arts and enriched by his experiences in Brussels, Turin and Paris, considered the machinery constructed by Haugwitz too cumbersome. He did not believe it expedient to remove the nobles from public affairs and to humiliate them in front of the bureaucrats. Neither did he think that the creation of a separate judicature made it necessary to combine administration and finance. In 1760 the political structure was crowned with a Council of State (*Staatsrat*), which assumed the functions previously exercised by the Privy Conference, but as a ministry with supreme authority. The membership of the Council of State was small. There were three representatives of the order of lords, which meant that the higher nobility would have new opportunities for advancement and could be more closely associated, through the ablest of its members, with the direction of the Empire. Only they would hold the title of Minister of State; their three colleagues, the *Gelehrte* or knights, were to be Secretaries of State.

The separation of administration and finance involved the suppression of the *Directorium in publicis et cameralibus*. In its place, a single chancellery for Bohemia and Austria provided the advantage of reviving the prestige of old institutions and at the same time bringing the kingdom and the archduchies under one administration. The Representation und Kammer was also to disappear to make way for provincial governments with increased powers and names which varied from one country to another: *Gubernium* in Bohemia and Moravia-Silesia, *Regierung* in Upper Austria and 'captainry' in Lower Austria, Carinthia and Carniola. There seemed no reason why the old dignities should not be restored to use and so the governor of Bohemia was awarded the traditional title of 'grand burgrave', which survived until 1848. Finances, now separated from administration, came under three supreme authorities: the Hofkammer for general financial administration, the

Generalkasse, responsible for accountancy, and the *Hofrechenkammer* or Audit Chamber, which maintained a check on the whole financial system and to which the Ministerial-Banco-Deputation was also subordinated.

Monetary innovations tended to render the general economy of the monarchy more flexible. In 1750 the monetary system was modified by the issue of silver coins of twenty gulden or ten thalers to the Cologne mark of 233·81 grams. Accepted by a convention signed by several states of the Empire, the new currency was often called 'convention coin' and was to remain in use until 1858. The beautiful Maria Theresa silver thaler with the effigy of the empress was sought even in the East. In 1762 the Bank of Vienna began issuing notes (*Zettel*) which did not bear interest but were accepted by the State treasury in payment of taxes; they were also used to a certain extent in private commercial transactions. These were the signs of a healthier economy in the monarchy as a whole.[28]

The renewed vigour of the House of Austria, manifested by the reorganization of the State, served to raise the prestige of Vienna and, to a certain degree, that of Prague in the intellectual circles of the Germanic Holy Roman Empire. The German universities, in particular those of Leipzig and Hall, were moving away from the old scholastic methods and adopting a new philosophy which two great figures had helped to elaborate and propagate: Christian Thomasius (1655–1728) and Hans Christian Wolff, a Silesian by birth (1679–1754). Both were disciples of Leibnitz and had studied the entire intellectual heritage of the seventeenth century: the jurists Grotius and Puffendorf, and the philosophers from Descartes to Bayle via Hobbes. It was their conviction that philosophy must be separated from theology. The exercise of human reason, freed from the shackles of authority, was to lead humanity to happiness. For Thomasius, the light of revelation and the light of reason were two distinct sources of knowledge: one enlightened the world of religion and the life beyond, the other made it possible to ensure the human race greater happiness in its earthly sojourn. The extension of knowledge in every field and exchanges among scholars, who could acquaint themselves with each other's hypotheses and conclusions in the *Acta eruditorum* founded by Leibnitz, were to rejuvenate thought, to fertilize and strengthen it.

Not all new ideas were received without question; atheism was feared and condemned no less than the vagueness of deism, but the belief was growing that a special vocation was reserved for the Germans. A disciple of Thomasius, Gottsched, the author of *Foundations of the German Language* and a German grammar, strove to purify and improve German, as the French had purified their language in the previous century, thereby ensuring themselves a vast audience in Europe.

Wolff inclined towards a Christian nationalism; in his view, the distinction between reason and faith should not cause them to be opposed to one another in a sterile conflict, but should lead them to harmony. Thus, the philosophy of Wolff, a Protestant who found himself more at ease in the relatively unregulated world of the Reformation than in the strict orthodoxy of Rome, did not exclude Catholic methods. Its following was concentrated in universities such as Salzburg, where it was regarded as an encouragement to the free and disinterested study of religion.[29]

In 1740 a Jesuit mathematician, Father Stepling, who was in communication with Wolff, agreed to assume a professorship at the university of Prague, on the condition that he would be free to teach what he thought: in his opinion, Aristotle's system of physics was outmoded, incompatible with the methods prescribed by the progress of mathematics and therefore incapable of providing a true exposition.

Some Jesuits were personally susceptible to the new ideas, but public opinion was turning against the Society, which was accused of being too formalist in its methods, insufficiently critical and predisposed to an excessively devotional, ritual religion that confined the mind to routine and enfeebled character. For a century the Jesuits had certainly wielded a profound influence, perhaps more profound than was realized, on the whole of Danubian society. They had not been alone in disseminating the ideas and in shaping the sensibilities of the Baroque period, for the other religious orders had embraced this movement and endowed it with their own particular traits. But the initiative for this activity was attributed to the Jesuits. Between the Society and the Benedictines a kind of rivalry developed. Benedictine scholars, reinvigorating the historic methods of erudition under the influence of the French monks of St. Maur, circulated from abbey to abbey, strengthening the links between their houses in Swabia, Salzburg and the Danubian countries. A monk of Zwiefalten, a Benedictine abbey in Swabia, came to Vienna in 1733 and made his influence felt at Melk, at Göttweig and at Břevnov, near Prague. The renewal of intellectual activity among the Benedictines was contemporaneous with the rebuilding of abbeys and abbey churches which took place when Baroque art was in full bloom. There was therefore no obvious incompatibility between this art and the new spiritual ideas. When it was desired to provide the young with a different form of education from that of the Jesuit colleges, it was the Benedictines who were asked to put forward proposals for reform. Both Benedictines and Carthusians inclined towards Augustinian notions of the kind which had been involved in the Jansenist controversy: they favoured a more interior, Christ-centred religion which, though definitely Marian and Tridentine, eschewed Ultramontane excesses and the delightful childishness of Baroque piety. Their ideas were shared by Maria Theresa's physician, Van Swieten, who had come from the Netherlands where he had lived in an atmosphere of hostility to the Society of Jesus. Van Swieten was convinced of the danger of too rigorous an education, especially where religion was concerned. His influence at the court was considerable, for the numerous births in the imperial household gave him an opportunity to display his medical knowledge and at the same time to expound his opinions. In the general reorganization of the administration there was need of a well-educated personnel. The problem of education was thus linked with the reform of the State. In January 1749, Van Swieten obtained the approval of the empress for a programme of reforms which reserved to the sovereign the right to appoint professors to the faculty of medicine and the dean in charge of studies at the university of Vienna. Three years later, the system was extended to the other faculties and a chair of German rhetoric, to be responsible for the teaching of language and literature, was created and entrusted to a Professor Popović (of Slovenian origin, let it be noted). Gottsched came to Vienna in 1749; he was received with sympathy and curiosity. When he was presented at court, the empress graciously apologized for her bad German. Although Vienna still did not possess an academy for the teaching of the German language, which Gottsched and then Klopstock had both considered desirable, the need to raise the quality of intellectual life throughout the country was widely felt among statesmen and in Austrian society, not only for cultural reasons, but also on political grounds, as a means of counterbalancing the prestige which the king of Prussia and his court now enjoyed in the Empire.

Prompted by her own good sense, Maria Theresa approved the creation of the new colleges of higher education which she was informed were necessary. An academy of oriental languages was founded for the training of the consuls who were to be responsible for commerce with Turkey and the East. An academy was created for indigent young nobles, a State-endowed institution with a teaching staff of salaried civil servants. A large part of the programme of this academy, which was inaugurated in 1746, in the palace of La Favorite, and called the *Theresianum*, was devoted to political economy and mathematics. In the faculty of law at Vienna the chairs of natural law and political economy, which were assigned to such eminent figures as Riegger, Martini and Justi, immediately acquired a great reputation.

Jesuits were no longer to be appointed as deans of faculties. This regulation had to be waived when Father Stepling was appointed to the university of Prague. When the Society was suppressed in 1773, a problem presented itself: what was to become of the Jesuit colleges and their pupils? Another order, a rival of the Jesuits, was ready to assume their role: the Piarists who, right up to modern times, were to wield such a powerful influence in Austria, and perhaps to an even greater degree in Hungary. Their methods were more practical than those used by the Jesuits; they aimed to train their pupils not as courtiers, but as good, solid Christians who would fulfil their duties in society. The regulations concerning education introduced in 1775 were the work of a Piarist, Father Gratian Marx; they struck a fairly happy balance between the practical disciplines, which had been neglected, and humanist culture, which was to be made less formal without being completely discarded: three classes were to be devoted to grammar and two classes to humanities (rhetoric and poetry). Instruction was to be given in German.

Elementary education had hitherto been the responsibility of the clergy, regular and secular, and had not been subject to State supervision. Some thought that it would be futile to attempt to organize education for the lower classes of society which, in their opinion, needed only the barest smattering of instruction: in this way, they argued, both the peace of mind of individuals and the order of society would be best served. But this timid view was outmoded. The royal commission formed to study these problems adopted the plan proposed by the abbot of Sagan, J. I. Felbiger. At the lowest level, in the village schools, children would receive instruction from the age of six to twelve years, without being obliged to go to school during the winter months. In Bohemia, classes were to be given in Czech in districts where this was the established language. Senior schools in the chief town of each Circle would teach the rudiments of Latin, history, geography, natural history and drawing. In these schools the language of instruction would be either German or Czech, according to the region. Finally, three training colleges were to be established, in Prague, Brunn and Vienna, with German as the language of instruction.

In this programme of intellectual and educational reform, two dominant ideas converged: the desire to reinvigorate the State and society by making people better able to fulfil their civic and moral obligations to both, and the respect for man's natural right to the enlightenment of reason.

While the seigniorial regime continued to prevail in the country areas, a transformation now took place in the towns of Bohemia as intellectual life assumed a greater intensity. Certain members of the aristocracy displayed their interest in culture and their generous concern for the common good by bold gestures: Count Kinský, general and director of the Military Academy at Wiener-Neustadt, had the family library transferred to the Clementinum; although he was not entirely free to dispose of the library (he was only the usufructuary of a *fideicommissum*), he made it available *ad usum publicum*. The interest in the life of the intellect was lowering social barriers, with the help of freemasonry, which was active in many different sectors of society.

In Prague, where the population rose from 38,500 to 77,500 in thirty years (1754–81), and in Brunn, societies of rural economy were formed for the purpose of studying and spreading the new techniques of crop-growing and stock-raising. A number of short treatises were published in German and in Czech. At Olmütz, in 1747, a citizen named Petrasch founded a society for scholars and men of letters, the *Societas incognitorum*, which was actuated by a rational rather than a sentimental Catholicism, concerning itself with benevolent works and the public good. Later, the *Prager Privatgesellschaft* came into existence, the distant forerunner of the Royal Society of Sciences and Arts of Bohemia, which survived until 1948.[30]

From Leipzig the cultivation of German language and literature spread to Prague and also became established at various intermediate points, such as the Piarist college of Kosmano in northern Bohemia. Seibt was educated at this college and then went to study at Leipzig; in 1764 he became the first professor at the university of Prague who was not a member of the Society of Jesus. His lectures, delivered in a very pure German, attracted noble and middle-class high society, persons such as the grand burgrave Egon Fürstenberg and the merchant Bolzano. In the salons of Bohemia it became the fashion to speak the language of Seibt: *seibtisch reden*.

It would not be true to say that Bohemia's past was now neglected. On the contrary, the Piarist Gelasius Dobner (1719–90) devoted his energies to a critical edition of the chronicler Hajek and spent twenty years on the *Monumenta historica nusquam ante hac edita*; Pelcl, the archivist of the Nostits, was responsible for the appearance in Czech of Balbín's hitherto unpublished *Defence of the Czech Language* and in 1783 conducted the first classes in national history at the faculty of philosophy in Prague. But at a time when the autonomy of the kingdom had dwindled almost to nothing within a centralized Austrian state, German established its preponderance everywhere as the language of educated circles and the active middle class. In applying the philosophy of the Enlightenment to the general policy of the State, the government of Vienna aimed to broaden recruitment to the world of commerce and industry, to swell the ranks of the military and civil engineers who improved the conditions of roads and regularized the system of rivers and canals, to stimulate economic progress in this agrarian and seigniorial society and to promote the rise, almost the irruption, of a middle class which, aware of its solidarity with the monarchy as a whole, would be conscious of being an Austrian middle class. Henceforth, German would seem the natural language on which social advancement would necessarily depend. Inevitably, the Czech language was in peril, for it was now only the language of the peasantry and the world of serfdom. The gravest danger lay in the fact that not all peasants were poverty-stricken: there existed a peasant élite which now began to find itself dissociated from the rest by the social success of its sons, for in order to become a burgess, acquire a position of social importance and rise to greater heights in the hierarchy, it was essential to speak German. The decrees of 1775 had allowed Czech no place in secondary education, not so much through deliberate hostility as through haughty indifference. Never had the language been in such dire jeopardy: those who spoke only Czech were prohibited from advancing beyond a certain social stage, while those who had advanced beyond that stage soon found the language incomprehensible. Around the year 1780 Prague, with a still powerful nobility and a rising middle class, was in the process of becoming a great German provincial city surrounded by a countryside whose inhabitants, loyal to the national idiom, were beginning to seem an alien people.

In Hungary the situation was not quite the same.[31] Here, the essential thing was that the hierarchy of the privileged orders should be respected by the queen. When her librarian, A. J. Kollár, of Slovak origin, published a work maintaining that in Hungary the legislative power belonged to the sovereign rather than to the Estates, and that the sovereign should impose taxes on the nobility and levy troops by his or her own decision, the book caused a scandal and was banned. There could therefore be no question either of modifying the fiscal and juridical privileges of the nobility, or of interfering with the administration of the counties where the *föispan*, the chief administrator, was to remain subordinate to the Estates and relatively independent *vis-à-vis* the Council of Lieutenancy which represented the absent queen. Institutions were left unchanged; the Banat of Temesvár and the zone enclosed by the military boundaries of the Danube, the Save and the Drave were reincorporated in the kingdom and divided once again into counties. The Council of State tried on several occasions, in the time of Kaunitz, to take an interest in Hungary, but could do no more than offer discreet advice. No minister or government department in Vienna was to be allowed to intrude into the kingdom's affairs. The queen was torn between two conflicting sentiments. She felt a genuine affection for the Hungarian nobles, among whom she found excellent officers such as General Hadik, whose troops entered Berlin during the Seven Years' War, and personal friends such as Count Grassalkovich, who afforded her the hospitality of his residence at Gödöllö. On the other hand, Maria Theresa was greatly upset by what she learned or observed of the lot of the peasantry. 'These poor people are bowed down by excessive burdens,' she would say; when the resistance of the Estates proved insurmountable, she would become angry: 'I must act according to my conscience; I do not wish to be damned because of a few magnates and nobles.' An ordinance issued in 1767, the *Urbarium*, prescribed that quit-rent contracts be renewed, that a maximum period for obligatory labour be fixed (an ambiguous measure, since, if the same rule were applied everywhere, the condition of some peasants would be improved, while that of others would be worsened), that the boundaries of peasant holdings be defined and that the prohibitions concerning freedom of movement be relaxed. But only the archbishop of Kalocsa and the bishop of Eger responded promptly to the demands of the queen, whose Christian sentiments they shared. It was easier to improve the personal condition of the peasants by issuing regulations directed at various particular problems: for example, it was forbidden to beat pregnant women, provision was made for free assistance to be given by midwives and for treatment to be given to persons bitten by mad dogs, orphanages were established (the Ursulines of Pressburg), restrictions were imposed on mendicity and an effort was made to establish the gypsies in settlements. That such measures should have been necessary shows how backward and wretched was the condition of the majority of the *jobbágy*. These reforms, although not applied uniformly in all counties, contributed to the personal popularity of Maria Theresa in Hungary.

The queen showed her solicitude for the prestige of her kingdom. From the Pope she obtained the title in Hungary of 'Apostolic Majesty', just as the king of France was 'His Christian Majesty', the king of Spain 'His Catholic Majesty', and the king of Portugal 'His Faithful Majesty'. She restored the position of the Virgin Mary as protectress of the country which had once been dedicated to her: *Regnum Marianum*. She ordered a venerable relic, the hand of St. Stephen, to be brought back from Ragusa to Buda. In the words of a Hungarian historian, 'nothing of this was the fruit of the philosophy of Enlightenment, but issued from the Baroque: indeed, it was only at this moment that our own Hungarian Baroque period achieved fulfilment, acquiring a social meaning which it had previously lacked'. At the same time, Hungarian Catholicism, permeating the countries of western and central Slovakia where it was to survive until the present day, became a more powerful force without, however, excluding a degree of genuine tolerance for other religions. Protestantism remained vigorous wherever it had taken root. In some towns on the plain, such as Kecskemet, the presence of the Catholic and Protestant churches on each side of the square symbolized the Hungarian tradition of religious tolerance.

The rivalry between the Jesuits and the other religious orders also manifested itself in Hungary. At Eger the Society had a flourishing college where the library was decorated with a fresco painted by Kracker, a magnificent composition with an explicit purpose: celebrating the Council of Trent, the fresco stressed the importance of extreme unction, order, the cult of the relics and the *Index Librorum*. But, in contrast with his distant predecessor Pázmány, the primate of Esztergom sought to eliminate the Jesuits from the seminaries and from the university of Nagyszombat. In 1777 the university was transferred to Buda, where it was provided with an observatory, scientific collections and a modern library. In Hungary, also, the suppression of the Society of Jesus was followed by a reorganization of the educational system. Maria Theresa adopted the programme entitled *Ratio educationis* which a former Jesuit, Urményi, had submitted to her. The territory of Hungary was divided into nine educational districts; as in Austria, secondary schools were to teach history (but in this case Hungarian history), natural history, with special emphasis on the mineralogy and flora of the country, and the sciences. In the village schools the local language was used for instruction: Magyar, German, Slovak, Croatian, Ruthenian, Illyrian or Wallachian. It was necessary to use these languages for teaching the rudiments, but in the secondary schools German alone was used. There were immediate protests, for Magyar, the national tongue of cultivated Hungarians, could claim equality of status. However, it was impossible to ignore the fact that German was commonly spoken in most towns and used among merchants not only at Pressburg, which lay near to Vienna, but also in the towns of the plain and the mountain regions.

The promulgation of the *Ratio educationis* was essentially a statement of principle and proved difficult to put into practice. Only a few hundred new schools were opened in a country which at this period numbered some nine million inhabitants. The school inspectors, among whom the clergy were deliberately left in a minority, did not succeed in organizing elementary education. One inspector declared that, as long as the counties refused to show interest, the reforms would have no effect. In the towns, on the other hand, the secondary schools (both Catholic and Protestant) proved quite successful. In 1763 a mining college was opened at Schemnitz.

Thus, in its institutions, its customs and its economy, Hungary was vastly different from the hereditary countries and much farther than mere distance would suggest from the Austro-Bohemian complex which had emerged from the reforms of Maria Theresa. As soon as the traveller found himself on the drier soil of Hungary, where the villages extended in long lines of low dwellings, and then in the boundless spaces of the plain, he was in a different world. The towns produced a no less striking impression, with their mosques converted for Christian worship and minarets which stood side by side with the bulbous towers of Baroque churches.

In both their architecture and their decoration the new residences of the aristocracy followed the prevailing fashion; indeed, they were almost in advance of Western style in their development of Baroque or Rococo art: the mansion of Ráckeve, for instance, which had belonged to Prince Eugene, or Eszterháza and Gödöllö, the latter with its graceful oval and the elegant curve of its fronton. These dwellings provided the setting for the extravagant entertainments, the house-parties lasting several days which were held in the hunting season, and the concerts at which Haydn conducted his early works. The small towns had never assumed a truly urban aspect: around the churches and the administrative buildings the village atmosphere still prevailed. The roads leading from one region to another were little more than tracks; in contrast, the Danube, Tisza and Maros flowed majestically across the plains, though they carried little traffic.

A mosaic of communities and languages characterized by contrasts of splendour and poverty, but in which there existed a common consciousness of belonging to the same state, an immobile society at the heart of a rapidly advancing Europe—such was the Hungary of the counties, which had been delivered from the Turks, but not yet assimilated by Western civilization, and which was proud of its individuality: *Extra Hungariam, non est vita. Si est vita, non est ita* (Outside Hungary, there is no life. If life there is, it is not of such a kind).

*

It was also considered important to rejuvenate, clarify and as far as possible unify jurisprudence. Commissions were instructed to examine the different customs prevailing in the Habsburg states and then to draw up and publish codes of law. The unification of the rules of law appeared essential to jurists like Martini, whose ideal was reason and justice considered in the abstract; it seemed less desirable to administrators such as the president of the High Court, Seilern, because of the complexity of customs in the different countries and because, in the field of civil law, there was a danger that the public might not receive the concrete benefits which reform was intended to bring.

This was indeed no easy undertaking and the *Codex Theresianus* was not published immediately. However, the *Constitutio criminalis Theresiana* appeared in 1768. Although its purpose was to humanize the penal system, this criminal code preserved many traditional forms of punishment: torture, with all its refinements of cruelty, corporal punishment and death by burning for incendiaries, homosexuals and those guilty of bestiality. Blasphemy, sacrilege, adultery, abduction, marriage with non-Christians and lapsing from the Catholic faith were all heavily punished. The bodies of suicides could not be granted the customary burial. On the other hand, the code relaxed the laws concerning sorcery and generally strengthened the royal authority in judicial matters, with the purpose of creating a more enlightened system of justice. Torture was abolished in 1777. The German translation of the treatise by Beccaria, *Concerning crime and punishment*, helped to persuade public opinion that punishment should not be an act of vengeance against the guilty person, but a means of redressing the wrong committed against society and a contribution to public morality.[32]

The authorities realized that, on the whole, agricultural methods were less than adequate, that the yield from seed sown was low and that general production suffered as a result. Everything was interrelated: to guarantee the State a good return from taxation, it was necessary that agriculture should not be overwhelmed with fiscal burdens; if industry was to find an internal market, only a certain degree of prosperity could create the necessary peasant clientele.

Inquiries such as that conducted by the Larisch commission, in three districts of Bohemia, led to some harsh conclusions. Peasant riots were occurring; since there had been trouble in one hundred and thirty-seven villages in Silesia, Count

Trautmannsdorf was appointed to carry out an inspection (1768). The empress was alarmed when she read his report; in certain respects the situation was even worse than it had been in Hungary. An attempt was made to rectify it by publishing a special corvée patent for Silesia.[33]

A few years later, however, in 1775, the kingdom of Bohemia witnessed its most serious insurrection since 1680. This particular revolt contained new elements. Bad harvests and epidemics in 1769 and 1770 had induced the royal government to intervene and to demand that the lords show their manorial registers to the authorities of the Circle. Very few lords complied with this request. The rumour spread that the queen had abolished the corvée and that the seigniorial administrations were refusing to publish the decree of liberation. The peasantry was not unaware of the mighty revolt of Pugachov which had spread across part of Russia and had been broken by the resistance of the towns. The insurrection of 1775 was not simply a riot provoked by poverty. It was planned in the region of Náchod, in north-eastern Bohemia, by a small rebel government headed by Anton Nydlt, the bailiff of the village of Rtyně. It is possible that *agents provocateurs* had been sent from neighbouring Prussian Silesia; this has been suggested but not proved. The insurgents were to arrive armed in Prague at the time when the peasant crowds would be assembled there for the annual pilgrimage of St. John of Nepomuk. But some rebels set off without waiting for the signal. Manors were burned and sacked; the peasants directed their offensive in particular against the stewards, compelling them to sign documents abolishing the corvée. At the same time, the scythes and crude hunting guns with which the rebels had armed themselves were soon replaced with good weapons; each village was forced to provide one combatant per house or per farm. In March, an army that had gathered round an educated peasant, Matthew Chvojka, known as 'the emperor of the peasants', attacked the seigniory of Chlumec but was routed in front of the town by the soldiers of the regular army. Another rebel force of fifteen thousand men marched on Prague at this same time; after the grand burgrave, Prince Egon Karl Fürstenberg, a humanitarian lord and disciple of Enlightenment, had tried to persuade the rebel leaders to disperse, the troops used side-arms to scatter the peasants and brought a large number of prisoners back to Prague. Sentences were pronounced and three rebels were executed, but on the whole there were no tragic reprisals. Marxist historians suggest that one of the reasons for the failure of the insurrection lay in the behaviour of the more prosperous peasants, who took part only under constraint and betrayed their class interests. And in fact class consciousness was both weak and divided, for side by side with the poverty-stricken day-labourers there existed peasants (the *sedláci*) who, though certainly hostile to the corvée, were not prepared to pay for its suppression by having their dwellings burned down and their granaries plundered. Thus, the same social group provided leaders for an organized revolt, men such as Nydlt and Chvojka, and also those who wished to come to terms with the authorities and improve their condition by means of better laws.[34]

Maria Theresa, who showed great personal concern in the insurrection, wondered if it would not be simpler to abolish serfdom and the corvée altogether. 'The oppression of the poor', she wrote, 'is an established fact', and 'people who have nothing to hope for have nothing to lose'.[35] But she was warned that such a measure might bring agricultural activity to an immediate halt and undermine the entire economy. It was considered more prudent to forestall the possibility of the peasantry refusing to give their labour at the peak of the season, which was imminent, by issuing a patent that would set more equitable limits to the institution of the corvée. The 'redeemed' peasants of the dominical were offered the opportunity of withdrawing from the seigniorial system by returning their lands to their lord, who would reimburse them in four yearly payments. For the peasants of the rustical, eleven categories of labour were established, according to the amount of State taxes which they paid. If the peasants found these new conditions no more favourable, they would be free to adhere to the old regulations, provided that these were henceforth faithfully observed. To discourage abuses and injustices, the patent laid down in minute detail the hours of labour, the compensations to be paid in the event of delay and the rate of remuneration for any extra hours of labour required; Sundays and feast-days were set aside as days of rest. This was an obvious improvement, but the principle of compulsory labour remained unchanged and continued to be held in execration by the entire peasant class.

During these same years, the reversion to the crown of the lands owned by the Society of Jesus provided further opportunities for experiment. Anton Raab, the official entrusted with the administration of these lands, gave the peasants the opportunity of redeeming themselves from the corvée and purchasing independent properties on the old domain. A measure of this kind was evidently a step towards peasant emancipation, the substitution of complete and individual ownership for the possession of lands within the framework of the seigniory. But the advantages which it offered were available only to peasants who were already comfortably situated, the petty capitalists of the agrarian communities. Raab expounded his ideas in a work entitled *Unterricht über die Verwandlung der Königlichen-Kaiserlichen böhmischen Domänen in Bauerngüter* ('The transformation of the royal domains of Bohemia into peasant possessions'). A patent issued in 1777 authorized the lords to apply this system on their estates; the experiment proved a success on one hundred and five royal, ecclesiastical and urban domains and on a few private seigniories.[36]

A policy which enabled a monarchy that had been disputed and attacked to resume the role of a great power in Europe, a reinvigorated military force, a series of reforms undertaken with patience and prudence which transformed the central region into a coherent state with a uniform administration and, above all, the aura of respect which now surrounded both the person of the sovereign and the dynasty, and which even drew Hungary, for so long a rebel, closer to the Danubian complex—achievements of this magnitude entitle the historian to speak of a great and fruitful reign. It is clear that the ideological and technical aspects of government, considered in isolation, were beyond the decision-making powers of a woman who was undoubtedly intelligent and industrious, but who lacked the imagination, the culture and the boldness of a true creator. But does this matter? Maria Theresa's ideology was the tutelary principle that constituted the essence of a patriarchal, even 'Baroque' conception of monarchy, a Christian fidelity in pursuing the achievement of her ancestors, which she could then transmit to her own descendants. Her technique was faithful activity in the service of her monarchy and the hope of easing the burdens of her peoples. Everything else she owed to the quality of her ministers, men as different from one another as Haugwitz, Van Swieten and Kaunitz, and to the army officers, bureaucrats and administrators who served her well. There were a few blemishes: the irreparable loss of Silesia, the annexation of the Polish provinces, which were attached to the Austro-Bohemian group of states as the kingdom of Galicia and Lodomeria, and the quite unnecessary annexation of Bukovina in 1774 as the price of mediation between Russia and the Porte (treaty of Kainarji). In 1765 the continuity of government was broken when the empress suddenly lost her companion and counsellor, Francis I. After considering the possibility of retiring to an abbey, she recovered her self-possession. She pursued the task for another fifteen years, associating her son, the Emperor Joseph II, with her government because he was her son and because this was the surest way of containing an impatience and intransigence in Joseph which she recognized as dangerous. From 1765 to 1780, Kaunitz and the emperor took the major initiatives in both foreign and internal affairs. Often Maria Theresa resigned herself merely to giving her approval. Yet no decision was taken without her knowledge. Although no longer the prime mover of her empire, she maintained a controlling influence. Historians have spoken of the 'Theresian era' just as they have spoken of the 'Victorian era': both were ordinary women in whom the grandeur of the royal function and the rise of a new age were reflected. The Baroque age was making way for the Enlightenment, but the queen-empress was in no sense the symbol of transition.

It has been seen earlier how great had been the successes of Baroque art in the period extending from the reign of Leopold I to that of Maria Theresa and how the hard years of the War of the Austrian Succession, with the heavier fiscal burdens necessitated by military requirements, had their repercussions on artistic activity. The construction of palaces and abbeys had then been interrupted, but in many cases was resumed when peace returned. Maria Theresa was herself a great builder: in Vienna (the Schönbrunn palace), Prague and Budapest she carried on her father's work and the royal residences, restored and transformed, owed their new aspect to her. Is one justified in speaking of a change of style? Perhaps Theresian Baroque, a term that may be used for chronological convenience, displayed less solemnity than the preceding phase, a greater concern for the regularity of façades and a greater rhythm and harmony in the proportions. The eloquence and majesty of Fischer von Erlach and his contemporaries made way for the more discreet elegance and delicate charm which Pacassi gave to the Schönbrunn palace and the castle in Prague. In the palace of the university of Vienna (now the Academy of Sciences) the French style was introduced by Jadot, the Lorraine architect employed by the Emperor Francis I. The interior decoration of the Schönbrunn palace revealed a new interest in oriental exoticism, with its lacquers and rosewood, the Chinese porcelain of the sitting-rooms and the Persian and Hindu miniatures. But this was a stylistic modulation rather than a revolution.

The great fresco-painters continued to enjoy the same favour; under the influence of their Italian contemporaries they gave their compositions a greater suppleness and their colours a greater brilliance and variety of nuance. The

Academy of Vienna shaped and guided artistic talent and its teachers were themselves great artists; these were the years of the finest works of Paul Tröger, its director from 1753 to 1759. The bronze statues of Raphaël Donner seemed to rediscover the purity of the Florentine Renaissance.

The portraitists Kupecký, a Hungarian of Slovakia, Meytens, a Swede, and Liotard, a Swiss, served the imperial family and the nobility with great success. The extent of royal, seigniorial and ecclesiastical commissions varied with the fluctuations of good and bad years and was also influenced by the social advancement and economic progress of the towns, which provided a middle-class clientele.

The imperial household had adopted the homely, patriarchal way of life of the Viennese middle class. Many a scene shows the family group at the fireside, the father in his dressing-gown, the mother serving tea or chocolate to her children. But the life of the court resumed all its splendour for ceremonial receptions and for the marriages of princes, celebrated with grand processions, fireworks, banquets, concerts and theatrical performances.

Music remained the most favoured art and the demands of its clientele kept composers continually occupied in producing new works; as each season went by, scores were left to accumulate in boxes with the result that the entire works of the greatest masters, their existence unrecognized by succeeding generations, were not gathered together until many years later.

The stunning fertility of talent of the Italian poet Metastasio, who lived in Vienna from 1730 until his death in 1782, provided subjects and libretti for operas and melodramas. Musical form and technique acquired a new diversity with symphonies, cantatas and concertos in which the violin, the harpsichord and the piano assumed a greater importance. Sacred music and secular music shared the same rich flowering, for the same artists composed for both categories. Boundaries of time or space did not exist. Neither Haydn, whom Beethoven was to call 'the father of us all', nor Mozart, nor Beethoven himself appeared from a void or by chance; they all evolved from their immediate predecessors, composers such as Fux and Dussek. The incomparable richness of Austrian art in the time of Maria Theresa is perhaps the major contribution made by Danubian civilization to that of Europe in general, and perhaps also the clearest manifestation of Danubian civilization as a supranational phenomenon which cannot be explained without taking into account the influences exerted by the various peoples who inspired this synthesis and who welcomed it with the same enthusiasm, despite differences of language, law and class. There was not a single country of the monarchy which did not make its contribution to this astounding fusion of diverse genius.

As Friedrich Heer observed, Austrian music is perhaps simply the expression of these contrary influences in an alliance which no philosophical or political system was able to overcome.[37]

NOTES

1. The palace of La Favorite in the Wieden district, the residence of the Empress Eleanor, widow of Ferdinand III, had been destroyed during the siege of 1683. Leopold had it rebuilt under the supervision of Ludovico Burnacini and it was then enlarged and embellished by Charles VI.

2. In 1709 the breweries at Hluboká brought their owner 19,716 gulden, those at Třeboň 13,037 gulden by comparison with 9,030 in 1677, and those at Jindřichův Hradec 20,009 gulden in 1730 by comparison with 20,698 in 1690 (from the table by Otto Placht, op. cit., pp. 238–9).

3. *Remarques historiques et critiques d'un voyage de l'Italie en Hollande dans l'année 1700.* Cologne, Jacques le Sincère, 1705, 2 vols., vol. I, p. 132.

4. *Československá Vlastivěda,* 1963 edn., chapter VII by J. Kočí, p. 521 *et seq.*

5. Prince Ferdinand Schwarzenberg (1652–1703), already mentioned in connection with the siege of Vienna, was a remarkable administrator of his estates. He coined money in his little imperial principality. His policy was continued by his son, Adam Francis (1683–1732), who inherited the possessions of the Eggenbergs and the title of duke of Krumlov.

6. Hugo Hantsch, op. cit., Erich Zöllner, op. cit., Ernst Hellbling, op. cit.

7. These two quotations are taken from dispatches from Mirepoix to Amelot: Paris, Affaires étrangères, C. P., Autriche, vol. 213, 1 January 1740, and ibid., vol. 222, 16 July 1739. (At the author's request, Mlle M. Foisil, doctor of history, kindly assembled the documents used here concerning the Austrian succession.)

8. Hugo Hantsch, op. cit., II, p. 148.

9. On the War of the Austrian Succession there is an anonymous contemporary work, *History of the Last Bohemian War,* Frankfurt, 1745. The work by J. Goll, *Válka o zemi koruny české 1740–1742,* I, 1915, is well-informed, intelligent and perspicacious. M. Sautai, *Les préliminaires de la Guerre de Succession d'Autriche,* Paris, 1907, and *Les débuts de la Guerre de Succession d'Autriche,* Paris, 1910. Fritz Wagner, *Kaiser Karl VII und die grossen Mächte 1740–1745,* Stuttgart, 1938.

   An excellent thesis for the '*diplôme d'études supérieures d'histoire*', presented by M. J.-F. Noël, at the Sorbonne in 1961 and hitherto unpublished (*L'affaire de succession de Bohême 1740–1743*), throws useful light on relations between the occupying power and the population of the kingdom.

10. On the role of France, in addition to the works mentioned in note 9, the author has examined portfolios 16 and 17, Frankreich, Varia, and 65, Frankreich, Weisungen; portfolio 16 had already been investigated by the Czech historian J. Goll in his research for the work indicated in note 9.

11. Cf. Hugo Hantsch, *Geschichte Österreichs,* II, p. 152; Denis Sinor, *History of Hungary,* p. 236: 'In fact, Hungary saved the Habsburg dynasty, a gesture she had every reason to regret in later years, but which ensured Maria Theresa's goodwill to the nation.' It is also interesting to observe how, in the time of Joseph II, an enlightened young noble gloried in the memory of 1741: 'Ein Zug in dem Character unsrer Nation, der ob ihn gleich kein Monument vergöttert in der ganzen Geschichte nicht seines gleichen hat.' ('A trait in the character of our nation which, though consecrated by no monument, is without equal in history.') This is quoted on p. 320 in the appendices of the work by Mrs. H. Balázs (Eva), *Berzeviczy Gergely a Reformpolitikus 1763–1795,* Budapest, 1967.

12. There exists no complete study of eighteenth-century international policy, a difficult subject but fascinating nevertheless. However, French historiography has made a valuable contribution with the works of Paul Vaucher, *Robert Walpole et la politique de Fleury, 1731–1742*, Paris, Plon, 1925, and M. Muret, whose article in *Peuples et civilisations*, vol. XI, entitled 'La prépondérance anglaise' (1936), was not justly appreciated in its day, because it did not accord with the ideas of the time and because the new light in which it presented foreign policy was not sufficiently recognized. The reader should also consult G. Zeller in *Histoire des relations internationales*, edited by P. Renouvin.

Two basic works for an understanding of the policy of Vienna and Berlin are: Reinhold Koser, *Geschichte Friedrichs des Grossen*, 4 and 5, Stuttgart, 1913, and Alfred von Arneth, *Maria Theresia*, 10 vols., Vienna, 1863–79, of which Hugo Hantsch has justly said that, although in some respects superseded by the many works written subsequently, it remains the basic study of Maria Theresa's reign. The Polish question was posed as early as the Seven Years' War. Augustus III, whose Saxon army had capitulated at Pirna, thus enabling the king of Prussia to occupy Saxony from 1756 to 1763, had fled to Poland, where he was confronted with anarchy among the nobility. Soon the intrigues of Prussia and Russia resulted in provisions being made for the dismemberment of Poland; the king's daughter-in-law, Princess Maria Antonia Walpurgis, informed Maria Theresa, predicting that she would find great difficulty in preventing the partition and might one day even be obliged to participate in it if she wished to avoid a new war (Vienna, Haus-Hof und Staatsarchiv, Familienkorrespondenz, portfolio 37, letter from Maria Antonia to Maria Theresa, not dated but certainly written in 1763). The death of Augustus III was followed in 1764 by the election of Stanislas Poniatowski, the client of Russia, who had to subscribe to the first treaty of partition in 1772.

13. On Maria Theresa, see the work by A. von Arneth mentioned above. Arneth edited Maria Theresa's copious correspondence with her children: *Joseph II*, 3 vols., 1867–8, and *Marie-Antoinette*, 1866. H. von Zwiedineck-Südenhorst, *Maria Theresia*, Leipzig, 1905. Eugen Guglia, *Maria Theresia, ihr Leben und ihre Regierung*, 2 vols., Munich, 1917. W. Andreas, *Maria Theresia, Geist und Staat*, 1922, 5th edn. 1960; *Das theresianische Österreich und das XVIII Jahrhundert*, Munich, 1930. H. Kretschmayr, *Maria Theresia* in *Die Deutschen Führer*, vol. III, Gotha, 1925; *Maria Theresia*, 1922, 5th edn. 1960. C. L. Morris, *Maria Theresia. The Last Conservative*, New York, 1937. Karl Tschuppik, *Maria Theresia*, Amsterdam, 1934, French translation 1936. J. A. Mahan, *Maria Theresia of Austria 1717–1780*, New York, 1932. J. Kallbrunner, *Kaiserin Maria Theresia's politisches Testament*, 1952.

On Francis of Lorraine: Caelestin Wolfsgrüber, *Franz I Kaiser von Osterreich*, 1899. Fred Hennings, *Und sitzet zur linken Hand*, Vienna, 1961. Hanns Leo Mikoletzky, *Franz I Stephan von Lothringen als Wirtschaftspolitiker* (Österreich Archiv), Vienna.

A highly esteemed but unpublished dissertation by Theophil Tromballa, *Franz Stephan von Lothringen und sein Kreis*. F. Walter, *Männer um Maria Theresia*, Vienna, 1951. Victor-L. Tapié, *Territoire et dynastie* (Bulletin de la Société d'histoire de France), 1966.

14. Here are two examples among many:

i. At the Staatsarchiv in Vienna, in the series Frankreich, Varia, portfolio 17, the author found an anonymous memorandum in French deploring certain abuses and annotated by Maria Theresa: 'Je l'ais ordonné et si ca (ça) n'est finis, je le veux qu'on le fasse d'abord et me rend conte pour quoi on ne la fait plutôt—a ca il y a a pourvoir parlez a Nesselrode. Je le veux absolument ca et Bartenstein m'en a at déjà parlée . . .'

ii. In Hennings, op. cit., p. 304, a note in Francis' handwriting: 'ma vivasité fig mir Kryl an et je vous dret (corrected to "voudroit" by Maria Theresa) ne la voyre (corrected to "l'avoyre" by Maria Theresa) pas fay pour bocoup (corrected to "fait et boucoup") das will nitt sagen et surtout visa vis de sa femme.'

15. Initially, freemasonry was not hostile to the Church. The emperor regarded it as a gathering of men concerned with the public good.

16. Hugo Hantsch, op. cit., II, p. 171.

17. This text is to be found in Dr. Otto Frass, *Quellenbuch zur österreichischen Geschichte*, 2, p. 309, from Kretschmayr, op. cit., p. 271.

18. Concerning Haugwitz and the first reforms of Maria Theresa: F. Walter, in *Die österreichische Zentralverwaltung*, vol. II/I, Vienna, 1938, and also his excellent exposé *Die theresianische Staatsreform von 1749* (Österreich Archiv), Vienna, 1958.

19. F. Walter, *Die theresianische Staatsreform* . . . , op. cit., p. 45 *et seq.*

20. Bohuslav Rieger, *Zřízení krajské v Čechách* ('Organization of the Circles of Bohemia'), Prague, 1889–1913; J. Kapras, *Právní dějiny zemi koruny české* ('History of the Law of the Bohemian Lands'), 1913; V. Vaněček, *Dějiny státu a práva v Československu* ('History of the State and the Law in Czechoslovakia'), 1964.

An excessively severe and historically unjust judgement of the policy of Maria Theresa towards the Czech state is to be found in the pamphlet by Edward Beneš, *Détruisez l'Autriche-Hongrie!*, Paris, 1916, which was a compendium of propaganda against the Dual Monarchy. 'By a decisive act of 1749, Maria Theresa completed the task which her house had set itself. By a unilateral and quite arbitrary article, she put an end to the existence of the Czech state.'

21. F. Walter, *Die theresianische Staatsreform* . . . , op. cit., p. 70.

22. Jaromir Neumann, *Hrad pražský*.

23. The chapter was accommodated in the old Rožmberk palace, which was given a new Baroque décor. When the Benedictine nuns of St. George were suppressed in 1781, the abbess of the *Damenstift* was accorded the privilege of crowning the queen of Bohemia. The last abbess (1918) was the Archduchess Maria Annunziata, sister of the Archduke Francis Ferdinand.

24. The allegories of the frescoes painted by Gugliemi in the Schönbrunn Galleries represent the gentle government of Maria Theresa (small gallery) and Austria during the Seven Years' War (great gallery).

25. J. Pekař, *České Katastry* ('Czech Cadastral Surveys'), Prague, 1915.

26. *Československá Vlastivěda* (1963 edition), chapter VII, pp. 562–5. A. Klima, *Die Textilmanufaktur in Böhmen* (in *Historica*, XV, 1968).

27. H. von Srbik, *Deutsche Einheit (Idee und Wirklichkeit von Heiligen Reich bis Königgratz)*, Munich, 1935.

Max Braubach, *Versailles und Wien von Ludwig XIV bis Kaunitz*, 1952.

In a letter to the British ambassador Keith, quoted in Guglia I, p. 134, Maria Theresa explained that she was not throwing herself into the arms of France, but was placing herself by the side of France, because Britain had been the first to abandon the old system by the alliance with Prussia.

On Kaunitz: Alexander Novotny, *Staatskanzler Kaunitz als geistige Persönlichkeit*, Vienna, 1947.

28. F. Walter, in the great work *Die österreichische Zentralverwaltung*, II/I (History of the central administration in the time of Maria Theresa 1740–80), Vienna, 1938, and also II/II and II/III (collections of documents).

On monetary reform: Maurice Fischel, *Le thaler de Marie-Thérèse*, Dijon, 1912.

29. E. Ermatinger, *Deutsche Kultur im Zeitalter der Aufklärung;* Robert A. Kann, *A Study in Austrian Intellectual History, from late baroque to romanticism*, New York, 1960; Hanns Leo

Mikoletzky, *Österreich—das grosse 18. Jahrhundert*, Vienna, 1967; A. Tibal, *L'Autrichien*, Paris, 1936; Mayer-Kaindl, *Geschichte und Kulturleben Österreichs von 1493 bis 1792*, 5th edn. 1960.

30. J. Prokeš, in *Československá Vlastivěda, Dějiny*, 1928 edn., studied these problems thoroughly.

31. Concerning Hungary at this time, consult: Homan-Szegfü, *Magyar történet*, vol. V; Stefan Janšák, *Slovensko v dobe uhorského feudalizmu hospodarské pomery od r. 1514*, 1848–1932.

   For eighteenth-century Pressburg: Dr. Eugen Forbát, *Die Geschichte des Handels und des Pressburger Handelsstandes in XVIII Jahrhundert*, Bratislava, 1930.

32. Concerning juridical reform, see Hellbling, op. cit., p. 301; Václav Vaněček, *Dějiny státu a práva*, p. 306.

33. K. Krofta, *Přehled dějin selského stavu* ('Historical Outline of the Peasant Condition'), 1919, p. 173 *et seq.*

34. For the revolt of 1775, see Svátek, *Dějiny Čech a Moravy* ('History of Bohemia and Moravia'); Václav Husa, 'Nevolnické povstání r. 1775' ('The Revolt of 1775'), in *Český lid*, XXXIX, 1932, and, under the same title, a work of 207 pages written in collaboration with J. Petřán, Prague, 1956; J. Fischer, 'Selské nepokoje na Moravě r(ku 1775' ('The Peasant Riots in Moravia in 1775'), in *Československý Časopis Historicky*, 1936, p. 163 J. Kočí, 'The peasant revolts in several Northern Bohemian domains in 1775' in *Československý Časopis Historický*, new series 1960, 5, p. 636.

   Václav Husa has studied the role of the prosperous peasants, their resistance and their 'class treachery'.

   The bibliography *Twenty-five Years of Czechoslovak Historiography, 1936–1960*, Prague, 1960, gives on p. 215 *et seq.* a list of works on this subject.

35. O. Frass, *Quellenbuch*, 2, p. 346, quotes from Guglia, *Maria-Theresia*, vol. II, p. 353, the letter of 1775 to the Archduke Ferdinand in which the empress declares that if the emperor (Joseph II) had been willing 'I will not say to support me, but simply to remain neutral, I could have achieved my object and abolished [*abzuschaffen*] serfdom and obligatory labour'. She complains of the landowning nobility, to which almost all the ministers belonged. The ministers, in particular Kaunitz, were not stubborn old men like their predecessors at the beginning of the reign, but in the matter of policy these men of the *Aufklärung* and the rational ideal were afraid to adopt the decisive measures which the empress, prompted by her Christian charity, would have wished to take.

36. K. Krofta, op. cit., p. 189 *et seq.*

37. *Histoire de la musique* (Encyclopédie de la Pléiade), vol. II, pp. 155–272; Heinrich von Srbik and Reinhold Lorenz, *Die Geschichtliche Stellung Wiens 1740–1918*, p. 10 *et seq.*; Friedrich Heer, *Europäische Geistesgeschichte*, p. 590.

8

Joseph II

THE REIGN OF Joseph II, the foundations for which had been laid during the period of his co-regency with his mother, was a brief but fruitful attempt to direct the Danubian monarchy along a course apparently necessitated by the general situation of Europe.

'Josephism was invented neither by Joseph II nor by the other personalities of Theresian or Josephian Austria,' writes F. Valjavec; 'It was the result of several spiritual currents and of efforts to establish a compromise between the old political and cultural conceptions, on the one hand, and the spirit of the *Aufklärung* and the tendency towards secularization, on the other.'[1]

Valjavec was thinking only of religious affairs, but his observation, and in particular the term 'compromise', could be applied to the general achievement of Joseph II. What was needed in 1780? In the European and world situation of this time, with the general progress of industrial production, the revival of agricultural activity and, in the political sphere, the rapid rise of two powers, Prussia and Russia, which were establishing themselves as the rivals of the House of Austria, nothing could have been more disastrous for the Danubian monarchy than a refusal to change. Maria Theresa had been a reforming sovereign. It was necessary to continue her work by introducing further changes. But how? The most awkward problem was to choose the right method. Joseph II was inclined by temperament to seek radical change and a break with the past. But in a political, economic and social organism as delicate and diverse as the Danubian monarchy, compromise was more effective than open rupture. Where the general trend is against uniformity and where it is necessary to ensure harmony and a balance of opposite forces, logic and reason cannot be applied too rigorously. It is wiser to canalize and discipline the forces of the past than to reject them. Compromise was perhaps the true vocation of the Danubian countries: in other words, it was a question of reconciling realities rather than applying principles. But Joseph II was concerned primarily with principles.

As early as 1764 the imperial coronation at Frankfurt had seemed to the new king of the Romans to be an outdated ceremony and had given him a poor opinion of the Empire. When he became emperor in the following year, on the sudden death of Francis I, he certainly did not regard this dignity as meaningless. He always took an interest in Germany, where he exercised the supreme judicial function and still possessed patrimonial territories (the Breisgau), and whose populations had such close ideological and linguistic links with the hereditary states. Yet the centre of gravity of his Empire remained the Danubian complex, although the importance of the external possessions of Lombardy and the Netherlands was not forgotten. Joseph II looked on all these lands as terrain for experiment, where he intended to introduce the new order at the expense of the old institutions. But he was too conscious of the medieval character of those institutions and unaware of the extent to which, despite their apparent outmodedness, they were still in harmony with the times and supported by public opinion.[2]

During his ten years of government, from 29 November 1780 to 20 June 1790, absolutism and tradition—one might say the philosophy of Enlightenment and the Baroque—were brought into confrontation. To suggest that the conflict resulted in the defeat of the former would be to over-simplify. Forces which did not depend on the will of the sovereign, even a sovereign as clear-sighted as Joseph II, combined to produce a natural equilibrium that enabled the monarchy to weather the storm of revolution and enter the industrial age.

Yet, initially, it was the traditional prestige of the royal function, with its patriarchal, quasi-religious authority, which guaranteed Joseph II the obedience of his subjects to the decisions that he was to take in the name of an abstract and desacralized state. The idea of the sovereign as the first servant of the State was not new—'It is not I who speak, but my State', said Louis XIII. In Joseph's mind, however, it assumed a more rigid and secular form and, consequently, could be understood and appreciated by an enlightened élite composed of great lords (both the truly convinced and the dilettanti), intellectuals, bankers and merchants. But the idea remained alien to the mass of the rural peoples who formed the bulk of the population of the emperor's states and who, though they still looked to the paternal justice of their prince, were anxious that the exercise of that justice should not conflict with everything they cherished. How imprudent it was to risk antagonizing the very people whose personal happiness the government was seeking to promote by its measures! And how strangely contradictory were this prince's scorn of the human element and his efforts to break away from the tradition of his predecessors, who had rarely ventured from the capital: often travelling incognito under the name of Count von Falkenstein, Joseph had visited Switzerland, Russia and France, ignoring royal courts and princely residences, interesting himself rather in the activity of the towns, the bustle of the great foreign ports and the behaviour of the bourgeoisie, and believed that he had thus acquired a depth of human experience. The comparison with Peter the Great is unavoidable. Historians have greatly exaggerated the backwardness of Russian civilization and society at the time when Peter the Great imposed the laws and customs of the West on the Russian nobility and on the towns of his empire. The fact remains, however, that the conditions peculiar to Russia, where peasant society lay scattered over vast spaces, enabled the tsar to establish a European-style administration on what was practically a *tabula rasa*. In the countries of the Habsburg monarchy, by contrast, ancient laws and traditions were still too strong and too efficacious to be swept away by decree.

For example, the Hungarian political nation, as represented by the privileged orders, remained keenly conscious of its historic laws and its juridical autonomy and considered the ceremony of coronation to be neither a formality nor a symbol, but an act indispensable to the normal organic life of the kingdom of Hungary. To bring the crown of St. Stephen back to Vienna as a museum piece, to accept the status in Hungary of a king 'in a hat'—in other words, an incomplete king whose authority was not formally ratified—was to commit a grave error and to invite a conflict with one of the countries whose support was most needed.

Despite this lack of insight, many measures were introduced that were to prove rich in results. Present-day Czech historians are justified in regarding the year 1781 as one of the most crucial in their country's past.[3] On 1 November 1781 a patent was issued for Bohemia and Moravia-Silesia which struck a blow at the old seigniorial system by suppressing personal servitude. In the offices of the Hof kammer and at the Diet there was much futile discussion about the nature of this servitude: was it a true serfdom or rather a contractual subordination of the tenant to the lord? The important thing was that the permission of the lord was no longer required for acts involving the freedom and dignity of the individual: henceforward the seigniorial administration would simply record any notifications of marriage and would automatically give a letter of authorization to peasants who wished to leave the estate of their own free will; children could enter into apprenticeship in accordance with their parents' wishes; no personal service could be demanded from orphans, except in cases where tutelage freely provided by the lord required compensation (such service was limited to three years). A second patent authorized 'redeemed' peasants to build and make other modifications on their holdings, which they were also allowed to sell or to mortgage (for up to a third of the value of the holding). 'Unredeemed' subjects received the right to acquire 're-deemed' status if this was to their advantage. The patents were of the utmost importance, for they guaranteed the mobility of a proportion of the peasantry in a country where the manufacturing industry was growing. The rise in the popula-tion of the towns during the years that followed was a direct consequence of these measures: there were now more people in the workrooms, factories and shops

The peasant's subjection to his lord was by no means completely abolished; the declared intention of the emperor was to establish a more moderate dependence of the kind prevailing in Austria, where the corvée was renowned for its relative mildness.

The patents of 1781 were followed by others and here the governmental method of Joseph II can be discerned, the patient preparatory work undertaken by depart-mental officials so that the imperial decision could be announced at the appropriate time, when the problem seemed to have been given sufficient deliberation. In 1783 the obligation to have corn ground at the lord's mill was abolished; later another patent defined the law of succession to prevent an excessive sub-division of peasant properties; in 1785 a tax of 5 per cent of the value of the relinquished property was imposed on peasants who wished to settle in Hungary. The purpose of this latter measure was to avert the danger of an exodus of workmen and artisans to a country where manpower was inadequate, for Austria and Bohemia were anxious to ensure that their factories enjoyed the benefits of social mobility.

To provide the State with a better fiscal system and to distribute taxes more equitably remained the administration's chief concern. In 1785 it was decided to undertake a new and more comprehensive revision of the lands of the monarchy. The survey was to be completed within four years: on this occasion, the whole cultivable area, and not only that already under cultivation, was to be measured. Each parcel of land would be given a number and the yield from its soil estimated. Part of the work of surveying was entrusted to the peasants, which indicates how highly their ability and trustworthiness were regarded, at least as far as the more advanced peasants were concerned. The authorities of the Circles passed the results to the various provincial governments, which then sent them to a royal commission. In Bohemia alone the survey estimated a taxable area of 15,568,000 arpents, while the survey undertaken in the time of Maria Theresa had produced only 10,305,000 arpents.

On the basis of the new survey the system of taxes was to be entirely reorganized. The patent of 10 February 1789 (*Steuer und Urbarialregulierung*) was the most revolutionary of Joseph's reign, providing for a general revision of the principles of taxation and of the entire seigniorial regime. A land-tax was to be exacted from all lands, according to their extent and productivity, without distinction between the dominical and the rustical. The peasant or cultivator was to retain 70 per cent of his revenue for subsistence and investments; State tax would not exceed 12/29 per cent and was fixed at 17/79 per cent for seigniorial land. The liberation of the peasantry was to be crowned by the abolition of the corvée. In fact, it was not abolished, but was to lose its obligatory, perpetual character from 1 November 1790: thenceforward, the conditions of labour would depend on an agreement freely concluded between the lord and the subject for a period of three years, at the end of which the contract could be renewed.

A Czech village notable named Vavák wrote in his register: 'I believe I am not mistaken in saying that we awaited All Saints' Day 1790 with the same joy with which our troops and our general Laudon must have awaited the fall of Belgrade. Oh, what rapture among the people of the villages when it was announced that no one would compel them any longer to go on forced labour with ploughs and animals or on foot! Those who have never felt the burden of forced labour could not understand.'[4]

It will be seen later, however, that general circumstances prevented the measure from being put into effect at the promised date. By All Saints' Day 1790 Joseph II was dead, and in the troubled condition of the monarchy it would have been dangerous to introduce such a major innovation in the social system. Consequently, the corvée continued to exist in the Danubian countries until 1848. Even today there are citizens in the People's Democratic Republics who in their childhood heard old men still talking of the labour imposed on their parents, as of a recent and detested memory.

The corvée was therefore to be retained in accordance with the ordinances of 1775 which, though generous by comparison with the past, now seemed hateful after hopes of total abolition had been raised. Yet so many other forms of rural

servitude had been suppressed that, despite the retention of the corvée, a larg
number of peasants found their personal and economic condition improved.

꩜

The religious reform on which the emperor decided, and which became one of th
most original elements of the Danubian system, was of no less importance, bot
in its immediate effects and in its consequences for the future. Here again, th
commonly accepted term 'Josephism' (*Josephinismus*) attributes too exclusive a
influence to the emperor himself.[5] In a reaction against the forms of religious prac
tice widespread in Germany and in the Austrian countries since the mid-seven
teenth century, a movement that favoured a more interior and less narrowly ritua
religion was taking shape in the dioceses and in many Benedictine monasterie
In certain educated circles, such as that which centred around Count Sporck,
collector of books and patron of the arts, in northern Bohemia, a keen interes
was taken in the works of the French Jansenists. Yet it would be an over-simplifica
tion to reduce these opposing influences to a conflict between the Jesuits and th
Jansenists, or to identify the Society of Jesus with Baroque piety and Jansenisn
with the philosophy of the Enlightenment. In their fine study of the Church and
popular devotions in the Baroque period, Veit and Lenhart showed clearly how
in central Europe, the devotional practices of that period were inspired as much b
the tradition of the Rhenish mystics as by the missions of the Counter-Reforma
tion. The atmosphere of religious strife and the false impression of appeasemen
given by the civil legislation issuing from the *Constitutio Westphalica* had encourage
a ritualism whose dangers had not escaped the attention of the ecclesiastica
authorities. But it was as difficult to condemn the intention as it was easy to perceiv
the excesses which distorted that intention. Pilgrimages and processions of th
Precious Blood aroused a moving collective fervour; but they were also the occa
sion for scenes of drunkenness and every kind of scandalous behaviour. The blaz
of candles and the myriads of votive statues, especially of the Virgin, which wer
dressed in sumptuous garments and bedecked with jewellery, bordered on idolatry
as if some form of latent paganism once more surrounded trees, springs an
flame.[6] It was feared that Eucharistic devotion might be debased by the practic
of holding the monstrance in front of accidental fires to ward off calamity, by th
excessive frequency of benedictions and by the idea that contemplation of the Hos
was almost as efficacious as communion.

On the other hand, any criticism of these excesses by educated persons induced
section of the clergy and, if not the entire Society of Jesus, at least some Jesuits, t
suspect heresy and, by a defensive reflex, to resort to prosecution and condemna
tion. On one side, there loomed the spectre of Jansenism, seen in even the mildes
plea for moderation; on the other, the spectre of the Jesuit peril, wherever piet
was evident. The men of the *Aufklärung*—Van Swieten, Kaunitz and, amon
Joseph II's advisers, the privy councillors Franz Kressl and Heinke, who wa
responsible for religious matters—were the adversaries of the Jesuits and regarde
expressions of popular fervour as crude superstition and stupidity. The suppressio

in 1773 of the Society of Jesus, decided by Pope Clement XIV and to which Maria Theresa consented, though not without regrets or misgivings, was seen as a first salutary step towards a purification of religious life. This decision, largely because of the manner in which it was interpreted, marked a major turning-point.

But the problem also had a political aspect. The Counter-Reformation had striven to re-establish the legal conditions of the past. The old religious boundaries which had existed before the great crisis had been reaffirmed, a procedure imposed moreover by the clauses of the treaty of Westphalia ordaining the restoration of the directorial year. The result was an institutional framework which no longer corresponded to reality or to the effects of population movements. Some dioceses remained disproportionately large, their boundaries straddling the frontiers of different states. The situation was obviously chaotic: in some regions parishes and monasteries were concentrated within a narrow area, while in others the number of churches was inadequate. Furthermore, the religious orders, which had contributed in so large a measure to the Catholic restoration by bringing the old religion back to Austria, Bohemia and faithful Bavaria, escaped the jurisdiction both of the diocesan bishop and of the State. The orders had penetrated the seigniorial system, regaining possession of vast domains and acquiring new ones, often well administered, and had set about rebuilding abbeys and abbey churches. The monasteries wielded a mighty influence over the entire surrounding region: persons engaged in a wide diversity of occupations (artists, artisans, cultivators and foresters) depended on them for their livelihood. A peasant was flattered to have a son who was a monk and who might, as frequently happened, become an abbot or prior. The numerical strength of the monasteries, as well as their wealth, was a cause for concern among the men of the *Aufklärung*. Nothing is more revealing in this respect than a memorandum submitted by Kaunitz to the Council of State in 1770, in which the institution of monasticism was the subject of an historical and rational critique.[7] According to Kaunitz, no one could claim that monasticism represented the essence of Christianity, since it had not existed in the early centuries of the Church. Judging by the kind of life led by so many monks, how could one pretend that their existence was really devoted to prayer, alms and meditation? The excessively large regular clergy could with great advantage be replaced by a smaller body of secular priests: it was therefore the responsibility of the State to modify their respective numbers in accordance with its own interests.

The religious orders also encountered the traditional hostility of the bishops, who found the authority which they exercised in their dioceses limited by monastic immunity. The bishops, moreover, deplored the fact that religious education and the guidance of souls were to a certain extent outside the control of the secular clergy.

In the seventeenth century the bishops throughout Europe had reluctantly tolerated the limitation of their rights by the Roman Curia and had refrained from holding the popes individually responsible for this process. The fear of schism induced them to remain fundamentally loyal to the Sovereign Pontiff. Despite the ardour of her Christian faith, Maria Theresa had been the first to engage in conflict with the Holy See. The clash had originated in Lombardy, where Rome exercised direct authority over the clergy and where ecclesiastical immunities rendered fiscal reform practically impossible. On the occasion of the reorganization of the *Giunta Economale*, in Milan, the department responsible for Italian affairs defined in strict terms the supervisory powers which that body was to exercise over ecclesiastical affairs in the interests of the State. It would be an exaggeration to say that, in signing a secret directive to the Giunta on 15 June 1768, Maria Theresa had unwittingly opened the door to a heretical conception of the relationship between Church and State, but she had certainly established principles from which 'Josephism' was to be derived.[8] Much importance has been attributed to the influence of a work which the auxiliary bishop of Trier, Nicholas von Hontheim, had published under the pseudonym of Febronius, *De statu praesenti Ecclesiae* ('Concerning the present status of the Church'), and to the general diffusion of Jansenism.

Many works of an Augustinian rather than a truly Jansenist character, such as the *Heures du cardinal de Noailles*, had for a long time figured in the libraries of private persons in Vienna and Prague. Similarly, in the masonic lodges, to which even ecclesiastics belonged, there was a desire to find a more interior and personal religion which would be less dependent on the Church and would seek to transcend the traditional forms of charity (alms-giving) in a grand humanitarian ideal. But perhaps it is more important to recognize not what was being advocated, but what was being rejected: hostility was directed chiefly against Rome and the monks, but also against the whole gamut of popular piety, which was regarded as an empty charade.[9]

The conflict soon set mother and son at variance. Maria Theresa accepted certain changes: during her reign the State had already established control over the monasteries' relations with the Holy See, foreigners had been prohibited from holding the office of abbot and a legal age-limit (24 years) had been fixed for religious profession. But these precautions were in no way directed against an alliance which Maria Theresa believed to be essential. Joseph II nurtured no deep ill will towards Catholicism. A deist, but also a Christian and Catholic, he considered religion and religious practice to be necessary to the good order and moral equilibrium of society. At the same time, he desired in his states a rationally organized Church that would provide a more effective support for his enterprise of enlightened despotism. He entrusted the task of reform to a special section of the Chancellery, the *Geistliche Rat in publico-politicis economicis*, under the presidency of Kressl. Not all the bishops refused to co-operate, but Migazzi, the cardinal-archbishop of Vienna, took fright and urged the empress to resist. There were two particular reforms which Maria Theresa was determined never to accept: a declaration of toleration, which would place all religions on an equal footing, and the secularization of the monasteries. A year after her death, both these proposals were put into effect.

The Patent of Toleration seemed to Joseph II to be the natural complement to the patent of personal liberty which he had promulgated. It was published on 20 October 1781 in the hereditary countries, on 26 October in Hungary, on 12 November in the Netherlands and on 30 November in Lombardy. Before the patent itself is considered, one point should be observed. A decision of grave importance had been taken which was to apply to a diversity of groups, Austrians, Bohemians (both Czechs and Germans), Hungarians, Croatians, Belgians and Italians, and which aspired to render a fundamental liberty to man, the subject of the emperor, irrespectively of the particular historical state to which he belonged. But the law required that a separate declaration be made for each country, which indicates how chancellery activity—in other words, bureaucracy—was expanding.

It is estimated that, during his reign of ten years, Joseph II published six thousand decrees and eleven thousand new laws. The application of these laws meant that an increasingly important role was to be assumed by a body of officials devoted to the service not of their own country, but of the State. The fatherland was identified with the whole complex of territories over which the sovereign exercised authority. All the subjects of the emperor were bound in solidarity one to another by the very fact of being his subjects. The ideal civil servant was defined in a memorandum of 1783 addressed to all the governors for the information of their administrative staff: 'The man who has no love for the service of his fatherland and of his fellow-citizens, who is not inflamed by a special fervour for the attainment of good, is not suited to public affairs and is unworthy to bear an official title or to receive a salary.'[10] Fatherland, fellow-citizen, public good—such terms had been in use for some time, but they now acquired a new significance. The service of the State—no longer simply devotion to the sovereign, the personal allegiance and lawful obedience owed to the Father-King—imposed a special conception of duty on each servant of the State, raising public office to the dignity of a vocation. Already the solid and faithful civil service which never ceased to expand, from the time of Joseph II to 1918, was taking shape. However routinist, servile or short-sighted it may have been, it was competent, assiduous and devoted to an ideal of professional honour: it was to guide the State safely through upheavals, territorial losses and all the legislative changes which a Czech politician, Rieger, was one day to call the 'grave-yard of constitutions'. Its work guaranteed the other citizens of the Empire a greater dignity and security in their daily life.

What were the benefits of the Patent of Toleration? Although it did not establish a general freedom of conscience, the subjects of the different countries were invited to declare to the seigniorial or communal authorities their adherence to one of the recognized religions. They were permitted to practise these religions in their respective places of worship, which did not obtain full equality of status with Catholic churches, since they were not permitted to have either towers or a main entrance opening on to the street. Nevertheless, a great many persons (eighty thousand is probably an acceptable approximation) opted for the reformed religions, embracing Lutheranism in the towns of Bohemia, Moravia and Austria, and Calvinism in the rural areas.[11] There was no shortage of German pastors, who came from Saxony and Prussia to take charge of the Lutherans; but the Calvinist churches had difficulty in finding pastors who spoke Czech, and were compelled to turn to the Slovaks of Upper Hungary. The patent did not recognize the legal existence of numerous dissident sects which the Catholic authorities had only recently been harrying, but which had found no difficulty in reorganizing themselves: Deists,

Abrahamists, Adamites, Sionists and even former Utraquists. Their number and diversity revealed a widespread unrest of soul in regions where guidance was lacking. Yet this spiritual disquiet aroused no sympathy in the emperor or his commission. Only the officially constituted churches were tolerated, offering guarantees to a religion of reason whose pastors were to teach basic Christianity and concern themselves with its moral and practical application. In this way, the people would learn to fear and honour God, to observe his commandments, to lead a just and simple life and to serve the emperor.

The good of the State demanded nothing more. Its interests were thus being served by both the Catholic and the Protestant churches. But in Hungary, Poland and Bukovina there existed Christians of yet another confession, the Eastern Orthodox Church. Maria Theresa had sought to reunite the Orthodox faithful with the Roman Church, to which they were close in doctrine, Eucharistic belief and devotion to the Virgin Mary, but from which they were separated by their liturgy and, even more important, by the memory of the passionate but not really fundamental differences between Rome and Byzantium. A number of Uniate churches (Catholic churches of the Greek rite) had consequently been established in the countries of the monarchy. Joseph II and his advisers were completely indifferent to oecumenism and to the reconciliation of the Catholic world. Since the Orthodox churches were traditionally well-disposed towards the authority of the sovereign and desired his protection, there seemed to be no reason to encourage a *rapprochement* with Rome. The Orthodox faithful could also be granted the benefit of toleration.

There remained the Jews, who were numerous in the towns, especially in Prague where they had their ghetto and had been closely associated with the entire history of the city and of Bohemia, and in Vienna where the Oppenheimers, the banking family, had rebuilt their fortune and continued to play an important role in the economic life of the country. The Patent of Toleration abolished certain forms of moral servitude which had weighed heavily on the Jews: they secured the right to purchase landed property and to practise the same trades as Christians, they were no longer compelled to wear humiliating distinguishing signs on their clothes and were allowed to send their children to non-Jewish schools wherever there existed no schools of their own religion.

On 29 November 1781 the great offensive against the monasteries began with the suppression of all religious communities which were not occupied either in teaching or in the care of the sick and which, it was claimed, made no contribution to the spiritual or material life of the population. However, the monks and nuns of the condemned communities remained free to join those orders that had not been affected by the decree.

The lands of the suppressed monasteries became the property of the State and were sold for the purpose of creating a 'religious fund', which was to be devoted to the reorganization of the Church as a public service. During the years that followed, a series of decrees was issued which resulted in the dissolution of a large number of orders and congregations: Carthusians, Camaldulensians, Cistercians, Carmelites, Poor Clares and Franciscan hermits. In Bohemia the number of religious fell from sixty million to twenty-seven million and more than seven hundred houses were closed. Some of these establishments were undoubtedly much less prosperous than others: throughout eighteenth-century Europe mysticism was on the wane and conventual life was losing its vigour. In general, buildings that were too large or in a poor state of repair would be put to better use if they were converted into manufacturing workshops, while lands would become more productive if more efficiently cultivated. The old division of dioceses and parishes no longer corresponded to spiritual needs and it seemed reasonable that their boundaries should be redrawn. On 4 February 1782 a decree was issued which concerned the creation and organization of new parishes. The 'religious fund' was to provide remuneration in keeping with the dignity of parish-priests, chaplains and curates, the *congrua* of 450, 300 and 150 gulden per year, respectively. This was indeed a profound change, for the clergy were no longer the holders of benefices, but the salaried servants of the State. The guiding principle behind the decree seemed sound enough and ensured a more effective organization of parish life, if it is true that in the time of Maria Theresa there had been one priest for eleven hundred souls and after the reform of Joseph II one priest for every six hundred. Similarly, the time was ripe for a rearrangement of the dioceses: the Austrian dioceses were freed from the tutelage of Passau and bishoprics were founded at Linz, St. Pölten, Laybach and Budweiss (České Budějovice, in Bohemia). To provide for the training of the clergy, twelve general seminaries were established in large cities: Vienna, Prague, Graz, Innsbruck, Olmütz, Pavia and Louvain; these central colleges made both the Roman college (*Collegium germanicum*) and the diocesan seminary quite superfluous. A common teaching programme was to be followed in the new seminaries; the purpose of this was to avert the danger of Ultramontanist doctrines being taught or of innovations being introduced by an over-zealous bishop or director, and to prevent the growth of divergent spiritual trends in the different countries. The bureaucratic, civil constitution of the clergy was not intended by its authors to exhaust the springs of spiritual life and, since it survived in some form into the nineteenth century, it clearly did not do this. On the other hand, it prepared the ground for too close an alliance between the civil power and the clergy, an alliance which it then served to perpetuate; even if the bishops and parish-priests did not become administrators first and foremost, they certainly could not entirely dissociate their religious and administrative functions. The new system encouraged too much quiet complacency and too great a fondness for inactivity among ecclesiastics throughout the countries of the monarchy.[12]

Numerous decrees relating to ceremonial and liturgical detail were promulgated. The procedure for burials was laid down: in the interests of hygiene, it was forbidden to bury persons in coffins or in churches; the dead were to be placed in sacks and buried in graves lined with lime. Altars not used for divine service were to be removed from churches. There were to be no more pilgrimages or processions (the only exception being processions of the Blessed Sacrament), no votive offerings of gold or silver, no vestments or jewellery on statues and no ringing of bells during a storm. The devotional embellishments of Baroque piety were condemned in their entirety.

In Rome, Pope Pius VI was more determined than his predecessor to defend Catholic tradition against the initiatives of enlightened governments. He thought that he would be able to preserve much by going to discuss the points at issue personally with Joseph II and his ministers. His journey and stay in Vienna occupied the months of March and April 1782. The emperor and Kaunitz were both ill at the time and were able to use this as a pretext for their attitude of almost insolent aloofness towards the person of the Pope. The people, by contrast, displayed immense enthusiasm. The acclamation which he received from the villages and the towns along the route was endorsed by the crowds that gathered daily in front of the Hofburg where, from his window, Pius VI blessed the kneeling faithful. During Holy Week the Pope followed the processions. On Easter Sunday he celebrated pontifical high mass at St. Stephen's and then went to give the apostolic blessing from the terrace of the Am Hof. He did not demand that the reforms be rescinded; his chief concern was to ensure that control of the clergy was not surrendered to the sole authority of the sovereign and that the papal bull *Unigenitus,* which had condemned Jansenism, continued to form part of the instruction given in the seminaries. As Joseph II fully realized, Pius VI attached significance to the bull not so much because of the propositions which it contained, but rather as a guarantee of obedience to the Holy See whenever the latter should make a doctrinal pronouncement. Perhaps he appreciated the full implications of Joseph II's measures and the advantages of the reorganization of dioceses and parishes. Later, the emperor paid a return visit to Rome.

Without pursuing their quarrels further, Pius VI and Joseph II concluded a *conventio amicabilis* which preserved the rights of the Church and at the same time, by means of ingenious half-measures, allowed the emperor control over the choice of bishops in Lombardy and in the Danubian countries.[13]

The two leading prelates of the monarchy, Cardinal Migazzi in Vienna and Cardinal Batthyány in Esztergom, were opponents of 'Josephism'. They were resolved to safeguard tradition and not to subordinate religious authority to the civil power. They therefore gave a free rein to any movement of public opinion that obstructed the application of the new regulations. Popular demonstrations were possibly more influential than doctrinal arguments in establishing a certain equilibrium and making the reforms acceptable. The peasants of Eisenkappel, in Carinthia, rose up in revolt when it was proposed to strip their shrine of the Virgin with Thorn: it was one thing to deliver the *coup de grâce* to an institution that was already tottering on the brink of ruin, but quite another to pronounce sentence of death on one that remained very much alive. Barely fifteen years previously Francis I and Maria Theresa had donated a large silver grille to the shrine of Mariazell in Styria. The altars of the transept at Maria-Taferl, beside the Danube, dated from 1775.

Baroque devotion had thus survived. In Prague the statuette of the Infant Jesus retained its imperial crown and its vestments, which were changed according to the liturgical calendar; statues of the Virgin still bore their mantles of brocade and their diadems; ornate, gilded altar-pieces and statues were still to be found, both at high altars and at altars declared superfluous for divine service. Just as a compromise had been reached between the ideal of Pius VI, who desired both theocracy and the doctrinal independence of the Church, and that of Joseph II, convinced of the necessity of the State's authority in religious matters wherever dogma was not at issue, so a compromise had enabled Joseph's reforms and Baroque piety to exist side by side: reform had been contained within certain limits and had perhaps rid piety of its excesses.

The process of transformation was indeed huge. Frequently the visitor to the Danubian countries discovers that a barrack, factory or hospital was originally a monastery which had been secularized by Joseph II. The Dorotheum in Vienna occupies an old monastery. In Prague, the church of St. George in the castle enclosure was taken from the Benedictines; the Bethlehem chapel, where John Huss had preached, was also deconsecrated at this time, as was the little church of Svatý Jan na Pradle (St. John on the Washing-place) beside the river; thirty years ago this last-named church was still being used as a forge. In Bohemia, at Zbraslav, the Cistercian monastery which V. V. Reiner and Palko decorated with their charming bright frescoes was converted into a factory and the monastery of Zlatá Koruna, a Gothic masterpiece, suffered the same fate. In Austria, the abbey at Wilhering was saved only at the very last moment, while the Benedictine abbey of Mondsee became a parish church, which it remains to this day. The abbey at Lilienfeld was secularized for two years and the abbey at Ossiach, in Carinthia, was permanently deconsecrated. Although these are but a few examples from many, they give an idea of the extent of secularization. On the other hand, the 'religious fund', constantly swelled by the proceeds of sales, provided the salaries which were paid to priests and also enabled new parish buildings to be erected. Although it was recommended that the furniture and venerated objects of the secularized monasteries be transported to these new buildings, countless art treasures were sold, dispersed or destroyed—paintings, statues, sacred vessels and antiphonaries, the relics of the Middle Ages and the more recent works of the Baroque period.

But if, against all this destruction, one sets the many works which survived and which preserved for the eyes of the modern world a Baroque art still full of life and untouched by two hundred years of changing tastes, one is better able to appreciate the vigour with which an imaginative, palpable and readily sensuous religion resisted the ideal of Josephism. Two spiritual forces had opposed one another: on the one hand, a tradition of sentimental and imaginative fervour and on the other, a rationalist and philosophical trend.

The organizing effort of Joseph II neutralized the anarchic element in the religious life of the Danubian countries. But it brought the risk of an iconoclastic holocaust that would have exhausted the springs of emotion and sensibility. The religion of the Danubian countries succeeded in preserving its ritual character, its attachment to images, brilliance and decorative intensity, qualities from which, in the nineteenth century and again in the present century, it was to derive the strength to resist other onslaughts, those of liberalism and naturalism. It was nourished by sources of inspiration of which music was to reap the benefit. If rationalism had emerged triumphant, among the élite of society and in particular among the masses, the achievement of Haydn, Mozart, Beethoven, Schubert and later Bruck-

ner would have been inconceivable. The fluid quality which has always characterized Austrian civilization, and which a superficial analysis attributes to Slav
influences or to a fusion of the genius of several different races, is to be explained
rather by sociological conditions that maintained Baroque art as a way of life.
The dreams and distractions of this art even played their part in everyday existence.
Yet historians were forgetful even of the names of the artists, whose activity,
sustained without interruption during the time of Joseph II, persisted well beyond
his reign. Today these artists are recognized to have been no less fertile than their
predecessors. In recent years the painter Maulbertsch has been the subject of a long
and worthy study by a Hungarian historian, Klára Garas. Born in Swabia in 1724
and trained at the Academy of Vienna, Maulbertsch painted over a period of fifty
years in all the countries of the monarchy, until his death in 1796. His style passed
from Baroque illusionism to a more airy and balanced composition, in which sky
and colour create a joyous mood, and then acquired a certain grandiosity, thus
following the path which led from Baroque to Rococo and Neo-Classicism. His
virtuosity and his facility for assimilation enabled him to execute a wide variety
of commissions; he painted for parish churches, abbeys, and the palaces and
cathedrals of the bishops. He extolled the enduring glory of St. John of Nepomuk
and painted a fine Baptism of Christ for one of the halls of the University of Vienna
and an Assumption on the dome of Maria Treu. He celebrated the history of the
former kings of Hungary and the renown of Maria Theresa. During the reign of
Joseph II he found himself at Pápa, Szombathely and Kalocsa, but was then called
to Strahov, near Prague, to the Premonstratensian abbey which Joseph's reforms
had left untouched and whose abbot, Mayr, while professing that his was not one
of the richest communities, commissioned him to paint the frescoes in the library.
The case of Maulbertsch bears witness both to the continuity of ecclesiastical
commissions, despite Joseph's reforms, and to the existence of artists whose reputa-
tions extended throughout the monarchy: art, rather than institutions, bound these
different countries together.[14]

Yet the liberation of the peasants and the reorganization of the Church were only
the basic elements in the vast programme of humanitarian and political reform by
which the emperor intended to transform the old monarchy into a rational and
prosperous state. Other measures were introduced to rejuvenate the administration.
A single Chancellery for Bohemia and Austria was entrusted with responsibility
for financial affairs; the *Hofrechenkammer* or Audit Chamber remained a separate
body with supervisory powers over all the financial organs of the hereditary states,
Hungary, the Netherlands and Lombardy. The process of regrouping and simplifi-
cation was extended further: the Chancellery of Transylvania was merged with
that of Hungary, while the affairs of Galicia were brought under the control of
the Austro-Bohemian Chancellery.

Budapest, owing to its central position, became the seat of the principal administrative departments of the kingdom of Hungary and was raised to the rank of

capital. But what was a capital of Hungary without a king or a palatine? An even bolder policy was adopted when, under the pretext that the counties were obstructing the decrees, it was decided to curtail their privileges and then to threaten their very existence by imposing a new administrative division of ten Circles, each headed by a royal commissary. Hitherto the *föispan* (*Obergespann*) had represented the king, but his activities had been restricted by the fact that he was also answerable to the county; the executive function had in fact been exercised by the *alispan*, appointed by the assembly of the nobles of the county. The 'king in a hat' was thus imposing his own administrators on Hungary, in a determined effort to promote efficiency but in contempt of the country's laws. For the same reason, and also because a modern language was better suited to general affairs than an archaic Latin, he issued a decree on 18 June 1784 which prescribed that the officials of the kingdom should use German: those who did not yet know the language would be allowed one year in which to learn it. The acts of the Hungarian Chancellery would henceforward be drawn up in German. In 1785 this measure was extended to Bohemia, where the use of Czech was similarly limited, and also to Galicia, where Polish was sacrificed, and to Goritz and Gradisca. It would be a mistake, however, to regard these measures as signifying a passion for Germanization. Joseph II himself spoke Czech and Magyar, but these languages did not seem to him to be appropriate to a modern state. As the historian Mitrofanov has pointed out, it was a matter of indifference to Joseph which language the Magyars or Slovaks of Hungary and the Rumanians of Transylvania used in the conduct of their private affairs.[15]

The reorganization of the municipal magistrates and the reform of justice in general was prompted by the same broad policy. Seigniorial justice was not abolished, but the judges paid by the lord were to be independent of him in the exercise of their duties. The courts of second instance or courts of appeal were established in a uniform system in 1783; the *Oberste Justizstelle* in Vienna remained the supreme court, to which there could be no recourse if the first two courts had delivered the same judgement.

The large-scale suppression of local or corporative tribunals shook the old feudal structure: even though special courts were retained for cases involving the army, commerce, exchange, the mines and, of course, ecclesiastical discipline, the spirit of a modern state had penetrated the judicial system. The same hierarchy of three courts was introduced in Lombardy.[16]

Here, also, the sovereign decreed from Vienna a reform which involved a major upheaval. The duchy of Milan, like the Netherlands, had not been simply annexed to the Danubian monarchy in 1713 by right of conquest. It had become part of the monarchy, but by juxtaposition and without losing its own institutions: its allegiance had merely shifted from Spain to Austria. In fact, it had hardly been aware of the change, which had only involved the appointment of a new governor as the representative of the duke of Milan. What did it matter if the duke was a Spanish Habsburg or an Austrian Habsburg?

Charles VI and Maria Theresa had improved the methods of the old institutions, reorganizing the tax system and provincial administration. Although they had undoubtedly aroused hostility, the old institutional framework remained. In the reign of Joseph II, however, it had already suffered from the decrees concerning ecclesiastical affairs and from the quarrel with Pius VI over the right to designate the archbishop of Milan. But everything was moving too slowly, in the opinion of the emperor and his Council of State. In 1786 the great change took place: the local Senate, which had existed for two hundred and fifty years as the embodiment of Italian liberties, was suppressed and replaced by a governing Council and specialized departments. A new rational order was substituted for the old chaotic situation: the separation of powers seemed likely to be fruitful and indeed it proved so. Hitherto the duchy of Milan had simply been an assemblage of patrician towns which had extended their power over the surrounding territory. It was now divided into new administrative areas of uniform extent under the authority of an officer appointed by the government in Vienna. The municipal authorities were granted wider powers in financial and economic matters, but lost their juridical function. The old aristocracy and the rich bourgeoisie which had come into existence with the economic revival of the eighteenth century, both stripped of their former responsibilities, were henceforth obliged to carry out orders decided in Vienna, many of which were prompted by wise judgement.

The Italian historian Francesco Valsecchi, in a fine book on enlightened despotism in Lombardy, has shown how, as if by magic, a great new edifice now came into being at the behest of an all-powerful will, a structure that bore the mark of a robust mind. But neither the architect nor the masons were Italians; instead of recognizing that, at the apex of the institutional pyramid, there existed the principle of sovereignty, the Lombards were merely conscious of the authority exercised by a master and his agents. For the first time Lombard society experienced the inconvenience of domination by foreigners—foreigners who were still barbarians when the Italians had ruled the world![17]

⁂

A centralized, modern monarchy was to be the guarantee of the well-being and prosperity of the Danubian peoples. The population had recovered from the devastation of the Thirty Years' War and in Bohemia, despite the epidemics of 1679 and 1713, had regained the level at which it had stood before the war. In Hungary the cessation of armed conflict and the influx of immigrants ensured the country's repopulation. But the general situation, though favourable, remained fragile. During the eighteenth century two scourges jeopardized the promise of progress in Bohemia: the Seven Years' War, not so much as a result of the battles fought as in its sociological consequences (increased prices, heavier taxes, undernourishment and disease), and the famine of 1771. Between the war and the famine the population had begun to rise again. From 1773 it resumed an upward trend and when Joseph II acceded to power the population of Bohemia was one-third higher than at the time of the 1754 census.[18]

When he travelled through his states the emperor observed the enormous differences of productivity and living standards between the western regions, where the rural areas showed signs of prosperity and the ability to recover quickly from a crisis and where factories were being established, and the eastern regions, where prosperity doubtless existed around the commercial centres and the mines, but where extreme poverty was to be found in certain unhealthy or isolated areas. And yet how abundant were the resources of the various countries of the monarchy! It was simply a matter of utilizing those resources, stimulating production and providing for the circulation of goods to the frontiers of the monarchy and to the Adriatic, where there was no shortage of ports. But things were not as simple as they appeared in theory to a man who believed that he could speak with authority and wisdom. In reality, the enterprise was of Herculean proportions, for it pre-supposed that all the obstacles presented by established routine, by private interests and by general conditions which lay beyond the reach of authority or persuasion, had already been surmounted. It was relatively easy to obtain results when it was a matter of large-scale building works or improvements in the road network. A surfaced road, the Via Josephina, was to link Karlovstvi in Croatia with Segna on the Adriatic coast, thus providing the Hungarian market with another outlet. A road was to connect Vienna and Prague, passing through Ihlava and Brünn (Brno) and enabling this latter city to expand as an industrial centre. The waterways of northern Bohemia were to be developed—the Elbe, the Sazava and the Vltava, which carried the rafts of floating logs that provided the factories of the region with fuel. A number of general measures were also to be introduced to improve the conditions of production and commerce. In 1783 internal tariffs and tolls were abolished in the hereditary states. The only duties allowed to remain were those which involved the public interest: for example, when roads or rivers passed through a seigniorial domain and thereby assumed the character of private property, tolls were maintained on condition that the proprietor of the adjacent land used the revenue for the upkeep of the road or bridge concerned. In 1784 the customs system was reorganized: duties were levied on the importation of foreign goods, especially textiles, so that the factories of the Danubian countries were obliged to increase their production and to achieve the same quality as their foreign competitors.

Towards the end of the eighteenth century cotton was being used to an increasing degree for the manufacture of light fabrics which could for everyday purposes be substituted for heavier and more expensive wool, and for linen, which did not offer the same resources to the various sectors of the clothing industry. Why should not linen and wool mills be adapted for weaving cotton? The raw material could easily be imported via Trieste, Fiume or Dubrovnik and the local workshops would not only produce for their customers within the monarchy, but could even compete with British textiles in countries that were relatively near and accessible, such as southern Russia where Catherine II was extending colonization and founding new towns. In fact, one of the best cotton mills was that operated by the firm of Koffiler and Zweickhardt at Brünn, which made fez for Istanbul.

In 1785 a decree was issued prohibiting the sale of foreign textiles on the internal markets of the monarchy, a measure which had various consequences: for instance, a number of British manufacturers settled in Austria so that they could put their own techniques into operation there (the firm of Stoke and Palm established a cotton mill at Warnsdorff). The manufacturers of northern Bohemia improved the quality of their production to such an extent that the inspectors believed the fabrics they seized on the Prague market to have been made in Britain and confiscated them until proof of their native origin was provided. The fiercest resistance came from merchants who had large stocks of foreign textiles and who were determined to dispose of them; consequently, the time-limit allowed by the decree had to be extended year by year until 1790.

The government was in fact being thwarted by the privileges of the merchant corporations, which monopolized the sale of goods and prevented the producers from dealing directly with customers. The merchants protested against the practice of hawking, complaining because itinerant tradesmen, generally Jews, Greeks or Serbs, who did not have the same expenses as themselves, were able to offer goods at a lower price. The customers were clearly quite satisfied, but the government could not antagonize the merchants. It was therefore decided that hawkers would only be permitted to sell products made in the hereditary countries: foreign goods, even those from Lombardy and the Netherlands, were rigorously excluded.[19]

It was certainly no easy matter to reform the entire economic system of the monarchy solely through the authority of the central power. Who in fact were the holders of capital? The general structure of the Danubian countries was agrarian: the greatest fortunes remained in the hands of the aristocracy, the owners of landed property. Although some families risked investments in manufactures or in new speculative enterprises, such as building projects in towns favoured by prosperity, the majority was more concerned to see the old economic practices preserved.

Where the linen industries had accumulated capital over a long period, there existed opportunities for purchasing machinery which, although expensive, made it possible to improve output. Progress was quite rapid. The three branches of the textile industry—linen, wool and cotton—expanded in northern Bohemia, which in the second half of the eighteenth century assumed the former role of the Silesian textile industry, now under Prussian control. Reichenberg (Liberec) and other towns in the Neisse valley became prosperous. The supply of energy posed a problem: wood was being consumed at such a great rate that there was a danger of forests being exhausted by wholesale plunder. An edict published on 21 March 1782, described with some exaggeration as the foundation charter of the industry, imposed restrictions on the exploitation of forests. At the same time, prospecting operations were conducted in search of coal, which in fact existed not far from the great textile centres. The industrial character of northern Bohemia thus became even more marked.

Manpower presented another problem. The legislation of 1784 paved the way for the extension of the wage-earning class. The Bohemian workman, whether German or Czech, was already becoming an indispensable element in the industrial economy, just as the peasant had been indispensable (and was to remain so for a long time yet) to the agrarian economy of the monarchy. But the working conditions of the wage-earner were increasingly harsh. The 'brazen law' of competition was having repercussions on the lot of the workman and was sowing the seeds of class struggle. Industry had its crises: as a result of the American war and its consequences for the textile market, the year 1787 saw the failure of a number of firms. The government did not intervene in these problems. During the reign of Maria Theresa it had quite readily granted subsidies or loans to firms in difficulty. Joseph II showed less generosity; he believed that it was in the public interest that the process of selection should be allowed to operate freely and that only the most solid and most efficiently managed concerns should be rewarded with survival. Owing to the lack of banks and of a well organized credit system, economic progress remained precarious; in particular, natural conditions and the consequences of a long-established order of things prevented some regions of the monarchy from participating in this progress.

The Tyrol found that membership of a great customs union offered few advantages: it was a region of transit where inn-keepers and carriers owed their principal revenues to the traffic between Italy and Germany, rather than to relations with the other Alpine countries or Bohemia. The condition of Hungary was even more singular, for this country was separated from Austria by a customs barrier and had very little to sell abroad: only grain, cattle, wine, tobacco, potassium and antimony. The industrial prosperity of the hereditary states tempted producers and merchants to seek an easy and immediate outlet in this agricultural country. This explains the attitude which induced Joseph II—also motivated by personal hostility towards a country whose nobility was recalcitrant in political matters and obstinate in clinging to the old economic routines—to allow Hungary to be treated as a colony of the Austro-Bohemian group. There can be no doubt that little or nothing was done to encourage the growth of a Hungarian industry: Hungarian merchants obtained their supplies in Vienna and the majority of them acted as the associates or agents of Viennese firms in Pressburg and even in Budapest. The imperial government did not scruple to declare, in the words of Kaunitz, that 'as long as the Hungarian nobility does not assume its share of general taxation, the interests of Austria and Hungary cannot be treated equally'. The president of the Hofrechenkammer also observed that Hungary, compelled to purchase goods because of the inadequacy of its own industry, provided the monarchy with much greater funds than any other of its provinces. In fact, only the nobles and the middle class of the principal towns could buy these goods, for in the country as a whole very little liquid money was available. If Hungary exported more than she imported, this was by no means a sign of health and progress: on the contrary, it was because she produced foodstuffs —cereals and meat—and lacked the resources and the affluent clientele necessary to enable her to become a buyer.

Yet Hungary's economic backwardness, though certainly exploited by the Austrians, could not be attributed solely to the policy of Vienna. Its causes lay much deeper. In the central part of Hungary, occupied by the Turks for a hundred and fifty years, it had not been possible to eradicate the aftermath of invasion within a period of seventy-five years. The process of repopulation, although spectacular in some respects, had nevertheless left large areas almost uninhabited; even with a rapid rate of population-growth, the void could only be gradually filled.[20] Consequently, agricultural production generally remained out of all proportion to the potential resources of the country. The political and administrative structure of the kingdom favoured the preservation of a noble rural class for which privilege consisted of fiscal exemption and the primacy of honour, and which remained untempted by industrial or commercial profit.

In the towns, and especially the mining towns, the corporations continued to cling jealously to their rights, resisting rather than encouraging industrial ventures. The great landed proprietors seemed much less favourably disposed to the introduction of factories than the landowners of Austria or Bohemia. It would not be true to say that factories were non-existent in Hungary, or that the few which were established proved unsuccessful. But if one considers the country as a whole, it is clear that Hungary, like Poland and Russia, was ill-suited to the development of industrial capitalism on the scale prevailing in the hereditary states, which were themselves much less advanced than the Western countries on which they had been modelled. Furthermore, the collective spirit of Hungarians accepted this state of affairs. Was not the Jewish usurer present at every level of society to alleviate financial crises? An indifference with regard to the future was sustained by a fondness for spectacle and music—always the same alliance of poverty and pride.

Although textiles and, to a lesser degree, metallurgy and mining constituted the principal industrial activity of the Danubian monarchy, a number of new industries proved quite prosperous; the paper industry, for example, was particularly in evidence in the region of Čáslav, in Bohemia: paper was produced for government offices and for printing and even blotting-paper was made, replacing the use of sand. The increased duties on luxury articles from abroad stimulated the manufacture of porcelain in Austria, Bohemia and Hungary, the production of Bohemia's glass industry, which was now competing with Venice, even on the external market, and the production of garnets and glass jewellery. The prohibition of cane-sugar, a measure that annoyed the Viennese public, which had acquired a fondness for coffee, encouraged the first attempts to develop the production of beet-sugar, undertaken by the Frenchman Joseph of Sauvaigne at the old monastery of Zbraslav. When the Emperor Joseph II observed from the official figures for 1787 that imports were only 7,250,000 florins in excess of exports, he rejoiced at what he regarded as a victory for his economic policy. It was pointed out to him that Hungary had been exporting more than she had been importing, but that this had not made her prosperous. Nevertheless, the progress of the general economy was incontestable.

❦

It was considered necessary to foster the spirit of the new order among the ranks of the civil servants and the middle class, now that they had been freed from the old traditions. Their instruction was to be relentlessly pursued, their sources of knowledge constantly supervised and purified. A vigilant watch was maintained over public education and censorship was reorganized. It has already been seen how Maria Theresa had devoted herself to education. She had also created a chastity commission to correct the excessive freedom of morals which had affected even Vienna, as the city grew in population and in brilliance. Finally, she had entrusted a commission of the Chancellery with responsibility for the censorship of books and other publications and for the preparation of a catalogue of forbidden books. The works of Voltaire and the French *philosophes* had been banned. During the first few weeks of his reign, in February 1781, Joseph II reshaped the commission of censorship; after making a few tentative changes, he detached it from the Chancellery and established it as a separate body with responsibility both for the censorship of books and for the supervision of educational problems. The new commission was given the title of *Studien und Bücherzensurhofkommission.*[21] It was, if not a ministry, at least a kind of superior council of culture. Owing to the diversity of languages, there could be no question of submitting for its examination all the books that might appear in the countries of the monarchy. Censors were therefore appointed to the governments of each country, a measure which reinforced administrative centralization and deprived the clergy of its traditional influence. But the provincial censors were urged to maintain the closest possible links with the Viennese commission, which was to serve as their model. The same recommendation was made to the Hungarian Chancellery, which had succeeded in preserving its autonomy and in establishing that works concerning the public law of Hungary could be justly assessed only by Hungarians; a special censorship commission was thus created at Pressburg. The Transylvanian Chancellery claimed that, owing to the wide diversity of religions in the country, persons with the qualifications necessary for the supervision of books could only be found in Transylvania itself; here, also, a separate censorship body was appointed, but, like the others, it was obliged to follow the directives of the commission in Vienna.

The central commission thus remained the most powerful and was alone capable of creating a harmony of national culture (*Nationalbildung*) throughout the monarchy. Its members were all disciples of the Enlightenment, men of cultivated and alert minds. Several were freemasons, which automatically made them the enemies not of the Catholic religion, but of the monks. In Cardinal Migazzi they found themselves dealing with an obstructive archbishop who was jealous of his authority and all the less inclined to look favourably on the censorship commission because, on the frequent occasions when he was attacked by pamphlets and journals, he found himself being feebly defended. Two censors distinguished themselves by their zeal: the president of the commission, Gottfried van Swieten, the son of Maria Theresa's counsellor, a man of great culture and a good musician who took Haydn, Mozart and later Beethoven under his patronage, but also a determined Voltairean and an admirer of the *Encyclopédistes*; and Joseph von Sonnenfels, who had taught literature at the Theresianum, an expert on Germany and a prominent theorist of Enlightenment. Would freedom of the press be granted? Would it be conceded that anything might be published or taught which, by rational criticism, contributed to the open discussion of principles, the progress of knowledge and the formation of judgement? The intention was clearly to develop a 'national' mentality, that is, one which accorded with the interests of the monarchy and the ideas of the emperor. The result was an extraordinary liberalism towards any attempt to criticize and even ridicule monastic life (the *Monachologie* of Ignatius von Born) or to satirize the behaviour of eminent persons. To the surprise and indignation of many, pamphlets attacking the emperor were allowed to circulate with impunity, not to mention numerous publications of a licentious nature. At the same time, works which had shocked the intellectually timid or the prudish found the censors more truly appreciative of their profound qualities. Goethe's *Werther* enjoyed complete freedom of publication after the report which it received from the censor Athanasius Szekeres, a secular priest and specialist in oriental languages, whom Joseph II always honoured with a special confidence. The same was true of works such as the *Histoire philosophique des deux Indes* by the Abbé Raynal, which was admired by some for its wealth of observation and disparaged by others for its liberty of judgement. Censorship was also exercised in the theatre, of which the emperor was especially fond and which seemed destined to replace the pulpit in the formation of opinion. But what was appropriate for the élite was not appropriate for the people and towards the end of Joseph's reign the censors, however liberal they might have been in other respects, condemned plays which revived memories disagreeable to the dynasty (*John the Parricide*) or which threatened to erode the prestige of the monarchic institution by showing royal persons, even those of the past, in tragic or humiliating situations.

The censorship commission did not escape criticism from the Church, from the Chancellery and the Council of State, and from many circles of society. It was accused of bias, culpable indulgence and complaisance towards everything that undermined the authority of faith and dogma and even that of the legitimate organs of power. In fact, it had opposed both Ultramontanist tendencies and the practices of religious life, which were in danger of encouraging excessive credulity and superstition. It regarded all forms of fanaticism as dangerous. When consulted by the censors of Prague, the abbot of Braunau, Rautenstrauch, a fervent supporter of the Enlightenment, had warned against the canticles of Luther on the ground that they might foster hatred between Catholics and Protestants and damage religious toleration. The censors had laboured with conviction to promote a religion that was humanitarian, spiritual and meditative rather than ritual and, at the same time, to inspire confidence in the emperor and in the decisions which he took in the public interest. Had they succeeded? Eventually even they hesitated when they saw the consequences of their activity, conscious of the awakening of a revolutionary spirit that might soon become a threat to the monarchy. They were working with an eye to the future. The attention of the government, in the spirit of Sonnenfels, was directed towards the universities, the secondary schools and the elementary ('trivial') schools. A number of new professorial chairs were introduced into the faculties of medicine, law and philosophy and were orientated towards the new disciplines—the sciences and philology. Joseph II reduced a number of small universities to the status of secondary colleges (*Lyzeen*); his preference was for a teaching programme that would produce technicians. Elementary schooling was made compulsory and the first to complain were the very people who ought to have derived the greatest benefit from education. The more prosperous peasants had been accustomed to supplementing the income of the local schoolmaster by gifts in kind, but they resented the obligation to provide him with a fixed salary in cash. The supervision of schools, no longer in the hands of the bishops and the clergy generally, was to be entrusted to the authorities of the Circle under the direction of the provincial governors. The officials of the State became unwelcome figures. Yet they were by no means sufficiently numerous to carry out the duties expected of them. It was not enough to rekindle their zeal with declarations of principle; it was necessary that they should be closely supervised in their turn. The police department, established at Vienna under the direction of Pergen, a man of very determined character, had its ramifications in the departments of the provincial governors. Spying and informing became common practice: suspicion, jealousy and imagination ran riot. The monarchy assumed the character of a police state, a fact which was even more distressing to outside observers than to the inhabitants themselves, many of whom accepted the situation, eventually coming to the conclusion that a modern state could not be governed in any other manner. But, like the emperor himself, the monarchy represented a curious mixture of liberty, humanitarian idealism and militarism, the desire to raise the individual dignity of man while employing for this purpose methods that seemed likely to make him more hypocritical and more servile.

Everywhere the grip of the State tightened. One of the sources of its strength was undoubtedly the quality of its army. From his mother's reign Joseph II had inherited the army which, over a period of forty years, had partially recovered the territory that had been threatened and had then protected it against further invasion. It was no longer the army of Prince Eugene, although its numbers matched the figure of one hundred thousand which the prince had recommended. It had been reorganized by Marshal Daun and then by Marshal Lacy, in his capacity as inspector general of the army and president of the Hofkriegsrat. It was recruited by conscription: one soldier was levied from each group of houses or farms. The person whom chance had designated could pay someone to take his place. Exemptions were so numerous—officials, doctors, citizens of the royal cities and merchants of certain privileged categories—that the burden of service fell once again upon the poorer peasantry, the journeymen and common labourers: as in the past, abhorrence of an unjust distribution of military service lay at the origin of many a peasant revolt. On their arrival in the army, however, the soldiers were placed in the charge of well-trained officers, the best of whom were former pupils of the military academies: the cadet college at Wiener-Neustadt and the college of engineers for the artillery and the engineer corps. The troops were accommodated in barracks and soldiers disabled in war could be admitted to the army pensioners' hospital. Joseph II founded a college of military surgery.

The regular army was supported by the army which guarded the 'Military Frontier', to the south of Croatia and Hungary, and which constituted a kind of militia.

The army was thus a professional force comprising men from every country of the monarchy, including Hungary, which still contributed the six regiments that it had provided since 1741 and also the Hungarian Guard, whose fine ceremonial uniforms delighted the Viennese crowds. Its language was German, which recruits had to learn, and its ideal the service of the sovereign above all individual and regional interests, of which the uprooted soldier ceased to be conscious. The army was becoming a fundamental institution of the Danubian system, by guaranteeing it the respect of foreign powers and by fostering a spirit of cohesion among the soldiers. A loyalty was evolving to a common fatherland which transcended territorial boundaries and traditional institutions.[22]

During the eighteenth century certain great minds had envisaged a perpetual peace among the states of Europe, an order of reason replacing the system of force and dubious juridical arguments which each government employed to justify its ambitions. But, like the king of Prussia, the rival whom he admired so greatly, Joseph II remained committed to the old ways.

He remained closely involved in the affairs of the Empire and at times wondered if his vocation lay in the renewal of Germany rather than that of his Danubian monarchy. But the first partition of Poland, which the Habsburgs had regarded merely as compensation for the loss of Silesia and as a means of recovering that country by exchange, had created a durable solidarity between the co-authors of partition: Prussia, the House of Austria and Russia. It had also reinforced the principle of European equilibrium, according to which the aggrandizement of one state was to be balanced by territorial gains on the part of its neighbours. When, at the end of a war against the Porte, Russia had secured new territories by the treaty of Kuchuk-Kainarji, the House of Austria had acquired in 1774 a small territory to the east of Transylvania, Bukovina, where the land was poor but of strategic importance, dominating the plain of the Pruth and Moldavia and providing a bridge between Galicia and Transylvania. Since it had reconquered Hungary and now found itself a great power bordering on an enfeebled Ottoman Empire, the House of Austria was obliged to maintain a close watch on events in the Balkan peninsula. In 1780 Joseph II met Catherine II at Mohilev, where they discussed the possibility of great changes: in the event of war and a joint victory over the Ottoman Empire, could not the provinces of Moldavia and Wallachia form a new and independent kingdom of Dacia, and if the Ottoman Empire were to collapse, could not a Christian empire even be re-established in its place? Could not the sovereign of this kingdom be the tsarina's second grandson, the one whom she had named Constantine, not without design, and who would thus found a secondary Romanov line in the Near East?

In these circumstances Austria would receive in compensation Serbia, Bosnia and Herzegovina, lands populated by Slavs of both the Orthodox and the Islamic creeds. Joseph's imagination was less vivid than Catherine's and he did not allow himself to be deceived by such prospects. Nevertheless, the situation which they had envisaged corresponded to a realistic view of the future. By the logic of events, the Balkan peninsula, once it was no longer dominated by the Ottomans, would fall into the orbit of the two Christian powers, whose association would then give way to rivalry. While the acquisition of Polish territories compelled them to present a united front to the other states of Europe, the East threatened to be the cause of their disunion. The proposals of 1780 contained the seeds of the rivalries that were to lead to the war of 1914. Joseph II realized that the partition of the Ottoman Empire was also of interest to France and Great Britain and at first he left Catherine II to pursue alone her acquisitions in the Crimea. In February 1788, however, he could not avoid joining with her in a new war against Turkey. During the difficult campaign that followed the Austrian troops recaptured Belgrade, but Joseph II, beset by internal problems, immediately entered into peace negotiations the conclusion of which he did not live to see.

Whatever its internal disposition, the monarchy could not escape one major difficulty: the necessity of conducting an offensive or safeguarding its defences on the western and eastern fronts simultaneously. In these circumstances, was the possession of Belgium really an advantage? Joseph II, who had visited this country, at first thought of developing its prosperity and ridding himself of a burden that had weighed heavily on him since the peace of Utrecht: the closure of the Scheldt and the blockade of the port of Antwerp. When he gave the order for a ship from Antwerp to sail out of the Scheldt into the open sea, the Dutch reacted with hostility and it seemed that war would break out. Joseph II preferred to negotiate through the agency of his ally, France, but achieved only partial success by the treaty of Fontainebleau in 1785. The problems posed by Belgium confirmed the emperor in his opinion that the possession of Bavaria would have been more advantageous to his monarchy. He had already thought along these lines during the period of his co-regency, when the elector had died without an immediate heir. He had sent troops into Bavaria and had claimed the electorate for his house. In retaliation, Frederick II had invaded Bohemia. This war (the fourth between Prussia and the House of Austria) brought no major battle, but the Prussian army made raids on crops and livestock in northern Bohemia and for a long time people spoke resentfully of the 'potato war'. Joseph II had to resign himself to the peace of Teschen and to a territorial compensation in the form of the Innviertel, which extended the western frontier of Upper Austria as far as the river Inn (1779).

However, a new vacancy of the electoral dignity in Bavaria coincided with the settlement of the Scheldt dispute. Joseph II suggested to the Wittelsbach heir, Maximilian Joseph of Zweibrücken-Birkenfeld, that Belgium should be exchanged for Bavaria. The proposal pleased no one. Even though Austria was an ally, France was unwilling to allow her to become too powerful in Germany. Frederick II of Prussia, for his part, claimed that Bavaria formed the only bulwark against a formidable Habsburg supremacy in the Empire! He assembled a League of Princes (*Fürstenbund*) and ordered troop movements in Bohemia. Joseph II had to renounce all hope of possessing Bavaria. Since he had never sought military glory or conquest, his foreign policy appears pale by comparison with his grand designs for the advancement of his empire. It was not the burdens of war which turned his subjects against him and brought failure on his reign, as had happened to so many other princes.

❧

The same philosophy of Enlightenment which inspired Joseph II to embark upon a programme of unification was also to awaken a new consciousness among the nations of the monarchy. This is not to say that men of learning were the first to oppose the emperor's policy: that role had been assumed by the members of the Diets, who adopted a more resolute attitude in the defence of privileges. On the contrary, the scholars flattered themselves that they were receiving encouragement from the prince and, when they protested their fidelity and their admiration of him, they were probably sincere.

The progress of historical science rekindled interest in the past of each individual country, as scholars devoted themselves to research, criticism and the publication of documents. In Prague the work of the Piarist, Dobner, who followed the method of the Benedictines, was pursued by his pupil Voigt, a specialist in numismatics, but who also published in German a work on the laws of the kingdom of Bohemia which showed the influence of Montesquieu and in which he lauded the old constitutions. In Vienna another Piarist, Rauch, edited the medieval chronicles (*Rerum austriacarum scriptores*) and, at Graz, Canon Aquilinus Julius Caesar composed annals of the duchy of Styria (*Annales ducatus Styriae*). How could such activities damage the cohesion of the modern state?

Similarly, no one could foresee that the interest taken by philologists in the archaic languages still in use in the different provinces might in any way endanger the unity of the monarchy. The study of these languages was motivated by scientific curiosity, by the desire to dismantle the philological mechanism; only later was it apparent that the question of language also presented a more immediate significance.

In the middle of the century the Hungarian historian Matthew Bel, of Slovak origin, had insisted on the antiquity of the Slav idiom which, he affirmed, remained in use, with differences only of dialect, from the Adriatic Sea to the Arctic Ocean: 'If, therefore, the glory of languages depended only on their use, the kinship of their dialects and their diffusion, the Slav language could be compared favourably with Latin.' This was merely a statement of principle and was, moreover, disputable. In contradiction, it was possible to argue the view put forward by the German jurist J. J. Moser in a study of the rights and duties of the Empire: 'Any reasonable man knows that language does not determine the nationality of a people, for the inhabitant of Montbéliard speaks French and is not thereby a Frenchman: he is in fact a German.'[23] Once it had been launched, the linguistic movement was to have consequences of a kind unforeseeable in its early stages.

In Hungary the Magyar language, which belongs to the Finno-Ugrian group and bears affinities to Turkish, Finnish and certain linguistic groups of Russia, could claim no kinship with the language of the neighbouring peoples. But its rights were defended by other arguments. The writer George Bessenyei, in the journal *Magyarság*, insisted that it was impossible for a national group to achieve intellectual progress unless it used the mother-tongue: 'Never has any nation in the world succeeded in attaining wisdom and depth of intellect unless knowledge has been introduced in its own language. It is in their own language that nations acquire learning, never in a foreign language' (1778). A few years later (1783) another man of letters, Nicholas Révai, published a journal in Magyar.

Thus the imperial decision of 1784, imposing the general use of German in the public departments of the monarchy, came at a time when a section of Hungarian opinion was intent on reviving Magyar and making it the language of a modern Hungary that would be stronger because better educated. Another writer, Alexander Baróczy, cited the example of the Czechs, who would rather throw themselves into the Vltava than abandon the language of St. John of Nepomuk.[24]

When the Croats heard talk of the ancient Slavs and of the community of race and language among Slavs, they recalled that, within the kingdom of Hungary, they still formed an historically and culturally autonomous group. No doubt, they remained Hungarians in their political allegiance, but they were not Magyars and had no reason to adopt the language of a section of their fellow-citizens. A situation of yet a different kind prevailed in the Slovakian valleys. The religious language of the Protestant communities and the cultural language of a large number of inhabitants was Czech. The people, however, spoke Slovak dialects which were all of ancient origin and differed little from one region to another. Would it not be possible to make these dialects literary languages? An attempt to do this was made by a Catholic priest, Bernolák, who published prayer-books and newspapers, the first manifestations of the revival, or rather the promotion, of the native idiom.

A similar situation was developing in Transylvania, where the Rumanian language was spoken neither by the Hungarian lords nor by the Germans of the towns, but only by the peasants. In all parts of the country the use of the ancestral tongue became an essential element of national sentiment, hitherto expressed only by the defence of juridical privileges or by devotion to a territory. The champions of linguistic renewal deplored the fact that the ruling classes had long since adopted a foreign language in which to give expression to their culture, regardless of the danger of thereby weakening both the national genius and the moral strength of their group.

A class problem was also unconsciously being posed, for it was the common people of the monarchy who, wherever the peasantry was not German-speaking, remained the exclusive depositaries of the ancient languages. It has already been seen how, in Bohemia, social advancement was accompanied by the risk of a loss of Czech consciousness. In Hungary, also, the Magyar language seemed to be in danger of vanishing, owing to its special character and its complexity. The forces of resistance to linguistic Germanization were shortly to find support from the Estates, alarmed by the threats to their political privileges.

In 1783, during a journey in Transylvania, the emperor was astounded at the miserable condition of the Rumanian serfs and reminded the intractable nobility that he had decreed the abolition of personal servitude throughout his states. At the same time, he ordered military registration in the villages along the frontier, which entailed the liberation of the registered peasants. In 1784, in the county of Hunedoara (Hunyad), the peasants flocked to obtain registration; when the authorities resisted, the peasants started sacking the houses of nobles, some of whom took fright and fled to Deva. But three strong peasant armies were on the march, spurred on by their popular chief, Horea (Horia-Hora), who had returned from Vienna claiming the emperor's protection against the lords. The rebels advanced on Cluj, Arad and Temesvàr, seeking to win to their cause the workmen of the mining towns. This mighty insurrection of serfs also assumed a national colouring: the Rumanian people of Transylvania against the Hungarian nobles. In the principality itself the Rumanians formed 63 per cent of the population and in the Banat 30 per cent. The Orthodox clergy supported their demands.

Joseph II hesitated, but it was difficult for him to break with the Hungarian nobility, which had already proved so recalcitrant. The army intervened and within a few weeks put down the revolt. Horea and his lieutenants, on whose heads a price had been placed, were delivered to the authorities and executed at Alba Julia in February 1785.[25] The rebellion had merely inflamed the quarrel between Hungary and the emperor. In the upper strata of society the nation was becoming increasingly conscious of its flouted independence. Who was this 'king in a hat' whose measures, decreed without the approval of the Estates, provoked social disorder everywhere? There was no king, no palatine, no Diet. Some talked of proclaiming the throne vacant and offering it to Frederick II of Prussia, always ready to defend the subjects of the Habsburgs against the injustices of their government, though in his own interests. As agitation grew, demands were made for the convocation of the Diet, alone capable of according the sovereign's decrees the sanction that endowed them with legal authority.

In the Austrian Netherlands, Joseph II considered that the governors who had been sent there, his sister Maria Christina and his brother-in-law the duke of Saxe-Teschen, were mistaken in following a traditional policy by seeking to gain the confidence of the inhabitants through respect for the old constitutions. In his eyes, this legacy of a medieval past could only prejudice the progress and the needs of a society. He intended to create an administrative council with a president designated by himself from Vienna. Meanwhile, discontent was spreading both among the middle-class élite and among the populace. In April 1787 the Estates of Brabant refused to vote taxes. On 20 May a riot broke out in Brussels. The general in command of the city's military forces did not even attempt to intervene, for the army was composed of Belgians who would not have fired on their compatriots.[26]

Two years later the news from France rekindled passions. The destiny of peoples was reverting to the peoples themselves: there was talk of dethroning the emperor and of establishing a Belgian republic. There was no longer any question of examining the measures taken by Joseph II to see if they were judicious and likely to be effective. This they were, no doubt, since several of them were to be adopted subsequently in the legislation of the kingdom of Belgium. The mere fact that they bore the stamp of a foreigner was sufficient to condemn these measures and render them hateful. Precisely the same reasoning had been adopted in Lombardy.

In Bohemia events had not yet reached this stage. But the Estates complained that the Diet was no longer convened: their prerogatives were being eroded as the interventions of the king became more frequent. The reshaping of legislation by decrees of the central power was destroying the old public order. The cadastral surveys and the proposed land-tax were depriving the Estates of their financial autonomy. The question of the coronation was also involved, for the royal oath taken at that ceremony would have reaffirmed the permanence of the state and of its constitution. The constitution of 1627 had admittedly been granted by the emperor, but it remained nonetheless valid. It had never been abolished and could not be abolished without perjury, since Ferdinand II, in according it, had also pledged his successors. The land-tax patent of 1789 and the abolition of the corvée were declared impracticable. It was now a matter of starting again.

In Vienna, two years previously, a curious pamphlet had been published under the title: *Why is the Emperor Joseph not loved by his people?* The author, with much skill, had drawn a contrast between the emperor's acts of beneficence, which should have won him the love of his subjects, and the unpopularity which they had in fact earned him. These cruel words recurred like a refrain: *and yet the people do not love him.* 'The freedom to think and to write are not favours conferred by the prince, but privileges of nature. For a long time those privileges had been withheld from the subjects by a misconceived maxim of state. No sooner was the helm of power in his hands than Joseph II restored them to the people, and yet the people do not love him.' Serfdom had been abolished, the parishes had been redistributed, seminaries had been established and facilities had been accorded to industry and commerce, 'and yet the people do not love him'. Why? Too many persons felt that they had been wronged by these wise reforms: the clergy, the civil servants who were compelled to work harder, the nobility and, to an even greater degree, those employed in the administration of the great domains who 'often more than the nobility itself tormented and tyrannized the peasants', and the merchants who served as intermediaries for foreign producers and found themselves deprived of their profits. The remedies which the pamphlet proposed, 'in accordance with the wishes of the élite of the people', were these: to provide civil servants with greater security in their employment, to separate the civil and the military, to relax police activity and spying, which were demoralizing society, and to encourage intellectual life. 'According to our state constitution, a people needs not only elementary schools, but also higher schools and scientific establishments.'[27] This was a middle-class programme of reforms put forward by a rising social group conscious both of its own needs and of those of the state. Unfortunately, however, Joseph II found no support from any social class or in any of his countries; everywhere he encountered not hatred, but simply resistance.

In the autumn of 1789 the recapture of Belgrade, which was the occasion of general rejoicing, brought the emperor a modicum of popularity for a few days. But the events in France had their repercussions in Belgium. The rebel armies which the Belgians had organized on Dutch territory boldly crossed the frontier, occupying Ghent and then Brussels, which the Austrians evacuated. The insurgents proclaimed the independence of Belgium and the deposition of the emperor. Was there still time to save Hungary? Joseph II announced that he would restore the administration of the kingdom to the situation of 1780, except only for the Edict of Toleration, the reorganization of the parishes and the liberation of the serfs. He ordered that the crown of Hungary be taken back to Buda. But Joseph was already ill and unable to make the journey for the coronation, which alone would have re-established his authority.[28] His reign was thus to end in general failure. The method of government which he had adopted for ten years, too arbitrary and too absolute despite the intention to be equitable, so lacking in a sense of proportion that its consequences incurred the disapproval of such resolute champions of reform as Kaunitz, eventually made his subjects everywhere 'unhappy under the government of a prince who never sought anything but their happiness', in the words of Pergen. Joseph's mistake was to have tried to achieve too much or achieve it too quickly, perhaps to have confused essentials with detail. His subjects forgot how much remained to his credit—above all, the liberation of man, the indispensable condition of future progress.

NOTES

1. Valjavec, *Der Josephinismus*, pp. 6–7.
2. On Joseph II, consult the correspondence published by A. von Arneth and A. Beer: *Maria Theresia und Joseph II, ihre Korrespondenz*, by Arneth, 3 vols., 1867–8; *Joseph II und Leopold von Toskana, ihr Briefwechsel, 1781–1790*, by Arneth, 1872; *Joseph II, Leopold II und Kaunitz, ihr Briefwechsel*, by Beer, 1873; *Joseph und Katharina von Russland, ihr Briefwechsel*, by Arneth, 1872. Also, the important work by P. Mitrofanov, translated from the Russian: *Joseph II, seine politische und kulturelle Tätigkeit*, Vienna-Leipzig, 1910; Professor S. K. Padover, *The Revolutionary Emperor*, 1934; Francis Fejtö, *Un Habsbourg révolutionnaire, Joseph II, portrait d'un despote éclairé*, Plon, 1953.
3. In the new Czechoslovak encyclopaedia (*Československá Vlastivěda*, 1963), under the editorship of J. Macek, 2nd part, *Dějiny*, vol. I, 'The Population of the Czechoslovak Territory in the year 1781.'
4. K. Krofta, *Přehled dějin selského stavu*, p. 207.
5. A bibliography on the religious reforms of Joseph II is to be found in Zöllner, *Geschichte Österreichs*, p. 694. The basic work is that of Ferdinand Maass, *Der Josephinismus*, 5 vols., 1950–9.

    E. Winter, *Der Josephinismus und seine Geschichte*, Brünn—Vienna, 1943; *Joseph II. Darstellungen auf der Kultur und Geistesleben Österreichs;* and *Tausend Jahre Geisteskampf im Sudetenraum*, Salzburg-Leipzig, 1938.

    An excellent work of synthesis: Fritz Valjavec, *Der Josephinismus. Zur geistigen Entwicklung Österreichs im 18 und 19 Jahrhundert*, Brünn-Vienna, 1944.

    A severely critical study, from the Catholic viewpoint, is to be found in Herbert Rieser, *Der Geist des Josephinismus und sein Fortleben, der Kampf der Kirche um ihre Freiheit*, Vienna, 1963, interesting for the development of Josephism in the lands of the monarchy. In the Fellner-Krestchmayr collection: *Die österreichische Zentralverwaltung*, II, vol. XII: 1st part, *Die Zeit Joseph II und Leopold II*, 1950, and vol. IV: a collection of the relevant documents, 1950.

    Of the many general works, the reader could consult *Handbuch der Deutschen Geschichte*, II⁴, and the study by Leo Just, *Der aufgeklärte Absolutismus*, Darmstadt, 1952. There are some excellent chapters by Prokeš in the first encyclopaedia *Vlastivěda (Dějiny*, 'History'), Prague.
6. L. A. Veit-Ludwig Lenhart, *Kirche und Volksfrömmigkeit im Zeitalter des Barocks*, 1956, and in particular chapter VIII, p. 209, entitled 'Romae non sic', from the words used by Pius VI in Vienna, when he saw the 'tombs' traditionally erected in churches on Good Friday.
7. F. Maass, op. cit.
8. H. Rieser, op. cit.

9. Joseph II expressed this clearly in a letter to Cardinal Hrczan (S. K. Padover): 'I have made philosophy the legislator of my empire . . . because I detest superstition and Sadducean doctrines and wish to deliver my people from them; with this aim, I shall drive out the monks and suppress their monasteries.'

10. Fellner-Krestchmayr, op. cit., II, vol. IV, Aktenstücke p. 123, no. 94, which contains the texts of the major patents.

11. E. Winter, *Tausend Jahre Geisteskampf im Sudetenraum*, p. 310.

12. One example among many of the long survival of Josephism: in his memoirs, *Kaiserhaus, Staatsmänner und Politiker*, Vienna, 1966, p. 154, the former minister Kielmansegg relates that, when he was *Statthalter* of Lower Austria, the Archduke Francis Ferdinand informed him of his desire that the Am Hof church, which had become a parish church in 1773, should be restored to the Jesuits. The church, says Kielmansegg, had long been a constant problem for the government, or rather for the 'religious fund', of Lower Austria; having only 5,000 parishioners, it demanded large subsidies every year from the fund. On the practical application of Josephism, see Rieser, op. cit.

13. F. Maass, op. cit.; also, a good exposé in Rieser, op. cit., p. 47.
    The journey of Pius VI to Vienna, studied by Schlitter in *Fontes Rerum Austriacarum*, II, 47[12], Vienna, 1892–1894, inspired numerous works of art, which reveal the public emotion aroused by the event. (Several interesting reproductions in the little book by F. Hennings, *Das Josephinische Wien*, Vienna, 1966.)

14. Klára Garas, *Franz Anton Maulbertsch 1724–1796*, Budapest, Academy of Sciences, 1960.

15. P. Mitrofanov, op. cit. (in note 2). H. Marczali, *Ungarisches Verfassungsrecht* and *Ungarische Verfassungsgeschichte*.

16. On Lombardy, F. Valsecchi, *L'assolutismo illuminato in Austria e in Lombardia*, 2 vols., 1931.

17. Ibid., vol. II, pp. 223–4.

18. This passage is inspired by the posthumously published book by Ludmila Kárníková, *Vyvoj obyvatelstva v českých zemich* ('Growth of the Population in the Czech Lands from 1754 to 1914'), p. 19 *et seq.*

19. For the economic policy of Joseph II: E. Benedikt, *Kaiser Joseph II und die Wirtschaft*; Kerner, *Bohemia in the 18th Century* (very interesting on customs policy); and much of the old work by Prášek, *Panování císaře Josefa II*, 1903.

20. At the beginning of the eighteenth century the total population of Hungary comprised 2,500,000 inhabitants (according to Szekfü, *État et Nation*, p. 190), of which Hungarian nationals (including those of Transylvania) constituted only 1,160,000, i.e. barely 45 per cent. Around 1790 it reached 8,500,000, including 3 to 3·5 million Hungarians, but 4 to 4·5 million immigrants or descendants of immigrants. But it must not be forgotten that the progress of the nationalities cannot be considered to be the result of natural demography. It was a phenomenon governed by human choice and, in a sense, by cultural adaptation.

21. On censorship in the time of Joseph II, the book by Oskar Sashegyi, *Zensur und Geistesfreiheit unter Joseph II*, Budapest, 1958, is a remarkable and excellently documented exposé of the question.

22. On the army, Mayr Kaindl, revised by Pirchegger, *Geschichte und Kulturleben Österreich von 1493 bis 1792*, 1960, p. 302 *et seq.*

23. J. J. Moser, *Von denen Kayserlichen Regierungs-Recten und Pflichten* (1774), p. 5.

24. J. Szekfü, *État et Nation*, Paris, 1945: chapter 1, *Le Hongrois langue d'État*, from which the quotations from Bessenyei have been taken.
    For the revival of Czech and Slovak, in addition to the useful chapters in vol. X,

Osvĕta, of the first encyclopaedia (*Československá Vlastivĕda*), there is the book by A. Pražák, *Národ se branil* ('The Nation has Defended Itself', the defence of the Czech nation and language from ancient times up to the present day), Prague, 1945, which contains some excellent texts.

25. Concerning the insurrection of Horea (Hora), see C. Daicoviciu and M. Constantinescu, *Brève histoire de la Transylvanie* (a French adaptation of 'History of Transylvania'), Bucharest, 1965, p. 156 *et seq.*, and bibliography p. 433. The consular correspondence of Trieste (consul Desjardins), in the French archives (A.N. Af. étr. B¹ 1086), relates that the rebel-leader invoked the emperor's promise to free the peasants from the juries of nobles: 'They were not rebels, but had taken up arms only to escape the harassments of the nobles and wished to recognize no master other than His Majesty.'

26. H. Pirenne, *Histoire de Belgique*, vol. V.

27. Pamphlet published in 1787 in Vienna (National Library, Vienna, 726–435 A), quotations pp. 10–60.

28. Eva Balász, in an appendix (p. 317) to her book on George Berzeviczy and the policy of reform of 1763–95 (Budapest, 1967), has published a memorandum by Berzeviczy in German on the principles applied by Austria in the government of Hungary, in which he explains at length the reasons for his disenchantment and passes harsh judgement on Joseph II who, he claims, had become a despot despite his noble character.

Part Three

❧ 9 ❧

Between Two Revolutions

JOSEPH II had accomplished a series of profound and lasting reforms, for many aspects of 'Josephism' were to survive him; but, at the same time, he had passed on to his successor a pre-revolutionary situation. Leopold II succeeded in restoring peace within the monarchy and in rebuilding the alliance between the dynasty and Hungary. His son, the Archduke Alexander Leopold (1772–95), who assumed the office of palatine, fully understood that he was not to act as a governor, but as the intermediary between Hungary and the sovereign. In his correspondence with his father he explained the spirit of the Hungarian constitution.[1] On the premature death of the young archduke one of his brothers, the Archduke Joseph, born in 1776, succeeded him. The Archduke Joseph remained palatine for half a century. He became a true Hungarian and attained a popularity to which his statue on a square in Pest still bears witness today; the inscription on the statue reads: 'He sacrificed his whole life to public affairs. He rebuilt Pest.' During these same years, however, the French Revolution was creating an international problem. Confronted with the disruption of the European monarchic order, Leopold, though prudent by nature, became one of the co-authors of the partition of Poland, with the king of Prussia and the empress of Russia, and the enemy of the new political system in which privileges were abolished and in which, without distinction of orders, the body politic comprised all the citizens, who substituted the common will for the authority of the prince. The war against the Revolution broke out several weeks after the death of Leopold II and the accession of his son, Francis II.[2] After fifty years of Austro-French alliance the whole of Europe was once more united against France, in a succession of alliances that were themselves to last for nearly twenty-five years (1792–1815).

Among the intellectual élite of Austria, Bohemia and Hungary the philosophy of the Enlightenment had aroused much sympathy for the French programme of reform. The example of the Revolution was to bring a new ideal to maturity. The yearning for freedom manifested itself everywhere, finding its most tragic expression in the conspiracy of the Hungarian Jacobins led by the abbot Martinovics (1795); the condemned men became figures symbolic of the nation. But the bloody nature of the events in France also gave rise to doubts. A young Hungarian noble, George Berzeviczy, while remaining faithful to the Enlightenment, deplored the execution of Louis XVI. But he also condemned the principle of the war of coalition as a terrible mistake. Convinced that force would never prevail over the ideas of a revolutionary people, he foresaw a succession of murders, injustices and iniquities.[3]

Among peoples for whom the monarchy still possessed a sacred character, the death of the king of France and then that of his queen provoked horror. 'At the very place where your archduchess fell, execute the last Frenchman!' threatened the polemist Haschka.[4] The articles of counter-revolutionary propaganda which appeared in the press were doubtless inspired by the government. But the partisans of reform and Enlightenment—in Bohemia, Bishop Kindermann, the ex-Jesuit Cornova and the popular writer Vavák—themselves became critical of the new French institutions. They came to the conclusion that the monarchic institution was beneficial in that it safeguarded the rights of the citizen. They warned against the dangers of an even more redoubtable tyranny, the tyranny of parties and sects, and implored the government to rectify abuses and deficiencies before calamities comparable with those in France were unleashed. The choice was between reform and Revolution. But the state of war in which the monarchy found itself prevented the introduction of radical reforms. The populations would have to supply the army with men and money. Troops were recruited by conscription and each rural or urban community was to provide its contingent (*Werbbezirke*). Since the same social categories remained exempt from military service—the nobles, unless they were professional officers, the clergy, civil servants, officials of seigniorial domains, doctors, the burghers of the royal cities and their sons, the proprietors or cultivators of a rural holding—the burden of service fell once again on the younger sons of peasant families and on peasants without land of their own. This was a detested obligation which some conscripts evaded by fleeing into the woods or taking up a life of vagrancy. In 1802 an attempt was made to alleviate the conditions of service, which had hitherto been practically for life: a limit of ten years was fixed for the infantry, twelve years for the cavalry and fourteen years for the artillery and the engineer corps; the successful soldier would also have the opportunity of contracting a new engagement on better terms. The Austrian army was in fact becoming a professional army, recruited among the lower orders of all the countries of the monarchy; as a whole, it proved its qualities of endurance and loyalty.

Money had to be sought from the Diets, in the form either of contributions or of loans. But, since revenues were insufficient to meet constantly increasing expenditure, the war could not have been pursued without the support of the bankers. The financial situation of the State thus worsened from year to year. The banknotes (*Bankozettel*) in circulation were worth only half of their nominal value by 1807, a quarter by 1810 and a tenth by 1811, when it was necessary to declare a state of bankruptcy. During this period, which was profoundly marked by the consequences of the Continental Blockade, the price of agricultural produce had risen continually and the peasants had made large profits. Just as this class of society was subsequently to benefit from a time of monetary crisis, the peasants now had unusually large funds at their disposal and could buy things of which their fathers had never dreamed—furniture, for example, and jewellery. At the same time, seigniorial dues weighed less heavily on them; some were able to extend their lands. Bankruptcy then reversed their situation, for the old paper-money was suppressed: it had to be exchanged at a disproportionately low rate for redemption notes or *Einlösungsscheine*, which the Czechs called *sajny*, and which henceforward were the only acceptable form of payment for seigniorial dues and taxes.

The Diets continued to discuss the redemption of the corvée. On certain estates peasants had already been allowed to buy their freedom by private agreement. But opinions were divided on the wisdom of this measure. The arguments used against it pointed to the monetary instability of the time and the danger of bringing chaos to the agricultural economy if the peasant were free to choose his own crops and livestock. There would be a shortage of horses if these animals were no longer required for draught labour. Once deprived of the corvée, which remained the only real link between the proprietor and the peasants of his estate, the seigniorial domains would lose their value and would no longer serve to guarantee the mortgages with which they had been encumbered, or even the debts which the nobles owed to numerous suppliers. Consequently, the corvée was retained and the peasantry, who no longer enjoyed the benefits of inflation, found its situation all the more irksome; many peasants experienced greater hardship in their daily existence. The war stimulated certain enterprises: metallurgy, textiles with its subsidiary industries of bleaching and dyeing, and food industries such as brewing (the Dreher brewery was opened at Schwechat at the end of the eighteenth century). The population of the towns increased.

The First Coalition was engaged far from Austrian territory: its armies were operating in Germany and in Belgium. Compromised after three years, when Prussia and Spain signed a separate peace, it was virtually brought to a halt by Bonaparte's dazzling campaign in Italy. The victorious French armies, advancing across Lombardy, the duchy of Milan and the quadrilateral of fortresses, reached Leoben in Styria. In this peaceful city, where attractive new houses bore witness to the prosperity of recent years, the first armistice was concluded. The treaty that followed (Campo Formio) resulted in the loss of Belgium, the cession of the left bank of the Rhine to the French Republic and that of the duchy of Milan to the new Cisalpine Republic. In compensation Austria received Venetia, her old rival, and the opportunity to dominate the Adriatic if peace was maintained.

An act of violence by Hungarian soldiers, who murdered the French plenipotentiaries at Rastatt, resulted in the formation of the Second Coalition, for which Great Britain had constantly been striving. Russia now joined the forces of the counter-revolution: the armies of Suvorov marched from Germany into Switzerland and Italy, the sign of a profound transformation in the power structure of old Europe. The presence of the tsar's soldiers in the West robbed Austria of the privilege of being the principal, and even the sole, defender of the old international political order against the Revolution. The support of the Russian armies had been indispensable to the Austrians in their campaign to regain Italy from France and to overthrow the sister-republics. But such alliances engendered rivalries. The discord between the Austrians and the Russians enabled the French generals to resume a victorious offensive (Masséna triumphed at Zurich). In the spring of 1800, Bonaparte, First Consul of France, gained a narrow victory at Marengo; by the treaty of Lunéville (1801) a part of Germany and of Italy returned to French domination.

How far did these wars—in the course of which the young brothers of the Emperor Francis, the archdukes Charles and John, had achieved some brilliant successes and, when fortune did not favour them, had at least averted catastrophe—help to resuscitate solidarity between the dynasty and its peoples? This is difficult to establish with certainty, but loyalty prevailed over resistance. The most serious consequence, however, was the radical transformation of the Holy Roman Empire. During the few months in which Europe seemed to have returned to a general peace (Great Britain had finally become reconciled with France) the Imperial Diet ratified the reorganization of Germany by the 'recess' of 23 February 1803. One hundred and twelve states of the Empire were abolished and numerous princes were 'mediatized', losing their territorial independence and entering into the allegiance of other states. In compensation for the territories ceded to France on the left bank of the Rhine, Prussia and other states of medium size were able to annex secular and ecclesiastical seigniories.

When it became known that the First Consul intended to ask the French nation to accord him the title of emperor—without yet abandoning the fiction of the Republic—the court of Vienna decided that, in order to strengthen the union of his independent hereditary states, Francis II would henceforth bear the title of emperor of Austria (as Francis I). For a time, at least, Francis combined in his person two imperial functions. Austrian historians are justified in associating this event with the decisions of the Pragmatic Sanction. Not only was the Danubian monarchy virtually detached from Germany, but its cohesion was augmented. The legitimacy of such a measure was immediately disputed. Nowadays, historians are inclined to attach little importance to the vain desire to bear a title equal to that of the sovereign of Russia or the head of the French Republic. The decision held a deeper and more real significance: for the first time the countries of the Danube received a common designation—though they did not lose their character of juxtaposed states, modern Austria had been born.[5]

In principle, therefore, there had been no modification of the traditional constitutions of the Danubian states, of the ancient privileges of Hungary or even of the hereditary states' membership of the Germanic Holy Roman Empire as long as the latter should survive. But the existence of Austria had been affirmed as an individual and more solid reality among the states of Europe. If war should be resumed, the government of this state would find circumstances as favourable to its military and fiscal needs as if it were a unified state. It has been suggested that the supranational, universal character with which the Holy Roman Empire had been endowed was now passing to the new Austria, which was about to discover its vocation: the grouping of states and nations under a sovereign who would be the guarantor of their common interests. That the imperial function should serve in Austria to bring different peoples into harmony without violating their individuality was not fully recognized until much later. For the time being its chief purpose remained dynastic prestige.

Germany was cut into two. A western Germany was to follow the destinies of France over the next ten years: certain regions were annexed to France as departments, while others existed as allied or subjected states with sovereigns who were under the patronage of France and who had family connections with her emperor. The other Germany, with Austria as its driving force, was to attempt to resist Napoleon. Furthermore, the German nation, as it became increasingly conscious of itself under the influence of writers who were not Austrians by birth, such as Fichte and Hegel, was to look on Austria as the country most interested in the general fate of Germany and the one predestined for its defence. But the Third Coalition, initiated by Austria, proved far from triumphant and brought a succession of reverses. The valley of the Danube, where Mack was taken by surprise at Ulm and forced to capitulate, became an easy invasion route through which the French advanced to Vienna.

The inviolable capital was occupied on 14 November. Napoleon then pursued the armies of the tsar and the Emperor Francis into Moravia, where at Austerlitz, on 2 December 1805, he gained the greatest victory of his career. Prussia, which had been preparing to rejoin the coalition, was compelled to sign a treaty of neutrality at Schönbrunn, while at Pressburg a treaty was concluded by which Austria abandoned Venice and Dalmatia, lost the Tyrol and Vorarlberg to Bavaria and ceded her German possessions to Württemberg and to the duchy of Baden.

Finally, on 6 August 1806, from the terrace of the church of the Am Hof, the dissolution of the Holy Roman Empire was proclaimed. In its place the Confederation of the Rhine was created with Napoleon as its protector. Prussia accepted the challenge on behalf of the German nation. But the Fourth Coalition brought new successes to the emperor of the French: the crushing defeat of Prussia, the continental blockade decreed at Berlin and, after the defeats suffered by the Russian army in the spring of 1807, the spectacular reconciliation with the tsar and the alliance of Tilsit: 'I hate England as much as you do,' said Alexander. France, in particular, was the object of unprecedented German hatred. Vienna became the meeting-point for all those awaiting the moment for a liberating offensive.[6] The publicist Gentz, after his wanderings in the spas of Bohemia, came back to the city to join such illustrious émigrés as Mme. de Staël, August and Friedrich von Schlegel, and Stein. Austrian intellectual circles were vigorously active. In the salons of Caroline Pichler, in the government departments, in the Chancellery headed by Stadion, among writers (the publicist Hormayr, a Tyrolean, founded *The Austrian Plutarch*), there was a growing conviction that the Austrian Empire would save the German nation and Europe. It would achieve this by regenerating the traditional forces of the past—devotion to the sovereign and to religion—and by rekindling the fervours of sentiment. A link was thus being established between the Baroque experience of earlier years and the Romanticism of the coming era. Even the French Revolution provided examples to follow: the Vendée, where both people and nobility had revolted, offered a model of resistance for the provinces whose faith and traditions were in peril. But the necessity to apply this stimulus to public morale did not deter the government from introducing practical reforms. The Archduke John secured the organization of a territorial reserve, the *Landwehr*, though only with some difficulty, for the idea of arming the people seemed revolutionary. He attempted by propaganda to prove that the lot of the inhabitants of Austria was a particularly happy one and that the government was gentle in its methods, guaranteeing everyone security in his possessions and in his work.[7] Educational reforms were undertaken and an attempt was made to provide society with a trained body of technicians (in Prague the first polytechnic institute was founded in 1806). Finally, preparations were hastened for the publication of the Civil Code which, although it did not in fact appear until 1812, was to ensure a more equitable exercise of justice and was to be extended, in a bold and efficacious enterprise of unification, to all the states of the empire except Hungary, which nonetheless felt the indirect benefit of its influence. It was hoped thereby to engender, above local patriotism, an all-embracing patriotism which, with the money of the provinces and the sacrifice of men's lives, would sustain the policy chosen by the emperor. Neither the Emperor Francis nor the Archduke Charles was yet ready to risk an offensive which they both believed to be premature. But they were surrounded by impatient and persuasive voices: the Archduke John and the Empress Maria Ludovica, a Modena, who was to inspire Goethe with the greatest admiration and was no less bellicose than Queen Louisa of Prussia had been in 1806. Great Britain added its own encouragements. Above all, the example of Spain, where Napoleon had suffered his first reverses, seemed to offer conclusive proof that a people convinced of its faith and its rights could, merely by its resistance, shake the invincible power of the colossus.

What then might a resolute and well-armed country achieve? It was decided to wage war and to attack Bavaria, the nearest neighbour in alliance with Napoleon. In the spring of 1809 the Emperor Francis was at Schärding, ready to assume the offensive, when he learnt of the popular rising in the Tyrol led by the innkeeper Andreas Hofer. But at the battle of Eckmühl the French armies again assured themselves access to the valley of the Danube. Vienna was occupied once more. However, at Aspern, in May, the onslaught of the Austrian army under the Archduke Charles inflicted a heavy defeat on Napoleon. He succeeded in regaining the advantage on the plain of Wagram. The war, begun too soon, was leading to yet another disaster for Austria.[8] A young Austrian named Staps tried to kill Napoleon during a review in the park of Schönbrunn, in the hope of ridding Europe of its tyrant. In Vienna a punitive peace was signed which accelerated the dismemberment of the old monarchy: southern Croatia, Istria, Carinthia and Carniola were taken from Austria to form together with Dalmatia the Illyrian Provinces, created by Napoleon to give France mastery of the Adriatic. Galicia was divided between the tsar and the grand duchy of Warsaw. Austria, burdened with a war indemnity of 85 millions, was compelled to adhere to the continental blockade. To make matters worse the Emperor Francis, despite his promise never to sign a peace unless the Tyrol was returned to Austria, had been forced to abandon Andreas Hofer and leave him to be shot on 20 February 1810. The new chancellor, Metternich, and the ambassador in Paris, Schwarzenberg, having sacrificed their fatherland, now consented to the sacrifice of the dynasty: since Napoleon had embarked on a search for a new wife, they gave him the eldest daughter of their emperor, the Archduchess Marie Louise. Metternich, a man of a practical nature, believed the Napoleonic Empire to be already solidly established and considered it expedient to seek an alliance to protect Austria against Russia. Never, until the explosion of 1918, was the Danubian monarchy subjected to such political humiliation.

When Napoleon engaged in the war with the tsar, Austria had to supply his armies for the Russian campaign. After the retreat, however, it found itself in such a position of advantage that the policy of Metternich appeared to have been justified. Owing to his family connections the Emperor Francis was better placed than any sovereign in Europe to persuade Napoleon to listen to counsels of moderation and wisdom. It should then have been possible to restore peace and forestall the possibility of Europe turning against France once more in a war of liberation that would bring further devastation and incite hatred among peoples.[9] But Napoleon repudiated the emperor's conditions and Austria thereupon rejoined the opposing coalition, taking part in the gigantic and baleful Battle of the Nations at Leipzig, where the French were crushed under the massed onslaught of their former allies. Throughout the next hundred years the memory of this battle was to nurture a spirit of conquest and revenge which made war and not peace the foundation of German solidarity. In the following winter the forces of the coalition invaded France, capturing Paris and securing the abdication of Napoleon: in the words of Georges Lefebvre, it was the Revolution itself which, in the person of Napoleon, was surrendering its sword.[10]

☙

The treaties of Vienna assured the revenge of the monarchic principle and the values of the old order, in so far as these had not been undermined by the upheavals of twenty years of war and revolutions.[11] The treaties proposed to guarantee the peace of Europe by establishing a balance between the great powers: Britain, Russia, Austria, Prussia and France. The situation of the Austrian Empire did not allow it to tolerate the expansion of Russia on the eastern littoral of the Black Sea, into which the Danube flowed, nor that of Great Britain in the eastern Mediterranean. In fact, Austria's acquisition of the Lombardo-Venetian kingdom and the former Illyrian Provinces (the coast of Dalmatia) made possible a return to an Adriatic policy of the kind adopted by Charles VI.

The preservation of the Ottoman Empire was the consequence of this policy, a singular reversal of circumstance, since the struggle against the Turk had constituted the basis of Austrian foreign policy for several centuries. The Ottoman Empire was now necessary to Austria. The Christian populations of the Balkans, for the most part devout in their faith under the guidance of their monks and parish priests, looked to the Orthodox emperor of Russia as their natural protector. The first Serbian insurrections had recently received the encouragement of Russia. The threat to the Austrian Empire, where the territory of Hungary had acquired a large Serbian population, was evident; but it was not yet as serious as the danger of agitation among the Greeks (the Greek merchants of Istanbul and the seamen of the islands), with whom Great Britain, established in Malta, might wish to enter into an economic alliance. An Eastern Question was reappearing in a form different from that of the past; it seemed to Metternich that the best remedy was to maintain the *status quo*. Even though Russia was a rival in the East and Prussia a rival in Germany, association with those countries was clearly necessary, since the three powers were still in possession of their Polish provinces. The partition of Poland continued to require the solidarity of its co-authors.

As for Germany, it was the view of Metternich that the Confederation would safeguard the prestige of the Habsburg dynasty, without necessitating the effort of a hegemony which neither its own resources nor the situation of the other powers rendered attainable or even desirable. The latent rivalry with Prussia was thus mitigated; Prussia was more truly German than Austria and therefore capable of attracting the hopes of the German nation, which had been reinvigorated by the wars of liberation and whose ideal, transcending the frontiers of states, aspired to territorial unification. This was a revolutionary desire in that it accorded primacy to the national ideal and no longer to allegiance to dynasties.

The situation of Italy was even more delicate. Here, public opinion, remembering the recent kingdom of Italy created by Napoleon, remained enamoured of liberty and resented the return of the Austrian administrators and the military, who spoke German and were regarded as Germans because of their status as Austrian citizens, although many were Bohemians and Slavs. Metternich considered that, if Venetia was to belong to Austria, Lombardy was no more than a military bulwark. Perhaps the line of the Adige would have sufficed for the defence of the Danubian system on its south-western front. But Milan had been regained. The prestige of possessing this territory gratified the dynastic pride of the Emperor Francis, but the price paid was heavy, for the emperor was obliged to hold in check a city where national consciousness was strong and society cultivated, and which was a natural hotbed of insurrection. The collateral branches of the Habsburg dynasty gained the throne at Modena and at Florence; the Empress Marie Louise secured the possession for life of the principality of Parma, which she considered by no means worthless. Naples had seen the return of the Bourbons, the natural enemies of the Revolution. The prophecy of Chateaubriand was thus fulfilled: Austria was occupying Italy by leasehold.

Ignaz Seipel suggested that the solution would have been to establish two federations of sovereign states, one in Germany, the other in Italy, each forming a league under the presidency of the emperor of Austria. In this way the supranational vocation of the dynasty would have been affirmed. The system could have been adapted to the hereditary states and three leagues would then have existed, offering their example as a model for the future of a reconciled Europe. The nobility of the ideal is evident, but was this not wishful thinking on the part of an historian judging *a posteriori*? Circumstances were not ripe for such an enterprise and the emperor of Austria did not dispose of the means with which to undertake innovations that would have constituted a 'conservative revolution'.

Metternich had glimpsed the advantages of associations of this kind, but he considered that in Germany a confederation of princes was preferable to a federation of states, which would have posed in a more acute form the problem of whether Prussia or Austria should exercise controlling authority. As for Italy, it seemed to him that the unity of that country could be achieved only in a republican form.[12] Consequently, the alliance with the sovereigns (the Pope included) would suffice for the preservation of order.

'The policy of Europe was henceforth to be guided by a universal principle, no less universal than its adversary, the great Revolution: the community of Christian states and their association founded on history.'[13] Since it was the responsibility of the sovereigns to guarantee that association, they became answerable to each other for the maintenance of order in their own states and in the event of the threat of revolution they could call on the assistance of their allies. It was this principle that led to the policy of the Holy Alliance and that of the Congresses, at which Metternich showed his astuteness, often in secret opposition to Russia and Great Britain: while the latter were conservative powers, they were ready to accept territorial changes or modifications of the European equilibrium, if this was to their political or economic advantage.[14]

The final resolution of the Congress of Vienna had contained clauses that could prove fruitful for the general progress of humanity. It condemned slavery and the slave system still in use in North and South America; it prohibited the negro slave trade, which continued to drain Africa of its ethnic substance. It also authorized the internationalization of the great waterways and thereby gave the industrial products of western Europe free access along the Danube to the Balkan peninsula and the Middle East.

The treaties of Vienna ensured Europe thirty-three years of peace, during which the development of science and technology brought economic progress and a better life for Europeans. Yet this system of an association of sovereigns, the general tendency towards the repression of the youngest and most idealistic sectors of opinion, was soon discredited, especially in the West. What has been called the 'Europe of Metternich' became, even during his lifetime, an object of detestation among the partisans of liberty and the younger generations.

Above all, the duel between Metternich and Italy was detrimental to Austria. The prestige of Italy's arts and the quality of its contemporary culture attracted France, Great Britain and a large part of Germany, as one of Goethe's most famous poems shows: *Kennst du das Land wo die Zitronen blühn?* It seemed that the brilliant and proud peninsula had been delivered into the hands of a barbarous soldiery. The Austrian troops were guilty of no particularly scandalous abuses, but the officers and soldiers appeared crude and arrogant and their behaviour formed too vivid a contrast to the irony, the suppleness and the nonchalance of the Italian character. In other words, the daily confrontation between the Danubians and the Mediterraneans fostered a kind of racial conflict, although this term was not used at the time. Europe judged Austria by what it heard of the misfortunes of Italy and showed little concern with the new problems that were beginning to make themselves felt within the monarchy.

The benefits which the slow but undeniable social progress of the eighteenth century had brought to the peoples of the monarchy, the contribution which the organization of schools in the time of Maria Theresa and Joseph II had made to intellectual development, were engendering a new ideal. The recovery of national consciousness and the 'awakening' now became manifest.[15] But, in societies accustomed to the plastic arts rather than rigorous reasoning, ideas could evolve only in an atmosphere of romanticism.

In Hungary, and a little later in Croatia and Bohemia, the memories of history became associated with existing concrete juridical realities. The old constitutions had never been abolished and the royal coronations testified to their perennial character. The uninterrupted tradition of each state thus survived in the new complex, the Empire of Austria.

The Polish provinces presented a special case. They had been detached from a state that had ceased to exist in international law, but their condition was so disgraceful that no one in Europe considered that partition could be either justified or permanent; furthermore, no one questioned the existence of the Polish people and nation.

The situation was different yet again when it was a matter of national groups which claimed the right to exist but which had never constituted an independent state (the unification of all Rumanians under Michael the Brave was an exceptional case). The sentiment which was now awakened was one of community of language and also of affection for a common territory. The yearning for a better and more just existence involved implicit social aspirations. People saw more clearly the harshness of their condition. They felt a greater sadness at being poor and oppressed and they found comfort and hope for the future in their more educated brethren, who were often also more favoured in their material circumstances and who spoke on their behalf—generally priests, pastors and the occasional person of eminence. Such was the situation of the Serbs, the Slovenes, the Rumanians of Transylvania and the Slovaks of the valleys of Upper Hungary. Religion had its part to play in their national solidarity.[16]

It is a mistake to include all these groups under the term of 'nationalities', which during the nineteenth century came to be used indiscriminately. Marx recognized this when he spoke of peoples having an historical past and peoples without such a past. At this stage of history a distinction should be made between 'state rights' and nationality; it was only later that the two ideas became merged. In what respects were they different? State rights represented an historical continuity of existence on a territory recognized by international treaties, irrespective of the ethnic origin or language of the inhabitants. This was the situation of the great countries of Europe. Mirabeau's description of pre-revolutionary France as a formless agglomeration of disunited peoples is obviously an exaggeration. But exaggeration must always originate in a basis of truth. In the juridical, economic and social conditions which characterized Europe at the end of the eighteenth century, what state did not consist of subjects of different languages and different customs? If it was quite natural that France should not yet be one and indivisible, that the kingdom should comprise Flemings, Bretons, Provençals and Alsatians, it was no more surprising that the kingdom of Bohemia should include both Germans and Czechs, or the kingdom of Hungary Magyars, Slovaks, Croats, Germans, Rumanians and Serbs. Thus, the use of a general historical term such as 'Frenchman' in France or 'Spaniard' in Spain signified that the different ethnic elements of the population belonged to the same state. All the subjects of the kingdom of Bohemia were *Bohemians*, the

Germans no less than the Czechs. All the subjects of the kingdom of Hungary were *Hungarians*, the Slavs no less than the Magyars. But, in order to be invested with its full force, the concept of state rights required the consent of all the inhabitants of a kingdom. The author, in his earlier days in Prague, received from his teachers so clear a consciousness of what state rights represented that for a long time he believed fervently not only in their efficacy but even in their contemporary significance. He is still convinced that the concept did represent something real, long after the rupture of 1848; moreover, as will be seen, the compromise of 1867, which lasted for fifty years, rested on this idea. Yet the notion of state rights was to a certain extent in contradiction with the ideal of nationalities and began to lose its vigour as soon as nationalities demanded to be recognized as such. It would not have been impossible to reconcile the two ideals. Men of sufficient wisdom and political imagination, provided that they were free of the prejudices of caste and intransigent nationalism, could have found satisfactory formulas. But people attached an ever greater importance to the conditions of their nationality; even those who invoked state rights did so in the interests of their particular group. The Czechs longed to restore the supremacy of their language in the kingdom of St. Wenceslas and looked on their German-speaking fellow-citizens as the descendants of intruders, of conquerors and of enemies. The Magyars sought to 'Magyarize' the entire kingdom of Hungary. National consciousness asserted itself as membership of a linguistic and ethnic group, even of a race, and, without ever denying historical and juridical tradition, henceforth accorded it less significance.

In these largely rural societies the love of the soil was almost an elemental force: a nation without its own territory was inconceivable. The territory and the devotion which it inspired in populations thus played an important role in the revival or the formation of national consciousness. But conditions were not the same everywhere. Those countries where the state possessed an ancient, traditional structure, with territorial boundaries fixed by history and by treaties, were easily identified. Notions became less clearly defined in regions which had never existed as states. Yet the inhabitants spoke the same language, which they had inherited from their fathers who, like their fathers before them, had lived and worked in the same region. A new idea was evolving: the idea that the territory belonged, by a moral rather than a legal right, to the linguistic community occupying it. A territorial fatherland was thus emerging on the fringe of formally constituted states. The Slovaks had never known any environment other than the counties of Upper Hungary, but the reality of a Slovak region, and therefore of a territorial Slovakia, existed nonetheless. Similarly, Transylvania, a historical principality governed by a Hungarian aristocracy, was regarded as Rumanian soil in those regions where the Rumanian-speaking rural populations had become conscious of their common character. Finally, in the annexed districts of the old kingdom of Poland, the Ukrainian or Ruthenian populations felt themselves to be morally the masters of their territory, which they looked on as their homeland. In certain extreme cases, the claims of nationality assumed an even more concrete character: the great proprietor, especially if he did not reside on his estate, became the intruder, while the one who cultivated the land became the legitimate master.

The population-growth and social progress of the nineteenth century occurred simultaneously with the evolution of these mental attitudes. Between 1819 and 1843 the population of the Austrian countries increased by 24 per cent; in 1846 i reached the figure of thirty-five millions. The expansion of the cities was considerable: by the middle of the century Vienna, which at the beginning of the French Revolution had a population of 235,098, numbered 400,000 inhabitants, in spite of a slight decline during the Napoleonic Wars (224,548 in 1810); Prague had 100,000 inhabitants and Trieste 80,000. Gathered together under the same hereditary dynasty, the countries of the House of Austria had never constituted a single state or a single nation. From a juxtaposition of states, they were to become a juxtaposition of peoples: nations and nationalities, impelled to remain together by diverse forces—the prestige and authority of the central government, the community of their economic interests and, unconsciously, the fact of their belonging to a common civilization. But, henceforward, each of these peoples recognized as its most cherished ideal the defence of its own individuality. The problem which until the final explosion, remained unsolved, if not insoluble, was the organization of their association. What institutional forms should this association assume? How could these peoples be persuaded to accept the sacrifice of part of their independence to the general obligations which remained essential to the existence of the system? What, in short, was to be the character of Austria?

It was always easy for an emperor to say 'My peoples' and to believe himself called to the vocation of a father. After all, Louis XIV had used this expression, which had not only accorded with the ideology of a monarch, but had also received the assent of his subjects.

It had been possible for the French Revolution to evolve, with the general consent of France, the idea of a nation that was one and indivisible, an idea which successive governments never called in question. But to reconcile the central principle of a common sovereignty with the subject peoples' desire for autonomy, an autonomy all the more difficult to recognize in that it presupposed the reconstitution of existing states or the promotion of national groups of recent development to the rank of nation or state—such was the formidable task confronting the rulers of Austria.

The problem was rendered even more complex by the fact that the Germans belonged to another great national community which lay outside the territory of the Austrian Empire and which was also seeking to establish itself as a modern state, a national unity founded both on history and on language; the more advanced spiritual and material civilization of the Germans had never ceased to offer a model and a stimulus to all. The tradition of the Germanic Holy Roman Empire, more durable than the Empire itself, continued to influence ideas and manners. The Austrian states had possessed territories extending into Germany; even with the more regular frontiers of the nineteenth century and Austria's withdrawal eastwards, several countries of the Austrian Empire still formed part of the Germanic Confederation of 1815. Although Austria was becoming more and more an individual reality, she remained partly German, and the Germanic element, especially in Vienna, continued to believe itself bound by ties of solidarity with other Germans. Furthermore, economic progress, instead of simplifying problems, added to their difficulty. Since the Elbe penetrated as far as Hamburg, providing German industrial production with access to the Danube, how could Austria break away completely from Germany?

New perspectives were emerging that were to constitute the fabric of nineteenth-century Europe: a Great Germany embracing all the territories of the House of Austria, including a Hungary averse to any form of foreign domination; or, alternatively, a juxtaposition and alliance of two states reconstructed in accordance with the liberal, constitutional ideal—a German Reich and an Austrian Empire, the solution adopted in 1879. But the constant preoccupation of this period was the attempt to solve, on the European and the international level, a central European problem which over the centuries had been inherent, though in a less acute form, in feudal and medieval law, in the ambiguous structure of the Germanic Holy Roman Empire and of the dynastic system of the Danubian countries.

In the nineteenth century, which saw the decay of the seigniorial system, the rise of the middle class, the development of capitalism and of industrial civilization, and the citizen's desire for autonomy substituted for the subject's duty of fidelity—all of these factors representing both cause and effect—the Danubian countries were to undergo a painful experience which can only be understood in the context of these general pressures. Yet it is often tempting to forget this and to explain everything in terms of incidental, regional problems which are treated as fundamental by historians with interests in a particular country. The result is a superficial view, though one supported by a host of arguments, of a struggle of oppressed peoples against a centralized despotism, as if it were simply a question of an arrogant policy of domination on the one hand and, on the other, national consciousness in revolt.

❧

Nothing in the existing order was to be changed—such, briefly, was the political formula adopted by the Emperor Francis I. This was somewhat surprising in a man who, as the son of Leopold II and the adopted son of Joseph II, was the pupil of two enlightened sovereigns. But his personal experience of the upheavals of the French Revolution had bound him for ever to the principles of a paternalist tradition. He was certainly not the most outstanding member of the large family that had issued from the marriage between Leopold II and a princess of Naples, a new alliance of Habsburgs and Bourbons. Of his brothers, the Archduke Charles surpassed him in military prestige, character and culture, and the Archduke John in intelligence, personality and readiness to accept progress; the Archduke Joseph, the Archduke Rainer and the Archduke Rudolf, the bishop of the family and the patron of Beethoven, were also men of no ordinary ability. Only the Archduke Louis and the Archduke Ferdinand of Tuscany were of a more modest mould.

The Emperor Francis I was cultivated, nevertheless, and possessed sufficient flexibility of mind to be able to judge men and to acquire, in the difficult exercise of the royal function, the prudence and the sagacity that made him one of the most skilful political tacticians of his house and of his time. He represented the transition from Maria Theresa, his grandmother, to Francis Joseph, his grandson. He sought to further his personal popularity by fostering a mood of kinship with the complex of societies which he governed: in the simplicity of his habits and his patriarchal way of life, appreciated more in the western states than in Hungary, many of his subjects were gratified to find a reflection of their own ideal and characteristics, which shows that shrewdness was not the least of his attributes. Vienna revered him and a host of contemporary portraits bears witness to its devotion. Thus, quietly but firmly, Francis I consolidated his dynasty. A good man with a great capacity for tender family relationships, manifested by his affection for his grandson, the duke of Reichstadt, and heedful of the sufferings of individuals, he knew how, by small, apparently insignificant gestures, to sustain the equivocal nature of his prestige. For he could also be reproached with frequent inconsistency of conduct and many a broken promise, a habit of governing on a day-to-day basis which provided a foretaste of *Fortwursteln*.[17]

Enlightened despotism was making way for a princely absolutism, which the personal character of the sovereign prevented from becoming a rigorous despotism. The particularism of states remained, but was gradually stripped of its efficacy: all power derived from the emperor and should therefore revert to him. In his paternalistic and aristocratic conception of his function, Francis I became increasingly accustomed to regard the Austrian Empire as 'a whole', according to the formula of Prince Eugene, but even more as a *fideicommissum*, a trust received from his ancestors which it was his duty to transmit to his successors. His fundamental benevolence towards his subjects did not induce Francis to improve their condition himself by introducing a programme of rational reform. In his eyes it was sufficient that they should be guaranteed the right to live in peace and order, *in Ruhe und Ordnung*. The deliberate paternalism of his policy thus depended on an increasingly meddlesome police system: liberty, the very name of which seemed tainted by the French Revolution, was regarded as suspect, as an invitation to rebellion.

At the same time, a vast bureaucratic machinery was gradually constructed in Austria by the introduction of new measures: the extension to the whole Empire of a system of civil legislation in accordance with the Code of 1812; a new tax system, for which yet another cadastral survey was made; the retention of the same currency after the bankruptcy and devaluation of 1811; and the creation in 1816 of a Ministry of Finances, by the merging of the old financial organs such as the Hofkammer and the Ministerial-Banco-Deputation into a new body, the General Chamber or *Allgemeine Hofkammer*.

The incessant modifications of detail introduced year by year reflected the irresolution of the emperor, who lacked the power of decision necessary for the rapid and permanent establishment of a new system such as Napoleon achieved. Issues were discussed by a conference of state at which the emperor took the final decisions, but on the basis of documents prepared by the various sections of the Council of State. Foreign affairs formed a separate domain, the Chancellery, over which Metternich exercised supreme authority.[18] In the field of internal affairs the most influential minister, though in no sense a prime minister, was a Bohemian noble, Count Kolowrat, who had replaced another Bohemian noble, Colloredo, and who symbolized the firmly established presence of the local aristocracies in the service of the emperor. But the position of at least a part of the nobility was changing. Fortified by their immense landed wealth, the nobles solicited and obtained the high offices in the army, the diplomatic service and the ecclesiastical hierarchy; in Vienna, marriages between different national groups, without extinguishing the pride of national lineage, diminished it somewhat, transforming the representatives of the old noble orders into a new society united in its deepest interests, its way of life and its common loyalty to the emperor and the Empire of Austria.

🐾

In general, it was a matter of administration rather than government. The increase in the number of officials, drawn from the expanding petty bourgeoisie, was slowly but surely breeding another vital force of the Danubian system: the civil service.[19] The service of the State—and henceforward this must be understood as the service of the Austrian Empire—was thus assured, as Joseph II had wished, by a conscientious, honest, self-effacing and increasingly efficient body of men.

Nothing was to be changed! This proved a hollow formula, for the period from 1815 to 1848, in the security of Metternich's peace, was one of frequent and irreversible changes. *Vormärz* or *Biedermeier*?[20] In other words, this period is commonly seen, according to the viewpoint of the historian, either as the development of the crisis that was to explode in the great upheavals of 1848, or as the era of a Romantic civilization characterized by charm and grace (*Gemütlichkeit*). Yet these were rather two aspects of the same reality. Economic progress brought with it the need to adapt countries of a traditional, rural character to an industrial activity characterized by the use of steam and steel, the reorganization of the mines, the substitution of metallurgy for textiles as the predominant industry, the erection of large factories in place of or side by side with the old workshops, and, with the rise of a new capitalism, the appearance of the proletariat.

At the same time, new forms emerged in art, in the theatre and in the decorative aspects of life generally. Baroque and Rococo were almost forgotten. Civil architecture looked to antiquity for its models, assuming a Neo-Classical style correct in its elegance, if limited in inspiration. This style is to be seen in the outer gateway of the Hofburg in Vienna, in the Customs House in Prague and in the colonnade of the Eszterházy residence at Eisenstadt.

But Neo-Classicism, which sprang from the rationalism of the *Aufklärung*, was balanced by another and more powerful trend—Romanticism. There can be no doubt that Romanticism blossomed more naturally in a world that had been subjected to strong Baroque influences and where music continued to nourish the faculties of imagination and sensibility. Beethoven died in 1827, but Schubert enjoyed three years of fertile genius and success in Vienna before he was laid to rest beside his master and idol in the cemetery at Währing.

Many features of the Baroque theatre were now to be found in the popular theatre of Vienna, in the varied and colourful productions of Fernand Raimund and Nestroy. In the theatres of Prague the works of Tyl and Klicpera delighted the public, while peasant humour and mischievousness inspired the puppet-theatre in which Kopecký, with his character of Kašparek, established a popular tradition that was to survive to the present day.

A more diversified clientele came into existence with the rise of new social strata and the greater prosperity of both town and country. While the painted chests and cupboards of peasant homes continued to show a predilection for bright shimmering colours and the floral stylizations of the Baroque period, the towns-folk chose for their furniture the light hues of maple and citrus-wood, inlaid with ebony or blackwood. A number of porcelain factories in Austria, Bohemia and Hungary provided the tables and cabinets of middle-class families with domestic crockery and ornaments, which represented the popular equivalent of the silver plate of the old noble households and an increase of material comfort by comparison with the crude pewter of the rural areas. The vogue of *genre*-painting, evoking somewhat affected rustic scenes of rocks, forests, waterfalls and flowers, explains the success of Ferdinand Waldmüller, the most popular Austrian artist of the period. The grandeur of Baroque and the exquisite grace of Rococo were thus replaced by a dangerously facile style, a certain sentimental flabbiness, though the technique of the artists lacked neither skill nor virtuosity. The need for an escapist art stimulated an attraction towards the Middle Ages and led to the troubadour style. At Laxenburg, on an island in the park, the Emperor Francis had a Gothic castle built.

More important was the tendency in intellectual circles to revive the prestige of the old languages and the national past. Scientific research and the fantasies of imagination developed side by side, as in the association between Dobrovský and Hanka.[21] Dobrovský, a former Jesuit and a disciple of rationalism and the *Aufklärung*, devoted himself to a rigorous study of the Slav languages and published in German a grammar and a history of the Czech language: *Ausfürliches Lehrgebau der boehmischen Sprache* (1809) and *Geschichte der boehmischen Sprache und älteren Literatur* (1819). His collaborator was Hanka, the editor of *Slavin*, a collection of linguistic studies the purpose of which was to strengthen the solidarity of the Slav peoples. In 1817 Hanka claimed to have made a dramatic discovery of manuscripts of medieval poetry, the manuscripts of Königinhof (Králové Dvur) and Grünberg (Zelená Hora), which seemed to establish proof of an ancient Czech literary culture. Palacký, a critical historian and archivist, used the documents for reference; Dobrovský expressed doubts which were ignored. Fifty years were to pass before the truth emerged, causing a scandal that divided opinion in a reinvigorated Czech nation. The manuscripts were fakes, a skilful, almost brilliant invention on the part of Hanka, who had believed at the time that he could further the glory of his nation by a fraud.[22]

The past of Austria—that is, of Austria considered as a whole—fascinated the noble imagination of Grillparzer. His admirable dramas and poems enriched German literature generally, but they bore the mark of the special genius of Austria. In his evocation of King Ottokar or of the fratricidal quarrel of the Habsburgs, Grillparzer grasped the true character of the history of these peoples, who had clashed one with another but had continued to live together, dimly conscious that their association was a condition necessary to their well-being.

The love of the fatherland and its history resulted, with the support of the Diets and the patronage of a few great lords, in the creation of the national museums: the Nemzeti Museum in Budapest, the Národní Museum in Prague and, in Graz, the Johanneum, founded by the Archduke John; learned institutions of an original character where collections of every kind—mineralogy, fossils, herbaria, archives, works of art, objects relating to folk-culture, old musical instruments—were assembled and preserved in order that the history of the particular country should be better known. Palacký, official historian of the kingdom of Bohemia, based his activities on the National Museum in Prague. He was not a professor at the university and it was only much later, when he had become famous, that he received the title of doctor *honoris causa*. From 1820 he was responsible for the publication of a scholarly review in the Czech language, *Časopis Českého Musea*, the first numbers of which contained academic eulogies of the Emperor Francis I.[23] There was nothing surprising in this, for the central government, far from organizing a systematic campaign of Germanization, itself took initiatives to encourage the teaching of the national languages. In 1803 the teaching of the Czecho-Slav language was authorized at the secondary college (*Lyzeum*) in Pressburg; in fact this was a religious rather than a national privilege, since Czech was the language of the Bible and of divine service in the Protestant communities of Upper Hungary. In 1816 and 1818 decrees were issued prescribing the study of Czech in establishments of secondary education and a knowledge of the language was henceforth obligatory for doctors, advocates and parish clergy.

Censorship was certainly still practised and Palacký was prevented from publishing a fifteenth-century text in its entirety because it contained ideas that were considered bold, though in fact they were quite harmless. The puerile timidity of certain traditionalist circles was curbing freedom of expression, without, however, halting a veritable intellectual revolution.

This revolution had its origins in Germany. The ideas which the Germans were propagating, and which they were rapidly putting into practice within the nation of Germany, were directed in the different Austrian countries towards the realization of a new ideal. Hegel had spread the idea of a necessary link between national existence and linguistic expression; Herder had stimulated an interest in the Slav world, its ancient linguistic forms and its dialects, the charm of its popular songs and the poetry of the rural communities. The consequences were twofold: on the one hand, a greater differentiation of Slav languages and, on the other, the sentiment of a legendary Slav brotherhood and the gradual awakening of a Pan-Slavism which, according to circumstances, either assumed a conscious, literary form or derived from a political Pan-Slavism. Germans, Slavs and Magyars, destined to clash several decades later in struggles which became increasingly bitter until the war of 1914, began by sharing a common enthusiasm for the elaboration of a national ideal. It is a curious fact that František Palacký was in communication with German patriots, such as Professor Luden of the university of Jena, and with numerous Hungarian patriots before he came to devote his energies to his historical studies and to his great theories concerning Czech history. In Hungary, the poet Vörösmarty celebrated the epic of King Matthias in a melodious and pure Magyar.

A Slovak, Kollár, composed a poem in Czech glorifying the Slavs: *Slavy Dcera* (*The Daughter of Slava*). This was not a politically motivated work, but an idealized image of the Slav peoples, of peoples enamoured of gentleness and justice and destined by their very virtues to the conquest of their more warlike Germanic neighbours. Čelakovský presented Slav songs as belonging to a single family of nations and stimulated interest in the poetry of the Russians and of the Austrian Slavs. Šafařík, a Moravian, pursued his philological studies of the old Slav languages.

Some Slav dialects of the Danubian empire were promoted, by the determined effort of small groups, to the rank of literary languages into which the great foreign works could be translated and which would serve for the publication of books and newspapers. Slovak claimed the right to exist independently of Czech. Many Slovaks still believed that the Czech language offered the Slovak populations the best instrument for their intellectual progress and that the spiritual unity of the two neighbouring Slav groups should be preserved and encouraged. This view, shared for a time by Palacký, a former pupil of the *Lyzeum* in Pressburg, suffered frequent periods of disfavour, but also times of renewed popularity. It lies at the root of Czechoslovak tradition and was to enjoy the ideological approval of President Masaryk.[24] But, in the opinion of others, the efforts of Czech grammarians and philologists to adapt their language to the practical needs of modern forms of expression did not appear entirely happy. The language thus modernized was encumbered with Germanic constructions and neologisms, while the dialects of the Slovakian valleys preserved a greater purity and beauty. It was argued, therefore, that these dialects should form the basis of a single common language for the Slovak group. The task of building up an independent Slovak language for use by the press and in literature was undertaken by men such as the udevít Štúr (1815–56), who occupied the chair of Czecho-Slav at the college in Pressburg—an attractive personality, a poet of grace and a general writer and journalist rather than a philologist; the young pastor Sládkovič, later recognized as the best of the Slovak poets; and Milan Miroslav Hodža (1811–70), a rigorous grammarian. What the parish priest Bernolák had attempted to achieve in the eighteenth century with the dialect of Trnava was now realized with the dialect of Turčanský Svatý Martin, in the central region at the foot of the Tatras mountains. *Nad Tatru sa blyska*! 'The lightning illuminates the Tatras', sang the poet Josef Matuška in a poem that was to become the national anthem of the Slovaks.[25] Meanwhile, the progress of the Czech language continued. Jungmann (1773–1847) devoted many years to the task of adapting it to modern civilization and patiently compiled his Czech-German dictionary. Byron and Chateaubriand kindled the inspiration of Karel Hynek Mácha, the author of the delightful idyll *Maj*, the first Czech work of a quality comparable with the European literature of Romanticism.[26]

Scholarly interest and the attraction of the southern Slavs' originality had induced a Viennese librarian, the Slovene Kopitar. to investigate the Slav dialects of Carniola, Carinthia and Styria. At the same time, the experience of the Illyrian Provinces, formed in the time of Napoleon, had generated an Illyrian ideal of fraternity among the Croats, the Serbs of Hungary and the Dalmatians, which made desirable a common literary language transcending differences of dialect. At Agram–Zagreb, a Croat, Ludevit Gaj, published a national Illyrian newspaper, *Ilirske narodne novine*. A writer and grammarian, Gaj intended to develop Croat as a literary language. Later, the identity of Croat and Serbian was to be recognized when a single language was established, but with two alphabets each related to a religious liturgy: Cyrillic for the Orthodox Serbs and the Latin alphabet for the Croats, who were devout Catholics. The Serbian language had also found itself a champion. Vuk Stefanović Karadžic, a Serb who had fled to Austria after the insurrection and the recapture of Serbia by the Turks, consulted Kopitar with the intention of methodically gathering together the songs sung in all regions inhabited by the Serbs, regardless of the political regime under which they lived. He composed a grammar (1814) and a dictionary of the Serbian language.[27] From 1826 to 1829 a Serbian almanach, *Danica*, was published in Vienna, further proof that there was no linguistic persecution of the Slavs. In the principality of Serbia itself, when the autonomy of the prince (*kniaz*) had been recognized, Miloš Obrenović and the Serbian clergy devoted themselves to establishing a literary language. Although the works of Kopitar, who had quarrelled with the prince, were banned, the metropolitan Petar nevertheless obtained from Austria and Russia the books which he needed to compose a Serbian grammar, 'of extreme necessity to his people'.[28]

Slovenian and Dalmatian continued to enjoy their own individual existence. The imperial government made no determined effort to oppose the progress of national languages, either because it attached an exaggerated significance to the loyalist declarations of writers, or because it believed that this Romantic attachment to local history, in a state which had never sought to merge its subjects into a single nation, nor even to impose the same laws on them, presented no danger to the system and might even be advantageous to the dynasty.

Thus, at a time when the Italians were suffering an offensive and often cruel police repression, an atmosphere of comparative tolerance prevailed in the Danubian countries, where intellectual life was allowed to develop peacefully and in a variety of forms. Nonetheless, if ideas seemed subversive, whatever the language in which they were expressed, they were seen as the occasion for alarm. In certain religious circles in Vienna a renewed effort was being made to revive the Catholic faith—which Josephism had threatened to enfeeble—by infusing it with a greater fervour, associating it more closely with Rome and Roman spirituality, and regenerating its doctrinal strength to counteract the trend towards the exclusive preoccupation with philosophy. The Emperor Francis I was no Ultramontanist and always respected Josephism for having made him the master of his clergy. Yet, when he piously performed the rites that would have caused displeasure to his uncle—devoutly following processions and washing the feet of the poor on Good Friday—he was participating in a resanctification of the imperial dignity and he happily reaped the benefits of a closer alliance with the Church. Moreover, among the common people of the rural areas and the provinces, there existed a devoutness the external manifestations of which surprised foreign visitors and irritated free-thinkers or those who were simply more critical.[29] Among the clergy there thus emerged two opposing currents, both of which sprang from the same desire to strengthen Catholic faith: one, which received the support of the papal nuncio Severoli, was concerned to propagate a self-contained system of irreproachable doctrine, to establish the primacy of Revelation and to maintain submission to the Pope and to Rome, while the other sought to revitalize faith by an alliance with reason, on which conviction was considered ultimately to depend. Associated with the first of these movements was the abbot Frint, subsequently made bishop of St. Pölten and who founded in Vienna an interdiocesan seminary, the *Frintaneum*, a rigorously orthodox establishment where a clerical élite was to be trained. In Prague, the Sunday sermons delivered in German by Bernard Bolzano, a pro-fessor of the faculty of theology, exerted the greatest influence on young people, both Germans and Czechs. Bolzano was a convinced Bohemian anxious to pre-serve a fraternal harmony between the two national groups. His sermons still possess the appeal of a persuasive faith and of a vibrant argumentation which called Holy Scripture to witness and which sought to bring the figure of Christ closer to people. He exhorted his young listeners to instruct themselves, never to lose through their own fault or negligence the benefit of the Christian education which they had received and to maintain a courageous virtue in their moral life. Never violent, but possessing a quiet warmth far removed from Baroque grandiloquence, his words invited them to a freely chosen adherence sustained by reason, and he did not hesitate to condemn the religious constraints of the past. Those who came under his influence retained something of his teachings throughout their lives, just as the disciples of Lammenais were affected by their master. But in Vienna, among the followers of Frint, it was thought that Bolzano accorded too much importance to reason and that his ideas were too closely akin to German philosophy and to Kantian idealism. He became the object of dissensions which, rather strangely, were tinged with an element of rivalry between Vienna and Prague. Chlumčanský, the archbishop of Prague, and Chotek, the grand burgrave, vouched for his religious orthodoxy and his loyalty; but the emperor's doctor, Stifft, persuaded Francis I that Bolzano was a dangerous agitator and a potential rebel. Bolzano was deprived of his professorial chair and the *Manual of Religious Know-ledge* which he had composed was banned on the ground of suspected heresy; the new archbishop of Prague, Anckvicz, was alarmed to learn that hundreds of copies of the book were being sold secretly. His disciples compromised him further by publishing his books and sermons in Germany, but Bolzano, unswerving in his fidelity to Rome and in his loyalty to the emperor, ended his days in meditation.[30]

In 1815 the Danubian monarchy remained a predominantly rural society of traditional habits: it comprised a few large towns, of a commercial rather than an industrial character, amid a countryside of manors, abbeys, villages and peasant farms. The previous fifty years had seen the development of industry, and especially of textiles, which employed a large, home-based labour force for the spinning of yarn and a small number of relatively simple machines in the factories. War, the continental blockade and successive territorial modifications had, over a period of twenty years, created a series of exceptional, fortuitous situations. With the return to a stable order, would the economy of the monarchy enter upon a new phase of growth? Economic conditions depended both on the social structure of the monarchy and on its position with regard to the other nations of Europe. In spite of the personal freedom which was now guaranteed to the peasantry, the retention of the corvée constituted an anomaly in the general system of labour and production. A century had proved insufficient for the restoration of Hungarian land to cultivation; although Hungary had been reintegrated and was active, the great plain still bore the traces of the long and disastrous Turkish invasion. The capital available in the countries of the Austrian Empire was inadequate for the large-scale industrial investment that would have been necessary to provide modern plant in territories which were by no means deficient in natural resources, and where the subsoil contained large deposits of metal and coal. It is also important to take into account the collective mentality of these peoples, which has not been sufficiently studied: cautiousness and respect for tradition were inevitably accompanied by a feebleness of enterprise, a tendency among peasant families to be too readily satisfied with the better living standard which they had already obtained, an attachment to the crafts and to the gradual social advancement which the most skilled artisans could be sure of securing for themselves by patience and thrift. Thus, societies characterized by prudence would not easily have been roused to enthusiasm for bold undertakings and the Danubian monarchy as a whole, owing to its very structure, could not emulate the rhythm of industrial production enjoyed by the states of western Europe, and in particular Great Britain.

General world conditions were also unfavourable to the Danubian countries. For example, Russia, which should have furnished a vast market for textiles and minerals, was protecting its own nascent industries and prohibiting imports from Austria. The re-opening of the Atlantic market and the revival of production in Great Britain, France and Germany resulted in the creation of new channels of circulation and competition in which Austria was not yet ready to participate. Consequently, even the disposal of Austrian agricultural produce—cereals and beet-sugar—presented difficulties and the exportation of Austrian textiles and manufactured articles was offset by the importation of these same goods from the West.

But there remained one factor which served to stimulate economic activity. The vocation of the Danubian monarchy in an industrial Europe was recognized as being to unite the mining regions of the Alps with the regions producing textiles, metals and coal, Bohemia, Moravia and Silesia (yet again the kingdom, with its rich soil and subsoil and its spirited peoples, was to play an important role); and to make Vienna the privileged commercial centre and driving force of the system. The Danube thus became the great transversal route from western to eastern Europe, affording access along its upper reaches to the industries of Germany and the West, and along its lower reaches to Hungary which, although an agricultural country, was itself to be industrialized; at the same time, roads and railways linked the Adriatic with the rivers flowing into the North Sea and the Baltic.

Nature had provided a vast domain of interconnected and complementary territories which justified the old aphorism of Hörnigk and which now needed to be adapted to the modern age. Industrial revolution was to be introduced, even if political revolution was rejected. However, there was still no question of a government programme: everything depended on individual initiatives and on the availability of capital.[31]

Capital was supplied by the great landowners, a number of whom set up factories on their estates, and, above all, by the banks. The creation in 1816 of a National Bank offered better facilities to the private sector, while the great banking-houses introduced in Vienna by the Rothschilds, Arnstein Eskeles, Fries and Geymüller, though they were not all established on equally solid foundations and were not yet mercantile banks in the strict sense of the term, began to give their support to great industrial enterprises.

It was necessary to increase production and productivity by the use of machines. The mechanization of textiles and the substitution of steam for the motive power hitherto provided by animals or water were dependent on the importation of machinery made either in Saxony or in Great Britain. Soon, however, though it was naturally impossible to dispense entirely with foreign machines, the Danubian countries began to make their own and to put new inventions into use. In 1826 the Veverka brothers invented the plough with moldboard; the engineer Ressel invented the propeller-driven boat and Madersperger a new machine for textiles (1830). The training provided by the higher technical colleges in Prague (1806), Vienna (1815) and Graz (1821) undoubtedly contributed largely to the process of technical discovery and to the industrialization of the Empire. Gerstner, the director of the college in Prague, played an important part in industrial initiatives and in the training of engineers.

Thus, between 1815 and 1848 the industrial revolution slowly penetrated the Danubian countries, in the patient and difficult struggle of progress against established routine, a struggle which created new social problems. In Bohemia, where textile factories continued to prosper in the region of Reichenberg (Liberec), the largest was that owned by the industrialist Liebig; the number of workers employed in cotton-spinning mills, roughly 40,000 in 1799, had fallen to 2,000 by 1830. In this same region the cloth factories, whose production rose from 35,534 pieces in 1790 to 58,000 pieces in 1832, employed only 8,985 persons by contrast with 30,000 in 1796. Naturally, new industries were being opened which required manual labour, but it is understandable that, locally, those workmen who found themselves deprived of their accustomed living should have looked on the machine as their rival and enemy and that, from time to time, panic should have driven them to acts of hostility against the engineers and mechanics of the new factories. Coal, which was being used industrially to an increasing degree—thus necessitating an acceleration in production—was competing with wood, the fuel hitherto supplied by the great landed proprietors. The first railways served initially to increase the efficacy of animal traction: in 1832 the line joining Linz (Upper Austria) and Budweiss (České Budějovice, in Bohemia), which covered a distance of eighty miles, provided the first link between the basin of the Danube and that of the

Vltava and the Elbe. But the carriers and the innkeepers, who had been dependent on road traffic, feared that the new mode of transport would destroy their livelihood.

Furthermore, working conditions were wretched, as they were throughout industrial Europe. The workers, at the mercy of foremen more inhuman than the seigniorial bailiffs, were still subjected to corporal punishment. In times of industrial crisis provoked by world conditions, they were thrown out on to the streets. Women and children worked in the mill for as much as thirteen hours a day. The slight increase of wages (an average of 24·6 kreutzers per day in Bohemia, 42 in Vienna and 40·6 in Lower Austria during the years 1837-42, by comparison with 23, 40·9 and 39·3 kreutzers for the years 1830-6) did not correspond with the rise in the price of grain (4·83 to 5·25 gulden per hectolitre of wheat, 3·62 to 3·69 gulden per hectolitre of rye, during these same years). As a result of unequal opportunities of employment and the inadequacy of wages, a sub-proletariat was coming into existence in the large cities, drifting from beggary to violence and forming the mobs of rioters which from time to time plundered markets, bakeries and butchers' shops.

Bad harvests brought food crises: 1840, 1842, 1845 and 1847 were harsh years with a very high cost of living. A general tax imposed on consumption in 1829 caused food prices to rise and from 1840 the increase in the cost of living was particularly marked. Moreover, since the brewing of alcohol had been made a State monopoly, part of the wheat and potato production was diverted from the food market.

Although buffeted, industrial progress was not brought to a halt. The industrial organization of the Danubian countries was being achieved by the creation of a railway network. The Rothschild bank obtained authorization to build a railway from Vienna to Brünn via Břecláv which, when it was extended as far as Bohumin, was to provide an outlet for the iron ore of Ostrava, the wheat of Hana, and the cattle and salt of Galicia. This line, the *Kaiser Ferdinand Nordbahn*, was also extended southwards; by 1841, ten thousand persons were travelling between Vienna and Wiener-Neustadt.

The large cities now saw the first locomotives, at Prague in 1845 and at Graz in 1846, and the population celebrated the event with a gay festival. At first, however, locomotives were imported from Great Britain. Soon, construction works were opened in Bohemia, near Prague, for the manufacture of Austrian locomotives. The steam-engine and the propeller made it possible to improve navigation on the Danube. In 1829 the Danube Steamship Company was founded (*Donaudampfschiffahrtsgesellschaft* or *DDSG*) and six years later, at Obuda, a shipyard was opened. The initial frustration provoked by competition soon gave way to a spirit of emulation: the *Kaiser Ferdinand Nordbahn* enabled Polish grain to be transported to Trieste more cheaply than Hungarian grain. Count Széchenyi attempted to improve flour production in Hungary by installing a steam-driven mill at Sopron. It was necessary to have access to the open sea and to accelerate the supply of raw materials (cotton and silk) to the textile mills: in 1845 there were more than 430 silk mills in Vienna. In 1832 several companies merged to form a powerful organization, the *Österreichischer Lloyd*, which possessed 26 ships by 1848. The success of Trieste might be thought to have given Venice cause for alarm. It has been suggested that the Austrian port was favoured to the detriment of the conquered city and that Venice was doomed to ruin. Nothing could be further from the truth: joined to the mainland by a bridge and linked with the Milan railway, Venice was making a rapid recovery.[32]

In this Empire of Austria, which in so many respects was in harmony with the progress of the Western countries, the extent of the nobility's domains was surprising, even if one bears in mind that the whole of Europe at this time was dominated by great landed proprietors. The seigniory remained a solid and apparently unshakeable structure. Although Sealsfield was perhaps jesting when he wrote that the prince of Liechtenstein could travel one hundred miles from Silesia to Lower Austria without leaving his lands, and that the revenues of Prince Eszterházy equalled the combined civil lists of the kings of Bavaria, Saxony and Württemberg, the important thing was that public opinion accepted this as fact. It is, however, true that in Bohemia alone Prince John Adolf Schwarzenberg possessed two estates of 49,125 and 45,714 hectares respectively, while Count Clam-Gallas owned 31,736 hectares at Friedland and 372 persons or communities held properties above 503 hectares.[33] On these vast estates, which were not all equally well administered, relations between the lords, the inhabitants of the towns and the peasants were not the same everywhere. Patriarchal traditions tended to operate in favour of the noble, for a certain pride was felt in being the subject of a powerful and illustrious personage, who was in many cases a benevolent landlord, if he was a disciple of Enlightenment, and a paternal one, if he was a good Christian. Social advancement was not impossible within the framework of the seigniory, for administrative opportunities were numerous and the peasant's first loyalty was patrimonial—a loyalty to the land which he cultivated and then to the seigniory on which his family had lived from generation to generation. Those who thought and felt in such a fashion were the more prosperous peasants whose peaceful way of life impressed foreign travellers. Unlike his ancestors of the seventeenth and eighteenth centuries, whose poverty had scandalized foreigners, the peasant of Bohemia and, to an even greater degree, the peasant of Austria appeared to the Englishman Turnhill to enjoy the same standard of living as the English peasant. Charles Sealsfield and Michel Chevallier insisted on the happy aspect of the rural populations and the signs of their prosperity. But they did not see the peasants of the Carpathians and of Bukovina. Everywhere the corvée was resented as an odious obligation. Even the administrators of estates doubted its efficacy. In 1823 the director of the estate of Křivoklát declared that the peasants sent their worst animals and equipment for labour and that the corvée was an obstacle rather than an advantage in the efficient management of the seigniory.

The general trend was towards the redemption of the corvée. But in 1821 a decree of the emperor discouraged this practice, which was virtually suspended on crown lands. The signs of discontent became more ominous: in 1821 the peasantry refused *en masse* to give its labour. At the time of the cholera epidemic of 1830 it was rumoured that the landlords had poisoned the wells; in 1846 an agrarian revolt broke out in Galicia and the government was compelled to tackle the problem once again. A law promulgated on 18 December 1846 confirmed the right of redemption by agreement freely reached between landowner and peasant. Various methods of redemption were authorized: an annual rent, an annual contribution of grain, the payment of a capital sum or the relinquishment of certain privileges on the estate, such as access to the pasture-land of the lord's demesne, the right to gather dead wood or the practice of exchanging lands. The measure was coolly received; although a book written by Brauner, a lawyer of Prague, urged them to redeem themselves from the corvée, many peasants continued to hope that it would be abolished without indemnity. Moreover, in the villages the very progress being made in the methods of cultivation accentuated the difference between the more prosperous peasants and their poorer brethren. The lowliest peasants, who had little or no land, found themselves in a situation of crisis: the inadequacy of their income and the illusion of prosperity in the towns induced them to swell the numbers of the urban proletariat.

In Hungary, also, where it could be seen that the peasant was still deprived of his personal freedom and was much more a slave than his counterpart in Austria-Bohemia, the peasant class comprised a diversity of gradations, from the *jobbágy* who occupied a complete or socage holding, to which he added land rented on the lord's demesne or allodium, to the agricultural labourer who had very little land, sometimes less than one-eighth of the normal serf holding, and who depended for his living on wages earned by working for the *jobbágy* or the landlord. The Hungarian Diets were also contemplating the redemption of the corvée. They improved the lot of the peasant by revising the conditions under which he could dispose of his property (he was allowed to mortgage his land without selling it). The sharp rise in the population (an average annual increase of 45,000 inhabitants) modified the proportion of peasants owning complete holdings (about 40 per cent in 1847) to the mass of agricultural labourers with insufficient lands (60 per cent).

The juridical and social conditions prevailing in Hungary made it difficult to adapt this country to a new economy. At the county assemblies and the Diets the minor nobles, who lived in penury, struggled for the preservation of their economic independence which, while ensuring their political privileges, was at the same time the cause of their enduring poverty. Among the upper aristocracy there existed men who were better acquainted with the times and who proposed radical reforms. Stephen Széchenyi, who had visited England, read Bentham, Bacon, Adam Smith, Montesquieu and Mme. de Staël. A Catholic of intelligent faith, Széchenyi detested social injustices. A patriot, he wished to see Hungary regain her place in a changing Europe. As a noble aware of the prestige and influence attaching to his rank, he considered it essential that the relics of feudalism should be removed so that labour and individual initiative might be liberated. In his book in Magyar entitled *Hitel* (*Credit*), he demanded the abolition of the *jus aviaticum*, which maintained the noble in the condition of a usufructuary and prevented him from exercising complete control over his possessions. The mobilization of land by the infusion of large quantities of capital from abroad seemed to him a fundamental condition of Hungary's economic growth. At the same time, he encouraged the formation of various societies for the promotion of the economy: a society for horse-breeding was founded in 1822 and the first races took place at Pozsony in 1826; another society financed the construction of a bridge across the Danube, the *Lánchíd*, built by the engineer Clarke, who was responsible for the Hammersmith Bridge in London.

It was necessary that Pest, like Vienna, should be organized as a centre for shipping on the Danube. A society founded in 1830 provided a regular service between Vienna and Pest. Steamboats also sailed on the Tisza and on Lake Balaton; railways linked Pest with Vacov and Solnok. This economic progress, however limited and however disproportionate to the country's resources and growth potential, was already transforming Pest. Opposite the royal citadel of Buda and the aristocratic quarter of the Vár, Pest became the city of the new epoch. The palatine, Joseph, supported the construction of a new quarter beside the river, just as the grand burgrave Chotek had encouraged the renovation of the old city of Prague. Count Széchenyi believed that Hungary could achieve economic prosperity only by maintaining a close association with Austria, for Vienna was the economic centre vital to the inseparable interests of the Danubian world. He also believed that the Magyars would take the initiative of economic reform; it therefore seemed only just that the study of the Hungarian language should be promoted and extended to the entire administration. But he was also anxious not to antagonize the Slav populations of Hungary, who had contributed to the defence of the kingdom and to its greatness. How many Croat and Slovak peasants had fought under Rákóczi in the war against Viennese hegemony! By contrast with this profoundly wise and discerning attitude, a more exclusive Magyar patriotism animated the minor nobility of the counties. These nobles were afraid of being submerged by the Slavs, who were proclaiming their ethnic kinship with foreign peoples; it was even wondered if the abolition of serfdom, by liberating more Slav peasants than Magyars, would not help to debase the national character of Hungary. Was economic progress inevitably to involve association with Austria? Could not Hungary emancipate itself to the extent of making Fiume, its port, the rival of Trieste? The most resolute Magyar patriotism found as its spokesman a remarkable orator, Louis Kossuth, who distinguished himself at the sessions of the Diet and who edited a newspaper, *Pesti Hirlap*. Opinions differed also on the political and administrative reforms to be adopted, and which were debated at the Diet of 1847: should the autonomy of the counties be strengthened, or should the kingdom be given a more centralized organization? It was not easy, moreover, to know which of these two solutions would offer non-Magyar Hungarians the best guarantees for their individual existence.[34]

If all these factors are considered in conjunction—a government preoccupied with its prestige in foreign policy and haunted by the fear of revolutionary propaganda, a government open to economic progress but no longer willing to take the initiative or to assume control of that progress, the necessity of industrializing a vast territory which lacked capital, the predominance of agriculture, but in a traditional, seigniorial form which impeded production, the growth of national consciousness among groups which asserted themselves through language, opposing the common language of the State and the prevailing methods of administration, the wretchedness of the working classes which accompanied the growth of factories in the towns, a Romantic effervescence in which sensibility enjoyed priority over logic—then it can be seen to what extent the birth of modern Austria was enveloped in contradictions.

To change nothing, when the general trend was one of change, was an impossible ideal. The demise of the emperor—Francis I died in 1835, at the age of sixty-eight— instead of bringing the younger generations to power, had resulted, rather curiously, in the establishment of a government of incompetent persons and old men. Metternich had nothing of the dictator in him, but the direction of Austria's destiny was superfluous to his designs for the better guidance of Europe and to the continued success of his chancellery schemes. Beside the new sovereign, the Emperor Ferdinand I, who was on the verge of mental deficiency, he had deliberately placed, not the Archdukes Charles and John, men of superior intelligence, character and experience, but their youngest brother, the Archduke Louis, because he was much less gifted and because his docility and lack of initiative guaranteed the preservation of established methods of administration.

Opposition thus grew, for the danger of inertia was obvious. Nothing is more characteristic in this respect than the correspondence of the young Count Leo Thun, a former pupil of Bolzano, with Alexis de Tocqueville, whose works he read in order to acquire a better understanding of the changing world. Thun declared that the government of Austria was an extremely complicated mechanism the component parts of which were essentially ineffectual. 'Unless considerable changes in the method of conducting affairs are made within a few years, unless it is possible to form ministries and a Council of Ministers acting according to fixed principles, we are going to undergo times of great peril either for the existence of the monarchy or for the state of society.'[35] This letter, dated 28 February 1846, anticipated by two years the repercussions of the French revolution of 1848, by comparison with which the reverberations of the revolution of 1830 had been easily contained. In cultivated circles, in the world of business and among young people in schools, the word 'constitution' assumed a magical significance, for it represented the end of patriarchal absolutism, which itself had been substituted for the attempt at enlightened despotism and government by the nobility. The upper strata of the peasantry, sensing that the seigniorial regime would inevitably be destroyed, rallied to this hope. The proletariat had not yet acquired a clear class consciousness. But the police had seized pamphlets which propagated socialist ideas. Strikes in the factories, called for the purpose of obtaining higher wages and legislation for more human working conditions, were a warning that riots might break out.

A feeling of solidarity with the Western countries, with Germany and northern Italy, ensured that a revolutionary movement would be welcomed as soon as the signal was given abroad. Of all the European revolutions of 1848, that which broke out in the Austrian Empire, when news was received of the events in Paris, developed a special character owing to the multitude of problems which it created, many of which had already been resolved in the West by earlier revolutions. There was agitation in the cafés and the streets, vehement articles in the press flouted censorship, the Diet of Lower Austria assembled in Vienna, passions rose in Budapest, where the poet Petöfi harangued the crowds and Kossuth demanded a modern constitution—but it was not proposed that the monarchy be overthrown.

Since the chancellor had fled, his influence eclipsed without detriment to Austria, the emperor received the advice of the best-informed members of his family: his uncle, the Archduke John, and his sister-in-law, Sophia of Bavaria, the wife of the Archduke Francis Charles. The liberals continued to appeal to him in their effort to obtain a constitution, or at least the authority to prepare one. The emperor formed a new government and promised an imperial assembly for all the hereditary states. From Hungary, deprived of the shrewdness and sagacity of the Archduke Joseph, who had died several months previously, a delegation of the Diet came to Vienna and asked the 'king' to form a government. Ferdinand agreed. The Hungarian government was composed of the most worthy figures in the country: Prince Louis Batthyány, the type of the liberal grand seigneur, Stephen Széchenyi, Kossuth, Eötvös, who was entrusted with the Ministry of Education, and the advocate Deák, who received the Ministry of Justice. Since the Diet continued to sit, it was in unison with that body that the government adopted in April 1848 a series of measures that transformed the Hungary of the aristocratic orders into a modern Hungary. All citizens were recognized as equal before the law, fiscal privileges were abolished and the rights of man were guaranteed—religious liberty, freedom of the press and the right of public assembly. A modern Parliament elected by a suffrage based on property-qualification would replace the old Diet. The independence of Hungary was asserted even more firmly by the existence of a Hungarian army which was distinct from the Austrian army and responsible to the Hungarian Ministry of War. The April laws, welcomed by western Europe as the happiest of innovations and as the sign of the victory of modern principles in a country of a medieval structure, received the royal sanction.[36]

In Prague, all classes of society were in ferment, from the liberal nobles to the lowliest artisans. But there existed no open hostility between Germans and Czechs. Young people of both ethnic groups fraternized with enthusiasm in the student corps, where the banners of each bore the same motto: 'Concordia, Svornost'. Citizens of Prague assembled in a room of the St. Wenceslas Baths and acclaimed the text of a petition which had been drawn up by the Czech advocate Brauner, and which demanded the equality of the two languages, the redemption of the corvée and the institution of a common Diet for the three provinces of the kingdom of Bohemia (11 March). The governor, Stadion, was absent from Prague, but he sent from Vienna a telegram drawn up in both German and Czech in which he announced that the constitution was proclaimed for all three provinces. When he returned to Prague, he skilfully sought to soothe the susceptibilities of all concerned; the discord which was already manifesting itself among Bohemians was between social classes rather than between Germans and Czechs. Prague was still a provincial city where the middle class—even the German-speaking middle class—remained favourably disposed towards the Czech intellectuals. To a certain degree, the citizens of Prague formed a harmonious group: they were all attached to their city and to their particular district, and the majority continued to live a patriarchal, simple existence.

By a decree of 8 April the government in Vienna guaranteed the equality of the two languages and also granted the convocation of a Diet of Bohemia, which was to be recruited on a broadened electoral basis and would discuss the redemption of the corvée. But it was to be the prerogative of the future imperial assembly, which was to meet in Vienna, to decide if the three Bohemian Diets would be merged into one, thereby confirming the political unity of the kingdom of Bohemia within the Austrian Empire. A national committee was formed in Prague to make preparations for the elections to the Diet and to the imperial assembly. The committee included both Germans and Czechs: the Germans were represented by the jurist Kliebert, the writers Meissner and Ebert, the author of *Vlast*, a poem which, under a Slav title (*Vlast* means 'fatherland' in Czech), proclaimed the equal devotion of the two peoples to their common country; the Czechs were represented by the lawyers Brauner and Rieger and the official historiographer of the kingdom, František Palacký, whose *History of the Czech People of Bohemia and Moravia*, already published in German, was also to appear in Czech.

A few years earlier, Michel Chevallier, observing the way of life of the Bohemian populations, had found them so loyal to the emperor that he thought revolution impossible in this country. In fact, revolution was to spring not so much from the internal problems of the Austrian Empire, as from its involvement with the affairs of Germany and Italy.

In Italy, the revolution had broken out in various parts during the first weeks of 1848. On the arrival of news from France, it acquired a greater momentum in Milan, where all social classes joined the insurrection, erecting barricades and driving the regular troops out of the city. The other Italian governments, coming to terms with public opinion, announced that constitutions would be granted. The king of Piedmont declared war on Austria, ordered his troops to enter Lombardy and invited all the states of the peninsula, and even the Pope, to take part in the campaign of liberation.

Events in Germany at this same time were assuming much broader dimensions. German economists had long deplored as obstacles to progress the fragmentation of Germany into states of small or medium extent and the archaic character of the Confederation, a society of princes in which the interests of peoples were excluded. It was necessary, above all, to achieve the economic unity of the Germanic territories. A customs association, the *Zollverein*, established since 1834 under the control of Prussia, represented the first stage towards unity. But this association had not yet been extended to the whole Germanic complex. Western Germany was one of the most advanced regions in Europe's capitalist and industrial system: here the revolution was to assume a social character. The demands of the working classes, elaborated under the influence of socialist writers, adopted the ideas of Marx and the Communist Manifesto.

The king of Prussia, after quelling the workers' riot in Berlin, appeared to reconcile himself to the liberal revolution that had spread over the whole of Germany. He did nothing to discourage the belief of one sector of opinion that he might become the sovereign of a renewed Empire. But the fundamental problem was plainly this: would Austria be included in the new German state that was to replace the condemned Germanic Confederation? Moreover, did the term 'Austria' signify only those Austrian territories which had formed part of the Holy Roman Empire, or the Austria as subsequently constituted, including the kingdom of Hungary and the Polish provinces, which had always remained external to and alien to the Holy Roman Empire? It might also be wondered how much longer the Austrian Empire would endure, in view of the many problems posed by its relations with the Italians and the Hungarians.

A committee of German patriots—the Committee of Fifty—had been formed in Heidelberg to make preparations for the elections to the Imperial Parliament that was to sit at Frankfurt and draft the constitution of the new Germany. The committee addressed itself to all those bodies which might be deemed legally representative of a country. The national committee of Prague was considered to be one such body and received an invitation from the Committee of Fifty to appoint deputies to the Frankfurt Parliament. This move resulted in a rupture between the Germans and Czechs of Bohemia. The Germans of Bohemia, imbued with the memory of the Holy Roman Empire, of which the kingdom had formed part, and mindful of the Germanic Confederation in which Austria had occupied a position of power, considered it quite natural that they should sit in the Parliament of the German nation. But the Czechs could not entertain similar sentiments: they had reason to fear that their national group, which was still fragile, would be absorbed and submerged by the new Germanic state. František Palacký replied to the Committee of Fifty in a letter which immediately became famous; in justification of his refusal he invoked history and expounded all the arguments in favour of an independent Austrian Empire.

The gist of Palacký's argument was that the kingdom of Bohemia had not been bound to the Holy Roman Empire by the same ties of allegiance as the other Germanic states. It was inhabited not only by Germans, but also by a Czech population of Slav origin. Along the Danube or in proximity to it, nature and history had determined the formation of peoples who did not belong to a single race, but comprised Germans, Slavs, Magyars, Latins and Greeks. In the prevailing situation of Europe these peoples found themselves threatened by the growth of two great empires: that of the tsars of Russia, which was moving towards universal monarchy, and that of the future Germany, which was already claiming as its own the territory of Czech Bohemia. In the face of this double peril, it was therefore in the interests of these peoples to join together in an independent state that would guarantee each of them autonomy for the present and opportunities for development in the future. 'Indeed,' concluded Palacký, 'if Austria had not existed for so long we would have been obliged, in the interests of Europe and even of humanity, to make every endeavour to create an Austria as soon as possible.' Tradition has given this cardinal idea a more concise form: if Austria had not existed, it would have been necessary to invent it.[37]

In fact, to a certain extent it was necessary to invent it, since only a reorganization of Austrian institutions would enable the mistakes of the past to be rectified. Palacký reproached the most recent Austrian governments, and in particular Metternich, with having disregarded the rights of the nations comprising the monarchy and not having recognized their equality. However, the Austrian state was to be reformed and to endure. It was not in the interests of its peoples that Austria should be deprived of its own army, necessary for their common defence, or that Vienna should cease to be its capital and be replaced by Frankfurt. There was one final reason, Palacký argued, why the union of Austria with Germany might be particularly dangerous. The character of the German revolutions suggested that the new German state would adopt a republican constitution. The Germans were entitled to choose the regime that suited them best. But, for Austria, the monarchy remained indispensable. 'Imagine', said Palacký, 'an Austria split into a number of republics, small or great—what a temptation for the foundation of a universal Russian monarchy!' Palacký was not mistrustful of the Russian nation, which was cherished by all its Slav brethren, but merely fearful of the despotic government of imperial Russia. In his opinion the ideal solution was the existence of two constitutional states, one German and possibly republican, the other Austrian and undoubtedly monarchic. These two states could then conclude a political alliance against possible enemies and an economic alliance in defence of their common interests.

In this springtime of peoples, Palacký's declaration might have been welcomed as a charter for the new Austria which would guarantee a new order in central Europe against revolutionary agitation. A few weeks after the letter was received, Palacký was summoned to Vienna by the president of the Austrian government, Pillersdorf, who offered him the Ministry of Education. Palacký declined the offer for fear of antagonizing the Germans of Bohemia. While the Czechs had enthusiastically subscribed to the message proclaimed by their historian, their German compatriots had repudiated it by electing their deputies to the Frankfurt Parliament. The kingdom of Bohemia was thus split into two groups, one Germanic, the other Slav, the first group attaching greater weight to the national ideal than to historical tradition. The two opposing groups soon came to hate each other. To this emotional division of Bohemia the different evolution of the two groups in the capitalist era was to add new causes of dissension. To a greater degree than contemporary observers realized or historians have subsequently recognized, the rupture between the Germanic and Slav elements in the kingdom which, by virtue of its demographic character and its economic potential, should have constituted the foundation of the new Austria, was one of the major events of the revolution.

Furthermore, the opposition encountered by the monarchy was too fierce to allow its regeneration by the harmony of its peoples, by the authority or power of persuasion of its rulers. The monarchy had needed the army to defeat the Italians and to maintain Lombardy as part of its system, when that country had begun to slip from its grasp. In May, at Santa Lucia, and in July, at Custozza, the army of Radetzky triumphed over Piedmont.

Grillparzer celebrated this military victory in enthusiastic verse:

> *Good luck, my hero, the task is yours!*
> *It is not only for the reflection of glory,*

275

Between Two Revolutions

In your camp is Austria,
Of which we are merely the scattered debris.

In deinem Lager ist Österreich... Was it then necessary that arms should also be turned against the internal revolution and that the hope of a liberal and peaceful Austria, such as Palacký desired, should vanish under the pressure of reality and civil war?

NOTES

1. *Sándor Lipót főherceg nádor iratai* ('Correspondence of the Palatine Alexander Leopold'), published by Elemér Mályusz, Budapest, 1926.
2. See the important biography of Leopold II by Adam Wandruszka, 2 vols., Vienna, 1964.
3. Eva Balász, *Berzeviczy Gergely a reformpolitikus 1763–1795* ('George Berzeviczy and the Political Reform 1763–1795'), Budapest, 1967, pp. 353–4.
4. F. Kutnar, *Veliká revoluce francouzská n naší soudobí kritice* ('The Great French Revolution in the Contemporary Criticism of Our Country'), ČČH, XL, pp. 33–79.
   The work by Haschka is entitled *Blutrache über die Franzosen*, Vienna, 1793.
   Květa Mejdřičká, *Čechy a francouská revoluce*, Prague, 1959, and Denis Silagi, *Jakobiner in der Habsburger Monarchie*.
5. Listchauer (*Kleine Geschichte Österreichs*, p. 215) quotes a fine passage by Ignaz Seipel in *Nation and Staat* (1916) on the universal, supranational character which the function of the new emperor was assuming at this time in an indivisible territorial monarchy, but which was not necessarily tending towards unification. H. Ritter von Srbik, in *Die Schicksalsstunde des alten Reiches* (Jena, 1937), stresses rather the separation from the German nation imposed by the French victories. See also: J. Redlich, *Das österreichische Staats- und Reichsproblem*, and the first chapter of Robert A. Kann, *Das Nationalitäten-problem der Habsburgermonarchie* (a revised and expanded translation of *The Multinational Empire*, New York, 1950), vol. I, *Österreich, der Name*.
   For the history of the revolutionary wars: H. von Srbik, *Deutsche Einheit*, vol. I, written from the 'Greater Germany' viewpoint; and the works of Hugo Hantsch and Erich Zöllner.
6. A. Robert, *L'idée nationale autrichienne et les Guerres de Napoléon*, Paris, 1933; J. Droz, *Le Romantisme allemand et l'État*, chapter III, *Le romantisme, mouvement national en Autriche en 1809*, p. 143 et seq.
7. Hugo Hantsch, op. cit., p. 283.
8. A. J. de Laborde, *Précis historique de la guerre entre la France et l'Autriche en 1809*, Paris, 1823, with atlas in folio.
9. On Metternich, the basic work is H. von Srbik, *Metternich, der Staatsmann und der Mensch*, Vienna, 1925; in contrast, Victor Bibl, *Metternich, der Dämon Österreichs*, Leipzig, 1936.
   Gentz observed that not everyone was capable of launching anew on the high seas and across reefs and the unfathomed depths a ship which for twenty years had been battered by wind and tempest (quoted by Srbik, *Metternich*, 1956, p. 13).
   G. Bertier de Sauvigny, *Metternich et son temps*, 1959.
10. G. Lefebvre, *Napoléon*, p. 564. Concerning Napoleon's effective administration in the Illyrian Provinces, consult Melitta Pivec Stelé, *La Vie économique des Provinces illyriennes (1809–1813)*, Paris, 1930.
11. On the Congress of Vienna, see the following general studies: *Histoire des relations inter-*

nationales, edited by P. Renouvin, vol. IV, *La Révolution française et l'empire napoléonien*, by André Fugier, vol. V, *Le XIXᵉ siècle, I*, 1815–1871, by Pierre Renouvin; Angeverg, *Le Congrès de Vienne et les traités de 1815*, 4 vols., Paris, 1864; Sir C. K. Webster, *The Congress of Vienna*, 1937.

In 1965 the 150th anniversary of the Congress was celebrated in Vienna by an exhibition. The review *Alte und moderne Kunst*, no. 81, July–August 1965, published the lecture delivered by the author at the opening of the exhibition and an article by Professor H. Benedikt. For Metternich's ideas on central Europe, consult Jacques Droz, *L'Europe centrale*, chapter I, p. 30 *et seq.*

12. Arthur Breycha Vaurthier, *Aus Diplomatie und Leben: Maximien des Fürsten Metternich*, 1964, p. 131.

13. H. von Srbik, *Metternich*, 1956, p. 15.

14. Jacques Henri Pirenne, *La Sainte Alliance*, 2 vols., Neuchatel, 1946; G. Bertier de Sauvigny, *Metternich et la France après le Congrès de Vienne*, vol. I, *De Napoléon à Decazes*, 1968; Josef Polišensky, *Opavsky Kongres r. 1820* ('The Congress of Troppau of 1820'), Prague, 1962.

15. Robert A. Kann, *Das Nationalitätenproblem*, I, chapter II, p. 40 *et seq.*

16. J. Mousset, *La Serbie et son Église*, Paris, 1938.

17. On the Emperor Francis: Viktor Bibl, *Kaiser Franz, der letzte römisch-deutsche Kaiser*, Vienna, 1937. Maynert, *Kaiser Franz I*, Vienna, 1872, and two curious contemporary studies of Austria and its sovereign: one written by Hormayr after his quarrel with the Austrian government, *Kaiser Franz und Metternich*, Leipzig, 1848, and the other by A. Sealsfield-Postl, *Austria as It Is*, London, 1828 (translated into German in 1919). Concerning internal administration: F. Walter, op. cit. (in chapter 7, notes 18 and 28), vol. II/I, *Die Geschichte der Zeit 1740–1848*; and Hellbling, op. cit., p. 323, *Der Vormärz und der absolutische Polizeistaat 1792–1848*. The word *Fortwursteln* ('marking time') was applied later to the policy of procrastination and composition in the time of Francis Joseph, by those who found that policy too timid and ineffectual.

18. F. Engel-Janosi, *Geschichte auf dem Ballhausplatz—Essays zur österreichischen Aussenpolitik, 1830–1945*, Vienna, 1963.

19. Some sound observations on this subject are to be found in F. Walter, op. cit., p. 350.

20. For the Biedermeier culture: R. Feuchtmüller and W. Mrazek, *Biedermeier im Österreich*, Vienna, 1963 (a copious bibliography), and the attractive and well-illustrated book by Mrs. Mělniková-Papoušková, *Praha před sto lety* ('Prague a Hundred Years Ago'), Prague, 1935 (this work is not easily accessible at the present time).

21. For the works published in 1953, on the occasion of the bi-centenary of the birth of Dobrovský, consult the bibliography *Twenty-five Years of Czechoslovak Historiography*, p. 231. The work entitled *Dobrowsky's Slavin von Wenceslas Hanka*, Prague, 1834, with the sub-title *Botschaft aus Böhmen an alle slawischen Völker* ('Message from Bohemia to All the Slav Peoples'), is a compilation of philological notes and observations on manners.

22. Concerning the dispute over the manuscripts, a scientific analysis is to be found in F. M. Bartoš, *Rukopisy Kralovédvorský a Zelenehorský* ('The Manuscripts of Kralové Dvůr and Zelená Hora'), Prague, 1946. There is no need to return to this affair, which has roused passions in Czech public opinion on several occasions. T. G. Masaryk gave space in his review *Athenaeum* to the articles of the philologist Gebauer, who challenged the authenticity of the manuscripts (1886). The ensuing controversy was fierce and was revived for political reasons on several subsequent occasions (1911, 1918 and 1937). But the manuscripts have been proved beyond doubt to be fakes.

23. J. Pekař, *Palacký* (1912).

24. T. G. Masaryk, whose father was of Slovak origin, had considered long before the 1914 war that the Czechs and Slovaks would gain by leaning on each other for support; while respecting, in the Republic which he founded, the Slovaks' right to retain their language as a national language (the second in the state), he did not attach primary importance to this question.

25. *Československá Vlastivěda* (1933), vol. VII (literature): *Literatura slovenská*, by A. Pražák, p. 209, and by the same author *Národ se branil* ('The Nation has Defended Itself'), p. 223 *et seq.* Dr. František Bokeš, *Dějiny Slovenska a Slovakov*, 1946. On Ludovit Štúr, J. V. Ormis, *Bibliografia Ludovita Štúra* (Turcanský Svatý Martin, 1958), and, in *Twenty-five Years of Czechoslovak Historiography*, p. 246, the long review by Ludovit Holotik concerning the present state of historical studies in Slovakia.

26. H. Granjard, *Macha et la Renaissance nationale en Bohême*, 1957. 'In spite of his ties with Germanic culture, he remained steadfastly and typically Czech', p. 103.

27. On the Illyrian movement and the linguistic awakening of the South Slavs, see Pypine and Spasovic, *Histoire des littératures slaves* (translated into French by E. Denis), 1881; B. Unbegaun, *Les Débuts de la langue littéraire chez les Serbes*, 1935; I. Popovic, *Geschichte der serbokroatischen Sprache*, Wiesbaden, 1960; A. Haumant, *La Formation de la Yougo-slavie;* J. Mousset, *La Serbie et son Église*, Paris, 1938; R. Kisszling, *Die Croaten*, 1956; J. Castellan, *En Serbie au seuil de l'indépendance, 1815–1839*.

28. J. Mousset, op. cit., p. 128.

29. Michel Chevallier, in an article in *La Revue des Deux Mondes* entitled *Du Gouvernement autrichien, 1842*, admits that he was disconcerted by the excessive nature of popular devotions, especially the cult of St. John of Nepomuk: 'This is not devotion, but adoration and idolatry.'

30. On Bolzano, apart from his own works (*Athanasia* and *Erbauungsreden*, 1839, are in the Bibliothèque nationale in Paris):
    E. Winter, *Bolzano und sein Kreis*, 1933, *Der böhmische Vormärz in Briefen B. Bolzanos an F. Prihonsky*, Berlin, 1956; *Bernard Bolzano, ein Denker und Erzieher im österreichischen Vormärz* (Österreichische Akademie der Wissenschaften, philosophisch-historische Klasse, Vienna, 1967), in collaboration with Paul Funk and Jan Berg.

31. For the whole of this period, in addition to the general works by Hantsch and Zöllner and the *Československá Vlastivěda* (vol. IV of the 1st edn. 1922; the 2nd edn. goes only as far as 1781):
    Slokar, *Geschichte der Industrie in Österreich und ihrer Forderung unter Franz I*, 1914. F. Engel-Janosi, *Über die Entwicklung der sozialen und wirtschaftlichen Verhältnisse in Österreich 1815 bis 1848* (Vierteljahrschrift für Sozial und Wirtschaftsgeschichte 17 1924). Kurt Kaser, *Der innerösterreichische Eisenhandel in der I Hälfte des 19. Jahrhunderts* Graz, 1927. B. Mendl, *Vyvoj řemesel a obchodu v městech pražských* ('Development of Trades and Commerce in the Cities of Prague'), Prague, 1947. Ludmila Kárníková *Uloha uhlí v průmyslovém rozvoji Čech do poloviny 19 stoleti* ('The Role of Coal in the Industrial Growth of Bohemia up to the mid-19th Century'), 78 pages, Rozpravy československé Akademie ved, 1958. Jaroslav Purš, *Průmyslová revolucev českych zemich* ('The Industrial Revolution in the Czech Lands'), Prague, 1960, which the author used for this chapter, together with an article by G. Merei, *Über einige Fragen der Anfänge der Kapitalistischen Gewerbe-Entwicklung in Ungarn* ('On Certain Problems in the Early Stages of Capitalist Industrial Development in Hungary'), in the collection entitled in French *Études historiques publiées en 1960 par la Commission nationale des historiens hongrois* vol. I, pp. 721–73, with a bibliography in Hungarian.

32. In the *Mémoires d'Outre-tombe* (ed. Levaillant, Édition du Centenaire, IV, p. 384)

Chateaubriand wrote a magnificent prose-poem on the decadence of Venice in 1833. In 1841 he added this fine sentence: 'L'Autriche a battu l'eau et tout s'est tu'—a beautiful turn of phrase, but unjust. In 1845, returning to Venice after twelve years, he recognized that the bridge which was to be built to link the islands with *terra firma* would not 'kill' the charm of the city, but that it would provide one more vein to bring blood to the heart of Venice. A. Valéry, in *L'Italie confortable*, Paris, 1847, observed that the city's population, then over 110,000, was increasing 'every day'. Venice had thus not been sacrificed.

33. Figures given in tables published in the appendix of an article by Oldřiška Kodedová, *Die Lohnarbeit auf dem Grossgrundbesitz in Böhmen in der zweiten Hälfte des 19. Jahrhunderts*, in *Historica*, XIV, Prague, 1967, p. 166 *et seq.*

34. L. Eisenmann, *La Hongrie contemporaine*; J. Szekfü, *Der Staat Ungarn 1918* and *État et Nation*, Paris, 1945; J. Varga, *Typen und Probleme des bauerlichen Grundbesitzes in Ungarn (1767–1849)*, Budapest, 1955; H. Schlitter, *Aus Österreichs Vormärz III*, Ungarn, Vienna, 1920; L. Kovács, *Gróf J. Széchenyi 1846–1848*, Budapest, 1889.

35. Christoph Thienen-Alderflycht, *Graf Leo Thun im Vormärz—Grundlagen der böhmischen Konservatismus im Kaisertum Österreich* ('Count Leo Thun in pre-March—Foundations of Bohemian Conservatism in The Empire of Austria'), Vienna, 1967.

36. The history of the events of 1848 is inevitably entangled in that of the different countries. The reader should therefore refer to the general histories—for Germany, the works of Veit Valentin, Srbik, Erich Brandenburg and Erich Marx; the collection published in Paris in 1948 and entitled *Actes du congrès historique du centenaire de la révolution de 1848*, to which F. Valsecchi (Italy) and D. Kosáry (Hungary) contributed; the collective work under the editorship of R. Kiszling, *Die Revolution in Kaisertum Österreich 1848–1849*, 2 vols., 1948; the chapter in Hugo Hantsch, *Die Nationalitätenfrage im alten Österreich*, pp. 36–49, entitled 'Das nationale Problem Österreichs im Revolutions-Jahr 1848'. In 1948, after the experience of the Second World War, historiography in general tended to adopt as its viewpoint the defence of liberty, which had been the objective of the 1848 revolution. Cf. Alexander Novotný, *1848, Ringen um Freiheit und Völkerfrieden*, Graz, 1948; and in Hungary, Francis Eckhardt (Eckhardt Ferencz), *1848, a szabadság eve* ('1848, the Year of Liberty') and the studies of Louis Kossuth by D. Kosáry. Historians then tended to move towards a Marxist interpretation and a unilateral viewpoint which placed economic and social causes in the foreground. This trend can be observed by referring to the work *Twenty-five Years of Czechoslovak Historiography* (p. 244 *et seq.* and p. 264 *et seq.*) and the bibliography of selected works of Hungarian historical science, 1945–59, published in an appendix to vol. II of *Études historiques*.

37. Palacký's letter was addressed to the president of the preliminary commission, von Sovion; the text was published by Palacký himself in his Memoirs (*Gedenkblätter*, Prague, 1874, p. 149). Large extracts have been translated into English in the book by S. Harrison Thomson, *Czechoslovakia in European History*, Princeton, 1953, p. 44, and extracts are also to be found in Robert A. Kann, *Das Nationalitätenproblem der Habsburgermonarchie*, 1964, vol. I, p. 172. Cf. Hugo Hantsch, op. cit., p. 593: 'ein glühendes Bekenntnis zur österreichischen Monarchie und ihrer europäischen Mission'.

❧ 10 ❧

From Austria to
Austria-Hungary

THE MOST SERIOUS problem remained that of relations with Germany, for the Parliament assembled at Frankfurt was entrusted with the mission of reconstructing the Empire and deciding in what manner Austria would participate in that Empire. A resolution of October 1848 proposed that only a simple personal union could exist between states not inhabited by Germans and the predominantly Germanic states of the new Empire.

Nothing could be more certainly guaranteed to bring about the disruption of the *Gesamtösterreich*, the Austrian Empire as it then existed, the constitutional organization of which would have been demolished by a system of simple personal union imposed from without. The solution favoured by Austria was a Greater Germany embracing both the old Confederation and the Empire of Austria, with the government of Vienna, and not that of Berlin, as its prime mover. A third possible solution was the formation of a Little Germany, that is, a unified German Empire that would exclude Austria—this was roughly the solution sought by Palacký and which Bismarck, for quite different motives, was to achieve after 1866, employing bellicose methods which the Bohemian historian had hardly contemplated. The Austrian government hoped that, once it had overcome its internal difficulties, it would be able to dictate to Germany the solution of its choice, or, failing this, that it would simply be able to restore the situation of 1815.

Hungary also presented problems.[1] The Hungarian Diet, composed of two Chambers and elected on a property-owning franchise (one million three hundred thousand electors for the Lower Chamber), was to resolve the agrarian question by suppressing feudal dues on an indemnity basis, to proclaim religious liberty and give children of all creeds access to existing schools and, finally, to define the rights of those inhabitants of the kingdom who were not of Magyar nationality. The Diet of Transylvania had voted in favour of union with the Hungarian Diet, but represented only the Magyar aristocracy of the principality. The religious authorities (the metropolitan Şaguna) and the middle class looked to Bucharest for support, envisaging the union of all Rumanians. The Serbs, under the leadership of the metropolitan Rajasić, wished to obtain a separate territorial status. Finally, the Croats, led by the ban Jellacić, pleaded their historic traditions in justification of their demand for the constitution of a kingdom of Croatia-Slavonia-Dalmatia uniting all the southern Slavs.

Complications had arisen as early as the summer of 1848. The minister Batthyány was not able to obtain the king's ratification of a law passed by the Parliament which ordered a levy of two hundred thousand men. The radicals protested, however, when it was proposed to send troops against the revolutionaries of Lombardy and Venetia: the cause of patriots was the same everywhere. Yet neither the secession of the Croats nor the danger of Wallachian and Serbian conspiracies on the Lower Danube could be tolerated. Amid this confusion, which was aggravated by agrarian disturbances in Transylvania and the Slovakian comitats, General Lamberg, sent by the king to take command of the army, was assassinated by fanatics in Pest on 28 September. The king placed Jellacić at the head of the army, but the Hungarian Diet pronounced the governor of Croatia a traitor to his country. A new war of independence was beginning. By a curious fiction, it was conducted for a time in the name of the king of Hungary against the imperial government, but on this occasion the subjects of the kingdom, Croats, Serbs, Transylvanians and Rumanians, placed themselves on the side of the emperor, trusting to him to ensure that their demands were satisfied.

Initially, events in Bohemia did not assume the same grave dimensions, but it was not long before developments in that country brought new misfortunes upon the population.[2] It was agreed that elections would be held to form a Constituent Diet of the kingdom. Thus, in the month of May 1848 the situation was this: a Parliament and constitutional government in Hungary, preparations for a Constituent Diet in Bohemia, and preparations for a Constituent Assembly which was to meet in Vienna and to define the general institutions of the Austrian Empire.

Poles and Croats then demanded that a congress of all the Slavs of the monarchy be convened in Prague. The congress, the counterpart to the assembly of all Germans at the Frankfurt Parliament, would affirm the solidarity of all Austrian Slavs. But the two assemblies were not of the same nature: the Prague congress had no precise political objective; its role was largely moral and, in present-day terminology, cultural. Authorization was granted. In order to avert any suspicion of Pan-Slavism, it was understood that only citizens of the monarchy would participate in the work of the commissions. Nevertheless, the invitation issued on 1 May ended with these words: 'If other Slavs living outside the territory of the monarchy wish to honour us with their presence, they will be our cordially welcomed guests.' Foreigners arrived at the congress as observers—a few Russians, including the revolutionary Bakunin, and even Germans and Magyars, who could claim no ethnic link with the Slavs.

During the first sessions of the congress, which was inaugurated by solemn High Mass on the horse-market (now St. Wenceslas Square), an emotional and aggressively romantic speech was made by Šafařík, who denounced 'the murderers of Slav souls' among the neighbouring peoples. The work of the congress was then distributed among several groups, Czecho-Slovaks, southern Slavs and Polo-Ruthenes. The possibility was considered of a federation of Slavs within the Austrian Empire—after all, the political boundaries of the Empire presented no real obstacle. Although authorized by the government, the congress conducted its deliberations under the supervision of regiments commanded by General Windisch-graetz. This loyal and stern officer was profoundly contemptuous and mistrustful of an assembly of civilians who, in his eyes, were all equally insignificant and merely trouble-makers. An incident between the troops and a procession of students led to riots in Prague. A revolutionary committee headed by the radicals immediately arrested the governor, Count Leo Thun, although he was a Bohemian patriot and a generous, conciliating man. Meanwhile, the National Guard and the students of the university, both of middle-class origin, mingled with the artisans and workers, helping to erect barricades in a national uprising against despotic power, a revolt of civilians against the army. General Windischgraetz withdrew his troops from the city and installed his artillery on the heights overlooking the left bank of the river. Prague was bombarded and several districts of the city caught fire. This was the first occasion on which modern tactics were employed by the army against citizens. The burgomaster was compelled to capitulate. Since the city was under martial law, there could be no question of resuming the sessions of the congress; neither was it possible to continue the elections for the Constituent Diet in the provinces. There remained only one platform from which Czech delegates could make themselves heard: the Constituent Assembly in Vienna. A delegation was sent to the capital.

The delegation was composed of the most enlightened Czechs, those who were the most competent to debate institutional problems, but also the most moderate in their social demands, the least disposed to violence and insurrection: Palacký, who had been alarmed by the events in Prague, Tomek, a professor, the lawyers Brauner and Rieger, and Karel Havlíček, the brilliant young editor of the news-paper *Národní Noviny*. These men were truly representative of the liberal 'intelli-gentsia'. Radicals such as Frič and Sabina, who would have gone much further in their demands, seeking support from popular movements, had been forced to flee from Prague, which was under martial law.[3]

At the Constituent Assembly in Vienna the Czechs met their German fellow-Bohemians, one of whom, Hans Kudlich, a Silesian, proposed and obtained approval of the great measure awaited by everyone: the abolition of the feudal system. Seigniorial rights were suppressed, but the lords were to receive compensation. Juridical and fiscal privileges were no longer to exist: all the citizens of the monarchy became free individuals and equal before the law (September 1848).

Meanwhile, events in Hungary provoked new disturbances. In October the workers of Vienna obstructed the departure of the regiments which were being sent to fight the Hungarians. Barricades were erected in the streets. The insurgents hoped that Hungarian troops would come to their assistance and that the revolution of the peoples would triumph over the authorities, the army and even the bourgeois Assembly. Hungarian regiments advanced as far as Schwechat, where they were halted by the Croats. General Windischgraetz then repeated the tactics employed at Prague: he bombarded Vienna and the rebellion was crushed.

The imperial family had escaped and taken refuge in Olmütz. The Constituent

Assembly found it impossible to continue its work in a city that was under martial law and still trembling from the recent riot. The government suggested that it move to Kremsier (Kroměřiže) and establish itself in the summer residence of the archbishop of Olmütz, where it could work in peace. Three hundred deputies assembled there and undertook to draft a constitution for the entire Austrian Empire; however, they did not admit Hungarians to their sessions, since Hungary was in revolt. They appointed a Constitution Committee which was divided into two sub-committees, one to define the rights of man and of the citizen, the other to draft the new political constitution of the Empire. The second of these sub-committees comprised five members: two Germans and three Slavs, including Palacký.

Although Palacký still attached prime importance to state rights and continued to think in terms of a united kingdom (Bohemia, Moravia and Silesia), he gave his support to a plan for a territorial division of the Empire according to national groupings. The German regions of Bohemia were to be granted autonomy, while the Czech districts were to be united with Moravia and Slovakia. At the Assembly, Tomek, a determined traditionalist, opposed the dislocation of the kingdom. But Palacký, after so many upheavals, was willing to make sacrifices so that the Empire might be regenerated. It was also essential that the new constitution should be as liberal as possible and should strike a balance between centralism and federalism. Would these hopes be fulfilled?

Another force was involved: the monarchic principle. No one was contemplating its abolition, but for some this principle was more than a tradition or a symbol: it was to be the indispensable factor in the reconstruction of the Austrian state. Prince Felix Schwarzenberg, appointed prime minister in November 1848, announced to the Assembly at Kremsier: 'We desire a constitutional monarchy genuinely and unreservedly.' But he was thinking primarily of a monarch with effective power and undisputed authority.

The intention was to strengthen a united Empire (*Gesamtösterreich*) that would not tolerate revolution on its territory, either in Hungary or in Italy. Austria could then decide the nature of its association with a Germany that had also been renewed. Thus, at Kremsier and at Frankfurt, where the Archduke John temporarily exercised the functions of imperial regent, two assemblies were striving to provide each state with a constitution. Any attempt to preserve the old order would have been sterile: reconstruction was essential.

New men were needed for the new order that was to be created. Schwarzenberg therefore advised Ferdinand I to abdicate. Although he was quite popular, the emperor was feeble in health, incapable of sustained effort and overwhelmed by events. A prince of a different kind was required for such a vast enterprise of regeneration, a young man uncompromised by his past whose youth would provide a guarantee for the future and whose personal destiny might thus be associated with that of the new Empire.

The choice fell on the eighteen-year-old Archduke Francis Joseph, the nephew of of the emperor and son of his brother Francis Charles. This was not the result of court intrigue; rather it was a revolutionary act accomplished for the safeguard of the monarchic institution. The imperial family gave its consent and the transmission of power took place at Olmütz on 2 December 1848.

An adolescent emperor, acceding to the throne when the future was so shrouded in uncertainty! Who could have foreseen that this was the beginning of one of the longest reigns in European history and that for sixty-eight years, in spite of changes, wars and social vicissitudes, the life of the emperor and that of the Empire were to be associated one with the other, as Schwarzenberg had hoped?[4]

Brought up by a mother who was intelligent and ambitious, but who knew when to retire into the background in the presence of ministers, Francis Joseph dutifully absorbed the lessons of Schwarzenberg. He served his apprenticeship submissively, but with profound conviction. It was in these early days that he acquired the elevated sense of duty which became his outstanding quality and from which he never deviated. He was endowed with robust health (his longevity was a remarkable biological achievement) and a sound intelligence which was by no means of a brilliant, imaginative kind. But it was in this that his strength lay, for, in the romantic atmosphere of the times, another prince of a more enthusiastic nature would have been tempted to embark on too bold projects and might, perhaps, have foundered. Over the years Francis Joseph, who never sought personal success, won the confidence and respect of his peoples. His reign marked a period of general technical progress, better living conditions for the majority of his subjects, the embellishment of cities and a blossoming of intellectual life and of the arts, achievements which, in another age, would have been accredited to his own person. At the same time, by a profound contradiction, every war of his reign brought military defeats, institutions were constantly called in question and hatred developed between the nations of the Empire, confronting the Austrian state with a peril even graver than the social question, which itself was becoming increasingly acute.

If Francis Joseph never discovered the secret of overcoming these growing difficulties, he became to an ever greater degree the man whose very presence averted catastrophes, the supreme arbiter in great crises: even the other states of Europe wondered anxiously what might happen if he were not there. At a time when, throughout Europe, the monarchic institution was losing its prestige, decaying or already dying, he embodied the virtues of that institution. He was, perhaps, the last true king in history.

Nothing of this could have been anticipated at the time of his accession. There was war in Italy and in Hungary. In Budapest a new revolutionary government had been organized by Louis Kossuth, who entrusted an emigrant Polish general, Bem, with the task of occupying and subjugating Transylvania. But the imperial army was advancing to the west of the kingdom; in December it occupied the capital. Windischgraetz then resumed his offensive, inflicting a cruel defeat on the Hungarians at Kápolna (21 February 1849). The young emperor himself took part in the battle of Raab; he was happy to give proof of his personal bravery, but did not yet understand that a sovereign should not seek such opportunities in combat against his own subjects.

In Italy, the king of Piedmont launched an offensive, but was defeated by Radetzky at Novara.

These military actions convinced Schwarzenberg that the revolts had been finally crushed and that new institutions could now be introduced. He proclaimed the dissolution of the Kremsier Assembly, whose debates he found confused, and at the same time promulgated a constitution (dated 4 March) for the whole Empire. By acting too hastily, he was jeopardizing its success. The very character of the new constitution indicated that the government did not propose to restore arbitrary rule or absolutism. It made the desired concessions to modern ideas, proclaiming the equality of all citizens before the law and recognizing the right of each nationality to use its mother tongue. But the document as a whole remained ambiguous. It contained no mention of 'nationalities' as such, but referred to 'groups of the people' (*Volkstamm*), as if the whole of Austria had been inhabited by a single people divided into different linguistic groups. The Empire formed one state: there was but one crown, that of the emperor of Austria. The territory of this state was divided, regardless of 'historic' rights, into regions the boundaries of which were approximately those of the principal nationalities; the Slovakian comitats or counties, Transylvania and Croatia thus found themselves in juxtaposition to a Magyar Hungary and no longer dependent on a Hungarian state. These new districts were to elect their Diets by a tax-qualification suffrage and the Diets, in their turn, were to send their deputies to an Imperial Parliament.

However, until the new institutions came into force, the government reserved the right to promulgate provisional laws (Article 86 of the constitution): in other words, there was to be a limited period of absolutism.

The manner in which the constitution was introduced, even more than its content, aroused indignation throughout the countries of the Empire. Admittedly, the peasant masses, which everywhere had been animated by hopes of agrarian reform and in Transylvania had been combated by military forces fighting for another form of revolution, were now relatively indifferent to institutional procedures: a whole revolutionary army had thus been drained of energy. In the cities, the working class was crushed, without leaders or groups to defend it. But the same mood did not prevail in middle-class circles, among jurists, intellectuals and merchants, all those who had a clear understanding of the concepts of liberty, public law and an order established by common consent. In their eyes, the dissolution of the Kremsier Assembly was a scandal and an affront. The deputies were their legitimate representatives and had only sought to create an equitable and just regime. The army was driving the deputies away and they were returning home empty-handed and dejected. The official press was adding its own sarcastic comments to their humiliation: to show its contempt of the deliberative assemblies, it spoke of *Finis Poloniae*. Karel Havlíček, accepting the challenge, seized on this insult in his newspaper *Národní Noviny*: 'No, we can agree only with the first word of the phrase. We do not yet know what should be put in place of *Poloniae*. The future will tell us this.'[5] Austria itself might well perish by rejecting the liberal ideal.

The proclamation of the constitution had even more serious consequences in Hungary. Never would the Hungary of the 'April laws', the national Hungary of Kossuth, allow its territory to be dismembered by a decision of Vienna which, depriving it of Transylvania, Croatia and the Banat, would reduce it to the status of a mutilated province. By what right did Vienna propose to act thus? The abdication of Ferdinand and the nomination of Francis Joseph were in themselves the height of illegality, for both had been accomplished without the consent of the Hungarians and outside Hungarian law. Consequently, there was no longer a king of Hungary. The representatives of the nation condemned the imperial government's repudiation of old pledges and pronounced the deposition of the dynasty. A republic was proclaimed under the presidency of Kossuth, who was appointed governor of Hungary. News of this event was warmly received in western Europe, where public opinion passionately supported the cause of Hungary, as it did that of Poland. The name of Kossuth became a household word, a symbol of liberty and fatherland under oppression.

The Hungarians were regaining their spirit; their armies, more resolute and better disciplined under the generals Georgei and Bem, found fresh vigour as they launched an offensive, compelling the Imperials to retreat and national groups to submit. Yet many people, even patriots, considered that this admirable revival brought with it terrible dangers: how long would a Hungary without allies succeed in maintaining its independence? Would it be possible to ensure the continued loyalty of the Slav and Rumanian national groups without according them the guarantees which they were demanding for their existence as free peoples?

Before there could be time to solve these problems, the government in Vienna turned to Russia for assistance in crushing Hungary. Francis Joseph appealed to the tsar in the name of order in Europe and the solidarity of thrones against the Revolution: 'Rebels of all nations are placing their hopes in Hungary and each success achieved by the Hungarians is hailed by the revolutionaries of all countries as a sign auguring the success of their own false causes.'[6] The tsar lent the emperor his troops. They were not particularly good soldiers, nor were they well armed, but the Hungarian forces, even less well equipped, were unable to hold out for long. Advancing along the passes of the Carpathians, the Russians penetrated into Hungary, captured Buda in May and then, on 13 July 1849, at Világos, forced General Georgei to capitulate. Yet again, heroic Hungary had been crushed.

Like Rákóczi in earlier times, Kossuth sought refuge in Turkey. With him went the principle of national independence. Reconquered Hungary, now at the mercy of the imperial army, was punished in atrocious fashion. Special courts were set up and delivered their sentences of death: Louis Batthyány was executed, by way of reprisal, on the anniversary of the murder of General Lamberg. Thirteen generals were shot at Arad. The troops of General Haynau, whose cruelties in Italy had earned him the nickname 'the hyena of Brescia', imposed a reign of terror in the comitats.[7]

The victory over the Hungarians—hardly a glorious one, since it had been achieved with foreign assistance against a people who were merely standing by their traditional rights—was interpreted as a victory over the international Revolution and gave Schwarzenberg complete freedom of manoeuvre in Austria and even in Europe. He could now dictate to Germany the policies of his choice. By threatening war, he dissuaded the king of Prussia from forming a restricted union of German princes for his own advantage; since no solution could be found that satisfied the needs of the time, the old Germanic Confederation was re-established. In Austria, a few months later, the constitution of 4 March was abolished. 'We have thrown all constitutions overboard and there is now only one master in Austria,' the young emperor wrote to his mother in 1851, with more enthusiasm than wisdom. Yet from the tumult of revolution, the sittings of the Constituent Assembly, the street-fighting, the pitched battles and the conquests of cities, two great and inviolable achievements emerged as the foundations of the new society: the abolition of serfdom and the equality of all citizens before the law. But, for the reconstruction of the political order, the only law was that which resided in the will of the sovereign.

§

Schwarzenberg was too intelligent to consider victory over the Revolution an end in itself.[8] He saw that victory only as an indispensable stage in the restoration of Austria's greatness in Europe. His ministry was composed of men of calibre and experience, such as Bruck, a great administrator of commercial affairs, and Alexander von Bach, a liberal by inclination who had been converted to the cause of authority by his abhorrence of riots. It was their intention that the return to order should open up an era of prosperity in Austria. The task was not an easy one, owing to the deficit of the State finances. But it was in the interests of the banks to save a system which alone seemed to guarantee the recovery and development of business activity: the way was thus open for capitalism and industry in a world which only recently had been totally committed to seigniorial agriculture. Although the land remained the source of income of the majority, it was henceforth involved in a new system of cultivation, that of individual enterprise.

The corvée had been abolished without redemption, since it constituted a personal servitude, but feudal or seigniorial dues—the quit-rents payable on holdings and numerous other dues imposed on the peasantry—were abolished only on an indemnity basis. These debts of redemption were divided into three equal categories: the first was immediately discounted, since it was included in the tax which the landlord had hitherto paid for his tenants; the other two categories were to be paid to the landlord in annual instalments, one by the peasant, the other by the regional administration. Capitalization was fixed at a sum twenty times that of the old dues; the peasant was to discharge his debt in twenty annual payments, for which he made a contribution to the exchequer every three months; the regional administration was to pay its share in forty annual instalments. In 1851 a redemption fund was instituted which issued to landlords bonds bearing interest at 5 per cent and payable by a system of drawing lots. The peasant's contribution was secured by a mortgage on the lands of which he now enjoyed complete ownership. By contrast with what had happened in France during the Revolution, when all indemnities had been suppressed by the law of 17 July 1793, the abolition of feudal dues in the Austrian Empire did not release large areas of land for purchase by the middle class or the peasantry. It is even possible that, as certain persons had predicted, the suppression of the corvée had a favourable effect on the productivity of the great domain. The sums received by the landlords in compensation could be invested in agricultural machinery or in various other forms of expenditure to ensure a better yield from cultivation. At all events, the abolition of feudal dues left the great families of the landed aristocracy in possession of their vast estates, some of which extended over thousands of acres, though large parts of these estates were covered by forests, ponds and waste land. Furthermore, as a result of the system of entail or *fideicommissum*, certain domains were inalienable and not liable to distraint. Such lands, held in usufruct by their proprietor, constituted a family possession that could only be transmitted from father to son or to the nearest heir. The magnitude of land revenues enabled proprietors to invest in industrial enterprises—not only textiles and the food industries (breweries and flour mills), but also the various branches of metallurgy: ironworks, mines and machinery.

One of the principal features of the new absolutism was the creation of the free commune as the base of the social structure; the commune administered its own affairs through elected representatives chosen by three classes of electors. Since the seigniory and its privileges no longer existed, the noble domain became dependent on the commune within which its lands lay, which meant that it came under the administration of several different communes. As this system tended to obstruct the efficient management of the estate as a whole, the old feudal lords, who were now simply great landowners, tried to evade the authority of the communal administration and to preserve their independence by making themselves responsible for the maintenance of public order and the upkeep of roads on their lands. Parishes were still under their control: they presented the candidates of their choice to the bishop, but in return provided for the upkeep of churches. Thus, the great noble domain retained its autonomy and its character of a little 'state'—but a little state which was also acquiring a modern aspect. On domains where the sumptuous Baroque edifices of the eighteenth century had not already been erected, manorial residences were rebuilt, sometimes in a pastiche of the Gothic style, as at Hluboká, the domain of the Schwarzenberg family. When the proprietor was in residence, the banner bearing his coat of arms flew from the top of the manor. At crossroads and along forest paths, signposts bore the name of the estate. At the eastern extremity of Lower Austria, almost on the frontiers of Hungary, the traveller of today can still see the escutcheons of the Frohsdorf estate, 'Herrschaft Frohsdorf', where the Comte de Chambord, the last king of France ('Henry V'), spent his melancholy years of exile. In the countryside of Bohemia, Austria, Galicia and Hungary the physiognomy of the old seigniorial system thus survived in the new order of capitalist economy and civic equality. The sons of many peasant families found ample opportunities for careers and social advancement in the employment of the great landowners, as domestic servants, coachmen, grooms, foresters of various grades, book-keepers, managers and even archivists. On efficiently administered estates, insurance agreements and pensions provided security in everyday life and for old age. The employees of the estate found themselves socially privileged and often took a pride in their allegiance to an illustrious family. They led an existence infinitely preferable to that of the ordinary labourer, enjoying a greater degree of material comfort than peasants who remained attached to the soil, cultivating inadequate plots of land. This system may have presented serious obstacles to the progress of the general economy, holding back the growth of production and, in many cases, perpetuating established routines and general stagnation, but there can be no doubt that it was acceptable and even positively beneficial to a large number of families.

The patriarchal, paternalist character of the noble domain remained an original feature of the rural society of the Empire until the partial reforms of the democratic republics and the profound revolution of the socialist regime, proof of a robust vitality which must be seen not merely as a survival, but as the result of a balance between technical progress and traditions which had not lost their efficacy.

Industrialization, which developed simultaneously with large-scale land-ownership, was, perhaps, the determining factor of the whole period.[9] For the historian viewing this period from a distance of a hundred years, the process of industrialization constitutes one of the major elements, if not the key element, of a complex phase in history, the entanglements of which can sometimes prove disheartening. It accorded both with a general philosophy and with a political ideal—the greatness of the Austrian system and of the dynasty. Manual labour, hitherto the instrument by which goods were produced and wealth was created, made way for the machine, whose potentialities were multiplied by the use of steam and then of electricity. The craft workshops and factories were replaced by large mills. Associated with the ideal of progress was the hope of personal enrichment through profit. The new freedom of labour fostered a mood of optimism among workers. The entrepreneurs, for their part, considered that development was possible only if society could be safeguarded against the risk of popular uprisings and attempts to undermine the new social order of liberal capitalism.

After the troubled years 1848 and 1849, the world of big business, and also that of the petty bourgeoisie and the artisan class, needed an assurance of tranquillity: the former therefore encouraged the establishment of a strong government and an efficient administration, which the latter accepted as necessary for the security of their daily life, even if this meant temporarily sacrificing the political ideal.

The conditions of economic progress corresponded more closely than ever with the character of the great territorial complex of the Austrian Empire. No longer was this a monarchy constituting 'a whole' (*ein Totum*) by virtue of a juxtaposition of states subject to the same dynasty, as in the time of Maria Theresa, but a modern association of complementary areas of production. From Poland to North Italy, from the mountains of Bohemia to the Save and the mountains of Transylvania, all the inhabitants of 'Austria', as the subjects of the emperor, enjoyed in principle the same rights and the same opportunities. But it remained to be decided whether central Europe, where economic development still lagged behind that of the Western countries, would find greater advantages for the future in union with Germany, in a customs bloc of seventy million inhabitants—a *Mitteleuropa* extending from the Baltic to the Adriatic which could send its products along the Danube to the Black Sea and to the Middle East.

Such was the conviction of Schwarzenberg's Minister of Commerce, Karl von Bruck. Born a German of the Empire and in the Protestant faith, this great merchant of Trieste, one of the founders of the *Österreichischer Lloyd*, possessed a fine intellect and a rare experience of commerce; he was therefore excellently suited to the task of guiding such a far-reaching programme of economic development. Jacques Droz, in his book *L'Europe centrale*, where he analyses the projects of the great expert, says that Bruck was more a German than an Austrian, a comment which should be understood as referring to the supreme goal of his enterprise.[10] The Dresden conferences marked the failure of that enterprise. Prussia, owing to its economic strength in the Rhineland region, one of the most industrialized in Europe, wished to dominate Germany through the *Zollverein* (Customs Union) and the alliance of that union with the coastal states of northern Germany; an alliance with the *Gesamtösterreich* bloc presented fewer advantages. Thus, on the economic plane as on the political plane, the rivalry of Prussia and Austria in Germany was leading to the co-existence of two great territorial complexes rather than their fusion. For the time being, an intermediate solution seemed to be the best—the conclusion of trade treaties such as Palacký, who was not an economist, had desired out of simple common sense.

It remained to establish the economic organization of *Gesamtösterreich*. Bruck now laid the foundations of a prosperity which, in spite of crises, the peoples of the Danube were to enjoy for nearly three-quarters of a century. He and Schwarzenberg, notwithstanding divergences of opinion, strengthened the solidarity of the countries of the Austrian Empire, a deep-rooted solidarity capable of resisting subsequent centrifugal tendencies and, despite numerous institutional modifications, of maintaining the Empire as a living community until the catastrophe of 1918. The combined efforts of the great aristocrat and the great bourgeois thus enabled Danubian society to make the necessary transition from the domanial, agricultural era to liberal capitalism and the industrial age. They were destined to provide only the initial impetus: Bruck resigned in 1851 and Schwarzenberg died suddenly in the spring of 1852.

In 1850 chambers of commerce and of crafts were established at the base of the new economic structure. There were sixty of these institutions in the various countries of the Empire, each comprising between ten and thirty members; their role was to serve as consultative bodies, supplying the government with information on which it could base its measures for the promotion of economic progress. In 1851 tariffs between Austria and Hungary were abolished and a uniform system of imposts was extended to the entire Empire. In 1859 the old corporations were finally suppressed: henceforward, any person could undertake any form of commercial or industrial activity simply by notifying the authorities. Restrictions on the manufacture or sale of goods were swept away. But it was permitted to form associations for the supervision of work contracts or the provision of insurance against sickness. In 1858 the monetary system was changed and the 'convention coin', which had lasted nearly a century, was abandoned.

These measures had immediate and diverse repercussions on the social structure of the Empire. The abolition of the tariff barrier was not wholly advantageous to

Hungary, although the Hungarian producer generally benefited like other producers from the facilities accorded to commercial undertakings. But Hungary was also becoming industrialized: during the preceding period it had increased the number of its steam-driven flour mills and it also possessed foundries and machine-construction workshops at Obuda. Its chief products, however, were cereals and meat. It was to the advantage of the much more industrially advanced western sector of the Empire to buy these goods and in return to sell its fabrics and machines to Hungary or to establish large works there such as sugar refineries. Hungarian historians are therefore justified in asserting that the development of textiles and metallurgy was retarded in Hungary by the influx of Austro-Bohemian products, while the predominance of the great domain, which was not directly counterbalanced by heavy industry, as in Austria and especially in Bohemia, contributed to the preservation of the old economic structures.

In Bohemia, progress was greater, bringing benefits both to the nobility and to the middle class. In a research organization known as the Industrial Unity of Bohemia the directorial posts were occupied by aristocrats such as Clam-Gallas, Salm and Chotek. Even in 1866 the noble families of Bohemia still possessed 500 of the country's 900 breweries, 300 of its 400 distilleries and 80 of its 120 refineries.[11] However, the middle class was the chief beneficiary of the system, establishing itself in the chambers of commerce and ensuring the Czech character of the Industrial Unity of Bohemia: the preservation of nationality, which had been encouraged by the reorganization of education (a subject that will be treated shortly), was henceforth closely linked with the class-consciousness of the bourgeoisie. Two conditions were indispensable to progress: a network of communications and a system of bank credit. Hitherto, bank credit had been available only for the benefit of the State and of commerce; it was now to be extended to finance industrial concerns.

At first, the railways had been State-controlled enterprises, but the State, encumbered with public expenditure greatly in excess of its resources, was in no position to contemplate further investment. To transfer the railways to private companies was a good solution which would bring money into the treasury and facilitate a more rapid industrial development of the territory. The Solomon Rothschild bank, the *Österreichische Nationalbank*, and the Péreire banking group were all involved in the operation, even competing against each other. Two great companies were formed within a few years, the Northern Railway Company (*Nordbahngesellschaft*) and the Southern Railway Company (*Sudbahngesellschaft*), which provided the great transversal route from the mountains of Bohemia to the port of Trieste and communication between the principal industrial regions. In 1851 a line was opened which ran between Prague and Saxony via Děčín and Podmokly, linking the coal-producing region with the textile region. In 1854 the obstacle presented by Bohemia's mountains was overcome: on 17 July the Semmering tunnel, a mighty undertaking by the engineer Ghega, was opened; another engineer, Engerth, had built a locomotive specially designed for the mountain railway. In 1858 the *Sudbahngesellschaft* absorbed the lines between Vienna and Trieste and extended its network into Carniola, Croatia, Slavonia and western Hungary

In Hungary, the railway which crossed the plain to the north of the Danube started from Pressburg; running via Galanta and Neusohl, it entered the river valley, which it then followed as far as Buda. Between 1849 and 1866 Hungary's railway network was extended from 178 to 2,158 kilometres. Finally, as a complement to this new railway system, the Danube was developed as a waterway. As a result of the progress of shipbuilding activity by the *Donaudampfschiffahrtsgesellschaft*, the great river enabled heavy goods and grain to be transported at reasonable prices. The Danube, swollen by the rivers of the Alps as soon as it reached the Austrian Empire, covered more than one thousand kilometres of Austrian territory as far as the Iron Gates and, although navigation was free on the river, its traffic was controlled to an increasing degree by Austria's rapid advance along the path of economic recovery. But beyond the Iron Gates the Danube became a Turkish river, which it remained as far as its mouth in the delta. In 1812, by the conquest of eastern Moldavia, arbitrarily named Bessarabia, Russia had extended its influence to a branch of the delta—yet another cause of rivalry between Russia and Austria, since earlier treaties with the Porte and the general stipulations of the Congress of Vienna had granted Austria the right of navigation as far as the Black Sea. By a special agreement between the two powers (St. Petersburg, 1840), Russia had been made responsible for the upkeep of the Sulina mouth of the delta and of a lighthouse which operated from March to December. In fact, there were two Danubes: a 'metropolitan' Danube, over which Austria exercised total control, and a 'colonial' Danube, where Russia, Turkey and soon other foreign powers had their interests.

The Congress of Paris (1856) placed this latter part of the Danube under the supervision of a European Commission. It was a natural weakness that the river which formed the axis of its territory should not belong in its entirety to Austria. But in the mid-nineteenth century the Lower Danube had still not been developed and the Iron Gates continued to form an obstacle to navigation. It remained an immense advantage to be in possession of this mighty natural waterway extending from Passau to the Iron Gates and it was in the interests of every country of the monarchy to provide for its upkeep and to develop its use.[12]

The provision of industrial plant depended on the credit which firms were to obtain from the great banking organizations. The chief producing regions were in northern Bohemia and in the other provinces of the kingdom, Moravia and Silesia, for it was here that the old textile workshops had been established and that the mining resources for metallurgy and the production of energy were to be found. But the financial centre remained Vienna, to which capital flowed both from the countries of the Empire and from abroad.

In 1856 the Rothschilds of Vienna founded the *Creditanstalt* with the assistance of the great landowners of Bohemia, the Fürstenbergs, the Schwarzenbergs and the Choteks. Agrarian wealth thus stimulated the industry of the Empire. It should be observed that this wealth was derived from land revenues and from the labour of the Czech peasant; it was therefore the peasant who, by the numerical strength of his group, by his diligent and patient toil, guaranteed the revival of the economy. But it was absolutely essential for the flexibility of the credit system that the Viennese banks should have branches or correspondents in the provinces. The

Creditanstalt was closely linked with a similar bank in Budapest, the *Tiszavidéki Vasuttarsasag*, and in 1857 it established a branch in Bohemia, the first joint-stock bank in the kingdom, which attracted largely German and Jewish capital. The Péreire bank, which had been the rival of the Rothschilds in the foundation of the Creditanstalt, gained its revenge by creating the General Austrian Land Bank (*Allgemeine Österreichische Bodencreditanstalt*), an institution like the French bank of similar title. This remarkable effort explains the upward movement of capitalist enterprise, the uninterrupted development (although curbed in certain sectors by an over-production crisis in 1857) of the Reichenberg-Liberec region, the growth of the suburbs of Prague (Smichov had a population of 2,608 by 1851 and 15,382 by 1869), the progress of Pest and the spectacular blossoming of Vienna.

At the end of 1857 the emperor, in a message addressed to the minister of the interior, gave the official order for the demolition of the old fortifications of Vienna. They had not halted the armies of Napoleon, but, after the upheavals of 1848, it had been the opinion of some that they might serve to protect the capital against riots in the suburbs. Since prosperity was becoming the guarantee of public order, the fortifications could now disappear. In their place a broad circular boulevard was to be laid: the Ring.[13]

The new boulevard, provided with barracks at strategic points, its width not exceeding the range of rifles, would ensure the internal security of the capital more effectively than the old walls. The buildings along the sides were to be constructed of hard stone in accordance with precise rules concerning stability. Public edifices were to be erected, either in open spaces or embellished with gardens: new wings for the Hofburg around a huge forum, the Heroes' Square, a new university, a new City Hall and later, when a constitutional regime had been re-established, a new Parliament, a new court theatre (*Burgtheater*) and finally, as the temple and symbol of the civilization of the Empire, the new Opera House. Not far from the Ring a votive church was built by subscription after the young emperor had escaped assassination. The architectural style displayed the broadest eclecticism. Reminiscences of Greek antiquity, the medieval art of Flanders, the Italian Renaissance and Baroque were intermingled to form an urban complex which, though possibly questionable in detail, possesses an undeniable attraction and majesty, chiefly because its proportions were not allowed to overshadow man or eclipse him under gigantic masses of masonry. Vienna, in the words of the journalist Jörgl, was at last to become what she ought to have been long ago: a 'Deutsch-Paris', a *Weltstadt* or 'world city'. The new complex was not built in a day: the work of construction occupied much of the reign of Francis Joseph. But the quality of civilization peculiar to Vienna, the crucible in which the different traditions and the diverse geniuses of the peoples of the monarchy were fused in the grandeur of an imperial capital, bestowed its charm on the Ring: even today, after so many vicissitudes and the bombardment of 1945, which it survived, it remains one of the most harmonious examples of urban construction in Europe.

After the death of Prince Schwarzenberg, Francis Joseph did not appoint a prime minister. Henceforward, the leading personality in the government was the minister of the interior, Alexander von Bach, who, though a liberal in his origins, had been converted since the Revolution to the methods of authority. Historians have spoken of these eight years of the Bach era as a period of blind political reaction, mechanical centralization and Germanization. But it has just been seen how great was the extent of economic progress during this period. It was the task of Count Thun, the minister of education, to reorganize the entire educational system so that, by the dissemination of knowledge, a social élite might emerge which would be sensitive to the requirements of the modern world, skilled in business affairs and, at the same time, loyal to the emperor and to the State. There was a need of engineers, civil servants, technicians and an expansion of the liberal professions. At the level of higher education, the universities were reformed and granted a greater degree of autonomy; the faculties of philosophy, comprising the humanists and the historians, occupied a special position. In general, the faculties recruited their teaching staff themselves and, in order to appoint the best specialists, they were permitted to turn to foreigners. The Austrian universities were thus entering into effective competition with the universities of Germany. Freedom of research was guaranteed, although limited in so far as nothing might be taught which was contrary to the principles of religion or of the State. Reorganization was directed principally towards secondary education. Grammar schools of eight classes provided a humanist education which included the teaching of Latin and Greek, while the *Real-gymnasien*, oriented towards the study of mathematics, the physical and natural sciences and modern languages, were to train a body of technicians for the world of business. Just as the grammar schools prepared pupils for the universities, these technical schools served as the training-ground for the higher institutes of commerce and industry. There can be no doubt that the benefit of these measures was enjoyed by the rising middle class and that the German language occupied a position of special favour: it was the chief language of the State, of the administrative institutions, the army and the business world. But it would be quite mistaken to suggest that the system sought to stifle the national languages. In towns and districts where the Slavs and Magyars predominated, their languages were used for general teaching purposes in secondary schools. In the primary schools, instruction was given in the language commonly spoken by the majority of the inhabitants of the commune.

Furthermore, during the following decades the national groups directed their wholehearted efforts towards the broadening of the system rather than its suppression: as they gradually became numerically stronger, they demanded a greater number of primary schools, and then secondary schools in which instruction was given in the national language, German having been relegated to the position of a second modern language. At a later stage, the governing classes of the nationalities were able to claim universities of their own. But the intellectual progress of the national groups was accomplished within the framework of Thun's legislation.

By founding an *Institut für Geschichtsforschung* (Institute of Historical Research) at Vienna in 1854, Count Thun created not a new teaching establishment, but a centre of studies where research historians from various universities of the Empire (Vienna, Prague, Budapest) would contribute their own conclusions in a united effort to analyse the positive aspects of the monarchy's history. The intention was to encourage both research into the history of the nationalities and a collation of the results of this research in order to obtain a better understanding of the profound nature of the association.[14]

Count Thun was in no sense a fanatic, but, like his contemporary, Thiers, and many others, he was convinced that a modern society could not be strong without solid religious foundations. He was prepared to sacrifice Josephism in order to give the clergy a more important position in public life. It was with this purpose that the Concordat with the Holy See was signed in 1855. The imperial *placet* was no longer necessary for the promulgation of papal bulls and direct communication could be established between Rome and the bishops. Divorce was not permitted for persons married according to the Catholic rite. The clergy were granted a right of supervision over public education at all levels, which severely restricted the freedom of teachers; moreover, religious instruction was obligatory in primary and secondary schools. The bishops presented to the emperor and to the local authorities their candidates for parishes and canonries, who were remunerated out of the 'religious fund'. This strengthening of the clerical framework of society was harshly criticized in liberal circles and was to be modified eighteen years later, by the laws of 1874. But it had many lasting results. No less than the Josephism which it was intended to combat, it reinforced the institutional status of the Catholic clergy in the life of Austria, giving priests a security untroubled by misgivings about loyalty to Rome. It certainly did not prevent the working masses from becoming increasingly alienated from the Church, as they found that religion gave them no moral support, nor did it prevent the middle class from adopting a formalism in which indifference or hypocrisy played a large part. But it did serve to maintain the venerable character of the Church and of religion, whose presence it established more firmly and on a greatly broadened basis. The ritual ceremonies, the great processions of the Blessed Sacrament held in the towns, with the assistance of the army and the civil authorities, the crucifixes placed in town halls, schools, courts and post offices, and which survived until the Second World War, even in the 'succession states', represent the original aspects of Austrian civilization and of a pervasive religious faith which explains how, even at the present time, staunch fidelity has on occasions been carried to the point of martyrdom.[15] During these same years, the religious rights of Protestants were confirmed and the Jews finally obtained complete equality with other citizens.

At the same time, the Bach regime was assuming the character of a police state. The police department had been detached from the ministry of the interior and placed under separate control. It was thus freer to exercise a meddlesome, humiliating and degrading surveillance over the whole of society, persecuting anyone suspected of liberalism. In Bohemia, the chief of police, Sacher Masoch, imposed a harsh yoke of oppression. Even Palacký was not spared. Rieger, who became Palacký's son-in-law in 1852, on his return from voluntary exile in France, encountered every kind of hostility during his defence of his doctorate thesis.

The journalist Havlíček, imprisoned at Brixen, contracted tuberculosis there and died in Prague. His funeral, supervised by the police, assumed the importance of a national demonstration and a woman placed a symbolic crown of thorns on the coffin. In the following year, Božená Němcová published a book which the censors passed and which enriched Czech literature with a masterpiece. Over the past hundred years and under successive regimes, generations of Czechs have read *Babička* (*The Grandmother*) and have loved this fundamental and vivid work. There could be no clearer assessment of its quality than that made by Arne Novák, a critic of the 1920s: 'The figure of Babička, in whom the Slav ideal of motherhood is embodied, shines like a gentle autumn sun. This blend of kindness and graciousness is reflected against the background of a nature no less maternal, in whose bosom man is born, grows up and dies.'[16] The love which Babička felt for her native country and for the Czech land, the memories of her distant childhood when she chanced to meet Joseph II, whom she saw as glorious and yet human, her devout religious faith, her generosity towards the infirm and those poorer than herself, the dignity of her bearing when she was greeted at the manor by the good countess, her wisdom and her simplicity—these are the qualities which form an exquisite image of a peasant woman both unworldly and yet vividly human, a portrayal illuminated by a quiet romanticism. The world of Babička, as Pekař was devoutly to write, bears testimony to the depths of the Czech soul and helps towards a better understanding of the contradictions which enveloped the Austrian monarchy and which did not permit the absolutist experiment to be prolonged beyond 1860.

Population-growth, the consequence of relatively favourable years and of the attenuation, if not the total disappearance, of the epidemics so long the scourge of the Danubian countries, swelled the numbers of inhabitants in the towns and the industrial centres, though the majority of the population still worked on the land. Even in 1869, out of 10,000 working persons, 5,229 were employed in agriculture by comparison with 2,916 in industry, 303 in commerce and 1,552 in other sectors.

The extent of great landed property can be illustrated by the figures for Bohemia, the most industrialized country, where 992 out of 640,000 properties (i.e. 0·16 per cent) remained in the hands of the great landowners, but these estates covered 34 per cent of the total land area. Between 1847 and 1857, the revenue from direct taxes in this same province had increased from 11,833,946 to 20,589,065 gulden and the revenue from indirect taxes from 19,566,498 to 37,697,241 gulden, which is clear proof of a general economic growth.

The condition of the working class was still wretched: the length of the working day varied between twelve and fourteen hours, women and children were employed in the mills, corporal punishment was still common and the workers were paid starvation wages, generally seventy kreutzers per day.

If, as Jan Slavík has written, the peasant of the great domain was more fortunate than the serf of the Middle Ages, it is easy to believe that he was also more fortunate than the worker in the capitalist mill. Both the liberated peasantry and the middle class—which in its lower strata was beginning to find opportunities for advancement and in its already flourishing upper strata felt an anxiety justified by competition and the sense of the fragility of its success—were alarmed by the constant increase of taxation, a favourable sign for the economy as a whole, but a burden on individual budgets, especially since the revenue from taxes was devoted neither to industrial plant nor to social improvements. Military estimates absorbed the largest proportion of State revenues (about one-third), consisting of one hundred and eleven millions compared with the thirty millions assigned to the ministry of commerce, while the police department received double the sum granted to the ministry of education. Civil servants earned a meagre salary, figuring as the poor relations of an increasingly middle-class society.

Moreover, the capital available within the Empire was inadequate and, in consequence, the general economy became more dependent on foreign capitalism, a factor that complicated the international situation. In order to maintain a position of equality with the great powers, Austria was obliged to keep a watchful eye on Prussia, her rival in Germany, to beware of the Near East, where Russia was feared by the whole of Europe because of the vast numbers of men which she could send into battle in the event of war, and, finally, to devote her attention to Turkey, which was becoming increasingly dependent on the financial support of the great powers. France and Great Britain had drawn closer to each other and were thus able to adopt a much more active foreign policy. In the Crimean War, set in motion when the Russian army invaded the Danubian provinces, Great Britain and France joined forces to defend the Ottoman Empire and to prevent Russia from dominating the Near East.[17] By its uncertainty, Austrian policy betrayed the weaknesses of a state where internal equilibrium had not yet been re-established after the upheavals of 1848. Austria intervened to obtain the evacuation of the Danubian provinces and mobilized her troops with the apparent intention of attacking Russia. In fact, she wished to remain neutral until peace had been restored.

Austria was unable to impose her arbitration. The Congress of Paris, held in 1856, saw the triumph of the France of Napoleon III and, to an even greater degree, the triumph of Great Britain. The Danubian provinces were made autonomous principalities. A state of Rumania was born, just as a principality of Serbia and a kingdom of Greece had already been formed.

An International Commission had been created to control navigation on the lower course of the Danube, down-river from the Iron Gates. The time of Prince Eugene was clearly past and Austria was no longer alone in her designs for expansion in the East: she now had to take account of the other European powers. Above all, she was finding it increasingly difficult to maintain her authority in northern Italy. The *Risorgimento* was developing as a movement, but Italian unity could only be achieved by opposition to Austria. If Piedmont had taken part in the Crimean War, this had been not so much for the sake of military victories (a few successes at the bridge of Traktir), as to secure the right to sit as a belligerent power at the Congress of Paris, where she could attract the attention of Europe. Henceforward, Piedmont was to assume the leadership of Italian independence. But, in order to attack Austria, she needed an alliance with Napoleon III. In the prestige policy which the emperor of the French was pursuing, and which he concealed under the pretext of redrawing the map of Europe more equitably by favouring the nationalities, the victory over Russia had been a first success. Napoleon III hoped to complete this success by a war against Austria, though he had no cause for dissension with that power. A new campaign, if it were to prove successful, would enable him to secure a rectification of frontiers and, for the satisfaction of public opinion, to obtain redress for the misfortunes of 1815. Since Great Britain would not promise him any assistance, Napoleon III decided to draw closer to Russia and to seek an alliance with that country, offering her advantages to the detriment of Austria. He encouraged Russia to hope for possession of Galicia and suggested that she should instigate a national uprising in Hungary. Such a project was far too revolutionary to tempt Russia to act. The tsar desired no new Polish territories; on the other hand, he valued the solidarity of interests maintained between the three northern powers by their common status as the co-beneficiaries of partition. In his eyes, a liberated Hungary in which Kossuth would be able to re-establish his influence was a disturbing rather than an alluring prospect. Austria's conduct during the Crimean War had grievously offended the Russian Chancellery which, right up to the war of 1914, nursed the memory of Austria's 'ingratitude', although political wisdom prevented it from seeking a vengeance that might prove costly.[18] France had to enter into the war of 1859, in support of Piedmont, without the assistance of the great powers and without any guarantee from the Hungarian revolutionaries: Kossuth realized that Napoleon III would not support to the end a new uprising in Hungary. In these circumstances, the emperor of the French, despite his brilliant victories at Magenta and at Solferino, was unable to fulfil the first part of his programme: the liberation of Italy from the Alps to the Adriatic. Austria was defeated nonetheless and compelled to sacrifice Lombardy. In compensation for the aggrandizement of Piedmont, France recovered Savoy and the county of Nice after favourable plebiscites had been held.

The loss of prestige which defeat always brings and the surrender of a province as rich as Lombardy, however recalcitrant and difficult to contain, forced Austria to seek a greater internal cohesion and thus to modify its form of government in order to gain the confidence of its subjects. Louis Eisenmann suggested that the constitutional changes effected in the Empire between 1859 and 1867 were necessitated by external circumstances rather than by the internal needs of the Austrian countries.[19] But the opinion of this profound observer of Danubian history requires qualification. Eleven years after 1848, the populations of the Empire had new reasons to be conscious of their solidarity, even if they were not particularly content with their lot.

It would be a mistake to attribute identical sentiments to the Italians, the Poles and the other Slavs of the monarchy. The Italian provinces considered themselves as subjugated, and economic advantages were of less importance to them than their aspirations for independence and union with their fellow-Italians of the peninsula. The Poles of Galicia cherished the same fervent loyalty to their old homeland, but they recognized—that is, the nobility and the middle class recognized—that, of the three co-authors of partition, Austria promised them the most tolerable conditions. In the common religion which they shared with Austria, they found one more reason for patiently awaiting the political advantages which would eventually come to them. The other provinces, though their nationalist claims were growing more urgent, were by no means separatists. They sought only the transformation of the political system and a greater measure of liberty. No one among the rising classes wanted the demise of an Empire that guaranteed order against the dangers of rioting and revolution and which seemed capable of diverting foreign war from the internal territory of the monarchy.

Yet the notion of fatherland (*Vaterland*) acquired a special significance for the subjects of the Austrian Empire. This sentiment was not one of attachment to the Danubian monarchy as a whole, nor even the Austrian patriotism of which Schwarzenberg had dreamed and which he perhaps confused with dynastic loyalty. It represented first and foremost the love of the native land and the mother tongue. which to an increasing degree was seen as the fundamental sign of nationality.

It was through love of their respective countries that the Danubian peoples showed an interest in the preservation of the Empire and the dynasty. Francis Joseph was held in quite high esteem in Vienna and his prestige was enhanced by the charm and youth of the beautiful empress, Elizabeth of Bavaria, whom he had married in 1854. But in the provinces which remained monarchist, respect for a traditional institution was doubtless a more influential factor than direct attachment to the person of the sovereign, which required a sanction other than the arbitrary power with which it had been invested since 1851.

❧

Regional patriotism comprised two distinct elements, which at times converged and thus reinforced each other, but which at other times found themselves in opposition: historic tradition and nationality. In those regions where historic tradition was of long standing, the centralist system of 1852 was accused of having disregarded and broken the continuity of that tradition; wherever nationality alone asserted itself, peoples demanded that it should be granted the sanction of the law and guarantees of future development.

Hungary, above all, rejected the new order, because it had abolished the kingdom's privileges, so fiercely defended as the political conquests of 1848, and because it had been founded on the defeat of 1849. Represented both by the upper nobility and by the counties, the aristocracy, which since the eighteenth century had become Magyar, demanded a return to the principle of state rights. Many politicians had disapproved of the radicalism of Kossuth and had believed that he was leading the country into unnecessary troubles. They doubted whether it would be possible to preserve a Hungary detached from Austria, when their country was faced with so many internal problems that were proving increasingly difficult to resolve. The Croats, who were also claiming their state rights, the Slovaks and the Rumanians had all derived great benefits from the material progress of the preceding ten years. Yet they were not fully satisfied, demanding further guarantees for their existence as nationalities and new personal liberties. The Magyar ruling classes considered that the demands of these groups should be taken into account and that they should be shown that a Hungary restored to its ancient rights could accord its Slav and Latin inhabitants greater advantages than Vienna.

In Bohemia, certainly, the opposition between Germans and Czechs was more intense than in 1848, for the progress of national language and consciousness could only be accomplished at the expense of German influence. This problem was still not insurmountable and the Czech political leaders were inclined to believe that a return to the principle of state rights would contribute to a reconciliation between national groups. For a number of reasons—pride in its ancient lineage, a repugnance to certain elements of individualism and free-thinking inherent in liberal doctrines —a part of the 'historic nobility' could not feel unmitigated enthusiasm for the institutions recently created by Vienna. These nobles would have preferred to cling to the traditional institutions of their ancient kingdom. The politicians of the Bohemian middle class, when they observed events in Hungary, were moved by a nostalgia which almost amounted to jealousy, because they had not hitherto been able to entrust the defence of their national cause to men of prestige. They lamented the fact that in Bohemia historical evolution and social habits had Germanized or at least 'Austrianized' the nobility. As a result of marriages with German women and the adoption of the German language in private life, the Bohemian aristocracy, even in families of Czech origin, did not possess the same national integrity that characterized its Hungarian counterpart. Nevertheless, its support could be usefully enlisted to the cause. Palacký expressed his own point of view effectively: 'We can never accept that the nobility possesses political privileges solely by birthright. But we shall welcome the nobility with joy, if it is willing to devote its activity, untrammelled by material cares and the obligation to work, to the greatness of the nation and to the safeguard of its political interests.'[20] Men such as Count Clam-Martinic and Prince Charles Schwarzenberg were prepared to respond to this appeal. However, the alliance between the leaders of the middle class and the aristocracy was leading towards a conservative policy which had already alarmed the more liberal elements.

The situation in Hungary became increasingly clear. In works written in German in order to reach a wider public, Stephen Széchenyi, Count Eötvös and Count Szecsen claimed that only a return to the historic rights of the Hungarian kingdom could ensure the solidity of Austria and that to insist on the fallacious pretext of equality would merely result in the oppression of one nationality by another. They maintained that it was dangerous to crush the individual beneath the weight of the mass: by disregarding Hungary's historic rights, Vienna had shaken the pillars of the monarchy. Finally, the economic benefits supposedly bestowed on Hungary since 1851 were illusory by comparison with the real needs of the country.[21] It was recognized in Vienna that the time had come to compromise with these diverse factors.

So that he might embark upon a new policy, the emperor discarded his German ministers and appointed a Polish noble, Count Goluchowski. He then enlarged his

Imperial Council, which he invited to join with him in seeking 'institutional forms which, by developing the unitary power of the Empire in accordance with the needs of modern times, will leave the particular customs of each race to blossom freely in the spirit of local traditions'. This view was shared by Eötvös: 'In earlier times, the different peoples of the Empire were bound together by their common hatred and fear of Turkey. Today, they should be bound only by the common possession of the same constitutional institutions.'

The Diploma of 20 October 1860 promised the transformation of the monarchy. It re-established the old Diets and provided for the creation of an Imperial Parliament (*Reichsrat*) composed of their delegates. It was warmly greeted in the provinces, because it diminished the influence of the central government and because, by restoring legislative authority to the Diet of each country, it encouraged hopes of a less burdensome and a more justly distributed fiscal system. To this extent the Diploma appeared liberal in character and the federalism which it heralded gave the nationalities reason to hope for guarantees for their advancement. But the conservative elements would inevitably constitute the majority in several Diets and their return to power alarmed the liberals, who regarded centralism as the prerequisite of economic progress. Moreover, the two concepts of Diet and nationality did not coincide. The Slovaks, for example, had failed to obtain a clearly demarcated territory in recognition of their nationality. And how would the Hungarian Diet react? Would it not consider the October Diploma inadequate, since it granted neither the restoration of the laws of 1848, nor the complete autonomy of the kingdom?

The Patent issued in February 1861, prescribing the conditions by which the principles of the October Diploma were to be implemented, thus marked a deviation towards centralism. It was the work of a new minister, Schmerling, a German liberal. The Imperial Parliament, whose legislative powers limited the powers of the Diets, consisted of two chambers: the House of Lords comprised the adult archdukes, high ecclesiastical dignitaries, members of the hereditary nobility and senators appointed for life by the emperor; the House of Representatives was composed of three hundred and forty-three deputies elected by the Diets, which in their turn were to be elected by four groups or 'curias' (the landed proprietors, the towns, the chambers of commerce and the rural constituencies); Hungary would be represented by eighty-five deputies (including nine for Croatia), Bohemia by eighty-two, Polish Galicia by thirty-eight and Venetia by twenty.

The most original feature of the February Patent concerned the two forms which the Imperial Parliament was to assume. The 'full' Parliament, which would include the Hungarian deputies, was to handle matters of common interest to the whole Empire; but the 'narrower' Parliament, which the Hungarian deputies would not attend, was to concern itself with the major problems of the other countries, in which Hungary had no direct interest. The system presented practical advantages and reinforced the solidarity of the western part of the Empire. But, at the same time, it established a general political institution above the Hungarian Diet and two such institutions above the other Diets. The regime created by the Patent, instead of satisfying opinion by its acceptance of liberalism and of the representative system, merely exacerbated regional opposition.[22]

꧁

The Hungarian Diet declared that it would never send its deputies to the 'full' Imperial Parliament, for it would not recognize any authority above itself, which was tantamount to saying that it would obstruct the functioning of the system. The nationalities intensified their propaganda. The various national groups, which had benefited from the economic situation, were ready to spend their money in the service of their patriotic cause. An interest was shown in all the media by which national consciousness could be expressed: newspapers, journals, books and schools. In Bohemia, in 1862, the doctors Scheiner and Tyrš founded a gymnastic society known as the *Sokoly* ('The Falcons'), with the intention of improving the health of the Czech race and developing its qualities of courage, endurance and loyalty. Subscriptions were opened to build a national theatre where dramas would be performed exclusively in the Czech language. It became customary to buy only Czech goods and to sell only to fellow-Czechs, even if this meant sacrificing quality to the national ideal. In Hungary, the Slovaks obtained their own secondary schools and founded an association, the *Matice Slovenská*, to subsidize the teaching of the national language. The teachers now possessed the materials necessary for instruction: grammars, dictionaries and reading-books. There was much generosity and idealism in all this activity; unfortunately, however, it was also breeding hatred between neighbouring national groups.

By this time, there no longer existed any real threat of persecution by the central government. Liberal ideas had acquired such great prestige that they were seen to be the natural attribute of all reasonable men in harmony with the times. Furthermore, the reputation of Austria, which had been accused of being a power of the past, reactionary, clerical and despotic, found itself re-established abroad by the promise of imminent constitutional reform. The provincial Diets were becoming platforms from which speakers could freely expound their patriotic themes.

Kossuth, in exile, condemned as treachery any attempt to seek a reconciliation with Austria and the dynasty. He was prepared to consider the possibility of a Danubian confederation, on condition that it was established by free peoples. But this would have required a maturity which the Danubian peoples had not attained. On the other hand, Count Julius Andrassy, who had taken part in the events of 1848 and had escaped the death penalty only by emigrating, took advantage of the amnesty and returned to Hungary. Together with Eötvös, Deák (Széchenyi had committed suicide in a fit of nervous depression) and the younger generation, represented by Albert Apponyi, he favoured a reconciliation with Austria. On Easter Monday, 11 April 1865, the Hungarian programme was presented by Deák in an article in the newspaper *Pesti Napló*. Deák defined the historic rights of Hungary, invoking the Pragmatic Sanction and the laws of 1848 as the foundations of the kingdom's independence. He acknowledged, at the same time, that it was not in Hungary's interests to exist in isolation from the other countries of the monarchy and that it would be to Hungary's advantage to reach an understanding with them for the management of their common affairs. The liberals of Austria realized that the time for peace and reasonable solutions was approaching.

Francis Joseph made a first journey to Hungary. He received the encouragement of the empress who, having only become a member of the family after the events of 1848, nursed no bitterness towards the Hungarians and appreciated both the great courtesy of Hungarian society and the nobility of its ideal of liberty. But a great deal remained to be done before agreement could be reached: '*Non est coronatus, non est unctus, non est rex noster.*' Francis Joseph was a king 'in a hat'. Until he was crowned, he would remain outside the law of Hungary.[23]

During the following weeks, political agitation was rife throughout the monarchy. In Croatia, the bishop of Diakovo, Mgr. Strossmayer, and Canon Racki, the founders of the South Slav Academy of Sciences, invoked their country's rights and the solidarity of Slavs. Their Slovene neighbours demanded electoral reform, while the Poles wanted an autonomous Polish administration for Galicia. In a single volume entitled *Idea státu rakouského* (*The Idea of the Austrian State*), Palacký published the articles which he had written for the journal *Národ* (*The Nation*). He was disturbed by the thought of a *rapprochement* between the Magyars and the Germans, fearing that the two strongest peoples of the monarchy would conclude an agreement giving them a position of supremacy and allowing them to treat the other peoples as servants. The Slavs could not resign themselves to such a prospect. Palacký declared: 'The day of the establishment of dualism will, by an ineluctable necessity of nature, bring the advent of Pan-Slavism in its least desirable form and the parents of the former will be the godparents of the latter. The result any reader can imagine for himself. We Slavs shall regard that day with sincere grief, but without fear. We existed before Austria, and we shall exist after her.' But he hoped that things would not reach this stage.[24]

The Slavs of Austria, who neither boasted the same past nor enjoyed the same standard of living and of culture, were in no position to undertake common action. As for the Slavs outside the Empire—in other words, the peoples of Russia —their Pan-Slavist ambitions gave grounds for alarm. The recent Polish insurrection in Russia, in 1863, had complicated matters further. It had attracted the sympathy of the Czechs, the Galicians and the Hungarians, who were always ready to show their friendship for the Poles and their hostility to Russia. Yet Palacký was afraid of alienating from the Czech cause the good-will of the tsar's government, which had just emancipated the serfs and from which other liberal concessions might be expected.

In September 1865 the emperor suspended the Patent of 1861; he initiated negotiations with the Hungarian Diet with a view to a constitutional reorganization which would then be submitted to the other Diets. That the Hungarians possessed highly skilful politicians is evident from the fact that the Croats and the Slovaks attempted to come to an understanding with them; the Czechs were content to demand at their Diet the coronation of Francis Joseph as king of Bohemia. In addition to Palacký's traditionalist party, the Old Czechs, there existed a more advanced and more boldly liberal group, the Young Czechs, who included Gregr and Sladkowský. But, in the circumstances, their attitude proved no more resolute —or, at least, no more effective.

⚜

During the years 1861–5, the situation of Austria in Europe had not improved. Since Bismarck had come to power in Prussia, with his carefully prepared plan for the realization of German unity to his own country's advantage, he had constantly sought to discredit Austria in Germany. He attempted to stigmatize Austria in liberal opinion by denouncing her as irreconcilable with modern ideas, incapable of emancipating the German nation and understanding its interests. In 1863 he thwarted the reorganization of the Germanic Confederation, which would have strengthened the authority of the emperor of Austria. In 1864 he drew Austria into the war of the duchies against Denmark, with the aim of creating complications which could be solved only by a new war, this time between Austria and Prussia. At a time when it needed all its strength to settle its internal affairs, the Empire was unable to avoid a conflict. Admittedly, it was still in alliance with the other states of the Germanic Confederation. But it was not a question of numbers. Prussia had at its disposal new armaments, including the rifle with firing-pin, and a highly experienced general staff that intended to use the railways for the mobilization of troops. Moreover, since the king of Italy had entered into an alliance with Prussia, Austria found herself compelled to fight on two fronts. The war of 1866 was short and cruel. The sudden offensive launched by the Prussians on Bohemian territory cost the Austrians thirty thousand men before a single major battle had been engaged. Field Marshal Benedek implored the emperor to sue for an immediate peace. But he was forced to join battle at Sadova and within a few hours was completely routed. On 3 July, in a new dispatch to Francis Joseph, he wrote: 'Today the catastrophe foreseen for the army the day before yesterday has been fully realized.' The successes of Archduke Albert at Custozza and the dazzling victory of Admiral Tegethoff at sea could not compensate for this disaster. The result was the loss of Venetia to Italy and the eviction of Austria from a Germany henceforth dominated by Prussia, which annexed several states of the northern plain and imposed its alliance on the southern states.[25]

The war had at least proved that the Austrian Empire still did not lack a moral cohesion, for the Danubian peoples, without possessing the same unanimity of patriotism as other states, had remained dedicated to the Empire, in the belief that its existence was necessary, if only for their own advantage. They had resisted attempts to dismember the Empire. An army of Hungarian volunteers under the command of General Klapka, which included liberated prisoners, advanced into Hungary without causing a general uprising. The Czechs were also courted by Prussia: 'Come to us as friends and you will find us your friends. If the just cause of Prussia is triumphant, the Czechs may again be offered the opportunity of freely deciding their own future.' In August, a pamphlet entitled *The Tears of the Crown of Bohemia* and printed in Berlin was distributed in Bohemia: 'Let us separate from Austria; let us lead our own independent life without her.' The pamphlet originated

from legitimist circles and was addressed to conservatives, whom it was intended
to move by invoking the ancient faith of Bohemians. At the same time, Bismarck
sent Frič, a radical of 1848, to the Young Czechs to suggest that they declare the
independence of the kingdom and elect as their king the prince of Savoy, Amadeus,
second son of Victor Emmanuel. This was an 'advanced' solution for the period.
The House of Savoy, as a result of its difficulties with the Pope and the representatives of the old dynasties, the Habsburgs and Bourbons, appeared modern and
liberal.

But the peoples of the Empire had more numerous reasons—some idealistic,
others practical—to remain faithful to Austria. In the rural regions, especially the
Tyrol, tradition, the permanence of simple values, duty towards God and the
prince, all operated in Austria's favour. In the towns, economic progress had continued to manifest itself during the previous fifteen years by the creation of new
firms and shops and by technical inventions such as gas-lighting and the extension
of the railway network. These were material achievements which their beneficiaries
were determined to preserve and for which the Austrian state appeared the surest
guarantee. Certain persons even reproached the Viennese with too great a material-
ism and with having too readily accepted defeat so that peace and the tranquillity
of daily life might be restored.[26]

'Above all,' Rieger declared in 1866, 'we wish to preserve the Empire, for we see
in its existence the guarantee of our national existence and that of the other small
nations which it embraces.' Ousted from Germany, dispossessed of its last Italian
province, Austria was now a state where the majority of the population spoke
Slav languages and proclaimed itself Slav. In Vienna, the Old Czechs Rieger,
Pražák and Brauner negotiated with the Polish and Yugoslav politicians. They all
believed that the Empire should be reorganized as a federation of historic countries:
German Austria, Bohemia, Galicia and Bukovina, and Hungary. What bound
them most strongly to Austria was the fear of Bismarckian Prussia and Russia
and the idea that security and progress could only be assured under the protection
of a common state, a super-state that would safeguard the free progress of the
historic states. The kingdom of Bohemia had its own greatness, its own authentic
and glorious history, which scholars of indisputable reputation such as Palacký,
Tomek and the young professor Gindely evoked in their works. Patriotism was
identified with the memories of Bohemia's grandeur. However, as society evolved,
the German middle class of the industrial regions of northern Bohemia became less
conscious of the state tradition and more aware of its economic solidarity with the
monarchy as a whole.

Furthermore, was the concept of state rights as clear in Moravia and Silesia as
it was in Bohemia? One of the weaknesses of the kingdom throughout its history
had been the absence of a common Diet and the virtual impossibility of creating
such a body.

It might seem surprising that Hungary, which at this time was neither the most
densely populated nor the most economically advanced country, should have assumed a greater importance in the destiny of the Empire than Bohemia, which
was more compact, richer, developing more rapidly and more closely linked to

the Alpine peoples and to the capital. It was men, rather than economic necessity, that proved the determining factor. The politicians of Hungary showed a greater cohesion. Their faith in their own cause was enhanced by the ingenious manner in which, turning historic memories, liberal aspirations and the progress of capitalism to their advantage, they were able to present themselves even to the German liberals as the most reliable partners, capable of joining with them in the reorganization of the Empire. A book published by a group of Hungarians in 1864, under the title *Drei Jahre Verfassungstreit*, contained this bold declaration: 'According to right and law, it is a question not of making concessions to the Hungarians, but of obtaining from them concessions for the monarchy.' Hungary had seized a position of advantage; no longer a suppliant, she awaited the entreaties of others.

When, after the defeat of 1866, Francis Joseph met Deák and asked anxiously 'What does Hungary want?', the 'old gentleman', as he was known familiarly by his admirers, replied with as much ingenuity as chivalry: 'Nothing more after Sadova than before!'

Francis Joseph had appointed to the ministry of foreign affairs the former minister of the king of Saxony, Count Beust, who was fiercely hostile to Prussia and desired, if not an immediate military revenge, at least the swift promotion of Austria's recovery. Rather like Prince Eugene in earlier times, he considered an immediate reconciliation with Hungary to be essential. In Count Julius Andrassy he found a persuasive negotiator. Moreover, he did not lack encouragement in Vienna. The result was the rapid conclusion of the Austro-Hungarian Compromise. But it should be said that the emperor did not adequately fulfil his role as arbiter. In effect, he sacrificed not only his own preference for a more broadly federal solution, but also the moral interests and susceptibilities of his other subjects, and in particular the Slavs.

The Compromise was one of the most astounding constitutional acts of the nineteenth century, both in its form and in its object. It was remarkable in form because it was presented not as a single act, a treaty signed by partners, but as a collection of laws bilaterally accepted by two constitutional governments and approved by two Parliaments—the one, in Hungary, being the Diet transformed into a modern Parliament of two chambers, and the other, in Austria, a Parliament elected on the model of the 'narrower' Parliament conceived by Schmerling in 1861. It was remarkable in its object because, nineteen years after the Revolution of 1848, it provided the problem of the Danubian monarchy with a solution destined to last as long as the monarchy itself. Many persons, especially abroad, regarded the agreement with Hungary as a liberal concession on the part of Vienna and as the end of Germanizing centralism. But they did not perceive that centralism had not disappeared, but was merely assuming a dual form. Hungary had regained the rank of a sovereign state. Francis Joseph and Elizabeth went to Budapest for the coronation. Nothing was omitted—the splendour of the religious ceremony with its Eastern liturgy, the solemn oath to respect the laws of Hungary, the king galloping up the hill and holding his sword towards the four points of the compass. All this was necessary so that the king might be legitimized and thus entitled to promulgate the laws which were to give effect to the Compromise.

Two constitutional states thus declared themselves bound one to the other by their history and by virtue of the Pragmatic Sanction, so that they would continue to have the same prince as their sovereign. The emperor of Austria was also king of Hungary. But it was no longer a question of a mere personal union, for the two states assumed common responsibility for foreign affairs and the army, which were entrusted to the supreme authority of the king–emperor. Both states contributed to the cost of maintaining these two departments, in proportion to their respective resources.

For the common affairs of the two states there were to be three ministers, nominated by the king–emperor: a minister of foreign affairs, a minister for the army and a minister of finance. The problem was to ensure that the Parliaments had supervisory control over these ministers To an even greater degree than Austria, Hungary was averse to any measure that might seem to create an organ of authority superior to its own institutions. It was therefore decided that each Parliament should nominate a Delegation and that the Delegations would sit alternately in each of the two capitals, on the same date, but without ever meeting in the same hall; they were to communicate with each other in writing. In this way, the sovereignty and independence of each state appeared to be firmly asserted.

Furthermore, the two states entered into an economic agreement renewable every ten years. They immediately adopted the same tariffs, the same currency values and a common postal system. Hungary's share of common expenditure was fixed at 30 per cent, but was liable to be modified subsequently. The National Bank of Austria became a common State Bank.

Thus, the old dynastic union which had existed since 1526 and the unified Empire desired by Felix Schwarzenberg were replaced by a perpetual association between two modern states: Austria-Hungary had been born.

Each state was to settle separately the problems of its national groups. Hungary concluded an agreement with the Diet of Croatia, the *Nagodba* of 1868. The kingdom of Croatia was placed in a subordinate but nonetheless advantageous position, within Hungary. It recognized the same sovereign, without insisting that a separate coronation should take place. It possessed its own Diet, the *Sabor*, which sat at Zagreb and decided internal affairs—administration, education, religion and justice. The executive power was entrusted to a governor, the *ban*, whose name was put forward by the Hungarian prime minister, but who was appointed and could be dismissed by the king. Croatia gave 56 per cent of its revenues to Hungary for the management of their common affairs. The Croat language (Serbo-Croat) was used in all official institutions. Just as, in the Imperial and Royal Army, whose language was German, Hungary had been able to establish a home-based reserve force speaking the Magyar language, so a Croat territorial army was created which spoke the Croat language. However, Croatia did not recover all the territories to which it could have laid claim, for Dalmatia was annexed to Austria and Fiume received a special status within the kingdom of Hungary. For the other nationalities, the Slovaks, the Serbs, the Rumanians of Transylvania and the Ruthenes of the old eastern comitats, the Hungarian Parliament introduced in 1868 a special law drafted by the shrewd Eötvös and Deák.

Since all Hungarian citizens were members of the one and indivisible Hungarian nation (*Magyar nemzet*), the fact of belonging to a particular national group could present no obstacle in obtaining any public office. Moreover, every citizen enjoyed the right to use his mother tongue in his private life, in religious worship, in the education of his children and, wherever general conditions permitted, in recourse to justice.

Nevertheless, since the unity of the state and the advancement of public life were of paramount importance, the Hungarian language alone would be employed in official acts and in administration. At the assemblies of the counties (the old comitats), if one-fifth of the members so desired, the use of a second language would be allowed for drawing up minutes; the commune assemblies enjoyed even more extensive language rights.

No nationality, apart from Croatia, could claim territorial autonomy. Transylvania was incorporated in Hungary, thereby losing any right to administer its own affairs. In connection with Slovakia, the ironic remark of a Hungarian statesman is often quoted: *Tót ember, nem ember* ('the Slovak is not a man'). In other words, the Slovak had no right to a civic existence, but was a Hungarian citizen of Slovak tongue. Certainly, the nationalities were not denied the right to use their language in developing their culture in harmony with the ideas of the times. The number of schools and colleges was to be determined and modified according to circumstances and the progress of the national groups. But the universities remained Hungarian. Chairs were founded at Budapest for the study of national languages and literatures, but for general teaching purposes Hungarian was to be used. Clearly, the chief intention was to allow no territorial separatism and to look to the time when the entire élite of the kingdom would speak the Magyar language, the symbol of the moral unity of the country. Once this had been achieved, the use of the other national languages would no longer pose a problem.

The rulers of Hungary could claim that this body of laws was liberal and equitable and that it reconciled the interests of a modern state with the personal rights of citizens. It remained to apply the laws faithfully. But they were by no means accepted unreservedly. Mgr. Strossmayer and his friends protested against the dismemberment of the historic territory of Croatia and attempted to revive a moral solidarity among all southern Slavs. To the Rumanians of Transylvania and the Slovaks, the absence of an administration of their own and of territories demarcated according to nationality seemed an injustice.[27]

The logical course would have been to settle the Bohemian problem at the same time as the Hungarian problem. The Compromise required the approval of the Austrian Parliament. Belcredi, the prime minister, had intended that this should be an 'extraordinary' Parliament, convoked for this particular purpose and elected in such a way as to give the Slav electors representation in proportion to their numbers. At the same time an agreement between Vienna and Prague was to have been concluded. But Beust, who was anxious to settle matters quickly and who looked on the Czechs with the traditional contempt of a German and a

Saxon, maintained the franchise fixed by the Parliament of 1861 and which left the Germans in the majority.

At the Diet of Bohemia, Rieger protested against these decisions. He affirmed that state rights were the guarantee 'of our political and national individuality' and announced that the Czechs would not attend the assembly in Vienna. In their absence and without their consent, the Parliament approved the Compromise and passed the new constitutional laws (the 'December laws') for the Empire of Austria. Henceforward, the Empire comprised seventeen kingdoms and countries represented in the Imperial Parliament. It was a question not so much of federation as of a fairly liberal division of administrative authority which recognized the existence of historic traditions and individual regional interests. In spite of differences of territorial extent and population, each country had its elected Diet, entrusted with local administration and empowered to nominate deputies to the Imperial Parliament (*Reichsrat*). The Parliament, composed of two chambers, exercised legislative power for Austria as a whole. The emperor appointed and dismissed ministers and each minister was responsible to the two chambers for the affairs of his own department.

The Czechs had grounds for discontent. Although the emperor continued to bear the title of King of Bohemia, their historic country had not been granted the status to which it was entitled. Bohemia, Moravia and Silesia were regarded as separate administrative districts, without a common Diet and without common institutions. The Czechs were consequently determined to assert their nationa consciousness in great demonstrations: the laying of the foundation-stone of their national theatre and popular pilgrimages (*tábory*) to places of historic fame, such as the hill of Říp in the environs of Prague, where one of the first Christian sanctuaries had been built.

At the same time, they sought to make themselves better known abroad and to assert their Slav character in order to counter the success achieved by the Germans and the Magyars. In 1867 a scientific congress held in Moscow gave Palacký and Rieger the opportunity to plead the cause of Slav solidarity to the Russians and to encourage them to show greater justice to the Poles.[28] They also turned to France, where they had friends. Louis Léger, with the assistance of Frič, had just published a highly informative book entitled *La Bohême historique, pittoresque et littéraire* (1867), which made the French public aware of the existence of the Czech nation and the nature of its problems.

In an article in *La Revue des Deux Mondes* (1869), Saint-René Taillandier gave Austria this solemn warning: 'From the top of the watch-tower, we repeat this cry of alarm which is brought to us by so many voices from the banks of the Moldau and the Danube: either Austria will be a federation, or there will no longer be an Austria.'[29]

Rieger came to Paris and, when he was received by Napoleon III, gave him a report on the situation of Bohemia. But opinion in France had been largely influenced by the internal transformation of the Danubian monarchy into a constitutional and parliamentary regime. The French considered this sufficient, especially since they suspected that these reforms had been effected only with a view to an early revenge for Sadova.

Napoleon III had vainly hoped that Prussia, in compensation for its territorial aggrandizements, would allow France to extend her eastern frontier. Disappointed and humiliated, the emperor of the French contemplated the conclusion of an alliance with Austria–Hungary. Conversations took place between the chiefs of staff, but with no positive results. Rather surprisingly, it was Hungary, so popular among the French, that expressed reservations concerning an alliance.

This was certainly not because the Hungarians did not reciprocate the affection in which they were held by France: on the contrary, they admired and loved France sincerely. But their rulers were cautious. They needed peace so that they might transform their kingdom into a modern state with a well-equipped economy and a better administration. A war would have jeopardized everything. Moreover, they nurtured no resentment towards Prussia—in fact, they were much more mistrustful of Russia. They even feared that a victorious war might strengthen the power of the Germans in Austria and destroy an equilibrium that was so much to their advantage. France thus had no alliance with Austria–Hungary when, in July 1870, she imprudently fell into the trap set by Bismarck and waged war alone against Prussia. The French were defeated at Sedan, their empire crumbled, Paris was besieged, an armistice was concluded and then the Commune revolt broke out. At Versailles, the German Empire was founded, within the limits of a Little Germany and to the advantage of Prussia.

In these circumstances, it became even more important that Austria should overcome its difficulties with the Czechs. This was Francis Joseph's personal wish. The policy of the liberal Germans (the Auersperg ministry), with its anti-clerical bias, annoyed the emperor in many respects. A man of tradition, Francis Joseph appreciated the historic prestige of state rights. During the summer of 1871 he changed his ministry, appointing an Austrian, Hohenwart, a German economist, Schäffle, formerly a professor at Freiburg, and two Czechs, Dr. Habětinek and the jurist Jireček. Negotiations were begun with the representatives of Bohemian state rights: Rieger, Clam-Martinic and Prince Charles Schwarzenberg.[30]

By a rescript published on 12 September, Francis Joseph promised that he would be crowned king in Prague. The negotiators then defined the terms of the agreement, the 'Fundamental Articles'. The Bohemian Chancellery was to be re-established. The Bohemian Diet would have control of justice, schools and regional finance. The common affairs which Bohemia shared with the other countries of the Empire—railways, the postal service, military defence and general finance—would be under the authority of the central Parliament, which would decide the formidable question of a common Diet for the three provinces of the kingdom: Bohemia, Moravia and Silesia.

A Law of Nationalities was to protect the language rights of the Germans in Bohemia. Finally, the Bohemian Diet was to give its sanction to the Compromise of 1867 and the Czechs would naturally attend the Imperial Parliament. This programme of legislation would crown the labours of many years and promised the Empire of Austria the internal peace necessary for its progress.

Yet, when so near to success, the project was wrecked by the opposition of the Germans and the Magyars, who put forward a variety of arguments. To submit the Compromise, four years after its conclusion, for the approval of the Bohemian Diet was to diminish, almost to deny, the authority of that body. It was asserted, moreover, that the autonomy of Bohemia would modify the Constitution of Austria, endowing it with a federal character, especially since the Austrian ministry would henceforth include representatives of the Diets. The Hungarians, for their part, suspected that foreign policy might assume too favourable a bias to Russia and the fear of Pan-Slavism became intensified. Finally, it was foreseen that the politicians who would reap the immediate benefits of the new system in Bohemia would be landed aristocrats and middle-class conservatives. Such a prospect alarmed the liberals. Robert A. Kann, an expert on the history of the nationalities, considers the liberals to have been justified on this point. He expresses astonishment at the fact that the economist Schäffle should have associated a programme of economic renewal with the recognition of state rights in Bohemia. Schäffle was disturbed by the consequences of economic liberalism. In the industrial sector, he feared the predominance of large-scale banking capitalism and the harmful effects of uncontrolled competition; he also disapproved of the preponderance of the great domain in the agricultural sector. He therefore considered that the autonomy of Bohemia and a Cisleithania steered towards federalism would provide favourable institutional and juridical bases for a new system of production and labour. His mistake, in the opinion of Kann, was to forget that state rights served first and foremost the economic interests of the nobility and landed property.[31]

Undoubtedly, a part of the Bohemian aristocracy expected moral and material advantages from the granting of state rights. But another group, which had the same economic and social interests and was known as the *Kaisertreu*, remained centralist and liberal. In fact, in Bohemia the concept of state rights enjoyed a broad and truly national support among the Czechs. It was rejected, according to some authors, by the Germans of Bohemia and the Austrians: 'We did not gain victory at Sedan to become the helots of the Czechs.' But were the Germans of Bohemia unanimous in opposition? Did they all share the ideas of their political leaders, men like Plener and Herbst? This has never been proved. What is certain, however, is that historians have tended to pay heed only to the voices of the extremists. It is commonly assumed that the Bohemian Germans of 1871 can be compared with the Sudetens of 1938. But, when one realizes that, between 1920 and 1939, many Bohemian Germans preferred Czechoslovakia to the risk of being absorbed by a Germany which had been reduced to economic ruin and then, after a brief respite, found itself lurching towards the Hitlerian adventure, it is tempting to believe that their ancestors had good reasons to accept the state rights of an autonomous Bohemia. Bohemian patriotism had not been entirely extinguished among the Germans of the country. The fever of speculation justly observed by Schäffle, the effects of which were bewilderingly evident in Vienna and Budapest, and were also spreading to Prague, gave cause for alarm to people who remained devoted to the traditional family business patiently and honestly managed. In the still romantic mood of the time, the coronation of the king might have aroused as much enthusiasm among the Germans of Prague as among the Czechs.

At least, the historian can argue *a contrario*. When the coronation and the application of the Fundamental Articles were postponed—to all intents and purposes abandoned—and the minister Hohenwart retired, the Czech nation was grievously disappointed. It felt that it had been the victim of a hoax, which it was never to forget. Between the Czechs and the Germans of Bohemia, who might still have been reconciled had promises been fulfilled, a rift had been created. Henceforward, Bohemia no longer consisted of a single bilingual people, but two national groups set one against the other, enemies in a common fatherland. The Czechs felt no real affection for the sovereign and the dynasty; indeed, by 1900, of all the nations of the Empire, they were undoubtedly the least devoted to the emperor.[32] Until the final explosion in 1918, the Bohemian problem remained the irremediable weakness of the monarchy; the threat which it posed to the equilibrium of the Empire, and even of Europe, brought benefit to no one.

The new generations, represented by the Young Czechs, denounced the incompetence of those who had failed, the Old Czechs. Yet, unless all idealism in history is to be condemned systematically, it must be recognized that—as has been well said by Jaroslav Prokeš, an historian of the period between the wars—the principles of these defeated men, 'founded on a mighty confidence in right and justice, attained a moral elevation from which the years of political militancy subsequently diverted the Czech nation and which was only reawakened by the struggle for independence during the First World War'.[33]

This testimony of a Czech can be compared with that of a Bohemian German, Rainer Maria Rilke, the spokesman of all those who, in their love of higher truth, free thought and artistic development, perceived to what extent these national conflicts, by the immeasurable injustice and hatred which they provoked, had jeopardized not only the benefits which one national group might expect from the other, but also the harmony necessary for the progress of each:

> *Es dringt kein Laut bis her zu mir,*
> *Von den Nationen wildem Streite,*
> *Ich stehe ja auf keiner Seite*
> *denn Recht ist weder dort noch hier.*

> (There comes to me no cry
> From the savage combat of the nations.
> I stand on neither side,
> For right is neither there nor here.)

NOTES

1. For every aspect of the problem of the nationalities, from 1848 to the present time, the work by Robert A. Kann, *The Multinational Empire*, New York, 1950, is of fundamental importance (translated into German, in a revised and expanded form, under the title

Das Nationalitäten-problem der Habsburgermonarchie, 2 vols., Graz-Köln, 1964); excellent bibliography.

Hugo Hantsch, *Die Nationalitätenfrage im alten Österreich*, 1953; E. Franzel, *Die Donauraum im Zeitalter der Nationalitätenprinzips*; J. Szekfü, *État et Nation*, Paris, 1945; F. Zwitter, *Les Problèmes nationaux dans la monarchie des Habsbourgs*, Belgrade, 1960.

For the history of the individual nationalities:

Bohemia: J. Pekař, *Československé Dějiny*, Prague, 1921, an outline really intended for secondary schools, but a useful summary of Bohemian history and its interpretation. *Československá Vlastivěda*, vol. IV, *Dějiny*; Václav Husa, *Dějiny Československá*, Prague, 1961. Foreign studies: E. Denis, *La Bohême depuis la Montagne Blanche*, 2 vols., 1903; S. Harrison Thomson, *Czechoslovakia in European History*, Princeton, 1953.

Hungary: in French, Francis Eckhardt, *Histoire de la Hongrie*, Paris, 1932; in Hungarian, the monographs on Kossuth by D. Kosáry (1946) and on Eötvös by I. Sötér (1953); A. Domanovszky, *Die Geschichte Ungarns*, Leipzig, 1923; L. Makkai, *Histoire de Transylvanie*, Paris, 1946; Daicoviciu and Constantinescu, *Brève histoire de la Transylvanie*, Bucharest, 1965; R. Kiszling, *Die Kroaten*, 1956.

Concerning the aspect of public law in the problems of the nationalities:

J. Redlich, *Das österreichische Staats- und Reichsproblem*, 2 vols., Leipzig, 1920–6; J. Kapras, *Právní dějiny zemi koruny české* ('History of the Law of the Lands of the Bohemian Crown'), from the viewpoint of state rights; V. Vaněček, *Dějiny státu a práva v Československu* ('History of the State and the Law in Czechoslovakia'), Prague, 1964; a Marxist interpretation. Professors Rauchberg and Peterka have presented the viewpoint of the Germans of Bohemia in an objective manner.

For Hungary: H. Marczali, *Ungarisches Verfassungsrecht*, Tübingen, 1911.

2. The Bohemian revolution has been studied by historians of various viewpoints: K. Kazbunda, *České hnuti z 1848* ('The Czech Movement of 1848'), Prague, 1928—a liberal interpretation; F. Roubik, *Český rok 1848* ('The Year 1848 in Bohemia'), Prague, 1931; Arnost Klíma, *Rok 1848 v Čechách* ('The Year 1848 in Bohemia'), Prague, 1943. In Russian: I. I. Udal'tsov, *Otcherki iz istorii natsional'no polititcheskoi bor'by v Tchekii v 1848* ('Aspects of the History of the National and Political Struggle in Bohemia in 1848'), Moscow, 1951.

J. Macůrek, *Rok 1848 a Morava* ('The Year 1848 and Moravia'). An important collection of documents, *Slovanský Szejd v Praze 1848* ('The Slav Congress of 1848 in Prague'), was published by Z. Tobolka and V. Žáček, Prague, 1952. Marxist historiography is severe on the moderate elements of Prague. It accuses the middle class of having preferred capitulation to the success of the popular revolution which the workers and the peasants of the provinces, already in revolt, were preparing to support. But this is not the real problem. After the bombardment of the city, all resistance was impossible. The origins of the riot are still shrouded in uncertainty. Undoubtedly, the incident that set it in motion occurred quite by chance: the encounter between the troops and a procession of students in Celetná Street, whereupon shots were fired, one of which hit the wife of General Windischgraetz, sister of Felix von Schwarzenberg, as she stood by her window. But among the foreign elements and probably also among the police there were persons determined either to provoke incidents and exploit them, or to repress liberal agitation by force.

3. V. Čejchan, *Český radicalism v létech 1848–1849* ('Czech Radicalism in the Years 1848–1849'), *Dějiny a přitomnost*, I, 1937, pp. 16–34.

4. Of the large number of works on Francis Joseph, the following are particularly worthy of mention: J. Redlich, *Kaiser Franz Josef von Österreich*, Berlin, 1929, and the three

volumes of Egon Conte Corti, 1951–5: *Vom Kind zum Kaiser, Mensch und Herrscher* and *Der Alte Kaiser*. Alexander Novotný, *Franz Joseph I*, Göttingen, 1968.

On the occasion of the fiftieth anniversary of the death of Francis Joseph, a very thorough iconography was published by Hans Pauer, *Kaiser Franz Joseph I. Beiträge zur Bild-Dokumentation seines Lebens*.

The best biography of the Empress Elizabeth, whose alluring personality also inspired men of letters (Barrès, *Amori et Dolori Sacrum*), remains that written by Corti, *Elisabeth*, Vienna, 1934.

5. On the Parliament of Kremsier: Otokar Odložilík, *Na Kroměřížském sněmu, 1848–1849*, Prague, 1947. On the constitutions: Fellner, op. cit. (in note 1, chapter 3).

Reprisals in Bohemia were of terrifying proportions: martial law was maintained in Prague for several years on the dubious pretext that a conspiracy was being organized, 28 death-sentences were pronounced and 51 sentences of imprisonment totalling 474 years. The death-sentences were then commuted to imprisonment and a general amnesty was granted in 1857.

6. A. Andics, *Die Habsburger und die Frage der Zarenhilfe gegen die Revolution* in *Études historiques* (see note 31, chapter 9), vol. II, p. 7.

7. On the war of 1848–9 in Hungary: J. Perenyi, 'Documents relatifs à l'intervention de l'armée russe en Hongrie' in *Revue d'histoire comparée*, 1946; D. Stremooukoff, 'La question allemande et l'intervention russe en Hongrie', *Actes du Congrès historique de la Révolution de 1848*, Paris, 1949; also, the old study by Mihail Horvath, *Magyarország függetlenségi harcának története* ('History of the Hungarian War of Independence'), 1871–3.

The Russian historian Tarlé, in his *Krimskaïa Voïna* ('The Crimean War', vol. I, p. 23), provides a revealing text concerning the poor equipment of the Russian army, which was nevertheless adequate to ensure victory over the Hungarians, even worse equipped.

8. On Schwarzenberg: R. Kiszling, *Fürst Felix Schwarzenberg*, 1952.

9. Concerning the industrialization of the Habsburg lands between 1851 and 1859, in addition to the great work *Geschichte der österreichischen Land und Forstwirtschaft und ihrer Industrie 1848–1892*, there is a basic bibliography including works published up to 1966 in Erich Zöllner, *Geschichte Österreichs*.

H. Benedikt, *Die Wirtschaftliche Entwicklung in der Franz Josef Zeit*, 1958.

For Bohemia, which by the mid-nineteenth century was the most industrialized country in the monarchy, consult the study by J. Purš, *Průmyslová revoluce v českých zemích* ('The Industrial Revolution in the Czech Lands'), Prague, 1960. For Hungary: V. Sandor, *Die Hauptmerkmale des industriellen Entwicklung in Ungarn zur Zeit des Absolutismus (1849–1867)* in vol. II of the collection *Études historiques* published by the Budapest Academy of Sciences, 1960; and, in another collection published by the same Academy, *Studien zur Geschichte der Österreichisch-Ungarischen Monarchie*, 1961, the articles by J. Kovachs on the peasantry in Transylvania and by J. Buszko on the economic development of Galicia.

10. Jacques Droz, *L'Europe centrale*, p. 94.

11. Jean de Bourgoing, *Andere Zeiten, Rückblick vor dem Abschied*, 1964, p. 70.

12. On the Danube: D. Sturdza, *Collection of documents concerning freedom of navigation on the Danube*, Berlin, 1904; V. Radovanovitch, *Le Danube et l'application du principe de la liberté de navigation fluviale*, Geneva, 1925; J. Duvernoy, *Le régime international du Danube*, law thesis, Grenoble; A. Heksch, *Die Donau von ihrem Ursprung bis an die Mündung*, Vienna, 1881; *Le Danube. Sa mission économique et civilisatrice dans l'Europe centrale et orientale* (Histoire collective), 1933.

13. F. Hennings, *Ringstrasse Symphonie*, vol. I, *Es ist meine Wille*.

14. A. Lhotsky, *Österreichische Historiographie*, Munich, 1962, and Victor-L. Tapié, *Méthodes et problèmes de l'histoire de l'Europe centrale* (Mélanges Renouvin), Paris, 1966.

15. Apropos of the Concordat of 1855, the *Memoirs* of Hübner, then Austrian ambassador in Paris, relate that the Empress Eugénie was astounded by the new treaty, which she considered 'medieval' (vol. I, p. 372).

16. Arne Novák, *Československá Vlastivěda*, vol. V, *Pisemnictví*. Several monuments in Czechoslovakia have been devoted to the figure of Babička.

17. On the Crimean War: V. Gitermann, *Geschichte Russlands*, 3 vols., Zurich, 1949; N. Potiemkine, *Histoire de la diplomatie*, 2 vols., Paris, 1946; Vernon John Puryear, *International Economics and Diplomacy in the Near East, 1834–1835*, Stanford University Press, 1935; *England, Russia and the Straits Question, 1844–1854*, Berkeley, California, 1951. Of particular value: E. V. Tarlé, *Krimskaïa Voïna* ('The Crimean War'); also, F. Valsecchi, *Il Risorgimento e l'Europa, l'Alleanza di Crimea*, Milan, 1948; A. Luzio, *La guerra di Crimea e la politica estera austriaca*, in *Studi e bozzetti*, Milan, 1927.

18. François Charles-Roux, *Alexandre II, Gortchakoff et Napoléon III*, Paris, 1913; Victor-L. Tapié, 'Le traité secret franco-russe de 1859' in *Études d'histoire contemporaine*, vol. V, Paris, 1953.

19. Louis Eisenmann, *Le Compromis austro-hongrois de 1867*, preface.

20. T. G. Masaryk, *Česká otázka* ('The Czech Question'), 1908, p. 190, quotes this passage from an article by Palacký in the newspaper *Národní listy*.

21. The text of Eötvös is quoted by the Baroness Blaze de Bury in *L'Autriche et ses réformes*, a little study that bears witness to the lively interest shown abroad in the reforming intentions of the Austrian government. In his work *Über die Gleichberechtigung der Nationalitäten in Österreich*, Pest, 1850, J. Eötvös had denounced the contradictions of the system of 1849, which claimed to be founded on the equality of rights among the nationalities. He asserted the necessity of returning to historic rights, maintaining that the patriotic sentiment with which the kingdom's best subjects had been imbued since youth should not be sacrificed to an artificial unity of state. An anonymous work inspired by Bach had based its argument on the economic progress accomplished in Hungary under the absolutist regime: *Rückblick auf die jüngste Entwicklungsperiode Ungarns* ('A Glance at the Last Period of Development in Hungary'), 1857. Stephen Széchenyi, challenging Eötvös' conclusions, replied with a 'look' at the latter's 'glance': *Blick auf den anonymen Rückblick*.

22. Concerning the Diploma and Patent, cf. Fellner, and Hellbling, op. cit., p. 357 et seq.

23. André Lorant, *Le Compromis austro-hongrois et l'opinion publique française en 1867* (supplementary thesis submitted for the 'doctorat d'État'), Paris, 1968.

24. Palacký, *Idea státu rakouského* ('The Idea of the Austrian State').

25. The battle of Sadova was the subject of an exhibition held in Vienna in 1966; the catalogue issued for the exhibition contains some valuable information: *Gedenkschrift 1966*, Vienna, 1966.

26. See in Hennings, *Ringstrasse Symphonie*, vol. I, p. 56, a cartoon of 1866 showing members of the middle class and the *demi-monde* in the cafés of Vienna, with this cruel caption: 'Do not such people deserve their fate?'

27. For the history and interpretation of the Compromise: J. Zolger, *Der staatsrechtliche Ausgleich zwischen Österreich und Ungarn, 1867*, 1911; L. Eisenmann, *Le Compromis austro-hongrois de 1867*, Paris, 1904; Friedrich Luckwaldt, *Liberalismus und Nationalismus*, *Propyläen Weltgeschichte*, VIII, 1930; F. Hartung, *Österreich-Ungarn als Verfassungstaat*,

Halle, 1918; J. Galantai, *Az 1867 es Kiegyezés* ('The Hungarian Compromise of 1867'), Budapest, 1967; H. Marczali, *Ungarische Verfassungsgeschichte*.

28. Louis Léger, *Le panslavisme et l'intérêt français*, Paris, 1917 (a war-time work of a rather tendentious nature), gives a long commentary (pp. 210–49) on the Congress of Moscow of 1867 and quotes extracts from Rieger's speech.

29. Louis Léger and Josef Fricz (Frič), *La Bohême historique, pittoresque et littéraire*, Paris, 1867. Cf. Ernst Birke, *Frankreich und Ostmitteleuropa im 19 Jahrhundert*, p. 272 *et seq*.

30. The rescript of 12 September 1871 began with this solemn promise: 'We recognize the rights of this kingdom and are ready to prove this by our coronation oath.' On the Fundamental Articles, apart from the general histories already mentioned, see Zd. Tobolka, *Politické dějiny československého národa od. r. 1848 až do dnešní doby* ('Political History of the Czechoslovak Nation from 1848 to the Present Day'), 5 vols., Prague, 1932.

   See also a collective work published in Vienna in 1961, *Das böhmische Staatsrecht*; and in the review *Bohemia*, vol. IV, 1963, an article by Rudolf Wierer, 'Der böhmische Staat und der Ausgleichsversuch des Ministerium Hohenwart-Schäffle'.

   However, in order to appreciate fully the spirit of 'state rights' and the sentimental value of this concept in the collective psychology of the Czechs, the reader should ideally immerse himself in the whole of Czech literature from 1871 to 1914 and even beyond. See J. Pekař, *Z České ,ronty* ('From the Bohemian Front'), vol. II.

31. Robert A. Kann, *Das Nationalitätenproblem der Habsburgermonarchie*, vol. II, p. 175 *et seq*.

32. The Czechs had irreverently applied to the Emperor Francis Joseph the nickname *Procházka*, which means 'walk', but is also frequently found as a Czech surname. In an article of reminiscences published by the *Vienna Gazette* on 19 November 1966 (a supplement devoted to the fiftieth anniversary of the death of Francis Joseph), Johannes Urzidil recounted how, during the emperor's visit to Prague in 1908, street-vendors began to move around the crowd as soon as the procession passed by, offering little paper sticks which they called '*hole na procházku*', meaning literally 'walking-sticks' but which could also be taken to mean 'sticks to beat *Procházka*'.

33. Jaroslav Prokeš, *Československá Vlastivěda*, vol. IV, p. 783.

❧ 11 ❧

The Era of Capitalism
and the Nationalities

THE TRAVELLER who visits Vienna and Budapest cannot fail to be struck by the ostentatious grandeur of the two Parliaments: one on the Ring, with its Hellenistic porticoes and pediment; the other, admirably situated beside the Danube, its Gothic style calling to mind the Houses of Parliament at Westminster.[1] The two buildings bear witness both to the prestige of representative institutions which were regarded as the expression of modern liberties and also to the material prosperity of the period and its uncertain artistic taste, which preferred pastiche to creative originality. In themselves they symbolize the liberalism and the economic strength of the two capitals. Henceforward, neither the Hofburg nor, on the hill of Buda on the other side of the great river, the royal palace with its dome crowning the façade added to the constructions of Charles III[2] and Maria Theresa, were the only centres of political life: it was the Parliaments that passed the laws.

In 1960, an old professor at the University of Budapest talked to the author about his youth and the hopes which he had cherished: 'I saw the king passing over the Lánchíd', he said. The king was Francis Joseph on his way between the palace, where he came to stay every year, and the Parliament, where the assemblies of the nation were held. The man whose reign had begun with absolutism had become a constitutional sovereign in each of his monarchies. In both countries the system of 1867 was liberal in that it recognized the equality of citizens, liberty of conscience, freedom of expression both in speech and in the press, and the right of every citizen to use his mother tongue and to ensure its use in the education of his children at the elementary level.

Political liberty was guaranteed, since neither in Austria nor in Hungary could the sovereign modify the constitution at will; in Austria, his right to invoke Article 14, which enabled him to promulgate ordinances of a legislative nature during the suspension of Parliament, was merely a temporary right and gave him no authority to change constitutional laws.

The system was not very different from that of the countries of western Europe. But the Parliaments of those countries had evolved from unified nations. In Germany, the *Reichstag*, elected on universal suffrage, represented the German nation, even if the other assembly, the *Bundesrat*, comprised the delegates of the different German states. Consequently, the Western Parliaments were concerned only with matters of general policy, internal or external: the Government, supported by the majority of parliamentary representatives, faced an Opposition guided solely by ideological preferences and economic interests. In Austria and in Hungary, the situation was less clear-cut, for it was complicated by the demands of the nationalities, who were dissatisfied with the general system. Nationalist claims were to assume increasing importance during this period and to present a formidable obstacle to the exercise of parliamentary life.

Yet it must be realized that many questions of fundamental importance for the populations of the Empire were debated in the Diets and by the regional and 'communal' authorities. Thus, the nationalities did not withdraw into permanent and immovable opposition, for they—or rather the élite among them—hoped to obtain more favourable legislative concessions through the intervention of their deputies at the Imperial Parliament. Doubtless, there were some die-hards who condemned any form of opportunism and co-operation. In Hungary, the supporters of Kossuth proved unyielding in their resistance, refusing to recognize the existence of the Compromise and to attend the Parliament in Budapest.

In Bohemia, the Czech members of the Diet declined to nominate deputies to the Imperial Parliament from 1871 to 1879, although their German colleagues naturally appointed their own deputies. The Rumanians of Transylvania, signatories to the Blaj declaration of 1868, repudiated the union of Transylvania and Hungary which had been approved by the Diet of 1865. They refused to recognize that their compatriots attending the Budapest Parliament were representative of the Rumanian nation.

But the die-hards were not in the majority, nor did they command lasting support; many of them resigned themselves to defeat. Among the more advanced nationalities a class of politicians had already been formed which could make its influence felt in the debates of the Parliaments. By consenting to sit in the assemblies in Vienna or Budapest, they were undoubtedly giving their sanction to the system of 1867, but they knew that they could turn it to the advantage of their national group and that it would bring them positive benefits.

Certain countries had more reason than others to play their part in the system. This was especially true of the Poles, not because they had lost their desire for a free and independent Poland, or consented to the scandalous negation of international justice inherent in the dismemberment of their homeland, but because, of the three conquering co-partners of partition, the Empire of Austria alone offered them equitable conditions of existence. Neither the yoke of the tsar nor the harsh regime of the king of Prussia could be compared favourably with the tutelage of the Austrian emperor, who included among his titles that of King of Galicia and Lodomeria. Although merely a country represented at the Imperial Parliament (like the sixteen other countries of Cisleithania), Galicia had been granted special privileges and a practically autonomous status by the ordinances of January 1867 and July and November 1868. Polish was the administrative language of the country and German was used only in relations with the central power. The governor of Galicia was always a Pole and a Polish minister traditionally held a position in the Cisleithan government. Two universities, at Lemberg (Leopold, Lwow) and at Cracow, ensured the development of higher education and scientific research. Finally, the common religion which they shared with Austria was all the more appreciated by the Polish Catholics of the Empire because the denominational and doctrinal question was, for their fellow-countrymen, one of the principal causes of dissension with Russia, officially intransigent in her Orthodoxy, and with Protestant Prussia.

As a result of the loyalty shown by the Poles of Austria, a number of Polish aristocrats—Goluchowski, Potocki, Belcredi, Badeni—were called to assume the presidency of the Austrian ministry in times of difficulty and especially when it was necessary to settle urgent problems with the Czechs, who were Slavs and Catholics like the Poles. Polish deputies, Franciszek Smolka and David von Abrahamowicz, held the office of president of the House of Representatives[3]; Abrahamowicz served for a period of thirty-seven years, from 1881 to 1918.

The political leaders of the Rumanians of Transylvania wavered between passivity and an active participation in affairs. But when in 1864 Francis Joseph had elevated Bishop Andrew Şaguna, a patriot and loyalist, to the dignity of metropolitan of the autocephalous Rumanian Church, he had not sought to buy a conscience. By releasing the Rumanian Orthodox from the obedience of the Serbian metropolitan of Hungary, he had given their national group a legitimate concession which was greatly appreciated.[4]

When a nationality was weak, it gained nothing by standing aloof and depriving itself of advocates in the assemblies of the Empire.

Each Parliament comprised two chambers: a Senate or House of Lords, where the adult archdukes, bishops and persons nominated for life by the emperor or king sat by right (Palacký was a senator), and a House of Representatives, who were elected.

In Austria, the deputies were nominated by the Diets, which were themselves elected by four 'curias' (great landowners, the towns, the chambers of commerce and the peasant communities). In addition to the obligation of being able to read and write, the right to vote was subject to a tax-qualification. From 1873, the electors of the curias designated deputies to the Austrian Parliament directly, without the intervention of their Diets.

In Hungary, where the franchise was granted to all male citizens of the Hungarian state who were at least twenty years old and economically and personally independent, the electorate was divided into a highly complicated system of thirty-seven categories, according to the nature and the amount of income (for example, the land of Transylvania was deemed to yield less than the Hungarian plain). The military, both officers and soldiers, had no vote. Thus, an electoral system based on tax-qualification existed everywhere. But it was gradually extended in Austria, until the introduction of universal suffrage in 1906. In Transleithania, on the eve of 1914, universal suffrage had still not been granted, although it had been much discussed. Throughout the Empire the old aristocracy continued to occupy an important political position which was linked with its economic power and its social prestige, still great despite the abolition of juridical privilege. But it was the middle class that derived the greatest advantage from the system, for success in business, which brought an increase of income and therefore of tax-liability, automatically ensured the right to vote. The distribution of electoral constituencies, ingeniously devised by the ministry of the interior in each state, continued to be denounced by the nationalities as a means of favouring the dominant groups, the Germans and the Magyars, to the detriment of the Slavs and Latins. In Bohemia, a country of fierce controversy, the Czechs constantly complained that their representation did not correspond with their real numerical strength in the kingdom and in the margraviate of Moravia. The 1870s saw a fierce struggle for the acquisition of large estates, for the nationality of a new proprietor could determine whether the Czechs or the Germans held the majority of votes in the curia of great land-owners.

When their province was integrated with the Hungarian state, the Rumanians of Transylvania formed only 15 per cent of the total population of Hungary and were alarmed to find how little influence they would have at the Parliament. In the old Diet, whose disappearance they deplored, they had outnumbered the Germans (the Saxons of Transylvania) and the Szekels. In each Parliament debates were held in the official language: German in Vienna, Magyar in Budapest. Since they belonged to a social élite, all deputies were accustomed to speaking in their respective official tongue. At the Diet of Bohemia discussions took place in both Czech and German; in Galicia and in Croatia only Polish and Serbo-Croat were used.

The system as a whole offered reasonable and tolerable conditions which could not, however, remain unchanged by the progress of national consciousness. This progress depended largely on two factors: natural population trends and freedom of opportunity. In Hungary, the legislative programme encouraged the diffusion of the Magyar language, without necessarily transgressing the Law of Nationalities of 1868. Magyar was made obligatory not only in the exercise of public office, but also in the practice of the liberal professions (medicine and law). Consequently, the opportunities available to persons of Hungarian nationality became increasingly numerous.

In the army, one of the institutional pillars of the Dual Monarchy, German was retained as the language of command. To choose a military career on land or at sea did not necessarily involve the loss of nationality, as is proved by two examples, one fictional, the other real: the hero of the novel by Zeyer, *Jan Maria Plojhar*, was a Czech naval officer, while Horthy, the last admiral of the Dual Monarchy, was a Hungarian; but whoever chose such a career thereby placed both himself and his family in a position where the interests of the 'common state' were to prevail over those of the national group to which he belonged by birth.[5]

Marriages and migrations within the monarchical territory often entailed a change of nationality; although language remained the fundamental mark of nationality, it was not always a determining factor. Foreign publicists and observers had difficulty in appreciating such distinctions, which could be clearly recognized by direct experience of life in Austria-Hungary.

In 1857 the monarchy as a whole, including Lombardy and Venetia, had numbered 32,261,000 inhabitants and twelve years later (1869), in spite of the loss of these two provinces, 35,812,000; by the end of the century its population had reached 46,974,000, excluding Bosnia and Herzegovina which were annexed in 1908. In 1910, including the annexed territories, Austria-Hungary formed a bloc of 51,390,000 inhabitants. This striking growth of population was well balanced between the two states, for Austria numbered 27,963,873 inhabitants and Hungary 20,900,000.

Between 1850 and 1880 the rate of European population-growth was as follows: 45 per cent in England and Wales, 39 per cent in Russia, 28 per cent in Germany and 23 per cent in Austria (24 per cent in Bohemia considered separately). The case of Bohemia during this period is fairly typical of the development of a country where industrial production was advancing. The group of Czech countries (Bohemia, Moravia and Silesia) reached a total population of 8,271,400 in 1880: within thirty years the population had thus increased by one-quarter. But the birth-rate had fallen since 1850. Between 1867 and 1873 the annual rate of marriages was roughly ten per thousand inhabitants; from 1873 to the war of 1914 it remained approximately 7·5 per thousand inhabitants.[6]

Marriages were more numerous in the agricultural regions than in the industrial areas (especially the textile areas). Infant mortality remained high, affecting mainly boys; on the other hand, the number of male births was greater than that of female births. A larger proportion of the female population reached an advanced age, despite deaths in childbirth, with the result that until the end of the century the Dual Monarchy comprised 10 per cent more women than men. It has often been said that feminine influence was a determining factor in the education of children and the orientation of their national consciousness. Although this problem has not yet been the subject of scientific research, it would appear that a numerically predominant feminine environment favoured the cohesion of the national group. It would be helpful to have more information than is available on the proportion of mixed marriages and to assess their consequences. But there can be no doubt that in Bohemia-Moravia the number of marriages was lower than it might have been. This is proved by the increase of illegitimate births, especially in the towns and during times of difficulty. The best years, the 1870s, years of external peace and internal prosperity, saw the number of marriages increase and the number of illegitimate births diminish. The rise of industry led inevitably to the growth of the towns. The population of Prague rose from 142,588 in 1857 to 162,323 in 1880. The heaviest influx affected the industrial suburbs of Karlín and Smichov. If these are included in the total population of the Bohemian metropolis, the figures for 1857 and 1880 become 234,007 and 356,246; the rate of growth between 1869 and 1880 was 29 per cent for the whole city, but 80 per cent in Karlín, 37 per cent in Smichov and only 3 per cent in Prague itself.

It was not only Prague or the industrial towns in the German districts of northern Bohemia that attracted new inhabitants. The development of the railway network made the other regions of the monarchy more accessible. The Vienna-Prague link had long been established by means of connecting lines that crossed Moravia and then the valley of the Elbe. In 1871 a more direct route was laid via southern and central Bohemia—Třeboň, Tábor, Benešov. Many Czechs left their country to look for work in the imperial capital. Around 1880, one-third of the population of Vienna, which (including the suburbs) rose from 431,147 to 827,567 between 1851 and 1890, consisted of Czech nationals—about 235,000 out of a total of 750,000. These Czechs were mostly the humble folk of the lower orders—shoemakers, tailors, joiners and domestic servants. The Germans of Bohemia, also attracted by the Vienna-Prague railway link, helped to swell the ranks of a higher category of the working class, that of the white-collar workers and school-teachers. For the Czechs of Vienna, the risk of absorption by Austrian society was considerable. Many Czech names can still be found on Viennese shop-signs and among doctors, intellectuals and artists. Today, in a climate more relaxed than that of the nationalist struggles, a certain tender nostalgia for the land of their ancestors can be observed among these citizens of Vienna. Yet the Czechs had their own schools and could therefore be sure of receiving their early education in their mother tongue; some of them, especially women, spent their entire adult life in Vienna without learning German, except for a few common phrases. 'Leave my Czechs alone', later said the burgomaster of Vienna, Karl Lueger, who had many Czechs among his electoral supporters and found himself having to defend them against the nationalist fervour of their German fellow-citizens.[7]

There can be no doubt, however, that these migrations significantly diminished the growth-potential of the Czech population; Bohemians were also emigrating to America, though in much fewer numbers than the inhabitants of the other regions of the Dual Monarchy—the Slovak districts of Hungary, for example. It is not difficult to believe that, as L. Karníková has suggested in a sound study of the subject, the population of Bohemia would have grown by one-third instead of one-quarter between 1850 and 1880, if these migrations had not taken place. Since the Czech population, still predominantly peasant, continued to show the highest fertility rate, its numerical progress would certainly have been assured. Although there has been much debate concerning points of detail, Austrian statistics in general were established on a sound basis. It can therefore be assumed that in Cisleithania the proportions of inhabitants in 1880 were 36·8 per cent Germans, 23·8 per cent Czechs, 14·9 per cent Poles, 12·8 per cent Ruthenes and 3·1 per cent Italians; the corresponding figures for 1910 were 35·6, 23, 17·8, 12·6 and 2·7 per cent. The resistance of the nationalities to assimilation thus remained strong, without causing any marked disturbance of the general equilibrium.

In Transleithania, on the other hand, the progress of the Magyar population was more rapid. In thirty years the proportion of Magyars rose from 41·2 to 48·1 per cent while that of the Germans dropped from 12·5 to 9·8 per cent and that of the Slovaks from 11·9 to 9·4 per cent—the decline shown by this latter figure was doubtless due to emigrations to foreign countries rather than to assimilation by the dominant group. The Slovak élite had asserted itself more strongly during this period and through newspapers, books and schools, despite the undeniable ill-will shown by the ruling power, it possessed more numerous means of protecting its nationality.

❦

Certainly, the favourable conditions of the early 1860s had encouraged the ruling classes to assure themselves solid political institutions and the Compromise had issued, to a certain degree, from a general desire for stability so that capitalist private enterprise might be developed. In 1862 a law had been promulgated which gave charters to the joint-stock companies. Until the crisis of 1873, their number grew from year to year. In 1867, the number of companies founded in Cisleithania was 154; in 1869, 113; in 1870, 74; and in 1872, 248. Bohemia played an important part in this sector: in 1867, 18 companies were established, including 16 at Prague; another 18 in 1869, 40 in 1870 and 59 in 1872, including 37 at Prague.

The countries of the monarchy formed one vast economic domain in which agriculture predominated and the textile industry traditionally occupied an important position, but mineral resources were sufficiently great and varied to facilitate the equipment of industry. The installation of the Bessemer converters at the iron-works of Vitkovice in Moravia in 1866 and of blast-furnaces at Kladno in 1860 made rapid progress possible in the production of cast iron. The need of agricultural machinery, both in Austria and in Hungary, and the construction of railways and rolling-stock provided the metallurgical industry with a home market whose demand it could not satisfy. Consequently, the economy of the Danubian monarchy remained largely dependent on imported materials. Foreign capitalists realized that they could make large and profitable investments in this vast, well-populated territory. These were new countries in search of rapid industrialization, where there existed solid traditions of labour, a body of well-trained engineers and a working class in which generations of craft activity had developed technical skill and a professional conscience. The conditions for success appeared to be at their peak. Furthermore, owing to their geographical situation, these countries could rapidly become the suppliers of regions even less industrialized than themselves—the first independent Balkan states (Serbia and Rumania), Russia, the Middle East and even more distant countries such as the East Indies and South America, which needed textiles. But capital was required. The largest fortunes belonged to the landowners, who preferred to invest in the food industries derived from agricultural production—sugar-beet refineries, flour mills, breweries. It was therefore necessary to drain the reserves of the liberal petty bourgeoisie and the peasantry and to provide credit so that, side by side with the large concerns, firms of medium size could more easily be established. Such, for example, was the role assumed by the Živnostenská Banka (The Bank of Light Industry), founded at Prague in 1869 and which immediately gained the confidence of Czech investors. This bank was to play a great part in the economic organization of Bohemia and in the consolidation of Czech nationality. But it was in Vienna that the most important affairs were still conducted and that the banks multiplied most rapidly—the fine buildings bordering the Ring (banks and the private dwellings of bankers) stand witness to their success and their power. Business expanded, as new enterprises sprang from existing ones.

Foreigners gave the system its impetus. Side by side with the directors of the *Anglo-Austrian Bank* and the Rothschilds, whose Viennese branch assumed Austrian nationality, there was Baron Hirsch, a Jew of Belgian birth who, among other things, financed the construction of railways in the Ottoman Empire. Success appeared to be confirmed by the trend of imports and exports. In four years, from 1869 to 1873, imports increased by 83 per cent by comparison with the preceding five years: imported raw materials for industrial use rose by 40 per cent and manufactured products by 131 per cent, but the export of raw materials dropped by 7 per cent, for a large proportion of these materials was now absorbed by local industries. On the other hand, the export of manufactured articles increased by 33 per cent, while exports as a whole rose by only 15 per cent. These figures all point to the growth of internal consumption. The average number of patents registered annually between 1867 and 1872 was 707, including 403 for Cisleithania; between 1862 and 1867 the average had been 578.[8]

Vienna became the centre of an International Exhibition, five years after the great success of the Paris Exhibition. But the mood of euphoria was brutally shattered. On 1 May 1873, convulsions at the Stock Exchange wrecked the economic situation, jeopardizing numerous business concerns, causing one bankruptcy after another, reducing families to ruin and heads of firms to suicide: over the whole of society a wind of panic blew which was long to be remembered. The years 1873–9 were years of recession and crisis. Yet these hard-working peoples did not abandon the struggle. Henceforth, they mistrusted dazzling promises and facile hopes, preferring to place their savings, which they patiently rebuilt, into the savings-banks and co-operative societies.

Circumstances began to improve again after 1879 and the return of prosperity was accompanied by a general abatement of political problems: a relaxation of tension among the nationalities (the Czechs returned to the Vienna Parliament), a more advanced social legislation which indubitably mitigated the wretched condition of the working classes and, in the field of foreign policy, the conclusion of the Dual and then of the Triple Alliance. Public opinion looked on the Triple Alliance as a guarantee against the danger of war, which had seemed imminent at the time of the Balkan insurrections and the Russo-Turkish war of 1877.

Inventions stimulated industrial production. In 1879 the Thomas Gillchrist process was used for the first time in the treatment of minerals in Bohemia; production increased steadily in the coal-mining and lignite industries. In 1884, the discoveries of the Czech inventor Křižík were put into practice with the introduction of electric lighting and electric equipment. Although the food industries maintained their advantage over the textile industries, in spite of a crisis in the refineries between 1883 and 1885, textiles managed to hold their own with the development of cotton goods and the use of jute. The leather industry was thriving and the Viennese glove trade, renowned for the elegance and fine quality of its products, even found a market in North America.

In the paper industry, wood and cellulose provided the mills with raw materials that could be obtained cheaply in these countries of forestland. A decline was to be observed in the craft workshops, where rags had been used to make the soft, thick sheets of paper which some shops in Vienna and Prague were still supplying to a clientele of connoisseurs right up to the troubled times of 1938 and 1939. The chemical industries, the manufacture of furniture, the glassware of Bohemia, porcelain and faience, all enjoyed increasing success. The construction of commercial buildings in Vienna, Wiener-Neustadt, Graz, Linz, Trieste, Leopold and Budapest—all cities were flourishing—stimulated various sectors of production and commercial enterprise. Nor should it be forgotten that musical instruments were being made in these countries whose love of the arts never diminished and where music conservatories, amateur societies, concerts, orchestras in cafés and restaurants existed in ever greater abundance.

Although heavy industry was largely concentrated in Lower Austria and especially in Bohemia (by the end of the century, of the 3,100 large concerns in Cisleithania, 1,846, i.e. over half, lay in Bohemia[9]), it was to be found in all parts of the Empire: in Styria, in Carinthia and even in Vorarlberg, around the large cities of the Hungarian plain, but also in the Banat, near Temesvár, in Transylvania, near the small Slovak towns, and in Poland. The economic map of the Dual Monarchy bears witness to the diffusion of its industries and the collective character of industrial effort. Yet, in the Europe of the time, Austria-Hungary was not a great industrial power. In 1900 the proportion of its population engaged in agriculture remained as high as 66·8 per cent by contrast with 35·2 per cent in Germany. The rhythm of production was more rapid in the Western states, where figures were higher both for production and in terms of money value. Austria-Hungary had difficulty in contending with such competition. The agricultural sector found its outlets imperilled by the arrival in Europe of vast quantities of American and Canadian cereals, while the progress of Russian production posed grave problems for Hungarian and Polish landowners. The exports of the German Reich were also penetrating into the Austrian Empire, in competition with home-manufactured products. The common customs policy of Austria-Hungary needed to resolve the conflict between the demands for protectionism made by the agriculturalists, and in particular those of Hungary, and the interests of the Austrian and Bohemian industrialists who, so that they could produce in larger quantities and more cheaply, remained committed to a policy of relative free trade.

The Dual Monarchy thus formed a highly complex economic system. On its territory, which was the largest in Europe after Russia and Germany, industrially advanced regions existed side by side with agriculturally backward regions. But it would be a mistake necessarily to identify industry with progress and agriculture with backwardness, for in certain agricultural sectors advanced techniques were being used, while in some forms of industry antiquated methods still persisted.

In recent years the historians of central Europe (Austrians, Poles, Czechoslovaks, Hungarians and Rumanians), though divided in their opinions and their methods, have agreed in recognizing that economic history had been neglected by earlier generations, who devoted their attention exclusively to political and national history. These historians have been striving to extend their research and to co-ordinate their findings, so that a clearer view of the general historical reality might emerge.

An important feature of Danubian economic history is the permanence of its structures throughout the progress of the era of liberal capitalism—approximately from 1867 to 1890—and even during the development of monopolistic capitalism up to the 1914 war. Industrialization advanced everywhere, but without any marked change in the relative economic strength of the different countries. For example, the horse-power employed in the Dual Monarchy increased between 1863 and 1900, but its territorial distribution remained roughly the same: in Bohemia, 35·8 per cent of the total in 1863 and 36 per cent in 1900–1; in the kingdom of Hungary, 18 and 19 per cent respectively; in the Austrian lands excluding Bohemia, 46·2 and 46 per cent (these latter figures are to be explained largely by the existence of the industrial complex around Vienna). But in forty years Bohemia's consumption rose from 20,728 horse-power to 604,510; that of Hungary, from 10,425 to 300,000, and that of the Austrian lands, from 26,735 to 772,490. The magnitude of Hungary's industrial effort is clear, but it was not sufficient to improve her position within the monarchy as a whole. In short, there was little difference in the comparative economic power of each country during this period, even if progress was general, as the Hungarian historian V. Sandor has observed.[10] The distribution of production between the two states which had been associated by the Compromise of 1867, and which formed a single customs territory, presented the same fundamental features. Hungary—the Hungary of the great landowners, but also the Hungary of the peasants, who did not have sufficient land (though this is another subject)—remained the chief supplier of cereals to the Austrian home market, while Austria provided Hungary with manufactured products. Some historians have suggested that Hungary, though politically independent, was still economically subordinate to Austria, in the position of a colonial or semi-colonial country. This view has been disputed, not without reason it would seem, for Cisleithania and Transleithania were not homogeneous blocs with a reciprocal system for the exchange of their products. Many parts of Cisleithania remained on the fringe of this interflow of trade in which industrial products and machines were sent to Hungary and large quantities of cereals were brought back to the great cities of Austria.

Nevertheless, the two states were complementary: the industrial strength of Austria and the agricultural strength of Hungary balanced each other, impelled by the same rhythm of production. Such a situation tended to favour the three groups in which capitalist organization was most highly developed—the Germans, the Czechs and the Magyars—while the other nationalities, especially in Hungary but also in Austria, found themselves less privileged, enclosed within their antiquated agrarian systems and retarded in their industrial development.

In 1913 Austria-Hungary came after Great Britain, Germany and France in European industrial production, to which it contributed a mere 6 per cent. It held third place in the production of coal and fifth place in the production of crude iron and textiles, behind Great Britain, Germany, France and even Russia, but ahead of Italy. Its contribution to European steel manufacture was 2·7 million tons (6·3 per cent).[11] Yet, throughout the period between the Compromise of 1867 and 1914, the economy of the Dual Monarchy never ceased to be dependent on foreign capital. On the eve of the First World War, foreign capital investment rose to ten thousand million crowns, of which six thousand millions came from Germany and three thousand millions from France, while Austro-Hungarian capital invested abroad amounted to only five hundred thousand crowns.[12] Austria-Hungary had not taken part in the colonial struggle and left the burden of industrializing Bosnia-Herzegovina to German capital. Such circumstances did not permit the Dual Monarchy to aspire to the role of a front-rank power in the international economic competition of the beginning of the twentieth century and they certainly had repercussions on its foreign and internal policy. Yet they did not prevent Austria-Hungary from being a great power by virtue of the size of its population, the quality of its civilization, the vastness of its territory and the variety of its agricultural and mineral resources. From this viewpoint, it was even reasonable to look on Austria-Hungary as a power of the future, a possibility which was obscured in the minds of many observers by the immensity of the monarchy's political problems. On the other hand, there could be no mistaking the signs of prosperity evident from the rise in the standard of living throughout the provinces of the monarchy—chiefly in the most industrially advanced provinces, but also in the most backward regions—the increase in the number of civil servants, which resulted from the extension of public administration, and the constant progress of rail and road communications. Since crises were by no means lacking, it was to these that the publicists devoted their attention, so that European opinion was less well informed about the positive aspects of life in Austria-Hungary.

※

The essential feature of the sociological evolution emanating from the industrial age was the growth in the numbers both of the wage-earning working class and of the middle class. It would be more accurate to speak of the middle classes, for the rising strata of society possessed, in schools and cultural associations, the means by which to preserve their respective national characters while attaining a higher social standing. For the Czechs, the capitalist and industrial development of Bohemia no longer involved the risk of loss of nationality which had been evident during the period of Joseph II, studied in an earlier chapter. In Bohemia there existed side by side, and even in confrontation, a German middle class and a Czech middle class, which itself comprised a variety of gradations, as in the countries of western Europe. In Hungary where, for the reasons already given, the process of 'denationalization' was more evident and was producing results, the Serb, Slovak and Transylvanian middle classes nevertheless gained in strength. Their political and cultural activity will be described at a later stage.

The formation of the working class posed a problem of a different kind.[13] While there is little difficulty in identifying the mass of wage-earners employed in the great mills as a proletariat, it is much less easy to establish a clear line of demarcation between the working class and the world of the small artisans, the journeymen of small enterprises and all those who, for one reason or another, found themselves attracted by opportunities for promotion to the middle class or bound in solidarity with their middle-class clientele, rather than involved in the great confrontation between capital and the working class. Moreover, the workers were recruited from the least favoured strata of the peasantry (other strata were in the process of forming a peasant social élite, even a rural middle class, a highly characteristic feature of Austro-Hungarian society), and their employment in mills involved migration and transplantation from their natural environment. It was generally recognized that the Czech was a good workman, sober-minded, industrious and honest. His labour was sought in all parts of the Dual Monarchy and he was to be found even in Transylvania. But, naturally, he was most strongly attracted to the industrial regions of northern Bohemia. Czech workers filled the textile mills and ironworks at Reichenberg and Gablonz. Working conditions remained Draconian: low wages, total lack of security of employment, corporal punishment and the disruption of family life caused by the employment of women and young children (children from the age of five were used for unravelling thread). The working class of Austria had to rely for its self-defence on the example and encouragement which it received from the proletariat of neighbouring Germany and, in particular, Saxony. With the creation of the First International in 1864, the meetings of the congress of Eisenach in 1869 and the foundation of the Social Democrat Party by Liebknecht and Engels in 1869, a workers' movement was taking shape in which the Cisleithan proletariat was to play an increasingly important part. This movement was divided into several different elements, one of which was the corporative element, represented by the mutual insurance societies and the production co-operatives. Once again, Germany served as the model, with the Schulze-Delitzsch societies. The rural credit societies established by Dr. Kampelik enjoyed great success in Bohemia. At the same time, the workers and artisans benefited from the development of the co-operatives for production, consumption and credit introduced by a Czech jurist, Dr. Ladislav Chleborad (1839–1911), the brother of a worker. In Prague, in 1868, a large crowd of workers which had assembled on the Žofín (Sophia) island approved the foundation of a production co-operative, the *Oul* ('The Hive'). Chleborad's programme was clear: 'The working class must help itself. We shall go neither with Schulze-Delitzsch nor with Lassalle, but by our own means, with the help of the Czechoslav nation.' This was the principle of *Selbsthilfe* ('self-help') propounded in Vienna by the Austrian socialists, Kessler and Max Menger. But Chleborad's activity was directed towards the particular interests of Czech workers. Since 1867 he had been publishing a Czech newspaper, *Dělník* ('The Worker'), and encouraging the Czech workers of the industrial regions of northern Bohemia in their opposition to their German employers. In his mind, the social question was inextricably interwoven with the national question. He was prepared to maintain, like Rieger, that things could not go well for the working class as long as they did not go well for the nation.

But this was to acknowledge the need to reach an understanding with a paternalist middle class and to admit that the support of the Czech middle class of Prague against the German middle class of Reichenberg could be of greater advantage to the proletariat than the struggle between the classes. Chleborad was to all intents and purposes denouncing German Jewish capitalism as the supreme and immovable enemy and looking to Czech capitalism as a more amenable adversary, if not a partner and ally. The national question apart, this position bore a certain similarity to that of the workers' movement in Lower Austria. In 1867 an imperial law had granted freedom of combination throughout Cisleithania, while prohibiting workers' associations from joining together in leagues or embarking on political action. On 15 December 1867 the first such association, the *Arbeiterbildungsverein*, was founded in Vienna. Many others were soon formed in all parts of the Empire. The law of 1867 proved advantageous to the co-operative societies: in 1871 there existed in Bohemia forty-nine exclusively working-class societies, eight of which were production co-operatives and thirty-six mutual benefit societies. Many members of societies such as the *Arbeiterbildungsverein*, which were organizations for culture and the defence of workers' professional welfare, embraced the cause of socialism. Yet the movement both enjoyed the patronage of the government and attracted the interest of the employers, who considered that it offered possibilities for an amicable understanding with the workers, a means of diverting them from strikes and violent action. It was the danger of absorption by the authorities and the threat to the workers' powers of self-protection that provoked a reaction from those elements committed to Marxist teachings and Social Democracy.

In fact, of these two elements, the disciples of Marx proved less numerous than the champions of Lassalle. Considered both as a whole and in its individual forms of national expression, the working-class movement in the Dual Monarchy bore the stamp of Lassalle rather than of Marx, at least until the congress of Hainfeld (1888). But the followers of Lassalle also opposed the concept of *Selbsthilfe*, which they considered to be tainted with liberalism. They organized workers' demonstrations and, in opposition to the *Arbeiterbildungsverein* or Workers' Cultural Union, founded the *Arbeiterverein* or Workers' Union. They penetrated into Hungary where the *Arbeiterbildungsverein* '*Vorwärts*' had been formed at Bratislava and where, in November 1866, a secret international congress was held.

A socialist newspaper, the *Wiener Arbeiter* ('The Vienna Worker') had been in circulation since 1868. The international socialists were mistrustful of nationalist preoccupations which, by intruding in the class struggle, threatened to undermine its character: 'In the workshops, the workers of the different nationalities work side by side in the same conditions. They are forced to submit to the same economic laws.' Nationalist ambitions, they declared, derived from liberal bourgeois ideology and the workers were urged not to dally with such notions, so that they might be better able to conduct the professional struggle. Strikes multiplied in Austria and in Bohemia, in the Liebig works at Gablonz, and produced results, sometimes in the form of wage increases of 10 per cent. On 13 December 1869 a great demonstration of several thousand workers took place in Vienna on the waste ground of the Paradeplatz, where the Parliament and Rathaus were subsequently built. The demonstrators sent delegates to the ministry of the interior with a petition demanding freedom of association and combination, freedom of the press (i.e. the removal of all remaining restrictions), universal suffrage and the replacement of the regular army by general conscription. In retaliation against this prematurely bold move, the government ordered the dissolution of the workers' unions, which then reorganized themselves as strictly professional unions. Agitation was not, however, allayed. But other factors were involved. The French experience of the Commune —the enthusiasm of the masses, the consternation of the lower and middle bourgeoisie, and the frightful manner of its repression—influenced men's minds in all sectors of society. Paradoxically, it served to strengthen the persuasions of both the radical and the moderate elements of the working class—the radicals assumed an even firmer revolutionary intransigence, while the moderates believed more than ever in the expediency of securing partial but immediate results. The co-operative societies continued to enjoy special favour, because the workers and artisans looked to them for guarantees of security and advancement. The partisans of Lassalle found a wider audience and maintained that, to combat the brazen law of wages and the incapacity of liberal capitalism to resolve the social question, it was essential to ask and, if necessary, insist that the government give its protection to the working class.

The economic crisis of 1873, more direct in its effects than the Commune, brought severe hardship to the workers of the Dual Monarchy. The manufacturers dismissed some of their employees and lowered the wages which they had only recently agreed to raise. Unemployment spread to all parts. In the heavy industry of Transylvania, fifteen thousand workers were dismissed between 1873 and 1879.

Strikes became more frequent and more desperate.[14] The army reappeared on the scene to restore order among the insurgent masses. In June 1875, in the textile industry of northern Bohemia, the workers of forty-two mills withheld their labour. Even if strikes finally brought concessions from the employers, the ringleaders often lost their jobs in the process. During this time of adversity for the working class, the Social Democrat movement did not abandon its activity. It attempted to gather its forces together at the congress of Neudörfl where, of the seventy-four delegates from the whole of Austria-Hungary, ten were Czechs and three Hungarians. Later, at the congress of Wiener-Neustadt, the more reformist resolutions of the congress of Gotha (1875) prevailed over the tradition of Eisenach.

In general, the Lassallian trend, which also proved more successful in Germany, remained stronger than Marxism in Austria-Hungary. Czech historians admit that Marxist ideas were almost unknown among the workers of their nation; the workers' newspaper published in Czech, *Dělnické Listy*, reflected the views of Lassalle. Marxism was disseminated by two young, educated working men: the tailor Ladislav Zapotocký (1852–1917), who translated the works of Engels,[15] and the blacksmith Bohuslav Pečka, who at one time had to emigrate to America. Their newspaper *Budoucnost* ('The Future') propagated scientific socialism. But the Lassallian trend still predominated at the congress held in 1878 at St. Margaret, near Břevnov, where the demands of the 'Czechoslav' workers' group were asserted. The Czech workers had no desire to be forgotten, but they still considered themselves closely bound to their German comrades. The Hungarian workers, after initially associating themselves with the general congresses, began organizing a Workers' Party in their own state (1880); the Slovaks and the Rumanians took part in this movement, for they were not yet able to contemplate independent action and, because of their professional contacts, were closer to their Hungarian fellow-citizens than to their fellow-Slavs of Cisleithania.

Social Democracy as a whole remained divided between those who sought to secure legislation that would reduce working hours, introduce universal suffrage and guarantee the educational rights of the working class, and those who saw illegal, revolutionary action as their sole means of salvation. The situation was all the more troubled during these years because, under the influence of Russian nihilism, anarchist tendencies were appearing which exerted a powerful appeal among certain young people.

The government attempted to alleviate the undeniable aggravation of the working-class problem by a programme of social legislation for which the Germany of Bismarck had already set an example. In 1887 the Imperial Parliament passed a law relating to insurance against industrial accidents and in 1889 a law for insurance against sickness, reforms that placed Austria in advance of many Western countries.

Among other circles of society, the attitude of the liberals who consented on rational grounds, but with reticence, to the intervention of the State in social matters was counterbalanced by a much bolder vision, which was chiefly concerned with the protection of the individual human being, the need to reconcile the Christian ideal with the economic conditions of the time. Christian Socialism was beginning to emerge. Its founder was Baron von Vogelsang, a German by birth who had entered the service of the Liechtensteins, Austrian great lords who had made themselves the princes of a little Alpine state, but who resided mostly in Vienna. A junior prince of the family, Aloys von Liechtenstein, was Vogelsang's collaborator. A younger man than the baron, he carried on and extended his activity. The new movement refused to become a party. At the time of the second *Katholikentag* at Vienna, in 1889, it invited the support of all persons of goodwill independent of political affiliations, urging them to form a Christian-Social (*christlich-sozial*) association for the enlightenment of public opinion. Young men joined the movement with enthusiasm—such as Frederick Piffl and Karl Lueger, who was later to become leader of the Christian Socialist Party, when it was finally organized as such, and also burgomaster of Vienna. The association's influence spread to hitherto conservative circles and even to members of the imperial family.

The immediate result was a renewed idealism in Austrian Catholicism, a clearer view of contemporary problems which was to leave a lasting mark on society and made experiments of outstanding originality possible. It is a pity that this generous endeavour was mingled with a ferment of anti-Semitism, explicable partly by the role played by a great many Jews in the excesses of liberal capitalism, but nonetheless unjustifiable. Like socialism, social Catholicism extended beyond the frontiers of nationalities, but it also had to face the same problem of knowing how to adapt itself to the particular conditions of each national group.

Neither the social policy of the government nor the appearance of a Christian-Social movement halted the revival of Social Democracy. At the congress of Hainfeld in 1888, a major date in its history, the Social Democrat Party adopted a programme which compelled attention by its forcefulness and coherence and heralded the victory of Marxism.

The principles of the class struggle and the objectives of a working class striving for the construction of a socialist world now emerged more clearly and more vigorously than ever before. Social Democracy proclaimed itself an international party recognizing no distinctions of race or country. Without illusions concerning parliamentary government, which it regarded as one of the forms of class domination, it demanded universal suffrage, the separation of Church and State, the secularization of education, the suppression of the army, which it considered one of the permanent causes of the threat of war and which it wished to see replaced by militias, and, in all things, the right of the working class to be defended only by its own qualified representatives.

This massive and constructive programme could not be implemented all at once. Inevitably, some of its proposals were taken up and defended by parties other than the socialists.[16] The congress of Hainfeld had at least resolved the conflict between the partisans of *Selbsthilfe* and the Lassallian champions of *Staatshilfe*, and even the conflict between the moderates and those of anarchist tendencies: it had established Marxist doctrine as the driving force of the working-class movement. The one delicate problem which it had evaded was that of the nationalities. It had been concerned first and foremost with the social revolution. The congress was soon followed by the great mass assemblies of workers, the Labour Days of 1 May 1890 and 1 May 1891. In Vienna, Prague and Budapest, as throughout Europe, people wondered what the morrow would bring. In fact, universal suffrage was an issue which brought the working class the support of a number of young intellectuals and of older people who still remembered 1848. In 1890 a Social Democrat Party was formed in Hungary. Like the Austrian party, it participated in the Second International formed in 1889. Gradually, however, two distinct trends became evident in Austrian Social Democracy. One was led by Victor Adler, intellectually the most outstanding representative of his group, who feared that the fragmentation of nationalities in the Empire of Austria might dissipate the forces of the working class. Adler was also conscious of the special characteristics of this multi-national state, which bore no analogy to the other countries of Europe. Consequently, he maintained the necessity of adapting Marxism to Austria and thus laid the foundations of Austro-Marxism. Such a position presupposed the conservation of the Austrian territorial complex and even of the monarchy itself, not that Adler had been converted to an institution which had issued from the aristocratic and bourgeois order and was associated with the domination of the upper classes, but because the monarchy was an established fact, a necessary condition for the continued existence of a vast economic domain, whereby the working class could best organize its own defence and the acquisition of power by the people. Adler thus became, as he whimsically described himself, the *Hofrat* or 'Court Councillor' of the Revolution. After an interview with him, Francis Joseph, with his very wide experience of things and people, declared without illusions of any kind, but with a certain satisfaction nevertheless: 'He certainly behaved with perfect correctness towards me.' Perhaps the emperor preferred Adler to certain liberals.

The other movement, though by no means wholly contradictory to the first, presented its own distinctive features and sometimes led to widely divergent standpoints. The congress of Brünn in 1899 declared that Austria should be transformed into a democratic state and a federation of nationalities, a programme that in no way conflicted with Austro-Marxism. But the Czech socialists now enjoyed their own individual existence, without severing their association with Austrian Social Democracy. Like the Austrians, they continued to participate in the Second International. Czech Social Democracy sprang into action with the publication of a new newspaper, *Právo Lidu*. It could not associate itself with the middle-class parties, since it remained loyal to the principle of the class struggle. However, under the influence of reformism, other Czech Socialists organized themselves as a national Socialist Party.

Hungarian Social Democracy, the foundation of which owed much to the worker Farkas, preserved its unity and comprised both a Slovak and a Rumanian section. Socialist newspapers appeared in each of the national languages (Serbo-Croat, Slovak and Rumanian) with the purpose of voicing the particular demands of each group and disseminating the Marxist doctrine common to all.

✥

The years 1866 and 1871 brought profound changes in the structure of Europe and in the relationships between the powers. Finally separated from the German Empire and with neither the intention nor the hope of revenge on Prussia, the Austro-Hungarian monarchy was henceforward interested primarily in the Balkan peninsula and the Near East, where its ambition was no longer territorial conquest, but the extension of economic influence.[17]

The Ottoman Empire had survived, a backward power rooted in its institutions, reluctantly tolerated by the Christian populations still under its subjection and compelled to have recourse to Western capital in its first attempts at modernization. For half a century it had been deprived of four states: the kingdom of Greece and the principalities of Serbia, Montenegro and Rumania. The Eastern Question was leading inevitably to a confrontation between Austria-Hungary and Russia. The Balkan peoples were Orthodox and mostly Slav. Constantinople still held an attraction for the tsar, both because of the prestige of the old Eastern Empire and because of the city's strategic position controlling the Straits, which afforded access to the Mediterranean from the Black Sea. In 1871 Russia had secured the abrogation of the clauses in the treaty of Paris (1856) which prohibited her from having naval dockyards in the Black Sea.

But Great Britain, her rival on the route to the Indies, was in no mood to permit Russia to send warships into the Mediterranean. The Balkan question, which involved not only the political organization of the peninsula but also navigation on the Danube, concerned powers other than Russia and Austria-Hungary. It was assuming an international character.

333

In the years immediately following 1871, the chancelleries of Europe were determined not to embark upon adventurous policies, in order to avoid another war. It was essential to maintain the *status quo*—in other words, to preserve the Ottoman Empire and to establish between Russia and Austria-Hungary, both of which would henceforth need to modify their ambitions for power, a reasonable understanding with regard to their respective interests in the East. The result was the meeting between the three emperors (the Tsar Alexander II, the Emperor William I and Francis Joseph) at Berlin in 1872, followed by talks between Alexander II and Francis Joseph at Schönbrunn in 1873 and then at Reichstadt, in Bohemia, in 1876.

Complications arose when the Christian populations of the Balkans revolted against the sultan in Bosnia-Herzegovina, on the threshold of Austria. Serbia went to war in support of its fellow-Slavs and co-religionists, was rapidly defeated, and was then saved by the diplomatic intervention of the powers. But, when the sultan failed to carry out his promises of reform and sent Asian troops against the Bulgarian populations of the northern provinces, Russia used this as a pretext for intervening in the Balkans. After several months of fierce combat the Russian armies, crossing the straits which had delayed them for so long, advanced on Constantinople. At San Stefano the sultan had to accept Draconian terms. A new state was created, a Great Bulgaria stretching from the Black Sea to the Aegean, coinciding roughly with the Orthodox exarchate and embracing Macedonia. It remained under the suzerainty of the Porte, but with a prince nominated by Russia. A Russian protectorate had practically been established over the eastern part of the peninsula, commanding the route between Serbia and Salonika.

Neither Great Britain nor Austria-Hungary could resign themselves to such a situation. The international crisis terminated in the Congress of Berlin (1878), at which Bismarck intervened as a conciliator, anxious to restore a European equilibrium that would be acceptable to all, at least for the time being.

The Ottoman Empire, though diminished in area, was preserved and regained Macedonia. All that remained of Great Bulgaria were the two autonomous but vassal provinces of Bulgaria and Rumelia. The other Balkan states were enlarged: Serbia acquired the region of Nish, Montenegro two ports on the Adriatic, while Rumania received Dobrudja, a barren region which it had to take in exchange for southern Bessarabia, assigned to Russia. But these three states were also granted full independence: Serbia and Rumania were soon to proclaim themselves kingdoms. The Great Powers secured important advantages: Great Britain had established herself in Cyprus and Russia in Bessarabia. The Congress of Berlin entrusted Austria-Hungary with the administration of the two provinces of Bosnia and Herzegovina and the military occupation of the sanjak of Novi-Bazar, wedged between the territories of Serbia and Montenegro.

At the Congress the Austro-Hungarian minister of foreign affairs, Count Julius Andrassy, had once again proved his ability as a negotiator and statesman. On intimate terms with Great Britain, where he had stayed during his exile, and fortified by the goodwill of Disraeli, he had achieved a great diplomatic success for his country. In his own words, he had given Austria-Hungary access to the East, both politically and materially. Nothing could henceforward modify the territorial order of the peninsula without the assent of Austria-Hungary, whose rights of economic penetration were also implicitly recognized. The possibility of the unification of Serbia and Montenegro had been averted and the preservation of Turkey guaranteed, until the latter could be replaced by something better. It was essential to prevent 'large Slav formations where Turkish domination is crumbling in ruin'.

The occupation of Bosnia-Herzegovina offered Austria-Hungary the advantages of annexation without its drawbacks. This hinterland of Dalmatia, an economically primitive mountain region, was inhabited by Slavs—Croats and Serbs, many of the latter descending from Croats who had become Serbs. The Orthodox religion predominated, but there were also Moslems, even among formerly Christian populations. Croatia—and therefore Hungary—continued to invoke ancient historic rights over these provinces. On the other hand, there was nothing to be gained at this stage by increasing the number of Slavs directly subject to the monarchy. Yet it was desirable that business circles should be offered opportunities for investment in this area. The solution was therefore accepted without too much opposition both by the Delegations and the two Parliaments.[18]

The negotiators at the Congress of Berlin had once again applied traditional methods, those adopted by the Congress of Vienna and even by the chancelleries of the eighteenth century. They had directed their attention to the interests of the powers, ignoring the interests of the peoples. Although the religious consciousness of all the Balkan population was clearly defined at this period, their national consciousness remained uncertain. It was awakening nonetheless, founded on an attachment to a legendary past and the hope of a new liberty which foreign propaganda was able to foster. Although she had emerged humiliated and dissatisfied from the Congress of Berlin, Russia still appeared to the Slav populations of the Balkans as a natural protectress, belonging to the same religion and race, related in language, an entity to whom they looked for their emancipation. In Sofia, as a symbol, a statue was erected to Alexander II, the Liberating Tsar.

The Congress had avoided a war in Europe, but had merely transferred to the Balkans the arena of potential conflict and, in particular, the rivalry between Russia and Austria-Hungary. The two powers appeared to reach an understanding on a division of influence, as Joseph II and Catherine II had done in earlier times. But they lacked sincerity, for each attempted to extend its authority in the Balkans to the detriment of the other.

For thirty years, from 1878 to 1908, equilibrium was on the whole maintained by means of agreements between chancelleries.

In Serbia, the native dynasty of the Obrenović reigned. The king, Milan, was a cynical person, corrupt and venal, who thought primarily of his own interests. He had married the daughter of a Russian officer, the beautiful Queen Natalya. But he had made an alliance with the Dual Monarchy. He could hardly have done otherwise at this period, for Serbia found itself bound by close economic ties with Austria-Hungary, selling agricultural produce and buying in return the majority of its manufactured goods. Serbia's loans inevitably came via the Stock Exchange at Vienna.

In Rumania, the situation was different. The sovereign, Charles I, a Catholic prince of the House of Hohenzollern-Sigmaringen, was a cultured man and a prudent politician. The aristocracy, of both native and Phanariot origin, and the humanist élite of the middle class showed to great advantage in international relations. In 1883 Rumania also concluded an alliance with Austria-Hungary and Germany, thereby creating a barrier between Russia and her principal dependency, Bulgaria. The two provinces of Bulgaria and Rumelia were to remain aloof from this alignment: they united and their successive princes, the vassals of the Sultan, alternated between Austrian and Russian protection.

The international situation in the Balkans depended chiefly on the great powers. On his western frontier Bismarck was disturbed by France's desire for revenge and feared a *rapprochement* between France and Russia. On 9 October 1879 he concluded with Austria-Hungary a treaty which represented the foundation-stone of the system of alliances that was to evolve in Europe during the next forty-five years. The alliance was defensive, providing for the possibility of one of the two powers being attacked by Russia, and it contained a promise of benevolent neutrality in the event of attack by another power.

In the opinion of Andrassy, this was sufficient to protect the Dual Monarchy against the threats of Russia, which would not risk an aggressive policy in the Balkans if she knew that she would thereby run the hazard of a war with Germany. At Germany's request, the Dual Alliance was then extended to include Italy. Bismarck did not intend that this system should cause a rupture with Russia, with which he renewed what he called the treaty of 'Reinsurance'. But Russia could not look without misgivings on the bloc formed by the Triple Alliance and the two Balkan allies of Austria-Hungary. She was Great Britain's rival on the route to the Indies. In western Europe, France found herself isolated, without allies.

In spite of the different political regimes of republican, petty-bourgeois France and autocratic Russia, the Franco-Russian *rapprochement* was the logical answer to the Triple Alliance. Thus, Europe saw the emergence of two opposing systems of alliances which, though political in origin, were to be rendered even more acutely antagonistic by the growth of large-scale capitalism.

In the view of Bismarck, the alliance with Austria-Hungary, founded on very positive motives, implied the abandonment of all propaganda favouring the union of all Germans in a single Empire. Henceforth, the Reich of the Hohenzollerns would have to respect the territorial integrity of its ally. It needed to be able to rely, in the event of war, on the support of the Austro-Hungarian army, which had been well organized through the efforts of the emperor, the Archduke Albert and the minister, Kuhn. The cohesion of this army depended on internal peace within the Empire. The Pan-Germanists, both in Germany and in Austria (the Schönerer movement), tried to spread their propaganda, but to no avail: people would not listen to them. It was even in Germany's interests that the political life of Austria should be as smooth as possible, so that the system might operate effectively. Thus, in spite of vicissitudes, the alliance between the two states was to be preserved until the war of 1914, in which they were jointly involved, and their collapse in 1918. By the force of circumstances, this alliance exerted a profound influence on the destinies and the way of life of the populations of the Dual Monarchy. By virtue of the juxtaposition of frontiers, the common language which Germany shared with a large part of Austria, and frequent economic exchange, it created something new which western Europe began to describe as 'the Central Empires', as if these states really constituted a single bloc. At the government level, the alliance brought more frequent contacts between military chiefs and statesmen. In Vienna, especially, but also in many other cities, it accustomed public opinion to look on Germany as a country from which manufactured products, technical processes, ways of life, information, arts and ideas were more readily accepted than from other countries. Under the semblance of providing the Dual Monarchy with security against Pan-Slavism and indirectly against Pan-Germanism, it promoted the infiltration of Germanic culture.

In the Austria of the closing nineteenth century, Germany thus assumed a place comparable with that occupied by Italy during the Baroque period. There can be no doubt that the whole of Austrian society now acquired a distinctive Germanic imprint. The non-Germanic nations did not escape the influence, at least not in the outward aspects of daily life. But they reacted all the more strongly in asserting their spiritual independence, their Slav or Latin character, with the result that the German alliance, by a recoil effect, also contributed to the disassociation of Austrian consciousness.

Relations with the Latin countries did little to counterbalance this Germanic offensive. The political alliance with Italy aroused many misgivings among Italians, for the memory of Austrian domination had not been extinguished. With the growth of nationalism and then the Irredentist movement, the Italians were primarily concerned with the welfare of those of their compatriots who lived in the Austrian Empire—in the Trentino and the southern Tyrol, along the Adriatic coast and Dalmatia, formerly a territory of the Venetian Republic. Contacts with France became less frequent. Whereas, after Sadova, circumstances had seemed propitious for an alliance between Austria-Hungary and France, the Triple Alliance had now placed Austria-Hungary in the same camp as France's principal adversary, the German Reich. Although France had not lost her prestige in public opinion, although the knowledge of the French language was still widespread in high society and in certain middle-class circles, and although French assumed the status of a second modern language in secondary schools (the *Lyzeen* and the *Real-gymnasien*), opportunities for interchange and personal meetings between the two countries became less frequent. The obstacle of distance was exaggerated by both sides, as prejudice and ignorance accumulated. Sometimes, a new fellow-feeling manifested itself—especially between French and Slavs—in reaction against the Germans, but a real understanding of situations became increasingly difficult.

Thus, the alliance with Germany, the effects of which extended far beyond its immediate political character, in a less easily definable and therefore more danger-ous manner, weighed heavily on the destinies of the Danubian peoples between 1879 and 1914.[19]

Relations with Russia remained stable until the end of the century. However, with the gradual evolution of industrial economy and the formation, both within the monarchy and in the Balkan states, of new middle classes whose financial interests lay in commercial competition, prestige was no longer the only cause of rivalries and the threat of war became more distinct. Neither Russia nor Austria–Hungary felt itself yet able to run the risk of conflict. By the agreements of 1897 and 1903, the two powers reaffirmed their balance of influence in the Balkans and their common interest in the preservation of Turkey. But for how long could they prevent the explosion of national forces in the little states of the peninsula?

The conclusion of the Dual Alliance and the return to economic prosperity were followed by a certain alleviation of internal strife in Austria and Hungary. In Hungary, it remained to put the Compromise into effect and to establish a modern administration. From 1875, this was the task facing the liberal government of Kálmán Tisza, which brought influence to bear upon the Hungarian Parliament by methods rather similar to those employed by Guizot in France and which consisted of securing a majority favourable to the government by means of favours judiciously bestowed. In Austria, a liberal experiment had been sustained since 1867, interrupted only by the Hohenwart ministry and its ill-starred attempt to reach an understanding with the Czechs. Paradoxically, the ministries known as the 'bourgeois ministries' were led by German lords of Bohemia, the Auersperg brothers. Their anti-clerical policy brought conflict with the Vatican and disturbed a large proportion of the population.[20] On the other hand, the liberals found difficulty in accepting Andrassy's foreign policy, which was too venturesome for their liking and involved a grave risk of war with Russia. They accused him of following the initiative of the Crown to the prejudice of Parliament and of burdening the budget with military expenditure.

The Germans of Austria by no means formed a unanimous body of opinion. The party 'loyal to the constitution' (*Verfassungstreu*) insisted that it was not a National German Party, but that it thought only of the higher interests of the Empire. It remained open to all and considered it dangerous to allow national questions to occupy the forefront of general policy. But other Germans, led by Schönerer, a landowner of the Waldviertel (a region of Upper Austria), were fomenting a passionate Germanic fervour among their compatriots. They wanted union with the German Empire and attacked the conservative elements in Austria, in particular the Catholic Church, which they denounced as an international force hostile to German interests.

Their attitude gave Francis Joseph yet another reason for desiring a *rapprochement* with the Czechs, whose return to the Austrian Parliament could re-establish a conservative majority there. The Moravians had already agreed to return to the Reichsrat, in 1874. The Old Czechs then consented to attend (1879) and to give their support to the Taaffe ministry, which enjoyed the personal confidence of the emperor. One member of their party, Dr. Pražák, a Moravian, was appointed a minister without portfolio, which made him the minister responsible for Bohemia, just as the cabinet also included a Polish minister for Galicia.[21]

How should the Czechs' reappearance at the Parliament be interpreted? Were they renouncing their state rights? Rieger had asserted those rights as an inviolable principle and Prince Charles Schwarzenberg, at the Bohemian Diet, had declared in a celebrated phrase that they would defend state rights even at the sacrifice of their heads and possessions. The Czechs were thus persevering in their demands, but they deemed it expedient to show less insistence for the time being. They thought that, by giving the sovereign the support which he was seeking, they would secure concrete advantages for the Czech nation and restore it to an active role in the political life of the Empire. Palacký had died in 1876, honoured by the entire Czech people as the father of the nation. Rieger was more closely associated with conservative circles, but was more familiar with parliamentary tactics. The Old Czech Party, of which he was leader, enjoyed a wider audience (especially in the provinces) than the liberal Young Czech Party, headed by Sladkowský and Gregr, the editor of the great Prague newspaper *Národní Listy*. Rieger was no longer a young man; disappointments had dampened his fighting ardour, but not his courage. An eloquent and moving orator, he believed that he could convince Parliament by persuasion and obtain substantial concessions for his country.

His most important achievement was to secure the creation in Prague of a separate Czech university in which the Czech language alone would be used for teaching purposes (1882). This was, without doubt, a very great victory. The old Charles University thus found itself divided in two, since the German university continued to exist. It was predicted that the Czechs would not be able to fill all the professorial chairs at their university, because they would not find enough Czech-speaking specialists. It was also feared that the new university would become the platform for an exasperated chauvinism. It was for this reason that the historian Gindely, whose Czech patriotism cannot be called in question, but who subscribed to the *Gesamtösterreich* idea, preferred to end his teaching days at the German university.[22]

The critics were proved wrong in both respects. The professorial chairs were filled. After some hesitation, a young *privat-docent* of Vienna, Thomas G. Masaryk, encouraged by his American wife, accepted the chair of philosophy in the hope of being able to lead student youth towards an ideal of liberty and justice. He soon gave proof of his independent and critical mind, attacking prejudices and commonly accepted ideas. He was no philologist and it was not he who discovered that the manuscripts of Hanka were fakes. But he gave space in his review *Athenaeum* to the articles of his colleague Gebauer, who was responsible for the discovery, and he defended the rights of truth scientifically established by proof. Masaryk remained insensible to calumny and resisted Rieger, who opposed the new interpretation of the manuscripts and invoked the memory of Palacký, who had believed in their authenticity.

The Czech university of Prague became the training-ground where the new critical methods were taught to a liberal generation that found itself broadly in sympathy with the Young Czech Party, provided that the latter showed a greater awareness of the problems of the day. Masaryk posed the Czech question in a new manner. He saw the true meaning, the 'logos', of the national tradition in Hussitism, the spirit of the United Brethren, the philosophy of Enlightenment and Protestantism. He wrote that politics were 'a matter of great importance for the nations, but not by any means the most important: their first and foremost concern must be spiritual politics, the intellectual and moral progress of society'. He took an interest in the social question which, he maintained, was linked with the Czech question. 'Which of you, if his son should ask for bread, would give him stones—and yet we are giving stones to the working class, in literature, in philosophy, in theology and in politics.' Masaryk admitted that Social Democracy regarded Marx as an incontestable authority and that he found this regrettable, for he felt he had no right to spurn proposals for justice and equity from whatever direction they might come. He even ventured to suggest that the 'Social Catholics' appeared to show a clearer appreciation of the social question than the Old Czechs and the Young Czechs. Finally, it was his view that the struggle between the Germans and the government should not be allowed to dominate the entire field of national politics. But his ideas seemed to be merely the theories of a professor: his time had not yet come. Public opinion showed a much keener interest in the debates at the Reichsrat.[23]

Since the local Diets had not been authorized—by the restoration of state rights—to settle the problems of the nationalities, the responsibility for resolving those problems fell upon the Parliament. The Czechs demanded guarantees for their fellow-countrymen in courts, in schools and in the general administration of Bohemia. The Taaffe government did not oppose their demands. But it would be necessary either for judges and officials to speak both languages, or for Bohemia to be divided into Czech districts, German districts and, where both groups lived in the same area, bilingual districts. In the Parliament the Germans—the Austrian deputies reinforcing the Bohemian Germans—rejected legislation which they deemed prejudicial to the Germanic group. The Czechs refused to approve measures which, by carving up their historic territory, would have destroyed the unity of the kingdom. All decision-making was blocked by competition for electoral popularity: the deputies were afraid of discrediting themselves in the eyes of their constituents by accepting compromises that would have been condemned as surrender. The constitutional and parliamentary system proved, in its functioning, fundamentally powerless to solve the situation. Without tracing in detail the passionate struggles that took place in the Reichsrat and at the Diet of Bohemia, it should be recalled that the battle for the rights of languages in Bohemia assumed an almost unbelievable importance in the public life of the Empire during the next twenty years, increasing in intensity from one legislature to another. The ordinances of the government were rejected or sabotaged. No sooner had the Old Czechs succeeded in coming to terms with the more reasonable Germans of Bohemia, in accordance with the wishes of the emperor, whom Rieger was anxious to satisfy, than the elections of 1891, held on this very issue, gave a majority to their opponents. The Young Czechs repudiated the agreement. But they proved no more able to achieve results.[24] In 1897 the Austrian prime minister, Count Badeni, formerly governor of Galicia and a Pole, put forward what was probably the most intelligent solution: all officials in Bohemia were to be obliged to have a knowledge of both languages. This could be interpreted as an indirect means of granting implicit satisfaction to the demand for state rights, since a single system of language was provided for the entire kingdom. But it rapidly became evident to what extent ethnic passions prevailed over historic memories, simple reason and clearly-perceived interests. The two groups clashed, both in the Parliament and at the Diet of Bohemia. The violence passed into the streets, as the phantoms of Pan-Slavism and Pan-Germanism were raised one against the other. Insults were hurled at the Czech people from Germany, by the great historian Mommsen, to whom the young historian Pekař replied in kind. The emperor had to suspend the parliamentary assemblies by invoking Article 14. The time had come for the economic agreement with Hungary to be renewed. But the Hungarians refused to take part in talks if, by the terms of the constitution, their only partners were to be the delegates of the Austrian Parliament. The ordinances had to be withdrawn and the Czechs sacrificed to the stability of the Empire.[25] The Czechs reacted violently but were then appeased, when the Young Czech leader, Karel Kramař, established his influence in the Parliament. Two Czechs, Dr. Kaizl and Dr. Albin Bráf, Rieger's son-in-law, were appointed ministers of finance in Austrian cabinets. However, the loyalty of the nation had been deeply hurt: prosperity could not induce the Czechs to forget their wounded patriotism and the injustice which they had suffered.

It so happened—fortunately for the peoples of the monarchy, who in their every-day existence gave more attention to their work than to the tumult of public life—that the periods of dissension and obstruction in the Hungarian Parliament and in the Austrian Parliament did not coincide. At the time of Badeni's ordinances, the Hungarians had recovered tranquillity after many troubled moments. The public was preoccupied with the celebration of Hungary's millenary (1896): the king and, in particular, the well-loved queen enjoyed a renewal of popularity.

❦

Hungary was confronted with two problems rather different from those of Cis-leithania: state rights and the nationalities.

The Compromise had recognized the state rights and independence of the kingdom. As far as state rights were concerned, the agreement concluded in 1868 with the Croats merely represented a concession by Hungary to a weaker country and involved no infringement of that principle. But, although there no longer existed any political authority above the Hungarian Parliament, there remained the 'common' army over which Francis Joseph, in his dual capacity of king-emperor, exercised command and which was seen as something exterior and even superior to Transleithan institutions, something over which the Hungarians did not have full control. The partisans of the Compromise resigned themselves to this situation. They were convinced that Hungary derived important advantages from its association with Austria, both in its military defence and in its economic development. This was the view of Deák and of Count Andrassy. The younger generation claimed that it could see further ahead. It found its spokesman in Count Albert

Apponyi (1846–1926), highly intelligent and a fervent, disinterested patriot who devoted his talents, fortune and whole-hearted energies to his country and who, as an old man, so nobly defended a vanquished and mutilated Hungary before the League of Nations. In the full vigour of his youth, Apponyi wished to assure his country a greater role in the Dual Monarchy and reproached the Tisza ministry with making too many sacrifices to Austria.[26]

Officers and soldiers had to swear an oath of personal fidelity to the king-emperor, the army's flags and insignia remained those of tradition and the language of command was German (except in the Hungarian reserve, the *honvéd*, which was poorly equipped). The Hungarian officers of the various imperial regiments thus had to speak in a foreign language. Most important of all, Hungarian recruits, instead of receiving a training that would strengthen their national consciousness, were learning to serve a territory much vaster than the kingdom of Hungary. In other words, Great Austria survived in and through the army. It was also true that the army chiefs—especially the Archduke Albert, who was the faithful soldier *par excellence* and had carefully reorganized Austria's military forces—remained too conscious of the memory of what they called the 'rebellion' of 1848 and sought to foster a supranational spirit among the troops. They imposed a constant check on all manifestations of Hungarian particularism and deliberately neglected the *honvéd*. The emperor looked on the army as the very foundation of the strength of his states, the institution that bound him more closely to all his peoples without distinction and, in turn, bound his peoples to his own person.

The demands of the Hungarian opposition led to a conflict with the sovereign. The debates on the military laws at the Hungarian Parliament (the mobilization of Hungarian contingents and the military budget) gave rise to some stormy sessions; it was in connection with these laws that the Crown Prince Rudolf had given his support to the opposition deputies a few days before his suicide.[27] Owing to the army question and the problem of national sovereignty which had been raised, the last years of the Tisza government proved fraught with difficulties (1886–90).

Yet Tisza made every effort to make his country economically stronger and more Hungarian. He encouraged the development of industry and commerce in all regions. It was even said that, since the partisans of Kossuth were to be found largely in the central plain, which was predominantly Magyar, Tisza looked for political support in the mountainous regions of the perimeter, where the non-Magyar nationalities lived. Yet, while he assisted the middle classes in their material success, he offended their patriotism, for he used the administrative system to 'Magyarize' them. It was considered essential that Hungary should be truly 'national', which she could not possibly be if too great an autonomy were granted to the individual nationalities. The claims of the national groups were regarded as a challenge to the integrity of the kingdom, a sign of treason. In view of the excessively imperious attitude of the Hungarian government, the leaders of the nationalities once again turned to Vienna and sought the protection of the emperor against the government of the king.

In 1892 a delegation of three hundred Rumanians of Transylvania appeared before Francis Joseph with a memorandum which he was to pass on to his minister for Hungary. Their action resulted in a dramatic high-treason trial. Nevertheless, the government had to allow the gathering in Budapest, in 1895, of a congress of nationalities (Serbs, Slovaks, Rumanians and Germans) whose programme comprised full freedom of expression for non-Magyar citizens, the use of the language of nationality in the comitats, the modification of the law of 1868, autonomy in education and religion, the right to combine in trade unions and leagues, universal suffrage and the secret ballot. At the time, there could be no question of making such far-reaching concessions. The millenary celebrations served as a diversion. In Austria, the economic agreement with Hungary was prorogued and the fear of not being able to renew it legally induced the opposition to moderate their demands. For some time the political structure of Austria-Hungary seemed to have been consolidated. The Hungarians accepted an increase in their quota of common expenditure, which was raised to 34·4 per cent. In return they obtained satisfaction on one important point. A number of common articles—beer, sugar, alcohol—had been subject to a consumption tax, the yield from which had reverted to the producer country. Austria had benefited more than Hungary from this arrangement and the Hungarians objected to paying a tax to the brewers of Vienna. Henceforth, the proceeds of the tax were assigned to the consumer country. However, the 'Party of Independence and 1848', founded in 1884 and which was later to be associated with the name of Kossuth's son, was making even more pressing demands over the military question. It even went so far as to insist that the officers of Hungarian regiments should all be able to speak Magyar, that the regiments should be billeted in Hungary itself, that Magyar should be made the language of command and, finally, that the military oath taken by Hungarian soldiers should be sworn to the Hungarian constitution. This amounted to a demand for an autonomous Hungarian army within the Imperial and Royal Army, whose supranational character would thus have been destroyed. Since an independent state bank was also being demanded and the possibility of a tariff barrier between the two countries was envisaged, the very principle of Dualism was at stake. The presence of the same sovereign at the head of each state would then have maintained a purely personal union between Austria and Hungary.

Francis Joseph could not give his consent. During the manoeuvres of September 1903, in the order of the day at Chlopy, he spoke as commander-in-chief: 'Common and one, as it now is, my army must remain, the solid force which defends the Austro-Hungarian monarchy against all enemies. Loyal to its oath, my entire army must continue on its way, fulfilling the most sacred of duties and imbued with a spirit of unity and harmony that respects national individuality and enables the qualities of each people [*Volkstamm*] to serve the good of the great whole.'

Not everyone was convinced that Hungary, because of its economic backwardness, which was to persist for several more years despite the rapid rate of progress, would not benefit by remaining within the vast economic complex of the Danubian monarchy. The 'common' state bank, in which Hungary was playing an increasingly important role, probably guaranteed the country greater discount facilities than a national bank, which would have been more limited in scope. Moreover, the autonomy of Hungary was affirmed by the existence of a separate currency, identical in value to the Austrian currency, and postage-stamps bearing an inscription in Magyar and the effigy of the king, wearing the crown of St. Stephen. But the question of the nationalities continued to present an obstacle to the regular and harmonious life of the country.[28]

In 1880 the Magyars formed 41·2 per cent of the population of the kingdom. As a result of the attractions which emigration offered to the rising classes and to Jewish businessmen, the proportion of Magyars had increased to 48·1 per cent by 1910, but this was still less than half the total population.[29] It is difficult to establish to what extent the middle classes of the different nationalities—Croats, Serbs, Slovaks and Rumanians—benefited from the incontestable growth of the economy, indicated by an increase of 120 per cent in the industrial production of Hungary between 1890 and 1913. The determination of the government to spread the Magyar language by enforcing its use in all schools and churches (without, however, suppressing the national languages) was resisted by the middle classes through their newspapers, their schools, their economic institutions (the Tatra Bank, founded in 1885, and the building societies) and in activities such as the exhibition of Slovak embroidery held at Turčánský Svatý Martin in 1887. Rivalry was fierce. In Croatia, Mgr. Strossmayer remained the great national figure until his death in 1895. His academy maintained intellectual contacts among all southern Slavs: Serbs, Croats, Dalmatians and even Slovenes. He was a champion of ecumenism and endeavoured to bring Catholics and Orthodox to consider those aspects of faith and liturgy which their Churches possessed in common, instead of thinking only of their ancient quarrels and the differences which separated them. On the other hand, the Hungarian governors of Croatia were fomenting rivalry between Serbs and Croats by favouring the Serbs. The Croat partisans of state rights (led by Starcevié) spoke of the restoration of the old kingdom of Croatia-Slavonia-Dalmatia and looked to Vienna for support, which Vienna would not grant them for fear of aggravating its difficulties with Hungary and weakening the Compromise. But the new, more democratic elements were in favour of taking advantage of a national programme and of existing circumstances, rather than remaining the prisoners of a historic tradition. Such was the tenor of the agreement reached at Fiume, in October 1905, when deputies from Dalmatia and the Küstenland (Trieste, Istria and Goritz)—in other words Cisleithans—made contact with Croats. They asserted the right of every nation to dispose freely of its own destiny. They were then joined by Serbs (the Declaration of Zara). Communication was established with the Hungarian Party of Independence. The intention was to make a common stand against the government in Budapest and the defenders of the Compromise. But the movement was led by intellectuals and a newly-rich middle class who concealed neither their hostility to ancient social traditions nor their anti-clericalism. Consequently, its influence was limited in Croatia, a Catholic country. Neither the advocates of state rights (led by Josip Frank after the death of Starcevié) nor the champions of peasant interests (the Radié group) joined the movement.

In Slovakia, the national cause received support from the Czechs. It was easy to invoke the intimate spiritual union that had existed, as has already been seen, between the Czechs and the Slovak Protestants in the comitats of Upper Hungary. But to associate the two movements more closely, to consider Czechs and Slovaks as a single people, proved less easy. Above all, if the Czechs were defending their own state rights, they could hardly attack those same rights in Hungary. The only persons in a position to do so were those who regarded the present wishes of the national group as more important than historic rights. Such was the standpoint of Professor Masaryk, who had not forgotten that he was of Slovak descent on his father's side. Masaryk made a habit of spending holidays in Slovakia in order to observe the state of mind and customs of the population, especially its lowliest strata, the people who represented the repository of the nation. His influence made itself felt among the intellectuals. The Slovak middle classes of Pozsony and of the other towns were determined to fight against Magyarization, but they continued to give their votes to those Hungarian parties (including the Catholic party of Count Zichy, founded in 1896) which offered them the greatest guarantees. At the same time, they sought an *entente* with the Rumanians of Transylvania.[30]

Although Transylvania remained a predominantly agricultural country (69·3 per cent of the population was still employed in agriculture) and, in certain districts, a very poor country (hence the departure of large numbers of emigrants), industrialization was advancing with rapid strides. Between 1900 and 1910 the number of firms rose from 477 to 791, under the stimulus of the Hungarian law for the promotion of industry. Even if industrial consolidation was accomplished with the aid of foreign capital and proved of greatest benefit to the large banks of Austria and Hungary, the number of banks and deposit-houses in Transylvania rose from 285 in 1899 to 463 in 1909. This economic advance proved favourable to the progress of intellectual circles—the lawyers, doctors and journalists. Admittedly, the Rumanians of Transylvania had not succeeded in obtaining complete control of the university of Cluj, where a chair of Rumanian existed, but they were benefiting from the intellectual progress of neighbouring Rumania and the activity of the Cultural League (*Liga culturala*). After the years of passivity that had followed the treason trial, the Transylvanians agreed to reappear at the Budapest Parliament. But the deputies of their national party found themselves in a small minority. They therefore joined with their Serb and Slovak colleagues to present their claims in unison. At least, on 28 July 1906 their leader, Julius Maniu, declared: 'The preservation of Hungary and of the Austro-Hungarian monarchy in general is a political and international necessity, for the Rumanians no less than for the Hungarians.' The hand of friendship had been proffered.[31]

Nevertheless, at the turn of the century, independent and shrewd minds were wondering if Dualism was still compatible with the preservation and development of Austria-Hungary. Was it not necessary, for the welfare of all, that a solution other than a dual centralism should be found for the problem of the nationalities?

Even in Austria the librarian of the Parliament, Karl Renner, published in 1902, under the pseudonym of Rudolf Springer, a study entitled *The Struggle of the Austrian Nation for the State* (*Der Kampf der Österreichischen Nation um den Staat*). Analysing the concepts of nation and state from a socialist viewpoint, he came to the conclusion that it was necessary to dissociate the national idea and the historicoterritorial idea. The monarchy should be safeguarded, but transformed into a federation of territories each of which would coincide with the area inhabited by a nationality and would enjoy administrative autonomy. But the right of belonging to a nationality was a personal right of man, as sacred as the right of choice in politics or religion. Owing to the migrations that resulted from industrialization, many citizens of the Empire found themselves separated from the territory of their nationality; they could not, however, be dispensed from the obligation of defending their nationality's cause, especially in cultural matters. The system proposed by Renner was two-dimensional: there would be a cadastral record of nationalities in which everyone would be registered, whatever his place of residence; each citizen would participate, by his votes, both in the administration of a territory and in the defence of a nationality. Thus, in an Empire that would continue to possess common institutions for general policy and the economy of the whole, the formidable contradiction between living on a territory and belonging to a nationality would be surmounted.

In 1903 a young French teacher, Louis Eisenmann, a jurist and *agrégé* in history, an expert on central Europe where he had studied, presented to the Faculty of Law at Dijon a thesis that proved to be a work of a powerful originality. A thorough critical analysis of the Compromise led him to the conclusion that a transformation of the system was desirable. He looked above all to the Hungarians to effect this transformation, because of their experience of representative institutions, but on condition that the aristocratic regime, in which the franchise depended on a tax-qualification, evolved into a truly democratic system and the spirit of chauvinism was tempered to allow a genuine understanding with the nationalities. Dualism would cease to be a dual centralism. Though socialist in his sympathies, Louis Eisenmann accepted the preservation of the monarchy. But what he desired was a 'monarchic Switzerland'. 'If this were to prove impossible, it would be a pity for Austria-Hungary and perhaps also for Europe.' During these years, when the imperialism of the great powers was reviving the danger of war, Eisenmann felt the necessity of appealing to the peoples against the military castes. He envisaged a United States of Europe, for which an equitable transformation of Austria-Hungary would provide a model worthy of imitation.[32]

No less significant was the title of a work published in 1906 by an intellectual of Transylvania, Aurel C. Popovici: *Die Vereinigten Staaten von Gross Österreich* ('The United States of Greater Austria'). Steeped in the foreign political thought of the last century (he quoted Sismondi frequently), heedful of the example of America and familiar with all that had been written on this subject in the Dual Monarchy, Aurel Popovici also put forward a federalist solution, but of a new kind.

Sacrificing the state rights of Hungary and Bohemia, he recommended the division of the Austrian complex into fifteen national territories, according to the numerical preponderance of the respective nationalities. Thus there would be a German Austria (absorbing the Tyrol and a part of southern Bohemia), a German Bohemia, a German Moravia (the north of the margraviate), a Bohemia embracing central Bohemia and the rest of Moravia, a Slovakia including Pressburg, a western Galicia including Cracow (and therefore Polish), an eastern Galicia (Ruthenian), a Hungary reduced to the Magyar-populated region, but larger than the Hungary created by the treaty of Trianon, a Transylvania repossessed of Bukovina, but with a Szekel territory to the east, a Vojvodina occupying the territory of the old Military Frontier, a Croatia enlarged by the addition of Dalmatia, a Slovene Carniola, a region of Trieste and an Italian Trentino. Naturally, enclaves of foreign minorities would continue to exist within these new territorial formations. But Popovici refused to allow the existence of such minorities to constitute an obstacle to a rational reconstruction of Great Austria. A small minority enclosed within a territory of a different language did not represent a true nationality, but merely a 'fragment' (*Bruchstück*), a 'splinter' (*Splitter*). To claim rights of autonomy for these minorities would be to make a mockery of the very concept of nationality. Each national territory would enjoy autonomy of administration and language. It would be represented at an Imperial Council responsible for the common affairs of the federation. The language of communication in the Empire would be German, which was to be the official language of the central departments in Vienna, the language of the Parliament (where the deputies could also use their national tongue) and, finally, the language for administrative correspondence between the different territories and in their official relations with the imperial government.

In the conclusion of his work, Aurel Popovici asserted the necessity of preserving the Danubian monarchy at all costs and of preventing its dislocation. 'Time is pressing,' he wrote; 'all the peoples are in the Austrian camp [*im Lager Österreich*, the phrase used by Grillparzer] and they are counting on their deliverance from the dualist yoke, on a liberating act by their emperor. This is an historic moment and will decide for evermore. The Empire of the Habsburgs must live or disappear. Good can still be accomplished, all can be saved. But it is now or never!'[33]

These various works have been criticized as Utopias, as fantasies contrived by intellectuals and professors. The solutions which they proposed inevitably called for many modifications of detail. The map drawn up by Popovici showed an alarming misappreciation of Czech feeling in Bohemia. But the real importance of these works lay in the testimony borne by men whose generation coincided rather curiously with the years of the Compromise (Popovici was born in 1863, Eisenmann in 1869 and Renner in 1870) and who all observed the rapid obsolescence of the Danubian system, a system no longer compatible with a society in which the accelerating growth of capitalist industry had brought far-reaching changes and such a strong consciousness among nationalities, both historic and new, that dual centralism appeared difficult to maintain. Like absolutism in the 1860s, it needed to be replaced in its turn. Did the Danubian monarchy possess the internal strength necessary to effect another such transformation?

NOTES

1. The Vienna Parliament was built between 1873 and 1883 by Theophil Hansen and the Budapest Parliament between 1883 and 1902 by E. Steindl.
2. The Emperor Charles VI was the third king of Hungary to bear this Christian name.

3. For details concerning the constitutions, see Hellbling, Kapras and Marczali, op. cit.; for Poland, R. A. Kann (an excellent chapter on the Polish question, vol. I, p. 214 *et seq.*), who on p. 229 quotes the comment of the deputy Wojciech Dzieduszycki (1883): 'The hunted stag has found his refuge in Austria.' The most recent study of the Polish administration is that of the Polish historian Klement Grzylowski, *Galicja 1848–1914*, Cracow, 1959.

4. *Brève histoire de la Transylvanie*, p. 277.

5. In the novel by the Czech author Julius Zeyer (1840–1902), the hero, a naval officer leaves the service after fighting a duel with a comrade in the land army who had been denigrating Prague. It might seem strange that a Czech should have chosen the navy as his career.

6. The publications of the Österreichische Statistik give the necessary information for all sectors: for example, analyses of each decennial census. *Die Ergebuisse der Volkszählung* (1880, 1890, 1900, 1910). For Bohemia, see the works (in German) of Professor H. Rauchberg (German University of Prague), *Der nationale Besitzstand in Böhmen*, 3 vols., 1905, and (in Czech) of A. Boháč, J. Auerhahn and especially L. Kárníková, *Vyvoj obyvatelstva v českých zemích 1754–1914* ('The Growth of the Population in the Czech Lands 1754–1914'), Prague, 1965; this latter work provides some highly significant tables and graphs and a penetrating study of Czech emigration to Vienna (p. 212), with a table indicating the districts around Vienna where the Czechs were to be found in large numbers (Hietzing, Korneuburg, Floridsdorf and Mödling) and also the rival trend of emigration to Germany from 1890 onwards. L. Kárníková shows how, after the agricultural crisis, the populations of southern Bohemia were drawn towards the capital.

7. 'Lasst mir meine Böhm' in Ruh' ', quoted by J. de Bourgoing, *Andere Zeit*, p. 291.

8. These figures are given by J. Purš in *Průmyslová revoluce v českých zemích* ('The Industrial Revolution in the Czech Lands'), Prague, 1960, p. 110.

9. Zöllner, op. cit., p. 453.

10. In the collection *Studien zur Geschichte der Österreichisch-Ungarischen Monarchie*, Budapest, 1961, there is an interesting article by V. Sándor, *Der Charakter der Abhängigkeit Ungarns im Zeitalter des Dualismus*, from which these figures are taken (p. 321).

11. Ibid., article by T. I. Berend and Ránki, *Das Niveau der Industrie Ungarns zu Beginn des 20 Jahrhunderts in Vergleich zu dem Europas*, p. 267, where the authors maintain that at this time the industrial development of Hungary, considered apart, was comparable with that of Italy.

12. It should be remembered that in 1892 Austria adopted the gold standard for the Austrian crown, the value of which was one half-florin.

13. Over the past twenty years a large number of books have been written on socialism in the lands of Austria-Hungary: Hubert Steiner, *Die Arbeitbewegung Österreichs 1867–1889*, Vienna, 1962, and *Bibliographie zur Geschichte der österreichischen Arbeitbewegung 1867–1918*, Vienna, 1962; Ludwig Brügel, *Geschichte der österreichischen Sozialdemokratie*, Vienna, 1922; F. Strohl, *Lehrheft zur Geschichte der österreichischen Arbeitbewegung*, Vienna, 1952.

   For Bohemia and Czech socialism: A. Horáček, *Počátky českého hnutí dělnického* ('The Beginnings of the Workers' Movement'), 1933; A. Klíma, *Počátky českého dělnického hnutí*, which a Russian historian, Rattner, reviewed in *Voprosy istorii*, January 1949, p. 135; R. Polin and J. G. Charon, *Les coopératives rurales et l'État en Tchéchoslovaquie et la Roumanie*, 1934; V. Husa, *Dějiny Československa*. There is much of interest in *Přehled Československ'ych dějin* ('Outline of Czechoslovak History'), I, II and III. Consult also *Twenty-five Years of Czechoslovak Historiography*. Z. Solle, *Die ersten Anhänger der Internationalen Arbeiter-Assoziation in Böhmen*, Historica, VII, 1963.

For Hungary: the collection already mentioned, *Studien zur Geschichte der Ö.-U. Monarchie*, contains a good article by E. S. Vincze concerning the ideological influence of the Germans on Hungarian socialism in the second half of the nineteenth century. Vincze mentions the work by D. Nemes, *Altalános Munkásegylet története* ('History of the General Union of Workers'), Budapest, 1952. In the same collection, p. 446, there is an article by J. Buszko on the workers' movement in Galicia from 1880 to 1916. In the *Brève histoire de Transylvanie*, p. 291 *et seq.*, there is a good outline of the subject and on pp. 434–5 a bibliography of works in Rumanian; see also, p. 292, a reproduction of a poster summoning the working population to a meeting at Temesvár in June 1870 (the poster is drawn up in four languages: Magyar, German, Serbian and Rumanian).

For Slovakia: Pavel Hapák, *Zu den Anfängen der Arbeiterbewegung in der Slowakei (1848–1890)*, Historica, XIV, 1967, pp. 51–122.

14. Jaroslav Purš, in an article in *Sborník Historický*, II, 12, Prague, 1964, entitled 'Situation of the working class and strikes in Bohemia during the industrial revolution', gives tables of figures for strikes in Bohemia before 1873: eight in 1867 and 1868, thirty in 1870 and forty-six in 1872. The increase in strikes during this period of prosperity was the sign of a stronger working-class consciousness and, at the same time, of concern over the question of wages.

15. The son of Ladislav Zapotocký was one of the Communist leaders during the first Czechoslovak Republic and became president of the Socialist Republic, between Gottwald and Novotný. His great culture and humanity, together with his profound knowledge of the different milieux of Czechoslovak society, ensured him a broader personal popularity than that enjoyed by his predecessor or his successor. During the period of the 'cold war' he has been almost totally forgotten in the West.

16. It is interesting to observe that the photograph reproduced in V. Husa, *Dějiny Československa* ('History of Czechoslovakia'), p. 267, with the caption 'Workers' demonstration of 1 May 1890 on the *Střelecký ostrov* in Prague', shows only the middle-class citizens of Prague, at least in the foreground: most of the men are wearing bowler-hats and the women are dressed comfortably, even elegantly. A demonstration against the prevailing system and in favour of universal suffrage was of interest not only to the proletariat, but also to the middle strata of society, which were to give their votes to the Young Czech Party and later to Masaryk's Realist Party.

17. Concerning Austria-Hungary's foreign policy, very thoroughly treated in the works of Hantsch, Zöllner and J. Šusta, *Světová politika v létech 1871–1914* ('International Policy 1871–1914'), Prague, see also: A. Pribram, *Die politischen Geheimverträge Österreich-Ungarns 1879–1914*, Vienna, 1920; T. Herkolovic, *Vorgeschichte der Okkupation Bosniens und der Herzegovina*, Agram, 1906; August Fournier, *Wie wir zu Bosnien kamen*, Vienna, 1909; Alexander Novotný, *Quellen und Studien zur Geschichte des Berliner Kongresses 1878*; id., *Österreich, die Türkei und das Balkanproblem im Jahre des Berliner Kongresses*, Graz, 1957; Robert William Seton-Watson, *The Role of Bosnia in International Politics 1875–1914*, London, 1931; P. Renouvin, *Histoire des relations internationales*, vol. IV.

18. J. Miskolczy, *Ungarn in der Habsburger Monarchie*, chapter IV, *Die Epoche des Ausgleichs*, p. 158 *et seq.*; the author, favourably disposed towards the principle of Dualism, analyses the reactions of Hungarian opinion to Habsburg foreign policy.

19. It is nevertheless a characteristic sign, from the point of view of cultural influence, that Germany provided 91·2 per cent of the foreign books and journals brought into Austria-Hungary in the early twentieth century.

20. Relations between Austria and the Vatican have been studied by F. Engel-Janosi in *Österreich und der Vatican*, 2 vols., Vienna, 1959.

21. There exists an abundance of historical works concerning Czech policy between 1879 and 1914, which are by no means free of tendentious interpretations. The return of the Old Czechs to the Imperial Parliament has been described as 'a Canossa'. It should be remembered, however, that the signing of the Compromise of 1867 had also been seen as a Canossa by Kossuth and the intransigent Hungarian patriots. The important question was to decide whether a militant policy would ensure immediate, concrete guarantees and advantages for the Czech nation and whether abstention from the Parliament would not condemn the Czechs to suffer the decisions of Vienna without any opportunity for discussion and control of those decisions. On the other hand, it cannot be accepted, as certain Marxist historians have suggested, that the ruling classes were guided solely by material considerations. Material interests played their part, consciously or unconsciously, but they certainly were not the principal factor in attitudes inspired primarily by a national ideal.

    The state rights of Bohemia were studied in a conference at Marburg, the proceedings of which were published under the title *Das böhmische Staatsrecht* (reviewed and discussed by Victor-L. Tapié in the *Revue historique*, Oct.–Dec. 1962, in an article entitled '*Le droit d'État du royaume de Bohême*').

    See also Z. V. Tobolka, *Dějiny české politiky nové doby* ('History of Czech Policy in the Contemporary Period'), which has been republished in several new editions, the last in 1932–3 under the title *Politické dějiny československého národa od. r. 1848 až do dnešní doby* ('Political History of the Czechoslovak Nation from 1848 to the Present Time'). The two-volume work by Ernest Denis, the French historian of Bohemia, remains a classic study: *La Bohême depuis la Montagne Blanche*, 1903, tracing the course of events up to 1901 (written from a nationalist viewpoint and Young Czech in its sympathies). For Czech policy within the general policy of Cisleithania: R. Charmatz, *Österreichs innere Geschichte von 1848–1895*, 3rd edn. 1968. Z. Tobolka, *Das böhmische Volk*, 1916, presents a well-informed tableau of all aspects of Bohemian national life up to the First World War.

    Czech opinion was particularly sensitive to the high-treason charges brought against the *Omladina* ('Youth') group in 1894. The most recent study of this subject is that by Jan Galandauer, *Politické dědictví Omladiny a pokrokové hnutí po roce 1897* ('The Political Heritage of the Omladina and the Progressist Movement after 1897') in *Československý Časopis Historický*, XII, 1964, 6. New Czech parties were formed: the Realist Party organized by Masaryk when he detached himself from the Young Czechs in 1893 (though the party had many sympathizers, it had few members, since its founder placed no great importance on numbers), the Agrarian Party, founded in 1899, the Independent or National Socialist Party (cf. Jan Mechyř, 'The Independent Socialists in the Workers' Movement in Bohemia at the Beginning of the 1890s', in Czech, ibid., XIII, 1965, 2); also, the Catholic Party and the Progressist Party of State Rights (Nationalist).

22. On the attitude of Gindely and his difficulties with his nationalist colleagues at the German University, see Kamil Krofta, *Byli jsme za Rakouska* ('We were under Austria'), p. 431: 'Antonin Gindely, the Czech question of 1879 and the division of the University of Prague in 1882'.

23. The paragraph on Masaryk is inspired by his book *Česká Otázka* ('The Czech Question') and the passage on the 'logos' is reproduced from words spoken by Masaryk during an

audience which the author had the honour of being granted in February 1934, in Prague Castle.

24. On the policy of Rieger, the memoirs of one of his daughters, Mrs. Červinková (the other daughter was the wife of Albin Bráf, the minister of finance in the Austrian government), and the unfinished work by J. Heidler should be consulted. In an excellent chapter in his *Memoirs and Commentaries*, entitled 'The Emperor and Dr. F. L. Rieger' (*Císař pan a Dr. Rieger*), p. 53, Viktor Dyk stresses the personal faith, in his opinion excessive, which the leader of the Old Czechs had in his sovereign: 'Everything remains in the balance and only this is certain: our affairs are gradually improving and will continue to do so, for *the emperor is more kindly disposed to us than ever.*'

25. B. Suttner, *Die Badenischen Sprachenverordnungen im 1897*, Vienna, 1960. It is rather strange that Count Thun, the governor of Bohemia, should have been extremely hostile to the ordinances, thinking that they would stir up hatred between the two groups, and that Badeni should have been able to say to the Germans that the ordinances would remove the danger of state rights for the future. However—and this was the eternal weakness in Bohemia's demands for state rights—Moravia and Silesia were not juridically associated with the kingdom.

26. J. Miskolczy, op. cit., p. 168, on A. Apponyi: Gróf Apponyi Alberto, *Emlékirataim. Ötven év* ('My Memoirs. Fifty Years'), Budapest, 1922–34, and J. Kristóffy, *Magyarország kalvariaja. Politikai emlékek* ('The Calvary of Hungary. Political Memoirs'), 1890–1926, Budapest, 1927.

27. The drama of Mayerling has been revived so frequently in literature that there is no need to go into detail here, except to say that, since the emperor reigned for nearly thirty years afterwards, the event of 30 January 1889 cannot be said to have had any political consequences. Portfolio 15 of the Nachlass of the Archduke Rudolf (in the Staatsarchiv of Vienna) contains the memorandum drawn up by Count Hoyos, under oath, in February 1889. Count Hoyos gives an account of his last conversation with the Kronprinz, who seemed quite calm at the time (the evening before his suicide). The archduke made a brief allusion to the Hungarian opposition, which had attempted to compromise him, but did not appear to attach any great importance to the matter; mental disequilibrium was the real explanation of his suicide.

28. On the nationalities: R. Kann, *Das Nationalitätenproblem* (op. cit.), which in vol. II, p. 390 *et seq.*, gives a table for the distribution of the nationalities in Austria-Hungary according to language. Id., *The Habsburg Empire, A Study in Integration and Disintegration*, New York, 1957.

Franz Zwitter, *The National Problems in the Habsburg Monarchy*, Belgrade, 1960, and the chapter entitled 'Die nationalen Fragen in der Ö-U. Monarchie, 1900–1914' in *Die nationale Frage in der Österreichisch-Ungarischen Monarchie, 1900–1918*, Budapest, 1966; R. W. Seton-Watson (Scotus Viator), *The Southern Slav Question and the Habsburg Monarchy*, London, 1911; R. Kiszling, op. cit.

As has been observed by Jacques Droz, *L'Europe centrale*, p. 200, it is regrettable that there should be no biography of Mgr. Strossmayer, but at least his correspondence has been published. See the bibliography in R. Kann, op. cit., II, p. 441.

L. de Vojnovic, *Histoire de Dalmatie*, 2 vols., Paris, 1934.

29. In their articles in the collective works already mentioned (*Studien, Études historiques*) present-day Hungarian historians (Sándor, Ránki and Berenyi) stress the differences between the various middle classes.

30. F. Eckhardt, *Histoire de Hongrie*.

31. L. Makkai, *Histoire de Transylvanie*; Daicoviciu, op. cit., p. 370. Jorga, *Geschichte des rumänischen Volkes, 1905*, and *Histoire des roumains de Bukovine à partir de l'annexion autrichienne 1775–1914*.
32. Louis Eisenmann, *Le Compromis austro-hongrois de 1867*, p. 680.
33. Aurel Popovici, *Die Vereinigten Staaten von Gross-Österreich*, p. 295, and Conclusion, p. 427.

✥ 12 ✥

Defence and Fall of
the Monarchy

A HUNGARIAN HISTORIAN, P. Hanák, has recently made the point that a great many
different forces were at work during the latter years of Austria-Hungary and warned
historians of all schools, liberal or Marxist, against the danger of oversimplifying
what is a highly complex problem.[1] This is to say, in the language of the present
day, that no 'unilateral' explanation can be accepted either for the preservation
of the system until 1914 or for its collapse during the course of the war. It cannot
be proved that its imminent downfall was inevitable, the consequence of a process
of internal disintegration, or, on the other hand, that its survival would have
been assured and the forces of cohesion destined to triumph, if the fatal blow had
not been struck from outside. It was almost in these same terms that the fall of the
Roman Empire was interpreted: did Rome succumb to her own exhaustion or was
she assassinated?

In the past, historians have frequently insisted on the factors which held the
Austrian Empire together: the personal prestige of the sovereign (thus implying
that all would collapse on his death), the army (whose defeat on the battlefields
would explain the crumbling of the system), the Church and the administration.
The present tendency is to seek causes in economic and social conditions. Thus
Austria-Hungary found itself wilting amid the competition of the international
market; the working class, as it progressed, was gradually replacing the middle
class, or rather the national middle classes, which had issued from capitalism. But
another aspect of the problem has been neglected. To what extent did there exist
at this time a civilization common to the different peoples of the Danubian monarchy, a civilization that could have held them together? Naturally, the author
can here only suggest a few starting-points for discussion.

The prosperity of the decades between 1867 and 1914, in spite of short periods
of crisis and hardship, manifested itself throughout the Empire in a greater and more
generally widespread affluence. (In the east, however, there still existed areas of
severe poverty from which the peasants emigrated in large numbers in the years of
bad harvests.) Statistical proof of this general improvement can be found in the
increased yield from consumer-taxes and income-tax, which was assessed on
declared incomes of one thousand two hundred crowns and above. The cities of the

Empire, especially the larger cities, made a striking impression on travellers by their fine layout and the agreeable quality of the life led by the citizens. In Vienna, towards the end of the morning, an elegant and select society would stroll along the Ring between the Schwarzenberg Platz and the Opera House, or would appear on the Prater in fine carriages, watched by a warm-hearted and happy crowd of ordinary folk. Budapest was equally alluring, with its arrangement of embankments and terraces contributing to the appeal of one of the most imposing riverside cities in Europe. In Prague, the old Horse Market had become St. Wenceslas Square (commonly known as the Vaclávák), a fine avenue planted with trees and dominated by the huge building of the National Museum and, in front of it, the equestrian statue of the saint by Myslbek. Following this avenue, the traveller passed from the prosperity of the new quarters, the Vinohrady with its impressive bourgeois edifices, to the historic setting of the Old Town and crossed one of the new bridges over the Vltava to the incomparable charm of Malá Strana, where the palaces and gardens had remained unchanged since the eighteenth century. But many other cities of the Dual Monarchy—Agram, Pressburg (Pozsony-Bratislava), Cracow, Lemberg, Cluj and Brasov—presented the same juxtaposition of picturesque old quarters and newly-built districts. Nearly every large town had for some years possessed its own fine buildings, erected to accommodate administrative departments and educational establishments.

Everywhere the symbols of tradition and the marks of a new order were to be found side by side. Architecture assumed a grand style, testifying to the power of the Austro-Hungarian state and its provinces and often also manifesting a stronger collective consciousness, for many buildings had been erected by national subscription, which had taken over the role of seigniorial patronage. The theatre in Prague prided itself in being the gift of the nation: *Národ Sobĕ*. A composite style was adopted which sought its inspiration in the Renaissance: arcades, loggias, faceted domes and statues in abundance. The architect Kirchner, in completing the façade of the Hofburg (looking on to St. Michael's Square), had followed the plans left by Fischer von Erlach, with slight modifications; for the other side of the palace his fellow-architects Simper and Hasenauer conceived a vast new structure of which only one wing was finished. This new edifice was to be extended beyond the Ring by the two museums, a majestic group representing a pastiche of the Italian Renaissance. Architects were returning to antiquity and to medieval art. For the buildings of the new quarters in Vienna, Budapest, Prague and Agram, they abandoned the coldness of the Empire style and the harmonious reserve of the *Biedermeier*, borrowing instead from the decorative traditions of Baroque and Rococo: atlantes supporting balconies, curved frontons, arabesques and *rocaille*-work in lavish profusion. Façades were often covered with a lightly-coloured distemper of green, ochre or yellow, which, however, soon acquired a dull and faded look. Creative imagination was lacking and artists had ample reason to criticize the philistines and officials responsible for this pretentious and pompous bourgeois style. The taste for Baroque splendour, adulterated in its adaptation to an age seeking its own artistic language, persisted in the Austria-Hungary of the later nineteenth century. Yet artists of undeniable quality, such as the painter

Makart, loved this eclectic extravagance. Makart introduced the fashion for interiors cluttered with tapestries, Eastern carpets, Greek bowls, large vases, trinkets and bronzes, among which palm-trees heroically but unavailingly sought the light. The procession which he organized in 1879, for the silver wedding of the imperial couple, was a stunning costume cavalcade which generations of Viennese were to remember as the most successful festival of the period.

It has already been said that Germanic influence extended over the whole of the Austro-Hungarian Empire. This influence was undeniable and assumed a variety of forms. However, the currents of innovation, breaking away from the official style of the Germany of Bismarck and William I, were greeted with sympathy and curiosity. In Vienna, especially, a civilization was evolving which borrowed from several sources, but only to distil from them a character of its own. Vienna has been severely reproached for its cosmopolitanism, for having detached itself from everything profound and wholesome and for having amalgamated Slav, Latin and Jewish influences in an incoherent, superficial and spurious hybrid. A great metropolis, inhabited by large numbers of foreigners and provincials, cannot escape this hazard. But who could fail to recognize the atmosphere of grace and the delicacy of taste of which Vienna held the secret, in the world of fashion, in the courtesy of its manners and in the refinement of its cuisine—a general mood of pleasurableness which was not to be found to the same degree in any other city of central Europe?

It is difficult to choose the right word to define this quality. *Gemütlichkeit* is untranslatable and, in any case, does not express the full reality: perhaps the French word *gentillesse* is the nearest. Vienna was echoing Paris, in a minor key. Though Paris lay far distant, its prestige remained powerful. Towards the end of the century Hungarian and Czech artists, perhaps dissatisfied with Vienna, made their way to France and found success there. Munkácsy won fame with his great tableau of Christ before Pilate. Mucha was appointed stage-designer to Sarah Bernhardt; he was one of the exponents of the *style nouveau* which, developing under the influence of Symbolism, had broken away from the servile and cruel imitation of nature and indulged in allegory and in variations on imaginary themes.

In Vienna, during these same years, under the influence of the painter Gustav Klimt, an artistic movement emerged whose character was defined in the review *Ver Sacrum* ('Sacred Spring') in 1898: 'We desire an art freed from bondage to the foreigner, but freed also from the fear or hatred of the foreigner. Foreign art must stimulate us, bring us back to ourselves; we wish to recognize and admire it wherever it so deserves, but not to imitate it . . . The goal for which to strive is the creation of a living national art, but which must not be merely a patriotic art.'[2]

The break with the official source of artistic inspiration was confirmed by the use of the magic word 'Secession'. This was not simply another 'school' which, like the others, would constrain and enslave the artist. Liberty would blossom in a quest for individuality and pure form, in a personal endeavour to wrest its secret from nature. A new exhibition pavilion was built, crowned by a hollow globe with interwoven leaves of gilded laurel; the pediment bore this inscription:

'To each age its art; to art its freedom' (*Der Zeit ihre Kunst. Der Kunst, ihre Freiheit*). The inscription was obliterated by the Nazis.

Klimt and Kokoschka were landscapists, portraitists and scene-painters. Fundamentally, they were poets and possessed a spiritual affinity with the poets of literature and music. Hugo von Hoffmannsthal was the great literary figure of the time, drawing his inspiration from antiquity and the Baroque and composing a diversity of works that included libretti for the operas of Richard Strauss, evocative of dreams and mysteries. The success of these artists was of a kind hardly conceivable elsewhere than in Vienna. Side by side with the high artistic quality manifested in their works, successes of a simpler though nonetheless delightful character were achieved. Vienna became the city of the waltz and the operetta. Johann Strauss (1825–99), the last and most famous of the family, assumed the status of a national figure in the Austria of this period. The rhythm of the *Blue Danube* seems to symbolize the inimitable appeal of Viennese life: a light, swirling flight in which there is no place for cares. The stunning technique of Franz Lehar, a Hungarian following in the wake of Strauss, conquered foreign audiences, as if these 'pom poms' were all that the Danubian countries had to contribute to general civilization. At a time when radio and records were still non-existent, such music was heard more frequently than the rich and sublime works of the two great rivals, Brahms and Bruckner.[3] Although Liszt, a Hungarian, had won a world-wide public, the two Czech masters, Smetana and Dvořák, were still not familiar to European audiences, whose preferences were divided between Wagner and the composers of Russia and France. Smetana had immediately found a patron in the Princess von Metternich who, after fulfilling her social and political role as ambassadress in Paris, held primacy of position in Viennese society. Dvořák also spent a long time in Vienna. Mahler, a Moravian by birth but Viennese by career, was director of the Vienna Opera at the time of his great creative activity. Bruckner, Smetana, Dvořák—names such as these may well illuminate a special characteristic of the spiritual and artistic life of Austria-Hungary. The high proportion of rural populations in the Empire of the nineteenth century is of significance not only for economic historians. A powerful peasant hereditary principle, the preservation of the link with the land, the people who lived on that land and their own profound sensibility, all help to explain the creative genius of the masters. Bruckner, the organist at St. Florian, impregnated with the religious beauty of the great abbeys, remained a peasant of Austria. The countryside of Bohemia, with its meadows, rocks and rivers is reflected in Smetana's symphonic poem *Má Vlast*, just as rustic life, naïve and yet cunning, inspired *The Bartered Bride*. As for Dvořák, his *Slavonic Dances* and *New World Symphony*, which was composed in America, are full of nostalgia for his country. It was this same communion with the native land and with the collective soul of the rural population that had given *Babička* its charm in earlier times. It would be a mistake, however, to think that this was simply a folk culture. The peasant tradition passes far beyond that level when it permeates the work of a great artist or writer and, by its human value, becomes capable of moving men's hearts outside the boundaries of individual countries and different eras.

A Hungarian critic, István Sötér, has demonstrated this fact with great shrewdness and thoroughness in a study of the problems of assimilation in the literature of his country. Taking music as his starting-point—the music of Béla Bartók—he writes: 'One of Bartók's most important sources was Hungarian peasant music. He is not a composer of folk-music, but in order to be able to express . . . thoughts which he addressed to the whole of humanity, he was destined by the force of circumstance to draw from peasant music . . . Bartók's attachment to peasant music is a fact that has its analogy in our poetry.'[4] The author was thinking of modern Hungarian poets, but his observation is equally applicable to those of the nineteenth century —Arany, for example.

The point made by Sötér could also be extended without distortion to other sectors of the artistic sphere and to other countries of the monarchy—to painting and sculpture, where traditional inspiration and the new mode of expression were also seen to meet. Yet these achievements were not crowned by the birth of an art that would have represented a common consciousness and expressed the supranational spirit compatible with the structure of the Danubian monarchy. In fact, the literatures of the different countries often assumed a tendentious character. Not that they were always polemical literatures. Some writers deliberately adopted this genre. A great many more, in their desire to express ideas concerning humanity and justice, chose themes that recalled the misfortunes and humiliations of their people and thus fostered a mood of hostility towards the ancestors of the ruling dynasty or towards the Church. The literature of the nineteenth century therefore helped neither to bring the peoples closer together nor to nurture the ideal of their future solidarity. It displayed other noble qualities: it served, for example, to sustain national pride, attachment to a territory, to a people and its history. But, in so doing, it cannot be said to have avoided rancour or to have encouraged union. This seems evident both from Czech literature, represented by the popular writer Aloís Jirásek, who revived Hussite fervour, and the poet Svatopluk Čech, a contributor to the review *Ruch* ('Movement') and the author of the beautiful *Songs of the Slave*, and also from Hungarian literature, with the novelist Mór Jókai (1825–1904) and the review *Nyugat* ('The West'), which published the first short story by Zsigmond Móricz (1879–1942). Neither did Austrian writers—the delightful story-teller Petr Rosseger, or Maria von Ebner-Eschenbach, a shrewd analyst of the society of his time who cherished memories of his native Moravia—attain a supranational plane. Perhaps, in contrast with these two authors, the case of Baroness von Suttner, *née* Kinský, should be mentioned. Her noble and moving book, *Die Waffen nieder!* ('Down with Arms!'), reconciled the hope of disarmament with a certain confidence in the policy of Austria. It enjoyed a great success and gained for its author the Nobel Peace Prize. But, while its pacifist inspiration and its just criticism of war touched many hearts, it also provoked antagonism, as was the case with the works of Romain Rolland. The book did not therefore arouse a general enthusiasm which could be described as 'Danubian', nor did it alleviate political or partisan conflicts.

Nonetheless, between 1867 and 1914 the intellectual life of the Dual Monarchy enjoyed a remarkable growth. The universities, where the German professors of the Second Reich felt themselves greatly honoured at being appointed to chairs, revised their methods and widened the field of research and discovery. A number of great names bear witness to this process: in biology, Mendl, in geography, Suess, in philosophy, Franz Brentano and, at the meeting-point of experimental science and psychology, Freud, who transformed man's vision of the inner world.

Everywhere, teaching staffs were of excellent quality. Seminaries and laboratories produced collective and individual works of high calibre. The universities thus formed an élite which contributed to the greatness of the Dual Monarchy as a whole, but which at the same time assured for each national group the conditions necessary for social advancement, the opportunity to acquire a clearer consciousness of its own particular destiny. After the disruption of the Empire, the 'succession states' were to receive the benefit of this activity.

In the early years of the twentieth century Austria-Hungary held its place as a great power in Europe: it had played a more than respectable part in the process of economic, social and spiritual change.

In its international situation, however, a time of new difficulties was approaching. Its resources were insufficient for the needs of industrial equipment, which the constant progress of techniques made it necessary to renew; moreover, Austria-Hungary was becoming increasingly involved in the development of the Balkan states. Although capital poured in from Germany, Vienna, the commercial and banking centre, continued to be the necessary channel for the transaction of business and the investment of funds. Thus, the solidarity of interests between the two allied states was reinforced, while Russia became more alarmed than ever at the progress of Germanic power. Austria-Hungary could not permit the Balkan peoples to be drawn by their economic interests into the sphere of protection of another country. The rivalry between Russia and Austria thus took a new course. No longer a question of prestige to be resolved by the chancelleries, it became a matter for banks and business circles and for local consular agents, whose role was difficult to define. Formerly, sovereigns and their ministers had alone been responsible for deciding on political action. They were now in danger of being impelled by other forces over which they had little control.

As far as Serbia was concerned, the situation had greatly changed. The immediate neighbour of Austria-Hungary, the little kingdom maintained close commercial relations with the Dual Monarchy, being the chief buyer of its grain and cattle and the almost exclusive supplier of its imports. In fact, a customs union between Serbia and Austria-Hungary appeared a reasonable solution on the economic plane.[5] The same was true, though to a lesser degree, of the kingdom of Rumania, the military ally of Austria-Hungary since 1883. But other factors intervened, for the ruling classes of Serbia and the new generation of Serbs resented the *de facto* tutelage of Austria. Their impatience had already manifested itself during the reign of the young Alexander Obrenović, the son of Milan and, like his father, dependent on Vienna. It showed greater intensity after the assassination of Alexander in 1903 and on the accession of Peter I Karageorgević, the son-in-law of the prince of

Montenegro; the new king was clearly inclined towards friendship with Russia and, having lived in France, had strong French sympathies. With politicians such as Pašić, Serbia was in a position to assume an international role which it had never previously held. Its ideal of a union of all Serbs in a single state induced it to seek influence over the Serbs of the Dual Monarchy. It supported these Serbs in their nationalist demands and established more intimate relations with the Croats, akin both in race and in language. In another direction, Serbia desired territorial aggrand-izement in the Turkish dominions inhabited by Serbs. Finally, Macedonia, popula-ted by Slavs of the Orthodox faith but of indeterminate nationality, became an object of dispute between Serbia and Bulgaria. The rulers of Bulgaria looked alternately to St. Petersburg and Vienna for support. As for Rumania, while the king, Charles, had every reason to remain faithful to the Austrian alliance, enlight-ened opinion felt a growing solidarity with the Rumanians of Transylvania, to whom it gave both encouragement and example. In two states adjacent to Austria-Hungary there thus existed forces of which one extreme consequence might be the disruption of the Dual Monarchy.[6]

At the turn of the century, the statesmen of Austria and Hungary were quite aware of the very real danger inherent in the Balkan situation. The time was long past when it was sufficient to maintain the *status quo*: henceforth, it was essential that the position of the Dual Monarchy in Europe should be consolidated. The Emperor Francis Joseph, prompted both by temperament and experience, hoped to achieve such a consolidation by judicious contacts with sovereigns and statesmen, just as he attempted to resolve the internal conflicts in his Empire by the discreet preservation of equilibrium. A different view was held by a prince of his family whom circumstances had made the second person of the dynasty and the state. After the death of the Archduke Rudolf, since the family decrees allowed no rights of succession to his daughter, the little Archduchess Elizabeth, the heir presumptive became the Archduke Charles Louis, the emperor's second brother. But this prudent and self-effacing prince did not interfere in politics. On his premature death in 1896, the situation changed with the advent of his eldest son. When he was quite young and far removed from the succession, the Archduke Francis Ferdinand had been chosen as heir by the last duke of Modena, in exile at Vienna, who had transmitted to him his fortune and the name of Austria-Este. Intelligent, strong-willed, serious, deeply religious and imbued with the grandeur of the monarchic ideal, the new heir, the *Thronfolger*, assumed a position of importance in the politics of Austria-Hungary. His strong personality was not generally appreciated.[7] Above all, he was loyal. He never sought to take his uncle's place or to create difficulties for him. He fulfilled his military functions with a devotion, a competence and a zeal that persuaded the emperor to entrust him over the years with the highest offices and finally to appoint him inspector-general of all land and sea forces. But, as the emperor grew old, the archduke began to think in terms of his approaching reign. His residence at the Belvedere became, not a hotbed of intrigue, but a centre of consultation where he received all those capable of inform-ing him about the state of the monarchy. Public opinion, in consequence, looked to the Belvedere, wondering what plans were being laid there. The archduke stood by two inviolable principles: the greatness of the monarchy as a whole, which was not open to question and which every good citizen, whatever his nationality, must serve; and respect for the Catholic religion. The archduke believed that no civil order could survive unless it was illuminated by fidelity to the Church, but he had no intention of interfering with the personal convictions or private life of anyone. His own private life was irreproachable, although he caused surprise by the marriage which he contracted in 1900 with a young woman of the Czech aristocracy, the Countess Sophie Chotek. The archduke solemnly promised not to transmit the rights of succession to his children, of lower birth than himself. These rights passed to his younger brother, the Archduke Otto, who died in 1906 and then to his nephew, who became the Emperor Charles in 1916. The Thronfolger never contemplated going back on his word.

The Archduke Francis Ferdinand had a poor opinion of Dualism, which he regarded as an unfortunate dismemberment of the monarchy, and he reproached Hungary for being governed by a nationalist aristocracy which, by not showing justice to the non-Magyar inhabitants, was allowing them to develop separatist sentiments. He therefore sought to win the sympathies of the opposition elements among the Croats (Dr. Frank), the Slovaks (Dr. Milan Hodža, a Protestant) and the Rumanians (Maniu and the patriarch Miron Cristea), promising them that he would not allow their legitimate rights to be forfeited. He disliked the parliamentary system wherever he found it, observing its impotence and the manner in which its energies were squandered in intrigue and speech-making. A man of agrarian and seigniorial tradition, he felt a certain repugnance for the capitalist system and liberalism, which were often accompanied by religious indifference, even anti-clericalism and atheism. He disliked the Jews because of their financial power and he regarded freemasonry as a baneful influence. On the other hand, he took an interest in the working-class question. He inclined towards Christian Socialism, for he could not accept that the enrichment of some should result in the enslavement and poverty of others. Such was the powerful personality of the man who intended to restore Austria-Hungary on monarchic and religious principles which, in the existing social structure of the Dual Monarchy, cannot be said to have been in contradiction either with the facts or with the aspirations of a large proportion of the population. The archduke was not popular. His coldness concealed a certain timidity and his dignified manner gave the impression of haughtiness. Everyone agreed in thinking that many things would change on his accession: some hopefully, others with apprehension.

Francis Ferdinand has been accredited with various projects, in particular 'trialism', which presented two possible forms. One would have been the restoration of the kingdom of Bohemia. That he loved Bohemia, where he often stayed in the palace of Konopiště, and that he never forgot that his children were half-Czech, is beyond doubt. But he mistrusted the policy of the Young Czechs, owing to their anticlericalism, their Hussitism and their Slav propensities, which he believed to be contaminated with Pan-Slavism. The other form of 'trialism', which he apparently preferred, would have involved the separation from Hungary of Croatia, which would have become the nucleus of a South Slav kingdom embracing

Dalmatia and Slovenia (both Austrian provinces) and, after the annexation of 1908, Bosnia-Herzegovina. Such a solution, which was much discussed, would have foiled Serbian ambitions and there can be no doubt that, as a result, certain Serbs looked on the Thronfolger as their most dangerous adversary.

Finally, the proposals put forward by Aurel C. Popovici engaged the attention of the archduke, who had long conversations with the author. But Francis Ferdinand had far too much political sagacity to draw up, years in advance, a plan which he would then put into operation *in toto* on the day of his accession. In his chancellery he gradually gathered together those persons capable of illuminating the decisions that he would take when he was finally empowered to do so. In the meantime, the most important thing was to strengthen the army so that Austria could command the respect of foreign countries and occupy the position in Europe to which it was entitled by the prestige of its past, the extent of its territory and the size of its population.

In the field of foreign policy, established alliances called for unswerving fidelity. The archduke, sure of the alliance with Germany, had less confidence in Italy, for he had misgivings with regard to the Trentino and Dalmatia. He desired a durable *entente* with Russia, even if only for the sake of monarchic solidarity and because reason required a fair balance of influence. Great Britain and France were more distant; in general, the Europe for which the archduke hoped was a Europe of states governed by wise and faithful rulers who would care for the well-being of their peoples and would respect the promises which they had given each other.

※

The years 1905–6 were years of extreme difficulty for Austria-Hungary. Yet, as most historians now recognize, the existence of the Danubian monarchy was not itself directly called in question; many foreign publicists failed to take a true measure of its strength and of the limits of its contradictions.[8] On this occasion, however, parliamentary turbulence coincided in the two states of Austria-Hungary and the question of the economic compromise led to a crisis of Dualism. The troubles of the Danubian monarchy were, at the same time, aspects of an international and social crisis that had affected the whole of Europe. The transformation of capitalism and the growth of monopolies were modifying the relative strength of the Great Powers.

Maritime and colonial rivalry between Great Britain and Germany was becoming more acute. Russia was allied with France, but Germany was attempting, if not to sever Russia from this alliance, at least to associate her with a policy hostile to Great Britain. On the other hand, France drew closer to Great Britain, forgetting old quarrels in order to have a free rein in Morocco, where she was encountering the hostility of Germany. Finally, Russia, having rashly engaged in the war against Japan which, it seemed, was diverting her attention from Balkan affairs, faced grave internal troubles. In the revolutions of 1905 against the absolutism of the tsar, both the middle class and the proletariat gave voice to their demands. The interplay of so many forces could not fail to have repercussions on internal events in the other countries.

In Austria, the problem of Bohemia remained the most serious, giving rise to violent debates both at the Imperial Parliament and at the Diet in Prague. It was recognized that an agreement between Germans and Czechs should have been reached much earlier, for the inflamed passions and stubbornness of the two groups now made an agreement very difficult to realize. Yet the proof that a solution was still not impossible was given in 1905 by the Diet of Moravia where, as a result of the establishment of a register of nationalities, a broadly equitable distribution of seats between Germans and Czechs was assured: each nationality could then assume a diversity of expression by choosing between its own political parties.[9] This solution was subsequently adopted by Bukovina and given favourable consideration in Galicia, where the Polish and Ruthenian groups were now in conflict. It was, perhaps, more difficult to apply in Bohemia, owing to the struggle for influence between the great landowners and the middle class. The nobility still possessed vast domains, which on the whole were well administered, and it was involved in numerous industrial concerns. Claiming, above all, to be loyal to the Empire and not interested in quarrels of language and nationality, it in fact showed its solidarity with the German group. The nobility did not wish to see the abolition of the electoral system, by which the Diet was chosen by 'curias' (a number of seats had already been allocated to universal suffrage), and it became the adversary of the Czech middle class, which was making constant progress, bringing in its wake the petty bourgeoisie, the rural bourgeoisie and a large proportion of the working class, and which represented the nation.[10]

A large Czech middle class, though lagging slightly behind the German middle class, henceforward played an important part in the Cisleithan economy, as can be seen from the presence of Czechs as ministers of finance in Cisleithan cabinets (Dr. Albin Bráf, for example). Although the Young Czech Party had to face competition from other Czech parties and had lost its numerical preponderance, its leader, Dr. Karel Kramář,[11] wielded real authority at the Reichsrat. He skilfully interested foreign opinion in the cause of the Czech nation and, under the name of *Austroslavism*, fostered cultural solidarity among all the Slavs of Cisleithania. He was anxious to demonstrate that the influence of the Slavs could modify the general policy of the monarchy, ensure a *rapprochement* with the Russian middle class and curb German political and economic expansion.[12] In the Empire of Austria, everything seemed to be dominated by the struggle between Czechs and Germans. The Germans formed only 35 per cent of the Cisleithan population and the Czechs (four millions in Bohemia alone, as against two million Germans) presented their blossoming nation as a model to the other nationalities of the Austrian state—the Poles, the Ruthenes, the Italians of the southern Tyrol and the Dalmatians. The upheavals at the Reichsrat resulted in changes of ministries and frequent recourse to Article 14, not to mention the suspension of the Prague Diet and, in the event of riots, the imposition of martial law—troubles serious enough to occupy the limelight in the press, even abroad, and to conceal the deep solidarity of interests which still existed.

Conditions were different in Hungary. As has been seen in the previous chapter, economic progress in the kingdom was pronounced and the rhythm of production extremely rapid. The production of Hungary's manufacturing industries rose by 120 per cent between 1898 and 1913. This represented an annual growth of 5·4 per cent, which was higher than the average rate of 4·6 per cent for western Europe. The increase in the production of the textile and leather industries was an annual average of 14·6 per cent, compared with 3·5 per cent in western Europe. The development of the railways in Transleithania represented a growth of 320 per cent between 1860 and 1890–1900, by which time the country possessed 20,988 kilometres of track.[13] The chief beneficiaries of this progress were the great manufacturers, mostly Magyars and Germans; but the middle strata of Hungarian society and the national groups also benefited, as is shown by the constant increase in the amount of deposits in savings-banks and the commercial banks. An economic and social transformation of this kind could not help but influence political life in Hungary.

As a result of the tax-qualification system, electoral pressures and the absence of a secret ballot, the Liberal Party had remained in power. It was composed of members of the great nobility and of the middle class; indeed, it is true that, to a large degree, the Austro-Hungarian Compromise represented a mutual arrangement between the Hungarian great landowner, who exported his cereals, and the Austrian industrialist, who supplied his manufactured products. The Hungarian nobility, by the extent of its properties and its extravagant way of life, occupied an even more privileged position in society than the Cisleithan nobility. But a section of the nobility and certain elements of the middle class had already joined the ranks of the opposition, the former on ideological grounds, the latter out of economic self-interest. They rebuked the Liberals for allowing the Cisleithan capitalists, both Germans and Czechs, to dominate the Hungarian market and economy and thus impede the industrialization of the country. The demands of the Hungarian opposition were still concerned with the army and the question of the language of command, but were also being directed in an increasing measure at the economic sector. Some desired full independence, with a separate tariff system and an autonomous state bank. Although the abolition of Dualism was not openly solicited, the changes that were being sought for Hungary's advantage might radically modify the very basis of the regime.[14] A political and social struggle now took place within the kingdom, among the Magyars, at a time when the working-class question and the problem of the nationalities were growing more acute. The middle-class strata of the national groups had little to expect from any success achieved by the 'Party of Independence and 1848' which, with its chauvinism, constituted a greater threat to them than did the Liberal Party, which had been responsible for the Law of Nationalities of 1868. But they believed that they would derive advantages from any form of democratic progress that might be achieved in Hungary. The elections held after the dissolution of the Hungarian Parliament in 1905 resulted in the triumph of the opposition parties, which formed a coalition: the Party of Independence, the Populist Party (many electors were Slovaks) and the Agrarian Party, which included both Slovaks and Rumanians among its supporters. The demands of the new majority led to a conflict with the Crown: the king could permit no infringement of the Compromise, the constitutional basis of the Dual Monarchy.

In Cisleithania, many persons were alarmed by the triumph of the Magyar nationalists, the most intransigent both in political matters and with regard to the economic relations between the two states. The Germans and the Czechs, though they were not thereby reconciled, joined in a harsh criticism of Hungarian methods. The chambers of commerce complained that the kingdom's administration was obstructing the rapid recovery of Cisleithan credit.[15] It was even said in Vienna that the Austrians had no worse enemies than the Hungarians. It was a question not merely of the juxtaposition of two parliamentary crises, but of a crisis for Dualism which derived to a large extent from the economic and social changes that had taken place during the past forty years. If the king-emperor did not wish to have recourse to the revolutionary solution, for which his advancing age, his temperament and his characteristic prudence gave him no inclination—in other words, if he was unwilling to impose his authority in order to transform his Empire into a federation of nationalities or states—then he would have to negotiate. He therefore sought, within the constitutional order, showing severity when necessary but without exceeding the strict limits of his rights, to restore tranquillity within each state so that the renewal of the ten-year economic agreement could be assured. This agreement was linked with the 'pragmatic' Compromise and its abandonment might jeopardize the entire system.

In Hungary, he tried at first to govern with a ministry of officials drawn from outside the parties. But organized resistance came from the comitats, which refused to pay taxes or to allow recruits to join the Hungarian contingent. In September 1905 the king had a brief meeting with the leaders of the coalition (Andrassy, Just' Francis Kossuth and Apponyi). On both sides it was clear on which points all bargaining became futile. The king would not give way either over the army question or over the Compromise. The minister of the interior, Kristóffy, even hinted that universal suffrage might be introduced in Hungary. But then both the coalition parties and the liberals would have been submerged under the mass of votes of the non-Magyar nationalities and the socialists. This was the period of the revolution of October 1905 in Russia, an event that encouraged the hopes of the 'advanced' parties.

At the beginning of 1906 the Hungarian House of Representatives was dissolved and Rumanian regiments entered the assembly hall to evacuate it. In such circumstances, it was a question either of engaging in civil war or of coming to terms with the king. In return for a few concessions concerning military organization, which involved no infringement of the army's unity, the members of the coalition agreed to join the new Wekerle ministry, which supported the Compromise.

Francis Kossuth was appointed minister of commerce and Apponyi minister of education. Kossuth was to watch over the interests of the Hungarian economy, while Apponyi was to introduce in 1907 an educational programme which, granting material advantages to teachers, also extended the obligatory use of the Magyar language to denominational schools and even to nursery-schools. The king had succeeded, though not without some difficulty, in removing the immediate threat posed by Hungary, a threat which, if it were allowed to develop, could lead to the secession of the kingdom.[16]

In Cisleithania, the last ministry had fallen as the result of a national issue, the Polish demand for greater autonomy in Galicia.[17] Was there no way of overcoming this apparently insoluble conflict by diverting public opinion towards other problems? Demonstrations in favour of universal suffrage were becoming more and more frequent. Was it wise to oppose these demands? Were the socialist parties more to be feared than the national parties? In Vienna, Francis Joseph had long refused to confirm the election as burgomaster of the Christian Socialist leader, Karl Lueger. But, since he had finally decided to do so, in 1897, he had been able to observe Lueger's extraordinarily effective management of affairs and his irreproachable loyalty to the Crown. On the other hand, Austro-Marxism as represented by the Social Democrats offered the monarchy guarantees, provided that it accepted reforms. In a highly industrialized territory, universal suffrage became a means of soothing discontent and obtaining a Parliament that would be concerned not so much with problems of nationality as with economic interests and that would accept the renewal of the Compromise.

The emperor entrusted the new government to a jurist, Baron von Beck, who proved himself a skilful parliamentary tactician and who, in the latter weeks of 1906, had the law introducing universal male suffrage passed by the House of Representatives and then by the more recalcitrant House of Lords.[18] In 1907 the elections gave 96 seats (out of a total of 516) to the Christian Socialists and 86 to the Social Democrats (of all nationalities): these were now the two strongest groups.

Although the socialists could be considered a supranational movement, deputies of the same nationality assembled in clubs to examine the questions of interest to their own country: the Czech Club comprised 82 members and the Polish Club 90. But the Ruthenes had 25 deputies and the Slovenes 18. Baron von Beck had made electoral reform conditional on the renewal of the Compromise. Negotiations were resumed between the two states and were fairly rapidly brought to a conclusion. Although he was no expert in financial matters, Beck was able to settle, by his personal arbitration, a number of delicate points which obstructed the progress of the two commissions. To satisfy Hungarian susceptibilities, it was decided that the customs union would henceforward be no more than a simple trade treaty and that the common tariff would in fact represent a juxtaposition of two individual but identical tariffs. The 'quota' was raised slightly and Hungary was granted parity in Austro-Hungarian banks. The major result was the salvation of the Dual Monarchy. The emperor, who had played a large part in this achievement, was able to refer in one of his speeches to 'the bond between the two states, a bond sanctified by an age-old community of destiny, reinforced by the Pragmatic Sanction and which will be transmitted intact to future generations'.

After the crisis of Dualism, the men who occupied the positions of power in the new ministries seemed determined to restore the prestige of the Dual Monarchy both abroad and at home. It was significant that Lieutenant Field-Marshal Conrad von Hoetzendorf was appointed Chief of the General Staff for the army and that Baron Lexa von Aehrenthal was made minister of foreign affairs, as successor to the cautious and peaceable Count Goluchowski.[19] Both men intended to serve Great Austria rather than the individual nationalities: they were preoccupied with its role as a great power in Europe. Although they agreed with the archduke-heir on principles, they differed from him in regard to the practical application of those principles. By comparison with these figures, in the full vigour of their manhood and strong in resolution, the emperor assuredly represented another generation, accustomed to a more sober approach and to a conscientious and patient search for solutions.

The Dual Monarchy found itself beset by increasingly numerous contradictions. The rise in the standard of living (impeded, however, by a constant rise in prices) gave an impression of well-being. But, in the international field, the position of Austria-Hungary was deteriorating. The tariff measures taken by Germany hindered the exportation of agricultural produce to the German market, while the proportion of German capital invested in Austria-Hungary, in the Balkan peninsula and in Turkey was constantly growing. Checked in its economic expansion to the west by the progress of its ally, Austria-Hungary also found Germany its rival in the Near East. Serbia was relying more and more on French and Russian capital for its railway materials and armaments, but looked to Germany and Great Britain for its imports. When the trade treaties of 1905 expired, Austria-Hungary wished to impose stricter conditions on Serbia. It was not simply a question of serving the interests of the Hungarian great landowners. As Hugo Hantsch has put it so well, what was at stake was 'the well-being or unhappiness of large numbers of peasants in both halves of the Empire, who would have been subjected to severe pressures by an inundation of cheap agricultural produce from overseas and from the Balkans'.[20] Consequently, the treaties were not renewed and a tariff war lasting several years was waged by the two states. At the same time, as technical progress brought higher agricultural production throughout the Balkan countries, the disposal of its produce became a matter of life or death for the peasantry.

The question of the railways assumed paramount importance. The Orient-Express went as far as Constantinople, via Vienna, Budapest and Belgrade. But preparations were being made for the construction of a transversal railway route from the Black Sea to the Adriatic, which would have diverted traffic from Austria-Hungary. Could not the Austrians, in retaliation, hasten the extension of their own lines and establish the link with the Turkish network, across the sanjak of Novi-Bazar and in the direction of Salonika? At all events, Austro-Hungarian capitalism, in which Czech capitalism occupied an increasingly important role, was interested in the economic affairs of the peninsula. A new company for trade with the Near East, the *Austro-orientalische Handelsaktiongesellschaft*, established branches in Alexandria and Smyrna and demanded from the government more effective support for its investments in Turkey and in the Balkan countries. At the beginning of 1908, Aehrenthal, the minister of foreign affairs, reminded the Delegations that 'the occupation of Bosnia-Herzegovina gives Austria-Hungary the right to consider itself a Balkan power' and that its task was 'to recognize the signs of the times and to take advantage of them'. The linking of the Bosnian network with that of the neighbouring countries would make it possible to direct Austro-Hungarian commerce towards the Aegean and the Mediterranean and to make this 'the shortest route from central Europe to Egypt and India'. It provided the means of safeguarding and reinvigorating the commercial position of the Dual Monarchy; at the same time, this route would clearly be used to transport not only the goods of Austria-Hungary, but also those of Germany, a larger producer. Their economic interests thus bound the two allies even more closely than the diplomatic and military agreement had done. Capitalism and imperialism were erecting a *Mitteleuropa* bloc; this Germanic expansion obviously presented great dangers for the culture and national consciousness of the Slav groups in the Empire. The Pan-Slav idea was gaining vigour among economic and political circles in Russia and a Russophil propaganda, hostile to Austria, was developing in Serbia. The hope of a Great Serbia filled young people with enthusiasm; since the Serbian government could not have tolerated movements that might aggravate what was already a difficult relationship with the neighbouring power, secret societies were organized. The Austro-Hungarian police uncovered revolutionary agitation among certain circles in Bosnia-Herzegovina.

When, in July 1908, the Young Turk revolution broke out, encouraged by pro-British business circles, Austria had reason to fear that its relations with the new government might prove difficult. The contagious effects of these disturbances could spread rapidly across the peninsula to Bosnia and Herzegovina. It was at this moment that the ministry of foreign affairs reconsidered a project that had already been examined several times: the annexation to the Austro-Hungarian monarchy of the two provinces with which it had been entrusted by the Congress of Berlin. But a state could not, by its own initiative, modify the nature of a mandate which it held from other powers. Furthermore, the recent agreements with Russia permitted no alteration of the status of the Balkans without previous consultation with Russia. Taking advantage of a visit by the Russian minister of foreign affairs, Izvolsky, to the spas of Bohemia, Aehrenthal invited him to a meeting, which took place in the mansion of Buchlovice, in Moravia, on 15–16 September 1908. The ground had already been prepared by an exchange of notes. In the course of these conversations, Aehrenthal obtained an assurance that Russia would not oppose an annexation. In return, Austria-Hungary would support Russia when the latter should seek to obtain passage through the Straits for her navy. In the conversations at Buchlovice neither the date nor the manner of annexation was specified. Izvolsky might well have believed that annexation would not take place immediately, nor without the assent of the other powers. However, on learning that Bulgaria intended to take advantage of events in Turkey by renouncing its vassalage to the sultan and by declaring its independence, Aehrenthal precipitated matters. On 7 October an imperial rescript and a proclamation to the Bosnian people announced the annexation of Bosnia and Herzegovina to Austria. As proof of goodwill, Austrian military forces evacuated the sanjak of Novi-Bazar, which thereby came under the sole control of Turkey. It was true, also, that the sanjak might become an object of dispute between two allied Slav countries, Serbia and Montenegro.

What was to be done with the new conquest? A population of a little under two millions (1,604,000 according to the estimates of 1895, 1,932,000 at the census of 1910, taken two years after the annexation) had become part of the Dual Monarchy. The Serbo-Croat element predominated (96·02 per cent), but was divided among three religious confessions: Roman Catholicism, Orthodoxy and Islam. Although many Moslems were descended from Croats who had been converted to Islam, they were nonetheless closely attached to the faith of the Prophet. In the name of ancient historic rights, Croatia, supported by a section of Hungarian opinion, would have readily claimed the annexation of the territory to Hungary. But the Magyars were alarmed at the prospect of thus swelling the Slav population of their kingdom. The best solution therefore seemed to be to establish a kind of 'Reichsland'—rather like Alsace-Lorraine in the German Empire—which the two states of the Dual Monarchy would administer jointly, but which would have a Diet elected by the local inhabitants.

The Delegations and the Parliaments approved the annexation in the autumn of 1908. The idea was put forward that the peoples of the monarchy were presenting this extension of territorial power to the king-emperor in honour of the sixtieth anniversary of his accession. In Vienna, at the beginning of December, a great festival was held in celebration of the old monarch's jubilee. But the Czechs did not attend the festivities and by their absence undermined any possibility of general harmony. Incidents had occurred at the Bohemian Diet in connection with the agreement between the Germans and the Czechs: Prague was under martial law. The annexation of Bosnia-Herzegovina represented a genuine success, but one fraught with dangers. Aehrenthal, for his part, had wished to prove that the monarchy was now capable of an independent foreign policy and bold initiatives.

Of the great powers confronted with this *fait accompli*, several gave their rapid consent: Germany, Italy and France. Great Britain showed greater reticence, feeling that an international conference should have been called. The tsar's government protested vigorously. Izvolsky complained that he had been deceived by Aehrenthal. Russia gave her full support to the resistance of Serbia, which declared its unwillingness to subscribe to the incorporation of its fellow-Slavs in the Dual Monarchy.

At the beginning of 1909, Turkey decided to recognize the annexation and signed a treaty with Austria-Hungary. Crisis then loomed once more, as a result of Serbia's increasingly vehement protests, encouraged by Russia. The Austrian military considered that the only way out of the impasse was a war against Serbia; business circles were divided in their views, some urging conciliation, others accepting the dangers of a conflict, even a conflict which, by the interplay of international alliances, might assume European dimensions. The Reichsrat approved estimates of mobilization. But Germany interceded with Russia, asking her to recommend moderation to Serbia. No longer supported by the great power without which it could not face a war against Austria-Hungary, Serbia gave way. The Belgrade government recognized the annexation unreservedly. A collision, the consequences of which could have spread to the two blocs of alliances, had only just been averted.

It thus seemed that the internal pacification of the monarchy had been crowned by a great diplomatic success. It was said that, in the twilight of the emperor's reign, the annexation had brought compensation for the Italian territories lost in the wars of 1859 and 1866. This compensation was merely apparent, for the Balkan provinces were comparable only in area with the rich lands, endowed with a great civilization and already advanced in their industrial progress, represented by Lombardy and Venetia at the time of their separation from the monarchy. Moreover, the pretence was a dangerous one: in the eighteenth century, the system of territorial barter had already proved disputable in principle and dubious in effect; the nineteenth century had gained little advantage by continuing to apply such methods. In the twentieth century, the territorial prestige of a dynasty counted for less and less amid material conditions and a social transformation which governments found difficult to control. Beneath what was regarded as another diplomatic flourish, the confrontation of imperialist forces had revealed itself with unmistakable clarity. Yet, in this entanglement of ambitious states, economic competition and collective passions which transcended individual desires, the role of personalities had been an important and positive one. The initiative in deciding for or against war had remained the responsibility of a few men.

Aehrenthal and Conrad believed that they were serving noble ends: the independence and greatness of their state. But Aehrenthal, though a man of honour and character, had sought success by the old Machiavellian methods. The brutality of his decision, his evasion of public law, which would have required a preliminary international *entente*, and his subterfuge in his conversations with Izvolsky justified the discredit in which he was held by the other countries of Europe. The press, which was assuming a determining influence in the formation of public opinion, had ample scope, wherever it was motivated by interests hostile to Austria-Hungary, for denouncing aggressive ambitions and the scandal of a powerful state that threatened a weaker neighbour. Considerations of this kind were sufficient to overshadow the no less dangerous imperialist ambitions of Russia and the veiled intrigues of the Serbs who were conspiring against the internal peace of Austria-Hungary.

Field-Marshal Conrad von Hoetzendorf worked with great zeal and competence to reorganize the army. He was determined to engage it in a preventive war in order to steal a march on the Serbs and the Russians, who had not yet made good their losses of 1905.

Yet, as long as the great international forces—the Church or Socialism—were not in a position to oppose those elements most likely to unleash a European conflict, the decision depended ultimately on the prudence and the moral courage of a few persons. It was not necessary that they should be great statesmen. President Fallières, for example, saw clearly that the Russian alliance could not be allowed to involve France in a foolhardy war, simply because of complications in the Balkans. Perhaps he was also mindful of the service that Austria-Hungary had rendered to peace in the settlement of the Moroccan question at the Conference of Algeciras (1906). King Edward VII, who in his discussions with Francis Joseph at Ischl, in 1908, had attempted in vain to guide Austria-Hungary's foreign policy in a direction more favourable to Great Britain, was a champion and architect of peace. William II, despite his outbursts and indiscretions, was still anxious at this stage to avoid a war with Russia.

The peaceful solution prevailed, but only for the time being. This was merely a respite. The risk of a European conflict had not been removed, since all the elements of a potential explosion still remained.

In all the countries of Europe the press found itself at the service of complex and contradictory economic interests of which its readers were unaware: they were susceptible to other arguments, such as the national ideal, but even then the press merely kindled passions. Dangerous blunders such as the Agram trial, in which proceedings were brought against alleged Serbo-Croat conspirators and in which the prosecution (that is, the Austro-Hungarian authorities) used documents of doubtful authenticity, caused very great damage to Austrian prestige. Each group tended to assume that its own cause enjoyed a monopoly of right and that all evil intentions could be attributed to its adversary.

$$\approx$$

The international climate became gradually more tense during the six years separating the crisis of 1908 and the war of 1914. The weakening of Turkey encouraged Italy's colonial ambitions in Tripolitania and, as a reaction, the growth of Irredentism, which directed its demands at the Trentino, Trieste and Dalmatia, traditionally countries of the Danubian monarchy but which comprised a large proportion of Italians. The outbreak of two wars in the Balkans, in 1912 and 1913, aggravated the danger of a general conflict. At the London Conference, in 1913, Serbia and Montenegro acquired a common frontier. Although Serbia received large territories in Macedonia, it failed to obtain access to the sea, owing to the creation of the state of Albania. Later, Bulgaria was obliged to give back a part of its conquests to the Turks and the Rumanians gained the region of Silistria, in Dobrudja. European Turkey emerged from the wars greatly diminished. Once again, Austria-Hungary found itself divided between the partisans of an immediate and preventive war and the advocates of a cautious policy. The archduke-heir, inspector-general of land and sea forces, was devoting all his energies to the military strength of the monarchy; but, in unison with Count Bertchold, the successor to Aehrenthal, who died in 1912, he did not wish to allow the generals to engage in war until internal order had been consolidated—a goal which he fully intended to attain.

A Czech historian, J. Křížek, has written: 'The extraordinary feature of Cisleithan political life is that, until the fall of the monarchy, hardly a single voice was raised against the monarchic principle and that the bourgeoisie, as a class, abandoned the republican concept of the State.'[21] There was nothing extraordinary in this. In fact, it was not simply that, as Křížek also claims, 'the national middle classes accepted the notion of a supranational attitude which had been adopted by the Crown' or that 'the middle class as a whole feared the advance of the working class'. In the consciousness of these peoples, and even in their collective subconscious, the much deeper forces of tradition and rural atavism were at work. For centuries, minds and hearts had been nurtured with respect for the monarchic institution, paternal and protecting. That institution was seen to be the consummation of a hierarchical society, founded on a broad peasant base and well suited to the needs of an agrarian world, in which each stage possessed its own special privileges and in which economic factors operated within a fairly limited area. The king was thus the supreme regulator, but accessible nonetheless. In the industrial age everything had changed with the transformation of economic relations and the extension of economic interdependence. The class struggle had emerged, the consequence in the field of labour and production of a universal liberty which, in the political field, implied the same rights for all individuals. The monarchic function was losing its intrinsic efficacy. But public opinion could not take cognizance of these gradual changes, while many characteristic aspects of the past still persisted in people's habits, especially in the country regions. It was therefore only to be expected that the monarchic sentiment should have survived. The Catholic Church and the Churches in general fostered this sentiment by preaching that it accorded with the divine order. Only in the case of Bohemia and Poland, two countries which considered themselves conquered territories (this was strictly true only of Poland), was loyalty passive, devoid of personal fervour for the sovereign and his dynasty.

In rather the same way, the peoples of the monarchy accepted the political regime, the association within the same state system of so many territories and nations which had traditionally striven to reconcile their individual existences with their community of destiny. In his *Diary of the Decisive Years*, Josef Redlich, an Austrian jurist and politician, put forward a view which, though in certain respects unjust, showed a profound understanding of the reality of the situation: 'How can this Empire, in which no one any longer has the sense of empire, retain its cohesion, how can it continue to exist, when one considers the present state of the administration, internal policy and diplomacy, the incapacity of the old sovereign, the indescribably difficult personality and position of the heir, the impracticability of the Dualism of 1867, the disheartening array of problems which present themselves on all sides, the avidity of the masses in national, financial and political matters, which finds its expression in a caricature of Parliament, both here and in Budapest? Nothing in all this justifies the hope of an amelioration. And yet, how and where could all these peoples, all these cultures, all these individuals exist, except in this impossible Austria-Hungary which has brought and still brings German culture to the Slavs and Magyars? How could one imagine an independent Hungary of Magyars, after the birth of powerful states among the southern Slavs? Where could the Czechs or the Poles find themselves better situated than in Austria?'[22]

When the festival held by the *Sokoly* ('The Falcons') at Prague in 1912 revealed to foreign visitors the strong, quiet consciousness of a nation in control of its own economy and culture; when, in this same year, the Eucharistic Congress drew to Vienna waggons of peasants in regional costumes and crowds of priests and nuns, and when, contrary to all expectation, thousands of persons who ordinarily had nothing but contempt for clericalism made of their presence a kind of civic act, it would have been difficult, had one not been mindful of the international situation, to believe in the reality of a decline and, even more so, in the inevitability of imminent disaster.

At the Parliament, in 1913, Professor Masaryk, a deputy and one of the most redoubtable members of the opposition, declared: 'Precisely because I have never let myself indulge in dreams about the fall of Austria, because I know that, good or bad, this Austria must endure, it seems to me that it is our duty to make something of it. Our plans for public law or administrative reform must not be allowed to weaken the others, but must fortify the whole.'[23]

Masaryk did not believe that this end could be attained by the methods contemplated by the archduke-heir—the strength of the army and the reinforcement of dynastic loyalty. But the existence of the monarchy seemed to him no more in contradiction with his evolving democratic ideal than it was with the socialist ideal of Renner. It was not here that the difficulty lay, but rather in the refusal or inability of politicians and nationalist movements to provide a positive programme of federation for the Austria-Hungary which they did not wish to see disappear and which they recognized as necessary. This task was being left to the scholars. Within the two centralist states, each group continued to resort to petty means in order to obtain modified advantages.

In Hungary, under the Stephen Tisza ministry, parliamentary life had resumed its course, after a fashion. This was not the case in Cisleithania, where experiments and ministerial crises followed one after the other, the government having frequent recourse to Article 14. In Bohemia, since 26 July 1913, the Diet had been suspended and the administration entrusted to a provisional Commission, the St. Anne Commission, on which both the Czechs and the Germans of Bohemia sat.

Daily life went on, nevertheless, for people had grown accustomed to difficulties.[24] Even working-class agitation showed no sign of becoming more acute. Suddenly, on 28 June 1914, in the euphoria of a fine, warm summer Sunday, the news of what had happened at noon in Sarajevo reached Vienna and spread throughout Europe. The archduke-heir and his wife, the Duchess von Hohenberg, who were visiting the city on their return from manoeuvres, had both been killed by revolver-shots fired by a young fanatic. The murders were the culmination of a plot hatched in Belgrade by the secret society *Narodná Obrana*, whose motto was 'Unity or Death'. Weapons and plans had been supplied in Serbia to a group of conspirators, Austrian subjects who had returned to Bosnia equipped with all the necessary instructions for the perpetration of the crime. The instigator of the conspiracy was a Serbian officer, Colonel Drajutin Dimetrijević, who in his secret activities bore the name of Apis. Neither the Serbian prime minister, Nicholas Pašić, nor the heir to the throne, Prince Alexander, who had just been appointed regent owing to the permanent illness of the king, Peter I, was aware of the plot. They were certainly not ignorant of the activity of secret societies or of the violence of nationalist pressures in their country, but they lacked the effective means of mastering these forces. Apis, passionately devoted to the Karageorgević dynasty, an ardent champion of Great Serbia, who obtained information from espionage agencies and was in contact with the Russian military attaché in Belgrade, was convinced that the archduke was the enemy of Serbia. He saw in Francis Ferdinand, largely because of the latter's policy favouring the formation of a South Slav state, the principal obstacle to the unification of the Serbian people.[25]

A few days before the assassination, the archduke had received the Emperor William II in his beautiful residence at Konopiště (Konopitsch). Ill-will has attributed a political character to this meeting. It has been said that plans for a war had been prepared. This is not true. No doubt, the two princes discussed the situation as they walked together in the rose-garden. That they should have done so was all the more natural because, less than two months earlier, the Emperor Francis Joseph had been dangerously ill. William II was chiefly concerned to persuade his host to show greater goodwill towards the Hungarian government and to Count Stephen Tisza. But the archduke, still under the influence of Maniu and of Vajda Vojevod, complained that the Rumanians of Transylvania were being oppressed by the Magyars. He did not conceal his dissatisfaction with the Italian policy of intriguing in Albania, nor his personal mistrust of King Victor Emmanuel.

The assassinations at Sarajevo ushered in the final period of the Habsburg monarchy. Encouraged to act by the Emperor William II, whose monarchic convictions had been shaken by the act of regicide, Austria-Hungary resolved to have done with Serbia once and for all. After the dispatch of an ultimatum, calculated by its intransigence to provoke a refusal, war was declared on 26 July. Undoubtedly, both in Vienna and in Budapest, where the Hungarian government had reluctantly subscribed to the ultimatum, it was still hoped that the war would be a limited one and that it would not unleash a European conflict. But such a hope was ill-founded. The personal weakness of the tsar, the determination of Russian ministers and generals to prove that Russia's protection was no empty thing, the attempt by Germany to intimidate France, the anxiety of the French government not to fail in the obligations of its alliance with Russia—all these were factors leading to the final catastrophe. Almost as if the disappearance of the archduke, unjustly accused of being a warmonger, had in fact removed the last obstacle to war, the conflagration flared: Austria-Hungary had given the signal for the European disaster in which it was to be engulfed.

❦

The author cannot here retrace the history of the First World War and its consequences. The eclipse of Austria-Hungary as a monarchic, supranational state was indubitably one of the major results of the conflict, but it is sufficient simply to single out those aspects essential to a deeper understanding of what happened.[26]

If the army constituted one of the foundation-stones of the system, the manner in which it conducted itself during the war poses one of the major problems of the war. It has often been suggested that, since it was composed of diverse nationalities, it must have lacked cohesion and discipline. It is easy to endow this army with the caricatured image traditionally represented by the Good Soldier Schweik.[27]

At the beginning of the war the Austrian infantry and cavalry were well trained and staffed, but, except for the artillery's 305 mortar, their equipment was not of the first order. The navy, with a total strength of 264,000 tons, comprised twelve battleships, seven cruisers, eighteen bombers, fifty-five torpedo-boats and six submarines. By the end of the war the army had lost 1,015,200 men on the battlefield and another 478,000 men had died in prisoner-of-war camps. Moreover, since the troops found themselves fighting their fellow-countrymen and their brothers in race (this was true of the Poles and the Serbs and, with the entry into the war of Italy in 1915 and of Rumania in 1916, the Italians and the Rumanians of Transylvania), their morale was attacked by internal dangers of a kind unknown by the other national armies.

Russia was able to appeal to the Czechs and the Slovaks in the name of Slav solidarity, to invite the enemy regiments to fraternize with her own and to tempt public opinion in the Slav countries by promising to support their demands for independence. In the autumn of 1914 the manifestos of the Russian generalissimo, the Grand Duke Nikolai Nikolaievich, were addressed to the nations of Austria-Hungary. In April 1915 a number of Czech regiments deserted (including the 28th Prague Regiment); at the time of the Brussilov offensive, in 1916, defections were so numerous as to help place between 265,000 and 300,000 Austrian prisoners in Russian hands. In Russia, a company of Czech and Slovak volunteers, the *Družina*, was organized as early as 1914; men also enrolled in the French Foreign Legion (the *Na Zdar* group). Subsequently, by active propaganda in the prisoner-of-war camps, soldiers anxious to uphold their oppressed nationality were persuaded to engage in the armies of the Entente against the Central Powers. It was as a result of this that the Entente decided in 1918 to recognize the National Councils of emigrants as *de facto* governments (the juridical formulae were varied). It thus avoided the accusation of having violated the laws of war by using prisoners in the struggle against their own country. The activity of the Czechoslovak Legion of Siberia in 1917 and 1918 exercised a great influence on the military situation during the latter months of the war and had important international repercussions. Finally, uprisings broke out on several occasions in Austrian regiments and in the navy—in February 1918 the naval units stationed at Cattaro revolted; although sporadic, these uprisings became more frequent in 1918.[28]

Yet it must be remembered that the Austro-Hungarian army as a whole fought with constant vigour: whatever their ethnic origins, its soldiers, bound by a personal oath of fidelity which they did not take lightly, proved their endurance and courage. The Austro-Hungarian military command was certainly not inferior to that of the other belligerents. Field-Marshal Conrad von Hoetzendorf, criticized in his own country, received the highest praise from his adversaries, who accredited him with exceptional qualities and considered him one of the outstanding army chiefs of the war.[29] Of the generals, the archdukes Frederick and Eugene and also Marshal Boroević gave proof of their great abilities. After a difficult first year of fighting (the fall of Lemberg and Przemysl in March 1915, the retreat after the first offensive in Serbia and the capture of Belgrade), the Austro-Hungarians gained very considerable successes from the beginning of August 1915, achieving within a few months the extension of the eastern front, from Czernovitz to Dunaburg, and the occupation of Serbia and Montenegro. The army had to fight on several fronts: in Italy, where eleven battles were engaged on the Isonzo, before the great offensive of autumn 1917 (Caporetto) which brought it from the Isonzo to the Piave; in Rumania, which was occupied as far as Bucharest, and later in the Ukraine.

But none of these campaigns brought the decisive victory that would have enabled Austria-Hungary to impose a cessation of hostilities. During the latter months of 1918 its armies suffered irreversible defeats and when the armistice was signed the forces of the Entente were on the point of invading its territory. Meanwhile, revolution had broken out at home while the Army of Italy was still fighting. The socialist Otto Bauer bears witness to this in his book *Österreichische Revolution*: 'Within, the Empire was already disintegrating; at the front, life still seemed to continue in the unity of any army embracing all the nations. The situation of summer 1848 appeared to have returned: *in deinem Lager ist Österreich.*' But this was merely an illusion, Bauer adds, for the army could not long remain untouched by the contagion of revolution.[30]

Surprising though this may seem, the military contingency was not in itself sufficient to bring about the downfall of the Dual Monarchy. The peoples had accepted mobilization and war with a quiet courage. J. Droz speaks of an 'Austrian patriotism'.[31] The truth, however, was of a more subtle kind. The sense of State and of civic duty was highly developed in the ideology and sensibility of the middle-class and national societies at the beginning of the twentieth century: duty was a meaningful concept. Consequently, manifestations of public censure were not carried to any great lengths. But a more obnoxious attitude was now taken by the military authorities who, seizing the initiative from the civil authorities, began to suspect all Slavs of treachery, simply because they were not Germans, and to bring proceedings against men highly esteemed by their fellow-countrymen —for example, the Czech deputies Karel Kramář and Aloís Rašín, who in 1915 were condemned to death (but not executed). In such circumstances, it was inevitable that national rancour should immediately become more bitter and that resistance should be organized.[32] Furthermore, though the Parliament continued to sit in Transleithania, the absence of parliamentary life in Cisleithania widened the gap between public opinion and the government. Above all, the economic condition of Austria, in relation to that of Germany and even Hungary, deteriorated rapidly as the result of the blockade. Hungary was better able to protect its food supplies because it was a more agricultural country. In Bohemia and Austria, the great cities had for a long time depended for their food not only on the produce of the neighbouring regions. The allied countries, Germany and Hungary, preoccupied with their own problems, were now giving Austria and Bohemia as little aid as possible. Hence, substitute foods had to be introduced—bread made with maize, ersatz coffee and stewed fruit, saccharine—and the slow but irremediable effects of malnutrition made themselves felt on people's health and nervous systems. Although these were countries of forestland, the shortage of coal was not compensated by the use of wood, for the railways had been requisitioned for the army and it was therefore difficult to transport wood. At all levels of society, the cold of the hard winters of 1916 and 1917 proved an even greater cause of suffering than hunger. In 1918 it was hoped that the conquest of the Ukraine would bring new supplies of cereals. The occupation of the Italian provinces alleviated the army's food problem. But the cities—Vienna, Prague and Graz—felt little benefit. With high prices, rationing and transport difficulties, the deprivations of urban life assumed tragic dimensions and strikes became inevitable. Everywhere, confidence in the competence of the public authorities dwindled. Salvation could come only from outside. The war had done much more than any form of political persecution to destroy the prestige of Austria in public opinion. The crisis of morale was even more formidable than the heroic effort which had been demanded of the soldiers.

The political situation merely multiplied the reasons for losing confidence in the very meaning of the struggle. One great unknown was the position of Italy, which had declared her neutrality at the outbreak of the war; but each of the two adversaries was eager to draw her into its camp. Italy could only be satisfied by prospects of territorial aggrandizement and all such aggrandizements were conceived to the detriment of Austria. Germany insisted that the Austrian Empire should agree to give the Trentino back to Italy and then Trieste, which would become a free city. The Entente, more generous, promised in addition to the Trentino the southern Tyrol, Goritz, Trieste, Istria and Dalmatia, though the latter comprised more Slavs than Italians (treaty of London, 26 April 1915). Italy, persuaded by this offer, entered into war against her former ally. In the following year, Austria was asked to renounce Transylvania in order to appease Rumania and it was understood that, in order to reconstitute an independent Poland that would fight against Russia, she should abandon Galicia. In short, to pave the way for victory, Germany was asking Austria-Hungary to make sacrifices that could hardly be greater even in the event of defeat.

The propaganda which had been calculated to strengthen the solidarity between the allies was failing in its object: large numbers of posters were being issued on which the helmeted and intrepid William II appeared to be protecting with his strength the Emperor Francis Joseph, shrunken and exhausted with age; Austria-Hungary's position as a second-rank power was thus merely underlined. At the same time, the prospects for the future put forward by publicists, even writers of great talent, left many persons unconvinced. In 1915 the German writer Frederick Naumann published a work that won immediate fame: *Mitteleuropa*.[33] He proposed a solution for the central European problem. Returning in a sense to Bruck's concept of a close economic alliance between the two great central powers, Naumann considered their destiny to be the intensive development of their own territory and of the Balkans, rather than the conquest of distant overseas markets. The awareness of a common economic interest, confirmed by the experience of the blockade, dominated all other considerations. The war had condemned the two powers to live in close union: after the war, they must continue to live thus, forming a single tariff bloc. By contrast with this programme, the Pan-Germanic ambition of imposing German culture on all the nationalities was pure fancy. Indeed, the strength of the system proposed by Naumann would rest on the independence guaranteed to each national group and on the respect shown to its individuality.

Naumann was thus advocating the construction of an *Oberstaat*, somewhat resembling the British Commonwealth, to which other countries (Poland and the Balkans) could be linked. The military alliance between two Empires, as realized by Bismarck, would be enlarged into a much broader system: *Mitteleuropa*, an economic and human reality, would be one of the elements of a world equilibrium. Naumann was also highly conscious of the problems of the working class, whose labour represented the mainstay of the whole structure.

It would be unjust to accuse Naumann of a Pan-Germanist intention or, at the opposite extreme, of a tendency towards defeatism simply because he abandoned the programme of sea-power and world expansion. He based his argument on concrete fact and on a real economic solidarity in central Europe. He showed his intellectual and moral courage by recognizing the right of all peoples to have their own independent culture. But, consciously or unconsciously, he considered the particular mission of *Gesamtösterreich* to be finished: he could not prevent the Germans from assuming the leading role in the new system and thus threatening the futures of the other nations (Hungary, Bohemia, Croatia, the southern Slavs and the Rumanians). A *Mitteleuropa* could be achieved only by the victory of Germany and, if it were not immediately founded on the humiliation of the non-Germanic nationalities, it would at least prepare the ground for their subordination to the authority of the victor. And yet, when his book was enjoying a resounding success, Frederick Naumann, who often visited Vienna, recognized that there were few men in Germany capable of embracing his project. The military and the industrialists, intent upon gaining victory and extending territorial conquests, controlled an even wider audience.[34] Peace might offer Austria-Hungary a means of escaping from the grip of Germany.

※

Undoubtedly, since the peace which terminates a war is always, to a certain degree, a compromise, any belligerent state, however resolutely it conducts the war, is anxious to know how it might become reconciled with the enemy or find a more amenable partner in an opposing coalition.

Although Austria-Hungary appeared to be responsible for the war, which it had indeed set in motion, the belief was held in France and in Great Britain that it would be relatively easy to detach Austria-Hungary from Germany and that this was what the Dual Monarchy really desired. The benevolent disposition of France and Great Britain was not unrecognized in Vienna and in Budapest, which justifiably saw Russia as its most redoubtable enemy. But, in consequence, the approaches made to or by Austria, with a view to the conclusion of a separate peace, proved more numerous than in the case of any other of the countries at war. It is not easy to establish to what extent these manoeuvrings, none of which was successful, helped to weaken the determination either of the government or of public opinion to continue the struggle on the battlefields. The idea soon became widespread that victory was doubtful and that negotiation presented the only means of salvation. Furthermore, Dualism was revealing its drawbacks. Hungary did not feel closely bound to Austria: as early as 1914, when their country was in danger of invasion by the Russians, the members of the Hungarian opposition had contemplated separate negotiations.[35]

In 1915 they took part in a private capacity in talks with Italian statesmen, and it is not an exaggeration to suggest that the policy of the Hungarian opposition played a part in the dissolution of the Dual Monarchy. Peace initiatives were taken by diverse groups; because of their former business or social relationships and their ideological sympathies (and here one can surmise the influence, difficult to define, not of freemasonry in general, but of freemasons as individuals), these groups were able to establish contacts with the emissaries of the opposing camp on neutral territory. Of these various peace offers, that made by the Emperor Charles I to France in the first months of his reign was reputed to have come the closest to success and was to be favourably remembered in certain French circles. The goodwill of the emperor, his Christian intention of halting the conflict and his love for his peoples cannot be questioned. The Archduke Francis Ferdinand believed that he had initiated Charles in his own policies. He even reassured himself by thinking that, in case of necessity, he would have in his nephew the successor capable of realizing those policies. But master and pupil were poles apart. Generous, but naïve and easily influenced, maladroit in the exercise of his rights, the Emperor Charles appears not to have taken true measure of his words and actions. Though sincere, he confused secrecy with secretiveness. He complained to his family of the manner in which the Germans of the Reich were managing the alliance. He said that he had been told by Francis Joseph himself that German pressure had pushed Austria-Hungary into declaring war and even, eight years earlier, into the annexation of Bosnia-Herzegovina.[36] The empress and, in particular, her mother, the duchess of Parma, were hostile to Prussia. It was from the family group that the initiative came for an approach to Poincaré, through the good offices of Prince Sixtus of Bourbon-Parma, the brother of the empress and an officer in the Belgian army. The French politicians believed in the possibility of success. The emperor offered to support the 'just claims' of France with regard to Alsace-Lorraine. Count Czernin, the minister of foreign affairs, was aware of the negotiations and took part in them, though without being informed of certain fundamental points. The negotiations were thwarted first of all by the resistance of the Italian minister Sonnino. Then, in the spring of 1918, Czernin committed the indiscretion of alluding in public to other secret negotiations with France and drew a stinging rejoinder from Clemenceau, who published details of the talks of 1917 and the letter of Charles I. The 'Sixtus affair' resulted in the emperor dismissing his minister and being obliged to make a public apology and reparation to the Germans. Charles I had to declare that Austria-Hungary was fighting to preserve Alsace-Lorraine for Germany. He found himself discredited, compelled to reinforce an alliance whose yoke he detested and soon to conclude an economic agreement, roughly along the lines of the *Mitteleuropa* project, which further diminished the independence of his own Empire.

Throughout Austria's negotiations with the belligerent powers there persisted the doubt whether it was a question of a separate peace or a general peace. Although Austria had made the initial advances, a peace would necessarily have involved Germany. The chances of success varied with the changes in the general military situation.

It is certain that neither Great Britain, France nor, later, America maintained the same determined attitude towards Austria as towards Germany. They did not desire the disappearance of Austria, an eventuality which they feared would confront them with an even more confused situation. For a long time they hoped that an agreement with Austria would hasten the end of the war. But naturally, if no solution could be found with the Austrian government, it would be necessary to look in another direction—to the National Councils which had been organized in Russia, Great Britain and France and which were appealing to the governments of the Entente to take the cause of the nationalities under their protection.[37]

The emigrant movement had originated in the Czech and Slovak colonies in Russia, as early as the summer of 1914. Two southern Slavs, Supilo and Trumbić, had gone to Italy, which was still neutral, to devote their energies to the destiny of Dalmatia. The census of 1910 had established the Italian population of Dalmatia as eighteen thousand, against six hundred and sixty thousand Serbo-Croats; but the Italians formed a powerful middle-class group and enjoyed the support of the Italians of the kingdom. Was there not reason to fear that, in their offers to Italy, the Allies might make promises with regard to Dalmatia? Supilo went to London and to Bordeaux, where the French government had established itself. Then he came up against the objection that the demands of the Yugoslavs counted for less than the million soldiers which Italy could supply to the Entente.

In London the national groups found their natural champions among liberal intellectuals, professors and journalists, men such as Wickham Steed and Seton-Watson, who possessed an expert knowledge of their problems. In the spring of 1915, Trumbić formed a Yugoslav Council, which proposed the constitution of a great South Slav state centred on Serbia and embracing the Banat of Temesvár, Bácska, half of Carinthia and also Styria. These were unreasonable demands, but Wickham Steed and Seton-Watson minimized their possible consequences in their consultations with the British government. The emigrants, who were in contact with the Serbian prime minister Pašić, could be of service. To draw Bulgaria on to the side of the Entente, it was necessary to persuade Serbia to cede to that country a few districts of Macedonia. In return, Serbia would be given Bácska, a Hungarian territory with a large Serb population.

Thus, the South Slav question in itself was still not being considered by the Allies. It was of interest only in so far as it affected relations with Italy, Serbia and Bulgaria. Nevertheless, a Yugoslav Council existed which the countries of the Entente were protecting and whose influence and possible future role they recognized.

A 'National Council of Czech Lands' (a vague term which could be extended to include the Slovaks) was formed in London, in November 1915. Its prime mover was Professor Masaryk, who had not emigrated at the beginning of the war, but had travelled in Holland, Switzerland and Italy. The Czech cause had found warm support in France, where the historian of Bohemia, Ernest Denis, a professor at the Sorbonne and an ardent patriot of Jacobin tendencies, had vigorously defended the Slavs of Austria-Hungary in a war that had placed Germans and Slavs in opposing camps. In 1915 he published a book which was well received by public opinion—*La Guerre*, in which he devised a map for the future Europe, the principal features of which were to be confirmed by the treaties of 1919.

Ernest Denis and Masaryk had known each other before the war. Renewing their old acquaintance, they now combined their efforts, publishing newspapers—*La Nation tchèque, L'Indépendance tchèque*—in which they attempted to initiate the public in the problems of Bohemia. Unlike many of his compatriots, who in the early months of the war had been awaiting the arrival of the Russians, Masaryk had only partial confidence in tsarist Russia. He confessed that he feared the installation of a grand duke in Prague as king of Bohemia.[38] His sympathies went to Great Britain, which he was convinced would emerge victorious. He saw the conflict as a revolution that was to lead to the triumph of Western democracy over the militarist and authoritarian regimes.

The National Councils received support and financial aid from their compatriots settled in America, many of whom had made their fortunes and had never ceased to show an interest in their old homeland, where in earlier days they had suffered too much not to feel bitterness towards the government and the whole system of Austria-Hungary. Through newspapers and lectures, an active propaganda movement was organized to influence public opinion in the Allied countries, while the leaders of the National Councils made themselves personally known to the journalists and politicians.

A young *privat-docent* of the University of Prague, Edward Beneš, a disciple of Masaryk who had also studied at Dijon and the Sorbonne, established himself in Paris, where he published the celebrated pamphlet *Destroy Austria-Hungary!* which made a dramatic impact on public opinion. Milan Štefánik, a young Slovak who had assumed French nationality and was an astronomer at the Paris Observatory, joined with Masaryk and Beneš. He was very different from them, of a more adventurous and romantic temperament. But he had many friends. In a war in which the West was invoking the liberty and independence of peoples, the liberation of the 'Czechoslovaks', considered as the two branches of a single nation, would surely find a place among the causes championed by the Allies. However, the lack of co-ordination and of sympathy between the group based in London and in Paris and the Czechs in Russia, who still put their trust in the tsar, persisted until the fall of tsarism in 1917 and the accession to power of the younger politicians. Masaryk, whose book on *Russia and Europe* had been banned by the tsarist censors, was a friend of Professor Miliukov, one of the new ministers. The whole body of Czechoslovak emigrants now rallied to him.

The governments of the Entente were thus protecting the National Councils and consenting to support their demands for autonomy, but in doing so they showed a certain caution in order not to block the way to a separate peace with Austria-Hungary. The National Councils, for their part, were maintaining relations with secret organizations formed within Austria-Hungary which kept them informed of events and to which they suggested general lines of policy. Here is revealed another essential characteristic of public opinion in Austria-Hungary during the war—a much broader awareness than in other countries of what was happening in the enemy camp and, despite the official anathemas hurled at the 'treason' of Masaryk, Supilo and Trumbić, despite the atmosphere of terror created by trials, a constant determination to find out the extent of the support which the emigrants could give to the national cause. There existed the conviction that the Austro-Hungarian regime would not survive in its pre-war form and that a new order would be instituted. This did not yet imply the abandonment of the monarchy or of the association of the Danubian peoples. Francis Joseph died on 21 November 1916. His death was surrounded by a mood of gravity and respect: but it was seen as a sign that the past had been extinguished. It almost coincided with the peace proposals made by the Central Empires, President Wilson's request to the belligerents to define their war aims, and the reply of the Entente, demanding the reconstitution of an independent Poland and urging that the Czechoslovaks, the Italians, the Rumanians and the Slavs of Austria-Hungary be liberated from foreign domination.

In Bohemia, the deputies of the Parliament had regrouped themselves in a 'Czech Union' (*Český Svaz*) which included representatives of all parties, even Social Democrats. At its head it placed a National Council whose chief spokesman was Antonin Švehla, of the Agrarian Party. The Czech Union declared that it repudiated the insinuation contained in the Allies' reply to President Wilson, 'for the nation envisages the conditions of its future development only under the sceptre of the Habsburgs'.

The new sovereigns had been crowned king and queen of Hungary in Budapest, in accordance with the old ceremonial and in the presence of deputations from every country of the Dual Monarchy. There was talk of a coronation in Prague, for which Professor Pekař prepared an address from the nation to its king.[39]

Censorship became more tolerant, without inspiring any new orientation of ideas: newspapers, pamphlets and books were filled with nothing but projects and allusions to change. The young emperor hesitated between two solutions: should he use his own authority to introduce a great programme for the reform of the Empire, or should he seek the sanction of the Parliaments? In the latter case, it would be necessary to reconvene the Austrian Parliament. Nothing had been set in motion or even promised when events suddenly gathered momentum— the declaration of an unlimited submarine war by Germany, which was determined to spare the neutral countries no longer, and the revolution in Russia.

The entry into the war of the United States in 1917 compelled the Central Empires to anticipate the time when the Americans would supply the countries of the Entente with armaments and men and thereby alter the balance of military power. It was thus essential to secure either a negotiated peace or a military victory in order to avert a catastrophe.

Even if the Kerensky government was determined to maintain its country's role in the war, the Russian revolution had modified the moral conditions of the conflict. The policies of governments were now confronted with the mighty hopes of the masses that their misery would shortly be at an end. New ideas were being disseminated: peace without annexation or indemnity, the right of peoples to govern themselves. How might such ideas be applied to the destinies of the nationalities in Austria-Hungary?

A decision of great importance was the convocation of the Austrian Parliament on 30 May 1917. The deputies did not inspire unanimous confidence in their constituents. It is of great significance that in Prague, where the hope of peace and renewal was intensely felt, people seemed to fear that the attitude of the deputies was not sufficiently firm. Articles in the press enthusiastically celebrated the Czech spring, while others, among them the articles of the historian Pekař, warmly defended the concept of state rights. In particular, a joint manifesto of writers created a sensation, calling upon the deputies either to defend the rights of the *Czechoslav* nation resolutely or to renounce their mandate. The use of the uncommon expression 'Czechoslav nation' was an allusion to a possible union with the Slovaks. At the Parliament the different national groups demanded the transformation of Austria, but at the same time renewed their declarations of loyalty to the emperor and the dynasty. The Czech Club, represented by the Agrarian deputy Staněk, insisted that the Habsburg-Lorraine monarchy become a federation of national states, free and equal in rights. For the Czech nation it claimed the historic territory of 'state rights' and union with the Slovaks: it was therefore requesting the preservation of the territorial association with the Germans of Bohemia, but also, by implication, the rejection of the Compromise, so that the Slovaks might join with the Czechs in a new national state.

The position of the Slovenes was also highly significant. The spokesman of the South Slavs—that is, the Slovenes, the Dalmatians and the Croats of Cisleithania—was a Slovene deputy, Fr. Korošec. The census of 1910 had recorded in Cisleithania a population of 1,249,448 Slovenes, concentrated chiefly in Carniola. Although a Slovene national middle class had emerged in the cities (Laybach, for example), where it found itself in competition with Austrians and Italians, the Slovenes were essentially a rural nation, devoted to the Catholic faith and to the monarchic tradition. The clergy was patriotic and there were Slovene bishops at Laybach (Mgr. Jeglić) and at Trieste (Mgr. Karlin). The population as a whole desired a close association with the Croats. Fr. Korošec therefore demanded the constitution of an independent state of Serbs, Croats and Slovenes, but under the sceptre of the Habsburg-Lorraine dynasty. What he was seeking was, in fact, the South Slav kingdom which Francis Ferdinand had contemplated. Once again, however, the break with the Compromise was implicit. But on 20 July 1917, at Corfu, the Serbian prime minister, Pašić, and Trumbić, representing the Yugoslav emigrants, concluded the pact which provided for the grouping of South Slavs around the kingdom of Serbia. The solution proposed by Korošec would involve a territorial modification of the Dual Monarchy, but not its disappearance. The second solution would not condemn the Dual Monarchy to total extinction, but would deprive it of all the South Slav populations.

The politicians wavered. In Croatia, at the reopening of the Diet, the Agrarian deputy Radić, who had wanted a separate coronation at Agram, declared that fidelity to the monarchy would not survive if the price was to be servitude. Each national group wished to obtain guarantees for its rights, but, in the new association, it intended to arm itself against any temptation to hegemony on the part of a neighbouring group.[40] The Social Democrats of Cisleithania had insisted on the convocation of the Parliament. They had made this a condition of the attitude which they would agree to adopt at the international conference in Stockholm, where they were to meet the socialists of the neutral countries. They consented (the Czechs included) not to repudiate the principle of a union of the Danubian nations in a federal state. They did not explicitly reject the monarchic form. In their view, the most important thing was to affirm the right of peoples to self-determination and the necessity of putting an end to the war by a peace without annexation or indemnity. At Stockholm, they made contact with emigrant Czech socialists. A striking feature of public opinion in Austria from 1916 onwards was that it expected a fundamental transformation of the State and was already preoccupied with the new order that would be introduced in Europe after peace had been achieved.

The climate was no longer dominated by the military and police dictatorship that had been rampant in the first two years of the war. Censorship still existed, but in a greatly relaxed form. In Vienna a review appeared, *Austria Nova* ('The New Austria'), which included among its contributors and patrons a number of persons close to the emperor, such as his adjutant-general, Prince Zdenko Lobkowicz, the Comte de Crenneville and Professor Lammasch. Works were being published which had the renewal of the Empire as their theme. In 1916 Ignaz Seipel, a professor of theology and the future chancellor of the Austrian Republic, published a vigorous study, *Nation und Staat*. Analysing these two concepts, he argued that the nation and the state were communities of a different character. He rejected internationalism and nationalism as extreme solutions, maintaining that only federation could guarantee the protection of common interests and satisfy the social, economic and intellectual aspirations of each group.

The titles of these works showed a certain similarity: *Österreichs Erneuerung* ('The Renewal of Austria'), published by Karl Renner in 1916; *Zur Wiederverjüngung Österreichs* ('For a Rejuvenation of Austria'), published in 1917 under a pseudonym, Austriacus Observator, who appears to have been a priest of the imperial entourage.[41] Early in 1917, resuming his work *The Struggle of the Austrian Nation for the State*, Karl Renner gave it a new title, *Das Selbstbestimmungsrecht der Nationen* ('The Nations' Right of Self-determination'). He asserted that the problem extended far beyond the framework of Austria and now involved the whole world. Austria, he said, despite the reactionary nature of its constitutions, had provided the first and the most convincing example of an international state, which now needed to be adapted to present conditions.

The war which had issued from the rivalries of capitalism and the political concept of the nation would lead to the triumph of internationalism, for which the new Austria would have presented the original model.[42] He counted eight nations within the Dual Monarchy. Each of these nations should be granted the right of self-determination on a particular territory (the 'circle') and the administration of its internal affairs. The citizens of the Empire would thus enjoy a twofold autonomy—territorial and national. The 'circle' would be the basis of the life of the state in its three dimensions—territorial, national and federal. The state would be the political and territorial federation of all the circles, the nation the federation of all the circles or parts of circles of any one ethnic group. All citizens, as members of the federation, would elect by universal suffrage a Federal Assembly, but it would be necessary to establish a fairly strong central government, for a simple personal union would be insufficient to guarantee the durability of the system.

Once again, Renner wished to set aside the historic claim of 'state rights' because, in his opinion, it did not make adequate allowance for the new national consciousness of the minorities; he also wished to overcome the obstacle of middle-class nationalism, a trend that seemed to be leading to the fragmentation of the Empire into little states which, by reason of their very weakness, would adopt a repressive policy towards their subjects. The first volume of his book appeared in 1918, at a time when events had already brought many changes. Renner described it as 'Kriegsarbeit' ('war work'). In reality, it was more like a buoy thrown in desperation into the sea. His project merited respect by the originality and power of its conception. It was not the work of a Utopian, for the subsequent career of its author, who on two occasions saved Austria's independence, gave ample proof that he was much more a statesman than a Utopian. But in 1918 Renner was confronted with the obstacle of national and social passions. He was asking too many sacrifices of the ideal of autonomy which, either in a traditional or in a democratic form, was becoming the lever employed by nations on the verge of total independence. The left wing of the Social Democrat Party rebuked him for clinging to Austro-Marxism and dreaming of a strong federal state; the socialist nations intended to determine their own destinies and to discover for themselves some new form of association.

※

The overriding and constant concern of the Emperor Charles was the restoration of peace. The reform of the Dual Monarchy seemed to him a means of attaining this goal, by satisfying the nationalities and gathering public opinion around himself. On 2 July 1917, after the Parliament had been reassembled, he granted a broad amnesty. Then, during the summer, he approached an Austrian deputy, Josef Redlich, with a view to the formation of a new ministry; Redlich was a member of the German Liberal Party, a man of wide experience and a skilful parliamentarian capable of rising above national prejudices. It was proposed that the new ministry would include representatives of the nationalities. Redlich was well acquainted with Professor Lammasch and a rich businessman, Julius Meinl, the director of a society for political research who had compiled some impressive reports on the economic condition of Austria. Lammasch and Meinl were in touch with foreign countries and had already made several peace soundings in Switzerland. In Hungary, the emperor planned to replace Tisza with Count Károlyi, a great lord of democratic sympathies, and to introduce universal suffrage. These were all men of high calibre whose very presence indicated that Austria-Hungary was not lacking in politicians. The programme was a bold and dangerous one, but worth attempting. The king-emperor, however, did not persevere in his plan, preferring ministries that would adopt a waiting policy to ministries led by daring personalities. Perhaps at this stage he was placing his hopes in the peace offers of Benedict XV.

The development of events merely reinforced the solidarity of the Central Empires and made it more difficult for Austria to embark on an independent policy. During the winter of 1917–18, the defeat of the Italians at Caporetto, the peace negotiations with Soviet Russia, the Ukraine and Rumania, and the occupation of new territories by the German and Austrian armies bound the destinies of the two Empires more closely than ever. Nevertheless, after President Wilson had published the Fourteen Points of his peace programme, the Emperor Charles entered into secret talks with him, attempting to persuade him that their objectives were not irreconcilable and that, once autonomy had been granted to the nationalities, a general peace would be more easily accomplished. But by this time the questions at issue had multiplied enormously and Austria's mediation seemed quite inadequate to settle them. The Austro-American negotiations were interrupted in the spring of 1918, when the clash between Clemenceau and Czernin compromised the prestige of the Austrian government.

The final part of the war was fought on the western front: the Central Empires were launching a new offensive in France. In these circumstances, the legions of volunteers and freed prisoners of war proved of great assistance to the Allied armies. They were good troops and the Czechoslovaks had distinguished themselves at Darney, on the Vosges front. In Russia, the Czechoslovaks formed an army for which Masaryk had secured recognition as an integral part of the French forces. He had then prepared the way for their evacuation via Vladivostok. In fact, during the summer of 1918 the Czechoslovak Legion, in its 'Anabasis', monopolized the Trans-Siberian railway line and thereby delayed the establishment of the Soviet regime.

In May a Congress of Oppressed Nations (that is, oppressed by Austria-Hungary) was held in Rome. A few weeks later, the French government recognized the Czechoslovak National Council as 'the future basis of an independent government and the trustee of Czechoslovak interests'. The solidarity of the Entente and the National Councils was intensified, as the chances of a separate peace with Austria-Hungary gradually faded. The idea gained ground that, since an agreement with the government of Austria-Hungary had not been realized, the time had come to hasten its downfall, which would also bring the downfall of Germany.

The internal situation of the Dual Monarchy was becoming increasingly grave. Only a small number of the Austro-Hungarian prisoners of war freed by the treaty of Brest-Litovsk had joined the Bolshevik army: a far greater number had engaged in the Czechoslovak Legion. But the large majority had poured back into their native country. They brought with them a revolutionary spirit, preaching peace without annexation or indemnity and social revolution. They found public opinion ready to listen. Poverty and starvation were to be found everywhere. The cereal harvest had dropped from 91 million quintals in 1913 to 49 millions in 1916 and 28·1 millions in 1917; the cost of living had increased to such an extent that the index for the average expenditure of a working family, taken as 100 in 1914, had risen to 312 by 1916, 616 by 1917 and 1,560 by 1918.[43] This was the time when the people of Prague set off in trainloads to look for food in the countryside of Bohemia and when the middle bourgeoisie of Vienna, whose savings had been sacrificed in war loans, found itself reduced to poverty. The situation was, perhaps, slightly less difficult in Hungary, where the harvest had been 98 million quintals in 1917, but it was serious nonetheless. Strikes followed one after another in the industrial regions and the troops refused to march against the strikers. In Prague, the May Day procession descended on Wenceslas Square behind a large banner bearing the inscription 'The Socialist Nation'. In Vienna, a campaign of calumny was being directed against the imperial family: there was talk of the 'treason' of the Italian empress and it was said that the incapable emperor was at the mercy of a cabal of priests and war-profiteers. And yet, when in the summer the military situation had begun to swing back in the Allies' favour and the rout of Germany had been set in motion, Charles I tried again to persuade America to bring a halt to the war on the basis of the Fourteen Points. In September, however, the collapse of the Bulgarian front brought the return of a new wave of demoralized soldiers, as the Austro-Hungarian units retreated under pressure from the Army of the East. In the streets of Vienna people shouted 'Long live peace! Down with the monarchy!' The ruling classes and the politicians feared that Bolshevism would spread throughout the Empire.

The dilemma was this: would the new order be that of the national ideal, represented by the middle class, in which the liberal intellectuals wielded as much influence as the industrialists and the bankers, or would it be that of the working class, the proletariat? At all events, the assault on the monarchic order of old Austria and on its traditional allies, the aristocracy and the Church, was being launched from two sides. On 16 October 1918, still with the intention of securing peace on the terms of President Wilson's programme, the emperor issued a manifesto in which he promised the transformation of the Empire of Austria into a federation of national states. He was thus accepting, amid chaos and disarray, the demands which had been put forward by the deputies of the Imperial Parliament in the previous year and which could have been realized by liberal ministries. Hungary was not included in the programme of reform. At the Social Democrat congress in Budapest, on 13 October, a delegate had declared that Austria-Hungary had ceased to form a political unity and that, henceforth, only the peoples possessed the right of decision-making. The Rumanians were demanding full independence for Transylvania, the Banat and Bukovina.

The National Councils in the various provinces admitted that they had more to fear from the blind anarchism of revolutionary upheavals than from the imperial government, which was now powerless. They were anxious to obtain a peaceful transmission of power and administration, so that they might be able, as the representatives of their liberated nation, to negotiate with the National Councils abroad and with the victors of the war. The Social Democrat leaders agreed to collaborate with them and to give them the support of the working class, which had rallied to the principle of the independent democratic state.

The emperor allowed K. Kramář to go to Switzerland to meet Edward Beneš. In the meantime, the independence of the Czechoslovak state had been proclaimed in Prague, on 28 October. The National Council of Agram declared the separation of the South Slavs from the Habsburg monarchy and their union with the kingdom of Serbia. On the same day, Count Károlyi, to whom the king had entrusted the Hungarian ministry, announced the full independence of Hungary and attempted to enter into negotiations with the high command of the French army, which was arriving in Belgrade.

To the emperor's request for an armistice President Wilson replied that the conditions on which his Fourteen Points had been based no longer existed and that it was for the nations of the monarchy to decide their own fate. In Vienna, on 21 October, the Austrian deputies had established a Council of State for the German-speaking countries, under the presidency of Renner. It was to Renner that the emperor's last minister, Professor Lammasch, handed over his powers on 31 October, after having ordered the commander of the Army of Italy to request an armistice. The emperor did not abdicate. He was content to renounce the exercise of his authority, on 11 November, but on the following day the Provisional Assembly of German Austria proclaimed the Republic. From Hungary, Count Károlyi begged the king to take no further part in the government, in the interests of the country.[44]

Thus the Habsburg monarchy, whose strength and prestige had shone over Europe for centuries, dissolved and vanished within a few days, having been asked to depart, rather than forcibly ousted, by the representatives of those nations whose territories it had gathered together under its sceptre, whose material existence and national reality it had protected at the time when it had been strong, and whose development it had tolerated as its own power weakened. But these nations were on the brink of the same violent social revolution that had been unleashed in Russia. New leaders, most of whom had received their training in the political struggles of the Dual Monarchy, were assuming the responsibility of representing the nations in negotiations with the victors and obtaining for them conditions of peace which, in the words of Renner, should not resemble those of Brest-Litovsk.

NOTES

1. *Die nationale Frage in der österreichisch-ungarischen Monarchie 1900–1918*, Budapest, 1966. This work contains the papers and discussions of the conference held in Budapest on 4–9 May 1964, concerning the problems of the Austro-Hungarian monarchy in the period 1900–18. The paper by P. Hanák is entitled *Einige Sozial-ökonomische Aspekte der nationalen Frage in der Österreichisch-Ungarischen Monarchie*, p. 319 *et seq.*, and begins with a good analysis of the interpretations of different historians. Hanák stresses the need

to study more closely the different social classes of the monarchy and the foundations for political changes which they were capable of providing. Pichlík, a Czechoslovak historian, offers some interesting observations along these same lines (ibid., p. 331). The young school of historians is anxious to break with the relics of nationalism, 'die Überreste des Nationalismus'; it shows a greater interest than its predecessors in the international trends of the working-class movement and, even for those who accept neither its ideology nor its method, opens up new and hitherto forbidden perspectives.

2. *Ver Sacrum:* 'Wir wollen eine Kunst ohne Fremdendienerei, aber ohne Fremdenfurcht und ohne Fremdenhass. Die ausländische Kunst soll uns anregen, uns auf uns selbst zu besinnen, wir wollen sie anerkennen, bewundern, wenn sie es wert ist, nur nachmachen wollen wir sie nicht,' 1898, I, a. p. 6. '. . . eine lebendige nationale Kunst sollte es natürlich sein, nicht *Heimat Kunst.*' Rainer Maria Rilke, Hugo von Hofmannsthal and Ricarda Huch joined the Secession movement.

3. Michel Lancelot, *Anton Bruckner*, Seghers, 1964, quotes on p. 162 this assessment made by Romain Rolland in 1908: 'We in France are familiar neither with the symphonies of Anton Bruckner, nor with any part of his copious achievement, nor with the engaging personality, gentle, mystical, modest, rather child-like, who throughout his life was overshadowed by the Brahms party and who, like Franck in our country, rallied around himself the forces of youth and originality against the official art of his time.' Wagner said of Bruckner: 'I know only one man who approaches Beethoven, and that man is Bruckner' (ibid., p. 58). Johann Strauss declared generously that, by comparison with Bruckner, he was merely a street fiddler; Bruckner, no less generous and knowing that the world has need both of grace and of grandeur, replied: 'I would give many symphonies for one waltz of Johann Strauss.'

4. István Sötér, 'The problems of assimilation in nineteenth-century Hungarian literature' in *Hungarian Literature, European Literature, Studies in Comparative Literature*, published by the Hungarian Academy of Sciences, Budapest, 1964, p. 355.

5. A customs union was contemplated by the Austrian government on several occasions. See Joseph Redlich, *Schicksalsjahre Österreichs 1908–1919*, vol. I, p. 166. Between 1895 and 1905 the Dual Monarchy provided 58 per cent of Serbia's imports and took 88 per cent of her exports.

6. D. Djordjevic, 'Movements for the national and economic independence of the Balkans up to 1914', *Acts of the International Congress of Historical Studies*, Vienna, 1965.

7. Of the great many works in French on the archduke, the reader could consult Maurice Muret, *L'archiduc François-Ferdinand*; also, the studies by Chlumecky, Eisenmenger, Soskony, etc. The most thorough work is that of R. Kiszling, *Erzherzog Franz Ferdinand von Österreich-Este*, 1955; rather curiously, one of the truest portraits of the archduke is to be found in a work of fiction by E. J. Görlich, *Der Thronfolger*, 1961. Jacques Droz, in *L'Europe centrale*, p. 181, says that the diversity of testimony with regard to Francis Ferdinand makes historians hesitate to give an opinion. But two points should be remembered: firstly, no serious study of the archduke is possible without having recourse to his archives, deposited by his eldest son in the *Staatsarchiv* in Vienna, and gathering together the testimony of persons who knew him well and many of whom are still alive today.

Secondly, Francis Ferdinand's strong personality will inevitably arouse sympathy or antipathy, according to individual temperament and opinion. Deeply loved by those close to him, the archduke was not at first an amenable person and he never courted popularity. As far as the 'judgement of history' is concerned, all that can be established with certainty is the respect which he commanded by his personal disinterestedness and his chivalrous loyalty.

8. A. Chéradame, *L'Europe et la question d'Autriche-Hongrie du début du XXᵉ siècle*, 1901; R. W. Seton-Watson (Scotus Viator), *Racial Problems in Hungary*, 1910; Wickham Steed, *The Habsburg Monarchy*, London, 1913.

9. On the Moravian Compromise of 1905, see R. Kann, *Das Nationalitätenproblem*, I, p. 200, and bibliography p. 401. Hugo Hantsch, *Die Nationalitätenfrage*, p. 62. This agreement seemed a good thing but was limited in its scope, since the problem as a whole could only have been settled if state rights had been granted earlier and had led to the creation of a common Diet for the kingdom of Bohemia.

10. In her little book *Prag*, Vienna, 1966, Johanna Herzogenburg gives some interesting eyewitness information concerning the way of life of the Bohemian nobility, still surrounded by a scrupulously observed system of etiquette which totally isolated it from the middle class.

11. Karel Kramář (1860–1937) was one of the principal political figures in Bohemia between 1891 and 1920. The leader of the Young Czech Party, he defended the doctrine, both political and cultural, of Austroslavism. Married to a Russian and himself possessing a large fortune, Kramář maintained contacts with the Russian liberals and the French republicans, with whom he found himself in sympathy. He was vice-president of the Reichsrat in Vienna. Arrested during the war, he was tried and sentenced to death (1915), but the death-sentence was postponed. Pardoned by the Emperor Charles, Kramář re-established contact with the emigrant movement and represented his country at the Peace Conference. He clashed with Masaryk and spent the rest of his life in opposition. There is no good biography of Kramář.

12. An article by J. Havránek, 'Social Classes, Nationality Ratios and Demographic Trends in Prague 1880–1900', *Historica*, XIII, shows clearly the difference in the standard of living of the German and the Czech middle classes in Prague between 1880 and 1900.

13. Figures provided by T. I. Berend and G. Ránki in their article *Das Niveau der Industrie Ungarns zu Beginn des 20. Jahrhunderts* in *Studien* (op. cit.), p. 275, and by J. Křížek (from details in the *Österreichisches Handbuch*, 1901) in 'La crise du dualisme . . .', *Historica*, XII, p. 87. It should be observed, however, that Cisleithania, which covered a smaller area, possessed 19,562 kilometres of railway track in 1901 and 22,749 in 1911, by comparison with 17,264 and 20,998 for these same years in Transleithania. Hungary was thus making a great effort in railway construction, though she still remained behind Austria.

14. This is the view taken by P. Hanák in his stimulating article *Probleme der Krise des Dualismus an Ende des 19 Jahrhunderts* in the collection *Studien* (op. cit.), p. 270.

15. Jurij Křížek, 'La crise du dualisme et le dernier Compromis austro-hongrois 1897–1907', *Historica*, XII (Prague), p. 117, note 107. An interesting article, which should be compared with that by P. Hanák, is to be found in the collection *Die nationale Frage* mentioned in note 1.
    Cf. the general article by F. Zwitter and that by L. Katus, *Über die wirtschaftlichen und Gesellschaftlichen Grundlagen der Nationalitätenfrage in Ungarn vor dem ersten Weltkrieg*, p. 149.

16. M. Paléologue, *Les Entretiens de l'Impératrice Eugénie*, Paris, 1921, states that the empress informed him on her return from Ischl in July 1906 that the Emperor Francis Joseph, strongly affected by the separation of Sweden and Norway in 1905, feared the secession of Hungary in the near future.

17. The Poles of Galicia were confronted with the obstacle of a growing Ruthene nationality even in their own territory. See R. Kann, op. cit., I, p. 322.

18. William A. Jenks, *The Austrian Electoral Reform of 1907*, New York, 1950. On Baron von Beck, see the biography written by his grandson, A. Allmayr-Beck, Vienna, 1959. Beck was a jurist and adviser to the Archduke Francis Ferdinand, who held him in high esteem. But the appointment of Beck as prime minister caused a rupture in their relationship. The archduke, under the influence of Kristóffy, accepted universal suffrage for Hungary. He considered that elections would favour the peasant masses, traditional and loyal to the dynasty, against the hegemony of the Magyar liberals and the Jewish businessmen. But in Austria, a heavily industrialized country, he feared that the effects of universal suffrage would be exactly the opposite, owing to the international character of Social Democracy. Moreover, in Bohemia and for the same reasons—socialism, the nationalism of the Czech middle class, and anti-Austrian Slavism—he did not wish universal suffrage to be granted for the elections to the Diet.

19. Marshal Conrad von Hoetzendorf published his Memoirs, *Aus meiner Dienstzeit*. There are biographies of him by Oskar Regele, *Feldmarschall Conrad*, Vienna, 1955, and in the *Neue Österreichische Biographie*, 1926. On Lexa von Aehrenthal, see J. Redlich in *Schicksalsjahren*, I, pp. 128–9; for the annexation, A. F. Pribram, *Austrian Foreign Policy, 1908–1918*, London, 1923, and Bernadotte E. Schmidt, *The Annexation of Bosnia and Herzegovina*, Cambridge, 1937.

    P. Renouvin, *Histoire des relations internationales*, vol. VI, 2.

    For an interpretation of the annexation in the general context of the situation of the Dual Monarchy, see the article by J. Křížek, 'Annexion de la Bosnie-Herzégovine', *Historica*, IX, Prague, 1964, p. 135, and the chapter by Hugo Hantsch, 'Austria and Europe', vol. IV of the collective work *The Europe of the 19th and 20th Centuries*, Milan, Marzoratti. Cf. Hugo Hantsch, *Leopold Graf Berchtold, grand seigneur und Staatsmann*, 2 vols., Vienna, 1963.

20. Hugo Hantsch, op. cit., p. 593.

21. J. Křížek, 'Crise du dualisme', *Historica*, XII, 1966, p. 108, note 81.

22. J. Redlich, op. cit., I, p. 166 (November 1912).

23. Masaryk quoted by Hugo Hantsch in *Nationalitätenproblem*, p. 66.

24. Erich Zöllner, *Geschichte Österreichs*, p. 427 *et seq.*

25. There exists a copious literature on the circumstances of the assassination. E. Zöllner, *Geschichte Österreichs*, gives a bibliography. The best documented work is that by Hans Uebersberger, *Österreich Zwischen Russland und Serbien*, Cologne, Graz, 1958. The Serbian government had no direct responsibility for the assassination. The crime was clearly committed by a fanatic, in execution of a conspiracy hatched by nationalists, and there is no need to attempt to explain it in terms of the class struggle or to make the assassins, whose act was to cost Europe and the world so much bloodshed, the heroes of the agrarian revolution and of the cause of the peoples. Police precautions were notoriously inadequate at Sarajevo, but this was simply a matter of negligence. The population of the city gave the archduke a warm welcome and the crowd wanted to lynch the murderer. The archduke, who had often been threatened with death in anonymous letters, was not unaware of the danger facing him when he visited Sarajevo, especially when, after a first unsuccessful attempt at assassination, he decided to go to the hospital to visit the wounded. It was on the way to the hospital that Prinzip awaited him. The duchess had refused to be separated from her husband.

26. The history of the war operations is clearly described in Zöllner, op. cit., French edn. p. 470. The short book by R. Kiszling, *Österreich-Ungarns Anteil an ersten Krieg*, Stiasny Verlag, 1958, offers an accurate account (96 pages) of the major actions fought on the different fronts.

27. 'The Adventures of the Good Soldier Švejk' (*Osudy dobrého vojáka Švejka*), by the Czech writer Hašek, is a satirical novel of military life in the Dual Monarchy.
28. R. Plaschka, *Cattaro und Prag. Revolte und Revolution*, Graz, 1963.
29. Oskar Regele, *Feldmarschall Conrad—Auftrag und Erfüllung*, Vienna, 1955. On p. 567 the author quotes the eulogies of contemporaries, even from the enemy camp: Lyautey, Gouraud, Lloyd George, Russkij, etc.
30. Otto Bauer, *Österreichische Revolution.*
31. J. Droz, *L'Europe centrale*, p. 227: 'A genuinely Austrian patriotism manifested itself at all levels of the population: the Slavs fulfilled their military duty like the Germans and the Magyars.'
32. Concerning the resistance of the Czechs and the Yugoslavs, see M. Paulová, *Dějiny Maffie* ('History of the Maffia'), Prague, 1937.
33. J. Droz has given an exposé of Naumann's doctrine, which he judges favourably, in chapter VII of his book *La Mitteleuropa de Friedrich Naumann et la fin de l'Autriche-Hongrie.*
34. Josef Redlich, *Schicksalsjahre*, vol. II, p. 71.
35. Leo Valiani, *La dissoluzione dell'Austria-Ungheria*, Milan, 1966. This is one of the best books on the disintegration of the Dual Monarchy. The author was able to have recourse to unpublished sources, such as the correspondence of the Italian politician Salvemini, and possesses an exhaustive knowledge both of the collections of documents published in the various countries and of the most recent articles by American, Austrian, Czechoslovak and Hungarian historians. Cf. Victor-L. Tapié, *L'éclatement de l'Autriche-Hongrie*, an article in *Revue de Paris*, October 1966.

    A large number of books have been written on the peace talks initiated by Austria-Hungary. Robert A. Kann has provided the most recent analysis of the affair involving Prince Sixtus of Bourbon-Parma: *Sixtus Affaire*, Vienna, 1967. Cf. Gordon Brook-Shepherd, *The Last Habsburg.*

    Professor Benedikt has devoted a remarkable study to the negotiations of the Julius Meinl-Lammasch group: *Die Friedensaktion der Meinlgruppe 1917–1918. Veröffest der Kommission für neuere Geschichte Österreichs*, 48, Graz, 1962.

    Cf. the work by Professor Engel-Janosi, an expert on the secret talks (the 'Revertera affair'): *Die Friedensaktion der Frau Hofrat Szeps-Zuckerkandl* in *Bausteine zur Geschichte Österreichs* (a miscellany published for the eightieth birthday of Professor Benedikt), Vienna, 1966.

    Frau Zuckerkandl was the daughter of the celebrated liberal journalist, Moritz Szeps, who was the friend and political adviser of the Crown Prince Rudolf. Another daughter of Szeps had married Clemenceau's brother. The attitude of Clemenceau in relations with Austria has frequently been studied without, however, being finally clarified. At first, Clemenceau appears to have had no objection to a separate peace. Then the undertakings given to the Czechoslovaks, whose military role on the French front had made a particularly strong impression on him, and a violent antipathy to the Habsburgs and the members of the Austrian government (Count Czernin) seem to have made him quite pitiless towards Austria during the peace negotiations.
36. According to Redlich, whose testimony can be trusted, op. cit., II, p. 214 (in his conversations with the Emperor Charles, who seemed determined to make Redlich his prime minister, 5 July 1917).

    On the Emperor Charles, see Reinhold Lorenz, *Kaiser Karl und der Untergang der Donaumonarchie*, Graz, 1959.
37. In addition to Valiani, op. cit., who throws light on the Yugoslav problem in particular,

see the memoirs of Masaryk, *Světová Revoluce* ('The World Revolution'), 1925, and Beneš, *Světová Válka a naše revoluce* ('The World War and Our Revolution'). J. M. Baernreither, *Der Verfall des Habsburgerreiches. Fragmente eines politischen Tagebuchs, 1897–1917*, Vienna, 1939. More recently: Z. A. B. Zeman, *Der Zusammenbruch des Habsburgerreiches*, 1963; and, of a more general character, Edward Crankshaw, *The Fall of the House of Habsburg*, London, 1963.

38. Karel Stloukal (1887–1957), *privat-docent* and then professor at the Charles University, published in 1930 an excellent study of the Czechoslovak state conceived by T. G. Masaryk during the war, with documents included in an appendix: *Československý Stát v představách T. G. Masaryka za války*, Prague, 1930.

   Masaryk believed for quite a long time that Czech (Czechoslovak) opinion would prefer that monarchic institutions should be preserved, even in an independent state. His own preference was for an English or Danish prince, who would be Protestant and would be able to offer greater facilities in relations with the German Empire, the ruin of which he considered by no means certain. He disliked the idea of a Russian monarch for reasons that were moral as much as political: he imagined a Russian monarch setting up a court in the royal castle, with French mistresses and champagne (Stloukal, p. 18, note).

39. In 1930, in the historical review *Český Časopis Historický*, nos. 3–4, J. Pekař published the address which he had prepared for King Charles III. This is a very fine text, based on the imprescriptible principle of state rights. Pekař was a monarchist like his master Goll, who had given the Emperor Charles history lessons when the latter was a young archduke. Both men refused to sign the writers' manifesto, because the right of self-determination threatened to contradict state rights and to justify the secession of the Germans of Bohemia. On the accession of Charles I a series of coronations was even envisaged: at Vienna, as emperor of Austria, at Agram, as king of Croatia (a proposal supported by Radić); it is difficult to say if such projects were merely outmoded fancies that would have been condemned to ridicule or if, on the contrary, they might have exerted an effect on public opinion.

   Concerning Czech opinion during the war, much useful information is to be found in the book by Viktor Dyk, *Vzpomínky a Komentáře* ('Memoirs and Commentaries'), Prague, 1927, the work of a nationalist historian of great talent.

40. Leo Valiani, *La dissoluzione*, p. 310 *et seq.*

41. The book by Austriacus Observator is distinctly hostile to the Slavs. The identity of the author seems to have been established by Reinhold Lorenz in an article in a collection published in honour of Professor Heinrich Benedikt's eightieth birthday (*Bausteine zur Geschichte Österreichs*, Vienna, 1966). Lorenz identifies the author as a German Benedictine, Fr. Wilhelm Schmidt.

42. Karl Renner, 'Das Selbstbestimmungsrecht des Nationen insbesonderer' in *Anwendung auf Österreich*, vol. I, *Nation und Staat*, Leipzig, Vienna, 1918.

43. Figures provided by Leo Valiani, op. cit., p. 290. Cf. J. Prokeš in *Československá Vlastivěda*, op. cit., p. 859 and V. Husa, *Dějiny Československá*, op. cit., p. 289 *et seq.*, very interesting on the question of strikes.

44. Franco-Hungarian conference of Paris, 1968; paper by Mme. Ormos.

Conclusion

AS THE MIDDLE AGES made way for the Renaissance, a family of great lords, who had gradually attained the dignity of sovereigns, had gathered the Danubian territories together, had defended them against the Turkish peril and had then sought to unite them more closely in a modern state: a monarchy as 'a whole'. Maria Theresa had attempted to make the concept of Prince Eugene a reality, which Joseph II then jeopardized by endeavouring to complete the task too rigorously and too hastily. Unity had thus not been accomplished. The Habsburg achievement was a feeble one by comparison with the achievements of other dynasties in other countries—the Capetians in France, for instance, and their successors, the Valois and the Bourbons. If the Habsburgs had failed, this was due partly to the perennial ambiguity of the system. Archdukes in Austria, kings in Bohemia, the Habsburgs were also elected emperors of the Germanic Holy Roman Empire and they held large fiefs in Germany, along the Rhine and the Danube. Endowed with the most illustrious title in Christendom, they were in a position to gather behind them the German lords, whom they could have either reduced to servitude or associated with their policies.

But the other Western powers, in particular France, which was better administered, more prosperous and, whether willingly or forcibly, more submissive to her princes, could not allow the Empire to become a hereditary possession, either *de jure* or *de facto*, of the House of Austria. Moreover, the territorial security of France required the restoration to the kingdom of lands formerly subinfeudated to France and which had recently fallen into the hands of the Habsburgs—Artois and Burgundy. The Thirty Years' War brought this rivalry to an issue: French hegemony was imposed on Europe and the House of Habsburg, restricted in Germany but not excluded from the Empire, felt its Danubian vocation to be more urgent.

Two factors had contributed to Habsburg power in Europe: the family alliance with the sovereigns of Spain and their fidelity to the Catholic Church. A territorial division had taken place as early as the reign of Charles V: the Spanish branch of the Habsburg dynasty acquired Spain, Flanders, the duchy of Milan and Naples, territories which gave it armies and markets and also the vast colonial domain of America, from which it obtained gold and silver.

While central Europe moved towards the Lutheran Reformation and Calvinism penetrated into Hungary, the Habsburgs had remained loyal to Catholicism and,

393

supported by Spain and by the Papacy, had undertaken to bring back to the Roman Church the peoples who had been won over to heresy. Unity of faith, according to the ideas of the time, guaranteed the political power of a prince. But this goal had not been fully realized. In a society of orders in which each group claimed its own privileges, adhesion to the Protestant Reformation was a means of resisting the royal power when the latter attempted to obtain the money contributions necessary for the upkeep of its army. Hence the Habsburgs' struggles against their own subjects: the harsh measures against the royal cities, the secessions of the nobility. If the war that followed the Defenestration of Prague resulted in the lasting establishment of absolutism in Bohemia in the religious sense, Hungary, where the nobility drew the peasantry into the *kuruc* wars, was still able to discuss the conditions of its return to allegiance, to negotiate on the basis of the preservation of its privileges.

At the same time, an economic evolution independent of the will of princes, but accelerated by the consequences of their policies, led to the weakening of the royal cities and their corporations and to the development of the great domain, to the advantage of the aristocracy. This was no longer an aristocracy of military men, but the aristocracy of the great landowners, whose wealth rested on the labour of the peasants, the corvée, rather than on the old feudal dues. Although, somewhat paradoxically, the great lords supported the sovereign with the money and the men which they contributed for 'general' expenditure and war, although they served him in the administration, in the army and in diplomatic offices, they presented an obstacle to absolutism by not permitting the sovereign to administer his lands effectively or to take advantage of all the fiscal resources that an independent policy would have offered. General prosperity had not benefited from the development of mercantilism, nor had it been possible to establish a fiscal system based on a better knowledge of the resources available and on a more equitable distribution of taxes.

In consequence, the illustrious Habsburg monarchy was, in the modern period, weaker than was admitted: its administrative capacity was limited and its financial resources inadequate for the role of a great power. The structure of the Danubian countries was thus unique in Europe: it could be defined neither as the different countries merged in a single state, nor as the different peoples gathered together in a single nation. The empirical, incomplete character of the Danubian system and its lack of tautness, though certainly prejudicial to the strength of the central power, tended to be beneficial to the peoples themselves, even in the servile condition in which the majority of the rural inhabitants found themselves. Naturally, they were deprived of the advantages which they could have enjoyed from a greater personal freedom of movement and initiative in a system with a less powerful seigniorial authority and a royal authority applied equitably to all subjects. But the individuality of each national group was undoubtedly better safeguarded. The history of the Danubian peoples evolved between these two poles: the community of nations considered as a whole and the particular character of each nation.

When, at the end of the seventeenth century, the danger of long and destructive wars was removed from the territory, Baroque civilization was free to blossom—a royal, but even more a seigniorial and peasant civilization. All the peoples participated in this culture, but the particular genius of each of them imprinted its own original character on works of art. The period from 1690 to 1740 represents half a century of Baroque achievement. The century of the Enlightenment and the positivist philosophy despised and disparaged the Baroque architecture, painting and sculpture with which it was confronted in such great abundance. At least, it is to the credit of the eighteenth century that it did not destroy these works. But it was ignorant and heedless of the long and intense effort of musical creativity which has only been brought to light in recent times and which explains why, in the late eighteenth and early nineteenth centuries, the flowering of the great universal geniuses of music should have taken place in the countries of the Danube.

Bound together also by the exchange of production (the wine and cattle of Hungary for the textiles and then the metal goods of Austria), these countries thus sought to establish the political conditions of their association. Fidelity to the monarchic principle and to the common sovereign was not in itself sufficient to resolve the political problem. Yet, although historians speak of the perpetual opposition between the dynasty and its peoples, it is interesting to observe the extent to which these peoples remained loyal throughout the fermentation of the revolutionary and Napoleonic period. On the other hand, the monarchy appeared to take this loyalty for granted. Later, the theorists 'discovered' the conciliating role incumbent on the emperor of Austria in his supranational vocation as ruler of a *Gesamtösterreich* where each state would find its proper place. In reality, however, the desire for internal harmony was overshadowed by the ambition for power, for the rulers of Austria continued to look towards Germany and Italy and were chiefly concerned to secure the resources with which to maintain an army that would guarantee possession of the Lombardo-Venetian kingdom and be able to intervene profitably in a European war.

Russia was feared. The double menace of Pan-Germanism and Pan-Slavism was already discernible before these terms acquired their full significance. But the Danubian monarchy found the justification for its existence in the very history of its peoples. Why should it allow itself to be sacrificed to the pretensions of the Germans of the Empire or those of the tsars, simply because it contained German and Slav populations to which it was expected to guarantee peace?

After 1848 the middle class of the Danubian countries assumed the role formerly played by the landed aristocracy, whose influence remained great even if it had ceased to enjoy pre-eminence. The middle class realized that its economic interests made association desirable, but, even with the Compromise, it did not succeed in establishing the conditions of the federative regime to which the majority of the population aspired. Just as the monarchy as 'a whole' had not been rendered a solid reality, so the constitutional and liberal order which issued from the industrial age failed to create a satisfactory system. Empiricism persisted during the nineteenth century, but the best guarantee of survival lay in economic and social progress. In these circumstances, to risk a war was dangerous. Even a short and victorious war would not have achieved much. But the long and exhausting conflict in which it engaged paved the way for the dissolution of Austria-Hungary. To an even greater degree than military disasters, internal difficulties and growing social misery brought about the collapse of the system.

When the monarchy had vanished, what remained? There remained an indisputable reality: the peoples of the Danube, moulded by a long history, each conscious of the will to exist, and which now became independent states.

It has often been said that the negotiators of the peace treaties at the Conference of Paris showed remarkable inconsistency by preserving a unified Germany, shorn only of Alsace-Lorraine and Poland, while committing themselves to the fragmentation of Austria-Hungary. But this is to evade the real problem.[1] As far as can be judged in the present state of historical knowledge, there are no grounds for believing that such a clear-cut programme of systematic destruction was adopted. It was a question, rather, of a lack of spokesmen and, in particular, of competent persons sufficiently enlightened to be able to overcome the private quarrels of the new states and to ensure that the independence of one state was not unacceptable to the others, or that their common interests were not totally disregarded.

Admittedly, a few broad principles were accepted: the right of peoples to govern themselves, their democratic organization and the noble doctrine of President Wilson's Fourteen Points. The difficulty was to make those principles a positive reality.

The peace-makers of 1918-19 took no interest in the problems of the Danubian world as such. They were content to include them as secondary considerations in their major preoccupations—their uncertainty with regard to Russia, the fear (at this time not unjustified) that social agitation might run amok and submerge public order even in the Western countries. Certain governments seemed to offer better guarantees for the construction of a democratic and liberal order, a greater capacity for reconciling justice and liberty with the regularity of administrative life. These governments had been formed by the alliance between the National Councils, recognized by the Entente, and representatives of their fellow-countrymen who had remained in the territories of the Dual Monarchy during the war, the interpreters of national opinion. In this way were formed the Czechoslovak republic, the kingdom of Serbs, Croats and Slovenes, and Great Rumania. Other governments— those of Austria and Hungary—inspired mistrust. Opinion had turned against them, for it was easier to suppose that they bore the original responsibility for the conflict, that they had been the 'prisons of peoples' (*Völkerkerker*) and that the new states had been liberated from their hold. They were now regarded as the vanquished, even as the guilty ones. From the vast mass of reports, often of a tendentious nature, and contradictory statistics accumulated by the commissions, the treaties of Versailles and of St. Germain (1919), followed by the belated treaty of Trianon with Hungary (1920), created a new central Europe, the principal features of which must now be retraced.

Galicia was detached from the former Austrian Empire and reunited with an independent Poland the proximity of which, through the centuries, had never been injurious to the Habsburg monarchy and which had even contributed to its salvation in 1683. Austria's role in the partitions of Poland could be explained, though never justified, by the prevailing situation of Europe. The Poles and the Ukrainians of Austria had regained their rightful place in a reconstituted fatherland. The problem had been equitably resolved, although the presence of a large Polish population in the region of Teschen in Silesia, and therefore in the former kingdom of Bohemia, immediately led to disputes and even to the risk of war between Poland and Czechoslovakia.

The new state of Czechoslovakia represented the association of the old kingdom of Bohemia with the comitats of Upper Hungary inhabited largely by Slovaks. During his years as an emigrant, Masaryk had given much thought to the possibilities of an independent economic existence for the Czech countries. He had sought the opinion of experts better acquainted than himself with such questions. He had come to the conclusion that the Czech countries could live on their own resources and bear the burdens of a fully independent state. But, naturally, this was to assume that the regions with a majority of German inhabitants, in the north, the west and the south, would remain part of the new state. Was there an injustice in this, a contradiction with the right of peoples to govern themselves? Did there exist an autonomous German nation, the Sudetens, which was to find itself forcibly incorporated into the Czechoslovak state? The term 'Sudeten', which was destined to acquire such a woeful significance, had already been employed by Pan-Germanic polemicists; but it was still not in common use, for it did not correspond to any true national consciousness. Admittedly, there existed several millions of Germans in Bohemia whose leaders attempted, in October and November 1918, to obtain their annexation to the new republic of Austria. Moreover, German opinion, confronted with the chauvinistic nationalism of certain Czech circles, feared that the new state might make reprisals against the Germans of Bohemia. There were a number of regrettable incidents. But there could be no denying the fact that the kingdom of Bohemia had for centuries enabled the two ethnic groups to live in co-existence, at times harmonious, at other times turbulent. For a Czech with any consciousness of his past, the reconstruction of an independent state was conceivable only within the historic frontiers and without any loss of territory. The Germans of Bohemia and the Czechs, associated by their history and in their daily life, even though they spoke different languages, had existed side by side, merged in the same civilization, benefiting from the same economic progress, having roughly the same way of life and, for the most part, emotionally attached to the same territory. This profound reality, which no one of good faith and free from prejudice could seriously have contested, fully justified the presence of the Bohemian Germans in the new Czechoslovak state. Unfortunately, however, the reality was overshadowed by the propaganda of the day and was dangerously misappreciated abroad. Within a few years it was to be more clearly recognized, with the result that German ministers were appointed in President Masaryk's republic. The economic argument, which maintained that Czechoslovakia could not be firmly established without the industrial regions, carried greater weight at this time, prevailing over historical and sociological arguments. Nonetheless, the manner in which Germans and Czechs would accommodate themselves to co-existence was to be the crucial problem for the new republic.

Conclusion

The newly constituted Czechoslovakia, extending over an area of about 55,000 square miles, comprised a total population of 13,613,172 in which the Czechoslovak element, considered as a single nation, numbered 8,760,937 inhabitants against 3,123,568 Germans and 745,431 Magyars (i.e. 65 per cent of the whole, against 23·7 and 5·6 per cent). Undoubtedly, the old problem of the nationalities, which had presented such a stumbling-block to Austria-Hungary, was now reappearing in the form of a problem of minorities. Although the Magyars did not constitute as large a non-Czech group as the Germans, they were certainly foreigners in the new state, both by their past history and by their present attitudes. Their presence was explained by strategic reasons.

By including Bratislava (Pozsony-Pressburg), a cosmopolitan city where the Slovaks had nevertheless enjoyed an important position for the past fifty years— rather as the Czechs had regained their place in nineteenth-century Prague— Czechoslovakia was solidly established on the Danube. The frontier then followed the river, which now became a barrier with Magyars inhabiting both banks. It brought within Czechoslovak territory towns such as Nové-Zámky, Rožnava and, above all, Košice (Kassa-Kachau), which were predominantly and perhaps even essentially Hungarian. Sub-Carpathian Russia (roughly 5,000 square miles and 606,568 inhabitants, the lowest population density in the state: about 120 inhabitants per square mile by contrast with about 310 in Bohemia and about 145 in Slovakia) was another Bosnia-Herzegovina entrusted to the administration of the Czechoslovak republic, which was thus burdened with heavy responsibilities towards a backward population. Territorially, it offered the advantage of present-ing a common frontier with Rumania.

The Rumania of 1919 was the realization of the dream of a union of all Rumanians which had been demanded in 1848 and then by the National Assembly held at Alba Julia in November 1918. Transylvania joined the Danubian provinces in an enlarged kingdom still ruled by the Hohenzollern-Sigmaringen (Ferdinand I, with his English queen, had succeeded Charles I). The Transylvanian territory still comprised a large proportion of Magyars, many of whom owned the most exten-sive properties, and also Germans and Szekels. Other territories inhabited by Rumanians (Bukovina to the north and the Banat of Temesvár to the south), but also by Magyars, completed the new state.

The kingdom of Serbs, Croats and Slovenes, as envisaged in the pact of Corfu, brought into existence, in an enlarged form, the South Slav state which the advocates of 'trialism' had hoped to create within the Danubian monarchy. The Dalmatian coast gave the state a long seaboard extending from Rjeka (Fiume) to Cattaro, an apple of discord with Italy, which retained Trieste and Istria. To the north, Bácska and the western part of the Banat of Temesvár had introduced Hungarian minorities into the Slav population of the new kingdom.

By contrast with these countries which had emerged from the upheaval aggrandized but by no means unified, Austria and Hungary were vanquished and humiliated countries where the memory of former greatness could not be eradicated, but whose rulers wondered, not without reason, if economic survival was possible. The Austrians had envisaged their union with Germany, since they had been refused association with the German districts of Bohemia. The people of Vorarlberg had sought in vain to obtain membership of the Swiss Confederation.

The southern Tyrol was allotted to Italy, in addition to the Trentino. As the result of a plebiscite, Austria had been allowed to keep northern Carinthia and had received the Burgenland, of which Hungary retained only the region of Sopron. The new Austrian republic, cut off from the sources of energy in the industrial regions of Bohemia, which hitherto had sustained the economic growth of the Vienna region, seemed a paradoxical relic of the old Empire, with an enormous and overpopulated capital. Certain neighbouring governments unthinkingly accepted the inevitability and imminence of its ruin—as if this great centre of civilization was not necessary for the equilibrium of Europe!

Hungary had been reduced to the territory inhabited by the Magyars: it now consisted of a mere 35,600 square miles and a population of only eight millions. In 1918 Count Károlyi, whose government had offered the Entente democratic guarantees, had attempted without success to safeguard the historic territory of his country, promising that the nationalities would be granted autonomy. Finding no support, he had then given a free rein to revolutionary expansion. For a few months a Republic of Councils (Soviets) was established, but was overthrown by the intervention of Czechoslovak and Rumanian regiments. Then there was constituted, with the consent of an unconvinced Entente, the reactionary government of Admiral Horthy, the regent of a monarchy whose king reappeared on two occasions in 1921, but only to find himself sentenced on the second occasion to deportation to Madeira. By the treaty of Trianon, Hungary had been forced to subscribe to the abandonment of its historic territories, because these were inhabited by non-Magyar peoples. For the next twenty years the assertion of national rights was to dominate the public life of Hungary. Albert Apponyi eloquently defended those rights before the League of Nations, rejecting with a haughty irony the idea that the newly established system would never change. National propaganda invoked the 'five Alsace-Lorraines'—Slovakia, Transylvania, Bácska, Temesvár and the Burgenland—and refused to recognize their mutilation. '*Nem! nem! soha!* No! No! Never!'

But Hungary thus found itself drawn into the camp of those powers which opposed the peace treaties and, later, into the orbit of the dictatorships—the Germany of Hitler and the Italy of Mussolini.

It was also necessary to settle the conditions for the utilization of the Danube, which all these states bordered. Had not the time come to create a Danubian Federation, with the great river as its axis, so that commerce and production might be stimulated in the different countries? In fact, the Danube was still not equipped to meet the needs of the European economy. Since 1878, Austria-Hungary had been entrusted with the mission of regularizing the course of the river in the region of the Iron Gates. Hungary had borne the brunt of the burden and the new channel had been officially inaugurated in 1896. Austria-Hungary's mandate had then been withdrawn. A convention signed on 23 July 1921 decreed that the entire course of the Danube was to be placed under the authority of an International Commission, which would have its headquarters at Bratislava and would exercise powers of administration and surveillance from Ulm to Braïla, while the old European Commission would continue to be responsible for the seaboard sector. But, in the conditions prevailing at this period, the utilization of the Danube could not constitute a sufficiently strong motive for solidarity, and even less for reconciliation, among the succession states.

Masaryk had envisaged a great economic federation stretching from the North Sea to the Aegean, another theoretical and premature project.

On the political plane, in 1921, the Little Entente was concluded, an alliance of the three principal succession states—Czechoslovakia, the kingdom of Serbs, Croats and Slovenes, and Rumania—to which the Western countries gave their patronage. The alliance in fact represented an insurance syndicate devised to prevent the revision of the treaties and the risk of a Habsburg restoration. There thus remained in the Danube basin a permanent hostility between an allied group of the three most powerful succession states and the two weakest states, isolated and not even bound one to the other: the heritage of the Habsburg monarchy, instead of offering a democratic guarantee for the peace of Europe, was becoming a source of future conflicts.

Some spoke of a 'Balkanized' central Europe. But such a suggestion seemed blasphemy to the champions of the new order and to the publicists responsible for justifying its existence. Nationalism was still rampant, both in the victorious countries, already disunited, and among the beneficiaries and the victims of the peace treaties. The organization of the League of Nations was fraught with difficulties. How could a wholly satisfactory solution have been found? It was true, however, that the new states had been brought into existence, forming a barrier against the advance of the socialist and working-class movement. In 1920 a strike had spread through Czechoslovakia and had been harshly suppressed by the troops, as in the time of Austria. In 1918, at the Assembly of Alba Julia which had founded Great Rumania, the Social Democrats had attempted to remove the dynasty and to obtain the introduction of republican institutions.

Yet a certain equilibrium had been established, the result of the presence in high offices of persons who had experience of Europe and had participated in the political debates of old Austria: in certain respects, the spiritual heritage of the past contributed to the rational reconstruction of the new central Europe.

Several of the most outstanding ministers in the succession states had been regular visitors to the Belvedere: Milan Hodža, in Czechoslovakia, and the Transylvanian Julius Maniu, who joined the pre-war and war-time Rumanian team of Bratianu and Jorga. Masaryk's abilities had been in evidence before he emigrated: he had been one of the most prominent personalities in the last Austrian Parliament, after the elections of 1911, and the great sagacity which he displayed in his relations with the politicians of the new states enabled him to prevent many excesses and blunders. When he spoke of 'de-Austrianizing' his country, he meant that he would encourage the diffusion of the democratic ideas of justice and liberty and that he would ensure the triumph of truth—*Pravda vítezí*—over passion. His first ministers of finance (Rašín and J. Preis, director of the Živnostenská Banka) did not shrink from taking severe measures in order to save a liberal economy. Rašín introduced an independent Czechoslovak currency and preserved his country from the galloping inflation that was submerging Germany and Austria. The purging of the monetary system paved the way for a new industrial boom in the country. Masaryk attached much importance to the religious idea. A Catholic who had been converted to Protestantism, he believed that Hussitism and the doctrine of the United Brethren represented the most authentic Czech tradition. In his eyes the Roman Church was suspect because of its alliance with the old regime and he certainly showed interest in the birth of a national Czechoslovak Church, which was short-lived. He quickly sensed, however, that anticlericalism would damage internal peace and bring difficulties with Slovakia, the rural populations of which were fervent in their faith and devoted to their priests. He preferred therefore to direct his efforts towards a *modus vivendi* with Rome and his policy of appeasement was crowned in 1929 by the celebrations of the millenary of St. Wenceslas. He sought justice for the minorities and contemplated the restoration of territories to Hungary. Above all, he maintained that, if international peace could be preserved for fifty years, a harmonious order would eventually prevail throughout central Europe. When, in 1930, there was talk in Geneva of a European Union, some considered that there could be no better president than Masaryk. But he was already eighty years of age and new perils were looming. The man who was to succeed him, Edward Beneš, had held a position at the League of Nations which was beyond his capacity and which had given him too much confidence in his abilities as a tactician. Of a less wide-ranging kind than Masaryk's and lacking the prestige enjoyed by his predecessor in public opinion, his optimism, whether sincere or affected, fostered dangerous illusions in Western Europe, both with regard to himself and with regard to the true balance of forces in the Danubian world. In particular, Beneš, in his attitude towards Hungary and especially towards Austria, nurtured a stubborn hostility and rancour which induced him to deny the obvious, whenever it conflicted with his own designs, and to prefer the worse alternative: 'Rather the Anschluss than the Habsburgs.'

On the debit side of the new central Europe must be set the difficulties that arose between those peoples related in race who had desired union in the same state and who now could not adapt themselves easily to their common existence. 'The new states,' wrote Roger Portal, 'in their victorious dynamism, did not resist the attempt which was made to impose a policy of assimilation just at the time when the increased media for education and the civilization of ideas were developing in the different ethnic groups a more vivid and a more exacting consciousness of their national originality.'[2] The problems of the nationalities had not been resolved, nor could they be resolved, merely by the change of the political system or by the abandonment of the common state. The vocabulary had changed: people spoke timidly of the 'minorities'. Inevitably, the most advanced group, the group with the greatest administrative experience, tended to impose its methods and ideology on the weaker groups, which then regarded themselves as oppressed. Thwarted in their daily habits, encountering wilful provocation, obstruction and constraint where they had imagined that they would enjoy total liberty, these groups denounced what they regarded as a new imperialism. Friction grew between Serbs and Croats, between Czechs and Slovaks. Anxious to prevent a secession, Alexander I hoped to cement the unity of Yugoslavia by a provisional dictatorship.

Among kindred peoples who had been united, but who now became adversaries and enemies, with greater or lesser violence according to their different temperaments, discord was intensified, exacerbated by propaganda from outside. Each new state needed to find its own equilibrium and, for the states as a whole, it was desirable that new forms of association should be discovered.

The Little Entente, initially directed against Hungarian revisionism and the restoration of Austria, was also to be confronted with a reawakening of German imperialism—the idea, taken up once more in various forms by the German theoreticians, that it was Germany's mission to direct the economic and political interests of the whole of central Europe.

Yet the consolidation of the new states was assured and a return of general prosperity became evident. During the time of the chancellor Ignaz Seipel, Austria obtained international financial aid.[3] It was able to reorganize its currency and build up its industry by utilizing its sources of energy—the immense water reserves of its mountains, the lignite of Styria and the oilfields discovered in the Waldviertel (33,000 tons in 1937). Czechoslovakia's foreign trade was 25 per cent higher in 1929 than in 1924. Prague was adapting itself to its new role as capital and intellectual life flourished there to an unprecedented degree. But how solidly the old values were also upheld in Vienna and in Budapest! Artistic and intellectual activity was manifested in all three capitals, in the lyrical works of the poets, the compositions of the musicians (Suk, Fibich and Martinů in Czechoslovakia, Alban Berg and Schoenberg in Austria, Béla Bartók and Zoltan Kodály in Hungary), the great acumen of critics in all these countries, and the birth of a proletarian literature which expressed the hope of the working classes that democracy would be crowned by socialism.

Could a closer economic association be established among the succession states, so that the production of complementary regions around the Danube might be co-ordinated? The relative euphoria of the years 1925–30 diverted attention from this problem. Not until the ominous signs of the world economic crisis became apparent was the question reconsidered. In 1931 Austria wished to conclude an economic *Anschluss* with Germany in order to stave off the threat that faced her, but The Hague Tribunal condemned such a solution as contrary to earlier agreements.

Schemes had also been elaborated by Czechoslovakia in an attempt to provide an economic counterpart to the political character of the Little Entente, but these too were directed against Austria and Hungary. A moderate agrarian reform had been achieved in Rumania and in Czechoslovakia and had given an impetus to Czech agriculture, in which the use of machinery was being developed. As the economic crisis began first of all to affect agricultural revenues, the Czechoslovak Agrarians, who now wielded a powerful influence in the government, had no intention of sacrificing their interests to those of the Yugoslav and Rumanian producers.

In these circumstances, it was the responsibility of the great powers which had taken the new order under their protection to recommend strongly to the countries of central Europe that they save the Danubian economy by their co-operation. Proposals were put forward by France, but received little support from Great Britain and Italy. Since the war, France had acquired a position of exceptional influence in the Danubian region. French groups had financial interests in the Škoda works in Czechoslovakia. The Czechoslovak army had been organized by a French military mission and its chief of staff was a Frenchman, General Faucher. French institutes and French language associations were flourishing in all the Danubian countries, even in Austria and in Hungary, where pro-French sympathies had remained strong in spite of events. The use of the French language, already stimulated by pre-war legislation, was spreading through the whole of society. The somewhat jealous reserve of Great Britain and Italy with regard to the French proposals heralded the disunity of the great powers. The effects of the crisis extended through the Danubian world, reaching industry and in particular the industrial regions of Czechoslovakia, where the German population—both the commercial middle class, threatened with ruin, and the working class, plunged into unemployment and lacking adequate financial assistance—presented an ideal target for Hitlerian propaganda, which at first assumed covert forms, but then became quite open. Among German intellectual circles was propagated the ideology of a Sudeten people of three millions which an alleged Czech imperialism wished to rob of its national consciousness. The climate of the worst pre-war years had returned. At the same time, the Communist Party, which had long been held in check by the socialist parties, was becoming more active and was winning the attention of the working masses.[4]

Just as the disasters of the war economy had struck the chief blow at Austria-Hungary, the economic crisis of the 'thirties was undermining the internal structure of each of the independent states of central Europe, which seemed not to recognize that they were threatened by a common peril.[5] Just as the nationalities of the Dual Monarchy had devoted their energies to fostering their mutual enmities rather than to seeking their salvation in a federation, so the succession states were incapable of attempting a reconciliation on the basis of national independence and democratic liberties. The results are well known—first the Anschluss, then Munich, a temporary, scamped solution in which Czechoslovakia was abandoned by her allies and in which no one appeared to perceive the scandalous mutilation of her historic territory. As the states of central Europe collapsed one after another, the whole of Europe passed under the Nazi yoke.

It needed four years and the alliance between Russia and America for the yoke to be removed. Yet the nations, in the struggle which they conducted both openly and underground, had proved to world opinion that they had evolved from a long history and were not factitious creations of the treaties of 1919. They represented collective realities which could not be ignored if Europe was to be reconstructed materially and spiritually.

But was Europe any longer the master of its destiny? Two colossal powers had emerged, the United States of America and the Soviet Union, which practically divided the world between themselves. What is known as the 'spirit of Yalta', as distinct from the letter of that agreement, gradually brought the countries of eastern and central Europe under Russian obedience. An Iron Curtain was lowered between the two halves of the old world. Meanwhile, a new battle, this time a battle of influence, was being fought over Austria and resulted in the only international treaty to issue from the Second World War: the treaty of Schönbrunn, signed in 1955.[6]

The little state whose future had appeared so uncertain in 1919 regained its independence, on the condition that it remained neutral and accepted certain economic obligations. Austria, situated in the centre of Europe, between the countries of the Atlantic Alliance and those of the Warsaw Pact, dominated by Russia, represented in status an extension of the Swiss Confederation. It formed a federal state. The prestige of Vienna enabled the old imperial capital to become a centre for culture and for international *rapprochements* and, in this new vocation, one of the places where the problems of world civilization and world organization could be most effectively studied.

This partial solution has not swept away uncertainties and dangers. The Danubian region still constitutes a weak and inadequately organized zone in the centre and east of Europe. As a result of being unable to gather its economic and political forces together in a reasonably vigorous whole, it has been and continues to be exposed to the dangers of tutelage or enslavement at the hands of a neighbouring great power.

In forms more numerous and more subtle than mere Pan-Germanism, the industrial Germany of the second half of the nineteenth century had established and held Austria-Hungary in its sphere of influence, thereby greatly restricting its political independence.

Hitlerian Germany regarded as essential to the foundation of its power the execution of the Anschluss and then the dismemberment of Czechoslovakia, which in practice amounted to annexation under the deceptive form of the two 'protectorates'. Similarly, in order to guarantee its strategic security and to maintain the cohesion of its ideological system, the U.S.S.R. has established its *de facto* domination over Danubian Europe, refusing to tolerate Hungary's attempt at emancipation in 1956 and then, twelve years later, the success of Prague in the spring of 1968, even though the desire of the Czechoslovaks to prepare the ground for a *rapprochement* with free Europe, by means of new economic relations and a greater freedom of thought, implied neither the abandonment of socialism nor the disruption of the Warsaw Pact. Thus, the consequences of the two world wars continue to weigh heavily on the nations of the Danube, delaying the time when they might determine freely among themselves how to establish the more harmonious relations which are the prerequisite of their progress. The ordeals which they have undergone have no doubt mollified the aggressive nationalism which, in the nineteenth century, raised these nations one against the other and which was one of the major causes of the collapse of the monarchy and its dismemberment. Those experiences have illuminated national sentiment among more numerous strata of society, which are also better informed of the real nature of problems. Attachment to collective and individual liberty has shown itself to be irreducible. All the struggles conducted over the past fifty years have been directed against tyrannies imposed from outside, however contradictory might have been the ideological systems for which they were fought. Here is revealed the indisputable strength of Danubian civilization. At each stage of transition, above the bloody confrontations and the public calamities, the words of Palacký affirming the vitality of these peoples are vindicated: 'We existed and we shall exist.' A faith of this kind can be asserted by every nation. History explains the reasons for this powerful consciousness, but it does not provide the key to a solution of the difficulties and misfortunes of the Danubian nations. As long as this key is not found, Europe will not be able to look to the future with confidence.

NOTES

1. P. Renouvin, *Histoire des relations internationales*, vol. VII, 1957, chapter VI: 'La conférence de la paix', pp. 154–89. The recent work by V. S. Mamatey, *The United States and East Central Europe 1914–1918*, Princeton, 1957, traces the evolution of the attitude and personal policy of President Wilson. Paul Mantoux, *Les délibérations du Conseil des Quatre*, 2 vols., Paris, 1955. Karel Pichlík, *První světová válka* '(The First World War'), Prague, 1968, the final chapter entitled 'Mir?' ('Peace?').
2. Roger Portal, *Les Slaves*, p. 376.
3. *Geschichte der Republik Österreich* ('History of the Republic of Austria'), a collective work under the editorship of Professor H. Benedikt, Vienna, 1954.
4. An outline of the history of the Germans in Czechoslovakia, interpreted from the viewpoint of the National Socialist ideology, is to be found in the short work by Josef Pfitzner, *Sudetendeutsche Geschichte*, Reichenberg, 1935. The author recognizes that the term 'Sudetendeutsch' came into use only at the beginning of the present century (p. 22), but he wishes the term to be understood as referring to the history of the Germans inhabiting the geographical area known as the Sudetenland. This highly tendentious book attempts to exploit the irenic views of Pekař and K. Krofta, but it is not separatist and accepts the necessity of a harmonious *entente* between Sudetens and Czechoslovaks.
5. M. Baumont, *La faillite de la paix*; J. B. Duroselle, *Histoire diplomatique de 1919 à nos jours*, 1957.
6. General Béthouart, *La bataille pour l'Autriche*, Paris, 1966.

Table of nationalities in Austria-Hungary at the census of 1910

(a) Empire of Austria: 28,572,000 inhabitants			(b) Kingdom of Hungary: 20,886,000 inhabitants		
		%			%
Germans	9,950,260	35·6	Magyars	9,945,000	48·1
Czechs	6,435,983	23·0	Germans	2,037,000	9·8
Poles	4,967,984	17·8	Rumanians	2,949,000	14·1
Ruthenes	3,518,854	12·6	Ruthenes	473,000	2·3
Slovenes	1,259,000	4·5	Slovaks	1,967,970	9·4
Serbo-Croats	783,334	2·8	Croats	1,833,000	8·8
Italians	768,442	2·7	Serbs	1,106,000	5·3
Rumanians	272,000	1·0	Poles	26,836	—
Magyars	10,974	—			
					97·8
		100·0			

(c) Kingdom of Bohemia within the Empire of Austria:			(d) Bosnia-Herzegovina: 1,923,000 inhabitants		
		%			%
	Bohemia: 6,781,997 inhabitants		Croats	400,000	21·0
			Serbs	850,000	43·0
Czechs	4,241,918	63·2	Moslems	650,000	34·0
Germans	2,467,700	36·8			
					98·0
		100·0			

Moravia-Silesia:
3,338,977 inhabitants

Moravia:

Czechs	1,868,971	71·75
Germans	719,400	27·69
		99·44

Silesia:

Czechs	180,300	24.3
Germans	325,500	43·9
		68·2

Number of Czechs in the entire monarchy in 1910	6,510,161
Number of Slovaks in the entire monarchy in 1910	1,968,613
Total	8,478,774

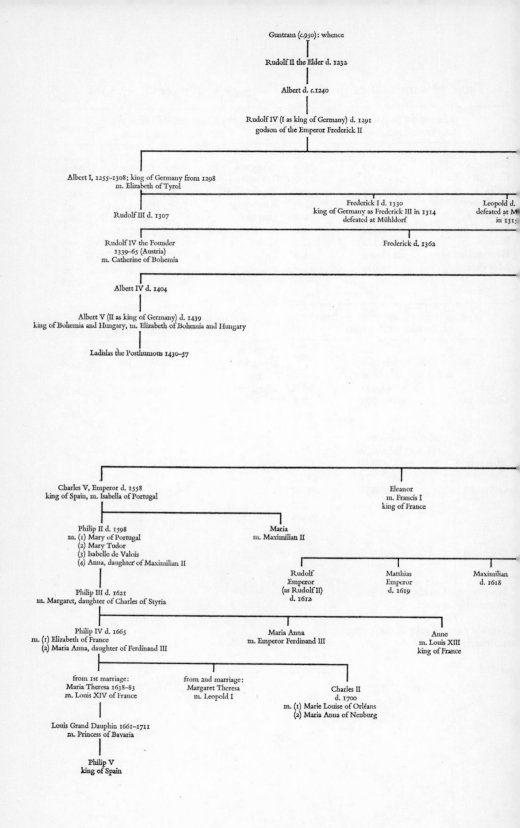

Guntram (c.950): whence

Rudolf II the Elder d. 1232

Albert d. c.1240

Rudolf IV (I as king of Germany) d. 1291
godson of the Emperor Frederick II

Albert I, 1255–1308; king of Germany from 1298
m. Elizabeth of Tyrol

Frederick I d. 1330
king of Germany as Frederick III in 1314
defeated at Mühldorf

Leopold d.
defeated at M
in 131

Rudolf III d. 1307

Rudolf IV the Founder
1339–65 (Austria)
m. Catherine of Bohemia

Frederick d. 1362

Albert IV d. 1404

Albert V (II as king of Germany) d. 1439
king of Bohemia and Hungary, m. Elizabeth of Bohemia and Hungary

Ladislas the Posthumous 1430–57

Charles V, Emperor d. 1558
king of Spain, m. Isabella of Portugal

Eleanor
m. Francis I
king of France

Philip II d. 1598
m. (1) Mary of Portugal
(2) Mary Tudor
(3) Isabelle de Valois
(4) Anna, daughter of Maximilian II

Maria
m. Maximilian II

Rudolf
Emperor
(as Rudolf II)
d. 1612

Matthias
Emperor
d. 1619

Maximilian
d. 1618

Philip III d. 1621
m. Margaret, daughter of Charles of Styria

Philip IV d. 1665
m. (1) Elizabeth of France
(2) Maria Anna, daughter of Ferdinand III

Maria Anna
m. Emperor Ferdinand III

Anne
m. Louis XIII
king of France

from 1st marriage:
Maria Theresa 1638–83
m. Louis XIV of France

from 2nd marriage:
Margaret Theresa
m. Leopold I

Charles II
d. 1700
m. (1) Marie Louise of Orléans
(2) Maria Anna of Neuburg

Louis Grand Dauphin 1661–1711
m. Princess of Bavaria

Philip V
king of Spain

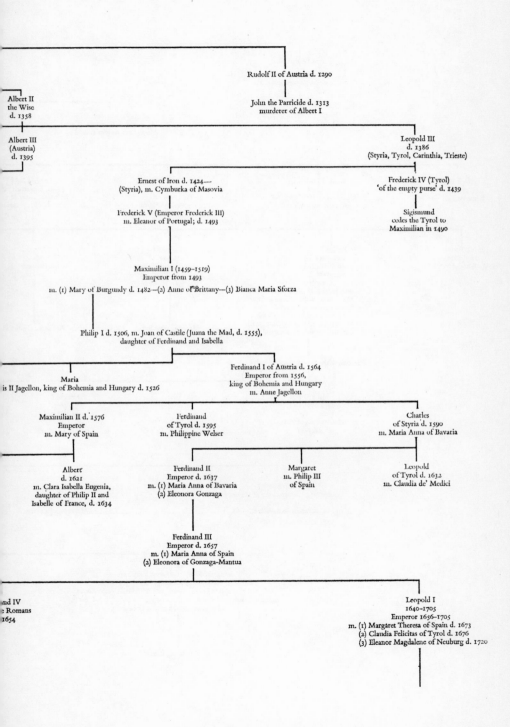

Rudolf II of Austria d. 1290

John the Parricide d. 1313
murderer of Albert I

Albert II
the Wise
d. 1358

Albert III
(Austria)
d. 1395

Leopold III
d. 1386
(Styria, Tyrol, Carinthia, Trieste)

Ernest of Iron d. 1424—
(Styria), m. Cymburka of Masovia

Frederick IV (Tyrol)
'of the empty purse' d. 1439

Frederick V (Emperor Frederick III)
m. Eleanor of Portugal; d. 1493

Sigismund
cedes the Tyrol to
Maximilian in 1490

Maximilian I (1459–1519)
Emperor from 1493
m. (1) Mary of Burgundy d. 1482—(2) Anne of Brittany—(3) Bianca Maria Sforza

Philip I d. 1506, m. Joan of Castile (Juana the Mad, d. 1555),
daughter of Ferdinand and Isabella

Maria
...is II Jagellon, king of Bohemia and Hungary d. 1526

Ferdinand I of Austria d. 1564
Emperor from 1556,
king of Bohemia and Hungary
m. Anne Jagellon

Maximilian II d. 1576
Emperor
m. Mary of Spain

Ferdinand
of Tyrol d. 1595
m. Philippine Welser

Charles
of Styria d. 1590
m. Maria Anna of Bavaria

Albert
d. 1621
m. Clara Isabella Eugenia,
daughter of Philip II and
Isabelle of France, d. 1634

Ferdinand II
Emperor d. 1637
m. (1) Maria Anna of Bavaria
(2) Eleonora Gonzaga

Margaret
m. Philip III
of Spain

Leopold
of Tyrol d. 1632
m. Claudia de' Medici

Ferdinand III
Emperor d. 1657
m. (1) Maria Anna of Spain
(2) Eleonora of Gonzaga-Mantua

...nd IV
...e Romans
1654

Leopold I
1640–1705
Emperor 1656–1705
m. (1) Margaret Theresa of Spain d. 1673
(2) Claudia Felicitas of Tyrol d. 1676
(3) Eleanor Magdalene of Neuburg d. 1720

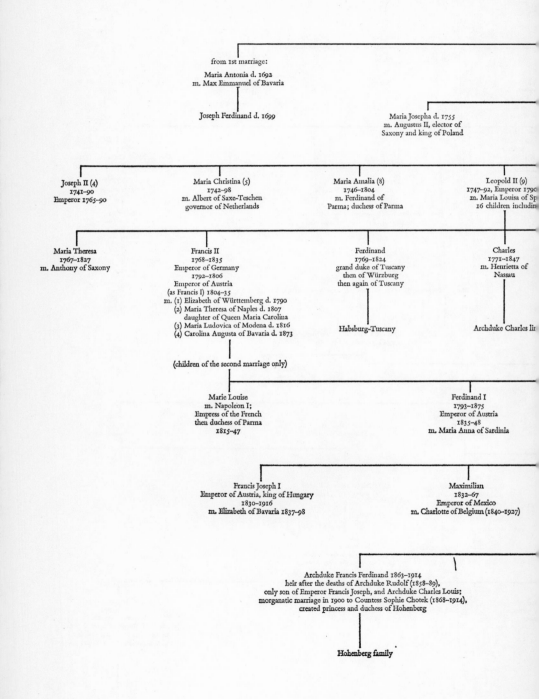

from 1st marriage:
Maria Antonia d. 1692
m. Max Emmanuel of Bavaria

Joseph Ferdinand d. 1699

Maria Josepha d. 1755
m. Augustus II, elector of
Saxony and king of Poland

Joseph II (4)
1741–90
Emperor 1765–90

Maria Christina (5)
1742–98
m. Albert of Saxe-Teschen
governor of Netherlands

Maria Amalia (8)
1746–1804
m. Ferdinand of
Parma; duchess of Parma

Leopold II (9)
1747–92, Emperor 1790
m. Maria Louisa of Sp
16 children includin

Maria Theresa
1767–1827
m. Anthony of Saxony

Francis II
1768–1835
Emperor of Germany
1792–1806
Emperor of Austria
(as Francis I) 1804–35
m. (1) Elizabeth of Württemberg d. 1790
   (2) Maria Theresa of Naples d. 1807
       daughter of Queen Maria Carolina
   (3) Maria Ludovica of Modena d. 1816
   (4) Carolina Augusta of Bavaria d. 1873

Ferdinand
1769–1824
grand duke of Tuscany
then of Würzburg
then again of Tuscany

Habsburg-Tuscany

Charles
1771–1847
m. Henrietta of
Nassau

Archduke Charles lir

(children of the second marriage only)

Marie Louise
m. Napoleon I;
Empress of the French
then duchess of Parma
1815–47

Ferdinand I
1793–1875
Emperor of Austria
1835–48
m. Maria Anna of Sardinia

Francis Joseph I
Emperor of Austria, king of Hungary
1830–1916
m. Elizabeth of Bavaria 1837–98

Maximilian
1832–67
Emperor of Mexico
m. Charlotte of Belgium (1840–1927)

Archduke Francis Ferdinand 1863–1914
heir after the deaths of Archduke Rudolf (1858–89),
only son of Emperor Francis Joseph, and Archduke Charles Louis;
morganatic marriage in 1900 to Countess Sophie Chotek (1868–1914),
created princess and duchess of Hohenberg

Hohenberg family

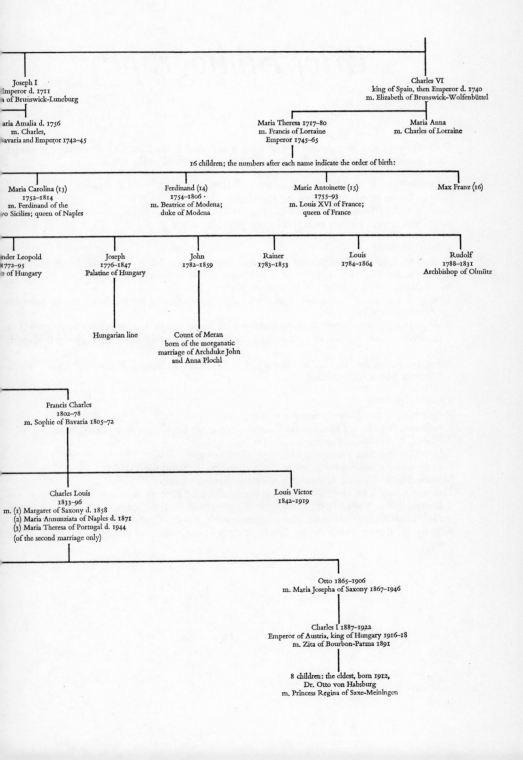

Joseph I
Emperor d. 1711
m. [...]a of Brunswick-Luneburg

Charles VI
king of Spain, then Emperor d. 1740
m. Elizabeth of Brunswick-Wolfenbüttel

[...]aria Amalia d. 1756
m. Charles,
[B]avaria and Emperor 1742–45

Maria Theresa 1717–80
m. Francis of Lorraine
Emperor 1745–65

Maria Anna
m. Charles of Lorraine

16 children; the numbers after each name indicate the order of birth:

Maria Carolina (13)
1752–1814
m. Ferdinand of the
[tw]o Sicilies; queen of Naples

Ferdinand (14)
1754–1806 ·
m. Beatrice of Modena;
duke of Modena

Marie Antoinette (15)
1755–93
m. Louis XVI of France;
queen of France

Max Franz (16)

[Alexa]nder Leopold
[1]772–95
[Palatin]e of Hungary

Joseph
1776–1847
Palatine of Hungary

John
1782–1859

Rainer
1783–1853

Louis
1784–1864

Rudolf
1788–1831
Archbishop of Olmütz

Hungarian line

Count of Meran
born of the morganatic
marriage of Archduke John
and Anna Plochl

Francis Charles
1802–78
m. Sophie of Bavaria 1805–72

Charles Louis
1833–96
m. (1) Margaret of Saxony d. 1858
(2) Maria Annunziata of Naples d. 1871
(3) Maria Theresa of Portugal d. 1944
(of the second marriage only)

Louis Victor
1842–1919

Otto 1865–1906
m. Maria Josepha of Saxony 1867–1946

Charles I 1887–1922
Emperor of Austria, king of Hungary 1916–18
m. Zita of Bourbon-Parma 1891

8 children: the eldest, born 1912,
Dr. Otto von Habsburg
m. Princess Regina of Saxe-Meiningen

Brief Bibliography

Only the principal introductory works are mentioned below; for further detail, the reader should refer to the numerous books and articles mentioned in the notes.

1 *Introduction—in the Collection 'Que sais-je?' (Presses Universitaires de France)*
Jacques Droz, *Histoire de l'Autriche*, No. 222
Henri Bogdan, *Histoire de la Hongrie*, No. 678
Pierre Bonnoure, *Histoire de la Tchécoslovaquie*, No. 1,301

2 *Bibliographies*
K. and M. Uhlirz, *Handbuch der Geschichte Österreichs und seiner Nachbarländer, Böhmen und Ungarn*, 4 vols., Vienna, 1927–44 (1 vol. republished in 1964)
A. Lhotsky, *Österreichische Historiographie*, Vienna, 1962
Twenty-five Years of Czechoslovak Historiography 1936–1960, Prague, Academy of Sciences of Czechoslovakia, 1960
Bibliography of selected works of Hungarian historical science 1945–1959, appendix of volume II of *Études historiques publiées en 1960 par la Commission nationale des historiens hongrois*, Budapest, 1960
Reviews: *Revue des Études Slaves* (Paris), *Acta Historica* (Budapest), *Historica* (Prague), *Studia Historica Slovaca* (Bratislava)

3 *General histories*
Roger Portal, *Les Slaves, peuples et nations*, 1965
J. Aulneau, *Histoire de l'Europe centrale depuis les origines jusqu' à nos jours*, Paris, 1926
A. Tibal, *L'Autrichien*, Paris, 1936
Adam Wandruszka, *Das Haus Habsburg*, Vienna, 1956
Paul Henry, *Le Problème des nationalités* (Collection Armand Colin)
Jacques Ancel, *Slaves et Germains* (Collection Armand Colin)
The major work on the history of the nationalities is: Robert A. Kann, *The Multinational Empire*, New York, 1950, revised and augmented in the German translation entitled *Das Nationalitätenproblem der Habsburgermonarchie*, 2 vols., Graz-Köln, 1964
Also by R. Kann, *The Habsburg Empire, a study in integration and disintegration*, New York, 1957

Index

Fiume, 152, 163, 227, 270, 398
Flanders, 10, 45, 46, 52, 156, 160, 393
Fleury, Cardinal, 181
Florence, 10, 26, 41, 252
Fontainebleau, 58, 235
Fontenoy, battle of, 185
Forgásch family, 75
France, 7, 9, 31, 36, 45–6, 58–9, 72, 91, 100,
    103, 105–7, 115–16, 118, 124–5, 130, 134,
    142, 144, 155–6, 159–62, 179, 180–1, 185,
    193–4, 213, 235, 238, 245, 247–51, 253,
    254, 256, 266, 297, 298, 309–10, 327, 336,
    337, 368, 369, 378, 379
Francesco V, Duke of Modena, 359
Franche-Comté, 45, 46, 47
Francis I, Emperor of Austria, 245, 248, 249,
    250, 251, 252, 257–61, 263, 264, 271
Francis I, Emperor of Holy Roman Empire,
    178, 185, 186–7, 189, 192, 206, 212, 222
Francis I, King of France, 1, 36, 52, 55, 58
Francis II, Duke of Brittany, 46
Francis II Rákóczi, 149, 159–60, 161, 270,
    286
Francis Charles, Archduke, 272, 283
Francis Ferdinand, Archduke, 359–60, 361,
    372, 373, 378, 382
Francis Joseph, Emperor, 258, 283–4, 286,
    287, 293, 294, 299, 300–10, 317, 318, 319,
    332–4, 338, 341, 343, 359, 365, 369, 373,
    376, 381
Frangepany, 143
Frank, Dr., 360
Frank, Josip, 344
Frankenberg, *Frankenberger Würfelspiel*, 98
Frankenthal, 98
Frankfurt am Main, 10, 90, 212, 275, 280,
    283
Frankfurt-an-der-Oder, 12
Franz, G., 119
Frederick II, Emperor, 37, 39–40
Frederick II, King of Prussia, 175, 178–80,
    185, 187, 193, 194, 195, 235, 238
Frederick III, Emperor, 24, 26, 40, 41–5, 88
Frederick IV, Elector Palatine, 87, 89
Frederick V, Elector Palatine, 90–1, 92, 93,
    97, 98, 99
Frederick, Archduke, 374
Frederick Augustus II, King of Prussia,
    273–4, 286

Frederick of Styria, 18–19
Frederick 'of the empty purse', 42
Frederick William, Elector of Brandenburg,
    115
Frederick William I, King of Prussia, 178
Frederick William II, King of Prussia, 245
Freiburg, 42
French Revolution, 36, 245–6, 249, 256,
    257, 258
Freschot, 175
Freud, Sigmund, 358
Frić, 282, 305, 309
Friedland, 101, 268
Friedland, Duke of, *see* Wallenstein
Fries, 266
Frint, Bishop of St. Pölten, 264
Frühwirth, 135
Fugger family, 52
Fürstenberg, Egon Karl, Prince, 199, 204
Fürstenberg family, 292
Füssen, peace of, 185
Fux, 207

Gablonz, 328, 329
Gaj, Ludevit, 263
Galanta, 144, 292
Galicia, 206, 224, 225, 234, 250, 288, 298,
    301, 303, 305, 318, 320, 339, 346, 362,
    365, 376, 396
Gallas, General, 105
Gallipoli, 21
Garas, Klára, 224
Gebauer, 339
Gentz, F. von, 249
George II, King of England, 193
George William, Elector of Brandenburg,
    103, 106
Georgei, 286
Georgius Agricola, 78
Gerson, 16
Gerstner, 266
Geymüller, 266
Géza, Duke of Hungary, 2
Ghega, 291
Ghent, 239
Gillchrist, Thomas, 324
Gindely, 305, 339
Glatz, 194
Glaz, 185

THE AUTHOR: Victor-L. Tapié is Professor of History at the Sorbonne. He has written many books on Central European history, including *Baroque and Classicism* and, with Professor Préclin, *Le XVIIe Siècle*. Professor Tapié is widely recognized as one of the most distinguished historians in France today.